THE ROUGH GUIDE TO

Wales

This eighth edition updated by

Tim Burford, Norm Longley and James Stewart

Contents

Introduction to
Wales

These are exciting times for Wales. Once overlooked and under-visited compared to its Celtic cousins Ireland and Scotland, this small country on the rocky fringe of western Europe has won accolades and then some in recent years. Barack Obama has praised its "extraordinary beauty, wonderful people and great hospitality", while National Geographic named Pembrokeshire the world's second-best coastal destination, and its coastal path second among the world's top ten long-distance paths. If the zeitgeist has swung Wales's way, it may be because it remains utterly authentic in an increasingly homogenized world, and despite the influx of goose-down duvets and gourmet menus, the essence of any visit remains unchanged. The solid little market towns and ancient castles reward repeated visits as much as the stirring mountains, gorgeous valleys and rugged coastline. The culture, too, is compelling, whether Welsh- or English-language, Celtic or industrial tradition, ancient belief or contemporary chutzpah. Even its comparative anonymity serves it well: while the tourist pound has reduced parts of Ireland and Scotland to Celtic pastiche, Wales remains brittle and brutal enough to be real, and diverse enough to remain endlessly fascinating.

Recent years have also seen a huge and dizzying upsurge in Welsh self-confidence, a commodity no longer so dependent on comparison with its big and powerful neighbour England. Popular culture – especially music and film – has contributed much to this revival, as has the arrival of a **National Assembly** in 1999, the first all-Wales tier of government for six hundred years. After centuries of enforced subjugation, the national spirit is undergoing a remarkable renaissance. The ancient symbol of the country, *y ddraig goch* or the **red dragon**, seen fluttering on flags everywhere in Wales, is waking up from what seems like a very long slumber.

As soon as you cross the border from England into Wales, the differences in appearance, attitude and culture between the two countries are obvious. Wales shares many physical

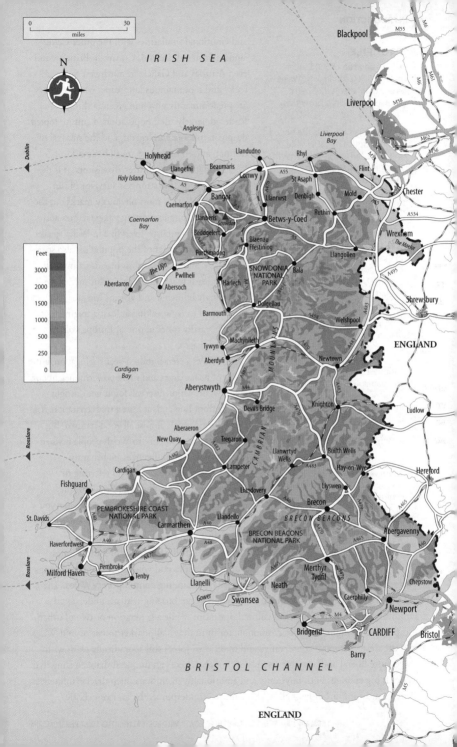

and emotional similarities with the other Celtic lands – Scotland, Ireland, Cornwall, Brittany, and even Asturias and Galicia in northwest Spain. A rocky and mountainous landscape, whose colours are predominantly grey and green, a thinly scattered, largely rural population, a culture rooted deeply in folklore and legend, and the survival of a distinct, ancient language are all hallmarks of Wales and its sister countries. To visitors, it is the **Welsh language**, the strongest survivor of the Celtic tongues, that most obviously marks out the country with tongue-twisting village names and vast bilingual signposts. Everyone in Wales speaks English, but a quarter of the population also speak Welsh: TV and radio stations broadcast in it, all children learn it at school, restaurant menus are increasingly bilingual and visitors too are encouraged to try speaking at least a fragment of the rich, earthy tones of one of Europe's oldest living languages.

After Wales' seven-hundred-year subjugation at the hands of its far larger and more powerful neighbour, many Welsh nationalists call for, if not outright divorce from England, at least a trial separation. The mutual antipathy is almost all good-natured, but often the greatest offence to Welsh people is when those very obvious differences are blatantly disregarded or patronized. Avoid referring to England when you really mean Britain or the United Kingdom, and **don't say English when you mean Welsh**: it is like calling a Kiwi an Aussie or a Canadian an American (probably worse).

Although it is the wealth of prehistoric sites, crumbling castles and wild landscapes that brings visitors here in the first place, they often leave championing **contemporary Wales**. The cities and university towns throughout the country are buzzing with an understated youthful confidence and sense of cultural optimism, while a generation or two of urban escapees has brought a curious cosmopolitanism to the small market towns of mid-Wales and the west. Although conservative and traditional forces still sporadically clash with these more liberal and anarchic strands of thought, there's an unquestionable feeling that Wales is big enough, both physically and emotionally, to embrace such diverse influences. Perhaps most importantly of all, Welsh culture is underpinned by an iconoclastic

democracy that contrasts starkly with the establishment-obsessed class divisions of England. The Welsh character is famously endowed with a **musicality**, lyricism, introspection and sentimentality that produces far better bards and singers than it does lords and masters. And Welsh culture is undeniably inclusive: anything from a sing-song in the pub to the grandiose theatricality of an **eisteddfod** involves everyone – including any visitor eager to learn and join in.

Where to go

Only 160 miles from north to south and 50 miles from east to west, Wales is smaller than Massachusetts and only half the size of the Netherlands. Most of its inhabitants are packed into the southern quarter of the country, a fact which will largely dictate where you travel and what you do. Like all capital cities, **Cardiff** is atypical of the rest of the country. Most

PREHISTORIC AND LEGENDARY WALES

Whether trudging through a dew-soaked field to some mysteriously inscribed **standing stone**, or catching the afternoon sun as it illumines the entrance to a cliff-top **burial chamber**, exploring Wales' prehistoric sites is thoroughly rewarding. At all but a few of the most popular, the bleating of sheep will be the only sound to break the contemplative silence of these spiritual places.

Prehistoric sites litter Wales. **Hut circles** defensively set atop windswept hills attest to a rugged hand-to-mouth pre-Celtic existence dating back four or five thousand years, while stone circles, intricately carved **monoliths** and finely balanced capstones set at crucial points on **ancient pathways** suggest the more spiritual life led by the priestly druids. Britain's greatest **druidic** centre was Anglesey, and the island is still home to many of Wales' best prehistoric sites, including the splendid chambers of Barclodiad y Gawres and Bryn Celli Ddu. Elsewhere, numerous standing stones and circles can be found on the mysterious slopes of the Mynydd Preseli in Pembrokeshire and in the area around Harlech in north Wales. Many sites take their names from great figures in Celtic history and folklore, such as Arthur and Merlin (Myrddin in Welsh); legends abound to connect much of the landscape with ancient tales.

national institutions are based here, not least the infant National Assembly, housed amid the massive regeneration projects of **Cardiff Bay**. The city is also home to the National Museum and St Fagans National History Museum – both excellent introductions to the character of the rest of Wales – and the superb Millennium Stadium, the home of huge sporting events and blockbuster gigs. The only other centres of appreciable size are loud-and-lairy **Newport** and breezy, resurgent **Swansea**, lying respectively to the east and west of the capital. All three cities grew as ports, mainly exporting millions of tons of coal and iron from the **Valleys**, where fiercely proud industrial communities were built up in the thin strips of land between the mountains.

Much of Wales' appeal lies outside the larger towns, where there is ample evidence of the warmongering which has shaped the country's development. Castles are everywhere, from the hard little stone keeps of the early Welsh princes to Edward I's incomparable series of thirteenth-century fortresses at **Flint**, **Rhuddlan**, **Conwy**, **Beaumaris**, **Caernarfon** and **Harlech**, and grandiose Victorian piles where grouse were the only enemy. Fortified residences served as the foundation for a number of the stately homes that dot the country, but many castles were deserted and remain dramatically isolated on rocky knolls, most likely on spots previously occupied by prehistoric communities. Passage graves and **stone circles** offer a more tangible link to the pre-Roman era when the priestly order of Druids ruled over early Celtic peoples, and later religious monuments such as the great ruined abbeys of **Valle Crucis**, **Tintern** and **Strata Florida** lend a gaunt grandeur to their surroundings.

Yet for all the appeal of its castles, megaliths or Dylan Thomas' home at **Laugharne**, many people find that the human monuments of Wales are upstaged by the beauty of the countryside, from the lowland greenery of meadows and river valleys to the inhospitable heights of the moors and mountains. The rigid backbone of the **Cambrian Mountains** terminates in the soaring peaks of **Snowdonia** and the angular ridges of the **Brecon Beacons**, both superb walking country and both national parks. A third national park follows the

LAND OF SONG

"Praise the Lord! We are a musical nation," intones the Rev. Eli Jenkins in Dylan Thomas' masterpiece, *Under Milk Wood*. It's a reputation of which the Welsh feel deservedly proud. Although plucky miners singing their way to the pithead was the dewy-eyed fabrication of Hollywood (*How Green Was My Valley*), Wales does make a great deal more noise, and makes it a great deal more tunefully, than most other small countries.

The country's male voice choirs, many struggling to survive in the aftermath of the decimation of the coal industry that spawned them, are the best-known exemplars of Welsh singing, but traditions go much further back, to the bards and minstrels of the Celtic age. Wales continues to nurture big voices and big talent: from the hip-swivelling Sir Tom Jones and show-stopping Dame Shirley Bassey (see below) to anarchistic rockers the Manic Street Preachers and young divas like Charlotte Church, Katherine Jenkins and Duffy.

Pembrokeshire Coast, with more Blue Flag/clean beaches than anywhere else in Britain and golden strands separated by rocky bluffs. Much of the rest of the coast remains unspoilt, with long sweeps of fine sand and the occasional traditional British seaside resort; places like the often-overlooked **Cambrian coast** and the superb **Gower peninsula**, the first region in Britain designated an Area of Outstanding Natural Beauty. The entire coast is now linked by the 860-mile **All-Wales Coast Path**; be sure to spend some time along its length.

When to go

The English preoccupation with the weather holds equally for the Welsh. The **climate** (see p.48) here is temperate, with Welsh summers rarely getting hot and nowhere but the tops of mountain ranges ever getting very cold, even in midwinter. Temperatures vary little, but proximity to the mountains is a different matter: Llanberis, at the foot of Snowdon, gets doused with more than twice as much rainfall as Caernarfon, seven miles away, and is always a few degrees cooler. For much of the summer, Wales – particularly the coast – can be bathed in sun. Between June and September, the Pembrokeshire coast, washed by the Gulf Stream, can be as warm as anywhere in Britain. The bottom line is that it's impossible to say with any degree of certainty that the weather will be pleasant in any given month. May might be wet and grey one year and gloriously sunny the next, and the same goes for the autumnal months – November stands an equal chance of being crisp and clear as being foggy and grim. If you're planning to lie on a beach, or camp in the dry, you'll want to go in **summer** (between June and September); book your accommodation as far in advance as possible for late July and August. For a chance of reasonably good weather with fewer **crowds** go in April, May, September or October. For **outdoor pursuits** you'll find June to October the warmest and driest for walking and climbing.

Author picks

During our authors' travels throughout the country, they have discovered their personal favourites among places, pubs, walks, nature reserves, beaches, railway journeys and much more.

Snowdonia's finest scramble Snowdon's splendid, but the north ridge of Tryfan gives wonderful exposure and views, and the scramble up borders on rock-climbing. See p.346

The grimmest beauty A dinky steam railway runs past Blaenau Ffestiniog's hard grey terraces nestled below great slopes of slate waste. See p.370

Sublime views Head to Beaumaris and settle down with a coffee to admire the superb view across the Menai Strait to the Snowdonian mountains. See p.418

Skeletal grandeur Ride Newport's Transporter Bridge, "A giant with the might of Hercules and the grace of Apollo", as it was described when it opened in 1906. See p.72

Birds flocking together Watch red kites swoop for their daily feed at Gigrin Farm near Rhayader. See p.233

Buy a pint from Bessie Spend an evening at the quirky *Dyffryn Arms* in bucolic Cwm Gwaun. See p.194

End of the world The Llŷn peninsula excels in escapism, whether the panorama from the summit of Tre'r Ceiri or the lovely seaside village of Aberdaron. See p.381

Coastal wonder Savour the glorious views of Worms Head and Rhossili Bay from the head of the Gower peninsula. See p.132

Our author recommendations don't end here. We've flagged up our favourite places – a perfectly sited hotel, an atmospheric café, a special restaurant – throughout the guide, highlighted with the ★ symbol.

FROM TOP MENAI SUSPENSION BRIDGE; HIKER DESCENDING GLYDER FACH TOWARDS TRYFAN

27

things not to miss

It's not possible to see everything that Wales has to offer in one trip – and we don't suggest you try. What follows, in no particular order, is a selective taste of the country's highlights, including beautiful beaches, outstanding national parks, fascinating wildlife encounters and unforgettable urban experiences. All highlights have a page reference to take you straight into the Guide, where you can find out more. Coloured numbers refer to chapters in the Guide section.

1

1 CONWY
Page 403
One of north Wales' finest walled medieval towns with over two hundred listed buildings as well as its castle, Conwy also exudes small-town charm.

2 CADAIR IDRIS
Page 281
The dominant mountain of southern Snowdonia, Cadair Idris is a magnificent beast chock-full of classic glacial features.

3 THE GOWER PENINSULA
Page 128
Beautiful beaches, open moorland, pretty villages and even a castle or two: there's a reason why this country in miniature was designated Britain's first Area of Outstanding Natural Beauty.

4 ABERYSTWYTH
Page 271

The capital of sparsely populated mid-Wales, Aberystwyth is a breezy and bright university and seaside town surrounded by luscious countryside.

5 MOUNTAIN BIKING AT COED Y BRENIN
Page 294

Some of Wales' finest singletrack and adrenalin-pumping descents through the forest combine with family trails, excellent running tracks and even geocaching.

6 FFESTINIOG RAILWAY
Page 370

Of Wales' many "great little trains", the Ffestiniog Railway, winding down through the Snowdonia mountains, is one of the best.

7 ST DAVIDS CATHEDRAL
Page 181

The heart of Welsh spirituality, St Davids Cathedral is at Wales' westerly extremity and has drawn pilgrims for a millennium and a half.

8 MAWDDACH TRAIL
Page 294

Ride or walk this easy trail beside Wales' finest estuary, the Mawddach, crossed by the 2253ft rail and foot bridge into Barmouth.

9 CARREG CENNEN CASTLE
Page 149

The most romantic ruin in Wales, Carreg Cennen Castle sits in glorious isolation amid pastures grazed by Welsh longhorns.

10 PEMBROKESHIRE COAST PATH

Break up this path around some of Wales' wildest coastal scenery into a series of day walks, or tackle the full 187 miles in one big push.

11 SNOWDON

Hike one of half a dozen demanding tracks to the top of Wales' highest mountain – or take the train and sup a beer at the summit café.

12 TRYFAN

Fabulous views along the Ogwen Valley in the wilds of Snowdonia are just one of the rewards for making the arduous ascent of Tryfan.

13 EDWARD I'S IRON RING

The might of the thirteenth-century English monarchy found its fullest expression in this chain of virtually impregnable fortresses, now evocative hollow shells.

14 CARDIFF BAY ARCHITECTURE

The wonderful Wales Millennium Centre and National Assembly Building are just two of many striking modern structures around the rejuvenated Cardiff Bay.

15 FESTIVAL NO.6, PORTMEIRION

An interesting programme of music and literature in the grandest folly of them all – Portmeirion is a superb backdrop for this leftfield festival.

10

11

17

18

 22 ABERGLASNEY
Page 148
Rescued from near-terminal decay, these formal gardens in the Tywi Valley are a perfect counterpoint to the nearby National Botanic Garden of Wales.

23 LLANWRTYD WELLS' MAD EVENTS
Page 225
Bog snorkelling, a Man versus Horse Marathon and a Real Ale Wobble bring a wonderful sense of lunacy to this quiet corner of mid-Wales.

 24 RUGBY
Page 44
Although Wales' standing in international rugby fluctuates wildly, the game remains nearly a religion here, never more so than when the national team is playing at Cardiff's awesome Millennium Stadium.

 25 LLANDUDNO
Page 398
North Wales' most genteel seaside resort, Llandudno spreads languidly around the bay beneath the ancient rock plug of the Great Orme.

 26 BRECON BEACONS
Page 201
The rambling moors of the Brecon Beacons are perfect for wild, lonely walks with thundering waterfalls and limestone caverns as destinations.

27 HAY-ON-WYE FESTIVAL
Page 223
Rub shoulders with the literati or just come along for music, a few book readings and a great time.

26

27

Itineraries

Our Grand Tour is ideal for a first visit to Wales, taking in a sampling of the best cities and towns, the country's industrial heritage and its superb mountain and coastal scenery. Fans of Neolithic cromlechs, ruined abbeys and stately homes should follow our Historic Buildings itinerary, while the more energetic will want to sample items on our Active Wales menu.

THE GRAND TOUR

If you've only got ten days and want to tick off Wales' acknowledged highlights, hit these.

❶ **Blaenafon** South Wales' industrial heritage: the powerful Big Pit mining museum and the evocative ruins of the Ironworks. **See p.106**

❷ **Cardiff** Ground-breaking architecture, top-notch culture and blistering nightlife in the cool Welsh capital. **See p.76**

❸ **Gower** Welsh natural heritage at its most stunning, the Gower peninsula boasts wide-open beaches, rocky bays and steep cliffs. **See p.128**

❹ **St Davids peninsula** Sample some of the finest sections of the Pembrokeshire Coast Path, and stay in delightful St Davids. **See p.181**

❺ **Cadair Idris** The folds of this fine mountain harbour old castles, churches and a steam railway, the Centre for Alternative Technology and the sublime Mawddach Estuary. **See p.281**

❻ **Snowdonia** Hard-working narrow-gauge railways, slate-mining heritage and nuggety villages in inspiring mountain scenery. **See p.332**

❼ **Portmeirion** The whimsical Italianate beauty of Clough Williams-Ellis' "home for fallen buildings". **See p.373**

❽ **Conwy and Llandudno** A domineering castle and ancient houses within an intact ring of walls make Conwy an essential stop, best

visited from Llandudno, with its grand seaside architecture, and blustery walks on the Great Orme. **See p.403 & p.398**

❾ **Llangollen** A canal aqueduct, a heritage railway, a hilltop castle, an abbey ruin and the home of the Ladies of Llangollen all wedged into a bucolic valley. **See p.312**

HISTORIC BUILDINGS

Edward I's massive castles across north Wales and the wonderful St Davids Cathedral are well known and covered; here are a few equally fascinating monuments which can be inspected in a week or so.

❶ **Tintern Abbey** Admire the wonderful roofless ruin that inspired Wordsworth's lines, by the placid River Wye. **See p.62**

❷ **Soar-y-Mynydd chapel** Wales' most remote chapel, in the wild countryside of Mynydd Eppynt. **See p.226**

❸ **Carreg Cennen** The most wonderfully sited of all the native Welsh castles, high on a cliff. **See p.149**

❹ **Pentre Ifan** Wales' largest burial stone with its 16ft-long top-stone precariously balanced on stone legs. **See p.193**

❺ **Penrhyn Castle, Bangor** Old masters in a grandiose Victorian mansion that loves to show off its slate-mining wealth. **See p.412**

ABOVE FROM LEFT MAWDDACH RAIL BRIDGE; SOAR-Y-MYNYDD CHAPEL, NEAR LLANDOVERY

❻ Plas Mawr, Conwy A superb example of an Elizabethan town house. **See p.406**

❼ Plas Newydd, Llangollen Fascinating mock-Tudor bolt hole of two aristocratic Anglo–Irish ladies. **See p.314**

❽ Erddig, Wrexham There is a *Downton Abbey* feel to the relationship between servants and masters at this stately home. **See p.309**

ACTIVE WALES

You'll enjoy that slice of bara brith or pint of Purple Moose all the more if you've earned it hiking, biking or surfing. Set aside a week or more.

❶ Whitewater rafting: Cardiff Abundant thrills and spills on these superb man-made rapids. **See p.87**

❷ Surfing: Gower Suit up and surf some of the UK's finest waves among the bays and beaches of the glorious peninsula. **See p.134**

❸ Coasteering: St Davids peninsula Jump off rocks into the sea, swim across bays and explore caves. **See p.183**

❹ Walking: Pembrokeshire Coast Path Spend a few hours or a few weeks exploring the gorgeous coves, windswept headlands and long beaches of this magical coastal walk. **See p.161**

❺ Mine exploring: Corris Get kitted out with harness and headlamp and listen to arcane tales of mining life in an abandoned slate mine. **See p.286**

❻ Mountain biking: Coed y Brenin Among the very best of many fine places to ride off-road in Wales. **See p.294**

❼ Rock climbing: Llanberis Pass The ultimate mountain challenge in the home of Welsh rock climbing; some climbers engage the guiding services of nearby Plas y Brenin. **See p.353 & p.345**

❽ Walking: Offa's Dyke Path Set aside a couple of weeks if you want to tackle the whole of this classic 177-mile long-distance walk, which largely follows the ancient earthwork along the English border. **See p.239**

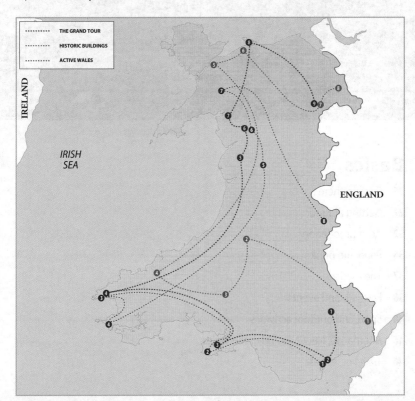

SNOWDON MOUNTAIN RAILWAY

Basics

Getting there

Wales is easily reached from the rest of the UK, Ireland and continental Europe with flights into Cardiff Airport. There are no direct flights to Wales from outside Europe, so you're best off flying to England and continuing overland from there. The widest choice is into London (City, Heathrow, Gatwick, Luton or Stanstead), though Manchester is better placed for north Wales and you might consider Birmingham for direct access to mid-Wales.

With most **airlines** nowadays, how much you pay depends on how far in advance you book and how much demand there is during that period – generally speaking, the earlier you book, the cheaper the prices.

If you're coming from elsewhere in Britain, or from Ireland, you can reach Wales easily enough by **train**, **bus** or **ferry**, though it may not necessarily work out cheaper than flying.

From England, Scotland and Ireland

The only airport of any size in Wales is **Cardiff Airport** (Wcardiff-airport.com), twelve miles southwest of the capital. There are very limited flights from the rest of the UK to Cardiff, with the airport currently only linked to Aberdeen and Newcastle with Eastern Airways (Weasternairways.com), Belfast with flybe (Wflybe .com), and Edinburgh and Glasgow with Cityjet (Wcityjet.com). Note that many of these routes mostly run business flights, timed and priced accordingly, and often not operating at weekends.

Crossing the border from England into Wales is straightforward, with train and bus services forming part of the British national network (see p.27). Fares on both can be very competitive if you book far enough in advance. The two roads providing the quickest access into the heart of the country are the **M4 motorway** in the south and the **A55 expressway** in the north. Both are fast and busy; minor routes are more appealing if you aren't in too much of a hurry.

From Ireland, there are flights from Dublin with Aerlingus (Waerlingus.com), though ferries are very frequent (see p.27).

From mainland Europe

Cardiff is also poorly served with flights **from mainland Europe**; presently, only KLM (Wklm.com) flies from Amsterdam, and Cityjet flies to Paris Orly. Alternatively, you could fly into Bristol airport just across the border, which has some excellent routings into mainland Europe. Birmingham, Liverpool and Manchester airports are handily placed for onward travel into mid- and north Wales respectively.

Alternatives to air travel are the traditional cross-Channel ferry services or the Channel Tunnel (see p.27).

From the US and Canada

Numerous airlines fly from both the **eastern and western US seaboards** to London, the principal gateway for visitors to Wales. You'll also come across useful direct flights to Manchester and Birmingham.

Low-season round-trip **fares** from New York, Boston and Washington to London start at around US$650, though US$800 is more normal, and through the summer you can expect to pay over US$1000 (add US$100–200 from other eastern cities). Low-season fares from the West Coast start at a little under US$950, though expect more like US$1400 in peak summer and around Christmas.

In **Canada**, you'll get the best deal flying to London from the big gateway cities of Toronto and Montreal, where fares are Can$1000–1200 round-trip. British Airways (Wbritishairways.com) flies direct to Heathrow from both Vancouver and Calgary while Air Canada (Waircanada.com) has nonstop links from Vancouver, Calgary, Edmonton and Ottawa. From the west, fares range from Can$1100 to Can$1600.

From Australia, New Zealand and South Africa

To get to Wales **from Australia**, **New Zealand** or **South Africa** you'll need to fly through London, or possibly Manchester in northern England.

Flights via Southeast Asia or the Middle East are generally the cheapest options, though fares vary little from between major **Australian cities**. The cheapest scheduled return flights are around Aus$1300 with Royal Brunei (Wbruneiair.com), though it takes a convoluted route via Brunei and Dubai. More direct routes cost Aus$2000–2400; good options include Etihad (via Abu Dhabi; Wetihadair ways.com), Emirates (via Dubai; Wemirates.com) and Malaysian (via Kuala Lumpur; Wmalaysiaairlines .com). Korean Airlines (Wkoreanair.com) flights are cheap but involve a twenty-hour stopover in Seoul. Singapore Airlines (Wsingaporeair.com), Qantas/

British Airways (🌐qantas.com.au), Thai (via Bangkok; 🌐thaiairways.com) and Cathay (🌐cathaypacific .com) are usually a little pricier but not always.

If travelling from **New Zealand** via Asia, you can choose between most of the carriers listed above, plus Air New Zealand (🌐airnewzealand.com) which flies to London via Shanghai. Prices via Asia are usually comparable with flights via North America. Air New Zealand flies to Heathrow via Los Angeles and does codeshares with United (🌐united.com), Continental (🌐continental.com) and others. Air Canada operates a route via Vancouver. Fares with Brunei, Malaysian and Korean typically cost around $2200–2500, with Air NZ usually NZ$2400–2700.

There are direct flights from **South Africa** to London Heathrow with South African Airways (Jo'burg and Cape Town; 🌐flysaa.com), British Airways (Jo'burg and Cape Town) and Virgin Atlantic (Jo'burg; 🌐virgin-atlantic.com). There are sometimes cheaper deals on indirect routes with Emirates (from Cape Town, Durban and Jo'burg via Dubai); Ethiopian (from Jo'burg via Addis Ababa); KLM (from Jo'burg via Amsterdam); and Lufthansa (from Jo'burg via Frankfurt; 🌐lufthansa.com). Return fares are generally in the ZAR7000–8000 bracket.

Package deals and tours

Although you may want to see Wales at your own speed, you shouldn't dismiss the idea of a **package deal**. Many agents and airlines put together very flexible deals, which are sometimes amounting to nothing more restrictive than a flight plus accommodation and car or rail pass, and these can actually work out cheaper than making the same arrangements yourself on arrival.

There are hundreds of **tour operators** specializing in travel to the British Isles. Most can do

packages of the standard highlights, but of greater interest are the outfits that help you explore Britain's unique points: walking or cycling trips, boat trips along canals, and any number of theme tours based around, for example, Britain's literary heritage, history, pubs, gardens, theatre, golf. A few of the possibilities are listed below.

TRAVEL AGENTS AND OPERATORS

North South Travel UK ☎ 01245 608 291, 🌐 northsouthtravel .co.uk. Friendly, competitive travel agency, offering discounted fares worldwide. Profits are used to support projects in the developing world, especially the promotion of sustainable tourism.

STA Travel UK ☎ 0333 321 0099, US ☎ 1800 781 4040, Australia ☎ 134 782, New Zealand ☎ 0800 474 400, South Africa ☎ 0861 781 781; 🌐 statravel.co.uk. Worldwide specialists in independent travel; also student IDs, travel insurance, car rental, rail passes and more. Good discounts for students and under-26s.

Trailfinders UK ☎ 020 7368 1200, Ireland ☎ 021 464 8800; 🌐 trailfinders.com. One of the best-informed and most efficient agents for independent travellers.

Travel CUTS Canada ☎ 1800 667 2887, 🌐 travelcuts.com. Canadian youth and student travel firm.

USIT Ireland ☎ 01 602 1906, Australia ☎ 1800 092 499; 🌐 usit.ie. Ireland's main student and youth travel specialists.

By train

We've covered details of train travel within the UK under "Getting around". What follows is a summary of services from Europe.

England has direct, high-speed passenger trains from France and Belgium via the Channel Tunnel with **Eurostar** (☎08432 186186, 🌐eurostar.com), which runs hourly between London (St Pancras) and Paris, Lille and Brussels. The cheapest return fares from Paris or Brussels to London start at around €85. Eurostar also offers frequent promotional fares,

---

FUN TOURS AND ADVENTURE TRIPS

If you're short on time or want to see the sights in the company of like-minded travellers, join a **guided tour**. Some of the best include:

Bus Wales ☎ 0800 328 0284, 🌐 buswales.co.uk. Wide range of backpacker and smarter tours, from day-trips (£50) to six- and ten-day trips (from £240 staying in hostel dorms to £1850 using five-star hotels).

Busy Bus 🌐 busybus.co.uk. Excellent outfit offering adventure day trips (£39) from Liverpool and Chester to North Wales, taking in Conwy Castle and Snowdonia National Park, among other places. They also operate cruise excursions from Holyhead (£49).

Dragon Tours ☎ 01874 658102, 🌐 dragon-tours.com. Similar to Bus Wales, with day-trips (£50), and six- and ten-day trips (from

£400 staying in hostel dorms to £3300 using five-star hotels); extra days available too.

Shaggy Sheep Tours ☎ 07919 244549, 🌐 shaggysheep.com. Great fun and hugely enthusiastic, the booziest backpacker tours around leave twice-weekly from London. Choose between the Merlin weekend trip (£118) or the four-day All-Wales Dragon trip (£148); adventure activities cost £40 extra. For independent travellers, there's also a handy jump-on, jump-off return bus service from London (£79) stopping at key destinations in Wales.

A BETTER KIND OF TRAVEL

At Rough Guides we are passionately committed to travel. We believe it helps us understand the world we live in and the people we share it with – and of course tourism is vital to many developing economies. But the scale of modern tourism has also damaged some places irreparably, and climate change is accelerated by most forms of transport, especially flying. All Rough Guides' flights are carbon-offset, and every year we donate money to a variety of environmental charities.

If coming from mainland Europe, ferries arrive at various **ports in England**. The shortest, most convenient route is the crossing from Calais to Dover with P&O ferries. Other useful crossings are Zeebrugge and Rotterdam to Hull, the Hook of Holland to Harwich, and Le Havre to Portsmouth.

For ferry routes and prices, contact the ferry companies direct or visit the excellent websites Seaview Ferries (Ⓦ seaview.co.uk/ferries) and Direct Ferries (Ⓦ directferries.co.uk).

FERRY COMPANIES

Irish Ferries ☎ 08717 300 400, Ⓦ irishferries.com.
P&O Ferries ☎ 08716 642121, Ⓦ poferries.com.
Stena Line ☎ 08447 707070, Ⓦ stenaline.com.

particularly for advance bookings, so it's always worth checking the website.

Drivers travelling between Calais and Folkestone can use **Le Shuttle** (from the UK ☎ 08443 353535, from France ☎ +33 (0)810 630304, Ⓦ eurotunnel .com), a vehicle-carrying train which whisks through the Channel Tunnel in 35 minutes. You can just turn up on the day you want to travel, but booking is advised and usually cheaper, especially at weekends. Return fares start from as little as €55 for a car and up to nine passengers.

By ferry

There are three **Welsh ferry ports** all serving Ireland with large, spacious vessels. Passenger fares are very competitive, with diverse special deals, and midweek and advance purchase offers. The busiest port is **Holyhead**, on the northwest tip of Wales, with ferries and fast catamarans from both Dublin and Dun Laoghaire (6 miles south of Dublin), though the fast cats often only run in the busiest summer months. **Fishguard** has ferries from Rosslare (just outside Wexford), supplemented by fast catamarans in July and August. The least busy port is **Pembroke Dock**, with ferry connections from Rosslare.

Getting around

The large cities and densely populated valleys of south Wales support comprehensive train and bus networks, but the more thinly populated areas of mid- and north Wales have to make do with skeletal services. Getting about by car is easy and, outside the cities, sheep and vehicles with agricultural equipment are likely to be a more persistent problem than other road users. Take the more scenic backroads unless you're in a real hurry. Information for cyclists is listed in the outdoor activities section (see p.40).

By train

The train is one of the best ways to get to and around Wales; the views are superb and the engineering often impressive. In addition to the main-line network, there are over a dozen **narrow-gauge trains** (see box, p.29). Britain's trains are run by a myriad of **operators**, but all are required to work as a single network with integrated ticketing.

FERRY CONNECTIONS FROM IRELAND

Route	Company	Frequency	Duration
Dublin–Holyhead (ferry)	Stena	4 daily	3hr 15min
Dublin–Holyhead (ferry)	Irish	2–3 daily	3hr 15min
Dublin–Holyhead (catamaran)	Irish	1 daily	1hr 50min
Dun Laoghaire–Holyhead (catamaran)	Stena	1 daily	2hr
Dun Laoghaire–Holyhead (ferry)	Stena	3–4 daily	3hr 15min
Rosslare–Fishguard (ferry)	Stena	2 daily	3hr 30min
Rosslare–Fishguard (catamaran)	Stena	1 daily	2hr
Rosslare–Pembroke Dock (ferry)	Irish	2 daily	4hr

Travelling to Wales, most use the fast, frequent service from London Paddington to **Newport** (1hr 45min), **Cardiff** (2hr) and **Swansea** (3hr), operated by First Great Western. Very few direct trains from England go beyond Swansea, although connections at Newport, Cardiff or Swansea link up with services to Carmarthen and stations in Pembrokeshire. The **north coast service** from London Euston to Holyhead (4hr), via Chester, also stops at Prestatyn, Rhyl, Colwyn Bay, Llandudno Junction and Bangor, and is operated by Virgin Trains. From other cities in England and Scotland, you'll probably need to change en route – at Bristol for the south coast line, at Crewe for the north coast.

Within Wales, services cover all the main cities and a seemingly random selection of rural towns and wayside halts. As well as the two major lines discussed above (which also have several slower services) there is the **Cambrian Coast line** from Birmingham and Shrewsbury through Welshpool, Newtown and Machynlleth, beyond which it divides at Dyfi Junction. The southern spur goes a few miles to Borth and Aberystwyth: the northern one crawls up the coast through Tywyn, Barmouth, Harlech and Porthmadog to Pwllheli. Even slower (but very picturesque) is the second route from Shrewsbury, the **Heart of Wales line**, which runs through Knighton, Llandrindod Wells, Llanwrtyd Wells, Llandovery, Llandeilo and a host of tiny halts on the way to Llanelli and Swansea.

Apart from the major inter-city services from England, all services are run by **Arriva Trains Wales** with timetables covered in detail on **Traveline Cymru** (see below) and on the useful See Wales by Bus and Train map, free from tourist offices.

Services on all but the main north and south coast train lines are infrequent, and are occasionally replaced by buses on Sunday. At many smaller stations, **ticket offices** close at weekends and in a lot of minor towns they've shut for good. In these instances, either use the vending machine on the platform, or if there isn't one, buy your ticket on board – but if you've boarded at a station with a machine or ticket office and haven't bought a ticket, you're liable for an on-the-spot fine.

TRAVELLING ON SUNDAYS

Throughout the guide we've given frequencies for trains and buses from Monday to Saturday. **Sunday** tends to have around 1–3 services, though the main routes have more and some routes have no Sunday service at all.

USEFUL CONTACTS FOR RAIL TRAVEL

Arriva Trains Wales ☎ 0870 900 0773, ⓦ arrivatrainswales.co.uk.

First Great Western ☎ 03457 000125, ⓦ firstgreatwestern .co.uk.

The Man in Seat Sixty-One ⓦ seat61.com. Superb site covering all aspects of British and European train travel.

National Rail Enquiries ☎ 08457 484950, ⓦ nationalrail.co.uk. Primary contact for all train timetables and booking.

The Train Line ⓦ thetrainline.com. Independent UK-wide online ticket retailer with a Best Fare Finder.

Traveline Cymru ☎ 0871 200 2233, ⓦ traveline-cymru.info. Integrated train and bus info, particularly useful for planning integrated journeys.

Virgin Trains ☎ 08719 774222, ⓦ virgintrains.co.uk.

By bus and coach

Inter-town **bus services** duplicate a few of the major rail routes, often at half the price of the train or less, but taking considerably longer. Buses are reasonably comfortable and on longer journeys there are refreshment stops.

WALES' BEST DRIVES

You can't go far in Wales without experiencing great views, but if you're set on seeking out some of the very finest scenery, try these drives:

Wye Valley Savour the wooded gorge of the River Wye on a journey from Monmouth past Tintern Abbey to Chepstow.

Gospel Pass Take the narrow road over the roof of the Black Mountains from Abergavenny past Llanthony Priory to Hay-on-Wye.

Elan Valley and Cwmystwyth From Rhayader take the mountain road past the reservoirs of the Elan Valley up to the blasted landscapes around Cwmystwyth and down past Devil's Bridge into the Vale of Rheidol.

Abergwesyn Pass Follow the ancient drovers' road the spectacularly remote moorland of the Cambrian Mountains from Llanwrtyd Wells to Tregaron.

Marine Drive A short but wonderfully scenic loop around the Great Orme.

Throughout Britain, long-distance bus (aka coach) services are almost all run by **National Express**, which serves most parts of Wales. The chief routes are from London to Cardiff; London to Milford Haven via Chepstow, Swansea and Pembroke Dock; London to Wrexham via Birmingham and Llangollen; London to Aberystwyth via Birmingham and Welshpool; from London along the north Welsh coast to Holyhead and Pwllheli, both via Birmingham; Birmingham to Cardiff, Swansea and Haverfordwest; Chester along the north coast to Llandudno, Bangor, Caernarfon and Pwllheli and Holyhead; and Chester direct to Holyhead.

Fares vary enormously with the cheapest tickets sold early. One-way London–Cardiff fares can be as little as £5. There are also numerous discount cards available (see box, p.30), while children under 3 travel free.

Low-cost inter-city services are also operated by **Megabus** (ⓦmegabus.com), with coaches running from a handful of UK cities to Carmarthen, Cardiff, Cwmbran, Newport, Swansea and Pembroke Dock; fares can be obtained from as low as £1 (if you book well in advance).

Much bus travel **within Wales** is provided by local bus services run by a bewildering array of companies: consult Traveline Cymru (see opposite) for details or visit ⓦshowbus.co.uk/timetables /wales.htm, which has links to all the major bus companies. Though services are more expensive and less frequent in rural areas, there are very few places without any service, even if it's only a private minibus on market day. All regions have their own detailed local **timetables**, easily obtained from tourist offices, libraries and bus and/or train stations. For occasional bus journeys, just pay as you get on, but good savings can be made with one of the various **bus passes** and combined bus and rail passes (see p.31).

In the **northern** half of Wales, Llandudno-based Arriva Cymru runs the majority of local services, but further south the system is far less unified, though most services west of Cardiff and south of Carmarthen are run by the Swansea-based First Cymru.

Cardiff Bus is the major company serving **Cardiff** and the Vale of Glamorgan. Various day, weekly and monthly passes are available, all of which can be bought aboard the bus.

The most important **medium- to long-range services** include: T2 from Bangor to Aberystwyth via Porthmadog; T4 from Cardiff to Newtown, calling at Merthyr, Brecon and Llandrindod Wells; 701 from Cardiff to Aberystwyth via Carmarthen; and X94 from Wrexham to Barmouth.

USEFUL CONTACTS FOR BUS TRAVEL

Arriva Cymru ⓦ arrivabus.co.uk/wales.
Cardiff Bus ⓦ cardiffbus.com.
First Cymru ⓦ firstcymru.co.uk.
National Express ☎ 08717 818178, ⓦ nationalexpress.com.
Traveline Cymru ☎ 01871 200 2233, ⓦ traveline-cymru .org.uk.

WALES' STEAM RAILWAYS: SIX OF THE BEST

With the rising demand for quarried stone in the nineteenth century, quarry and mine owners had to find more economical means of transport than packhorses to get their products to market, but in the steep, tortuous valleys of Snowdonia, standard-gauge train tracks proved too unwieldy. The solution was rails, usually about 2ft apart, plied by steam engines and dinky rolling stock. The charm of these **steam railways** was recognized by train enthusiasts, and long after the decline of the quarries, they banded together to restore abandoned lines and locos. Most lines are still largely run by volunteers, who have also started up new services along unused sections of standard-gauge bed.

Tickets are generally sold separately, but ten railways (including all those listed here) operate as **The Great Little Trains of Wales** (GLT: ⓦgreatlittletrainsofwales.co.uk) and offer a Discount Card (£10; valid 1 year), giving you twenty percent off the cost of the return journey on each of the GLT railways.

The railways below are listed north to south:
Snowdon Mountain Railway Llanberis. See p.349.
Welsh Highland Railway Porthmadog. See p.370.
Ffestiniog Railway Porthmadog. See p.370.
Llangollen Railway Llangollen. See p.314.
Talyllyn Railway Tywyn. See p.288
Vale of Rheidol Railway Aberystwyth. See p.277.

TRAIN AND BUS PASSES AND DISCOUNTS

Ordinary standard-class fares on UK trains are high and **first-class** costs an extra 33 percent, but there are various ways to save money. Off-peak and **advance-purchase** fares are much cheaper, **railcards** can save you a third off the price and there's a huge array of **rail passes** that cover all of Britain, just Wales or smaller regions.

TRAIN TICKET TYPES

Up to two children under 5 travel free with each adult-fare-paying passenger, while those aged 5–15 inclusive pay half the adult fare on most journeys. Bicycles are generally carried free with restrictions (see p.42).

As a guide to **prices**, a standard-class one-way ticket on the London–Cardiff route might cost £15 (Advance), £44 (Off-Peak) or £95 (Anytime).

Anytime Fully flexible ticket allowing travel on any train at any time within a month after purchase. Expensive.

Off-peak Return off-peak fares cost about a third of the price of Anytime fares, though one-way fares are seldom much cheaper than returns. If you're doing a lot of travelling on one-way journeys, rail and bus passes make a lot of sense. You generally cannot travel during weekday peak hours (these vary by route and company) and must complete outbound travel on the date shown on the ticket: the return portion is more flexible with the possibility of breaking the journey. At any station outside the morning rush hour, you'll routinely be sold an off-peak ticket.

Advance Advance-purchase tickets are the cheapest available, with no refunds and generally only valid on the train(s) you've booked. They must be bought at least the day before you travel and they're generally cheaper the further in advance you book. These are usually sold as single tickets, making planning a series of one-way journeys realistic if you are prepared to book ahead.

RAILCARDS

You can save a third on fares with one of several **railcards**, all of which cost £30 for a year (Ⓦrailcard.co.uk): the 16–25 Railcard; the Senior Railcard, for British residents over 60; the Family Railcard, for use by up to four adults travelling with up to four children (aged 5–15), who get sixty percent off; and the Two Together Railcard, for two named people travelling together. Children aged under 5 travel free at all times. Railcards also give a third off Explore Wales passes.

NATIONAL EXPRESS COACHCARDS

You can save a third on fares with one of several **coachcards** (Ⓦnationalexpress.com): the 16–26 Coachcard (£10); the Senior Railcard (£10) for those over 60; and the Family Coachcard

By car

If you want to cover a lot of the countryside in a short time, or just want more flexibility, you'll need your own transport. The **M4 motorway** (from London to Cardiff and Swansea) makes the most dramatic entry into Wales, across the graceful Second Severn Crossing bridge (£6.40 toll westbound only; no footpath or cycle lane). A few miles north, the M48 links England and Wales over the smaller, but original Severn Bridge (same toll; footpath and cycle lane available). Neither bridge accepts credit cards; check conditions and closures at Ⓦseverbridge.co.uk. The only other fast road into Wales is the **A55 expressway** running along the north Wales coast to the Ireland-bound ferries at Holyhead. An extensive network of dual carriageways and good-quality roads links all major centres, including the **A5** through Llangollen into Snowdonia and the **A40** into the Brecon Beacons. In rural areas you'll often find yourself on winding, sometimes hair-raisingly narrow, single-track lanes with slightly broader **passing places** where two vehicles can squeeze by – with this in mind, you might want to select a compact rental car. In very remote areas, you may still occasionally have to open gates designed to keep sheep from straying.

As in the rest of the UK, you **drive on the left** in Wales. **Speed limits** are 30–40mph (50–65km/hr) in built-up areas, 70mph (110km/hr) on motorways (freeways) and dual carriageways, and 60mph (97km/hr) on most other roads. Be alert to posted signs as **speed cameras** are everywhere.

(£8), which allows one child to travel free with a full paying adult. The Brit Xplorer Pass offers unlimited travel on consecutive days on the National Express network for 7 days (£79), 14 days (£139) or 28 days (£219).

RAIL AND BUS PASSES: BRITAIN AND WALES

All-Line Rail Rover Ⓦ nationalrail.co.uk. Unlimited travel on almost the entire network throughout England, Scotland and Wales (including the Ffestiniog Railway) for 7 consecutive days (£478). Available within Britain from larger train stations.

BritRail Pass Ⓦ britrail.net. Foreign visitors planning on several long-distance trips through other parts of Britain might consider purchasing a BritRail Pass online, which must be bought before you enter the country. A range of passes is available for unlimited travel in England, Scotland and Wales over various combinations of consecutive days or a certain number of days over 2 months, plus discounts for child (aged 5–15; half-price) and youth (under 26;

20 percent) passengers. One child can travel free on each adult pass (other children travel at half-price).

Explore Wales Pass Ⓣ 0870 900 0773, Ⓦ arrivatrains wales/ExploreWalesPass.co.uk. Eight consecutive days' bus travel and four days' rail travel within the same period (£94). Covers all of Wales and extends to Crewe, Shrewsbury and Hereford in England. Includes a fifty percent discount on the Ffestiniog narrow-gauge railway, twenty percent discounts on many other narrow-gauge railways, and reduced entry to CADW and National Trust properties. The pass can be bought at most staffed train stations.

RAIL AND BUS PASSES: NORTH AND MID-WALES

Explore North & Mid Wales Pass Same deal as the Explore Wales Pass but only covers the northern half of Wales (£64).

North Wales Rover All-day pass on all trains and most buses in north Wales and down the Cambrian Coast to Aberystwyth. The area is divided into seven zones and you can choose to travel within two

zones (£10), three zones (£15) or all zones (£27). Buy at the train stations.

Red Rover All-day bus travel throughout northwest Wales for £6.80. Buy on the bus.

Snowdon Sherpa Day Ticket All-day travel on the routes immediately surrounding Snowdon for £4. Buy on the bus.

RAIL AND BUS PASSES: WEST AND MID-WALES

Cambrian Coaster Day Ranger One day's train travel between Aberystwyth and Pwllheli (£11.10), valid after 9.15am and all weekend. There's also an Evening Ranger (£6.60; valid after 6.30pm). Buy at any station.

Heart of Wales Line Circular Day Ranger One day's unlimited train travel on the route Shrewsbury–Llandrindod

Wells–Swansea–Cardiff–Hereford–Shrewsbury with as many breaks as the timetable will allow (£35).

West Wales Day Ranger All-day train travel in Pembrokeshire, west of Carmarthen (£10.20). Valid after 8.45am weekdays and all weekend. Buy at the station.

RAIL AND BUS PASSES: SOUTH WALES

Explore South Wales Pass Same deal as the Explore Wales Pass but only covers the southern half of Wales (£64).

First Day Ticket Ⓦ firstgroup.com/ukbus/south-west-wales. A range of all-day bus passes using First company buses, for

example Swansea Bay area (£4) or Pembrokeshire (£5.50).

Valley Lines Explorer One day's Cardiff and Valleys bus and train travel. The Day Explorer (£11) is valid after 9.15am weekdays and all weekend; the Night Rider (£5.50) is only available after 6.30pm.

Road signs are pretty much international ("Give Way" means "Yield"), and road rules are largely common sense. Many road signs give instructions in English and in Welsh. You are not permitted to make a kerbside turn against a red light and must always give way to traffic (circulating clockwise) on a **roundabout**. This applies even for mini-roundabouts, which may be no more than a white circle painted on the road.

Petrol (gas) is sold in litres (a UK gallon = 4.56 litres, a US gallon = 3.8 litres), and at the time of writing, was around £1.30 per litre. Diesel costs slightly more.

The Automobile Association (AA; breakdowns Ⓣ0800 887766, Ⓦtheaa.co.uk), the Royal Automobile Club (RAC; breakdowns Ⓣ0800 828282, Ⓦrac .co.uk) and Green Flag (breakdowns Ⓣ0800 0510636, Ⓦgreenflag.com) all operate 24-hour emergency

breakdown services. You may be entitled to free assistance through a reciprocal arrangement with a motorizing organization in your own country – check the situation before setting out. You can call the breakdown numbers even if you are not a member, although you'll be charged a substantial fee.

Most foreign nationals can get by with their **driving licence** from home, but if you're in any doubt, obtain an **international driving permit** from a national motoring organization. All foreign vehicles should carry vehicle registration, ownership documents and **insurance**, so be sure to check your existing policy.

Hitchhiking and lift-sharing

You might get lucky **hitchhiking**, though it's rarely done nowadays, and a safer and more reliable alternative is **lift-sharing**, whereby you share the travel costs with someone already going in your direction. One of the best ways is through web-based agencies such as Carpooling (Ⓦcarpooling.co.uk) and Freewheelers (Ⓦfreewheelers.co.uk), where you register (free) and enter your desired route so that the database can come up with suitable matches. You then contact the resulting matches by email and make arrangements.

Car rental

Car rental is best booked online. You can expect to pay around £110 a week for a small hatchback. **Automatic transmissions** are rare at the lower end of the price scale – if you want one, you should book well ahead and expect to pay at least £170 a week for a slightly bigger model. Damage Liability Waiver (aka Collision Damage Waiver) is often included but still leaves you liable for the first several hundred pounds; this can be eliminated by paying roughly £10 a day. Most agencies offer vehicles with **diesel** engines, which give better overall economy despite the slightly more expensive fuel.

You'll also need to show your **driving licence**: few companies will rent out cars to drivers with less than one year's experience, and most will only rent out to people between 21 and 70 years of age. Some charge an additional fee for under-25s.

North Americans might want to contact the independently owned Europe by Car (US Ⓣ1 800 223 1516, Ⓦeuropebycar.com), which has good deals on short and longer-term rentals.

PAY AND DISPLAY

You often have to pay for **parking** in towns and at popular beaches, many of which are tucked into folds in the mountains or wedged below cliffs, giving little space for parking on the road.

At most pay-and-display car parks, tickets are issued by machine (you may have to type in your car registration number). Some shopping centres may require you to pay for parking, though you usually get your parking costs redeemed at the check-out if you make a purchase.

Parking prices are typically 50p to £1 an hour, though some places charge a flat fee of up to £5. It's definitely an incentive to use public transport – some eco-oriented attractions even give discounted entry to those arriving without a car.

Motorbike rental

A motorbike is a pleasurable way to see the Welsh countryside, but ludicrous insurance premiums mean that the few **motorbike rental** outlets in the UK charge at least £350 a week for powerful tourers. Try London-based Raceways (Ⓣ020 7237 6494, Ⓦraceways.net) or Manchester-based New Horizons (Ⓣ07907 304479, Ⓦnewhorizonsbikehire.co.uk).

Accommodation

Tourist accommodation in Wales is constantly improving, with top-rank international hotels, farmhouse accommodation, hostels, restaurants-with-rooms and the ubiquitous B&Bs. The growing array of farmhouse B&Bs and country houses typically offer a genuinely warm welcome, informal hospitality and quality home cooking. If you want to ensure you're staying in places where Welsh is spoken, check out Ⓦgwyliaucymraeg.co.uk, covering accommodation, pubs, cafés and restaurants.

Hotels and B&Bs

Bed & Breakfasts (B&Bs; in Welsh Gwely a Brecwast) may be anything from a private house with a couple of bedrooms set aside for paying guests to a small, stylish boutique establishment. **Guesthouses** tend to be larger, usually with around half a dozen rooms plus a guests' lounge, and can vary from homely to very flash. In both places you'll get a room with TV, tea- and coffee-making facilities and, usually, your own en-suite bathroom, for £25–45 per person (sometimes a little less out of season or in less popular areas). We always mention if a place has rooms without a private bathroom (though usually with a sink in the room) for which you'll pay slightly less. Many places have free wi-fi.

In the countryside you're more likely to find places described as a **farm** (essentially a B&B on a working farm) or an **inn** (usually village pub with rooms above). As visitor expectations and the demand for weekend breaks increase, some places in all the above categories are ramping up the standards, with sumptuous furnishings, better food and those little touches which make your stay special. Of course, you pay considerably more for such pampering. Most places accept credit

TOP 5 COUNTRY HOTELS

The Grove Narberth. See p.157
Llangoed Hall Bronllys. See p.213
Llwydiarth Fawr Anglesey. See p.416
Tyddyn Llan Llandrillo. See p.321
Ynyshir Hall Machynlleth. See p.286

cards, but at lower-end B&Bs you might have to **pay in cash**.

In town centres, B&Bs and guesthouses are supplemented by **hotels**, which can range from anything from rooms above a noisy bar to larger places that can be the grandest in town.

Wherever you stay, **breakfast** will almost certainly be included in the price. This may just be continental (orange juice, cereal, toast and tea or coffee), but more often will also include a full cooked breakfast of eggs, bacon, sausage, fried tomato etc. In fancier places there'll be a choice of juices, fresh fruit, yogurt and smoked fish, and perhaps Welsh dishes like Glamorgan sausages and laver bread.

A couple of free **publications** are well worth looking out for: the *Great Little Places* booklet (available online at ⓦlittle-places.co.uk), which features around fifty of the best small hotels, country inns and farmhouse B&Bs in Wales; and *Welsh Rarebits* (ⓦrarebits.co.uk), a similarly select listing of more substantial hotels and country mansions. Both websites give full coverage of all listed establishments and you can pick up the booklets at bigger tourist offices. There are also Visit Wales' comprehensive *Where to Stay* and *Farm Stay Wales* brochures, which can be ordered through its website ⓦvisitwales.co.uk.

Reservations can be made directly or through the local **tourist office** (£2 booking fee), though they will only provide information on "verified" accommodation (see box, p.34), and can

sometimes be reluctant to divulge details of places that don't advertise in the official local guide: if you don't see something suitable in the guide itself, don't be afraid to ask if there's anywhere else that matches your requirements for price and location.

Hostels and bunkhouses

Wales has 35 **hostels** operated by the **YHA** (reservations ☎0800 0191700, ⓦyha.org.uk). A few of these places are spartan establishments of the sort traditionally associated with the wholesome, fresh-air ethos of the first hostels, but many have moved well away from this institutional ambience. Welsh hostels range from some remote, simple barns in the wilds of mid-Wales and Snowdonia to relatively swanky centres in places such as Cardiff and Conwy. The greatest concentration of hostels is in Snowdonia, with smaller clusters around the Pembrokeshire coast and in the Brecon Beacons.

Prices vary according to demand, but in summer dorm beds range from £14 to £24 per night per person, with the majority around £15–20. Most hostels have self-catering facilities and many also serve breakfast (around £5); some, too, will offer a three-course dinner (around £12), as well as packed lunches (around £6). Most hostels close from 10am to 5pm and have an 11pm curfew.

Bed prices quoted in this book are for **members**: non-members are welcome but you'll be charged an extra £3 a night (£1.50 for under-18s). One year's membership of the England and Wales YHA, which is open only to residents of the EU, costs £15 per year (£5 for under-26s; £25 for two adults living at the same address), and can be obtained online or in person at any YHA hostel. Members gain automatic membership of the hostelling associations of the ninety countries affiliated to Hostelling International (HI). Visitors who are not members of the

---

ACCOMMODATION PRICES

Throughout this guide, hotel and B&B **accommodation prices** have been quoted based on the lowest price you would expect to pay per night in that establishment for a **double room in high season**, but not absolute peak rates (such as at certain bank holidays). For hostels and bunkhouses we've listed the price of a **dorm bed**, plus the price for any double or twin rooms (for YHA hostels, prices quoted are for members – non-members pay an extra £3 a night). **Campsite** prices are either listed per person, or per pitch based on two people in one tent. **Single occupancy** rates vary widely. Though typically around three-quarters of the price of a double, some places charge almost the full double rate and others charge only a little over half that.

Many establishments offer **discounts** for multiple-night stays, and/or drop their rates considerably (or offer special deals) outside the late May to early September summer season.

HI organization in their own country can join for £10 a year at any hostel.

It's always best to **book ahead**, particularly at Easter, Christmas and from May to August. If you're tempted to turn up on the spur of the moment, bear in mind that few hostels are open year-round and several have periods during which they take only group bookings.

YHA hostels still outnumber **independent hostels**, though there are a growing number of non-affiliated places offering similar facilities to YHAs, though often with a less regimented regime and no curfews or lockouts. We've mentioned the best of the independent hostels in this book but it is worth consulting ⓦindependenthostelguide.co.uk or buying *The Independent Hostel Guide* (£5.95).

These resources also list **bunkhouses** – typically more primitive affairs close to the mountains designed for hikers, climbers, mountain bikers and the like. The flashest are up to hostel standards, but many are little more than barns with toilet, shower and basic cooking facilities, starting from around £10. Bunkhouses may give preference to group bookings, and some purely cater to groups. See also ⓦbunkhousesinwales.co.uk.

Camping, caravanning and self-catering

Wales has hundreds of **campsites**, charging from around £3 per person per night for a spot in a field with a tap and a toilet, to upwards of £20 for a two-person tent at the plushest sites, where you'll find amenities such as laundries, shops and sports facilities; such places are typically used both by campers and **caravans**.

Some hostels have small campsites on their property, for which you'll pay roughly half the indoor fee. Farmers without a reserved camping area may let you pitch in a field if you ask first, and may charge you nothing for the privilege; setting

> ### TOP 5 CAMPSITES
> **Cae Du** Llangelynin. See p.292
> **Caerfai Farm** St Davids. See p.184
> **Gwern Gôf Uchaf** Ogwen Valley. See p.348
> **Rynys Farm** Betws-y-Coed. See p.342
> **Three Cliffs Caravan Park** Gower. See p.133

up a tent without asking is an act of trespass and won't be well received. Note that **wild camping** is illegal in national parks and nature reserves.

As a hangover from the days when thousands of holiday-makers from northern England and the Midlands decamped to the Welsh coast for a fortnight, many of the traditional seaside resorts are enveloped by camp upon camp of **permanently sited caravans**, rented· out for self-catering holidays. Although these can certainly be cost-effective, with facilities such as bars, shops and discos thrown in, many people prefer self-catering holidays in self-contained **cottages**, **farms**, **townhouses** or **apartments**. The usual minimum rental period is a week, though long-weekend breaks can often be arranged out of season. In midsummer or over Christmas and New Year, **prices** start at around £400 for a place sleeping four, although in winter, spring or autumn they can dip towards £250 for the same property. Some companies specializing in Welsh holiday cottages are listed opposite; tourist offices throughout Wales also have lists of self-catering holiday options.

The best of the detailed annual **directories** of Wales' camping and caravan sites are: the AA's *Caravan & Camping: Britain & Ireland*, which lists their inspected and graded sites, and *Cade's Camping, Touring and Motor Caravan Site Guide* (ⓦcades .co.uk). More niche alternatives include Rough Guides' *Camping in Britain* and the independent *Cool Camping: Wales* (ⓦcoolcamping.co.uk), both

---

THE ACCOMMODATION GRADING SYSTEM

Visit Wales operates a **grading system** for accommodation, assigning them a minimum of one star (seldom used) to a maximum of five stars, largely based on amenities rather than subjective impressions such as the general atmosphere of the place or the friendliness of its owners. Hotels are subdivided into five categories: country house hotel, small hotel, town house hotel, metro hotel and budget hotel. The term "Guest Accommodation" covers B&Bs, guesthouses, farmhouses, inns and restaurants with rooms.

To achieve a star rating, an establishment must be "verified" by Visit Wales inspectors, which ensures that you shouldn't be short-changed. For various reasons, some wonderful establishments choose to remain outside the official verification system, so the absence of a rating alone needn't be a deterrent.

with in-depth reviews of some superbly situated tent-oriented campsites.

SELF-CATERING AND FAMILY ACCOMMODATION

Asheton Eco Barns ☎ 01348 831781, ⓦ eco-barns.co.uk. Five very comfortable, low-impact units (each sleeping 4–7) fashioned from a traditional stone barn in Pembrokeshire.

Brecon Beacons Holiday Cottages ☎ 01874 676446, ⓦ breconcottages.com. Over three-hundred cottages and other buildings, some decidedly quirky, in the Brecon Beacons National Park and Wye Valley.

Coastal Cottages of Pembrokeshire ☎ 01437 765765, ⓦ coastalcottages.co.uk. Dozens of cottages, chalets, flats and houses – some with impressive leisure and activity facilities – around or near the Pembrokeshire coast.

Landmark Trust ☎ 01628 825925, ⓦ landmarktrust.org.uk. Over a dozen self-catering properties around Wales, from a seventeenth-century rural farmhouse sleeping two to a tower in Caernarfon's town walls (sleeps 5).

National Trust Holiday Cottages ☎ 0844 3351287, ⓦ national trustcottages.co.uk. Around fifty beautiful cottages all over Wales, usually with a three-night minimum. Prices vary widely through the year.

North Wales Holiday Cottages & Farmhouses ☎ 01492 582492, ⓦ northwalesholidaycottages.co.uk. Extensive array of cottages in the Snowdonia National Park and throughout the northern half of Wales, both on the coast and in the countryside.

Powell's Cottage Holidays ☎ 01834 812791, ⓦ powells.co.uk. Concentrates on properties in Pembrokeshire and the Gower.

Quality Cottages ☎ 01348 837871, ⓦ qualitycottages.co.uk. Over three-hundred cottages throughout Wales, mostly coastal.

Under the Thatch ☎ 0844 500 5101, ⓦ underthethatch.co.uk. A select choice of cottages and cabins, many beautifully restored; while most are traditional Ceredigion thatched cottages, there are also Romany caravans and yurts. Lets are generally weekly or half-weekly and most are in Pembrokeshire or the southern part of the Cambrian coast.

Wales Holidays ☎ 01686 628200, ⓦ wales-holidays.co.uk. A varied selection of over five-hundred properties all over Wales.

Food and drink

Wales is now home to some truly world-class food festivals, restaurants, farmers' markets and producers – part of the general renaissance of British cuisine combined with an increasing focus on fresh local produce. The country's natural larder includes freshly caught fish, tender local lamb and a smorgasbord of cheeses. These staple ingredients are used in everything from traditional dishes to fusion creations in some of the cities' most cosmopolitan restaurants.

Eating

Wales' culinary landscape has changed beyond all recognition in recent years, and while there are still many cafés, restaurants and pubs where you can get chips with everything, the overall standard of dining has improved dramatically. Native **Welsh cuisine** is frequently rooted in economical ingredients, but an increasing number of menus make superb use of traditional fare, such as salt-marsh lamb (best served minted or with thyme or rosemary), wonderful Welsh black beef, fresh salmon and sewin (sea trout), frequently combined with the national vegetable, the leek. Specialities include **laver bread** (*bara lawr*), edible seaweed often mixed with oats then fried with a traditional breakfast of pork sausages, egg and bacon. Other dishes well worth investigating include **Glamorgan sausages** (a spiced vegetarian combination of Caerphilly cheese, breadcrumbs and leeks), cawl (a chunky mutton broth) and cockles, trawled from the estuary north of the Gower.

The best-known of Wales' famed **cheeses** is Caerphilly, a soft, crumbly, white cheese that forms the basis of a true Welsh rarebit when mixed with beer and toasted on bread. Creamy goat's cheeses can be found all over the country, such as the superb Cothi Valley goat's cheese, as well as delicacies like organic Per Las blue cheese and Collier's mature cheddar.

Other dairy products include ice cream, which, despite the climate, is exceptionally popular, with numerous companies creating home-made ices, such as the Swansea area's Joe's Ice Cream or north Wales' Cadwaladr's.

Two traditional **cakes** are almost universal. *Welsh cakes* are flat, crumbling pancakes of sugared dough (a little like a flattened scone), while *bara brith*, a popular accompaniment to afternoon tea, literally translates as "speckled (with dried fruit) bread".

Menus featuring Welsh dishes can be found in numerous restaurants, hotels and pubs, many of which are part of **Wales the True Taste** (Cymru y Gwir Flas; ⓦ walesthetruetaste.com), a government scheme to encourage local cuisine.

Where to eat

If you're staying in a hotel, guesthouse or B&B, a hearty cooked **breakfast** (generally served 8–10am) will usually be offered as part of the deal, and may well get you through the greater part of the day. Evening meals are served from 6 to 10pm, though in rural areas – especially early in the week – you may find it difficult to get served after 8.30pm.

Cafés and **tearooms** (the terms are used pretty much interchangeably) can be found everywhere, and are generally the cheapest places to eat, providing hearty, cholesterol-laden breakfasts, a solid range of snacks and full meals for lunch (and occasionally, evening meals). Wales' steady influx of New Agers has seen the cheap and usually vegetarian **wholefood café** become a standard feature of many mid- and west Welsh towns. Cafés and restaurants are also increasingly equipped with espresso machines, though that doesn't necessarily always equate to great coffee.

Food in **pubs** varies as much as the establishments themselves, and while relatively few Welsh hostelries have done the full gastropub conversion, the standards in some pubs can now be very high. Most serve food at lunchtime and in the evening (usually until 8.30 or 9pm), and in many towns, the local pub is the most economical place (and, in smaller towns, sometimes the only place) to grab a filling evening meal.

Such places, along with **bistros** and **restaurants**, sport menus that rely extensively on fresh local produce. They can often tell you which farm the beef came from, and in coastal areas the chef may even know the fisherman. The standard of eating in Wales is also reflected in the number of restaurants holding a Michelin star, which currently stands at three.

Decent **ethnic restaurants** are still difficult to find, even in the bigger centres, though there are a clutch of outstanding Indian places in Cardiff and Swansea.

In pubs and cafés you can expect to **pay** £6–10 for a main course, closer to £15 in good restaurants and around £20 in the very best places; sample prices are given for each review.

Drinking

As elsewhere in Britain, daytime cafés are not usually licensed to sell alcohol, and though restaurants invariably are, **pubs** remain the centre of social activity. The legal drinking age is 18, though an adult can order alcohol for someone aged 16 or 17 who is dining. Some places offer special family rooms for people with children, and beer gardens where younger kids can run free.

Pubs

Welsh pubs vary as much as the landscape, from opulent Edwardian palaces of smoked glass, gleaming brass and polished mahogany in the larger towns and cities, to thick-set stone barns in wild, remote countryside. Where the church has faltered as a community focal point, the pub often still holds sway, with those in smaller towns and villages, in particular, functioning as community centres as much as places in which to drink alcohol. Live music – and, this being Wales, singing – frequently round off an evening. As a rule of thumb, if a pub has both a **bar** and a **lounge**, the bar will be more basic and frequently very male-dominated, while the lounge will tend to be plusher, more mixed and probably a better bet for a passing visitor.

Opening times vary but typically are Monday to Saturday 11am to 11pm, Sunday noon to 10.30pm, with many quieter places closed between 3 and 6pm, particularly throughout the week. "Last orders" are called by the bar staff about fifteen minutes before closing time. Liberalization of licensing laws has allowed pubs to stay open later, but with the exception of city centres most places stick close to the standard hours.

What to drink

Beer, sold by the pint (generally £2.50–3.50) and half pint (half the price), is the staple drink in Wales, as it is throughout the British Isles. Traditionalists drink **real ale**, an uncarbonated beer, usually hand-pumped from the cellar but sometimes served straight from the cask; it comes in many varieties (some seasonal), including the almost ubiquitous deep-flavoured **bitter**, but sometimes mild, or **dark** as it is often known in Wales. **Lager**, which corresponds with European and American ideas of beer, is also stocked everywhere. Also quite common is the sweeter and darker **porter**. Irish **stout** (Guinness, Murphy's or Beamish) is widely available.

There's been a real renaissance in the Welsh brewing industry in recent years, and you can now find some superb independent **breweries** right

TOP 5 FOOD PUBS

Bunch of Grapes Pontypridd. See p.112
Felin Fach Griffin Brecon. See p.210
Tŷ Gwyn Betws-y-Coed. See p.343
The White Eagle Rhoscolyn. See p.426
Y Polyn Nantgaredig. See p.146

across the country. The most widely known is Cardiff-based Brains, whose heady brews include SA and Dark, while, also in the south, there's Llanelli-based **Felinfoel**, with Double Dragon Premium bitter the aromatic ace in their pack. Others worth looking out for include the Tomos Watkin brewery in Swansea, Evan Evans from Llandeilo, and Otley from Pontypridd. There's no shortage of great breweries in mid- and north Wales either, with Monty's from Montgomery, and Purple Moose from Porthmadog currently going great guns.

Many pubs are owned by large, UK-wide breweries which sell only their own products, so if you are interested in seeking out distinctive brews, choose your pub carefully. The best resource for any serious hophead is the annual *Good Beer Guide* produced by **CAMRA** (the Campaign for Real Ale; ⓦ camra.org.uk): if you see a recent CAMRA sticker in a pub window, chances are the beer will be well worth sampling.

As in other Celtic regions, **cider** has a huge following; look out for Orchard Gold (a traditional farmhouse apple cider) and Perry Vale (pear cider), both made by the Welsh Cider and Perry Company (Gwynt y Ddraig).

Pubs and off-licences (liquor stores) increasingly stock a growing range of Welsh **spirits**; the biggest recent success story is the Penderyn distillery on the southern edge of the Brecon Beacons National Park, which produces signature single malt whiskies as well as Merlyn (cream liquor), Five (vodka) and Brecon gin.

There are also a number of Welsh **wines** available, though you rarely see these offered on restaurant wine lists. Wines sold in pubs have improved considerably in recent years, although the best world selections tend to be found in the places serving good food. Few restaurants have a good selection of wines by the glass, generally offering little more than a house white and a house red.

The media

The media that you will encounter in Wales is a hybrid of Welsh and Britain-wide information. Although the London-based UK media attempts to cover life in the other corners of Britain, few people would agree that Wales receives a fair share of coverage in any medium. Of all the solely Welsh media, newspapers are probably the weakest area, and periodicals and TV coverage the strongest and most interesting.

Newspapers and magazines

The **British daily newspapers** are all available in Wales, but news of Wales is not terribly well covered – even the goings-on at the Welsh Assembly in Cardiff are rarely analyzed, let alone any other area of Welsh life. The only quality **Welsh daily** is the *Western Mail* (ⓦ walesonline.co.uk), a sometimes uneasy mix of Welsh Assembly, wider Welsh and British news and a token smattering of international affairs coupled with populist lifestyle pap and features on celebrities. From the same stable is Wales' national **Sunday paper**, *Wales on Sunday*.

What the *Western Mail* is to south Wales, the *Daily Post* (ⓦ dailypost.co.uk) is to the north of the country, with a fairly decent spectrum of news and features that marks it out from other local dailies. All areas have their own long-standing **weekly papers**, generally an entertaining mix of local news, parish gossip and events listings.

Go into any bookshop in Wales, and you'll be surprised by the profusion of Welsh **magazines**, in both English and Welsh. For a broad overview of the arts, history and politics, it's hard to beat *Planet* (ⓦ planetmagazine.org.uk), an English-language bimonthly that takes a politically irreverent line, combining Welsh interest with a wider cultural and international outlook. The more serious English-language quarterly *New Welsh Review* (ⓦ newwelshreview.com) is steeped in Wales' political, literary and economic developments, while *Poetry Wales* (ⓦ poetrywales.co.uk) is an excellent publication of new writing. The bimonthly glossy *Cambria* (ⓦ cambriamagazine.com) subtitles itself as "Wales's Magazine", an epithet that it's doing its best to fulfil with sparky writing on all matters Cymric, together with superb photography. For a wider view of Welsh social issues, with insights into "alternative" culture and news, pick up the weekly *Big Issue Cymru*, sold by homeless vendors on the streets of major towns and cities. If you're half-proficient in Welsh, the weekly news digest *Y Cymro* is an essential read, although younger, funkier features can be found in the weekly glossy *Golwg*, and more political topics are chewed over in the monthly *Barn*. If you're attempting to master the language, try *Lingo Newydd* magazine, aimed at learners at all levels.

Television and radio

In marked contrast to the London-centric print media, **TV and radio** are wholeheartedly moving out of southeast England. Cardiff is home to the Welsh branches of devolved broadcasting organizations including the BBC and ITV, and indigenous Welsh operators such as S4C.

The state-funded BBC (Wbbc.co.uk/wales) operates two **TV** channels in Wales – the mainstream **BBC One Wales** and the more esoteric **BBC Two Wales**. They may sound avowedly Welsh, but the vast majority of programming is UK-wide, with Welsh programmes, principally news and sport, but also features, political and education programmes, slotted into the regular schedules. This is even more the case with the determinedly populist **ITV Wales** (Witv.com/wales).

The principal **Welsh channel** is **S4C** (*Sianel Pedwar Cymru*, verbally "*ess pedwar eck*"; Ws4c .co.uk), which has grown from shaky beginnings (see box, p.445) to become a major player, sponsoring diverse projects including Welsh animation and feature films. These include the Oscar-nominated films *Hedd Wyn* and *Solomon a Gaenor* and the terrifically tasteless prehistoric cartoon *Gogs*. It now broadcasts solely in Welsh and each weeknight includes a dose of the BBC's longest-running TV soap, *Pobol y Cwm* (*People of the Valley*). The sister English-language Channel 4 is also available throughout Wales.

The BBC is also a major player in **radio**, with five UK networks, all broadcasting in Wales: Radio One combines pop with a slick interpretation of youth and dance culture; Two is pop and rock skewed to those in their 30s and 40s; Three is classical and jazz; Four offers a passionately loved ragbag of magazine shows, current affairs, drama, arts and highbrow quizzes; and Five Live broadcasts a constant, entertaining mix of news and sport. The BBC also operates two stations in Wales alone: **BBC Radio Wales**, a competent, if gentle, English-language service of news, features and music, with occasional dashes of élan, and **BBC Radio Cymru**, a similarly easy-going mix in the Welsh language. Both can often be more entertaining in the evening and at weekends, away from the daytime tyranny of rolling news, sport, weather and traffic congestion.

Of the commercial stations, the brashest is Radio One soundalike **Capital FM**, serving Cardiff, Newport and around, together with **Capital Gold**, its twin for news, features and the greatest hits and oldies music. Also in the capital and along the south coast is **Heart Radio** with its twin station, **Heart North Wales**, operating out of Wrexham; both are good for music, sport and phone-ins. **Kiss 101**, meanwhile, provides dance, hip hop and drum n' bass for the masses. **Swansea Sound**, whose reception extends west towards Pembrokeshire, is solid and frequently interesting. There are bilingual services from **Radio Ceredigion** and **Radio Pembrokeshire** on the west coast, **Radio Carmarthenshire** inland and **Champion FM** around Caernarfon and Bangor.

Festivals and events

Ranging from the epic to the absurd, Wales' wealth of festivals sees all walks of life partying in muddy fields across the country. Many of the events on the nation's annual calendar are uniquely Welsh with an ancient pedigree, notably eisteddfodau – age-old competitions in poetry and music – that still form the backbone of national culture.

Many towns and cities now have annual **arts festivals** of some kind, mentioned throughout the Guide, and, in the case of the major events, in the list below. There are numerous other events with a distinctly surreal edge – from the Cilgerran **coracle races** (see p.268) to bizarre happenings like peat-bog snorkelling competitions in Llanwrytd (see p.225), and parading around Llangynwyd village (see p.118) with a horse's skull to welcome in the new year (the Mari Lwyd). Wales is now host to some of the UK's best summer **rock and pop music festivals**, in addition to some excellent **DJ-led events** and New Age **fairs**; these are usually publicized by handbills, posters in wholefood shops and cafés, and word of mouth.

Events calendar

Visit Wales maintains a fairly comprehensive events list at Wvisitwales.com, and we've covered folk festivals in Contexts (see p.455).

JANUARY–APRIL

Mari Lwyd (Jan 1; Wfolkwales.org.uk/mari.html) At Llangynwyd, near Maesteg, the most authentic survivor of the ancient Welsh custom of parading a horse's skull through the village streets.

Six Nations rugby championship (Feb–March) Wales plays five matches, two or three of which are played in the Millennium Stadium; Wales last won the championship in 2013.

St Davids Day (March 1) Wales' national day, with *hwyrnos* (late nights) and celebrations nationwide.

Wonderwool Wales (Late April; ⓦ wonderwoolwales.co.uk) At the Royal Welsh Showground in Builth Wells, this two-day gathering showcases the best of Welsh wool and wool products, from raw materials to designer fashion – with plenty of sheep on show too.

MAY

Tredegar House Folk Festival (Early May; ⓦ tredegarhouse festival.org.uk) A weekend of international dance, music and song at this grand seventeenth-century mansion.

Hay Festival (Late May to early June; ⓦ hayfestival.com) One of the most feted literary festivals in the world; this huge gathering has also spawned a dedicated festival for children and HowTheLightGetsIn, a unique festival of philosophy and music. (see p.223).

St Davids Cathedral Festival (End of May to first week in June; ⓦ stdavidscathedralfestival.co.uk) Superb setting for classical and contemporary concerts, and recitals over ten days.

Urdd National Eisteddfod (Last week of May; ⓦ urdd.org) Vast and enjoyable youth eisteddfod – one of the largest youth festivals in Europe – that's held in a different part of the country each year.

JUNE

Great Welsh Beer & Cider Festival (Early June; ⓦ gwbcf.org.uk) Three days to sample from nearly three hundred ales and two hundred ciders (the majority from Welsh breweries) in the Millennium Stadium.

Cardiff Singer of the World competition (Mid-June; ⓦ bbc .co.uk/cardiffsinger) Huge, televised week-long festival of music and song held in odd-numbered years, with a star-studded list of international opera and classical singers.

Criccieth Festival (Mid-June; ⓦ cricciethfestival.co.uk) Music, theatre and art around the Llŷn town.

Gregynog Festival (Last half of June; ⓦ gwylgregynogfestival .org) Classical music festival in the superb country house surroundings of Gregynog Hall near Newtown, Powys.

Gŵyl Ifan (Mid-June; ⓦ gwylifan.org) A weekend of folk-dancing workshops, displays and processions in various locations in and around Cardiff.

Man Versus Horse Marathon (Mid-June; ⓦ green-events.co.uk) A 22-mile race at Llanwrtyd Wells, Powys, between runners and horses with both equine and human winners in its time.

Pembrokeshire Fish Week (end June; ⓦ pembrokeshirefishweek .co.uk) Guided beach walks, boat trips, snorkel safaris and learn-to-fish sessions, alongside all manner of other coastal jollity at this week-long festival.

Cardiff Festival (June–Sept; ⓦ cardiff-festival.com) Broad-brush festival encompassing theatre, sport, the Cardiff Food and Drink Festival, and lots more.

JULY

Beyond the Border (Early July; ⓦ beyondtheborder.com)

Three-day international storytelling festival at the fairy-tale setting of St Donat's Castle, Vale of Glamorgan, held every even-numbered year.

Cardigan Bay Seafood Festival (Early July; ⓦ aberaeron.info /seafood) At Aberaeron, Dyfed, some of Wales' best chefs whip up delicious morsels.

Gower Festival (First half of July; ⓦ gowerfestival.org) Two weeks of mostly classical music in churches around the Gower.

Llangollen International Eisteddfod (First or second week in July; ⓦ international-eisteddfod.co.uk) Over twelve thousand participants from all over the world attend, including choirs, dancers, folk singers, groups and instrumentalists (see box, p.312).

Wakestock (Mid-July; ⓦ wakestock.co.uk) Big, bold three-day wakeboarding and music festival in north Wales, attracting up to ten thousand bleached-haired punters for cutting-edge headline acts, top DJs and spectacular wakeboarding.

Really Wild Food & Countryside Festival (Late July; ⓦ really wildfestival.co.uk) St Davids comes alive for a weekend of rural traditions, music, storytelling and great food.

Royal Welsh Show (Late July; ⓦ rwas.co.uk) Europe's largest agricultural show and sales fair at Builth Wells; an absolute Welsh institution and a top day out. You can watch the ultra-serious judging of prize farm animals, competitive sheep-shearing or wood chopping, displays of falconry and craftsmanship, or simply feast on farm-fresh produce. Hundreds of stallholders sell everything from artisan products to agricultural equipment (see p.228).

Snowdon Race (Late July; ⓦ snowdonrace.co.uk) A ten-mile race from Llanberis to the summit of Snowdon and back down again; attracting masochists from across the world, the best runners record times of just over an hour.

The Big Cheese (Late July; ⓦ caerphilly.gov.uk/bigcheese) Tasting aside, this massive town festival – taking place mostly within the grounds of Caerphilly Castle – features re-enactments, craft stalls, a traditional fun fair and a Big Cheese Race (see p.110).

AUGUST

Royal National Eisteddfod (First week in Aug; ⓦ eisteddfod.org .uk) The centrepiece of Welsh culture (originally meaning "a meeting of bards"), this is very much a Welsh festival (largely conducted in Cymraeg) and is Wales' biggest single annual event. The vast maes (field) hosts art, craft, literature, rock music, Welsh-language lessons, theatre and major music and poetry competitions. Venues alternate each year.

Brecon Jazz Festival (Mid-Aug; ⓦ breconjazz.co.uk) Three-day jazz festival widely regarded as one of the best in Britain.

Croissant Neuf Summer Party (Mid-Aug; ⓦ partyneuf.co.uk) Small, friendly and green weekend festival near Usk that's always fun and especially good for families.

Green Man Festival (Mid-Aug; ⓦ greenman.net) Near Crickhowell, this is one of the UK's premier music festivals, featuring an always sparkling line-up (see p.214).

Pride Cymru (Mid-Aug; ⓦ cardiffmardigras.co.uk) Cardiff's lesbian and gay festival takes over Coopers Field with live music, market stalls and bars.

Gŵyl Machynlleth (Late Aug; ⓦ momawales.org.uk) Wide-ranging arts festival, with a solid programme of chamber music at its core.

Llandrindod Wells Victorian Festival (Late Aug; ⓦ victorianfestival.co.uk) A week of family fun, street entertainment and Victorian costumes rounded off with a fireworks display.

World Alternative Games (Aug; ⓦ worldalternativegames .co.uk) Set up in response to the London Olympics in 2012, this two-week event (every two years) features utterly bonkers events like gravy wrestling, synchronized bath-tubbing and wife carrying.

World Bog Snorkelling Championships (Aug Bank Holiday Sun; ⓦ green-events.co.uk) Muddy swim-off along a 180ft-long bog course at Llanwrtyd Wells, Powys.

SEPTEMBER

Festival No6 (beginning Sept; ⓦ festivalnumber6.com) Superb, sophisticated new festival set in atmospheric Portmeirion, with a typically wide ranging selection of music, from the Manic Street Preachers to the Welsh Male Voice Choir. DJs, comedy, film and poetry too.

Abergavenny Food Festival (Mid-Sept; ⓦ abergavenny foodfestival.com) This weekend chow-down is Wales's premier gastronomic event ., with a smorgasbord of fresh food showcased by celebrity chefs.

Tenby Arts Festival (Late Sept; ⓦ tenbyartsfest.co.uk) Well-established week-long arts romp in Tenby, with a lively fringe too.

OCTOBER

Swansea Festival of Music and the Arts (Oct; ⓦ swanseafestival.org) Two weeks of stellar quality music, theatre, dance and art throughout the city.

Sŵn (Mid- to late Oct; ⓦ swnfest.com) Superb four-day happening showcasing the best in new music in Wales; takes place at various venues around Cardiff.

NOVEMBER–DECEMBER

Bonfire Night and Lantern Parade (Early Nov) Superb procession in Machynlleth, culminating in fireworks and performance.

Dylan Thomas Festival (Early Nov; ⓦ dylanthomas.com) Celebrating their hometown son, there are talks, performances, exhibitions, readings and music throughout Swansea.

Real Ale Wobble (Mid-Nov; ⓦ green-events.co.uk) Non-competitive mountain biking and real-ale drinking over 15, 25 or 35 miles at Llanwrtyd Wells, Powys.

New Year's Eve celebrations (Dec 31) New Quay in Dyfed is *the* place to party on New Year's Eve.

Sport and outdoor activities

With craggy mountains, large areas of moorland, a deeply indented coastline, wide beaches and fast-flowing rivers, Wales makes a fabulous outdoor playground – you're never far from a stretch of countryside where you can lose the crowds on a brief walk or cycle ride. The short day-hikes are some of the best anywhere, while keen walkers can hike a skyline ridge or tackle a long-distance path over a couple of visits or in one epic tramp. Mountain bikers coarse around the popular forest bike parks, while road options include many wonderfully scenic, little-frequented back roads. Elsewhere, the mountains and cliffs provide scope for fabulous rock climbing and thrilling coasteering trips. Along the coasts, watersports prevail, notably surfing, but also the growing sports of kiteboarding and wakeboarding. And there are plenty of fine beaches for less structured fresh-air activities.

Walking

There isn't a built-up area in Wales that's more than half an hour away from some decent walking country, but three areas are so outstanding they have been designated **national parks**. Most of Wales' northwestern corner is taken up with the **Snowdonia National Park**, comprising a dozen of the country's highest peaks separated by dramatic glaciated valleys, and laced with hundreds of miles of ridge and moorland paths. From Snowdonia, the Cambrian Mountains stretch south to the **Brecon Beacons National Park**, with its striking sandstone scarp at the head of the south Wales coalfield and

---

SAFETY IN THE WELSH HILLS

Welsh **mountains** are not high by world standards, but they should still be treated with respect. The fickle weather makes them more dangerous than you might expect, and you can easily find yourself disoriented in the low cloud and soaked by unexpected rain. If the weather looks like it's closing in, get down fast. It is essential that you are properly equipped – even for what appears to be an easy expedition in apparently settled weather – with proper warm and waterproof layered clothing, supportive footwear, adequate maps, a compass, food and water. Always tell someone your route and expected time of return – and call when you get back so that they know you're safe.

TOP 5 WALKS

Aberglaslyn Gorge Beddgelert. See p.362
Cwm Idwal Ogwen Valley. See p.347
Dinas Head Newport. See p.151
Port Eynon to Rhossili via Worms Head
Gower. See p.132
Precipice Walk Dolgellau. See p.294

lush, cave-riddled limestone valleys to the south. One hundred and seventy miles of Wales's south-western peninsula make up the third park, the **Pembrokeshire Coast National Park**, best explored along the **Pembrokeshire Coast Path**, one of Wales's wonderful designated **long-distance paths** (see p.42).

Unless you're doing your walking on out-of-season weekdays, don't expect to have the major trails in the national parks to yourself. Many of the best one-day walks in the country are detailed in this Guide, but for more arduous mountain treks, you'll benefit from bringing a specialist walking guidebook (see p.464), which are widely available. You can get more information from The Ramblers' Association (☎029 2064 4308, ⓦramblers.org.uk /wales), Britain's main countryside campaigning organization and self-appointed guardian of the nation's footpaths and rights of way.

Rights of access

Although they are managed by committees of local and state officials, all three Welsh national parks are predominantly privately owned. Until recently it was the goodwill of landowners that gave access to much of the land, but the 2005 **Countryside and Rights of Way Act** (CRoW) gives open access on foot (but not generally by bike or horse) to "all land that is predominantly mountain, moor, heath or down" across Wales. Such areas (almost a fifth of the country) are marked on all new Ordnance Survey maps, and at boundaries you'll see a brown "walking man" sign. Landowners are, however, allowed to restrict access for a number of reasons and signs are posted locally.

Access to other land is restricted to **public rights of way**: **footpaths** (pedestrians only; yellow waymarkers), **bridleways** (pedestrians, horses and bicycles; blue waymarkers) and **byways** (open to all traffic, but generally unsurfaced; red waymarkers) that have seen continued use over the centuries. Historically, these are often over narrow mountain passes between two hamlets, or linking villages to mines or summer pastureland. Rights of way are marked on Ordnance Survey maps (see p.50) and

are indicated from roads with signposts, and inter-mittently waymarked across the countryside; any stiles and gates on the path have to be maintained by the landowner. Some less scrupulous owners have been known to block rights of way by destroying stiles – and with some walkers wilfully straying from official rights of way, some resentment is perhaps understandable. Disputes are uncommon, but your surest way of avoiding trouble is to meticulously follow the right of way on an up-to-date map.

Ordnance Survey maps also indicate routes with **concessionary path** or **courtesy path** status, where access is given over private land at the goodwill of the owner; though these are usually open for public use they can be closed at any time.

Some places to stay that are particularly geared to walkers display a "Walkers Welcome" sticker in their window and on their website.

WALKING HOLIDAY OPERATORS

Celtic Trails ⓦ celtic-trails.com
Contours Walking Holidays ⓦ contours.co.uk
Drover Holidays ⓦ droverholidays.co.uk
Footpath Holidays ⓦ footpath-holidays.com
Walkabout Wales ⓦ walkabout-wales.com
Walkalongway ⓦ walkalongway.com

Rock climbing and scrambling

As well as being superb walking country, Snowdonia offers some of Britain's best **rock climbing** and several challenging **scrambles** – ascents that fall somewhere between walks and climbs, requiring the use of your hands. One or two of the tougher walks included in the text have sections of scrambling, but for the most part this is a specialist discipline, well covered in books available locally.

The scale may not be huge (the highest route only takes you up 800ft), but the quality is excellent, and there's an astonishing variety of routes in a small area. In fact, the term "cragging" comes from *craig*, Welsh for cliff. **Llanberis**, at the foot of Snowdon, is the home of Welsh climbing, with routes ranging from easy hands-on scrambles up

TOP 5 MOUNTAIN HIKES

Glyder Traverse Ogwen Valley. See p.347
North Ridge Tryfan. See p.346
Pen y Fan/Corn Du Brecon Beacons.
See p.206
Pony Path Cadair Idris. See p.294
Snowdon Horseshoe Snowdon. See p.354

mountain ridges to impossibly difficult climbs only achievable by the world's best climbers.

Further south, the pick of the crags are the limestone sea cliffs along the **Pembrokeshire coast**: the bulk of the action happens near Bosherston. The military ordnance testing areas of Range East and Range West here mean that parts of the coast are off limits, but there are plenty of areas with much freer access. Further east, the Gower peninsula is also ringed by tempting sea cliffs.

Beginners should contact Plas y Brenin: The National Mountain Centre (Ⓦ pyb.co.uk) or the British Mountaineering Council (Ⓦ thebmc.co.uk), which can put you in touch with climbing guides and people running courses.

Cycling

Wales now ranks as one of Britain's premier **cycling** destinations, with a complex web of traffic-free bike paths, off-road tracks and low-traffic cycle routes, plus some excellent mountain bike parks. Back road routes along river valleys and over mountain passes have a sufficient density of pubs and B&Bs to keep the days manageable, and while steep gradients can be a problem, ascents are never long, with Wales' highest pass barely reaching 1500ft. In urban areas, though, cyclists are still largely treated with disrespect by many motorized road users and by the people who plan the country's traffic systems. If you plan to ride in built-up areas, get a **helmet** and a secure **lock**.

Transporting your bike by **train** is a good way of getting to the interesting parts of Wales without a lot of stressful pedalling. Bikes are generally carried free on suburban trains outside the weekday rush hours of 7.30 to 9.30am and 4 to 6pm. On most routes in Wales there is only space for two bikes and you are expected to make a reservation (free; ☎ 0870 9000 773), though they'll accept unreserved bikes if there is space. On inter-city routes, say from England into Wales, space is still very limited but free reservations are accepted. Arriva's free *Cycling by Train* brochure (downloadable from Ⓦ arrivatrainswales.co.uk/Bicycles) and *National Rail Cycling by Train* (from Ⓦ nationalrail.co.uk) are both useful resources.

Bike rental is available at bike shops in some large towns (outlined throughout the Guide) and many resorts, and the quality of bikes is improving. Expect to pay in the region of £20–25 per day, or more for specialist off-road machines with suspension.

Places to stay that are particularly geared to cyclists often have a "Cyclists Welcome" sticker in their window and on their website.

Cycle touring routes

The best of Wales's narrow lanes, disused railway lines and forest paths have been linked together to

---

HEROIC HIKES AND LENGTHY RAMBLES

Wales is traced by a spider's web of over a dozen wonderful long-distance paths (LDPs). Three of these – the Pembrokeshire Coast Path, Offa's Dyke Path and Glyndŵr's Way – are additionally designated National Trails, waymarked at frequent intervals by an acorn symbol. The following is a brief rundown of the most popular LDPs.

All Wales Coastal Path (870 miles) Opened in 2012, the coastal path (Wales is the only country in the world to provide a dedicated footpath along its entire coast) links Chepstow (Severn estuary) in the south with Queensferry in the north; it's split into eight geographical areas, and incorporates many already established paths like the Pembrokeshire Coast Path, the Llŷn Coastal Path and the Anglesey Coastal Path.

Cambrian Way (275 miles; Ⓦ cambrianway.org.uk) The longest, wildest and most arduous of the Welsh LDPs, cutting north–south over the remote Cambrian Mountains.

Glyndŵr's Way (135 miles; Ⓦ nationaltrail.co.uk /glyndwrsway) A lengthy meander among the remote mountains and lakes of mid-Wales, visiting sites associated with the great fifteenth-century Welsh hero. See p.238.

Landsker Borderlands Trail (60 miles; Ⓦ ldwa.org.uk) Gentle waterways, quiet villages and easy trails characterize this slightly contrived circular walk around the Landsker region in Pembrokeshire.

Offa's Dyke Path (177 miles) The classic Welsh LDP, running from Prestatyn in the north to Chepstow in south Wales, tracing the line of the eighth-century earthwork along the English border for a third of the way. A blend of wooded lowland walking and higher hilltops, with exhilarating open territory through the Black Mountains. See p.239.

Pembrokeshire Coast Path (186 miles) Almost all within the Pembrokeshire National Park, this hugely rewarding coastal trail dips into quiet coves and climbs over headlands, with sweeping ocean views and plenty of birdlife on the cliffs and offshore islands. See p.161.

Wye Valley Walk (136 miles; Ⓦ wyevalleywalk.org) A lovely, sylvan, sea-to-source trek following the River Wye from Chepstow to Plynlimon, beginning with a long section through a dramatic wooded gorge. The English section visits Ross-on-Wye and Hereford. See p.61.

form **cycle routes** as part of the National Cycle Network created by **Sustrans** (W sustrans.org.uk). Set up in 1977, this charity promotes sustainable transport, principally by developing cycling routes – over 10,000 miles have been created, 1200 of them in Wales, of which a quarter are traffic-free. The entire network is covered in the official *Cycling* handbook *in the UK* (£20).

Three major cycling routes cross Wales. The main north–south **Lôn Las Cymru** (the Welsh National Route; Route 8) was opened in 1996 and covers 250 hilly miles from Anglesey, through Snowdonia, the Brecon Beacons and the industrial valleys of the south, to the Severn Bridge. Sustrans publishes two maps of the route (£7 each), one covering Holyhead to Builth Wells and the other from Builth Wells to Chepstow and Cardiff. **Lôn Geltaidd** (Celtic Trail East; Route 4; map £7) traverses 186 miles across the south of the country (seventy percent of it traffic-free) from Fishguard to the Severn Bridge. Along the north coast the busy roads are avoided on the **North Wales Coast Route** (Route 5). In addition there are numerous other local routes, sometimes on dedicated traffic-free paths but often directed along quiet lanes; free leaflets available locally are easy to follow. Areas worth considering are the Gower peninsula, Pembrokeshire, Anglesey, the Llŷn and the supremely unspoilt and fairly challenging three-day **Radnor Ring**, near Llandrindod Wells.

Mountain biking

Since the 1990s, the forests of Wales have gained an enviable reputation for top-class **mountain biking**. Every weekend mud-splattered bikers weave along miles of single-track at the thirteen dedicated **bike parks** dotted along the mountainous spine of the country – from the Gwydyr Forest just outside Betws-y-Coed to Cwm Carn in the Valleys northwest of Newport. There's something to suit everyone, from beginners to hardened speed freaks. There's no charge for using them (though there may be a small parking fee), and though bike rental facilities are improving, you may be better off bringing your own machine or renting one from a nearby town.

Elsewhere, off-road cycling is allowed along designated bridleways (waymarked with blue arrows), including the Snowdon Ranger, Rhyd Ddu and Llanberis paths up Snowdon (see p.354), but conflict between hikers and bikers has led to the creation of the **Snowdon Voluntary Cycling Agreement**, which limits the hours riders can use

them. Anytime in winter (Oct–April) is OK and you can ride before 10am and after 5pm throughout the summer: slog up in the pre-dawn cool for that summit sunrise, or head up for sunset and a nerve-wracking dusk descent.

If you really fancy a challenge, make for **Sarn Helen**, an epic route across the country through Snowdonia and the Brecon Beacons, loosely following an old Roman route. At 270 miles long – running from Conwy to Gower – it's reckoned to be the most ambitious off-road ride in Britain and is likely to take over a week.

Footpaths, unless otherwise marked, are for pedestrian use only, and even on bridleways you should always pass walkers at a considerate speed and with a courteous warning of your presence.

For more **information** check out: W mbwales .com, which concentrates on the main bike parks, or W mtbtrailfinder.co.uk, which has excellent articles on routes, along with groups where you can hook up with other riders. Local bookshops and bike stores stock relevant guides.

The CTC and holidays

Britain's biggest **cycling organization**, the Cyclists' Touring Club (CTC: W ctc.org.uk), supplies members with touring and technical advice as well as insurance. Its website has a wealth of information, including dozens of routes through Wales.

If you want a guaranteed hassle-free **cycling holiday**, various companies offer easy-going tours where you ride from hotel to hotel, and a van carries your bags. Some give you an arranged itinerary, while others guide you.

CYCLE TOUR OPERATORS

Bicycle Beano T 01981 560471, W bicycle-beano.co.uk. Book well ahead to join Bicycle Beano on three-day (Northern Welsh borders; £420) and week-long cycling holidays (Snowdonia; £780). They pedal along with you and rides include accommodation and all meals (except lunch). They're a lot of fun, good value for money and the cooking is vegetarian (and often organic).

Crwydro Môn T 01248 713611, W angleseywalkingholidays .com/cycling.html. Tailored, week-long, self-guided packages (from £325) around Anglesey with bike, B&B and luggage transfer included.

Drover Holidays T 01497 821134, W droverholidays.co.uk. Over a dozen guided and self-guided bike tours all over Wales with everything organized and even the option of an electrically assisted bike to help with the nastier hills.

Wheely Wonderful Cycling T 01568 770755, W wheely wonderfulcycling.co.uk. Several self-guided tours around wonderfully rural sections of mid-Wales and the borders, from a weekend to a week (£185–640).

TOP 5 BEACHES
Barafundle Bay Pembrokeshire. See p.160
Porth Dinllaen The Llŷn. See p.384
Rhossili Bay Gower. See p.132
Tresaith near New Quay. See p.260
Ynyslas near Borth. See p.280

Coastal activites

Wales is ringed by fine **beaches** and **bays**, many of which are readily accessible by public transport – though some tend to get very busy in high summer. With most of the Welsh coast influenced by the currents of the North Atlantic Drift, water temperatures are higher than you might expect for this latitude, but only the truly hardy should consider swimming outside summer. For swimming and sunbathing, the best areas to head for are the Gower peninsula, the Pembrokeshire coast, the Llŷn and the southwest coast of Anglesey. Though it has more resorts than any other section of Wales' coastline, the north coast certainly hasn't got the most attractive beaches, nor is it a particularly alluring place to swim. **Wild swimming** is popular all over Wales, the country's many wonderful lakes and rivers providing ample opportunities for a refreshing dip.

Wales' southwest-facing beaches offer the best conditions for **surfing**, **windsurfing** and **kiteboarding**. The water may not be that warm, but great sweeping beaches lashed by strong, steady winds off the Atlantic make for some excellent spots. Key centres are Rhosneigr on Anglesey, Aberdyfi along the Cambrian coast, Whitesands Bay (Porth-mawr) near St Davids, and Rhossili on the Gower peninsula near Swansea. All these places have shops selling gear and offering lessons. Kiteboarding isn't exactly an easy sport to learn, but a class can get you body-dragging (more fun than it sounds) inside a day, and actually riding a board in a couple of days. For surfing information, contact the Welsh Surfing Federation Surf School (☎01792 386426, ⓦwsfsurfschool.co.uk) on the Gower peninsula.

If you'd rather surf indoors, Swansea's state-of-the-art LC leisure complex (☎01792 466500, ⓦthelcswansea.com) features the "Board Rider" surfing wave machine, with beginner, intermediate and advanced surfing lessons available; there are similar facilities at Cardiff's superb International White Water Centre (☎029 2082 9970, ⓦciww.com).

Wales may not be at the cutting edge of adventure sports, but it led the way with **coasteering**, an exhilarating combination of hiking, coastal scrambling, swimming and cliff-jumping. Clad in a wetsuit, helmet and buoyancy aid, you aim to make your way as a group along the rugged, wave-lashed coastline. It was pioneered by St Davids-based TYF Adventure (see p.183), which runs a range of trips, from the relatively tame to full-on blasts along the coast and even eco-trips suited to families.

Kayaking and rafting

Board riders constantly have to compete for waves with the surf ski riders and **kayakers** who frequent the same beaches. Paddlers, however, have the additional run of miles of superb coastline, particularly around Anglesey, the Llŷn and the Pembrokeshire coast. The best general guide is the encyclopaedic *Welsh Sea Kayaking* (£20) by Jim Krawiecki and Andy Biggs.

Inland, short, steep bedrock rivers come alive after rain. As equipment improves, paddlers have become more daring, and Victorian tourist attractions such as Swallow and Conwy falls, both near Betws-y-Coed, are now fair game for a descent. Most of the kayaking is non-competitive, but on summer weekends you might catch a slalom or freestyle kayaking event at the National Whitewater Centre (☎01678 521083, ⓦukrafting.co.uk), outside Bala, or at the Cardiff International White Water Centre. In both places you can ride the rapids in rafts. The best whitewater resource is ⓦcanoewales.com.

Pony trekking

Wales's scattered population and large tracts of open land are ideal for **pony trekking**. Don't expect too much cantering over unfenced land: rides tend to be geared towards unhurried appreciation of the scenery from horseback and are often combined with accommodation on farms. Rates are typically around £20 for the first hour and £10–15 for each subsequent hour.

Mid-Wales has the greatest concentration of stables, but there are places all over the country, amply detailed in the brochures supplied by the Wales Trekking and Riding Association (☎01497 847464, ⓦridingwales.com).

Rugby

Rugby (the "Union" variety) is a passion with the Welsh and their national game. Support is strongest in the working-class valleys of south

Wales, where the fanaticism has traditionally been fuelled by the national side's success. Welsh rugby saw its glory days in the 1970s, when Wales turned out some of the best teams ever seen. The scarlet jerseys regularly dominated the annual **Five Nations Championship** (now superseded by the Six Nations Championship, with the addition of Italy), winning six out of the ten championships – three of them **Grand Slams** (where every match is won). This formidable side included fearless fullback J.P.R. Williams, the elusive and magical outside-halves Barry John and Phil Bennett, and the dynamic scrum-half Gareth Edwards.

The 1980s and most of the 1990s were barren times, but when rugby turned professional in 1995, it was able to coax back players who had defected to the rival code, rugby league. Although Wales generally struggled to keep up with the standards of arch adversary England throughout the 1990s, let alone the all-conquering southern hemisphere sides, the recruitment of New Zealander Graham Henry in 1998, and the building of the new 72,500-seater **Millennium Stadium**, coincided with a gradual reversal in the national side's fortunes.

Although Wales only managed to get to the quarter-finals of the 1999 and 2003 Rugby World Cups, 2005 saw a massive turnaround and the national team lifted the **Six Nations trophy** with a Grand Slam. The next couple of years saw poor results culminating in an abominable 2007 Rugby World Cup when the national team failed to progress to the quarter-finals. Under another Kiwi coach, Warren Gatland, the national side rebounded in 2008 with a massive **Grand Slam**, conceding just two tries in the process. Results ebbed thereafter, but they were superb during the 2011 Rugby World Cup, being robbed of a place in the final after a dubious sending off of captain Sam Warburton against France. With Gatland still in charge, another Grand Slam followed in 2012 and expectations are high for the 2015 World Cup.

To see an **international game**, you'll have to be affiliated to one of the Rugby Union clubs or be prepared to pay well over the odds at one of the ticket agencies. Most tickets are allocated months before a match and touts are often found selling tickets for hundreds of pounds outside the gates on the day.

Away from the international arena, a thriving rugby scene exists at **club level**, with upwards of a hundred clubs and forty thousand players taking to the field most Saturdays throughout the season (from September to just after Easter). The upper tier is known as the Pro 12, with four Welsh teams – Cardiff Blues, (Llanelli) Scarlets, Newport Gwent Dragons and (Swansea) Ospreys – playing against the top teams from Ireland, Scotland and Italy. Of the Welsh sides, Ospreys are by far the most successful, having won the league four times.

It's often worth going to a match purely for the light-hearted crowd banter – if you can understand the accents. Check with individual clubs for fixtures and ticket prices, which start at under £15 (though £20–25 is typical).

Football

Though **Welsh football** (soccer) is seen as a minority sport, it has just as many participants as rugby. Moreover, the emergence of both Swansea and Cardiff as Premiership sides in recent years has galvanized the sport in the principality. Although Swansea has retained its spot in the elite division since arriving in 2011, Cardiff was relegated back down to the Championship after just one season, in 2014. Both sides have fared well in the cups recently, with Swansea winning the League Cup in 2013 – its first major piece of silverware – and Cardiff reaching the FA Cup Final in 2008, the first Welsh club to achieve this since doing so itself in 1927. Traditionally, Wrexham is the third team in Wales, though its 87-year stay in the Football League came to an end in 2008, and it has remained a non-league team since. The rest of the clubs play in the lacklustre **Welsh Premier League** (Ⓦwelshpremier.com). For more on the Welsh game, check the website of the Football Association of Wales (Ⓦfaw.org.uk).

In contrast to the rude health of Welsh club football, the national side continues to struggle. After a brief period of success between 2002 and 2004 under the stewardship of Mark Hughes, it endured a lacklustre spell under John Toshack, who remained in charge for six years.

The shocking suicide of the next manager, Gary Speed, in 2011, led to Chris Coleman taking over, but results have remained poor, and the club still waits to qualify for its first tournament since 1958. However, with the likes of Gareth Bale, now starring at Real Madrid, and Aaron Ramsey, at Arsenal, hopes are once again high for the future.

Alternative, New Age and green Wales

Possibly more than any other part of Britain, Wales – the mid and west in particular – has become something of a haven for those searching for alternative lifestyles. Permanent testimonials to this include the Centre for Alternative Technology (CAT), near Machynlleth, now one of the area's most visited attractions, and Tipi Valley, near Talley, a permanent community living in Native American tepees who run a regular public sweat lodge. Both institutions were founded in the idealistic mid-1970s and have prospered through less happy times. For the most part, it's been a fairly smooth process, although antagonism between New Agers and local, established families does break out on occasion.

For visitors, the legacy of this "green" influx is evident throughout Wales. Even in some of the smallest rural towns, you'll often find a health-food shop, wholefood café, somewhere flogging esoteric ephemera or an alternative resource centre. Any of these will give you further ideas and contacts for local happenings, places, groups and individuals.

There's also a plethora of good **festivals** from spring to autumn, ranging from big folk and blues bashes to smaller gatherings in remote fields, with little more than a couple of banging sound systems. Information travels best by word of mouth, so keep your eyes and ears peeled for information and don't hesitate to ask around.

For ecologically minded tourists, there are now numerous package deals that include walking, cycling, dancing and healing holidays, and **retreats** in remote centres, usually with vegetarian and vegan food as part of the deal. Some of these are static, many are in temporary sites, while others keep you on the move.

RETREATS AND WORKSHOPS

Buckland Hall Bwlch, near Brecon ☎ 01874 730330, ⓦ bucklandhall.co.uk. Beautiful hall and gardens hosting holistic lifestyle courses and workshops.

Cae Mabon near Llanberis, Gwynedd ☎ 01286 871542, ⓦ caemabon.co.uk. Stunning Snowdonia setting for residential courses, storytelling and arts events, with accommodation in roundhouses, a hogan and benders.

> **TOP 5 INDUSTRIAL HERITAGE SITES**
>
> **Clywedog Valley** Wrexham. See p.308
> **Colliery Museum** Cefn Coed. See p.120
> **Ironworks and the Big Pit** Blaenafon. See p.106
> **Llechwedd Slate Caverns** Blaenau Ffestiniog. See p.365
> **National Slate Museum** Llanberis. See p.351

Centre for Alternative Technology Llwyngwern, near Machynlleth, Powys ☎ 01654 705982, ⓦ cat.org.uk. Residential courses on green themes such as self-build homes and organic gardening.

Dance Camp Wales Pembrokeshire ⓦ dancecampwales.org. Ten-day participatory dance festival held in July or August in a beautiful location, with about five hundred participants.

Healing Tao Britain Conwy ☎ 01492 515776, ⓦ healingtao britain.com. Residential weekend workshops on meditation and Chi Kung, most of which take place in Colwyn.

Spirit Horse Powys ☎ 07882 522878, ⓦ spirithorse.co.uk. Camps to celebrate ancient ceremonial and cultural traditions in a stunning, secluded setting.

Vajraloka Buddhist Meditation Centre Corwen, Denbighshire ☎ 01490 460406, ⓦ vajraloka.org. Regular retreats, either men-only or mixed.

Travel essentials

Costs

Wales is certainly not a cheap destination, but prices are generally lower than in many parts of England, particularly London.

The **minimum expenditure**, if you're camping and preparing most of your own food, would be £20–25 per day, rising to £35–40 per day if you're using the hostelling network, some public transport and grabbing the odd takeaway or meal out. Couples staying at budget B&Bs, eating at unpretentious restaurants and visiting a couple of tourist attractions are looking at £60–70 each per day – if you're renting a car, staying in comfortable B&Bs or hotels and eating well, you should reckon on at least £80–90 a day. Single travellers should note that single rooms often cost more than half the price of a double, making them relatively expensive.

VAT

Most goods in Britain, with the chief exceptions of books and groceries, are subject to a twenty percent **Value Added Tax** (**VAT**), which is almost always included in the quoted price. Visitors from non-EU countries can get a VAT refund when leaving the country on goods bought through the **Retail Export Scheme**; participating shops have a sign in their window; see Ⓦhmrc.gov.uk/vat for details.

Student and youth cards

The various official and quasi-official **youth/ student ID cards** are of relatively minor use in Wales, saving only a few pence for entry to some sites. If you already have one, then bring it, but if you don't, it's barely worth making a special effort to get one.

Full-time students are eligible for the International Student Identity Card (ISIC; Ⓦisic.org), while anyone under 26 can apply for an International Youth Travel Card, which carries the same benefits; both cost £12. A university photo ID might open some doors, but is not as easily recognizable as the ISIC cards.

Tipping and service charges

In restaurants a service charge is sometimes included in the bill; if it isn't, leave a tip of 10–15 percent unless the service is unforgivably bad. Taxi drivers expect a tip in the region of ten percent. You do not generally tip bar staff – if you want to show your appreciation, offer to buy them a drink.

Tourist attractions

Many of Wales' most treasured sites – from castles, abbeys and great houses to tracts of protected landscape – come under the control of the privately run UK-wide **National Trust** or the state-run **CADW**, whose properties are denoted in the Guide by "NT" and "CADW".

Both organizations charge an entry fee for most places, and these can be quite high, especially for the more grandiose NT estates. If you think you'll be visiting more than half a dozen NT places or a similar number of major CADW sites, it's worth buying an **annual pass**. Membership of the National Trust (❶0844 800 1895, Ⓦnationaltrust .org.uk; £58, under-26s £27, family £98) allows free

TOP 5 GARDENS

Bodnant Conwy. See p.407
Colby Woodland Gardens Amroth. See p.160
Dyffryn Gardens Barry. See p.99
National Botanic Garden Tywi Valley. See p.147
Powis Castle Welshpool. See p.248

entry and parking at its properties throughout Britain. Sites operated by CADW (❶01443 336000, Ⓦcadw.wales.gov.uk; £40, seniors £26, ages 16–20 £22, under-16s £16, family £66) are restricted to Wales, but membership also grants you half-price entry to sites owned by English Heritage and Historic Scotland. CADW also offers the Explorer Pass, which allows free entry into all CADW sites on three days in seven (adult £17.50, family £36.80), or seven days in fourteen (£26/£51.20). Entry to CADW sites is free for Welsh residents over 60: check their website to obtain a pass.

Many other old buildings are owned by the local authorities, and admission is often cheaper. Municipal **art galleries** and **museums** are usually free, as are sites run by the National Museums and Galleries of Wales (Ⓦmuseumwales.ac.uk), including the National Museum and St Fagans National History Museum, both in Cardiff. Although a donation is usually requested, **cathedrals** tend to be free, except for perhaps the tower, crypt or other such highlight, for which a small charge is made. Increasingly, **churches** are kept locked except during services; when they are open, entry is free. You'll normally be able to find a notice in the porch or on a board telling you where to get a key if the church is locked. Wales also has a number of superb showcases of its **industrial heritage**, mostly concerned with mining and mineral extraction.

Keen birders might consider joining the **RSPB**, where membership (Ⓦrspb.org.uk; £36 a year) gives you free entry to its reserves throughout Britain.

Entry charges given in the Guide are the full adult rates, but the majority of the fee-charging attractions located in Wales have 10–25 percent **reductions** for senior citizens and full-time students, and 20–50 percent reductions for under-16s – under-5s are admitted free almost everywhere. Family tickets are also common, usually priced just under the rate for two adults and a child and include up to three kids.

Finally, visitors planning on seeing more than a dozen stately homes, monuments, castles or gardens might find it worthwhile to buy a **Hudson**

TOP 5 CASTLES

Beaumaris Castle Beaumaris. See p.418
Caernarfon Castle Caernarfon. See p.356
Caerphilly Castle Caerphilly. See p.109
Carreg Cennen Castle Llandeilo. See p.149
Conwy Castle Conwy. See p.404

AVERAGE MONTHLY TEMPERATURES AND RAINFALL

CARDIFF

	Jan	Feb	Mar	Apr	May	Jun	Jul	Aug	Sep	Oct	Nov	Dec
Max/min (°C)	8/2	8/2	11/4	13/5	17/8	19/11	21/3	21/13	18/10	15/7	11/4	9/3
Max/min (°F)	47/36	47/36	51/40	55/41	62/47	67/51	71/55	71/55	65/50	58/45	51/40	48/38
Rainfall (mm)	119	91	89	65	65	66	61	90	104	117	117	128

DOLGELLAU

	Jan	Feb	Mar	Apr	May	Jun	Jul	Aug	Sep	Oct	Nov	Dec
Max/min (°C)	6/1	6/1	8/2	11/4	14/6	16/9	18/11	18/11	16/9	12/7	9/4	6/2
Max/min (°F)	43/34	43/34	47/36	51/40	57/43	61/48	65/51	65/51	61/48	54/45	48/40	43/34
Rainfall (mm)	172	156	116	96	104	83	90	81	99	187	147	184

Explorer Pass (£79 for 3 days, £79 for 7 days, £109 for 14 days, £179 for 28 days; ⓦ hudsonsheritage .com), which gives free admission to over two hundred sites throughout the UK, a good number of which are in Wales.

Electricity

In Britain, the **current** is 240V AC at 50Hz. North American appliances will need a transformer, though most laptops, phone and MP3 player chargers are designed to automatically detect and adapt to the electricity supply and don't need any modification. Almost all foreign appliances will require an adapter for the chunky British three-pin electrical sockets.

For details of how to plug your **laptop** in when abroad, phone country codes around the world and information about electrical systems in different countries look at ⓦ kropla.com.

Emergencies and police

As in any other country, Wales' major towns have their dangerous spots, but these tend to be inner-city housing estates where you're unlikely to find yourself. The chief risk on the streets – though still minimal – is **pickpocketing**, so carry only as much money as you need, and keep all bags and pockets fastened. Should you have anything stolen or be involved in an incident that requires reporting, go to the local police station. The ☎ 999 (British) or ☎ 112 (pan-European) numbers for police, fire and ambulance services should only be used in emergencies. There is also a non-emergency number for the police ☎ 101 (10p per call).

Entry requirements

Citizens of all European countries – other than Albania, Bosnia Herzegovina, Macedonia, Monte-negro, Serbia and most republics of the former Soviet Union – can enter Britain with just a passport, generally for up to three months. US, Canadian, Australian and New Zealand citizens can travel in Britain for up to six months with just a passport. All other nationalities require a **visa**, available from the British consular office in the country of application.

For stays longer than six months, check details on the Home Office website (ⓦ gov.uk/visas -immigration), where you can download the appropriate form. Do this before the expiry date given on the endorsement in your passport. **Embassy contact details** are listed on ⓦ gov.uk.

FOREIGN EMBASSIES IN BRITAIN

Foreign embassies are all found in London.

Australia ☎ 020 7379 4334, ⓦ uk.embassy.gov.au.

Canada ☎ 020 7258 6600, ⓦ canada.org.uk.

Ireland ☎ 020 7235 2171, ⓦ embassyofireland.co.uk.

New Zealand ☎ 020 7930 8422, ⓦ nzembassy.com.

South Africa ☎ 020 7451 7299, ⓦ southafricahouseuk.com.

USA ☎ 020 7499 9000, ⓦ usembassy.org.uk.

Customs and biosecurity

Travellers entering Britain directly from another EU country do not have to make a declaration to **customs** at their place of entry, and can effectively bring in almost as much wine or beer as they like. It is supposed to be for personal use, so if you have more than 90 litres of wine and 110 litres of beer you may be questioned. If you're travelling from a non-EU country duty-free allowances are as follows. **Tobacco allowances** are: 200 cigarettes, or 100 cigarillos, or 50 cigars, or 250g of loose tobacco.

Alcohol allowances are: four litres of still wine, plus one litre of drink over 22 percent alcohol, or two litres of alcoholic drink not over 22 percent, or another two litres of still wine. You're also allowed other goods (including perfume) to the value of £390. For details, contact HM Revenue & Customs (ⓦ hmrc.gov.uk).

Biosecurity is also an issue. It is illegal to import meat, milk and other animal products from outside the EU: see Ⓦdefra.gov.uk for more details. The website also has details of the fairly strict PETS scheme, which allows pet **cats** and **dogs** to enter Britain without quarantine.

Gay and lesbian Wales

Homosexual acts between consenting males were legalized in Britain in 1967, but it wasn't until 2000 that the age of consent for gay men was made equal to that of straight men, at 16. Lesbianism has never specifically been outlawed, apocryphally owing to the fact that Queen Victoria refused to believe it existed. In December 2005, civil partnerships between same-sex couples were legalized – marriage in all but name. The most significant step, however, came in 2014, when **same-sex marriage** was finally legalized.

With such a rural culture, it's perhaps not surprising that Wales is less used to the lesbian and gay lifestyle than its more cosmopolitan English neighbour. That said, there's little real hostility, with the traditional Welsh "live and let live" attitude applying as much in this area as any other. Several Welsh celebrities have come out in recent years, and it's barely caused a stir.

The organized gay scene in Wales is fairly muted. The main cities – Cardiff and Swansea – have a number of pubs and clubs, with Cardiff especially beginning to see a worthy and confident gay scene – a Mardi Gras festival in August included – more in keeping with the capital's size and status. The best resource for gay and lesbian events in the capital is Ⓦcardiff.gaycities.com.

Beyond the two big cities, gay life becomes distinctly discreet, although university towns such as Lampeter, Bangor and Wrexham manage support groups and the odd weekly night in a local bar, while Aberystwyth is a significantly friendly milieu. There are some informal but well-established networks, especially among the sometimes reclusive alternative lifestylers found in mid- and west Wales. **Border Women** (Ⓦborder women.org) is a well-organized lesbian network for mid-Wales and the Marches.

Health

No vaccinations are required for entry into Britain. Citizens of all EU countries are entitled to free **medical treatment** at National Health Service hospitals; citizens of other countries are charged for all medical services except those administered by accident and emergency units at National Health Service hospitals. Thus a US citizen who has been hit by a car would not be charged if the injuries simply required stitching and setting in the emergency unit, but would be if admission to a hospital ward were necessary. Health insurance is therefore strongly advised for all non-EU nationals.

Pharmacies (known generally as chemists in Britain) can dispense only a limited range of drugs without a doctor's prescription. Most pharmacies are open during standard shop hours, though in large towns some may stay open as late as 10pm. Doctors' surgeries tend to be open from about 9am until early evening; outside surgery hours, you can turn up at the casualty department of the local hospital for problems that require immediate attention – unless it's a real **emergency**, in which case ring for an ambulance on ☏999 or ☏112.

Insurance

Even though EU health-care privileges apply in the UK, it's a good idea to take out **travel insurance** before travelling to cover against theft, loss and illness and injury. For non-EU citizens, it's worth checking whether you are already covered before you buy a new policy. If you need to take out insurance, you might want to consider the travel insurance deal we offer (see box below).

ROUGH GUIDES TRAVEL INSURANCE

Rough Guides has teamed up with WorldNomads.com to offer great travel insurance deals. Policies are available to residents of over 150 countries, with cover for a wide range of adventure sports, 24hr emergency assistance, high levels of medical and evacuation cover and a stream of travel safety information. Roughguides.com users can take advantage of their policies online 24/7, from anywhere in the world – even if you're already travelling. And since plans often change when you're on the road, you can extend your policy and even claim online. Roughguides.com users who buy travel insurance with WorldNomads.com can also leave a positive footprint and donate to a community development project. For more information, go to Ⓦroughguides.com/travel-insurance.

A typical travel insurance policy usually provides cover for the loss of baggage, tickets and – up to a certain limit – cash or cheques, as well as cancellation or curtailment of your journey. Most of them exclude so-called dangerous sports unless an extra premium is paid; in Wales this can mean whitewater rafting, windsurfing and coasteering, though probably not ordinary hiking. If you take medical coverage, ascertain whether benefits will be paid as treatment proceeds or only after return home, and whether there is a 24-hour medical emergency number. When securing baggage cover, make sure that the per-article limit – typically under £500 – will cover your most valuable possession. If you need to make a claim, you should keep receipts for medicines and medical treatment, and in the event you have anything stolen, you must obtain an official statement from the **police**.

Internet

Cybercafés (where you can expect to pay £2–3 an hour) are now few and far between, as most cafés and bars now offer **free wi-fi**, though you will be obliged to buy a drink. Free wi-fi is also now very common at B&Bs and hotels, even in the most remote areas.

Alternatively, almost all public libraries now have free **internet access** with several computers and wi-fi.

Mail

Virtually all **post offices** (*swyddfa'r post*) are open Monday to Friday 9am to 5.30pm, Saturday 9am to 12.30pm. In small communities, you'll find sub-post offices operating out of a shop, but these work to the same hours even if the shop itself is open for longer. Stamps can be bought at post office counters and from a large number of newsagents and other shops, although often these sell only books of four or ten stamps. A first-class letter to anywhere in Britain (up to 100g) costs 62p and should arrive the next day; second-class letters cost 53p, taking two to four days to arrive. Prices to Europe and the rest of the world vary depending on the size of the item and how quickly you would like it delivered. For parcel rates visit ⓦ royalmail.com.

Maps

Most bookshops have a good selection of **maps** of Wales and Britain, though the best can be found in specialist travel bookshops. Virtually every petrol station in Britain stocks large-format **road atlases** produced by the AA, RAC, Collins, Ordnance Survey (OS) and others, which cover all of Britain at a scale of around three miles to one inch and include larger-scale plans of major towns. The best of these is the OS road atlas, which handily uses the same grid reference system as their accurate and detailed folding maps.

For hiking, go for the widely available maps by **OS** (ⓦ ordnancesurvey.co.uk), renowned for their accuracy and clarity. The 204 maps in its 1:50,000 (a little over one inch: one mile) Landranger series (£6.99 each) cover the whole of Britain, while the more detailed 1:25,000 Explorer series (£7.99 each) also covers the whole country, has field boundaries to aid navigation, and is at an ideal scale for walkers. They also have an OS MapFinder app, whereby you can download high resolution maps to your smart phone or tablet.

Measurements

Like the rest of Britain, Wales is in very slow transition from **imperial** to **metric** measurements. Groceries are sold in packets quoted in grams and litres but usually in portions equivalent to a pound or a pint. Maps show mountain heights in metres but road distances are in miles and speeds in miles per hour. Petrol is sold by the litre. In pubs, beer is still sold in pints.

Money

The British **pound sterling** (£; *punt* in Welsh, and informally referred to as a "quid") is divided into 100 pence (p; in Welsh, c for *ceiniogau*). Coins come in denominations of 1p, 2p, 5p, 10p, 20p, 50p, £1 and £2. Notes come in denominations of £5, £10, £20 and £50. Shopkeepers carefully scrutinize any £20 and £50 notes tendered, as forgeries are not uncommon. For the latest exchange rates, check the useful website ⓦ xe.com.

Most hotels, shops and restaurants accept the major **credit**, **charge** and **debit cards**, particularly Access/MasterCard and Visa/Barclaycard. American Express and Diners' Club are less widely accepted. Cards are accepted at most B&Bs, though you should check beforehand.

Almost every Welsh town has a branch of at least one of the major **banks**: NatWest, Halifax, HSBC, Barclays and Lloyds TSB. As a general rule, opening hours are Monday to Friday 9 or 9.30am to 4.30 or 5pm, and branches in larger towns are often open on Saturday from 9am to 1pm. Post offices charge no commission, have longer opening hours, and are therefore often a good place to change money and cheques.

Opening hours and public holidays

General **shop hours** are Monday to Saturday 9am to 5.30/6pm, although there's an increasing amount of Sunday and late-night shopping in the larger towns, with Thursday or Friday being the favoured evenings. The larger shopping malls tend to stay open until 8 or 9pm from Monday to Saturday, and from 11am to 5pm on Sunday, as do many of the big supermarkets. Note that not all **service stations** are open 24 hours, although you can usually get fuel around the clock in the larger towns and cities. Also, most fee-charging sites are open on bank holidays, when Sunday hours usually apply.

Phones

Public **payphones** are still to be found in most places, but the near-ubiquity of mobile phones means they are seldom used. **Call costs** vary greatly depending on whether you are calling from a private landline, public pay-phone or the mobile network you are on. We've given call cost guidelines below.

To **call Wales** from outside the UK, dial the international access code (☎011 from the US and Canada, ☎0011 from Australia and ☎00 from New Zealand), followed in all cases by 44, then the area code minus its initial zero, and finally the number.

If you're bringing your own **mobile phone/cellphone** with you to Wales, check with your service provider whether your phone will work abroad and what the call charges are. The cost of calls within the EU has decreased significantly within recent years, but calls to destinations further afield are still unregulated and can be prohibitively expensive.

The **GSM system** used in Britain is compatible with other European and Australasian systems, though most North American single-band phones don't work here. A better bet might be to bring your phone and buy a new pre-pay SIM card for it (under £5). With no contract you simply top up your account as you need to. If your phone doesn't work on UK frequency bands you may need one that does. These are available from the numerous high-street outlets from as little as £15.

There's frenetic competition between the main operators – Vodafone (Ⓦvodafone.co.uk), O2 (Ⓦo2.co.uk), Orange (Ⓦorange.co.uk) and T-mobile (Ⓦt-mobile.co.uk) – so shop around.

Beware of **premium-rate numbers**, which are common for pre-recorded information services – and usually have the prefix ☎09.

Shopping

The quintessential Welsh memento is a **lovespoon** – an intricately carved wooden spoon that in centuries gone by was offered by suitors when courting. The meanings of the various designs range from a Celtic cross (symbolizing faith/marriage) to vines (growing love) and a double spoon (commitment), with dozens of others available. Prices range from a few pounds for a small version, to several hundred pounds for a large, elaborate spoon by a well-known carver. You'll find them in craft shops all over the country, including some dedicated solely to these ornaments.

Other unique items include some superb paintings, jewellery, leatherwork and screen-printing from **arts and crafts** galleries throughout Wales. Some are run by the artists themselves, and you can watch them at work. Given that Wales has an estimated three to four times as many sheep as humans, it's not surprising that there are some wonderful **woollen products** available.

A good online resource is the Wales Crafts Council (Ⓦwalescraftcouncil.co.uk).

PUBLIC HOLIDAYS

New Year's Day January 1.
Good Friday late March to mid-April.
Easter Monday late March to mid-April.
Early May Bank Holiday first Monday in May.
Spring Bank Holiday (sometimes referred to as Whitsun) last Monday in May.

Late summer Bank Holiday Last Monday in August.
Christmas Day December 25.
Boxing Day December 26.
Note that if January 1, December 25 or December 26 falls on a Saturday or Sunday, the next weekday becomes a public holiday.

Studying in Wales

There are numerous places around Wales where you might attend full-day or multi-day courses (residential or otherwise) to pursue all manner of interests. Some of the most interesting are:

Nant Gwrtheyrn 10 miles north of Pwllheli ☎ 01758 750334, Ⓦ nantgwrtheyrn.org. Extensive range of Welsh language courses run for everyone from complete beginners to near-fluent speakers.

Plas Menai: The National Watersports Centre near Caernarfon ☎ 01248 670964, Ⓦ plasmenai.co.uk. All manner of predominantly two- and five-day courses covering sailing, windsurfing, kayaking and jet skiing in a beautiful location on the Menai Strait.

Plas Tan y Bwlch near Porthmadog ☎ 01766 772600, Ⓦ plastanybwlch.com. Snowdonia National Park Study Centre, which runs residential courses focusing mainly on the environment and appreciation of the countryside. They extend to landscape photography, botanical painting, mushrooms and toadstools, drovers and drovers' roads, heritage railways and much more. Many are taught in Welsh or bilingually, and are suitable for Welsh-language beginners.

Plas y Brenin: The National Mountain Centre Capel Curig ☎ 01690 720214, Ⓦ pyb.co.uk. This internationally recognized outdoor training centre runs a huge range of residential courses and samplers at all levels up to expert, plus expedition training. Typical courses include a Navigation Skills course for hill-walkers, an Advanced Scrambling week, a weekend introduction to rock climbing, a five-day introduction to sea kayaking, and a multi-activity weekend. Also offers qualification courses for all levels of instructors. See p.345.

Time

Greenwich Mean Time (GMT) is in force from late October to late March, when the clocks go forward an hour for British Summer Time (BST). GMT is five hours ahead of New York, ten hours behind Sydney, and twelve hours behind New Zealand.

Tourist information

Wales promotes itself enthusiastically through **Visit Wales** (aka Croeso Cymru: Ⓦ visitwales.com), which operates a central information service that's excellent for pre-trip planning, with a detailed website and plenty of free brochures which can either be downloaded or sent by mail.

Tourist offices (usually called Tourist Information Centres or TICs) exist throughout Wales, and are usually very well stocked with information on the local area and elsewhere throughout the country – you'll find contact details and opening hours of all TICs throughout the Guide. The average opening hours are much the same as standard shop hours, though in summer they'll often be open on a Sunday and for a couple of hours after the shops

have closed on weekdays. Opening hours are generally shorter in winter, and in more remote areas the office may well be closed altogether. All centres offer information on accommodation (which they can often book), local public transport, attractions and restaurants, as well as town and regional maps.

Areas designated as national parks (the Brecon Beacons, Pembrokeshire Coast and Snowdonia) also have a fair sprinkling of **National Park Information Centres**, which are generally more expert in giving guidance on local walks and outdoor pursuits.

Travellers with disabilities

Visitors with **disabilities** generally fare pretty well travelling in Wales, though many older buildings (and especially cheaper places to stay) are difficult or impossible to adapt and it always pays to call ahead to check the situation. Disabled parking spaces are common; new buildings (including accommodation) are required to make appropriate provision; and a fair number of existing hotels, B&Bs and restaurants are retrofitting accessible bathrooms and ramps. Some YHAs also have disabled facilities.

Public transport companies are now making more of an effort to accommodate passengers with mobility problems. Some rail services now cater for wheelchair users, and assistance is usually available at stations if you call at least 24 hours in advance; call National Rail Enquiries (see p.28) to get the number of the appropriate rail company. You may be eligible for the Disabled Persons Railcard (£20 per year; Ⓦ disabledpersons-railcard.co.uk), which gives a third off most tickets for you and a companion.

The link for "Passengers with disabilities" at Ⓦ nationalrail.co.uk has information for journey planning, including maps identifying stations that have access to platforms without steps. There are no bus discounts for disabled passengers who are not Welsh citizens. Rental cars with hand controls are rare and expensive.

Access to **monuments and museums** is improving all the time. The National Trust (see p.47) produces a downloadable sheet detailing accessibility to NT properties in Wales; disabled visitors must pay entry fees, but they can bring a friend or carer in to assist them free of charge. CADW allows wheelchair users and the visually handicapped, along with their assisting companion, free entry to all monuments. You can download a booklet with detailed site access details.

Some **public toilets** are kept locked, but some local authorities have joined the National Key System (NKS) in which disabled people can gain access to facilities via a standard key (contact RADAR, see below). Some tourist offices also hold a key that you can borrow.

CONTACTS

Access-Able Ⓦ access-able.com. Online resource for travellers with disabilities.

Disability Rights Ⓦ disabilityrightsuk.org. Campaigning organization that's a good source of advice on holidays and travel in the UK.

Disability Wales Ⓦ disabilitywales.org. Welsh equivalent of Disability Rights (see above).

Mobility International USA Ⓦ miusa.org. Information and referral services, access guides, tours and exchange programmes.

Open Britain Ⓦ openbritain.net. Excellent online resource listing a whole range of accessible travel related information, from accommodation to attractions.

Society for Accessible Travel and Hospitality (SATH) Ⓦ sath .org. Long-standing non-profit educational organization with useful travel tips and access information on its website.

Tourism For All Ⓦ tourismforall.org.uk. Offers various guides and advice for access throughout Britain.

Wales Council for the Blind Ⓦ wcb-ccd.org.uk. Though not specifically set up with visitors in mind, it does provide a good contact point.

Wales Council for the Deaf Ⓦ wcdeaf.org.uk. Also not specifically set up with visitors in mind, but provides a good contact point.

Southeast Wales

KAYAKERS ON RHOSSILI BEACH

1

Southeast Wales

Home to some sixty percent of the country's population, the southeastern corner of Wales is one of Britain's most industrialized regions. Both people and industry are most heavily concentrated around the sea ports and former mining valleys, though quiet hills and beaches are only ever a few miles away. Wales unfolds from the English border in a beguilingly rural manner. The River Wye flows forth from its mouth at the fortress town of Chepstow, where you'll find one of the most impressive castles in a land where few towns are without one. In the Wye's beautiful valley lie the spectacularly placed ruins of Tintern Abbey, downstream from the old county town of Monmouth. Industrialization intensifies as you travel west to the River Usk, which spills out into the Bristol Channel at Newport, Wales' third-largest conurbation, and home to the remains of an extensive Roman settlement in adjacent Caerleon.

To the west and north are the world-famous **Valleys**, once the coal- and iron-rich powerhouse of the British Empire. This is the Wales of popular imagination: hemmed-in valley floors packed with seemingly never-ending lines of slate-roofed terraced houses, slanted towards the pithead. Although all the deep mines have closed, the area is still one of tight-knit towns, with a rich working-class heritage displayed in some illuminating museums and colliery tours, such as the **Big Pit** at Blaenafon and the **Rhondda Heritage Park** in Trehafod. The valleys follow rivers coursing down towards the coast, where great ports shipped their products all over the world. The greatest of them all was **Cardiff**, once the world's busiest coal port, now Wales' upbeat capital. Stellar museums, a storybook castle, exciting rejuvenation projects and Wales' best cultural pursuits make the city an essential stop.

Immediately west of the capital, and a world away from the industrial hangover of the city and Valleys, is the lush **Vale of Glamorgan** and **Glamorgan Heritage Coast**, which stretches 28 miles westwards to include the neighbouring county of Bridgend. The entire area is dotted with stoic little market towns and chirpy seaside resorts – most notably **Barry** in the east and **Porthcawl** in the west.

West again is Wales' second city, **Swansea**. Bright, breezy and brash, Swansea is renowned for its nightlife and is undergoing rapid development, particularly along its historic waterfront. Like Cardiff, Swansea grew principally on the strength of its now revitalized docks, from where the coast arcs round from the **Port Talbot** steelworks in the east to the elegant holiday town of **Mumbles** on the jaw of the magnificent **Gower peninsula** in the west. Gower was Britain's first-ever designated Area of Outstanding Natural Beauty, and remains a microcosm of rural Wales, with its grand beaches, rocky headlands, ruined castles and bracken heaths roamed by wild horses.

Highlights

❶ Tintern Abbey Get your poetic juices flowing at Tintern's towering ruins, romantically situated in the Wye Valley. **See p.62**

❷ Transporter Bridge, Newport Check out this remarkable feat of engineering by climbing up to the walkway – though a head for heights is required. **See p.72**

❸ Caerleon Contemplate whether Wales' best-preserved Roman remains were the site of King Arthur's fabled court, Camelot. See **p.74**

❹ Cardiff Dazzling architecture, a city-centre castle and some cracking nightlife mark the Welsh capital out as a must-visit destination. **See p.76**

❺ National History Museum, St Fagans Take a free and fascinating amble around this wonderful ensemble of Welsh buildings from the past. **See p.95**

❻ Blaenafon Strap on a hardhat and head-lamp and follow ex-coal miners into the Big Pit – one of the country's most poignant and powerful museums. **See p.107**

❼ Rhossili beach Surf some of Britain's best waves where the Gower peninsula ends in a flourish. **See p.132**

HIGHLIGHTS ARE MARKED ON THE MAP ON P.58

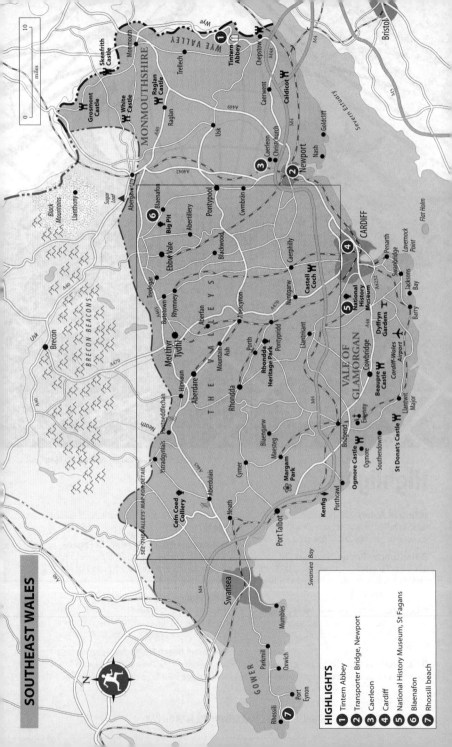

SOUTHEAST WALES

HIGHLIGHTS
1. Tintern Abbey
2. Transporter Bridge, Newport
3. Caerleon
4. Cardiff
5. National History Museum, St Fagans
6. Blaenafon
7. Rhossili beach

Bristol

Wye

WYE VALLEY

Monmouth
Skenfrith Castle
Grosmont Castle
White Castle
Raglan Castle
Tintern Abbey
Caldicot
Chepstow

MONMOUTHSHIRE

Trellech
Raglan
Usk
Caerwent
Goldcliff
Nash

Abergavenny
Blaenafon
Big Pit
Abertillery
Pontypool
Cwmbran
Caerleon
Christchurch
Newport

Black Mountains
Sugar Loaf
Llanthony

Ebbw Vale
Blackwood
Caerphilly
Castell Coch
CARDIFF
Penarth

Tredegar
Butetown
Rhymney
Bedwyn
Nantgarw
National History Museum
Swanbridge
Jacksons Bay
Lavernock Point
Flat Holm

BRECON BEACONS
Brecon
Usk

Merthyr Tydfil
Hirwaun
Aberdare
Mountain Ash
Pontypridd
Dyffryn Gardens
Cardiff-Wales Airport
Barry

THE VALLEYS

Ystradgynlais
Pontneddfechan
Cefn Coed Colliery
Aberdulais
Neath

Rhondda Heritage Park
Porth
Llantrisant
VALE OF GLAMORGAN
Cowbridge
Beaupre Castle
Llantwit Major
St Donat's Castle

Blaengarw
Maesteg
Cymer
Rhondda

Ogmore Castle
Ogmore
Southerndown

Bridgend
Ewenny

Margam Park
Kenfig
Porthcawl
Port Talbot

Swansea Bay

Swansea
Mumbles

GOWER
Parkmill
Oxwich
Port Eynon
Rhossili

SEE THE VALLEYS' MAP FOR DETAIL

0 ___ 10 miles

By car Southeast Wales is by far the easiest part of the country to travel around. Swift dual carriageways connect with the M4, bringing all corners of the region into close proximity.

By bus and train Public transport is similarly thorough:

this is the only part of Wales with a half-decent train service, and most suburban and rural services interconnect with Cardiff, Newport or Swansea. Bus services fill in virtually all of the gaps, though often rather slowly. See "Getting around" in Basics for discount fares and passes.

The Wye Valley

Only in the local government reorganization of 1974 was the **Wye Valley** finally recognized as part of Wales; before this, the area was officially included as part of neither England nor Wales, so that maps were frequently headlined "Wales and Monmouthshire" (the county name). In this easterly corner, the two main towns are decidedly English in flavour: **Chepstow**, at the mouth of the Wye, with its massive castle radiating an awesome strength; and **Monmouth**, sixteen miles upstream, a spruce, old-fashioned town with the lingering air of an ancient seat of authority.

Six miles north of Chepstow, on the banks of the Wye, stand the inspirational ruins of the Cistercian **Tintern Abbey**, while across the river the southern segments of the **Offa's Dyke** earthworks are shadowed by a long-distance footpath (see box, p.239).

Chepstow

Of all the places that call themselves "the gateway to Wales", **CHEPSTOW** (Cas-Gwent) – the first Welsh town on the main road into the country – has probably the strongest claim. Situated on the western bank of the River Wye, just over a mile from where its tidal waters recede into the Severn estuary, Chepstow is an easy-going and engaging place, and worth a stop to visit its ancient castle.

Chepstow's position as a former river port is evident in the thirteenth-century **Port Wall**, encasing the castle precincts and the town centre in their loop of the river. The fifteenth-century **West Gate** marks the southern end of the **High Street**, a handsome thoroughfare sided by Georgian and Victorian buildings and sloping down from the gate towards the river. Here, the elegant five-arch cast-iron **Old Wye Bridge**, built in 1816, is still in use for cross-border traffic into England. This section of the Wye is tremendously tidal, with a mighty 49ft difference in the water level between high and low tides – one of the world's highest tidal drops. A short street with a riverside esplanade, The Back, runs southeast from the bridge; a plaque on the wall of the *Riverside Wine Bar* commemorates the quay as the site from which the three leaders of Newport's Chartist March of 1839 were dispatched to Van Diemen's Land (now Tasmania), in Australia.

A five-minute walk up the hill from The Back, **St Mary's Priory church** was founded at the same time as the castle, in around 1072, as a Benedictine priory. Much of what survived has been modernized over the centuries, but today you can still see its Norman origins, including an intricate arched eleventh-century doorway.

Chepstow Castle

Bridge St • March–Oct daily 9.30am–5pm, July & Aug till 6pm; Nov–Feb Mon–Sat 10am–4pm, Sun 11am–4pm • £4.50; CADW • ☎ 01291 624065

The strategic location of **Chepstow Castle** could scarcely be bettered. Built tight into a loop of the River Wye, it guards one of the most important routes into Wales. Chepstow was the first stone castle to be built in Britain, with its first Norman incarnation, the Great Tower keep, rising in 1067, just one year after William the Conqueror's victory at Hastings. William had realized the importance of subduing the restless Welsh, creating borderland Marcher Lordships and encouraging the title

1

WALES COAST PATH IN MONMOUTHSHIRE

As well as being the starting points for both the Offa's Dyke and Wye Valley walks, Chepstow is now also the official, if unlikely, starting point for the newly inaugurated **Wales Coast Path**; the path begins in Riverside Gardens near the Old Wye Bridge, before cutting inland across fields and then meeting up with the Severn Estuary; some thirteen and a half miles of the path is covered within Monmouthshire.

holders to expand into Welsh territory: a succession of Chepstow's lords attempted this, necessitating the renewed and increasingly powerful fortification of their castles over the next two hundred years.

The walled castle comprises three separate enclosures, the largest of which is the Lower Ward, dating mainly from the thirteenth century. Here, you'll find the **Great Hall**, which has been colourfully re-created as the Earl's chamber, and a fine vaulted cellar.

Twelfth-century defences separate the Lower Ward from the Middle Ward, which is dominated by the still-imposing ruins of the **Great Tower**, whose lower floors include the original Norman keep. Beyond the Great Tower is the far narrower Upper Ward, which leads up to the Barbican **watchtower**. From here, there are superlative views back over the castle and down the cliff to the mud flats of the river estuary.

Chepstow Museum

Bridge St • July–Sept Mon–Sat 10.30am–5pm, Sun 2–5pm; Nov–Feb Mon–Sat 11am–4pm, Sun 2–4pm; Oct & March–June Mon–Sat 11am–5pm, Sun 2–5pm • Free • 🕿 01291 625981

Opposite the castle, a cream-painted Georgian town house contains the **Chepstow Museum**. Staid but comprehensive displays cover pretty much every aspect of local life over the years, with nostalgic photographs and paintings of the trades supported in the past by the River Wye, including records of Chepstow's brief spell as a shipbuilding

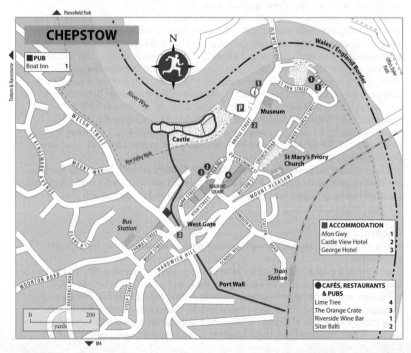

centre in the early part of the twentieth century. The mock-up hospital ward, meanwhile, harks back to the days when the house functioned as a Red Cross hospital during World War I, and then the district hospital until 1976. Take a look upstairs, too, at the rather fine eighteenth-century topographical prints of Chepstow Castle.

The Wye Valley Walk and Chepstow Racecourse

From Chepstow, you can follow the first section of the fairly challenging, two-and-a-half-hour **Wye Valley Walk** to Tintern Abbey, which starts from the castle car park. A map – or the official route guide (£7.95), available from the tourist office – is advisable, as the path tucks and meanders around and above the twisting Wye. The walk brushes past the picturesque old estate of **Piercefield Park**, a mile north of town, part of which has metamorphosed into **Chepstow Racecourse** (☎01291 622260, ⓦchepstow-racecourse .co.uk), one of the country's premier racing venues, with regular, year-round meets, culminating in the Welsh National in December. The entrance is off the A466 north of town. You could return along the other side of the river on the Offa's Dyke Path, which passes the dramatic viewpoint of Devil's Pulpit (just off the B4228) and reaches its southern end at Sedbury Cliffs, a mile or so east of town on the English side of the border.

ARRIVAL AND INFORMATION   CHEPSTOW

By train Trains between Cardiff and Birmingham stop at Chepstow's train station, 5min walk south of the High St.
Destinations Cardiff (every 30–60min; 40min); Gloucester (every 30–60min; 30min); Newport (every 30–60min; 25min).
By bus The bus station is on Thomas St, near the West Gate.
Destinations Bristol (hourly; 50min); Caerwent (hourly; 15min); Cardiff (every 30min–1hr, 1 change; 1hr 20min);

Monmouth (hourly; 50min); Newport (every 30min; 25min–1hr); Penhow (hourly; 20min); Tintern (4–8 daily; 20min); Usk (5 daily; 35min).
Tourist information The TIC is in the castle car park, off Bridge Street (Mon–Fri 10am–1pm & 2–4pm, Sat & Sun 9.30am–1pm & 2–5pm; ☎01291 623772, ⓦchepstow towncrier.org.uk); it's well stocked with local walking guides, and staff can also book local accommodation.

ACCOMMODATION

Afon Gwy 28 Bridge St ☎01291 620158. In a plum location perched on the banks of the River Wye, the seven crisply decorated rooms in this restful, three-storey guesthouse are right on the mark. **£70**
Castle View Hotel 16 Bridge St ☎01291 620349, ⓦcastleviewhotel.com. Bags of charm in this seventeenth-century building, with a grand oak spiral staircase leading off to twelve cosy rooms featuring

crooked floors, thick oak beams and exposed stone walls; some have castle views. Good value. **£72**
George Hotel Moor St ☎01291 625363, ⓔchepstow @paritybars.com. A hostelry of sorts for several centuries, the *George*'s large, simply furnished, and occasionally careworn rooms sit above a ground-floor bar and restaurant, though they are reasonably well insulated. Fairly priced. Breakfast is extra. **£50**

EATING AND DRINKING

Boat Inn The Back ☎01291 628192. Convivial waterside pub, with black timber beams, bare brick walls and a warm, welcoming atmosphere. There's a decent selection of ales and a vegetarian-friendly menu. Mon–Thurs & Sun 9.30am–11pm, Fri & Sat 9.30am–midnight.
Lime Tree 24 St Mary's St ☎01291 620959, ⓦlimetreecafebar.com. Two-floored café/bar, with burgundy walls covered in local photographs, leather sofas and softly lit corners where you can browse the newspapers; a good spot for breakfast (pancakes, smoothies) or lunch (burgers, filled breads, tapas). Daily 8.30am–11pm.
The Orange Crate 9 Beaufort Square ☎01291 630153, ⓦtheorangecrate.co.uk. Breezy, all-orange juice bar and health-food café whose jolly staff whizz up all manner of fresh fruit and veg drinks, which you can enhance with a

shot of garlic, beetroot or ginger; there are soups, salads and wraps too. Mon–Sat 8.30am–4.30pm.
Riverside Wine Bar 18a The Back ☎01291 628300, ⓦtheriversidewinebar.co.uk. Cracking location aside, this handsome riverside restaurant offers super tapas and modern Mediterranean cuisine, such as paella, and chicken and bacon skewers; a good selection of gluten-free dishes too. Tapas £3.95, mains £10–15. Daily 10.30am–11pm, Fri & Sat till midnight.
Sitar Balti The Cellar, Beaufort Square ☎01291 627351, ⓦsitarbalti.co.uk. Well-regarded Indian restaurant in the basement of a town house, specializing in balti lamb and chicken dishes; the fish dishes, including one with trout and another with sardines, are particularly worth a punt. Mains £8–12. Daily 6pm–midnight.

1

Tintern Abbey and around

March–Oct daily 9.30am–5pm, July & Aug till 6pm; Nov–Feb Mon–Sat 10am–4pm, Sun 11am–4pm • £5.50; CADW • ☎ 01291 689251

Six miles north of Chepstow, the roofless ruins of **Tintern Abbey** are spectacularly sited on one of the most scenic stretches of the River Wye. The abbey and its valley have inspired writers and painters ever since the Reverend William Gilpin published a book in 1782 extolling their picturesque qualities, and the "tall rock/The mountain, and the deep and gloomy wood" written about by Wordsworth are still evident today. Such is the abbey's enormous popularity, however, that it can get murderously busy, so it's best to go out of season or at the beginning or end of the day when the crowds have thinned out.

The best way to appreciate the scale and splendour of the abbey ruins is by walking along the opposite bank of the Wye. Just upstream from the abbey, a bridge crosses the river, from where a path climbs a wooded hillside. Views along the way and from the top are magnificent. The abbey makes a fitting venue for the annual **Tintern Sacred Site and Sound Festival** each July.

Brief history

The abbey lasted as a monastic settlement from its foundation by the Cistercian order in 1131 until its dissolution in 1536, and the original order of monks was brought wholesale from Normandy, its members establishing themselves as major local landholders and agriculturalists. This increased the power and wealth of the abbey, attracting more monks and necessitating a massive rebuilding and expansion plan in the fourteenth century, when Tintern was at its mightiest. Most of the remaining buildings date from this time, after which the influence of the abbey and its order began to wane. Upon dissolution, many of the buildings were plundered and stripped, leaving the abbey to crumble. The fact that the ruins have survived at all is largely thanks to their remoteness, as there were no nearby villages to use the stone for rebuilding.

The church

The centrepiece of the complex is the magnificent Gothic **church**, built at the turn of the fourteenth century to encase its more modest predecessor. At more than 230ft in length, it retains an extraordinary sense of grandeur, despite, or perhaps because of, being completely roofless. Much of the rest of the building remains intact, including the remarkable tracery in the west window and intricate stonework of the capitals and columns. On the neatly carpeted grass floor, meanwhile, lie pieces of the former pulpitum, an enormous decorative screen that once ran across the width of the nave.

The monks' quarters

Around the church are the less substantial ruins of the **monks' domestic quarters**, mostly reduced to one-storey rubble. Rooms are easily distinguishable, however, including an intact serving hatch in the kitchen and the square of the monks' **cloister**. The course of the abbey's waste disposal system can be seen in the **Great Drain**, an irregular channel that links kitchens, toilets and the infirmary with the nearby Wye. The **Novices' Hall** lies close to the Warming House, which, together with the kitchen and infirmary, would have been the only heated parts of the abbey, suggesting that novices might have gained a falsely favourable impression of monastic life before taking their final vows. In the dining hall, you can still see the **pulpit door** that would once have led to the wall-mounted pulpit, from which a monk would read the scriptures throughout each meal.

Tintern village

Now cluttered with teashops and overpriced hotels, the tiny village of **TINTERN** (Tyndyrn), immediately north of the abbey, is strung along a mile or so of the A466 around a loop of the river. Some 200yd along the road, by the small stone arch bridge, the **Abbey Mill** centre (daily 10.30am–5.30pm) houses a restored nineteenth-century water wheel – which springs into action at half past each hour – as well as craft shops and a coffeehouse. Further along Monmouth Road, bibliophiles will want to browse through the collectable and out-of-print titles – including some particularly rare children's titles – at Tintern's wonderful **bookshop**, Stella Books (Mon–Fri 10am–5.30pm, Sat & Sun 9.30am–5.30pm).

ARRIVAL AND INFORMATION

TINTERN

By bus The #69 bus between Chepstow and Monmouth stops at the abbey, the Abbey Mill, the visitor centre and several other points along the main village road.
Destinations Chepstow (Mon–Fri 8 daily, Sat 6, Sun 4; 20min); Monmouth (Mon–Fri 8 daily, Sat 6, Sun 4; 40min).
Tourist information The excellent Old Station visitor centre (daily: April–Sept 10.30am–5.30pm, Oct

10.30am–4pm; ☎ 01291 689566) is located another few hundred yards towards Monmouth in the former Tintern station; two refurbished carriages house an exhibition on the Wye Valley, while you can pick up leaflets on local walks, including the surrounding wildflower meadows and cliff rambles above the river. For kids, there's a play area and a miniature railway (£1) that operates most Sundays.

ACCOMMODATION AND EATING

Kingstone Brewery Opposite the Old Station ☎ 01291 680111, ⓦ kingstonebrewery.co.uk. Small microbrewery currently producing seven ales, the pick of which is the Kingstone Gold; brewery tours (£5) and ale-tasting are available, and in summer, light lunches are offered in their café. Tues, Wed, Fri & Sat 10am–4pm.
Old Station Behind the Old Station visitor centre ☎ 01291 689566. The former waiting room of the old Tintern station is now a quaint Victorian-era tearoom, with a selection of sandwiches and cakes, and hot and cold drinks; the grassy lawn in front is a delightful spot for a picnic. Tents can be pitched in the paddock behind the Old Station (booking essential); the only facilities are toilets and washbasins. Tearoom:

April–Oct daily 9.30am–5.30pm; closed Nov–March. Camping **£4**/person
Parva Farmhouse North of the abbey off the main road ☎ 01291 689411, ⓦ parvafarmhouse.co.uk. Restful B&B accommodation in this pretty seventeenth-century farmhouse, with en-suite, mostly river-view rooms; downstairs there's an honesty bar and a cosy restaurant warmed by a beamed fireplace and serving a three-course dinner menu for £21. **£78**
Royal George Monmouth Rd ☎ 01291 689205, ⓦ bw -royalgeorgehotel.co.uk. Located opposite the Abbey Mill, this neat, if slightly old-fashioned, hotel has modern, ground-level and first-floor rooms in a chalet-style building facing a large, willow-fringed garden. **£80**

Monmouth

Bordered on three sides by the rivers Wye and Monnow, elegant **MONMOUTH** (Trefynwy) retains the quiet charm of its days as an important border post and one-time county town. The centre of the town is **Agincourt Square**, a large and handsome open space at the top of the wide, shop-lined Monnow Street, gently descending to a distinctive thirteenth-century bridge over the River Monnow.

Shire Hall

Agincourt Square • Daily 10am–4pm, Oct–March closed Sun • £2, including audio visual guide • ☎ 01600 775257, ⓦ shirehallmonmouth.org.uk

The cobbled square is dominated by old coaching inns, flanking the arched Georgian **Shire Hall**. Built in 1724 as a Court of Assize, it was here, in 1839, that the Chartists' trial was held, which resulted in the death penalty for its three ringleaders – Frost, Williams and Jones – though this was later commuted to transportation (see box, p.70). The hall continued to function as a court until 2002, and you can still see the original courtrooms, as well as the holding cells below.

In the foyer, the exhibition Dig Monmouth is worth a peek for its small but intriguing archaeological finds, in particular a collection of Victorian clay pipes, and an exquisite medieval comb, flute and oddly shaped twelfth-century bone dice.

The hall's facade includes an eighteenth-century statue of the Monmouth-born King Henry V, victor at the 1415 Battle of Agincourt, which brought Normandy (and soon afterwards France) under the rule of the English Crown. In front is John Goscombe's

1

florid statue of another local, the Honourable Charles Stewart Rolls, cofounder of Rolls-Royce. A pioneer aviator too, in 1910 Rolls became the first man to pilot a double-flight over the English Channel, though barely a month later, he had the misfortune to become the first Briton to be killed in a plane accident.

The Castle and Regimental Museum

Regimental Museum: Castle Hill • April–Oct daily 2–5pm; Nov–March Sat & Sun 2–4pm • Free • ☎ 01600 772175, ⓦ monmouthcastlemuseum.org.uk

The **castle**, founded in 1068, was rebuilt in stone in the twelfth century and almost annihilated in the Civil War. The only notable remains are the Great Hall and Great Tower, the former little more than several chunks of wall, the latter featuring a fine traceried window; it was here, too, that Henry V is thought to have been born in 1387. Adjacent, the gracious seventeenth-century **Great Castle House**, built from castle bricks from the old Round Tower, has variously served as an Assize court, judges' lodging and a girls' school. These days it serves as the headquarters of the Royal Monmouthshire Royal Engineers, whose distinguished history is celebrated in the **Regimental Museum**. Formed in 1539, the regiment is the most senior in the British Army Reserve (Territorial Army), and unique for having the word "Royal" in its title twice.

Nelson Museum and Local History Centre

Priory St • Mon–Sat 11am–1pm & 2–5pm, Sun 2–5pm; Nov–Feb until 4pm • Free • ☎ 01600 710630

The market hall complex contains the **Nelson Museum and Local History Centre**, an attempt to portray the life of the great admiral through his personal artefacts – sword, medals, intimate letters and china – together with pictures, prints and naval equipment of the day. Charles Rolls' mother, Lady Llangattock, was an ardent admirer of Nelson and a voracious collector of related memorabilia, and it is her collection now on display in the museum.

Monnow Bridge

At the bottom of Monnow Street, a couple of hundred yards from Agincourt Square, the road narrows to squeeze into the confines of the fortified **Monnow Bridge** and its hulking stone gate, dating from 1262. This served both as a means of defence for the town and a toll collection point and is now the sole remaining medieval fortified river bridge in Britain where the gate tower actually stands on the bridge. Look up at the medieval garderobe (toilet), which originally emptied straight into the river below; it's now in this position because of the need to create pedestrian passageways through the gate in the nineteenth century owing to the increase in traffic.

The Kymin and Round House

Kymin Daily dawn–dusk • Free • ☎ 01600 719241 • **Round House** Easter–Oct Mon, Sat & Sun 11am–4pm • £3 • NT • ☎ 01600 719241

Just over a mile east of Monmouth, a steep road climbs up to **The Kymin**, a fine viewpoint over the town and the Wye Valley. It's crowned by the crenellated Georgian **Round House**, built as a banqueting hall, and a Neoclassical **Naval Temple**, constructed in 1801 to cheer Britain's victories at sea. Fittingly, Nelson, and his wife Lady Hamilton, visited the temple a year later.

ARRIVAL AND DEPARTURE
MONMOUTH

By bus Buses operate from the bus station at the bottom of Monnow Street.

Destinations Abergavenny (6 daily; 50min); Chepstow (hourly; 50min); Newport (hourly; 1hr); Raglan (hourly; 20min); Ross-on-Wye (9 daily; 35min); Tintern (4–8 daily; 35min); Usk (hourly; 30min).

INFORMATION AND ACTIVITIES

Tourist information The TIC is in the foyer of the Shire Hall (daily 10am–4pm, Oct–March closed Sun; ☎ 01600 775257, ✉ monmouth.tic@monmouthshire.gov.uk).

Canoeing The Monmouth Canoe & Activity Centre

(☎01600 713461, 🖳monmouthcanoe.co.uk), right by the Wye in Castle Yard, offers canoe and kayak rental, plus

instruction if needed, and guided river trips. Advance booking required.

ACCOMMODATION

Bistro Prego 7 Church St ☎01600 712600, 🖳pregomonmouth.co.uk. Eight tightly packed en-suite rooms in a cosy B&B located above the town's finest restaurant. There's also a comfortable residents' lounge with wide-screen TV, sofas and skylight. **£65**

The Coach House St John's St ☎01600 775517, 🖳thecoachhousemonmouth.co.uk. Three crisp, white-coloured en-suite rooms in this sweet little family-run guesthouse just a short walk down from the Shire Hall. **£65**

Punch House 4 Agincourt Square ☎01600 713855, 🖳sabrain.com/punchhouse. The refurbished, generously

sized rooms above this popular tavern look the part now, manifesting grey-painted timber beams, contemporary furnishings and mirrored walls, while the uneven floors and doors lend further character. **£70**

CAMPING

Monnow Bridge Campsite Drybridge St ☎01600 714004. Simple, clean and convenient town-centre site with no facilities save for toilets and showers; to get there, cross Monnow Bridge, turn right and it's behind the pub *Three Horseshoes*. **£10**/pitch

EATING AND DRINKING

★**Bistro Prego** 7 Church St ☎01600 712600. The best place to eat in town, this sprightly bistro offers separate lunch and dinner menus, with imaginative Italian-influenced dishes like tagliatelle with venison ragu (£12.50), and hake with aubergine caponata (£13). Peroni on tap too. Daily 11am–10pm.

Gate House Old Monnow Bridge ☎01600 713890. Occupying an enviable spot by the medieval bridge, and with a veranda perched over the water, *Gate House* is one of the most agreeable spots in town for a pint on a warm summer's day. Excellent draught beer, including Director's. Daily 11am–11pm.

Punch House 4 Agincourt Square ☎01600 713855. Standing adjacent to the Shire Hall, the Tudor-looking *Punch House* is the town's most popular hostelry, a rambling, reputedly haunted inn serving mainly Brain's beers; it's popular with the breakfast and mid-morning coffee crowd

too. Daily 8.30am–11pm, Fri & Sat till midnight.

Robin Hood 126 Monnow St ☎01600 713240. Diagonally across from *Gate House*, but a far more traditional boozer, this centuries-old inn is where Shakespeare is believed to have once drunk; decent beers and a fun, relaxed atmosphere. Daily 11am–11pm.

★**Stonemill** Just beyond the village of Rockfield, 2 miles west of town on the B4233 ☎01600 716273, 🖳thestonemill.co.uk. Fine dining with seasonal menus created using locally sourced ingredients, most gathered from the surrounding woodland; treats include rack of new-season lamb with buttered curly kale and confit garlic (£19.95), and roast breast of pheasant with cream sprouts and pancetta (£18). The restaurant itself, in a sixteenth-century barn with thick brick walls and chunky oak beams, looks gorgeous. Set menus £15.95–£25. Tues–Sat noon–3pm & 6–11pm, Sun noon–3pm.

The Three Castles

The fertile, low-lying land north of Monmouth, between the Monnow and the River Usk, was important as an easy access route into the agricultural lands of south Wales, and in the eleventh century the Norman invaders built a trio of strongholds here – **Skenfrith**, **Grosmont** and **White castles** – within an eight-mile radius of each other.

The castles' size and splendour demonstrate their significance in protecting the borderlands from the restless English, as well as the disgruntled Welsh, who first attacked nearby Abergavenny Castle in 1182, prompting King Ralph of Grosmont to rebuild the three castles in stone. In July 1201, all three were presented by King John to Hubert de Burgh, who fought extensively on the Continent and brought back sophisticated new ideas on castle design to replace earlier models with square keeps. He rebuilt Skenfrith and Grosmont, and his successor as overlord, Walerund Teutonicus ("the German"), worked on White Castle. In 1260, the advancing army of Llywelyn ap Gruffydd threatened the king's supremacy in south Wales, and the three castles were refortified in readiness.

Gradually, as the Welsh began to adapt to English rule, the castles were used more as living quarters and royal administrative centres than as military bases. The only return to military usage came in 1404–05, when Owain Glyndŵr's army pressed down to

1

Grosmont, only to be defeated by the future King Henry V. The castles fell into disrepair, and were finally sold by the Duchy of Lancaster to the Duke of Beaufort in 1825. The Beauforts sold the castles off separately in 1902, the first time since 1138 that the three had fallen out of single ownership.

White Castle
April–Oct daily 10am–5pm • £3 (generally free access rest of year); CADW • ☎ 01600 780380

Named for its white rendering (a few patches remain on the exterior walls), **White Castle** (Castell Gwyn) lies about eight miles west of Monmouth, and a mile south of the village of Llanvetherine. The most dramatic of the three castles, it's situated in open, rolling countryside with some superb views over to The Skirrid mountain (see p.220). From the grassy Outer Ward, a bridge leads over the moat into the dual-towered Inner Gatehouse, where the western tower, on the right, can be climbed for its vantage point. Here, you can appreciate the scale of the tall twelfth-century curtain walls in the Inner Ward. Of the domestic buildings within the walls, only the foundations and a few inches of wall remain. At the back of the ward, there are massive foundations of the Norman keep, demolished in about 1260 and unearthed in the early part of the twentieth century. The southern wall that took the place of the keep was once the main entrance to the castle, as can be seen in the postern gate in the centre, on the other side of which a bridge leads over to the Hornwork, one of the castle's three original enclosures, although now no more than a grass-covered mound.

Skenfrith Castle
Open access • Free; NT

Seven miles northeast of White Castle, alongside the River Monnow in the pretty border village of **SKENFRITH** (Ynysgynwraidd), is the thirteenth-century **Skenfrith Castle**, dominated by the circular keep that replaced an earlier Norman incarnation.

The castle's walls are built of sturdy red sandstone in an irregular rectangle. In the centre of the ward is the 21ft-high, roofless round keep, raised slightly on an earth mound to give archers a greater firing range, while below here are the vestiges of the great hall and private quarters. The Hall Range of domestic buildings includes an intact thirteenth-century window, complete with its original iron bars.

Grosmont Castle
Open access • Free; CADW

Five miles upstream of Skenfrith, right on the English border, the most dilapidated of the Three Castles, **Grosmont Castle** (Castell y Grysmwnt), sits on a small hill above the village of **GROSMONT**. Entering over the wooden bridge above the dry moat, you first pass through the ruins of the two-stage gatehouse. This leads into the small central courtyard, dominated on the right-hand side by the ruins of a large Great Hall, dating from the first decade of the thirteenth century. The village **church** is also worth a look, with some impressive Norman features, most notably the nave arches and the font. A memorial in the nave is popularly believed to be of John Kent, a fifteenth-century bard and magician believed by some to have been Owain Glyndŵr in hiding.

GETTING AROUND   THE THREE CASTLES

By bike You can drive around all three castles in a couple of hours, though it's much more enjoyable to cycle or hike the nineteen-mile circuit of paths, which are detailed in a booklet (£3.95 from Monmouth tourist office).

ACCOMMODATION AND EATING

The Bell Skenfrith ☎ 01600 750235, ⓦ skenfrith.co.uk. Opposite the castle, this sumptuous sixteenth-century riverbank inn accommodates eleven thoughtfully styled rooms, with pure wool Welsh blankets, gorgeous linens and roll top baths; most look out either over the hills or the river. *The Bell*'s well-regarded restaurant sources ingredients from

OPPOSITE PUB SIGN IN THE RHONDDA (P.116) >

The
Colliers

1

its organic kitchen garden, providing elegant dishes like fillet of bream with radish, artichoke and dandelion risotto (£15). In warmer weather pick a table on the terrace. Daily noon–2.30pm & 6.30–10pm. **£110**

Hunter's Moon Inn Llangattock Lingoed ☎01873 821499, ⊕hunters-moon-inn.co.uk. Four floral (but not too floral) en-suite rooms are complemented by the intimate thirteenth-century pub (stone-flag flooring, bare brick walls and low ceilings) serving good food and superb guest ales. Daily noon–11pm. **£75**

Mid-Monmouthshire

The disputed past of mid-Monmouthshire, between Chepstow and Newport, is obvious from the yet more castles that dot the landscape, such as that at **Caldicot**, just off the M4 near the southern Severn Bridge. Nearby **Caerwent** is now a quiet village which was once a great Roman town.

To the north is an undulating land of forests and tiny villages, crisscrossed by winding lanes that offer unexpectedly delightful views – and quaint pubs – around each corner. The contours shelve down in the west to the valley of the **River Usk**, the former border of Wales as decreed in the sixteenth century by Henry VIII. Today, the A449 roars through the valley, bypassing lanes, villages and the peaceful small town of **Usk** before joining the A40 near the spectacular ruins of **Raglan** castle.

Caldicot Castle

April–Oct daily 11am–5pm • Free • ☎01291 420241, ⊕caldicotcastle.co.uk • Buses from Chepstow and Newport stop at The Cross in the village, from where it's a five-minute walk

Wedged between the M4 and the railway, **CALDICOT** (Cil-y-coed) is the first sight of Wales for train travellers using the main line from London and drivers using the second Severn bridge crossing from Bristol.

Contained within a densely wooden country park on the eastern side of the village, the heavily restored **castle** dates from the twelfth century – one of the Norman Marcher castles built to keep a wary eye on the Welsh. The castle crumbled in the years leading up to the 1800s, before being rebuilt by a wealthy Victorian barrister, Joseph Cobb. The only original parts are a large fourteenth-century round tower and elaborate gatehouse, situated either side of a grassy courtyard, whose centrepiece is one of Nelson's battle cannons from his flagship *Foudroyant*. The tower contains a smattering of furniture and an intriguing collection of Cobb family photos.

Caerwent

Two miles northwest of Caldicot lies the historic village of **CAERWENT**. Almost two thousand years ago, the village was known by the Romans as Venta Silurum, the "market town of the Silures", a local tribe forcibly relocated here from a nearby hillfort by the conquering Romans in around 75 AD, after 25 years of battle.

The most notable remnants of the Roman town are the crumbling **walls** which form a large rectangle around the modern village. Access is easiest from the steps in front of the *Coach and Horses* pub, leading you up onto stone ramparts that command melancholic views around the quiet valley – a leisurely stroll around the walls should take no more than forty minutes. The South Wall is the most complete, still maintaining its fourth-century bastions. Follow the South Wall as it continues around to the old West Gate. Halfway along, a lane cuts up towards the village **church**: maps and diagrams in the porch explain the site of the village, and you can also see two inscribed stones, one a dedication from the Siluri tribe to their Roman overlord, Paulinus, and another, dedicated to Ocelus Mars, demonstrating the odd merging of Roman and Celtic gods for worship. Opposite the church, on the village's main street, the shin-high, rectangular outline of a Roman temple has been excavated.

Usk

Bypassed by the main A449, the quaint town of **USK** (Brynbuga) straddles the river of the same name. The town's hub is **Twyn Square**, where pastel-painted houses, flower boxes, shops and pubs make for an exceptionally pretty picture. At the top of the square – beyond the handsome clock tower – is a thirteenth-century **gatehouse**, once part of a Benedictine nunnery, and now guarding the passage to the impressive twelfth- and thirteenth-century church. Surviving features from its days as a nunnery in the 1200s include the nave and tower.

Usk Castle

Daily dawn–dusk • Free; donation requested • ☎ 01291 672563, ⓦ uskcastle.com

Looming up on a hilltop five minutes' walk from the centre of town stand the ivy-clad ruins of **Usk Castle**. Central to this eccentric little twelfth-century structure, which formed the backdrop to the Battle of Usk in 1405, are three impressive towers: the French-influenced Garrison Tower, the Great Tower with two fine intact Norman windows, and the more complete Dovecote Tower, with niches set inside for nesting birds. Meanwhile, geese and chickens roam freely among the vegetable, herb and flower gardens.

Usk Rural Life Museum

New Market St • April–Oct Tues–Sat 10.30am–5pm • Free • ☎ 01291 673777, ⓦ uskmuseum.org

At the bottom of Bridge Street, just before the bridge, the illuminating **Usk Rural Life Museum** is housed in a converted eighteenth-century malt barn. Aspects of farming are explained in a pleasantly haphazard way, and everything from animal-castrating implements to re-creations of domestic and farming interiors (including a dairy, stables and a cobbler's workshop) are packed into every available corner, while adjoining covered barns continue the exhibition with a vintage collection of tractors, ploughs and stagecoaches. Look out for Saunderson's superb Model G, which sold so well upon its initial production that it enabled the company to become the largest tractor manufacturer outside America.

ARRIVAL AND DEPARTURE
USK

By bus Buses pull in at the top of Twyn Square.

Destinations Monmouth (hourly; 30min); Newport (hourly; 30min).

ACCOMMODATION AND EATING

Glen-yr-Afon House Pontypool Rd ☎ 01291 672302, ⓦ glen-yr-afon.co.uk. An elegant and gracious country house, a 5min walk west of town across the river, with rooms of differing architectural design, though all are furnished to a high standard and have appealing garden views. **£136**

King's Head 18 Old Market St ☎ 01291 672963, ⓦ kingsheadusk.com. This centuries-old inn, a couple of minutes' walk down from the museum, doesn't look especially appealing, but the rooms are surprisingly modern and retain a certain character; there's a hearty breakfast to boot. **£65**

La Cantina 61 Bridge St ☎ 01291 673433. A smart, bare-brick bistro where Mediterranean food, and in particular fish, is the order of the day, like plaice in a lemon butter sauce with new potatoes (£16.95). The all-day menu offers smaller, bite-size dishes like German sausages with home-made tomato sauce, for £5–7. Mon 10am–4pm, Tues–Sat 10am–11.30pm, Sun 10am–5pm.

Nag's Head Twyn Square ☎ 01291 672820. The most enjoyable of the town's pubs is this engagingly cluttered space with local memorabilia and brass plates scattered around the bar; dishes like home-made rabbit pie and guinea fowl complement the terrific selection of real ales. Daily 9.30am–2.30pm & 5–11pm.

Three Salmons Bridge St ☎ 01291 672133, ⓦ threesalmons.co.uk. A hotel of sorts for some four hundred years, this striking listed building conceals the most contemporary rooms in town, each with fabulous beds, smart flat-screen TVs and DVD players, and sparkling bathrooms. The cool, handsome restaurant serves a lot of the wet stuff (fillet of halibut with beetroot and white bean cassoulet, £15), though locally sourced game is never far from the menu. Accomplished wine list too. Daily noon–2.30pm & 6.30–11pm. **£100**

1

Raglan Castle

March–Oct daily 9.30am–5pm, July & Aug till 6pm; Nov–Feb Mon–Sat 10am–4pm, Sun 11am–4pm • £4.50; CADW • ☎ 01291 690228 • Bus #60 (every 30min) from Monmouth, as well as hourly buses from Usk

Seven miles north of Usk is the village of **RAGLAN** (Rhaglan), lorded over by its glorious **castle**. The castle's ornate style and comparative intactness set it apart from other more crumbling Welsh fortresses. The late medieval castle was constructed on the site of a Norman motte in 1435 by Sir William ap Thomas. Various descendants added to the castle after his death, and building carried on into the late sixteenth century.

The **gatehouse** is still used as the main entrance, and the finest examples of the castle's showy decoration appear in its heraldic shields, intricate stonework edging and gargoyles. Inside, stonemasons' marks, used to identify how much work each man had done, can be seen on the walls. Ap Thomas' grandson, William Herbert II, was responsible for the two inner courts, built in the mid-fifteenth century around his grandfather's original gatehouse, hall and keep. The first is the cobbled **Pitched Stone Court**, designed to house the kitchen and servants' quarters. To the left is **Fountain Court**, once surrounded by opulent residences that included grand apartments and state rooms. Separating the two are the original 1435 **hall**, the **buttery**, the remains of the **chapel** and the **cellars** below.

Off Fountain Court, through the South Gate, is the pristine **bowling green**, standing on 12ft-high walls above the Moat Walk, and reached by a flight of stone steps from the green. The moated yellow ashlar **Great Tower**, off Fountain Court, manifests Continental influences in its construction, and has a surprisingly contemporary appearance. Two sides of the hexagonal tower were blown up by Cromwell's henchman, Fairfax, after an eleven-week onslaught against the Royalist castle in 1646. Climbing the tower gives you some marvellous views of the complex and surrounding countryside.

Newport and around

Wales' third-largest urban area, lively, gritty **NEWPORT** (Casnewydd-ar-Wysg) grew up around the docks at the mouth of the Usk and was finally granted city status in 2002. Evidence of Newport's rich history was largely erased by unfortunate twentieth-century development, but a massive **regeneration project** is having a transformative effect on many parts of the city. Its **sporting links** have helped too; the staging of the Ryder Cup golf tournament at nearby Celtic Manor in 2010 did much to raise Newport's profile; its rugby team, the Newport Gwent Dragons, is the source of much local pride; and the national velodrome is located here.

Vestiges of the city's history do remain, however, particularly along the river by the monumental **Transporter Bridge**, while there are also the scant ruins of a riverside **castle** and, high on a hill above town, the **Newport Cathedral** of St Woolos, King & Confessor. The city's superb **museum**, meanwhile, explores Newport's vibrant past.

THE CHARTISTS

In an era when wealthy landowners bought votes from the enfranchised few, the struggles of the **Chartists** were a historical inevitability. Thousands gathered around the 1838 People's Charter that called for universal male franchise, a secret (and annual) ballot for Parliament and the abolition of property qualifications for the vote. Demonstrations in support of these principles were held all over the country, with some of the most vociferous and bloodiest taking place in the radical heartlands of industrial south Wales. On November 4, 1839, Chartists from all over Monmouthshire marched on Newport and descended Stow Hill, whereupon they were fired at by soldiers hiding in the *Westgate Hotel*, killing around 22 protesters. The leaders of the rebellion were sentenced to death, which was commuted to transportation, by the wealthy leaders of the town. Queen Victoria even knighted the mayor who ordered the arbitrary shooting.

The heart of the city is **Westgate Square**, overlooked by the now defunct Westgate Hotel, an ornate Victorian successor to the hotel where soldiers sprayed a crowd of Chartist protesters with gunfire in 1839, killing nearly two dozen – the hotel's original pillars still show bullet marks. At the bottom of Commercial Street, **John Frost Square** (named after a former mayor and one of the 1839 Chartist leaders) is home to the Kingsway Centre, which, among other things, incorporates the city museum. The surrounding area is at the heart of the city's current redevelopment programme, the most obvious sign of which is a mega shopping and entertainment complex, which should come to fruition by the end of 2015.

The riverfront

Scything the city in two is the River Usk, whose tidal waters flow to the Severn estuary, three miles away. Between the rail and main road bridges are the risible remains of the town's **castle**, first built in 1191, rebuilt in the fourteenth century, sacked by Owain Glyndŵr in 1402 and refortified later in the same century.

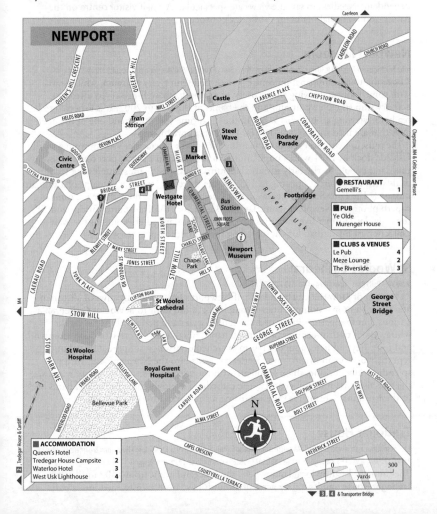

NEWPORT

RESTAURANT
Gemelli's — 1

PUB
Ye Olde
Murenger House — 1

CLUBS & VENUES
Le Pub — 4
Meze Lounge — 2
The Riverside — 3

ACCOMMODATION
Queen's Hotel — 1
Tredegar House Campsite — 2
Waterloo Hotel — 3
West Usk Lighthouse — 4

1

On the other side of the Newport Bridge, a walkway leads along the riverbank past Peter Fink's giant red sculpture, **Steel Wave**, a nod to one of Newport's great industries. Nearby, building work in 2002 revealed the remains of a medieval ship (see below).

Transporter Bridge

April–Sept Wed–Sun 10am–5pm (last crossing west to east is 4.30pm) • Car toll £1, free for cyclists and pedestrians; walkway £2.75; visitor centre free • ☎ 01633 656656, ⓦ newport.gov.uk/heritage

Dominating the Newport skyline is the magnificent **Transporter Bridge**, built in 1906 to enable cars and people to cross the river without disturbing shipping, by hoisting them high above the Usk on a dangling blue gondola. One of only six such bridges still in operation in the world, its comical, spidery legs flare out to the ground, connecting Brunel Street on the west bank and Stephenson Street opposite. The ride is smooth and the two-minute crossing has cut commuting times since the bridge was reopened in the mid-1990s. If you've got a head for heights, it's also possible to climb the 177ft (or 270 steps) up to the walkway, though this is, as you might imagine, very weather-dependent. Needless to say, the views are spectacular. A small **visitor centre** on the river's west bank elaborates on the bridge's history.

Newport Museum

John Frost Square • Tues–Fri 9.30am–5pm, Sat 9.30am–4pm • Free • ☎ 01633 656656, ⓦ newport.gov.uk/heritage

Above the tourist information centre is the enlightening city **museum**, which starts with some footage showing the recovery of a remarkably well-preserved fifteenth-century ship (the Newport Ship) on the banks of the Usk in 2002. It is expected to be ready for viewing around 2015, but in the meantime you can attend one of the open days that are held throughout the year (see ⓦ newportship.org).

The museum continues by documenting Newport's spectacular growth from a small Uskside dock in 1801 with a population of a thousand to a grimy port town of seventy thousand people by the early twentieth century. Perhaps the most interesting section deals with the Chartist uprising in 1839, while there are some fine remains of a Roman mosaic ("The Four Seasons") excavated at Caerwent. On the floor above are some superb photos of Newport's iconic landmarks, such as the Transporter Bridge and TJ's, the legendary former live music venue. The top-floor art gallery contains the **Wait Collection** of Edwardian kitsch, including three-hundred-plus teapots.

St Woolos Cathedral

Stow Hill • Daily 8am –6pm • Free • ☎ 01633 212077

At the top of **Stow Hill** you'll find one of Newport's few remaining rows of Victorian and Georgian town houses. A ten-minute walk uphill leads to **St Woolos Cathedral**, a curious, but fascinating jigsaw of architectural styles and periods. Entry is via the whitewashed twelfth-century St Mary's Chapel, notable for its pre-Conquest stonework and font. Beyond here, a superb Norman arched doorway – supported by columns reputedly of Roman origin from Caerleon – leads into the Norman nave, with its splendid timber ceiling, thick set pillars with rounded arches, and clerestory windows; the two aisles are fifteenth century. The cathedral's jarringly modern chancel harks back to these original Norman features, sporting a circular marble east window.

Tredegar House

2 miles southwest of Newport, just off M4 junction 28 • **House** Easter–Sept Wed–Sun 11am–4pm • House tour & gardens £7.20; NT • **Park** Daily 9am–dusk • Park and gardens free • ☎ 01633 815880 • Buses #15 and #30 from Newport

The home of wealthy local landowners, the Morgan family, from 1402 until 1951, **Tredegar House** and its ninety acres of grounds have been transformed into a park complete with boating and fishing lake and craft workshops. The seventeenth-century red-brick house replaced the Morgans' earlier home, and its interior is far more lavish than its unassuming exterior suggests. Of its thirty rooms open to the public, most memorable is the first-floor **Gilt Room**: an explosion of glittering fruit bosses, an intricate gilded marble fireplace, mock-walnut panelling and an elaborately painted gold stucco ceiling. The formal walled **gardens** behind the housekeeper's shop have been relaid in patterns culled from eighteenth-century designs.

ARRIVAL AND INFORMATION   NEWPORT

By train The train station is on Queensway at the top of the High Street.
Destinations Abergavenny (every 30–60min; 25min); Bristol (every 30min; 40min); Caldicot (hourly; 15min); Cardiff (every 15–30min; 15min); Chepstow (hourly; 20min); London (hourly; 1hr 50min); Swansea (every 30–60min; 1hr 20min).
By bus The bus station is on Kingsway, just down from John Frost Square.

Destinations Abergavenny (hourly; 1hr); Abertillery (every 30min; 1hr); Blaenafon (every 15min; 50min); Brecon (every 2hr; 2hr 20min); Caerwent (hourly; 40min); Cardiff (every 30min; 30min); Chepstow (every 30min; 50min); Monmouth (hourly; 1hr); Raglan (hourly; 40min); Usk (hourly; 30min).
Tourist information The TIC is in the museum complex on John Frost Square (Mon–Fri 9am–5.30pm, Sat 9am–4pm; ☎01633 842962, ⊚newport.gov.uk).

ACCOMMODATION

Queen's Hotel 19 Bridge St ☎01633 844900, ⊚jdweatherspoon.co.uk/home/hotels/the-queens-hotel. Despite its location above a busy, youthful pub, this is a very good-value central hotel, with modern, appealing rooms furnished in dark blue and burgundy tones. Breakfast costs extra (£7). **£50**
Tredegar House 2 miles southwest of Newport ☎01633 815600. Picturesque, well-equipped and family-friendly campsite within the grounds of Tredegar House. Open all year. Pitch **£21**/pitch
Waterloo Hotel 113 Alexandra Rd ☎01633 264266, ⊚thewaterloohotel.co.uk. Opposite the Transporter Bridge, this landmark turreted red-brick building has been a hotel/hostelry of sorts since 1870, when it

functioned as a docks pub (and brothel). It's slightly more refined these days, with the likes of underfloor heating in the bathrooms. Most rooms have dramatic views of the floodlit bridge by night, though for something a little special, take one of the two tower rooms, which have four-poster beds. **£90**
West Usk Lighthouse Five miles south of Newport ☎01633 810126, ⊚westusklighthouse.co.uk. Beyond the suburb of Duffryn, this place is set inside an 1821 lighthouse (decommissioned in 1922) at the mouth of the Usk on its western bank, with four exquisite nautical-style rooms, holistic therapies including a flotation tank, and a life-size Dalek at the entrance signed by the third Doctor Who, John Pertwee. Not cheap, but it is a bit special. **£145**

EATING AND DRINKING

Gemelli's 42 Bridge St ☎01633 251831, ⊚gemelli newport.co.uk. Run by chirpy Italian brothers Pasquale and Sergio, the food in this informal, artfully decorated restaurant is both inviting and authentic. Specialities include home-made tagliatelle with Welsh lamb sauce (£10.50), and mushroom- and herb-stuffed ravioli. A gluten-free menu is also available. Mon–Sat 9.30am–3pm & 6.30–10pm.

Ye Olde Murenger House 53 High St ☎01633 263977. Dating from 1530 and featuring a beautiful Tudor frontage and inviting lamplit interior, this great old stager offers Sam Smith's beers as well as some good guest ales. Local photos, as well as many of Dylan Thomas, look down from the walls. Mon–Sat 11am–11pm, Sun noon–2.30pm & 7–10.30pm.

NIGHTLIFE AND ENTERTAINMENT

Le Pub 1 Caxton Place ☎01633 221477, ⊚lepub .co.uk. A rip-roaringly fun music bar, with decent-quality live bands and DJs most Fridays and Saturdays, as well as comedy on Thursdays. Wed–Sun 8pm–1am, Fri & Sat till 3am.
Meze Lounge 6 Market St ☎01633 211432. Newport remains one of the centres of the buoyant Welsh rock and dance music scene. The city's best live music is the preserve

of this hip venue, with a prolific roster of indie-rock bands and some premier DJs.
The Riverfront ☎01633 656757, ⊚newport.gov.uk /theriverfront. The city's principal entertainment venue, staging everything and anything, from theatre, dance and comedy to contemporary and classical music and cinema – watch out too, for unplugged sets by local artists in the café.

1

Caerleon

Predating Newport by at least a thousand years, **CAERLEON** (Caerllion) is northwest of the town bridge over the River Usk (Wysg), which gave Caerleon its old Roman name of Isca. Its well-preserved remains constitute one of the most important Roman military stations in Britain, but it's best known for its reputed association with King Arthur.

Brief history

This was a major administrative and legionary centre built by the Romans to provide ancillary and military services for smaller, outlying camps in the rest of south Wales. An enormous garrison housed up to five thousand members of the Second Augustan Legion in a neat, rectangular walled town. Its only near equivalents in Roman Britain were Chester, servicing north Wales and northwest England, and York, dealing with the Roman outposts up towards Hadrian's Wall and beyond.

Although the settlement gradually decayed after the Romans left, there were still some massive remains standing when itinerant churchman Giraldus Cambrensis visited in 1188, chronicling the "immense palaces, which, with the gilded gables of their roofs, once rivalled the magnificence of ancient Rome". Today, the remnants of the Roman town lie scattered throughout the present-day centre, including the excavated bathhouse and preserved amphitheatre, both of which retain a powerful sense of ancient history.

The fortress baths

High St • April–Oct daily 9.30am–5pm; Nov–March Mon–Sat 9.30am–5pm, Sun 11am–4pm • Free; CADW • ☎ 01633 422518

Atmospheric and cleverly presented, the superb Roman **fortress baths** date from around 85 AD. Used by soldiers and their families as a place to unwind, the baths were the most important social places of the time, though the men bathed separately from the women and children. The greater part of the excavations uncovered a wonderfully intact communal pool, which is where people would go after visiting the cold hall baths (frigidarium), sections of which adjoin the main pool – the warm and hot hall baths are believed to be still buried under the town.

Also clearly visible are the foundations of the heated changing rooms - in the form of stacked tiles – and the drain, in which a hoard of gemstones (see opposite), as well as teeth, buttons and food remnants, were found. Judging by the splendid mosaic fragments on display, it would seem that the baths were richly decorated too.

KING ARTHUR

The name **King Arthur** is ubiquitous in Wales – in history, folklore books and dozens of place names (only the Devil has more places named after him across Britain). He has become one of the greatest Celtic allegories, a figure to be invoked for all manner of causes and one claimed by almost every part of the British Isles, but the earliest and strongest evidence for the reality of Arthur comes indisputably from Wales.

The first mention of King Arthur was around 800 AD in the *Historia Britonum* (History of the British), by the Welsh monk Nennius. Three centuries later, his compatriot Geoffrey of Monmouth used this work, among others, as the source material for his magisterial twelve-volume *Historia Regum Britanniae* (History of the Kings of Britain), in which he writes that Arthur was a sixth-century Celtic British king who defeated the invading Saxon army in the turbulent decades after the departure of the Romans. From sparse, semi-factual beginnings, epic stories developed. Arthur became an idealized medieval European knight, a totem of Celtic resistance and supernatural powers.

Caerleon is widely believed to be the location of Arthur's court, **Camelot**, although other claims place Camelot near Llangollen, in England at Glastonbury and in Cornwall, and in Brittany in France. Wales, however, remains perhaps the strongest contender; dozens of areas throughout Wales have Arthurian associations, and there is a plethora of books on the subject, such as Laurence Main's *In the Footsteps of King Arthur*, which has some great walks to get you to remote spots of Arthurian significance.

National Roman Legion Museum

High St • Mon–Sat 10am–5pm, Sun 2–5pm • Free • ☎ 01633 423134, ⍟ museumwales.ac.uk

A Victorian Neoclassical portico is the sole survivor of the original **National Roman Legion Museum**, now housed in the modern building behind. There are hundreds of artefacts dug from the remains of Isca and a smaller fortress at nearby Burrium (Usk): coinage, tools, pottery and glassware, military fittings and, best of all, some ninety beautifully carved gemstones retrieved from the fortress bath drain. No less impressive is a collection of chunky funerary and dedication stones, though perhaps the most curious exhibit is a sandy-coloured stone coffin with bone fragments, discovered in 1995 when digging ground for the University of Newport.

The amphitheatre

Broadway Lane • Daily 9.30am–5.30pm • Free

Opposite the museum, Broadway Lane leads down to the Roman **amphitheatre**, one of the best preserved in Britain, which was hidden under a grassy mound called King Arthur's Round Table until excavation work brought it to light in the 1920s. The amphitheatre was built around 80 AD, the same time as the Colosseum in Rome; legions of up to six thousand would sit tightly packed on the grassy stepped walls to watch the gory combat of gladiators, animal baiting or military exercises. It is still occasionally used for events and re-enactments, though of a somewhat less bloodthirsty kind. Over the road, alongside the school playing fields, are the extensive foundations of the legion's **barracks** (also called the Prysg Field), the only Roman barrack blocks still visible in Europe; you can easily make out the circular ovens and latrines.

Ffwrwm Centre

High St • Most shops daily 9.30am–5.30pm • ☎ 01633 430777, ⍟ ffwrwm.co.uk

Within the **Ffwrwm Centre** are crafts workshops, an art gallery and a fine bistro. Scattered around this eccentric cobbled courtyard – where, it is alleged, Tennyson came to investigate rumours that Caerleon was the seat of King Arthur's court (see opposite) – are dozens of sculptures inspired by ancient Celtic and Arthurian lore, while you can also clasp the gold horns of a Welsh fertility bull, an act that is supposed to lend you untold powers of procreation. It is also home to the largest-ever Welsh lovespoon (see p.51), carved from a 44ft cedar trunk.

ARRIVAL AND INFORMATION

CAERLEON

By bus From Newport, take bus #28 or #270 and get off by the post office on the High Street. Returning to Newport, catch the bus from the same spot or from the *Hanbury Arms*.

Tourist information The TIC is beside the Legionary Museum on the High Street (daily: April–Oct 10am–5pm, Nov–March 10am–4pm; ☎ 01633 422656, ✉ caerleon .tic@newport.gov.uk).

ACCOMMODATION AND EATING

Hanbury Arms Uskside ☎ 01633 420361. Located at the bottom of the High Streert, by the River Usk, the whitewashed *Hanbury* dates from the sixteenth century and is where Tennyson spent several weeks in 1856 writing *Idylls of the King* – seek out the plaque. Beers include Brains and a selection of guest ales, and there's live jazz most Sunday evenings. Daily 11.30am–11pm, Fri & Sat till midnight.

Pendragon House 18 Cross St ☎ 01633 430871, ⍟ pendragonhouse.co.uk. Listed house near the baths, with three fresh white-on-white en-suite rooms, with super beds, cool linens and flat-screen TV/DVD players. A warm welcome guaranteed, too. **£70**

Priory Hall High St ☎ 01633 421241, ⍟ thepriorycaerleon.co.uk. A long, low stone-built twelfth-century building opposite the baths, this quiet, rambling place has reasonably decent, restful rooms in both the hotel itself and the adjoining annexe. **£85**

Radford House Broadway ☎ 01633 430101, ⍟ radfordhouse.co.uk. Opposite the museum, this grand Georgian guesthouse has three brilliantly conceived rooms, each one furnished in a different architectural theme: Georgian, Roman (with canopied bed) and Art Deco. There's also a handsome communal drawing room with plenty of books and a log fire. Affordable luxury. **£85**

The Snug Ffwrwm courtyard ☎ 01633 430238,

1

Ⓦthesnugcaerleon.co.uk. Warm, friendly daytime café which on Friday and Saturday evenings serves full meals, typically of an Italian bent, or like veal parcel with mushrooms Parma ham and mozzarella cheese in red wine (£18), and the Sunday lunch is always a hit. There's outdoor seating in summer and a roaring log fire in winter. Daily 8.30am–4pm, plus Fri & Sat 7pm–midnight.

Cardiff

Official capital of Wales only since 1955, the buoyant city of **CARDIFF** (Caerdydd) has over the last fifteen years witnessed a remarkable evolution from a large town to a truly international city, with massive developments in recent years in the centre as well as on the rejuvenated Cardiff Bay waterfront.

Cardiff first gained significance in the nineteenth century with the international rise in importance of coal and iron – it was ideally located as a port for shipping these worldwide; the civic charter incorporating the city dates from 1905. The city's political profile since then has gone from strength to strength, particularly since devolution in 1999. With a reputation as a mighty party town, allied to lots of top-class sport and a cultural reawakening, it's little surprise that Cardiff has become one of the UK's most enticing destinations.

Cardiff's sights are clustered around fairly small, distinct districts. Easily navigable on foot, the **commercial centre** is bounded by the River Taff – source of the nickname of generations of expatriate Welsh – on the western side. The Taff flows past the high stone walls of Cardiff's **castle** and the **Millennium Stadium**, the city's two defining landmarks. Near the southeastern tip of the castle walls is Cardiff's main crossroads, where the great Edwardian shopping boulevards Queen Street and High Street conceal a world of arcades, great stores and run-of-the-mill malls. North of the castle, a series of white Edwardian buildings is home to the **National Museum and Gallery**, **City Hall** and **Cardiff University**.

Heading northwest out of the centre, the well-heeled suburb of **Pontcanna** is home to the city's best restaurants, beyond which is the village-like suburb of **Llandaff**, built around the city's patchwork **cathedral**.

A mile south of the commercial centre is **Cardiff Bay**, the whole area utterly revitalized since the construction of a barrage to form a vast freshwater lake; home to the **National Assembly** and **Wales Millennium Centre**, among many other attractions, it's a bona fide destination in its own right.

Brief history

Cardiff's origins date back to Roman times, when tribes from Isca settled here, building a small village alongside the Roman military fort. The fort was largely uninhabited from the Romans' departure until the Norman invasion, when William the Conqueror offered Welsh land to his knights if they could subdue the local tribes. In 1093, Robert FitzHamon built a simple fort on a moated hillock that still stands today in the grounds of the castle. A town grew up in the lee of the fortress, developing into a small fishing and farming community that remained a quiet backwater until the end of the eighteenth century.

Industrial expansion

The **Bute family**, lords of the manor of Cardiff, instigated new developments on their land, starting with the construction of a canal from Merthyr Tydfil (then Wales' largest town) to Cardiff in 1794. The second Marquis of Bute built the first dock in 1839, opening others in swift succession. The Butes, who owned massive swathes of the rapidly industrializing south Wales valleys, insisted that all coal and iron exports used the family docks in Cardiff, and it subsequently became one of the busiest ports in the world. By the beginning of the twentieth century, Cardiff's population had soared to 170,000 from its 1801 figure of around 1000, and the ambitious new Civic Centre in Cathays Park was well under way.

Changing fortunes

The twentieth century saw the city's fortunes rise, plummet and rise again. The dock trade slumped in the 1930s, and the city suffered heavy bombing in World War II, but its elevation to status of Wales' capital in 1955 suffused Cardiff with a renewed sense of purpose. This optimism and confidence has blossomed further still since the inauguration of the National Assembly in 1999, which has coincided with many government and media institutions relocating from London and elsewhere; the recent creation of the BBC Drama Village, alongside the opening of Pinewood Studios, both down by the bay, is latest proof of Cardiff's burgeoning appeal.

The city centre

The city's main north–south thoroughfare is **the Hayes**, dominated on one side by the **St Davids Centre**, a gargantuan complex incorporating over 180 shops, as well as the **St Davids Hall** concert venue. The major point of interest in the Hayes, however, is **The Old Library**, home to both the enlightening **Cardiff Story** and tourist information centre.

On the north side of the St Davids Centre, pedestrianized **Queen Street** is Cardiff's most impressive shopping street, with many of its fine nineteenth-century buildings spruced up, albeit many now effaced by typical chain-store frontages. At the western end of the street, a statue of **Aneurin Bevan**, postwar Labour politician and classic Welsh firebrand, stands aloof from the bustle.

Hidden away between the Hayes and **St Mary Street** – another flush with ornate Victorian and Edwardian shop frontages – are Cardiff's wonderful **arcades**. Beyond here, the High Street presages **Cardiff Castle**, the city's premier tourist hangout, while the magnificent **Millennium Stadium** close by is well worth visiting for a guided tour.

The Old Library and Cardiff Story

The Hayes • Mon–Sat 10am–4pm • Free • ☎ 029 2078 8334, ⍟ cardiffstory.com

At the top of the Hayes is the beautifully colonnaded frontage of the **Old Library**, home to the city's tourist office and the **Cardiff Story**. Utilizing artefacts, hands-on gizmos and audiovisual displays, it's an enlightening romp through the city's colourful history, with particular emphasis on how Cardiff has been shaped by the docks and the local coal industry. While here, don't miss the stunning **tiled corridor**; something of a hidden gem, this was the original library entrance, its ornate floor-to-ceiling tiles produced by Maw & Co in 1882.

The arcades and Cardiff Market

Secreted away between the Hayes and St Mary Street and High Street are some half a dozen renovated Edwardian arcades, concealing some of the city centre's most interesting shops. Of these, the **High Street** and **Castle arcades** are the most rewarding, packed with great clothes shops, quirky gift shops, fab little coffee houses and a range of esoteric emporia. Another worth seeking out is the glorious **Morgan Arcade**, with original 1896 detailing and Venetian windows. Here, you'll find **Spillers Records**, which was founded in 1894, making it the world's oldest record shop; you can easily spend a few hours browsing among its hard-to-find tracks of all genres, including loads of local releases. Just off the High Street is the elegant Victorian **indoor market**, great for fresh food and specialist bric-a-brac stalls.

Cardiff Castle

Daily: March–Oct 9am–6pm; Nov–Feb 9am–5pm • £12 admission includes an audio guide; £3 extra for house tour; £4 extra for clock tower tour (weekends only) • ☎ 029 2087 8100, ⍟ cardiffcastle.com

The geographical and historical heart of the city is **Cardiff Castle**, an intriguing hotchpotch of remnants of the city's past. Having been the seat of several powerful families over the centuries, its most intense phase of development came under the ownership of the Bute

CARDIFF

■ **ACCOMMODATION**

Avenue Guest House	4
Beaufort Guesthouse	9
Cardiff Caravan Park	2
Cardiff University	5
Hotel One Hundred	7
Jolyons at no.10	11
Lincoln House	6
Nomad	10
SACO Apartments	3
Town House	8
YHA Cardiff	1

● **CAFÉS & RESTAURANTS**

Cibo	6
Conway	4
Fish at 85	5
Migi	3
Mint and Mustard	1
The Smoke House	7
Waterloo Gardens Teahouse	2

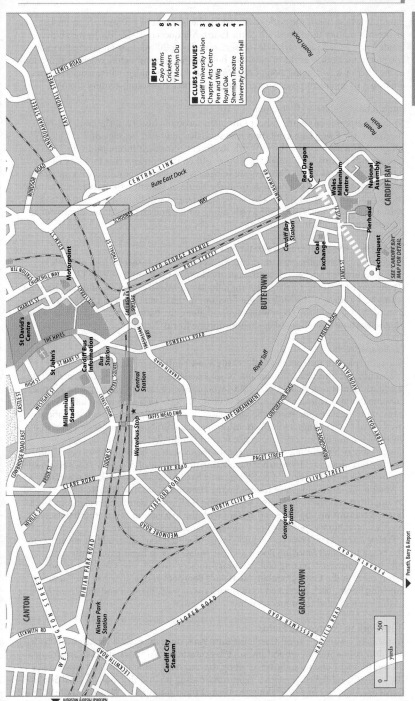

PUBS
- Cayo Arms — 8
- Cricketers — 5
- Y Mochyn Du — 7

CLUBS & VENUES
- Cardiff University Union — 3
- Chapter Arts Centre — 9
- Pen and Wig — 6
- Royal Oak — 2
- Sherman Theatre — 4
- University Concert Hall — 1

family, in whose hands the castle remained for the best part of 150 years, from the late eighteenth century until the death of the fourth Marquess in 1947. The fortress hides inside a vast walled yard, each side measuring well over 200yds long and corresponding roughly to the outline of the original fort built by the Romans. Before entering, take a look at the exterior wall running along Castle Street to the river bridge, where stone creatures are frozen in impudent poses, a rather tongue-in-cheek nineteenth-century creation.

Interpretation centre and exhibition

In the **interpretation centre** a short film offers a concise history of the castle. In the basement, the **Firing Line exhibition** relays the distinguished heritage of The Queen's Dragoon Guards and The Royal Welsh Regiment since their inception in the late seventeenth century – although the former gained their present title in 1959, the latter as recently as 2006. Cabinets are stacked with all kinds of military memorabilia garnered from numerous conflicts, from the Battle of Waterloo to more recent ventures in Iraq and Afghanistan. Here, too, is the sole reminder of Roman presence hereabouts, with a few dozen yards of exposed **wall**, along with some excellent three-dimensional murals depicting life in a Roman fort.

The Norman keep, battlements and tunnels

Perched atop a smooth grassy motte in the northwestern corner is the handsome, though much remodelled, eleventh-century **Norman keep**, built of Blue Lias limestone. At the top there are terrific views of the silky lawns spread out below and the gleaming white steel girders of the Millennium Stadium in the distance. From the North Gate immediately behind the keep, walkways lead along the **battlements**, underneath which are the **wartime tunnels**, used as shelters during World War II.

Castle apartments

The centrepiece of the complex is the **castle apartments**, dating in part from the fourteenth and fifteenth centuries, but much extended in Tudor times. Ultimately, it was the third Marquess of Bute (1847–1900) who lavished a fortune on upgrading his pile, commissioning architect and decorator William Burges (1827–81) to aid him. With their passion for the religious art and the symbolism of the Middle Ages, they systematically overhauled the buildings, radically transforming the crumbling interiors into palaces of vivid colour and intricate design, a style termed Gothic Revival. In all the rooms, fantastically rich trimmings complement the gaudy style so beloved of two nineteenth-century eccentrics, and it's worth remembering that, as one of over sixty residences owned by the Butes in Britain alone, Cardiff was only lived in for several weeks of the year.

Among the most impressive rooms are the **Drawing Room**, the **Arab Room**, decorated by imported craftsmen, the grand **Banqueting Hall**, which dates originally from 1428, but was transformed by Bute and Burges with the installation of a riotously kitsch fireplace, and **library**, possessed of a similarly fanciful chimneypiece.

Paying a little extra gives you a guided tour of all the above plus additional access to the fabulous **Winter Smoking Room** and the **Nursery**, with hand-painted tiles and silhouette lanterns depicting contemporary nursery rhymes. The Clocktower tour (also extra) takes in the **Clock Chamber**, **Bachelor's Bedroom** and, above that, the **Summer Smoking Room**, both decorated in rich patterns of gold, maroon and cobalt, with many of the images culled from medieval myths and beliefs.

Bute Park to Pontcanna Fields

Immediately west of Cardiff Castle lies **Bute Park**, once the private estate of the castle, and now containing an **arboretum**, superb flowerbeds, a stone circle, the remains of an old priory and some pleasant walks along the Taff banks. The main road crosses over the river at Cardiff Bridge, with a right turn leading up into the coolly formal **Sophia Gardens**. A quarter of a mile along the river is the multipurpose **Welsh Institute of Sport**

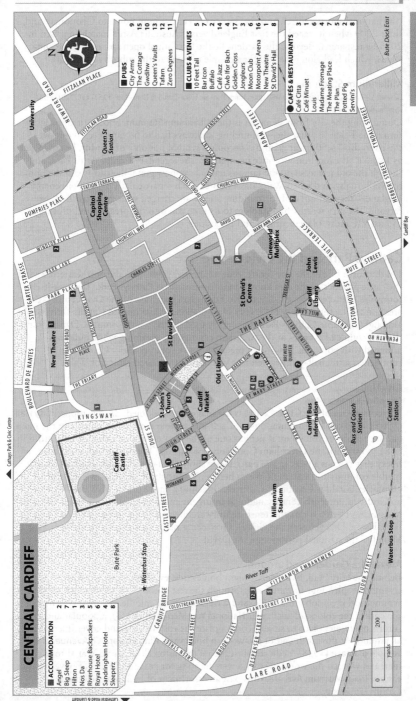

CENTRAL CARDIFF

■ ACCOMMODATION
Angel	2
Big Sleep	7
Hilton	1
Nos Da	3
Riverhouse Backpackers	5
Royal Hotel	6
Sandringham Hotel	4
Sleeperz	8

■ PUBS
City Arms	9
The Cottage	15
Gwdihw	10
Queen's Vaults	13
Tafarn	12
Zero Degrees	11

■ CLUBS & VENUES
10 Feet Tall	5
Bar Icon	7
Buffalo	2
Café Jazz	14
Clwb Ifor Bach	4
Golden Cross	17
Jongleurs	3
Moon Club	6
Motorpoint Arena	16
New Theatre	1
St David's Hall	8

● CAFÉS & RESTAURANTS
Café Citta	3
Café Minuet	1
Louis	6
Madame Fromage	4
The Meating Place	5
The Plan	7
Potted Pig	2
Servini's	8

1

(the national sports centre), and the Swalec cricket stadium, home to Glamorgan and, since 2009 when it staged the first England versus Australia Ashes match (reprised in 2015), a test arena. Beyond the gardens lie the less formal open spaces of **Pontcanna Fields**, which lead along the Taff for a couple of miles to the suburb of Llandaff.

Millennium Stadium

Westgate St • Daily tours (starting from the WRU store), hourly Mon–Sat 10am–5pm, Sun 10am–4pm • £9.50 • ✆ 029 2082 2228, ⓦ millenniumstadium.com

Dominating the city from all angles is the **Millennium Stadium**. Shoehorned so tightly into its Taff-side site that the surrounding walkways had to be cantilevered out over the river, this 74,500-seat giant has become a symbol not only of Cardiff, but of Wales as a whole. The location was once occupied by the legendary Cardiff Arms Park, and though the old terraces and the famous name have now gone, the turf is still the home of Welsh rugby, and when Wales has a home match – particularly against old enemy England – the stadium and surrounding streets are charged with good-natured, beery fervour. The very worthwhile **Stadium tours** take you into the press centre, dressing rooms, VIP areas, players' tunnel and pitchside.

Cathays Park and the Civic Centre

On the north side of the city centre, only a hundred yards from the northeastern wall of the castle precinct, is the area known most commonly as **Cathays Park**. The park itself forms the centrepiece for the impressive Edwardian buildings of the **Civic Centre** – the area containing the County Hall, City Hall, National Museum and Cardiff University – although the name Cathays Park is generally used for the whole complex. Dating from the first couple of decades of the twentieth century, the gleaming white buildings arranged with pompous Edwardian precision speak volumes about Cardiff's self-confidence, a full half-century before it was officially declared capital of Wales.

City Hall

Cathays Park • Mon–Fri 9am–5pm

The centrepiece of the Civic Centre is the magnificent, domed, dragon-topped **City Hall** (1905), an exercise in ostentatious civic self-glory. Note the Peace sculpture in the main entrance lobby as you go in: it depicts one of the women who marched from Cardiff in 1981 to establish the Greenham Common peace camp. The ornate interior is a riot of finery that reaches a peak in the particularly showy first-floor Marble Hall: all Sienese marble columns and statues of Welsh heroes. Among the figures are twelfth-century chronicler Giraldus Cambrensis, thirteenth-century native prince of Wales, Llywelyn ap Gruffydd, fifteenth-century national insurgent and perpetual hero, Owain Glyndŵr, Welsh king Henry Tudor and tenth-century architect of Wales' progressive codified laws, Hywel Dda (Howell the Good). Overseeing them all is the figure of Dewi Sant himself – the national patron saint, St David.

Alexandra Gardens and around

Behind the City Hall, two ruler-straight boulevards, evidently designed with ceremonial splendour in mind, run through the rest of the Civic Centre, arranged in symmetrical precision around **Alexandra Gardens** in the middle. At the very centre of the park is the colonnaded circular **National War Memorial** (1928), a popular and surprisingly quiet place to sit and contemplate the rush of civic and governmental duty all around. At the north end of the western boulevard, **King Edward VII Avenue**, is the **Temple of Peace** (1938), dedicated just before the outbreak of World War II to Welsh men and women the world over who were fighting for peace and relief of poverty. The eastern road, **Museum Avenue**, runs past an assortment of buildings belonging to Cardiff University.

National Museum and Gallery

Cathays Park • Tues–Sun 10am–5pm • Free • ☎ 029 2057 3000, ⓦ museumwales.ac.uk

Housed in a massive domed Portland-stone building, the exceptional **National Museum and Gallery** attempts to tell the story of Wales and reflect the nation's place in the wider, international sphere. Occupying the ground floor is the "Evolution of Wales" exhibition, on either side of which are the natural history galleries, and the "Origins" archeological exhibition. The upper floors are devoted to the museum's exceptional art galleries.

Evolution of Wales gallery

The museum's most obvious crowd-pleaser is the epic **Evolution of Wales** gallery, a natural history exhibition packed with high-tech gizmos and a staggering amount of information. It starts with a stirring large-screen video presentation, *Dyma Gymru* (This is Wales), full of stunning aerial footage taken over mountains, waterfalls and other natural wonders. It then goes on to explain, through fossils, rocks and footage of volcanoes, earthquakes and the galaxies, the slow beginnings of life on earth. Dinosaurs and the early mammals get a good look-in, including a terrific Tyrannosaurus rex skull.

Natural History galleries

The environmental education continues in the adjacent **Natural History** galleries, with a magnificent collection of sparkling crystals, re-creations of assorted environments – mountain, wetland, seashore, dunes – and some great interactive technology and interpretive boards. It then heads upstairs with a display entitled "Man and the Environment", featuring numerous animals and their habitats, and culminates in the world's largest leatherback turtle, caught off Harlech in 1988.

Origins archeology gallery

Trumping both the above is the **Origins archeology gallery**, a dazzling assortment of mostly Bronze Age and Iron Age treasures. Pride of place, however, goes to the **Red Lady of Paviland Cave**; discovered in 1823 on Gower (see p.132), the red-stained skeleton was later revealed to be that of a young man dating from around 26,000 years ago, which makes it the earliest-known burial in Britain. Among the most impressive artefacts is the superb **Caergwrle Bowl**, a boat-shaped gold votive container, more than three thousand years old and made of tin, shale and gold. No less exciting is the **Capel Garmon Firedog**, discovered near Conwy in 1852; originally one of a pair, this beautifully crafted Iron Age hearth stand with horned animals' heads most probably inhabited a chieftain's roundhouse. Heading towards the back, there's some exquisite Celtic jewellery, as well as an inspirational collection of stones and casts, spanning the earliest carved fragments (around the fifth century), through Celtic and early Christian standing stones to the more elaborate examples of the early medieval age.

Galleries 1 to 10: Historic Art

Galleries 1 to 10 examine Wales' artistic heritage, with a particularly strong collection from the **eighteenth century**, an era that was perhaps the heyday of Welsh art, with its three main protagonists – Richard Wilson, William E. Parry and Thomas Jones – well represented. Unsurprisingly, the Welsh landscape is to the fore, with the enlightening **Welsh Landscapes** in Gallery 7 well worth consideration. Here, Wilson's skill in capturing Wales' unique light can be seen to lustrous effect in his studies of castles at Caernarfon, Dolbadarn and Pembroke, as well as more emotionally intense pieces such as the beautiful *Pistyll Cain*. One of Wilson's protégés, William Hodges, also makes an appearance, most notably in his gentle evocation *Llanthony Priory*. While the equally prolific Jones also dealt in landscapes – look out for *A View in Radnorshire* and his evocative images of Naples – his most notable offering is *The Bard*, a dramatic historical piece based on Thomas Gray's tale of Edward I's massacre of the Welsh bards. The **Faces of Wales** in Gallery 5 features an intriguing collection of portraits and photos of various

1

esteemed natives, such as the travel writer Jan Morris. There's also a superb collection of **ceramics**, one of Wales' most prolific areas of applied art.

Welsh Sculpture

In the rotunda beyond Gallery 15 is a fabulous **sculpture** collection, dominated by the celebrated one-man Welsh Victorian statue industry, Goscombe John. Far better here than on the dreary municipal plinths they usually adorn, his male studies verge on the homoerotic and his female forms are exquisite. Look out for the moving *Parting*, while, inevitably, there's a nod to Celtic mythology, in the shape of the playful, Rodin-esque *Merlin and Arthur*.

Galleries 11 to 15: Impressionists and Modern Art

Galleries 11 through to 16 is where the real action is, with many works given at the bequest of two local wealthy sisters, Margaret and Gwendoline Davies. Gallery 11 is dominated by nineteenth-century French Art, featuring the likes of Millet (the haunting, unfinished *Peasant Family* and lovely, pastoral *Goose Girl at Gruchy*), the watery landscapes of Boudin, and numerous works by Manet, including the intricately observed *Effect of Snow at Petit Montrouge*. Neighbouring Gallery 12 concentrates on **Modern Art from the 1930s onwards**. Highlights include some stunning and wild pieces by Welsh supremo Ceri Richards, surrealists such as Magritte (*The Empty Mask*) and Trevelyan. Some sculpted pieces reside here too, including fine works by Henry Moore, among them *Upright Motif*, and Barbara Hepworth's haunting *Oval Sculpture*. Gallery 14, entitled **Art After Cézanne**, features a couple of pieces by Picasso, as well as sculptures by Matisse and Epstein, while in Gallery 15, the emphasis is very much on British art around 1900, with the likes of Walter Sickert, Sylvia Gosse and Gwen John, and Harold Gilman's colourful London scenes (*Café Royal* and *Mornington Crescent*).

Gallery 16: Impressionists and Post-impressionists

Gallery 16 is unquestionably the museum's star room, owing to its fabulous collection of works by the **Impressionists and Post-impressionists**. Dominating the room are several pieces by Monet, including an uncharacteristically grey *Thames at London*, whose work sits alongside artists such as Cézanne, Sisley (including his views of Penarth and Langland Bay), Carnière, Degas, Pissarro and Renoir; his coquettish *La Parisienne* is a real standout. The centrepiece here, though, is Van Gogh's stunning *Rain at Auvers* – angry slashes of rain run across the otherwise harmonious canvas – which was painted just weeks before his suicide. Mesmerizing pieces by Rodin also pepper the gallery, where there's a version of *The Kiss* and his original *Eve*.

Cardiff Bay

Although the bay is an easy half-hour stroll from the city centre, the most relaxing way to reach it is by waterbus (see box, p.89), train (every 15min from Queen Street station) or the #6 Baycar bus from outside Central station (every 10–15min; £2 return)

A must-see part of any Cardiff tour, **Cardiff Bay** has become one of the world's biggest regeneration projects, the downbeat dereliction of the old docks having been almost completely transformed into a designer heaven; the arrival of the BBC's Drama Village – where both *Doctor Who* and *Casualty* are shot – has served to further enhance the Bay's appeal. In times gone by, when the docks were some of the busiest in the world, the area was better known by its evocative name of **Tiger Bay**, one that was immortalized by locally born chanteuse Shirley Bassey.

Ever-expanding, the Bay area now comprises four distinct parts, situated either side of **Roald Dahls Plass**, the main square named after the Cardiff-born children's author (1916–90) best known for his 1964 classic, *Charlie and the Chocolate Factory*: on the eastern side lie the swanky civic precincts around the glorious **Wales Millennium Centre**; north of here the **Drama Village** and the new **Doctor Who Experience**; to the west, the shiny **Mermaid Quay**, which is effectively the bay's retail and leisure complex; and finally, set back from the water's edge, the somewhat down-at-heel, but increasingly gentrified, Taff-side suburb of **Butetown**.

The Wales Millennium Centre

Bute Place • Guided tours: daily 11am & 2.30pm • £6 • ☎ 029 2063 6464, Ⓦ wmc.org.uk

Dominating the whole area is the mesmerizing **Wales Millennium Centre**, a vibrant performance space for theatre and music, and the resident home to many of Wales' premier arts organizations. Likened by critics to a copper-plated armadillo or aardvark, the WMC soars over the Bay rooftops, its exterior swathed in numerous Welsh building materials, including different slates, wood and stone, topped with a stainless-steel shell tinted with a bronze oxide to resist salty air.

Writ large across the frontage in 7ft-high letter windows, the inspirational bilingual **inscription** was crafted by poet Gwyneth Lewis; the phrases read downwards – in English "In these stones, horizons sing" and in Welsh "Creu gwir fel gwydr, o ffwrnais awen" ("Creating truth like glass, from the furnace of inspiration") – but, ingeniously, they also read across each line, in two languages, and still make crystal-clear poetry.

The grace and style continue throughout the interior, fashioned from materials that hark back to Wales' mineral-extracting past, from the native oak, ash, beech, sycamore,

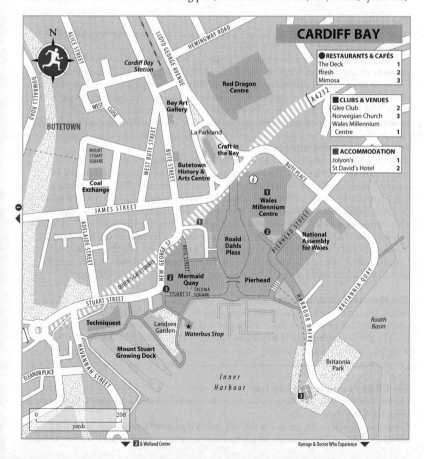

1

alder, birch, chestnut and cherry woods to the riveted steel and coal-like pillars.
Guided tours of the building allow complete backstage access, as well as intimate
views of the main auditorium, the acoustically sensational Donald Gordon Theatre.

The ground floor houses the main box office, music shop, souvenir shop, and the
excellent bar and brasserie *ffresh* (see p.92). Daily **free performances** of anything from
poetry to hip-hop take place in the WMC foyer, usually at lunchtime and 6pm.

The Pierhead

Daily 10.30am–4.30pm • Free • ☎ 0845 0105500, ⓦ pierhead.org

The most obvious, and evocative, reminder of the Bay's shipping heritage is the
magnificent red-brick **Pierhead Building**, which has beckoned vessels into Cardiff port
since its construction in 1897. A typically ornate neo-Gothic terracotta pile, it was
built for the Cardiff Railway Company – formerly the Bute Dock Company which
burnt down in 1892 – and perfectly embodies the wealth and optimism of the Bute
family and their docks. It now houses a surprisingly enjoyable **exhibition** documenting
the rise and fall of the coal-exporting industry hereabouts; the building became the
administrative centre for the Port of Cardiff in 1947, and the last shipment of coal left
here in 1964. There's also an exhibition on the genesis of the nearby **National Assembly
for Wales**, a striking building designed by Richard Rogers.

The Norwegian Church

Harbour Drive • Mon–Fri 11am–4pm, Sat & Sat 10am–4pm; opening hours can vary depending on special events • ☎ 029 2087 7959,
ⓦ norwegianchurchcardiff.com

A short walk around the Bay stands the gleaming white **Norwegian Church**, an old
seamen's chapel built in 1868 on land donated by the Marquis of Bute. Once one of
the most important Scandinavian missions in Britain – it regularly served up to seventy
thousand sailors per year – the building is more well known for being the place where
Roald Dahl – whose parents were Norwegian – was christened. Its role today is as a
prominent arts and performance centre, while there is also a charming little café here.

The Doctor Who Experience

Discovery Quay • Daily 10am–5pm • £15 (£13 online) • ☎ 0844 801 3663, ⓦ doctorwhoexperience.com

A five-minute walk north of the Norwegian Church, a large, humpbacked-shaped
hangar houses the **Doctor Who Experience**, devoted to the cult BBC programme that
was first aired in 1963, and most of which has been filmed in Cardiff since its relaunch
in 2005. While you don't necessarily have to be a fan to enjoy this, it does help; the
visit begins with a cleverly conceived, multi-sensory "journey through time", in which
you join the Doctor in confronting various adversaries. Thereafter, you're free to
wander around the two floors of original props and artefacts, which include the
costumes of all twelve Doctors to date, the Tardis interior, and the Doctor's many
arch foes, such as Davros, the Cybermen and, of course, the iconic Daleks.

The Mermaid Quay district

Across from the Pierhead, **Mermaid Quay** is an airy jumble of shops, bars and
restaurants that on a warm day is a fine place to hang out and watch the world amble
by. The city's **waterbuses** and **bay cruise** operators leave from here (see box, p.89),
with information boards carrying details of a variety of boat-rental opportunities to
get you out onto the water.

Cardiff Bay Barrage and Bay Trail

Daily 7am–10pm • Free • ☎ 029 2087 7900, ⓦ cardiffharbour.com • Waterbuses run between the waterfront and the southern end of the
barrage daily 10.30am–4.30pm (£4 return)

Central to the whole Bay project is the half-mile-long **Cardiff Bay Barrage**, built right
across the Ely and Taff estuaries, which transformed a vast mud flat into a freshwater lake

and created eight miles of useful waterfront. Despite its controversies, the barrage is a phenomenal bit of engineering, and it's well worth having a wander along the beautifully landscaped embankment to see the lock gates, sluices, fish path and stunning views; there's a great kids' play area and skate park too. For something more strenuous, you could tackle the 6.2mile **Bay Trail**, a circular path for walkers and cyclists that wends its way around the bay and across to Penarth. If you don't fancy walking, note that yellow waterbuses shuttle between the waterfront and the southern end of the barrage at Penarth.

The Wetlands Centre

Jutting out over the water like an ocean-going liner, the **St Davids Hotel**, east of Mermaid Quay, acts as a stylish full stop to the sweep of the bay. From its car park, a path leads a couple of hundred yards to a 20-acre **wetland reserve**, created partly to help offset the loss of wading-bird habitats when the barrage was built and the Bay flooded. It's a surreally peaceful spot in which to have a picnic or just stop and let the world go by for a while.

Cardiff International White Water

Watkiss Way • Mon, Tues, Thurs & Sat 9am–5pm, Wed & Fri 9am–8pm, Sun 9am–4pm • ☎ 029 2082 9970, ⓦ ciww.com • Bus #7 from Cardiff Bay

Rounding off the waterfront's varied attractions is **Cardiff International White Water**, located within the International Sports Village down by the mouth of the River Ely. The main attraction here is the indoor simulated surf machine, but the rapids course is hugely popular too, accommodating a number of adrenaline-fuelled watersports, including rafting, canoeing, kayaking and hydro-speeding. The variable river flows make it suitable for everyone, including beginners.

Butetown

The area immediately inland from the Bay is the salty old district of **Butetown**, whose inner-city dereliction is still evident among the rampant gentrification that has taken place here and the surrounding area over the past couple of decades. James Street is the main commercial focus, while to its north are the cleaned-up old buildings around **Mount Stuart Square**, now mostly accommodating offices and the occasional art studio.

Coal Exchange Building

Mount Stuart Square • ☎ 029 2049 4917, ⓦ coalexchange.co.uk

By far the most impressive of any of the buildings in Butetown is the mammoth **Coal Exchange Building**. Built in the 1880s as Britain's central Coal Exchange, the building was used as a base from where trade negotiations for the south Wales coal mining industries could take place; it also saw the world's first £1 million cheque signed in 1908. The old trading hall retains its splendid Corinthian columns and wood-panelled walls, though the building is currently closed pending major restructuring work.

Butetown History & Arts Centre

4/5 Dock Chambers, Bute St • Tues–Fri 10am–5pm, Sat & Sun 11am–4.30pm • Free • ☎ 029 2025 6757, ⓦ bhac.org

The enthusiastically run, community-based **Butetown History & Arts Centre** aims to record and celebrate the remarkable multicultural pedigree of a district that is home, for example, to one of the oldest black communities in Britain. To that end, the centre mounts rotating exhibitions (with particularly strong photographic shows), offers guided tours, stages cultural events and maintains a growing archive.

Craft in the Bay

The Flourish • Daily 10.30am–5.30pm • Free • ☎ 029 2048 4611, ⓦ makersguildinwales.org.uk

Set out rather stylishly at the southern end of Lloyd George Avenue, one block further east of Bute Street, is **Craft in the Bay**. Occupying an old maritime warehouse, this fabulous, sheer-glazed building exhibits a range of contemporary applied art and craft from practitioners the length and breadth of Wales, as well as some from overseas. Many of the products can be purchased and there's a cute café here too.

Llandaff Cathedral

Cathedral Rd, Llandaff • Cathedral: daily 8am–7pm; garden open access • Free • ☏ 029 2056 4554, ⓦ llandaffcathedral.org.uk • Bus #33 or #33A from Cardiff bus station

A small, quiet ecclesiastical village, **Llandaff** lies two miles northwest of the city centre. The church that has now grown up into the city's **cathedral** is believed to have been founded in the sixth century by St Teilo, but was rebuilt in Norman style from 1120 well into the thirteenth century. From the late fourteenth century, the cathedral fell into disrepair, hurried along by the adverse attention of Cromwell's soldiers during the Civil War. In the early eighteenth century, one of the twin towers and the nave roof collapsed. Restoration only began in earnest in the early 1840s, and Pre-Raphaelite artists such as Edward Burne-Jones, Dante Gabriel Rossetti and the stained-glass firm of William Morris were commissioned to provide colourful new windows and decorative panels. In January 1941, a German landmine destroyed whole sections of it, but faithful and painstaking restoration was finally completed in 1960.

The fusion of different styles and ages is evident from outside, especially in the mismatched western towers. The northwest tower is by Jasper Tudor, a largely fifteenth-century work with modern embellishments, while the adjoining tower and spire were rebuilt from nineteenth-century designs.

The interior

Inside, Jacob Epstein's overwhelming *Christ in Majesty* sculpture, a concrete parabola topped with a circular organ case on which sits a soaring Christ figure, was the only entirely new feature added in the postwar reconstruction, and dominates the nave today.

At the west end of the north aisle, the **St Illtyd Chapel** features Rossetti's cloying triptych *The Seed of David*, whose figures – David the shepherd boy, David the King and the Virgin Mary – are modelled on Rossetti's Pre-Raphaelite friends. Along a little further, in the south presbytery, is the tenth-century Celtic cross that is the cathedral's only pre-Norman survivor. At the far end of the cathedral is the elegantly vaulted and beautifully painted **Lady Chapel**, notable for its gaudy fifteenth-century reredos on the back wall that contains, surrounded by golden twigs and blackthorn in each niche, bronze panels with named flowers (in Welsh) in honour of Our Lady. Over two dozen flowers take their Welsh names from the Virgin Mary.

The walled garden

While you're here, it's worth having a quick look at the medieval **walled garden** of the Llandaff Bishops' Palace on the Cathedral Green. With herbaceous plants arranged according to medieval patterns, it makes a pleasant – and fragrant – place to sit for a few minutes.

ARRIVAL AND DEPARTURE   CARDIFF

By plane Cardiff international airport (☏ 01446 711111, ⓦ cardiff-airport.com) is ten miles southwest of the city on the other side of Barry. The most direct way to reach the city centre is by Express bus T9, which runs every 20min (£5) and takes you from the main terminal into the city in 30min. Alternatively, you can take a shuttle bus from the main terminal to Rhoose Cardiff International Airport train station and then a connecting train (Mon–Sat hourly, Sun every 2hr; £3.70 combined ticket). A taxi from the airport to Cardiff Central will cost around £30.

By train Cardiff Central train station handles all inter-city services, as well as many suburban and Valley Line services. Queen Street station, at the eastern edge of the centre, is for local services only, including those to Cardiff Bay.

TRIPS AND TOURS

Open-top, hop-on hop-off **sightseeing bus tours** (daily, every 30min: April–Oct 10am–5pm, Nov–March 10am–3.30pm; 24hr-ticket £12) start from outside the castle and carve a circuit around the city and Cardiff Bay, allowing you to hop on and off at will. For something a little more energetic, Cardiff Walking Tours (☎07905 923421, ⊚cardiffwalkingtours.com) operates a range of interesting **walking tours**, including city strolls, history walks and a bay ramble, typically around an hour and a half long and costing £6.

A scenic **waterbus service** (hourly 10.30am–4.30pm; £4 one-way; ☎029 2034 5163, ⊚aquabus.co.uk) operates between Bute Park, near Cardiff Castle, to Mermaid Quay in the bay, though occasionally (depending on the river flow), the service will only run as far as Taff's Mead Embankment, diagonally across from the Millennium Stadium. Bay Island Voyages (☎029 2078 2733, ⊚bayislandvoyages.co.uk) offers various boat trips out to Flat Holm island (see p.98), plus high-octane trips in a rigid-hulled inflatable boat around the Bay.

Destinations Abergavenny (every 45min; 40min); Barry Island (every 20–30min; 30min); Bristol (every 30min; 50min); Caerphilly (every 15min; 20min); Carmarthen (hourly; 1hr 45min); Chepstow (every 30–60min; 40min); Crewe (mostly hourly; 2hr 30min); Haverfordwest (9 daily; 2hr 30min); Holyhead (6 daily; 5hr); Llanelli (every 30–60min; 1hr 10min); Llantwit Major (hourly; 40min); Llwynypia (every 30min; 50min); London (every 30min; 2hr); Manchester (mostly hourly; 3hr 10min); Merthyr Tydfil (every 30min; 1hr); Neath (every 30min; 40min); Newport (every 15–30min; 15min); Penarth (every 15min; 15min); Pontypridd (every 15min; 30min); Swansea (every 30min; 1hr); Trehafod (every 30min; 35min); Ystrad Rhondda (every 30min; 50min).

By bus The main bus station is in front of Cardiff Central train station.

Destinations Abergavenny (hourly; 2hr 20min); Barry Island (every 30min; 1hr); Blaenafon (hourly, 1 change; 1hr 30min); Brecon (8 daily; 1hr 35min); Bristol (8 daily; 1hr 20min); Caerphilly (every 20min; 40min); Cardiff–Wales Airport (every 20min; 30min); Chepstow (every 30min–1hr, 1 change; 1hr 20min); Cowbridge (every 30min; 40min); Llantwit Major (6 daily; 45min); Merthyr Tydfil (every 20min; 55min); Nelson (hourly; 35min); Newport (every 30min; 40min); Penarth (every 15min; 20min); Pontypridd (every 15min; 30min); Senghenydd (hourly; 50min); Swansea (every 20min; 1hr).

INFORMATION

Tourist information Housed inside the Old Library on The Hayes, the tourist office (Mon–Sat 9.30am–5pm, Sun 10am–4pm; ☎029 2087 3573, ⊚visitcardiff.com) stocks a welter of information, on Cardiff and further afield. Tickets for the theatre and other events can be purchased here, and staff can book accommodation. You can pick up a copy of *Buzz*, a free monthly guide to arts and events in the city. There's also a visitor centre in the Millennium Centre in Cardiff Bay (daily 10am–6pm).

GETTING AROUND

On foot Cardiff is an easy, flat and compact city to walk around; even the Bay area is within a 30min stroll of Central station.

By bus Out of the centre, there's an extensive and reliable bus network operated by the Cardiff Bus (Bws Caerdydd) company. A one-way fare anywhere in the city costs £1.80 (payable on the bus, exact money only). The last buses generally leave the city centre at around 11.30pm. Various travel passes offer good savings: a "Day to Go" ticket (£3.60) gives unlimited bus travel around Cardiff and Penarth for a day, a range which can be extended to Barry and the Vale of Glamorgan with the "Day to Go Plus" ticket (£4.90). The Network Dayrider ticket (£8) covers all the above plus much of the rest of southeast Wales. A "Weekly to Go" ticket (£15) is good for seven days' unlimited travel around Cardiff and Penarth,

while the "Weekly to Go Plus" ticket (£19) covers the entire Cardiff area network. All are available from the ticket office in the library on the Hayes (Mon, Tues & Thurs–Sat 11am–5pm; ☎029 2066 6444, ⊚cardiffbus .com) or on board buses themselves; you can also buy the "Day to Go" tickets from the tourist office.

By taxi There are taxi ranks at Central station, Queen Street station, Duke Street by the castle and St Mary's Street; try Capital Cabs (☎029 2077 7777) or Dragon Taxis (☎029 2033 3333).

By bike Pedal Power offers an excellent bike rental scheme (and guided tours), with outlets at *Pontcanna Caravan Park* and at a kiosk just beyond the Norwegian Church in Cardiff Bay (☎029 2039 0713, ⊚cardiffpedalpower.org; £7/hr, £20/day).

1

ACCOMMODATION

Cardiff has a reasonable, though by no means extensive, stock of **accommodation**. The centre, in particular, is surprisingly lacking in good-quality establishments, while the more interesting places, including a well-established belt of Victorian guesthouses, are located 15min walk northwest of the centre along leafy Cathedral Road, towards the suburb of Pontcanna. There's a decent spread of hostels, most of which are centrally located. Be aware that **prices** for all forms of accommodation are ramped up hugely during rugby weekends.

HOTELS AND GUESTHOUSES

CITY CENTRE

Angel Castle St ☎ 029 2064 9200, ⓦ thehotelcollection .co.uk; map p.81. Much-restored Victorian bauble occupying a prime city-centre location between the castle and the Millennium Stadium; although the building looks slightly jaded from the outside, the air-conditioned rooms are large and modern enough. **£75**

Big Sleep Bute Terrace ☎ 029 2063 6363, ⓦ thebigsleephotel.com; map p.81. Snazzy budget option occupying a former 1960s office block turned retro designer hotel; the vivid, blue-shaded rooms are available in doubles, triples and family rooms, which double up for disabled guests. **£70**

Hilton Kingsway ☎ 029 2064 6300, ⓦ hilton.co.uk /cardiff; map p.81. Cardiff's most agreeable high-end hotel, offering warmly decorated, generously sized rooms, and sparkling bathrooms with large walk-in showers; some overlook Castle Park. First-rate facilities include a heated lap pool, spa and gym. **£110**

Royal Hotel 88 St Mary St ☎ 029 2055 0750, ⓦ royalhotelcardiff.com; map p.81. Despite its air of faded grandeur, this Victorian building conceals a modern interior; the bold red-and-black furnished rooms and limestone-finished bathrooms are well appointed, if somewhat devoid of charm. Given that it's on one of the city's busiest streets, it's surprisingly quiet. Some good advance rates are available too. **£59**

Sandringham Hotel 21 St Mary St ☎ 029 2023 2161, ⓦ sandringham-hotel.com; map p.81. Pleasantly old-fashioned, family-run hotel offering plain but clean decor, good service and a friendly atmosphere. One of the better value for money places in the city. **£40**

★ **Sleeperz** Station Approach ☎ 029 2047 8747, ⓦ sleeperz.com; map p.81. Cleverly utilizing the architectural space in between the rail line and two roads, this funkily designed hotel has light-filled rooms in breezy white/orange and black/grey colour schemes; the corner cabin bunk rooms are particularly neat. Terrific value. Breakfast is extra. **£55**

CATHEDRAL ROAD

Avenue Guest House 163 Cathedral Rd ☎ 029 2023 2855, ⓦ theavenueguesthouse.com; map pp.78–79. A very reasonable family-run Victorian-style place with six fresh, sunny rooms, some en suite, all of which are individually styled. **£60**

Beaufort Guesthouse 65 Cathedral Rd ☎ 029 2023 7003, ⓦ beauforthousecardiff.co.uk; map pp.78–79. One of the most gracious Victorian guesthouses along this strip, with classic period furnishings in all ten rooms, a great-looking dining room and secure parking. **£82**

★ **Jolyon's at No. 10** 10 Cathedral Rd ☎ 029 2009 1900, ⓦ jolyons10.com; map pp.78–79. There's no scrimping on style at this gorgeous boutique hotel, which accommodates 21 handsomely presented rooms (eight of which are larger suites) manifesting Italian/French-inspired furnishings; ask for a room overlooking Bute Park. **£99**

Lincoln House 118 Cathedral Rd ☎ 029 2039 5558, ⓦ lincolnhotel.co.uk; map pp.78–79. The most upmarket accommodation in the upper reaches of the road, this small Victorian hotel has rooms furnished with button-leather couches and heavy brocade. There's also a comfortable lounge bar for residents. **£90**

Town House 70 Cathedral Rd ☎ 029 2023 9399, ⓦ thetownhousecardiff.co.uk; map pp.78–79. One of the more modern guesthouses along Cathedral Road, this restored Victorian house has stained-glass windows and a mosaic-tiled hall, and offers eight en-suite rooms, a residents' lounge and better-than-average facilities. **£65**

EAST OF THE CENTRE

Hotel One Hundred 100 Newport Rd ☎ 07916 888423, ⓦ hotelonehundred.com; map pp.78–79. It's not the most flattering location in the world, on one of the busiest roads into the city, but this appealing seven-room bed and breakfast offers bespoke beds, crisp linen, and neat extras like DVD players and iPod docking stations. **£75**

CARDIFF BAY

Jolyon's 5 Bute Crescent ☎ 029 2048 8775, ⓦ jolyons .co.uk; map p.85. Sister hotel to *Jolyon's* on Cathedral Road, this exquisite boutique hotel in a former seaman's house has seven beautifully conceived rooms, each unique, perhaps with a wrought-iron or antique carved wooden bed, Indian teak fittings or slate-tiled bathroom walls; one even has its own roof terrace. **£85**

St Davids Hotel Havannah St ☎ 029 2045 4045, ⓦ thestdavidshotel.com; map p.85. An air of cool sophistication pervades this business-minded hotel whose waterfront location is unmatched anywhere in the city; encircling the vast, sunny atrium are a choice of rooms, though nearly all have floor-to-ceiling windows and balconies from which to take in the views. Top-notch spa facilities to boot. **£100**

HOSTELS, SELF-CATERING AND CAMPING

Cardiff Caravan Park Pontcanna Fields ☎029 2039 8362, ⓦcardiff.gov.uk; map pp.78–79. Very good council-run caravan park, an easy 25min walk from the city centre, with limited tent pitches, two service blocks, laundry and dishwashing facilities. The entrance is from Pontcanna Fields or at the end of Dogo St, off Cathedral Road. Open all year. **£6**/person, **£3**/car

Cardiff University Cathays Park ☎029 2087 4616, ⓦcardiff.ac.uk/conferences. Thousands of en-suite student rooms near the city centre are available from around 20 June to 10 Sept on a B&B or self-catering basis. A good, cheap option. Breakfast available Mon–Fri only. **£55**

Nomad 11 Howard Gardens ☎029 2025 6826, ⓦnomadcardiff.co.uk; map pp.78–79. In a Victorian terrace building a 5min walk from the centre, this youth-orientated hostel has small and large dorms; facilities include lounge with Sky TV, bar and games room with pool table. Dorms **£18**

Nos da 53–59 Despenser St ☎029 2037 8866, ⓦnosda .co.uk; map p.81. Hip hostel/budget hotel on the riverbank opposite the Millennium Stadium. Accommodation is in singles, doubles (some en suite) and four- to ten-bed dorms, with avant-garde decor like outsized artwork that flips down and transforms into beds. Also home to the popular bar *Tafarn* (see p.93). Dorms **£21.50**, doubles **£44**

★**Riverhouse Backpackers** 59 Fitzhamon Embankment ☎029 2039 9810, ⓦriverhouse backpackers.com; map p.81. Cosy, contemporary backpackers' hostel in a 120-year-old Victorian villa with mixed and female-only dorms and twin rooms, as well as a self-catering kitchen, welcoming dining/lounge area and a sunny wraparound garden terrace. Dorms **£18**, doubles **£44**

SACO Apartments 76 Cathedral Rd ☎011 7970 6999, ⓦsacoapartments.co.uk; map pp.78–79. Elegant one- and two-bedroom apartments in a large town house with full kitchens, washer/dryers, internet and private parking. **£90**

YHA Cardiff 2 Wedal Rd, Roath Park ☎0870 371 9311, ⓦyha.org.uk; map pp.78–79. Large, purpose-built building just underneath the A48 Eastern Ave flyover at the top of Roath Park, almost 2 miles from the city centre and reachable via bus #28, #29 or #29B from the station (get off at the bus stop for Wedal Rd/Lake Rd West). No curfew. Dorms **£16**, doubles **£36**

EATING

The city's long-standing internationalism, particularly its Italian influence, has paid handsome dividends in its range of **restaurants** and **cafés**. That said, there's a paucity of top-drawer restaurants in the centre itself, and you'll have to head a little further out to sample the best of Cardiff's food, in particular to Pontcanna to the northwest, where there's a coterie of outstanding restaurants. Mermaid Quay in Cardiff Bay is now home to a staggering number of restaurants, though many of these are the ubiquitous chain affairs.

CITY CENTRE

CAFÉS

★**Madame Fromage** 21–25 Castle Arcade ☎029 2064 4888, ⓦmadamefromage.co.uk; map p.81. A small slice of Paris at this delightful corner café-cum-deli where cheese is king – the menu offers a lot more besides, however, from tartlets and quiche to lamb cawl and charcuterie platters. Afterwards, or alternatively, make a beeline for the shop's tempting stock of jams, pickles and chutneys. Mon–Fri 10am–5.30pm, Sat 9.30am–5.30pm, Sun noon–5pm.

★**The Plan** 28–29 Morgan Arcade ☎029 2039 8764; map p.81. Without question, *the* place in Cardiff to come for coffee, a great-looking two-floored café with floor-to-ceiling windows, offering a super range of drinks as well as light meals (breakfasts, baked potatoes, toasties and salads) made using locally sourced organic produce.

Mon–Sat 8.45am–5pm, Sun 10.30am–4pm.

Servini's 6–10 Wyndham Arcade ☎029 2039 4054; map p.81. Secreted away down another arcade, this cheery family-run local serves a wide variety of filling sandwiches and baguettes, among them some great veggie choices; there's a cracking all-day breakfast on offer too. Eat in or take away. Mon–Sat 8am–4pm.

RESTAURANTS

Café Citta 4 Church St ☎029 2022 4040; map p.81. A friendly, laidback pizzeria straight out of Italy, with a fine little log-burning oven knocking up freshly cooked pizzas (£7–8) using dough and sauces made on the premises, and locally sourced ingredients. Ideal spot for either a quick lunch or a quiet evening meal. Tues–Sat 11am–11pm, Sun noon–6pm.

CARDIFF FARMERS' MARKETS

If you're looking to pack a picnic, you could do a lot worse than head to one of Cardiff's terrific **farmers' markets** (ⓦriversidemarket.org.uk), where you can pick up some great local produce and sometimes other knick-knacks. The biggest and best is the Sunday **Riverside Market**, opposite the Millennium Stadium on Fitzhammon Embankment (10am–2pm). On Saturdays (9.30am–1pm) the **Roath Market**, at the Mackintosh Sports Club on Keppoch St, in Roath, also has an arts and craft bazaar.

★Café Minuet 42 Castle Arcade ☎029 2034 1794; map p.81. Cheap, cosy and delightfully odd restaurant, whose hearty, authentic Italian regional cooking has been attracting a loyal band of locals for years. Park yourself at one of the check-clothed tables or out in the arcade itself, where there's a tiny hatch for takeaway snacks. Mains £6–8. Mon–Sat 11.30am–4.30pm.

Louis 32 St Mary St ☎029 2022 5722; map p.81. This place won't win any prizes for glamour, but it's a wondrously cheap and old-fashioned restaurant serving great heapings of well-cooked, traditional British comfort food such as steak and kidney pie (£6). Mon–Fri 8.30am–8pm, Sat 8am–7pm, Sun 9am–4pm.

The Meating Place 40 St Mary St ☎029 2022 4757, ⓦthemeatingplace.co.uk; map p.81. The clue is in the name at this sparkling grill house where you can choose from a concise menu of gut-busting meat dishes, though it's the restaurant's signature hanging skewers, marinated and cooked on an open charcoal barbeque, that really pull in the punters. The two-course express menu (£9.95) is good value. Mon 5.30–11pm, Tues–Sat noon–3pm & 5.30am–11pm, Sun 10.30am–4pm.

★Potted Pig 27 High St ☎029 2022 4817, ⓦthepottedpig.com; map p.81. This venue – in the reconditioned vaults of a former bank – is a terrific spot to tuck into all things piggy, like potted pig with toast and pickles, or roast belly of pork (£12), though there's much more besides, such as crab, rabbit and duck. The wine list complements the food brilliantly. Just the place for a romantic liaison. Tues–Sat noon–2.30pm & 7–10pm, Sun noon–2pm.

CARDIFF BAY

CAFÉ

★The Deck 20 Harrowby St ☎029 2115 0385; map p.85. Outstanding neighbourhood coffeehouse and cakery whose genial staff delight in serving some of the best coffee in the city, alongside baked goodies, sandwiches and breakfasts. The Vintage High Tea (£14) is a lot of fun. Mon 9.30am–4pm, Tues–Sat 9.30am–5.30pm.

RESTAURANTS

ffresh Wales Millennium Centre ☎029 2063 6465; map p.85. Deservedly a big hit with pre-show diners, this is as fresh as its name suggests. Nicely crafted lunch and dinner menus, featuring the likes of pan-fried sea trout with sauté potatoes, samphire and shrimp butter (£15.50). Meanwhile, the crisp, minimalist lounge bar serves scrumptious burgers with onion marmalade and potato chips. Restaurant Tues–Sat noon–2.30pm & 5–9.30pm, Sun noon–3.30pm; bar Tues–Sat 10am–11.30pm, Sun & Mon 10am–5pm.

Mimosa Kitchen & Bar 9 Mermaid Quay ☎029 2049 1900, ⓦmimosacardiff.com; map p.85. The Bay's most rewarding restaurant, sporting a simple but striking design with a brushed steel bar, deep brown leather seating and slate flooring. The Welsh-oriented menu features the likes of Perl Las chicken with cauliflower fritters and sautéed spinach (£12.50), while the gut-busting gourmet burgers are a real standout. Mon–Thurs 10am–11pm, Fri & Sat till midnight, Sun till 10.30pm.

OUT FROM THE CENTRE

CAFÉS

★Milgi 213 City Rd ☎029 2047 3150, ⓦmilgilounge .com; map pp.78–79. Quirky, boho-chic café where (veggie) food, art and music all have equal sway. Weekly and monthly events here include the supper club, the art and curry club, and the Northcote Lane vintage market every third Sunday of the month. The Sunday veggie roast is superb and the yurt out back is a perfect spot for a cool drink. Daily 11am–12.30am.

Waterloo Gardens Teahouse 5 Waterloo Gardens ☎029 2045 6073, ⓦwaterlootea.com; map pp.78–79. Upmarket teahouse, a 20min walk north of the centre in Roath, whose reputation for artisan teas and home-made cakes (including gluten-free ones) is unrivalled anywhere in the city. Sample one of fifty or so loose-leaf teas alongside a slice of courgette and lime cake. Well worth the short trek. Mon–Sat 8am–6pm, Sun 9am–6pm.

RESTAURANTS

Cibo 83 Pontcanna St, off Cathedral Rd ☎029 2023 2226, ⓦcibopontcanna.com; map pp.78–79. Small, tremendously busy but always welcoming Italian whose best aspect is its fragrant garden; here you can enjoy focaccia sandwiches, fresh pasta and proper pizza (including takeaways), alongside a blackboard of daily specials and desserts. Mains £8–10. Mon–Fri noon–11pm, Sat & Sun 10am–11pm.

Conway 58 Conway Rd ☎029 2022 4373, ⓦknifeandforkfood.co.uk; map pp.78–79. Fine gastropub with a daily blackboard menu offering a mix of upmarket pub classics (such as beer-battered fish and chips) alongside more polished dishes like pan-roasted fillet of gurnard on minted peas (£12). The living-room-style dining area, surrounding a central fireplace and shelves of books, is delightful. Daily noon–11pm.

★Fish at 85 85 Pontcanna St ☎029 2023 5666, ⓦfishat85.co.uk; map pp.78–79. Wholesalers, fishmongers and restaurant all in one, and quite brilliant it is too. The "Catch menu" allows customers to pick something from the counter, which could be, for example, brill, snapper or red mullet, along with an accompanying sauce, and then it'll be cooked just the way you like it. Alternatively, just select something from the menu, like whole roasted Sand sole and brown shrimp *beurre noisette* (£18.50). Tues–Sat noon–3pm & 6–10pm.

Mint and Mustard 134 Whitchurch Rd ☎029 2060 0333, ⓦmintandmustard.com; map pp.78–79. Don't let the dull, rather distant location put you off: this is the city's finest Indian restaurant, with a menu as brilliant as it is bold; try the pan-fried Tiffin sea bass on a bed of curry mashed potato (£13.95) or one of the many exceptional vegetarian dishes – the melt-in-the-mouth Bombay chaat is sensational. Daily noon–2pm & 5.30–11pm.

★**The Smoke House** 77 Pontcanna St ☎029 2034 4628; map pp.78–79. Lunchtime deli foods are laid out in crates on the counter (check out the pig pie), then, in the evening, the American barbeque – dry rubbed using naturally smoked spices and seasoning – takes over, rustling up a sizzling array of meats (ribs, patties, steaks) served on heavy wooden boards with hand-cut chips, pickled gherkins and red cabbage slaw. Wash it all down with a Honker's craft beer. The rustic interior, replicating a US-style farmhouse, looks terrific. Deli Mon–Fri 11am–2.30pm; restaurant Tues–Sat 6.30–10.30pm, plus Sat & Sun noon–2.30pm.

DRINKING

Cardiff's **pub life** has expanded exponentially in recent years, with chic cosmopolitan bars jostling for space alongside the more traditional Edwardian palaces of etched smoky glass and deep-red wood. You'll find plenty of both in the very centre, particularly along Mill Lane, Greyfriars Road and Westgate Street – weekend nights are legendarily raucous in Cardiff, during which time the city centre is not for the faint-hearted. The most agreeable pubs, however, are located out on the margins, notably along Cathedral Road in the direction of Pontcanna, with more out towards the student quarter around Cathays.

CITY CENTRE

★**City Arms** 10 Quay St ☎029 2064 1913; map p.81. Opposite the Millennium Stadium, this no-nonsense boozer is always popular, especially on international match days and before gigs at *Clwb Ifor Bach* just around the corner. Brains beers as well as some choice guest ales. Mon–Thurs 11am–11pm, Fri & Sat till 2.30am, Sun noon–10.30pm.

The Cottage 25 St Mary St ☎029 2033 7195; map p.81. Traditional Edwardian pub with cheerful staff serving some of the best Brains in the city centre, alongside good cask options and a range of decent home-made pies. Daily 11am–11pm, Fri & Sat till midnight.

★**Gwdihw** 6 Guildford Crescent ☎029 2039 7933, ⓦ gwdihw.co.uk; map p.81. Pronounced "goody-hoo", this is a wonderful little corner café/bar, its exterior painted bright orange and the interior decked out with stripped wood flooring, odd bits of furniture and retro-style accoutrements. Daily happenings include alternative film, poetry recitals, micro-festivals and regular bouts of live music on the dinky little stage. Mon–Wed & Sun 3pm–midnight, Thurs noon–midnight, Fri & Sat noon–2.30am.

Pen and Wig 1 Park Grove ☎029 2064 9090; map pp.78–79. Large boozer in a quiet residential street, popular with local professionals and students for the fine selection of very reasonably priced guest ales. Unspoilt flagstone-floored interior and decent beer garden. Mon–Fri 10am–midnight, Sat 10am–1am, Sun noon–11.30pm.

Queen's Vaults 29 Westgate St ☎029 2022 7966; map p.81. Cavernous rugby-memorabilia pub across from the Millennium Stadium, with antique fittings, large TV screens and pool tables, hence its enormous popularity with local sports fans. Mon–Thurs & Sun 10am–11pm, Fri & Sat till midnight.

Tafarn 53–59 Despenser St, Riverside ☎029 2037 8866; map p.81. Part of the hostel *Nos da*, with a heated outdoor deck overlooking the Taff, a cantina serving locally sourced meals and bar snacks, and an impressive range of Welsh beers, ciders and spirits. Occasional live music too. Daily noon–11.30pm.

Zero Degrees 27 Westgate St ☎029 2022 9494; map p.81. Shiny microbrewery in a lino-clad converted garage with friezes made from heat-compressed Wellington boots and discarded mobile phones. The £4 beer sampler lets you

---

SPECTATOR SPORT IN CARDIFF

Cardiff's sporting pedigree is strong and it now boasts several world-class sporting arenas. Inevitably, **rugby** takes centre stage, and there are few more atmospheric places to be than Cardiff on international match-day at the magnificent Millennium Stadium. The city's club side, **Cardiff Blues** (☎0845 345 1400, ⓦ cardiffblues.com), plays in the Pro 12 league at Cardiff Arms Park, which adjoins the Millennium Stadium.

Despite playing second fiddle to rugby, **football** remains popular in the city, thanks to the recent success of **Cardiff City** (☎0845 365 1115, ⓦ cardiffcityfc.co.uk), who were promoted to the Premier League for the first time in 2013, though they were relegated the following season. Cardiff's **cricketing** profile has increased massively in recent years, thanks to the staging of test matches at the Swalec Stadium in Sophia Gardens, which is also the home of **Glamorgan**, Wales' sole first-class cricket team (☎029 2040 9380, ⓦ glamorgancricket.com). The stadium has also staged two England versus Australia Ashes test matches, in 2009 and 2015.

taste all six of its house brews, including mango and a couple of wheat beers. Great gourmet pizzas too. Daily noon–midnight.

OUT FROM THE CENTRE

Cayo Arms 36 Cathedral Rd ☎029 2023 5211; map pp.78–79. Within a six of the cricket ground, two conjoined Victorian town houses have formed this large, busy and proudly Welsh pub, with Tomos Watkin beers, decent food and a lively crowd. Mon–Sat noon–11pm, Sun noon–10.30pm.

Cricketers 66 Cathedral Rd ☎029 2034 5102; map pp.78–79. Set in a gorgeous Victorian town house, this combines a sunny interior – big sofas from which to admire the cricketing memorabilia – with lively beer gardens front and back. The Welsh cask-conditioned beers are some of the best in Cardiff, and the food is very creditable too. Daily noon–11pm.

★**Y Mochyn Du** Sophia Close, off Cathedral Rd ☎029 2037 1599; map pp.78–79. Right in the shadow of the cricket ground, this old gatekeeper's lodge is a fine place to sup a pint of Welsh brewed beer, either in the conservatory or outside among the greenery. Popular with Welsh-speakers. Mon–Fri noon–11pm, Sat till midnight, Sun till 10.30pm.

NIGHTLIFE AND ENTERTAINMENT

There's plenty of choice when it comes to **nightlife** in Cardiff, whether your tastes run to banging clubs, sweaty rock gigs (in English or Welsh), or a night of soothing jazz or classical music. Despite the healthy state of Welsh music, there is a dearth of small- to medium-sized gig venues in the city, a situation not helped by the closure of a number of well-established places in recent times. In addition to the places listed here, Cardiff Castle and the Millennium Stadium stage major events, particularly the latter, which is usually on major acts' world tours. **Theatre** in Cardiff encompasses everything from the radical and alternative at the smaller venues, to big, blowsy productions and West End spectaculars at the Wales Millennium Centre, home of Welsh National Opera (⊛wno.org.uk). The WMC and St Davids Hall are the main venues for classical music.

CLUBS

Buffalo 11 Windsor Place ☎029 2031 0312, ⊛buffalocardiff.com; map p.81. Upbeat, retro bistro-cum-cocktail bar/club manifesting fabulously quirky decor and a cool vibe from lunchtime until the wee hours. Electronica is Buffalo's real forte, though there's plenty else happening, including experimental art and fashion parties. Daily 11am–4am.

Cardiff University Union Park Place ☎029 2078 1400, ⊛cardiffstudents.com; map pp.78–79. With four venues under one roof, there's much going on here, from assorted dance nights to big-name live bands. Open to non-students.

Clwb Ifor Bach 11 Womanby St ☎029 2023 2199, ⊛clwb.net; map p.81. Widely known as the "Welsh club", due to the prevalence of Welsh-language acts and punters, this is a sweaty and massively fun live music and dance club on three floors with nightly gigs, sessions or DJs, including 70s and funk nights. Tues–Sat 10pm–3am.

LIVE MUSIC VENUES

10 Feet Tall 11a Church St ☎029 2022 8883, ⊛10feettall.co.uk; map p.81. Perennially popular tapas-cum-cocktail bar that rocks hard most nights of the week, but the vibe is ramped up a notch when the basement club *Undertone* – hosting gigs and various themed nights – clicks into gear. Daily noon–3am.

Café Jazz 21 St Mary St ☎029 2038 7026, ⊛cafejazzcardiff.com; map p.81. Unassuming but popular venue, below the *Sandringham Hotel*, hosting a diverse range of jazz concerts Mondays to Fridays; electric blues, funk, swing, gypsy jazz and the like. Entrance typically £3–6.

Moon Club Womanby St ☎029 2037 3022, ⊛themoonclub.net; map p.81. This superb club has really come to the fore recently for its prolific roster of gigs (typically three or four a week) by both domestic and foreign bands, with affordably priced tickets (£5–6).

Motorpoint Arena Mary Ann St ☎029 2022 4488, ⊛livenation.co.uk/cardiff; map p.81. Large concrete venue rising high over the city centre's southern streets and playing host to major rock and pop gigs, classical concerts, opera and comedy.

Norwegian Church Harbour Drive ☎029 2045 4899, ⊛norwegianchurchcardiff.com; map p.85. Venue for all kinds of musical and performance evenings, though typically of a classical or operatic bent.

Royal Oak 200 Broadway, Newport Rd, Roath ☎029 2049 6628; map pp.78–79. Renowned music pub with acoustic and electric jam sessions on Wed, starting from 9pm (free). Occasional bands too.

St Davids Hall The Hayes ☎029 2087 8444, ⊛stdavidshallcardiff.co.uk; map p.81. Part of the huge St Davids shopping centre, this venue is home to visiting orchestras and musicians from jazz to opera, and is frequently used by the excellent BBC National Orchestra of Wales. The lunchtime concerts are well worth attending.

University Concert Hall Corbett Rd, Cathays Park ☎029 2087 4816, ⊛cardiff.ac.uk/music; map pp.78–79. Between October and May, this impressive performance space hosts public concerts by university and local orchestras, jazz groups and easy-listening ensembles.

Wales Millennium Centre Roald Dahls Plass, Cardiff Bay ☎029 2063 6464, ⊛wmc.org.uk; map p.85.

Stunning performance space that's home to Welsh National Opera, along with various other music and dance companies. Also used for touring West End and other mega-productions.

GAY AND LESBIAN NIGHTLIFE

Cardiff's gay scene is far from massive, but robust all the same; the city's premier event is Pride in August (ⓦpridecymru.co.uk). Otherwise, it doesn't take too much effort to discover what's going on, as the principal venues are on Charles Street, just off Queen Street in the city centre. The venues below are for men and women.

Bar Icon 60 Charles St ☎029 2066 6505; map p.81. Trendy bar, with muted, comfy decor and a tendency to get funky towards the weekend; live DJs on Saturdays. Mon–Thurs noon–midnight, Fri & Sat till 2am.

Golden Cross 283 Hayes Bridge Rd; map p.81. Laidback restored Victorian pub, rich in atmosphere and with some beautiful tiled pictures of yesteryear Cardiff. Camp entertainment a speciality, as is the cheap food. Daily noon–midnight.

THEATRE AND COMEDY

Chapter Arts Centre Market Rd, Canton ☎029 2030 4400, ⓦchapter.org; map pp.78–79. Although best known for its art-house movies, this superb multifunctional arts complex also hosts comedy, local and touring theatre and dance companies, and art exhibitions; invariably there's a strong Welsh theme to events here.

Glee Club Mermaid Quay, Cardiff Bay ☎029 2023 0130, ⓦglee.co.uk/cardiff; map p.85. Cardiff's best comedy club, with appearances by some of the biggest names on the British stand-up circuit; occasional live music too, featuring some well-established artists.

Jongleurs Oceana Club, Greyfriars Rd ☎0870 0111 960, ⓦjongleurs.com; map p.81. More corporate than the *Glee*, but dependable for decent comedy; shows on Fridays and Saturdays with four acts each night.

New Theatre Park Place ☎029 2087 8889, ⓦnewtheatrecardiff.co.uk; map p.81. Splendid Edwardian city-centre theatre playing host to big shows, musicals and pantos.

Sherman Theatre Senghennydd Rd, Cathays ☎029 2064 6900, ⓦshermancymru.co.uk; map pp.78–79. An excellent two-auditorium repertory theatre known for its strong line-up of plays in both Welsh and English. New and translated classic Welsh-language pieces, stand-up comedy, children's entertainment, drama, music and dance.

DIRECTORY

Hospital In the first instance, phone NHS Wales Direct on ☎0845 4647. The city's main hospital is the University Hospital of Wales, Heath Park (☎029 2074 7747).

Internet Cardiff Central Library (Mon–Wed & Fri 9am–6pm, Thurs 9am–7pm, Sat 9am–5.30pm; free for 30min); TIC (Mon–Sat 9.30am–5pm, Sun 10am–4pm; £1/30min).

Left luggage There are left-luggage lockers at the tourist office (£4–10).

Police Cardiff Central Police Station, King Edward VII Ave, Cathays Park (☎029 2022 2111); Cardiff Bay Police Station, James Street (same phone number).

Post office Inside the Queen's Arcade, St Davids Centre (Mon–Sat 9am–5.30pm).

Castell Coch

March–Oct daily 9.30am–5pm, July & Aug till 6pm; Nov–Feb Mon–Sat 10am–4pm, Sun 11am–4pm • £5.50; CADW • ☎029 2081 0101 • Bus #26A from Cardiff bus station

Above the village of **TONGWYNLAIS**, four miles north of Llandaff, the coned turrets of **Castell Coch** rise mysteriously out of a steep wooded hillside. A ruined thirteenth-century fortress, Castell Coch was rebuilt into a fantasy castle in the late 1870s by William Burges for the third Marquess of Bute, complete with a working portcullis and drawbridge. Numerous similarities with Cardiff Castle include the lavish decor, culled from religious and moral fables, that dazzles in each room. Lady Bute's bedroom, at the top of one of the three towers, incorporates a fabulously painted double dome, around which 28 panels depict frolicking monkeys, some of which were considered lascivious for their day. However, the castle was hardly ever lived in and sees more life today, especially the tearoom situated in what was once the valet's room.

St Fagans National History Museum

St Fagans • Daily 10am–5pm • Free • ☎029 2057 3500, ⓦmuseumwales.ac.uk • Buses #32 and #320 from Cardiff bus station

Separated from Cardiff by a sliver of greenery, the village of **ST FAGANS** (Sain Ffagan), four miles west of the city centre, has a rural ambience only partly marred by the

1

busloads of tourists that regularly roll in to visit the unmissable **St Fagans National History Museum**.

The castle and grounds

The museum is constructed on grounds near **St Fagans Castle**, a country house built in 1580 on the site of a ruined Norman castle and furnished in early nineteenth-century style, complete with heavy oak furniture and solemn portraits. Surrounding the castle are the formal gardens, from where grassy terraces slope down to a chain of eighteenth-century fishponds, which have also been restored to something akin to their original design. It's a lovely spot for a picnic.

Open-air museum

Beyond this parkland area is the **open-air museum**, an outstanding collection of period buildings – houses, shops, dwellings, churches – garnered from all corners of Wales and faithfully rebuilt on this site. There's much to see, and many of the structures can be entered, so give yourself a good couple of hours to take it all in.

Many of the domestic structures are farmhouses of different ages and styles – compare, for example, the grandeur of the seventeenth-century red-painted **Kennixton Farmhouse** from Gower or the homely Edwardian comforts of **Llwyn-yr-Eos Farm** with the threadbare simplicity of the Gwynedd farmworkers' **Llainfadyn Cottage**. An interesting variety of workplaces on the site include a **tannery**, a **pottery**, three **mills** and a **smithy**, most of which house people demonstrating the original methods. Indeed, the early twentieth-century **bakehouse** is still in good working order and you can purchase various goodies here.

The best demonstration of how life changed over the years for a section of the Welsh population comes in the superlative **Rhyd-y-car** ironworkers' cottages from Merthyr Tydfil. Built originally around 1800, each of the six houses, with their accompanying strip of garden, has been furnished in the style of a different era – stretching from 1805 to 1985. Even the frontages and roofs are true to their age, offering a wade through working-class Welsh life over the past two centuries. Next door are the Victorian **Gwalia Stores** from the mining community of Ogmore Vale; the smell of polished mahogany is as evocative as the starchy-aproned assistants and the jars of boiled sweets that they sell. In between the cottages and the store, take a quick look at the wonderfully grand Victorian **urinal**.

Other buildings to look out for include the diminutive whitewashed 1777 **Pen-Rhiw Chapel** from Dyfed, which is still used by a small Unitarian community, the pristine and evocative Victorian **St Mary's Board School** from Lampeter, and the ordered mini-fortress of a 1772 **Tollhouse** that once guarded the southern approach to Aberystwyth.

The Vale of Glamorgan

South of the capital, the **Vale of Glamorgan**'s rich pastoral landscapes and cliff-fringed coastline, broken by long, sandy beaches, are often overlooked by visitors, though they are worth at least a couple of days' exploration. Lively seaside resorts at **Porthcawl** in the west and **Barry** in the east contrast with the more refined atmosphere of **Penarth**, clinging to the coat-tails of Cardiff. In between lie yawning wide bays and tumbledown castles, linked by bracing coastal walks along spectacularly stratified cliffs. Inland, the lower parts of the Vale's urban features – such as Wales' international **airport** at Rhoose and occasional looming factories – are set against rolling green pastureland sprinkled with charming, low-key market towns like **Cowbridge**, **Llantrisant** and **Llantwit Major**.

FROM TOP DETAIL ON CARVED SEAT, CAERLEON (P.74); THREE CLIFFS BAY, GOWER (P.131) >

GETTING AROUND — THE VALE OF GLAMORGAN

By train and bus The Vale's proximity to Cardiff makes it easy to explore using public transport. The main-line train route through the Vale has a stop at Bridgend, a handy interchange for bus services to the coast and some of the larger inland settlements, while the Vale of Glamorgan line, an alternative route from Cardiff to Bridgend, has stops at Rhoose and Llantwit Major. Barry and Penarth, almost suburbs of Cardiff, are easily reached by bus and train.

Penarth and around

An easy and enjoyable day out from Cardiff, the increasingly upmarket Victorian seaside town **PENARTH** lies just across the Barrage from Cardiff Bay. Upon arrival, most people make a beeline for the tidy esplanade, presided over by its newly renovated pier, while the town centre manifests plenty of fine Edwardian and Victorian architecture.

Turner House Ffotogallery and Alexandra Park

Plymouth Rd • Tues–Sat 11am–5pm • Free • ☎ 029 2070 8870, ⊛ ffotogallery.org

The fine red-brick **Turner House**, on the opposite side of the tracks, is home to the small but engaging **Ffotogallery**, which stages contemporary photographic and other lens-based media exhibitions, as well as artist talks and multimedia events. Running down the left-hand side of Turner House, the Dingle path leads into showy **Alexandra Park**, emblemizing the spirit of Penarth with its flowerbeds and bandstand.

Penarth Pier and Pavilion

Mon–Wed 10am–5pm, Thurs–Sat till 8pm, Sun till 6pm • Free • ☎ 029 2071 2100, ⊛ penarthpavilion.co.uk

Continuing down the hill brings you onto the charmingly fusty **Esplanade**, a surprisingly short, but tidy promenade that's had new life breathed into it courtesy of the newly restored **pier and pavilion**. Originally built in 1895, the pavilion fell into serious disrepair in the 1990s, but has recently been brilliantly restored to its original Art Deco state, and now houses a seventy-seater boutique cinema, café and exhibition space.

Lavernock Point and Flat Holm

Jutting out into the Bristol Channel two miles due south of Penarth, **Lavernock Point** provides a forlorn setting for assorted campsites and pubs, but is notable as the place in which conversation was first heard by means of radio waves. This – as a plaque on the wall of the Victorian church notes – took place on May 11, 1897, when Guglielmo Marconi sent the immortal words "Are you ready?" over to his assistant George Kemp on the island of **Flat Holm** (Ynys Echni), three miles out in the channel, officially Wales' most southerly point.

Over the years, Flat Holm has been used as a Viking anchorage, a cholera hospital and a lookout point. Today it's an interesting and beautifully remote **nature reserve**, the nesting place of thousands of gulls and shelducks. It's possible to visit the island (see below), though visits from Cardiff are restricted to once a fortnight because of the tides; once on the island, you are met by a warden who will offer a guided tour (included in the price) of the island's history, flora and fauna. Alternatively, you can hire a commercial boat from Cardiff Bay, though this is expensive.

ARRIVAL AND DEPARTURE — PENARTH

By foot One of the most agreeable ways to reach Penarth is by foot, which is done by crossing the Cardiff Bay Barrage and following the signs for the Wales Coast Path.

By train From the train station on Station Approach, a path on the right leads up to Stanwell Road, which continues into the town centre.

Destinations Cardiff (every 15min; 15min).

By boat to Flat Holm Boats are run by MW Marine (☎ 01934 636734, ⊛ mwmarine.org; £24, plus a £5 landing fee), which operates out of Weston-Super-Mare, and call in at Cardiff fortnightly throughout the year; book well in advance.

ACCOMMODATION AND EATING

Fig Tree Esplanade ☎ 029 2070 2512. The interior is a bit charmless, but the balcony terrace fronting this ornate Victorian building is a neat spot to rest up and try some Pembrokeshire mussels (£11) or the Fig Tree fish pie with mashed potato and Welsh cheddar (£17). In summer, the roof terrace is an even more attractive proposition. Tues–Sat noon–3pm & 6–11pm, Sun noon–4pm.

Foxy's 7 Royal Buildings ☎ 029 2025 1666. Opposite the train station, this sunny deli makes for an ideal lunch stop; stuffed panini, warm salads, mouth-watering cakes and a shop stacked with great local produce. The Friday night gourmet meal (£21 for three courses) is fun. Mon–Thurs & Sat 8am–6pm, Fri 8.30am–9pm, Sun 10am–4pm.

Pier Hotel Esplanade ☎ 029 2032 9549, ⓦ thepierhotelandcafebar.co.uk. Although somewhat plain-looking from the outside, this comely little hotel smack-bang on the seafront has six polished rooms, three of which possess expansive sea views, hence cost a little extra. The wood-decked terrace is a good spot to kick back with a beer and soak up the rays. **£79**

Barry and around

Six miles southwest of Penarth, **Barry** (Barri) is the quintessential Welsh resort of old. Until the 1880s, when it was developed as a rival port to the Bute family's Cardiff, the main centre for activity, **Barry Island** (Ynys y Barri), was indeed an island due to its position on the tidal estuary, but the docks' construction saw the river diverted. Today, the "island" fronts Whitmore Bay, an expansive Blue Flag **beach**, behind which runs a cheerful promenade.

In recent years, the town has returned to its traditional roots as a family resort, with a **Pleasure Park** (April–Sept Sat & Sun, daily during school holidays 12.30–8pm) full of fairground attractions, crazy golf course on the prom (£4) and, inevitably, a handful of tacky arcades. One of these, as well as many other attractions hereabouts, trades on the back of the hit TV sitcom *Gavin & Stacey*, which was mostly filmed in Barry. If you're seeking a bit more solitude, head east around the headland to Jacksons Bay.

Dyffryn Gardens

Dyffryn, 7 miles north of Barry • Daily: March–Oct 10am–6pm (house noon–4pm); Nov–Feb 10am–4pm (house noon–3pm) • £7.40; NT • ☎ 029 2059 3328

In the hamlet of **DYFFRYN** are the magnificent **Dyffryn Gardens**, set around the Victorian home of a local merchant. Seldom busy, the gardens offer everything from formal lilyponds and billiard-table-smooth lawns to joyous bursts of floral colour and the russets, golds and greens of an arboretum.

St Lythan Long Cairn and Tinkinswood Long Cairn

Open access • Free • St Lythan Long Cairn is just south of the gardens; Tinkinswood Long Cairn is on the other side, beside the wooded lane between Dyffryn and St Nicholas, a village on the A48 two miles from Cardiff's Culverhouse Cross roundabout

By the lane junction just south of Dyffryn Gardens is the **St Lythan Long Cairn**, over four thousand years old. It's nowhere near as impressive, however, as its near neighbour, the **Tinkinswood Long Cairn**, a huge, capstoned burial chamber, around 4500 years old. Legend has it that anyone who sleeps beneath the fifty-ton monolith for a night will either die, go raving mad or become a poet – a threat commonly ascribed to other megalithic sites in Wales.

Llanerch Vineyard

4 miles northwest of St Nicholas and 1 mile south of M4 junction 34 • Daily 10am–5pm • Self-guided tours £7.50 • ☎ 01443 222716, ⓦ llanerch-vineyard.co.uk

Among rolling hills, **Llanerch Vineyard** is Wales' most successful winery, producing around ten thousand bottles of white and rosé Cariad wine each year, most of it sold within Wales. On a self-guided tour, you can nose around the vines and a patch of ancient woodland before sitting down to a taste of the finished product. Also on site is a wine shop, restaurant and bistro/café, accommodation (see p.100) and a cookery school.

ARRIVAL AND DEPARTURE

By bus Buses drop passengers on Friars Road, just above the promenade.
Destinations Cardiff (every 30min; 1hr).

By train Trains from Cardiff rattle through Barry Docks and Barry stations before terminating at Barry Island.
Destinations Cardiff Queen Street (every 15min; 35min).

ACCOMMODATION AND EATING

Acorns Guesthouse 17 Romilly Rd ☎01446 743238. While the rooms in this pleasant little B&B are decidedly average (and there are no en suites), they do have a TV, fridge and microwave, and it is the cheapest place in the area. **£45**

Cadwaladers 11 Paget Rd ☎01446 736486. A welcome reprieve from the surrounding tack, this smart little café, just behind the Pavilion, offers a range of light bites, but the best reason to pop by is the good strong coffee and marvellous ice cream. Mon–Thurs 9am–7pm, Fri–Sun till 8pm.

Llanerch Vineyard Hensol ☎01443 222716, ⓦllanerch-vineyard.co.uk. Smart, contemporary accommodation just outside Barry, with ten studio-style rooms overlooking the vineyard and in the farmhouse. The fabulous-looking restaurant knocks up home-cooked seasonal food like game pie with sweet potato mash (£18); while the adjoining bistro/café is a lovely spot for coffee or a glass of wine. **£80**

New Farm Port Rd West between Barry and Cardiff Airport ☎01446 735536, ⓦnewfarmbarry.co.uk. A welcoming early seventeenth-century farmhouse B&B whose six cosy rooms have some nice touches, though not all are en suite. The farmhouse breakfast will set you up nicely for the day. **£55**

The Vale coast

West of Barry, the **Vale of Glamorgan** coast alternates between craggy cliffs and wide, white-sand beaches. Considering its location between Wales' two great cities, it's surprisingly quiet, as most of the old-fashioned little towns and seashore villages seem to have escaped the effects of the surrounding industrialization.

Llantwit Major

At first glance, **LLANTWIT MAJOR** (Llanilltud Fawr) appears to be all modern housing estates and rows of shops, but at its heart is a tiny kernel of winding streets. This is where, in around 500 AD, the scholarly St Illtud educated a succession of young men at his monastery, giving the town the chance to claim the title of Britain's earliest centre of learning. Among Illtud's pupils were St David as well as St Patrick, who was abducted from the monastery by Irish pirates to become the patron saint of Ireland.

A miniature fifteenth-century **town hall** sits just before the quaint town square and serves as an informal **visitor centre**. From here, Burial Lane winds its way past the village square and down to the front of the magnificent **parish church**, sheltering in a hollow next to the trickle of the Col Huw River.

St Illtud's church

Burial Lane • Daily 8am–6pm • ☎01446 795551

The first thing that strikes you about this superb church is its size: it is, in fact, two churches joined at the tower. The older west church, nearer the stream, dates from around 1100; aisles were added in the twelfth and thirteenth centuries to transform it into the nave of a new church. Tagged on to the rear of the west church is the beautifully restored Galilee Chapel, though the original whitewashed stone walls sit somewhat incongruously with the modern glass windows and tiled flooring; the chapel keeps a fine collection of decorative Celtic crosses and stones. Prize among these is the **Illtud Cross**, an exquisitely carved eighth-century boulder, on which the letters ILT and half of a U (remains of ILLTUD) can still be made out; similarly impressive is the Houelt Cross, one of the finest examples of a wheel cross anywhere in Wales. The east church is notable chiefly for some fresco remains, the most impressive being the one of St Christopher on the north wall, dating from around 1400.

The beach

At the junction at the top of Burial Lane, Colhugh Street descends for a little over a mile along the scrubby valley of the Col Huw River to the rocky **beach**, popular for surfing and a great starting point for some wonderful walks along the caves and inlets of the stratified cliffs and back into the rolling countryside. There's a tidy little beach café here too.

St Donats Arts Centre

01446 799100, ⓦstdonats.com

From the beach, the clifftop path runs for two miles westwards to reach **St Donat's Bay**, dominated by a mock-Gothic castle, dating back to the fourteenth century, that was bought and restored by US tycoon William Randolph Hearst in the 1930s, and is now the international Atlantic College and multipurpose **arts centre**, at the forefront of Welsh efforts to internationalize local culture. As well as music, theatre, film, dance, exhibitions and community outreach, the centre hosts the excellent **Beyond the Border Storytelling Festival** (ⓦbeyondtheborder.com) during the first weekend of July, with typically over one hundred performances. The *Glass Room Café* is a delightful spot to while away an hour or so.

ARRIVAL AND INFORMATION LLANTWIT MAJOR

By bus Buses drop passengers behind the modern shopping precinct, from where it's a short walk down East Street into the town centre.
Destinations Barry (Mon–Sat 6 daily; 30min); Cardiff (Mon–Sat 6 daily; 1hr).
By train The train station on the Vale line is just above the

bus stop.
Destinations Barry (hourly; 10min); Bridgend (hourly; 20min); Cardiff (hourly; 45min).
Tourist information The TIC is in the town hall on Church Street (April–Sept Sat 10am–12.30pm & 2–4pm, Sun 2–4pm; 01446 796086).

ACCOMMODATION AND EATING

Acorn Camping Ham Lane South 01446 794024, ⓦacorncamping.co.uk. Large, well-shaded site a mile or so south of town with excellent modern amenities, including a shop, laundry, indoor games and children's play area. **£15**/pitch

Illtud's 216 Church St 01446 793800, ⓦilltuds216 .co.uk. Satisfying restaurant with a menu drawing together some exceptional meat- and seafood-based dishes, such as slow-roasted stuffed belly pork with rosemary mash (£14). Once beyond the front bar, you enter

a seductive, hall-like interior graced by candle-topped tables, high ceiling drapes and splashes of artwork. Tues–Sat noon–2.30pm & 6–11pm, Sun noon–5pm.

The Old Swan Inn Church St 01446 792230. Dating back to the twelfth century, Llantwit's oldest public house is the most agreeable place for a pint. The sociable bar/dining room offers a better-than-average blackboard menu and a choice selection of beers sourced largely from local brewers. Mon–Sat noon–11pm, Sun till 10.30pm.

Southerndown

West of Llantwit Major, the coast ducks and dives past remote cliffs and sandy beaches. **SOUTHERNDOWN** is a diffuse holiday village of touristy pubs and one excellent restaurant. However, the real reason to come here is **Dunraven Bay**, a beautiful, wide beach backed by jagged cliffs of perfectly defined layers of limestone and shale.

Heritage Coast Centre

Opening times erratic but usually Mon, Thurs & Fri 9am–3pm • 01656 880157, ⓦvaleofglamorgan.gov.uk

In the busy car park by Dunraven Beach is the **Heritage Coast Centre**, a small information point about walks and drives along this splendid section of the south Wales coastline. Dunraven is at the western end of a magnificent fifteen-mile **coastal walk**, dipping down into tiny, wooded valleys and up across wide stretches of cliff and sand.

1

Porthcawl

One of Wales' most enduring family resorts, **PORTHCAWL** possesses a quaint village centre, several sandy beaches and some fantastic **surf**, making it a great sojourn along the coast. The town also attracts large numbers of golfers, here to test themselves on the magnificent Royal Porthcawl course, consistently ranked one of Britain's finest.

The Esplanade and beaches

John Street, the main pedestrianized thoroughfare, extends down to the **Esplanade**, Porthcawl's extensive seafront promenade which stretches the full length of the town and changes its name throughout. The Esplanade comprises a typical array of Victorian and Edwardian hotels along the rocky beach, where you'll find the domed **Grand Pavilion** (☎01656 815995, ⍵grandpavilion.co.uk), home to assorted seaside entertainment shows and pantomimes. Eastwards, the Esplanade runs to a lifeboat station at the harbour before veering north alongside the coast under the name of Eastern Promenade, the home of Porthcawl's solid seaside attractions: the **Coney Beach amusement park**, behind whelk stalls and candy-floss shops looking out over the popular **Sandy Bay** and neighbouring **Trecco Bay**.

Porthcawl Museum

John St • Tues–Sat 10am–noon & 2–4pm • Free • ☎01656 786639

Housed inside the town's Grade II-listed Old Police Station, the small but engaging **Porthcawl Museum** documents the deeds of local folk, though the emphasis is on the role that Porthcawl's men played during World War I. The town and surrounding area was one of Wales' key recruiting areas, as well as an important training centre, during the war. On display are campaign medals, diary entries, and some cleverly conceived "trench art": items created from bullets and shell casings, like an ashtray and coal scuttle.

The Simon Tucker Surfing Academy

Rest Bay • Tuition £30/hr, board rental £10, wetsuit rental £5 • ☎07815 289761, ✉simon@surfingexperience.com

On the northwest side of town, a twenty-minute walk from the centre, is the far quieter and more beautiful **Rest Bay**, locally famed as a swimming and **surfing beach**. The Simon Tucker Surfing Academy, run by the former champion surfer, operates from the beach and offers tuition, board and wetsuit rental, plus loads of information on the local scene.

ARRIVAL AND INFORMATION   PORTHCAWL

By bus Buses set passengers down on John Street, from where it's a two-minute walk down the pedestrianized section of this same street into the town centre.
Destinations Cardiff, via Cowbridge (every 30min; 1hr 35min); Swansea (hourly; 30min).

Tourist information There's no tourist office in town, but you can get (limited) info from the library on Church Place, just around the corner from the bus stop (Mon–Sat 9.30am–1pm & 2–6pm; ☎01656 754845, ⍵welcometoporthcawl.co.uk).

ACCOMMODATION AND EATING

Accommodation in Porthcawl is plentiful, good value and concentrated around Esplanade Avenue, Mary Street and along the promenade in its various guises.

Fairways Hotel West Drive ☎01656 782085, ⍵thefairwayshotel.co.uk. Popular with visiting golfers to nearby Royal Porthcawl, this medium-sized shoreline hotel is one of the town's fancier options, accommodating smart, decently sized rooms, some with sea views. The orangery is a cool spot to take breakfast. **£110**
Foam Edge 9 West Drive ☎01656 782866, ⍵foam -edge.co.uk. Despite the nondescript exterior, this is a cheerful, family-run guesthouse with two warm and

beautifully decorated rooms, one with an enclosed balcony, but both with sensational sea views; and there's a hearty cooked Welsh breakfast to round things off. **£80**
Olivia House 44 Esplanade Ave ☎01656 789022, ⍵oliviahouse.com. On the road running up from the pavilion, this town house has been converted into a showy boutique hotel sporting six lavish, individually styled rooms, with thoughtful touches given to each. Breakfast typically consists of kippers or smoked salmon and scrambled egg. **£75**

ALL SHOOK UP

Each year, on the last weekend of September, Porthcawl becomes the unlikely destination for one of Europe's largest **Elvis Presley** celebrations (W elvies.co.uk). This rip-roaring festival sees the town overrun with thousands of Elvis impersonators keen to outdo each other in a host of tribute shows taking place at the Grand Pavilion and other venues throughout town. The somewhat more refined **International Jazz Festival** takes place at the end of April (W porthcawl-jazz-festival.com).

CAMPING

Brodawel Moor Lane, Nottage ☎ 01656 783231, W brodawelcamping.co.uk. About a 15min walk north of town, this is a simple field site with reasonable, well-kept facilities, including showers, laundry, utility room, and a cool play area for kids. Closed Nov–March. **£15.80**/pitch

EATING AND DRINKING

Rava 29 Mary St ☎ 01656 773888. Atmospheric, family-run restaurant dishing up good value Italian fare, and there's invariably a cracking catch of the day. The two-course early evening menu (6–7pm) is terrific value (£11.95). Tues–Sat 6–11pm.

A Touch of Class The Esplanade ☎ 01656 771383. Busy coffee house near the Pavilion that also does pancakes and waffles for breakfast, and sandwiches and wraps for lunch; the two-course evening menu is a steal at £9.99. Tues–Sat 8am–11pm, Sun & Mon 8am–5.30pm.

The inland Vale

The Vale of Glamorgan's hinterland is speckled with some intriguing towns and villages, notably Llantrisant and Cowbridge, alongside ruined castles, and all connected by narrow, winding, high-hedged lanes.

Llantrisant

Ten miles west of Cardiff **LLANTRISANT** perches dramatically between two peaks which rise sharply from the rivers Ely and Clun. It was once encircled by fortifications to exploit its natural position as a watching post over the Vale of Glamorgan, and it retains a charmingly quaint atmosphere reminiscent of a French hilltop town.

The town centre is focused on the **Bull Ring**, where there's a suitably wild-eyed statue of **Dr William Price** (1800–93), dressed in his favoured druid's outfit of moons, stars and a fox fur on his head. Dr Price subscribed to radical beliefs for his time – vegetarianism, nudity, republicanism, the unhealthiness of socks, anti-smoking and free love – as well as pointing out the potential environmental disasters of mass industrialization. He is best remembered for burning the body of his dead infant son, Iesu Grist (Welsh for "Jesus Christ"), in an oil drum on Llantrisant Common in January 1884. He was arrested and, in a sensational trial in Cardiff, acquitted, after which cremation was made legal in the UK.

Clustered around this comely little square are a handful of quirky, artisan shops and craft outlets. A short walk from the square is the old guildhall, dating from 1733, the last remaining tower from the thirteenth-century castle and, 100yds along the lane, the parish church, offering glorious views across the Vale.

ARRIVAL AND DEPARTURE   LLANTRISANT

By bus Buses set passengers down by the Bull Ring.

Destinations Cardiff (hourly; 45min); Pontypridd (every 20min; 20–40min).

Cowbridge

High-class boutiques and restaurants line the long and handsome main street of **COWBRIDGE** (Y Bont Faen), Wales' wealthiest town. On the south side of the High Street, Church Street leads under the narrow gatehouse that is the sole survivor of the four that once punctuated the town's fourteenth-century walls.

1

Old Beaupre Castle
Daily 10am–4pm • Free; CADW • ☎ 01443 336000

A little more than a mile south of town, down St Athan Road, a quiet lane fringed with high hedges, there's a tiny lay-by opposite the Regency finery of Howe Mill. A path opposite leads along the bank of the River Thaw for a quarter of a mile to the gauntly impressive ruins of **Old Beaupre Castle**, largely an Elizabethan manor house. Built by the local noble family, the Bassetts, Beaupre is a huge shell of ruined Italianate doorways and vast mullioned windows in the middle of a quiet Glamorgan field.

ARRIVAL AND DEPARTURE COWBRIDGE

By bus Buses set passengers down by the Town Hall on the High Street.

Destinations Cardiff (every 30min; 50min); Porthcawl (every 30min; 50min).

ACCOMMODATION AND EATING

Bear Hotel High St ☎ 01446 774814, ⓦ bearhotel .com. An upgraded, long-established coaching inn now harbouring supremely comfortable, individually designed rooms, though all are typically furnished in classical style and some have four-poster beds. **£110**

Huddart's 69 High St ☎ 01446 774645, ⓦ huddartscowbridge.co.uk. Upmarket, fairly formal, family-run restaurant where you can expect tempters like honey duck salad, and pan-fried guinea fowl on a sultana and cinnamon potato cake (£16.50). Tues–Sat noon–2pm & 6.30–10pm, Sun noon–2pm.

Market Place 66 High St ☎ 01446 774800, ⓦ the -marketplace.co.uk. Beautiful restaurant divided into different sections, with the graceful bare-brick interior of the listed seventeenth-century dining room contrasting with the modern garden terrace and mezzanine bar. Exceptional menu featuring the likes of pan-fried cod with braised fennel and red pepper sauce (£17.95). Tues–Sat noon–11pm, Sun noon–3pm.

★**The Quarter Penny Café** 54 High St ☎ 01446 774999, ⓦ quarterpennycafe.co.uk. Park yourself in one of the little brick alcoves of this superb café and enjoy a smoked salmon and cream cheese sandwich with a glass of Prosecco. Early birds can tuck into the Quarter Penny Big Breakfast (£7.95). The summery terrace out the back is delightful. Mon–Sat 8.30am–5pm, Sun 9am–4pm.

The Valleys

No other part of Wales is as instantly recognizable as **the Valleys**, a generic name for the string of settlements packed into the narrow cracks in the mountainous terrain to the north of Newport, Cardiff and Swansea. Coming through Monmouthshire, the change from rolling countryside to sharp contours and a post-industrial landscape is almost instantaneous, though the greenery evident today is a far cry from the slag heaps and soot-encrusted buildings of a mere three or so decades ago.

Each of the valleys depended almost solely on coal mining (see p.108). This nearly defunct industry has left its mark on the staunchly working-class towns, where row upon row of brightly painted terraced houses, tipped along the slopes at incredible angles, are broken only by austere chapels, the occasional remaining pithead or the miners' old institutes and drinking clubs.

Although not traditional tourist country, this is without doubt one of the most fascinating corners of Wales. Some of the former mines have reopened as gutsy and hard-hitting museums, notably the absorbing **Big Pit** at Blaenafon and the **Rhondda Heritage Park** at Trehafod. You'll also gain a deeper impression of valley life from less conventional attractions such as the Utopian workers' village at **Butetown** and the iron gravestones of **Blaenafon**, as well as the dignified memorials, found in almost every community, to those who died underground – or, in the heart-rending case of **Aberfan**, while simply going about their daily lives. South Wales, perhaps more than any other part of Britain, demonstrates the true human cost of the world's first industrialized nation. In addition to the Valleys' industrial landmarks, there are some older historic sights here, notably the vast **Caerphilly Castle** and the sixteenth-century manor house of **Llancaiach Fawr**.

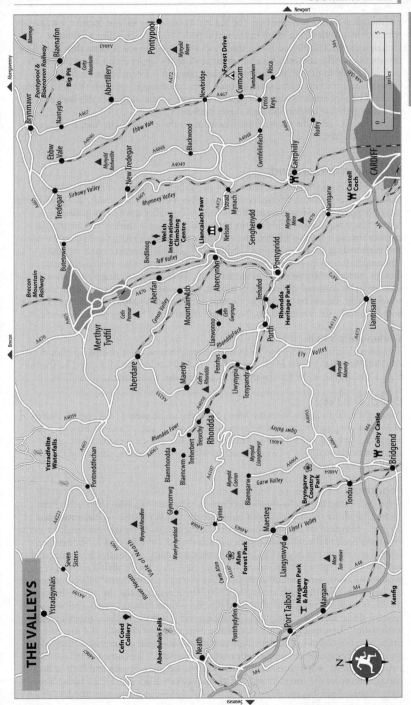

THE VALLEYS

1

Although now much cleaned up, the Valleys still combine unique sociological interest with scenic qualities. As a result of the formidable terrain, each valley was almost entirely isolated. Canals, roads and train lines competed for space along the valley floor, petering out as the contours became untameable at the upper end. Connecting roads were built only in the 1920s, and even today transport is frequently restricted to the Valleys' outer reaches, with roads and train lines radiating out through the south Wales coalfield like spokes on a giant wheel. The Valleys also offer unforgettable **walking** holidays; paths are best on the high ridges between valleys.

This section covers the valleys from Blaenafon in the east to Cwm Afan and Port Talbot in the west.

Blaenafon and around

Situated in the northeastern extremities of the Valleys is the iron and coal town of **BLAENAFON** (sometimes referred to by its English spelling, Blaenavon). Its lofty hillside position makes it feel less claustrophobic than many valley towns, but its decline is testified by a population of little more than five thousand, a third of its nineteenth-century size. It remains a spirited and evocative place, a fact recognized when the town and surrounding landscape gained UNESCO World Heritage Site status in 2000.

Blaenafon is perhaps best known for its **Big Pit**, an old coal mine-turned-museum, though the former ironworks is no less gripping, while there are vestiges of the town's industrial past scattered all over town. Indeed, the town's attractions could easily detain you for a day. This all comes together in the town's **World Heritage Day** at the end of June, with live music, street entertainers, Victorian fun fair and a heritage costume parade.

Working Men's Hall

The town's Victorian boom can be seen in its architecture, most notably the florid **Working Men's Hall** on the High Street. Built in 1895, miners used to pay a halfpenny a week for the use of the library and other recreational and educational facilities.

Church of St Peter

Across the road from the Working Men's Hall, the much older (1805) parish **church of St Peter** is a good example of what became known as Enginehouse Churches – an engine house being the sole type of building familiar to local masons. Contact the tourist office if you'd like to see the interior with its tomb covers, pillars and font, all fashioned out of iron.

Ironworks

North St • April–Oct daily 10am–5pm; Nov–March Fri & Sat 9.30am–4.30pm, Sun 11am–4.30pm • Free; CADW • ☎ 01495 792615

About 700yds up the hill on North Street are the town's remarkable **ironworks**, one of the most complete extant sites of its period in the world. Although iron smelting in the area dates back to the sixteenth century, it wasn't until three Midlands businessmen formed the Blaenafon ironworks in 1789 that the industry took off. Limestone, coal and iron ore – ingredients for successful smelting – were locally abundant, and at peak production there were five furnaces here. The Blaenafon works grew to become one of the largest in Britain, finally closing in 1900. The remains of the site offer a thorough picture both of the process used to produce iron – three furnaces and a cast house remain, alongside the hulking water balance tower – and the workers' lifestyles that went with it. Entering the cast house, you're greeted by the clanking and roar of a furnace accompanied by dramatic light and smoke effects in a very well-conceived multi-sensory experience entitled, appropriately enough, "Welcome to Hell".

Across from the water tower stand the whitewashed Stack Square and Engine Row cottages, built for the foremen and craftsmen between 1789 and 1792, though they were inhabited until as recently as 1971. Two of these neat, four-room abodes remain

1

in situ, with another housing an exhibition on the history of iron- and steel-making, and a model of how the site would have once looked. The neighbouring Truck Shop (truck meaning "exchange") was where miners would go to purchase goods, albeit at deeply inflated prices (there were no other shops in town); however, given that workers were invariably paid late, and therefore had little or no money to pay for these goods, these arrears were docked from their pay, ensuring that they were permanently in debt.

It was here, too, that the hit BBC docu-drama *Coal House* was filmed, with families trading twenty-first-century life for the conditions of the 1920s.

Blaenafon Community Heritage & Cordell Museum

Lion St • Mon, Tues, Thurs & Fri 10am–1pm & 2–3.30pm, Sat 10am–1pm • £1.50 • ☎ 01495 790991

Adjoining the town library, the tiny **Blaenafon Community Heritage & Cordell Museum** proudly documents the roles played by various groups throughout the community. More absorbing are the exhibits on the life and works of author Alexander Cordell (1914–97), including his books, typewriter and Tippex-splattered desk. Born in Ceylon (now Sri Lanka), Cordell developed a deep affinity for Wales and its industrial past during the many years he spent living in the area, a theme which manifested itself in his renowned 1959 novel, *Rape of the Fair Country*; it was eventually translated into seventeen languages. Also available here are details of four local driving tours around "Cordell Country".

Pontypool and Blaenavon Railway

Easter–Sept: Sat & Sun 11am–4pm, plus Wed in summer school holidays, and on special days • £7 return (ride all day) • ☎ 01495 792263, Ⓦ pontypool-and-blaenavon.co.uk

Between Easter and September, steam-train buffs can ride on the **Pontypool and Blaenavon Railway**, which shunts between the Furnace Sidings (signposted just off the B4248 between Blaenafon and Brynmawr) and the *Whistle Inn*, before heading down to the Big Pit Halt (near the museum) and Blaenavon High Level station, where there's a small **museum** detailing the history of the line. Railway fanatics may also want to visit the Railway Shop, in Brownings bookshop at 33 Broad Street (Mon–Fri 10.30am–5.30pm, Sat till 4pm), which has some wonderful exhibits, as well as trains and other accessories to buy.

Big Pit

Signposted on west side of town, off the B4246 • Feb–Nov daily 9.30am–5pm, hourly tours 10am–3.30pm; Dec & Jan call for tour times and availability • Free, car park £3 • ☎ 029 2057 3650, Ⓦ museumwales.ac.uk • #30 bus (hourly) from Newport stops outside the entrance

Three-quarters of a mile west of the town lies the marvellous **Big Pit National Coal Museum**, occupying a former colliery which opened in 1880 and closed exactly a century later. One of the largest coal-mining sites in the South Wales Coalfield, it employed some 1300 men at its peak.

The Pit

Of all the mining museums in south Wales, Big Pit brings you closest to the experience of a miner's work and life, as you descend 300ft, kitted out with lamp, helmet and heavy battery pack into a labyrinth of shafts and coal faces. The guides are ex-miners, who give you a personal insight into mining life as they lead you through examples of the different types of coal mining, from the old stack-and-pillar operation, where miners would manually hack into the coalface before propping up the ceiling with a wooden beam, to more modern mechanically worked seams. Constant streams of rust-coloured water flow by, adding to the dank and chilly atmosphere that terrified the small children who were once paid twopence for a six-day week (of which one penny was subtracted for the cost of their candles) pulling the coal wagons along the tracks. Just as integral to the working of the mines were the pit ponies, hardy creatures who worked at Blaenafon until 1972; you also get to see the now forlorn-looking stables.

1

The Pithead Baths

Back on the surface are the superbly preserved pithead baths, dating from 1939 and just about the last ones surviving anywhere in the country. Beyond the rows of lockers, some of which contain miners' belongings, several rooms offer a compelling and moving insight into the lives and times of the miners and their families. The plight of women is given due prominence, with emphasis on their role during the miners' strikes, when they organized food parcels and soup kitchens, and in many cases joined their men on the picket lines. The exhibition concludes with coverage of the explosive 1984–85 strikes; look out for the series of feisty testimonies from the miners made redundant here.

ARRIVAL AND INFORMATION   BLAENAFON

By bus The town's main bus stop is at the top High Street, which runs parallel to Broad Street, the main focus of activity in town.

Destinations Newport (every 10min; 1hr).

Tourist information The Blaenavon Heritage Centre is on Church Road (Tues–Sun: April–Sept 9am–5pm, Oct–March 9am–4pm; ☎01495 742333, ⓦvisitblaenavon .co.uk). Also here is an enlightening exhibition on the history of the town's coal-mining and ironworking industries, as well as a café.

ACCOMMODATION AND EATING

Coffi 1860 76 Broad St ☎01495 790127. There are very few places to eat or drink in Blaenafon, but this charmingly staffed coffee shop more than compensates; park yourself at one of the stripped wooden tables under the building's original green and cream tiling and tuck into a home-made pastry washed down with a steaming cup of coffee. Mon–Sat 7.30am–4pm, Sun 9am–3pm.

Lion Hotel Broad St ☎01495 792516, ⓦthelionhotelblaenavon.co.uk. The town's one hotel is a bright affair, its twelve deep-burgundy-coloured rooms comprising warm fluffy carpets, cool fabrics, and sparkling, marble tiled bathrooms; somewhat surprisingly, there's a

---

THE WELSH COAL INDUSTRY

The land beneath the inhospitable hills of the south Wales valleys had some of the world's most abundant and accessible natural seams of **coal**, as well as iron ore. During the boom years of the nineteenth and early twentieth centuries, wealthy English capitalists came to Wales and ruthlessly stripped the land of its natural assets, while paying paltry amounts to those who risked life and limb in the mines. The mine owners were in a formidably strong position – thousands of Welsh working class, bolstered by their Irish, Scottish and Italian peers, flocked to the Valleys in search of work and some sort of sustainable life. The Valleys – virtually unpopulated at the start of the nineteenth century – became blackened with soot and packed with people, pits and chapels by the beginning of the twentieth.

By 1920, there were 256,000 men working in the 620 mines of the south Wales coalfield, providing one-third of the world's coal resources. Vast **miners' institutes**, paid for by a wages' levy, jostled for position with the Nonconformist chapels, whose muscular brand of Christianity was matched by the zeal of the region's politics, trade-union-led and avowedly left-wing. Great socialist orators rose to national prominence, and even Britain's pioneering **National Health Service**, founded by a radical Labour government in the years following World War II, was based on a Valleys community scheme run by Aneurin Bevan.

Over half of the original pits closed in the harsh economic climate of the 1930s. World War II saw a brief respite in the closure programme, which continued even more swiftly in the years immediately after. As coal seams became less economical (due to the additional distance to reach the coalface from the pitheads), and the political climate shifted, the number of people employed in the industry dipped down into four figures in the aftermath of the 1984–85 miners' strike. No coalfields were as solidly behind the strike as south Wales, whose workers and families responded wholeheartedly to the call to defend the industry, which their trade union, the **National Union of Mineworkers** (NUM), claimed was on the brink of being decimated. The year-long war of attrition between the Thatcher government and Arthur Scargill's NUM was bitter, finally seeing the government victorious as the number of miners returning to work outnumbered those staying out on strike. Over a quarter of a century on, all but a few privately run south Wales pits have now closed.

sauna and steam room here too. £85

Rifleman's Arms Rifle St ☎ 01495 792297. A 10min walk north of town on the Abergavenny road, the friendly

Rifleman's offers five decent en-suite rooms above its pub, though it's by no means noisy. £65

Abertillery

It's worth taking a short detour down the Ebbw Vale Valley to Abertillery, ten miles southwest of Blaenafon, where the **Guardian monument** pays tribute to fallen miners of the Six Bells colliery disaster. In 1960, 45 miners were killed here by an underground explosion, an event commemorated some fifty years later with the unveiling of this, the largest memorial in the Valleys. The 40ft-high statue of a miner was constructed from some twenty thousand individual slices of steel, while the names of the victims are cut into the handsome sandstone plinth on which the miner stands.

Cwmcarn Forest

8 miles south of Abertillery • Forest drive April–Aug daily 11am–7pm; March, Sept & Oct daily 11am–5pm; Nov–Feb Sat & Sun 11am–4pm • £5/car • Visitor Centre Daily 9am–5pm • ☎ 01495 272001, ⊛ cwmcarnforest.co.uk

Offering plentiful opportunities for cycling and walking, the **Cwmcarn Forest** is best seen along the **Cwmcarn Forest Drive**. Setting out from the visitor centre, the seven-mile figure-of-eight drive takes in superb scenery, as well as kids' play areas, an Iron Age hillfort and numerous mountain bike trails of varying difficulties. There are some half a dozen waymarked walks, too, the longest and most strenuous of which is the twelve-mile Raven Walk, which circles the Sirhowy and Ebbw Valleys, affording terrific views of the Seven Estuary and the Brecons. Information about all of these trails can be obtained from the visitor centre, which also has walking maps and guides, and a pleasant café.

GETTING AROUND	CWMCARN FOREST
By bike If you need to rent a bike, you can do so from PS Cycles (☎ 01495 246555, ⊛ pscycles.co.uk) in	Abercan, one mile north of Cwmcarn.

ACCOMMODATION

Forest Drive campsite Next to the visitor centre. The very small, but neat and grassy campsite also has nine wooden	pods each sleeping three to four people; there are cooking and shower facilities for use by all. £15/pitch, £40/pod

Caerphilly

Now almost a suburb of Cardiff, just seven miles north of the capital at the foot of the **Rhymney Valley**, the town of **CAERPHILLY** (Caerffili) is wrapped around its staggering moated **castle**, the largest in Wales and the second largest in the UK after Windsor Castle. Caerphilly was also the birthplace of legendary comedian Tommy Cooper, a large bronze statue of whom stands opposite the castle.

The castle

April–June, Sept & Oct daily 9.30am–5pm; July & Aug daily 9.30am–6pm; Nov–March Mon–Sat 10am–4pm, Sun 11am–4pm • £5.50; CADW • ☎ 029 2088 3143

Built on the site of a Roman fort and an earlier Norman fortification, the present **castle** was begun in 1268 under Gilbert de Clare, who wanted to protect the vulnerable coastal plains around Cardiff from Llywelyn ein Llyw Olaf (Llywelyn the Last).

For the next few hundred years, Caerphilly was given at whim by various kings to their favourites – most notably by Edward II to his minion, and some say lover, Hugh le Despenser, in 1317. The Civil War necessitated the building of an armoury, which prompted Cromwell to seize it, drain the moat and blow up the towers. By the early twentieth century, the castle was in a sorry state, sitting amid a growing industrial town

1

THE BIG CHEESE

In addition to its castle, Caerphilly is also synonymous with its crumbly white **cheese**, which has inspired the vibrant **Big Cheese festival** (ⓦcaerphilly.gov.uk/bigcheese), held over three days in late July in the shadow of the castle. Lots of events take place, from street theatre to concerts, a funfair, falconry, historical re-enactments and craft market, a cheese race and, of course, a food market selling cheese along with all manner of local produce. Throughout the rest of the year, the only place in town to buy actual Welsh Farmhouse Caerphilly cheese (rather than those made elsewhere but still carrying the Caerphilly label) is the visitor centre.

---

that saw fit to build in the moat and the castle precincts. It was during the late 1920s, under the supervision of the fourth Marquess of Bute, that the castle underwent an extensive period of restoration, followed, in 1958, by the demolition of houses and shops so that the moat could be reflooded.

The castle grounds

You enter the castle through the much-restored great **gatehouse** that punctuates the barbican wall by a lake. From here, a bridge crosses the moat, part of the wider lake, to the outer wall of the castle itself, behind which sits the hulking inner ward. Located here is the massive **eastern gatehouse**, which includes an impressive upper hall and oratory and, to its left, the wholly restored and reroofed **Great Hall**, largely built around 1317 by Hugh le Despenser. Running round from the eastern gatehouse, behind the Great Hall and down to the southwestern tower, is an elevated walkway. Walking along here, you'll pass the iconic southeastern **leaning tower**, with a dramatic cleft in its walls where Cromwell's men are said to have attempted to blow it sky-high (though the tilt is more likely due to simple subsidence). With the exception of the ruined northeastern tower, the other corner turrets have been blandly restored since the Civil War, though the northwestern tower houses a reasonably interesting exhibition on the castle's restoration. A platform behind the barbican wall exhibits medieval war and siege engines, pointing ominously across the lake.

ARRIVAL AND INFORMATION   CAERPHILLY

By train From the station, it's a five-minute walk up Cardiff Road to the centre of town and the castle.
Destinations Cardiff (every 15min; 20min); Rhymney (hourly; 40min).
By bus Buses stop alongside the train station.

Destinations Cardiff (every 15min; 25min).
Tourist information The town's red-brick visitor centre is just along from the castle entrance on Twyn Square (daily 10am–5.30pm; ☎029 2088 0011, ⓦvisitcaerphilly.com).

EATING AND DRINKING

Glanmors Tearooms Castle Court Precinct ☎029 2088 8355. For a spot of refreshment after visiting the castle, pop into this wonderfully genteel tearoom, with table

service and tea served in china pots and teacups. Light lunches also available. Mon–Sat 8.30am–5.30pm.

The Rhymney and Sirhowy valleys

Following the traditional border between the former counties of Glamorganshire and Monmouthshire north of Caerphilly, the Rhymney Valley is light on worthwhile sights, and becomes increasingly industrialized as it steers past a seamless succession of small towns. That said, there are one or two points of interest if heading this way, as there are in the similarly low-key Sirhowy Valley across to the east.

Winding House

Cross St, off White Rose Way, New Tredegar • Tues–Sun 10am–5pm • Free • ☎01443 822 666 • 10min walk south of Tir-phil train station

Ten miles up the valley from Caerphilly is **NEW TREDEGAR**, where the **Winding House**, with its gleaming Victorian-era steam engine that once powered the colliery's

1

high-speed lifts, is worth a visit. The engine usually runs only on bank holidays, though other dates are sometimes scheduled in. Otherwise, there's an enlightening exhibition on the history of Caerphilly and its surrounds.

Butetown

At the head of the valley, a mile beyond Rhymney town and just short of the A465 Heads of the Valleys road, tiny **BUTETOWN** (Drenewydd) was constructed as a model workers' estate in 1802–03 by the idealistic Marquess of Bute, a member of Wales' richest land- and minerals-owning family, although only the central grid of houses was ever built. There's an enlightening heritage trail ("A walk around Bute Town"; available via app on ⓦbutetownhistory.info), which brings to life some of the town's most prominent buildings.

Tredegar

A mile east of Butetown, at the head of the Sirhowy Valley, the little town of **TREDEGAR** boasts **Bedwellty House and park**, a Georgian mansion built for the Homfray family, cofounders of the Tredegar ironworks. With major restoration work now complete, it is possible to visit, but only as part of a group; still, there is a lovely tearoom (daily 10am–4.30pm) on site, and in the grounds (unrestricted access; free) you'll find an arboretum, ice house, and the world's largest lump of coal, a fifteen-ton block exhibited as part of the 1951 Festival of Britain. If you've time, head up into the centre to view the very fine cast-iron **town clock**, erected in The Circle in 1858.

The Taff and Cynon valleys

Like the River Rhymney, the River Taff also empties into the Bristol Channel at Cardiff, after passing through a condensed 25 or so miles of industry and population that obscure the former **china works** at Nantgarw. The first town in the Taff Vale is **Pontypridd**, one of the most cheerful in the Valleys, where the Rhondda River hives off west. Continuing north, the river splits again at **Abercynon**, where the Cynon River flows in from **Aberdare**. Just outside Abercynon is the enjoyable seventeenth-century **Llancaiach Fawr** manor house, while to the north, the Taff is packed into one of the tightest of all the Valleys, passing **Aberfan** five miles short of the valley head town of **Merthyr Tydfil**.

China Works Museum

On the A470 • Wed–Sun 10am–4.30pm • Free • ☎ 01443 841703

Barrelling north along the A470, you'd never suspect that the **China Works Museum** is tucked behind a thicket of trees just by the junction for **NANTGARW**. For less than five years in the 1810s, the pottery here produced some of the finest porcelain in the world, the few florid examples on display only serving to whet your appetite for the extensive collection in the National Museum and Gallery in Cardiff. Master porcelain painter William Billingsley set up the works with high ambition using Valleys coal and Cornish clay, but the extremely difficult "soft paste porcelain" process resulted in just a ten-percent firing success rate and the enterprise soon folded. One of the firing kilns has now been rebuilt and the main building contains small displays on the process and the history of the site.

Pontypridd

Home town of crooner Tom Jones, **PONTYPRIDD** is today rapidly gentrifying as Cardiff commuters move in, but retains its own unique spirit. Arriving in Pontypridd, you're greeted by the town's distinctive arched **bridge** of 1775, once the largest single-span stone bridge in Europe. Featuring three holes either side to lessen the bridge's overall weight and allow gusty winds through, it was built by local amateur stonemason William Edwards, whose previous attempts crumbled into the river below. Wednesdays and Saturdays are good days to be here, with the old-fashioned **market** spilling out onto Market Street and the surrounding squares.

1

Ynysangharad Park

On the far side of the river from the town centre is **Ynysangharad Park**, established after World War I as a memorial park, but now the town's popular green space. The focal point of the park is the recently restored Pontypridd lido, a grade II-listed building originally constructed in 1927 but which closed in 1991. Here, too, you'll find Sir W. Goscombe John's cloying allegorical statue and tomb in honour of Pontypridd weaver Evan James, who in 1856 composed the stirring *Hen Wlad Fy Nhadau* (*Land of My Fathers*), which subsequently became the Welsh national anthem.

Pontypridd Museum

Taff St • Mon–Sat 10am–5pm • Free • ☎ 01443 490748

Right next to the bridge, the **Pontypridd Museum** is housed in what was one of the town's great chapels. Built in 1861, it has been lovingly restored, and boasts unusually ornate ceiling bosses, pillars, pulpit, stained-glass window and organ that all contribute to the reverential atmosphere. The centre's contents are a real treasure-trove of photographs, video, models and exhibits that succeed in painting a warm picture of the town and its outlying valleys. Tom Jones and local opera star and actor Sir Geraint Evans are also celebrated among the exhibitions here.

World of Groggs Shop

159 Broadway • Mon–Fri 9am–5pm, Sat 10am–5pm • ☎ 01443 405001, ⓦ groggs.co.uk

A ten-minute walk southeast of Pontypridd's elegant and impressive train station, the wonderfully quirky **John Hughes' Grogg Shop** has been producing figurine caricatures of Welsh rugby stars, as well as other sporting and world celebrities, for some 45 years. Also on display are photos, rugby shirts and memorabilia donated by some of those who've been made into a "Grogg", and an autograph wall signed by various stars. It's well worth a visit even if you don't plan on buying anything.

ARRIVAL AND INFORMATION   PONTYPRIDD

By train The train station is a 10min walk south of the old bridge on The Graig.

Destinations Abercynon (every 15min; 10min); Aberdare (every 30min; 35min); Cardiff (every 20–30min; 30min); Merthyr Tydfil (every 30min; 35min); Treherbert (every 30min; 40min).

By bus The bus station is directly above the old bridge on

the western bank.

Destinations Abercynon (every 15min; 10min); Aberdare (every 15min; 50min); Caerphilly (every 30min; 30min); Cardiff (every 15min; 35min); Merthyr Tydfil (every 15min; 25min).

Tourist information The TIC is inside the Pontypridd Museum (Mon–Sat 10am–5pm; ☎ 01443 490748).

ACCOMMODATION AND EATING

Blueberry Hotel Market St ☎ 01443 485331, ⓦ blueberryinn-pontypridd.co.uk. Appropriately appealing name for this sparkling little hotel, whose nine rooms are fashioned in one of two styles: cool, crisp white-on-white, or classic French. Breakfast is extra. **£69**

★**Bunch of Grapes** Ynysangharad Rd ☎ 01443 402934, ⓦ bunchofgrapes.co.uk. A terrific combination of restaurant and pub, whose imaginative menu (pan-fried guinea fowl with home-smoked new potato and caramelized pumpkin; £15) is the best for miles around. There are typically more than half a dozen real ales on at any one time, while the festival bar testifies to the many regular beer events held here. Located in a residential

street beyond the park and A470 flyover. Daily 11am–11pm.

Clwb-y-Bont Off Taff St ☎ 01443 491424, ⓦ clwbybont .net. Down a narrow lane just behind Boots, this thick-set building is the town's principal club and live music venue, with open mic evenings, and acoustic, jazz and blues concerts. Mon–Thurs 6.30pm–11am, Fri 6.30am–1am, Sat noon–1am.

Llanover Arms Bridge St ☎ 01443 403215. Retaining a certain worn charm, the stone-fronted *Llanover*, situated right by the bridge, is one of the town's better watering holes. The beer is good too, with a couple of decent guest ales. Daily noon–11pm.

1

> ## PONTYPRIDD'S MALE VOICE CHOIR
>
> Pontypridd boasts one of the country's finest **male voice choirs**, and visitors are welcome to watch rehearsals, which take place down in the basement of the museum on Sunday evenings at 6pm; access is via the stone stairs to the right of the museum entrance. Concerts are at the Tabor Hall on Vaughan Street (in the Pwllgwaun neighbourhood); the tourist office has schedules.

Llancaiach Fawr Manor

Just north of the village of Nelson • Tues–Sun 10am–5pm (last admission one hour before closing) • £7.50 • ☎ 01443 412248, ⓦ llancaiachfawr.co.uk • Bus #X38 from Pontypridd (Mon–Sat hourly)

The river divides at **Abercynon**, four miles up the Taff Valley, with the Cynon River flowing in from Aberdare in the northwest. Two miles east of Abercynon is **Llancaiach Fawr Manor**, a Tudor house built around 1530 which has been transformed into a living-history museum set in 1645, the time of the Civil War, with guides dressed as house servants and speaking seventeenth-century English. Although the whole experience could easily be nightmarishly tacky, it's actually very deftly done, with well-researched period authenticity and numerous fascinating anecdotes from the staff.

The three-floored residence – reputedly one of Britain's most haunted – was originally built for the Prichard family, erstwhile Sheriff of Glamorgan and Justice of Peace, the latter a position he held throughout the Civil War. During the tour you get to view the kitchen and dining room, the Great Hall (which was used as a courtroom), the bed chambers and counting house (an arms store). Special tours are also available, including seventeenth-century-themed evenings, and, between October and March, ghost and candlelit tours.

Aberfan

North of Abercynon, the Taff Valley village of **ABERFAN** contains one sight that's impossible to forget: the two lines of arches that mark the **graves** of the 144 people killed in October 1966 when an unsecured slag heap slid down a hill and onto the Pantglas Primary School in the village. The death toll – including 116 children – is beyond comprehension. Official enquiries revealed the sorry inevitability of the disaster, given the cavalier approach to safety so often displayed by the coal bosses. Over four decades later, the tragedy lives on in the memory of the thousands of people from all over southeast Wales and beyond who came to help recover the bodies.

Aberdare

Eight miles northwest of Abercynon, towards the top of the Cynon Valley, is the sprawling town of **ABERDARE** (Aberdâr). The town was built on the local iron, brick and brewing industries, in addition to playing a prominent role in the development of early Welsh-language publishing. Aside from the rows of terraced houses, the centre offers a handful of good shops, **cafés** and **pubs**, such as the lively *Yr Ieuan ap Iago* on the High Street.

Cynon Valley Museum & Gallery

Depot Rd • Mon–Sat 9am–4.30pm • Free • ☎ 01685 886729

A short walk from the train station brings you to one of the Valleys' best museums, the **Cynon Valley Museum & Gallery**, housed in an old tram depot next to the Tesco superstore. Exhibits convey the social history of the valley, from the appalling conditions of the mid-nineteenth century, when nearly half of all children born here died by the age of 5, to stirring memories of the 1926 General Strike and the 1984–85 miners' strike. Alongside are some videos and displays on Victorian lantern slides, teenage life through the ages, the miners' jazz bands and the local publishing industry. To round things off, there's also a bright art gallery and decent café on site.

Dare Valley Country Park

Visitor centre: April–Sept Mon–Fri 9am–5.30pm, Sat & Sun till 7pm; Oct–March daily 9am–4pm • ☎ 01685 874672,
ⓦ darevalleycountrypark.co.uk

On the western flank of town is the **Dare Valley Country Park**, where you can participate in one of three waymarked trails, ranging between two and four miles. There's good birdwatching here, too, with a platform to view nesting peregrines, while the chain of small lakes harbours moorhen, little grebe and coots. The **visitor centre** has an exhibition on the park's formation, in addition to the inevitable café; it's also the starting point of the 32-mile **Glamorgan Forest Way** to Afan Argoed and Margam Country Park (see p.120). Bike rental is available between April and September.

Merthyr Tydfil

On the cusp of the grand, windy heights of the Brecon Beacons to the north and the industrial valleys to the south, the fortunes of **MERTHYR TYDFIL** (Merthyr Tudful) have risen and fallen more than once. Merthyr's strategic location was first exploited by the Romans as an outpost of their base at Caerleon. In 480 AD, Tydfil, Welsh princess and daughter of Brychan, Prince of Brycheiniog, was captured as she rode through the area, and murdered for her Christian beliefs. She became St Tydfil the Martyr, and her name was bestowed on the area. Merthyr was at the heart of Wales' industrial might in the early nineteenth century, with Cyfarthfa and Dowlais among the largest ironworks in the world at the time. Following the decline of the ironworks, renewed impetus was provided by the steel and coal mining industries, though their subsequent demise has seen high unemployment and deprivation ever since. That said, its relatively cheap house prices have made it an attractive proposition for commuters from Cardiff.

Cyfarthfa Castle

Just beyond the A470 Brecon road • **Castle** April–Sept daily 10am–5.30pm; Oct–March Tues–Fri 10am–4pm, Sat & Sun noon–4pm • £1 •
☎ 01685 727371, ⓦ cyfarthfa.com • **Railway** April–Sept Sat & Sun noon–5pm, daily during school holidays • £1.25

Cyfarthfa Castle, located north of the centre, is Merthyr's key site. Built in 1825 as an ostentatious mock-Gothic castle for William Crawshay II, boss of the town's original ironworks, it's set within an attractive, 160-acre **park** that slopes down to the river and once afforded Crawshay a permanent view over his iron empire.

Cyfarthfa's current incarnation, however, is as a museum, and a great one at that. You start in a well-re-created traditional Welsh Valleys café on the ground floor, then go downstairs into the old wine cellars for a gutsy history of the town. Starting with tales of the martyr Tydfil, the Penydarren Roman fort and ruined Morlais Castle, the narrative soon leads into Merthyr's industrial and political heritage. Merthyr's place in working-class history is well examined, with an interesting set of panels and pamphlets on the 1831 riot. Other exhibits examine Aberfan, the 1984–85 miners' strike, pubs and the temperance movement, as well as the beleaguered 1980s Sinclair C5 car, constructed here at the Hoover plant – "built by Hoover, driven by suckers" as the local phrase memorably had it.

Upstairs, the castle's opulent main rooms, all chandeliers and acres of curtains, house a superb collection of Welsh and international **art**. Welsh highlights include an uncharacteristically gentle study of *The Elf* by monumental sculptor Goscombe John, and works by local painters Penry Williams, Augustus John, Cedric Morris, Kyffin Williams and Alfred Jones, whose double portrait of Salome is mesmerizing.

The surrounding **park** contains landscaped walks, a plant nursery, café, bowling green, tennis courts, and a stage set next to the main lake. Best of all, is the **miniature railway**, delighting adults and kids alike as it runs a loop around the lake, island and castle.

Joseph Parry's Cottage

Chapel Row • April–Sept Thurs–Sun 2–5pm • Free • ☎ 01685 727371

Tucked among modern houses just off the A4102 (Bethesda Street), alongside the River Taff, is **Chapel Row**, a line of cottages built in the 1820s for skilled ironworkers.

1

One of these is **Joseph Parry's Cottage**, where the composer was born, though this mini-museum is most interesting as a social record of slightly better-than-average workers' domestic conditions of the nineteenth century. Parry's music, including the national favourite *Myfanwy*, is piped between rooms, and the upstairs section of the house is given over to a display of his life and music.

ARRIVAL AND INFORMATION

MERTHYR TYDFIL

By train Merthyr's train station lies east of the town centre, a minute's walk from the High Street.
Destinations Cardiff (every 30min; 1hr); Pontypridd (every 30min; 30min).
By bus The bus station is right in the centre on Wheatsheaf Lane.

Destinations Brecon (every 1–2hr; 40min); Cardiff (every 20min; 50min); Swansea (6 daily; 1hr 10min).
Tourist information The TIC is behind the bus station at 14a Glebeland Street (Mon–Fri 9.30am–4pm; ☎01685 379884, ✉ tic@merthyr.gov.uk).

ACCOMMODATION AND EATING

Grawen Farm Cwm Taf ☎01685 723740. Located four miles north of town on A470, this family-run farm has modern, well-equipped facilities. Closed Nov–March. **£14**/pitch
Redhouse Cafe High St ☎01685 384111. Inside the beautifully renovated Old Town Hall – itself now a fine exhibition and performance space – this bright and breezy café is comfortably the best place in town for cake and

coffee, as well as something a little bit more substantial. Daily 8am–5.30pm, Fri till 7pm.
Tregenna Hotel Park Terrace, next to Penydarren Park ☎01685 723627, ⊛ tregennahotel.co.uk. It's far from inspiring, possessing an austere exterior and rather dated rooms, but this low-rise hotel is in a quiet location and is just about the cheapest place in town. Rooms also available in an annexe. Breakfast is extra. **£45**

The Rhondda

The twin valleys of the **Rhondda** – Rhondda Fach (Little Rhondda) to the east and Rhondda Fawr (Great Rhondda) to the west – are each sixteen miles long yet less than a mile wide. Between them they once formed the heart of the massive south Wales coal industry. Hollywood romanticized the area in the 1947 Oscar-winning weepie *How Green Was My Valley*, although the story was based on author Richard Llewellyn's early life in nearby Gilfach Goch, outside the valley.

Early records show that in 1841 the Rhondda had a population of under a thousand, but that exploded with the discovery of coal and, by 1924, 167,000 people had squeezed into the available land in ranks of houses packed around sixty or so pitheads. Poverty and hardship were rife, but so were pride, self-reliance, radical religion and

---

THE MERTHYR RADICALS

In the seventeenth century, Merthyr became a focal point for Dissenters and Radicals, movements which, through poverty and oppression, gained momentum in the eighteenth century as the town's four massive ironworks were founded to exploit locally abundant seams of iron ore and limestone. Merthyr became the largest iron-producing town in the world, and by far the most populous settlement in Wales: in 1831, the town had a population of sixty thousand, more than Cardiff, Swansea and Newport combined. Workers flocked from all over Britain and beyond, finding themselves crammed into squalid housing, while the ironmasters built themselves great houses and palaces nearby. Merthyr's **radicalism** bubbled furiously: it was here that the red flag was first raised, when rioters in 1831 gathered around a standard dipped in the blood of a killed calf; another martyr, union organizer Dic Penderyn, was hanged unjustly for his role in the riots. Later, the town saw the election of Britain's first-ever socialist MP, Keir Hardie, in 1900.

Merthyr's precipitous development saw it peak and trough earlier than anywhere else: of its four mighty ironworks, only one was still open at the end of World War I, and that closed in the 1930s. In 1939, a Royal Commission suggested that the town be abandoned and the inhabitants shifted to the coast. The plan was forgotten when war broke out.

firebrand politics. The Communist Party ran the town of Maerdy (nicknamed "Little Moscow" by Fleet Street in the 1930s) for decades. The 1984–85 miners' strike saw solidarity in the Welsh pits on a greater scale than any other part of Britain until the Rhondda's last pit closed in 1990. Aside from the excellent **Rhondda Heritage Park**, there's some rewarding hillwalking, with astounding views over the densely packed houses below.

Rhondda Heritage Park

Daily 9am–4.30pm, closed Mon Oct–March; tours 10am, noon & 2pm • £5.60 • ☎ 01443 682036, ⊛ rhonddaheritagepark.com • Trehafod train station is a 5min walk from the Heritage Park

The Rhondda starts just outside **Pontypridd**, winding through the mountains alongside railway, road and river to **Trehafod** and the colliery museum of the **Rhondda Heritage Park**. Although the first pits were sunk here in 1850, it wasn't until William Lewis (later Lord Merthyr) reopened the site in 1880 that the pit began to prosper, and by 1900 some five thousand men were producing in excess of a million tons of coal a year. Production at the Lewis Merthyr colliery ceased in 1983, seven years before the last pit closed in the Rhondda. Wandering around the yard, you can see the 140ft-high chimney stack, which fronts two iconic latticed shafts, named Bertie and Trefor, after Lewis's sons.

Guided tours take you through the engine winding houses, lamp room, fan house and a simulated "trip underground", with stunning visuals and sound effects, re-creating life (and death) in the late nineteenth century and 1950s through the eyes of colliers.

Rhondda Fach

The Rhondda's two valleys divide at the bustling town of **PORTH** ("Gateway"), a mile beyond the Rhondda Heritage Park, from where the Rhondda Fach (Little Rhondda) River twists its way northwards through the smaller and frequently forgotten valley of the same name, passing endless archetypal Valleys towns like Ynyshir, Pontygwaith, Tylorstown, Ferndale and Maerdy – row after row of tiny houses clinging to sheer valley walls.

Rhondda Fawr

The **Rhondda Fawr** (Great Rhondda) stretches from the outskirts of Pontypridd to Blaenrhondda and is blessed with a train line, a decent road and most of the sights. The first notable settlement is **Tonypandy**, followed a mile later by **Llwynypia**, wedged in between walkable, forested hillsides. From here, a steep two-mile climb leads up to **Mynydd y Gelli**, where the remains of an Iron Age hut settlement and a Bronze Age burial chamber and stone circle can be seen.

Treorchy

The road, river and train line wind tortuously past an endless stream of towns to **TREORCHY** (Treorci), best known internationally for its famed **Treorchy Male Choir**, Wales' oldest, formed in 1883 (⊛ treorchymalechoir.com). Visitors are welcome to rehearsals, which usually take place at 7pm each Monday and Thursday at Treorchy primary school on Glyncoli Road; phone ahead for confirmation (☎ 07849 466080). Most concerts by the choir take place at the splendid **Parc and Dare Theatre** on Station Road (☎ 08000 147111), a multipurpose arts venue that's always busy, though the choir performs all over the country, as well as internationally.

Treherbert

North of Treorchy, at the top of the Rhondda Fawr, is **TREHERBERT**, its straggle of houses continuing up the valley at **Blaencwm** and **Blaenrhondda**, two communities effectively bypassed since a new road was built in the 1930s by unemployed miners, connecting Treherbert to the forests and lakes of Hirwaun Common en route to Brecon.

By train A train line, punctuated with stops every mile or so, runs the entire length of the Rhondda Fawr from Pontypridd to its terminus at Treherbert.

By bus Buses also cover the route; change in Merthyr Tydfil for connections to the Brecon Beacons.

The Ogwr, Garw and Llynfi valleys

To the southwest of the Rhondda, the Ogwr, Garw and Llynfi valleys are different to their bigger, better-known neighbour: the contours are slightly softer, the open spaces wider and the towns less bustling.

The Ogwr Valley

South from Treorchy, the **Ogwr Valley** plunges through the Rhondda Fawr to the ancient settlement and now county town of **BRIDGEND** (Pen-y-bont ar Ogwr), itself a useful transport interchange. Just over a mile northeast of the town are the substantial remains of **Coity Castle** (free access; CADW), built around the end of the twelfth century by one of the earliest Norman knights in the area. Bridgend is also handy for Porthcawl (see p.102).

The Garw Valley

The dead-end **Garw Valley** consists of a road, river and the disused railway crammed in on the valley floor, before they all peter out into wooded hillsides. Most of the scars of the valley's mining past have now been levelled and landscaped, leaving it surprisingly pretty, and, as it's well off any tourist track, very rewarding for walks and congenial company in local pubs and shops. At the southern end of the valley, the **Bryngarw Country Park** (daily dawn–dusk; free, but charges for special events) is a pleasant diversion, with landscaped gardens, exceptional flower collections and mature woodlands gathered around the restored Bryngarw House, which now houses a bistro and conference centre.

The Llynfi Valley

Stretching up from Bridgend and Tondu along the A4063 is the broad-bottomed and leafy **Llynfi Valley**, the main settlement being **MAESTEG**, from where the main road links up with the A4107 at Cymer, for Cwm Afan. On top of the mountain to the south of Maesteg is the beautiful village of **LLANGYNWYD**. Birth- and burial-place of bard Wil Hopcyn, it has an ancient atmosphere in stark contrast to the ex-mining towns below. The splendid pub *Yr Hen Dt* is said to be the oldest inn in south Wales, where revellers traditionally congregate on New Year's Day for the hallowed Welsh custom of the **Mari Llwyd** (Grey Mare), during which a horse's skull is paraded through the village to ward off evil spirits during the forthcoming year.

MALE VOICE CHOIRS

Although Wales' **male voice choirs** can be found all over the country, it is in the southern, industrial heartland that they are loudest and strongest. The roots of the choirs lie in the Nonconformist religious traditions of the seventeenth and eighteenth centuries, when Methodism in particular swept the country, and singing was a free and potent way of cherishing the frequently persecuted faith. Throughout the breakneck nineteenth-century industrialization in the Valleys, choirs of coal miners came together to praise God in the fervent way that was typical of the packed, poor communities. Classic hymns like *Cwm Rhondda* and the Welsh national anthem, *Hen Wlad Fy Nhadau* (*Land of My Fathers*), are synonymous with the choirs, whose full-blooded interpretations render all other efforts insipid.

Despite the collapse of coal mining in the twentieth century, most choirs continue to perform in Wales and abroad. Each small Valleys town has its own choir, most of whom happily allow visitors to sit in on rehearsals. Ask at the local tourist office or library, and take the chance to hear one of the world's most distinctive choral traditions in full, roof-raising splendour.

Cwm Afan

Winding its way between the top of the Llynfi Valley and the coast at Port Talbot, the main attraction in bucolic **CWM AFAN** is the **Afan Forest Park**, whose 9000 acres of hilly forest has become one of the country's premier mountain-bike destinations.

Afan Forest Park Visitor Centre

Visitor centre April–Sept Mon–Fri 9.30am–5pm, Sat & Sun till 6pm; Oct–March Mon–Fri 9.30am–4pm, Sat & Sun till 5pm • Free; parking £1; museum £3 • ☎ 01639 850564, ⓦ afanforestpark.co.uk • **Afan Valley Bike Shed** Rental from £20/half day • ☎ 01639 851406

Situated three miles west of little **CYMER**, the excellent **Afan Forest Park Visitor Centre** houses the small **South Wales Miners' Museum**, where a mock-up miners' tunnel leads through to all manner of mining-related memorabilia, such as equipment, documents and photographs. The centre is the starting point for some nine walking trails, as well as five waymarked **mountain bike** trails, which are fairly demanding, so not best suited to families or those seeking a gentler time of it. Bikes can be rented from Afan Valley Bike Shed, just below the visitor centre.

Glyncorrwg Ponds Visitor Centre

Visitor centre May–Oct daily 8am–5pm, till 8pm Wed & Thurs, till 10pm Fri & Sat, Sun 9am–5pm; Nov–April daily 9am–4pm • Free; parking £3 • ☎ 01639 851900, ⓦ glyncorrwgpondsvisitorcentre.co.uk • **Skyline Cycles** From £30/day • ☎ 01639 850011, ⓦ skylinecycles.co.uk

Some five miles further up the valley, the **Glyncorrwg Ponds Visitor Centre** is a dedicated biking centre, and the starting point for half a dozen trails, all between difficult and severe; bikes can be rented from Skyline Cycles, just below the café. Other facilities include a bike shop, bike park, jet wash, showers and camping.

ACCOMMODATION	**CWM AFAN**
Afan Forest Park campsite ☎ 01639 851900. The campsite has shower and toilet facilities; fires are also permitted. Closed Oct–March. **£3.40**/person	alpine chalet dedicated to mountain bikers; many of the bright, cool a/c rooms have fantastic views down towards the lush forest. Bike wash and lock-up available. **£80**
Afan Lodge Duffryn Rhondda ☎ 01639 852500, ⓦ mountain-bike-accommodation.com. On the main road between the forest park visitor centre and Cymer, this former miners' institute building has been converted into a superb	**Glyncorrwg Ponds campsite** ☎ 01639 851900. Level pitches look out over a picturesque landscape, though facilities are limited to a shower and toilet block. Open all year. **£5**/person

Pontrhydyfen

The valley descends for a couple of miles towards the village of **PONTRHYDYFEN**, picturesquely sited at the confluence of the Afon and Afon Pelenna rivers. Slicing through the village are two monuments that further testify to the region's proud industrial heritage: a magnificent four-arch aqueduct dating from 1827, and, a little further downstream, an equally impressive nine-arch viaduct, built in 1898. The village is best known, however, as the birthplace of actor Richard Burton, who was born in a house (unmarked) at the foot of the aqueduct. From here, roads either side of the river continue south to the industrial sprawl of **PORT TALBOT**, still dominated by its massive steelworks.

Margam

A couple of miles southeast of Port Talbot, on the other side of junction 38 of the M4, **MARGAM** was originally a Cistercian settlement and later the home of various industrial magnates. The first left turn after the motorway junction leads to the arcaded twelfth-century **abbey church**, the sole remaining Cistercian house of worship in Wales.

1

Margam Stones Museum

April–Sept Wed–Sun 10.30am–4pm; Oct–March Wed & Fri by appointment only • £2.10; CADW • ☎ 01443 336000

Within a nineteenth-century schoolhouse is the little-known **Margam Stones Museum**. Often bypassed in the rush to get to the neighbouring country park, this outstanding collection of memorial stones, sculptured crosses, grave slabs and tomb covers dates mostly from Celtic and medieval times. The most prized exhibit is the tenth-century Cynfelin (or Conbelin) stone, an intricately carved wheel-headed cross. Take a close look, too, at the figures and gargoyles from destroyed Welsh churches and monasteries.

Margam Country Park

Castle and grounds April–Aug daily 10am–6pm; Sept–March park only Mon & Tues 1–4.30pm, Wed–Sun 10am–4.30pm • Free; miniature railway £1.80; parking £4.50 • ☎ 01639 881635, ⓦ margamcountrypark.co.uk • Bus #1 (from Bridgend or Swansea) stops outside the entrance

The 850-acre **Margam Country Park** has enough to see and do to keep you occupied for the best part of half a day, longer if the weather is kind. The park is centred around the nineteenth-century Gothic pile of **Margam Castle**, much of which was gutted by fire in 1977. It's essentially off-limits, but you can still wander into the lobby and peer up the octagonal lantern tower and see a few models and photos. One of these is of Eisenhower, taken when he visited American troops stationed here during World War II.

Down from the castle, and tucked in by the abbey church walls, are the impressive remains of the original Cistercian **abbey**, most notable for the vaulting of its twelve-sided chapterhouse, which survived the dissolution of the monasteries only to have its roof collapse under the weight of weeds in 1799. Alongside is Margam's showpiece **orangery**, a splendid Georgian outhouse, built in 1790 and, at 327ft long, reputedly the longest in Britain. There's plenty for kids to do here, including a miniature railway (which runs from the entrance up to the castle), a "fairyland" play area, an adventure playground, a farm trail and, for older kids, a Go Ape centre.

Vale of Neath

Although the town of **NEATH** (Castell-Nedd) is not particularly worthy of a visit, the **Vale of Neath**, spearing northeast, boasts several fascinating remnants from both the Industrial Revolution and the coal-mining industry.

The Aberdulais Tinworks and Waterfalls

2 miles northeast of Neath • Feb, March & Oct daily 11am–4pm; April–Sept daily 10.30am–5pm; Nov–Jan Fri–Sun 11am–4pm • £4.80; NT • ☎ 01639 636674 • Bus #154 from Neath & #158 from Swansea

Aberdulais was once one of the world's largest tinplate manufacturing centres, thanks largely to its position at the confluence of the Dulais and Neath rivers. Its **waterfalls** have been harnessing hydroelectric power here since the sixteenth century – initially for the manufacture of copper – though the present-day water wheel was installed in 1982. Among the impressive extant remains is the tinning house and chimney stack; the old smithy building now accommodates an illuminating exhibition on the industry. The falls themselves provide a picturesque backdrop to the site. There's also a tempting tearoom.

Cefn Coed Colliery Museum

A4109, 3 miles north of Aberdulais • May–Sept daily 10.30am–5pm • Free • ☎ 01639 750556 • Bus #158 from Neath and Swansea

What was once the world's deepest anthracite mine is now the **Cefn Coed Colliery Museum**. Dubiously nicknamed "The Slaughterhouse" – owing to the extreme dangers faced by miners working at depths in excess of 2250ft – the colliery closed in 1968, with workers transferred to the nearby Blaenant drift mine, which subsequently closed in 1990. This is more low-key than many of the Valleys' other heritage sites, but a walk around the mining gallery and boiler house through to the magnificent steam winding engine gives yet another stark reminder of a region's once proud but now lost way of life. Crowning the site are the colliery's iconic latticed steel pithead frames.

Swansea

Over half a century ago, Dylan Thomas dubbed his native **SWANSEA** (Abertawe) an "ugly, lovely town" – a scathing but affectionate epithet which was once well deserved, although the famous poet probably wouldn't recognize the place these days. The city was devastated by bombing in World War II and hastily rebuilt, but since the turn of the millennium has been undergoing something of a renaissance, with bright, bold new developments springing up across the city.

Swansea's wide seafront overlooks the huge sweep of **Swansea Bay**, the focal point of much of the redevelopment, particularly around the old docks, and the city now boasts some of the best-funded **museums** in Wales. The seafront arcs around to the Gower peninsula, with the elegant but relaxed seaside resort of **Mumbles**, as well as some of Britain's best **surfing**, on its doorstep.

Brief history

The city's Welsh name, Abertawe, refers to the settlement at the mouth of the River Tawe, now being coaxed back to life as part of Swansea's redeveloped waterfront after centuries of use as a repository for Swansea's metal trades. The English name derives from Viking sources, suggesting that a pre-Norman settlement existed in the area. The first reliable records of Swansea date back to 1099, when a Norman castle was built here as an outpost of William the Conqueror's empire. A small settlement subsequently grew near the coalfields and the sea, developing into a mining and shipbuilding centre that, by 1700, was the largest coal port in Wales.

Metal-smelting days

Copper-smelting became the area's dominant industry in the eighteenth century, soon attracting other activities to pack out the lower Tawe Valley. Drawn by the town's flourishing activities, a swiftly growing port and the arrival of the Swansea Canal, thousands of emigrants moved to the city from all over Ireland and Britain; by the nineteenth century, the town was one of the world's most prolific metal-bashing centres.

Decline and revival

Smelting was already on the wane by the beginning of the twentieth century, although Swansea's port continued to thrive. Britain's first oil refinery was opened on the edge of the city in 1918, with dock developments growing up in its wake. Civic zeal, best exemplified by the graceful 1930s Guildhall, was reawakened after the establishment of an important branch of the University of Wales here in 1920. Swansea was devastated during World War II, however, when thirty thousand bombs rained down on the city in just three nights in 1941. Initial rebuilding left the city disjointed, although now, with a population of around two thousand hundred, Swansea boasts resurgent music, club and surf scenes, and some spirited rebuilding and redevelopment. Moreover, the recent success of the city's **football club**, now Premier League regulars, has energized Swansea even further.

Castle Square and around

Very much the heart of the city centre, **Castle Square** is a pleasant amphitheatre of steps surrounding a fountain, albeit slightly ruined by an unnecessarily large TV screen. Standing somewhat incongruously on the east side of the square are the **castle ruins**, the most obvious landmark being the semicircular arcades, built into the wall between 1330 and 1332 by Bishop Gower to replace a Norman predecessor.

1

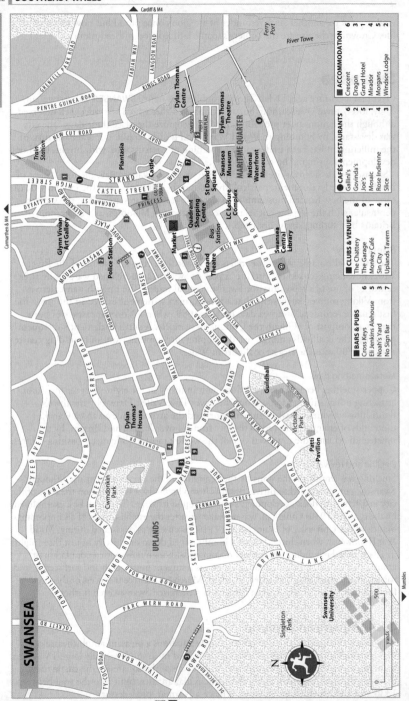

▲ Cardiff & M4

Ferry Port

River Tawe

MARITIME QUARTER

SWANSEA

ACCOMMODATION
Crescent	6
Dragon	3
Grand Hotel	1
Mirador	4
Morgans	5
Windsor Lodge	2

● CAFÉS & RESTAURANTS
Gallini's	6
Govinda's	2
Joe's	5
Mosaic	1
Rose Indienne	4
Slice	3

■ CLUBS & VENUES
The Chattery	8
The Garage	9
Monkey Café	1
Sin City	4
Uplands Tavern	2

■ BARS & PUBS
Cross Keys	6
Eli Jenkins Alehouse	5
Noah's Yard	3
No Sign Bar	7

Dylan Thomas Centre
Dylan Thomas Theatre
Swansea Museum
National Waterfront Museum
Swansea Central Library
St David's Square
LC Leisure Complex
Quadrant Shopping Centre
Bus Station
Grand Theatre
Market
Castle
Plantasia
Glynn Vivian Art Gallery
Police Station
Train Station
Dylan Thomas' House
Guildhall
Victoria Park
Patti Pavilion
Cwmdonkin Park
Swansea University
Singleton Park

Train Station

▲ Camarthen & M4

COMMERCIAL RD
AMBERLAN PLACE

STRAND
CASTLE STREET
HIGH STREET
DYFATTY ST
NEW CUT ROAD
PENTRE GUINEA ROAD
GRENFELL PARK ROAD
FABIAN WAY
LANGDON ROAD
KINGS ROAD
QUAY PARADE
ALEXANDRA RD
ORCHARD ST
CASTLE SQUARE
PRINCESS WAY
WIND ST
ST MARY ST
SINGLETON STREET
GROVE PLACE
MOUNT PLEASANT
MANSEL ST
THE KINGSWAY
OXFORD STREET
CROMWELL STREET
TERRACE ROAD
WALTER ROAD
ST HELEN'S ROAD
WEST WAY
ARGYLE ST
BEACH ST
OYSTERMOUTH ROAD
WESTERN STREET
DYFED AVENUE
PANT-Y-CELYN ROAD
PENLAN CRESCENT
DONKIN RD
UPLANDS CRESCENT
BRYN-Y-MOR ROAD
KING EDWARDS ROAD
ST HELEN'S AVENUE
EATON CRESCENT
BRUNSWICK ST
BERNARD STREET
GLANBRYDAN AVENUE
SKETTY ROAD
GLANMOR ROAD
GLANMOR PARK ROAD
PARC WERN ROAD
TOWNHILL ROAD
COCKETT RD
TY-COCH ROAD
VIVIAN ROAD
GOWER ROAD
DE LA BECHE ROAD
BRYNMILL LANE
MUMBLES ROAD
BRYN ROAD

UPLANDS

N

0   yards   500

▼ Gower
▼ Mumbles

Running south from the castle is **Wind Street** (so named because it's winding – or at least gently curving), nocturnal Swansea's main drag, chock-full of bars, pubs and restaurants; evenings are quite something along here. The remaining streets hereabouts are largely the preserve of shops, with just the occasional place of interest for the visitor.

Swansea Indoor Market

Oxford St • Mon–Fri 8am–5.30pm, Sat 7.30am–5.30pm • ☎ 01792 654296, ⓦ swanseaindoormarket.co.uk

There has been a **market** here or hereabouts since the mid-eighteenth century, though this current glass-roofed incarnation – Wales' largest – has been here since 1961. It's a lively bustle of colourful stalls, fresh flowers and freshly baked food, including local delicacies like laver bread (made from laver, aka seaweed), as well as cockles trawled from the nearby Loughor estuary, traditional Welsh cakes, fish and cheeses. You'll also find stalls selling clothing, jewellery and gifts.

Plantasia

Parc Tawe • Daily 10am–5pm • £3.95 • ☎ 01792 474555

Possibly of greater interest to kids than adults, the retail park on the Strand, Park Tawe, includes the great pyramidal glasshouse of **Plantasia**, comprising a tropical hothouse with exotic plants and tamarin monkeys, a birdhouse with parakeets and numerous insects, an aquarium and a 20ft Burmese python.

Glynn Vivian Art Gallery

Alexandra Rd • Tues–Sun 10am–5pm • Free • ☎ 01792 516900, ⓦ glynnviviangallery.org

A short walk north of Castle Square brings you to the **Glynn Vivian Art Gallery**, a delightful Edwardian venue housing an inspiring collection of Welsh art including works by Gwen John, her brother Augustus (whose mesmerizing portrait of Caitlin Thomas, Dylan's wife, is a real highlight) and Kyffin Williams; the grimy mining portraits of Josef Herman; and a whole room of huge, frantic canvases by Ceri Richards, Wales' most respected twentieth-century painter. In the early nineteenth century, Swansea was a noted centre of fine porcelain production, of which the gallery houses a large collection, together with pieces of contemporary work from Nantgarw, near Cardiff. Note that the gallery is undergoing a major renovation project (it's due to reopen late 2015), so some of the above may have changed.

The Maritime Quarter

The spit of land between Oystermouth Road, the sea and the Tawe estuary has been christened the **Maritime Quarter**, with its vast centrepiece marina surrounded by contemporary apartments, cafés, shops, museums and a leisure centre. Entering the quarter from the east, the main road bridge over the Tawe is guarded by a World War II ack-ack gun, which stands as a memorial to the Luftwaffe decimation suffered by Swansea.

Swansea Museum

Victoria Rd • Tues–Sun 10am–5pm • Free • ☎ 01792 653763, ⓦ swanseamuseum.co.uk

Founded in 1835 as the Royal Institution of South Wales, **Swansea Museum** is Wales' oldest public museum. Much of it is still appealingly old-fashioned, with a wizened Egyptian mummy, lots of archeological finds, and local porcelain and pottery. More interesting is the Cabinet of Curiosities room, full of glass cases stuffed with all sorts of oddments such as offbeat household items, memento moris – miniature shrines containing photos and models of the deceased – and some intriguing local photos, including several of Winston Churchill taken during his visit to the city in World War II. There's also a marble bust of Gower son, Edgar Evans, who perished with Scott in Antarctica in 1912.

1

Dylan Thomas Centre

Somerset Place • Daily 10am–4.30pm • Free • ☎ 01792 463980, ⓦ dylanthomas.com

In the former nineteenth-century guildhall is the **Dylan Thomas Centre**, where a superb exhibition offers a compelling insight into his life and times. Entitled "Man and Myth", it has some unique archive material on display: original worksheets, bar tabs, the writer's only known painting, and the last photos of Thomas before his death, taken, appropriately enough, in a New York bar. Also here are the doors of the shed in which Thomas wrote at Laugharne. In the meantime, a fascinating video on his life and work plays continuously. Look out for the many terrific literary events taking place here throughout the year.

National Waterfront Museum

Oystermouth Rd • Daily 10am–5pm • Free • ☎ 01792 638950, ⓦ museumwales.ac.uk

Down by the marina is the fine **National Waterfront Museum**. Carved out of the shell of the old Industrial and Maritime Museum, the original building has been stunningly extended to accommodate wide-ranging exhibitions on Wales' history of innovation and industry. The museum is divided into fifteen zones, each with an interactive take on topics such as energy, landscape, coal, networks and money. Much else besides is celebrated here, such as Wales' success in the field of sport and its contribution to the music industry, with coverage of the much loved colliery brass bands, awards won by the likes of the Super Furry Animals and a pair of bejewelled wellies worn by Dame Shirley Bassey at Glastonbury in 2007. Look out too for the many superb heritage pieces, such as the 1907 Robin Goch (Redbreast) monoplane, one of the very few pre-World War I planes still in existence.

West Swansea

Aside from being one of the greenest parts of the city, thanks to a generous spread of parks and gardens, the area west of the centre counts a few worthwhile attractions in the shape of some architectural gems, a couple of fine little museums, and Dylan Thomas' birthplace.

The Guildhall and Brangwyn Hall

St Helen's Road dips down to the seafront near the tall white tower of the **Guildhall** – a soaring piece of 1930s civic architecture. Within the Guildhall, **Brangwyn Hall** takes its name from Sir Frank Brangwyn, who painted the eighteen enormous British Empire panels lining the hall. Its function today is as one of the city's premier classical concert venues, and it really comes into its own during the Swansea Festival of Music and the Arts (see box, p.126).

Patti Pavilion

Immediately behind the Guildhall, down by the coast road, the most prominent feature of **Victoria Park** is the **Patti Pavilion**, a graceful green-roofed, glass-paned hall that was a gift from the nineteenth-century Spanish opera singer Adelina Patti, brought here from her home at Craig-y-nos in the Brecon Beacons. Today the pavilion is home to a function hall and Indian restaurant.

Ceri Richards Gallery and Egypt Centre

Swansea University, Mumbles Rd • **Ceri Richards Gallery** Mon–Fri 10am–6pm, Sat 10am–4pm • Free • ☎ 01792 295526 •
Egypt Centre Tues–Sat 10am–4pm • Free • ☎ 01792 295960

Along the coast road, the **Swansea University** campus affords a commanding view over the bay stretching to Mumbles Head. On site is an imaginative performance space, the **Taliesin Arts Centre**, which also incorporates the **Ceri Richards Gallery**, specializing in touring exhibitions by contemporary Welsh and Celtic artists.

Also housed here, the **Egypt Centre** is Wales' pre-eminent Egyptology display, part of the collection of eminent pharmacist Sir Henry Wellcome. The collection is split in two: The House of Death, with its funerary paraphernalia (look out for the beautiful painted coffin of a lady musician from Thebes), and The House of Life, covering day-to-day existence, although most of the artefacts come from tombs.

Cwmdonkin Park

In the Uplands area, a thirty-minute walk from the city centre, shaded avenues rise up the slopes past the sharp terraces of **Cwmdonkin Park**, where there is a memorial to Dylan Thomas inscribed with lines from *Fern Hill*, one of his best-loved poems.

Dylan Thomas' birthplace

5 Cwmdonkin Drive • Daily 10.30am–4.30pm • £8 • 📞 01792 472555, 🌐 5cwmdonkindrive.com

On the eastern side of Cwmdonkin Park, a blue plaque at 5 Cwmdonkin Drive denotes this solid Victorian semi as **Dylan Thomas' birthplace**. Thomas actually lived here until he was 20, and while nothing remains from his time, the house has been sympathetically restored to re-create the atmosphere of early twentieth-century life in Swansea. In-depth **guided tours** of the surprisingly spacious interior take in the house's many rooms, including the grand lounge, his father's study, the kitchen and Thomas' boxy bedroom. It's even possible to sleep here, but to do so you must contact the house well in advance. There isn't always someone present at the house, so you'd do well to call in advance.

ARRIVAL AND DEPARTURE | SWANSEA

By train Swansea is the main interchange station for services out to the west of Wales and for the slow but scenic line across the middle of the country to Shrewsbury in Shropshire. The train station is at the top end of the High Street, a 10min walk from Castle Square.
Destinations Cardiff (every 30min; 55min); Carmarthen (hourly; 50min); Ferryside (11 daily; 40min); Haverfordwest (9 daily; 1hr 30min); Kidwelly (11 daily; 30min); Knighton (4 daily; 3hr); Llandeilo (4 daily; 1hr); Llandovery (4 daily; 1hr 20min); Llandrindod Wells (4 daily; 2hr 20min); Llanelli (hourly; 20min); Llanwrtyd Wells (4 daily; 1hr 45min); London (hourly; 3hr); Milford Haven (9 daily; 1hr 50min); Newport

(every 30min; 1hr 20min); Pembroke (5 daily; 2hr 5min); Tenby (6 daily; 1hr 40min); Whitland (hourly; 1hr 10min).
By bus Swansea's enormous bus station is in the centre of the city on The Quadrant.
Destinations Aberdulais (every 45–60min; 45min); Aberystwyth (3 daily; 2hr 45min); Brecon (5 daily; 1hr 35min); Cardiff (every 30min; 1hr); Carmarthen (every 30min; 1hr); Dan-yr-ogof (5 daily; 1hr); Merthyr Tydfil (5 daily; 1hr 15min); Mumbles (every 10min; 15min); Oxwich (9 daily, 1 change; 1hr); Pennard (hourly; 30min); Port Eynon (9 daily, 1 change; 1hr 15min); Porthcawl (hourly; 1hr 20min); Rhossili (10 daily; 1hr).

GETTING AROUND AND INFORMATION

By bus Getting around Swansea is easy, but the thorough bus network is useful for further-flung areas, including the suburbs near the University such as Uplands and Sketty (a bracing half-hour walk from the centre) and Mumbles and Gower. A day ticket covering the city centre area is £4, while the Swansea Bay day ticket (covering southern Gower to Rhossili) is £4.70. Weekly tickets are £19 and £21 respectively.
By bike Excellent bike rental is available at Action Bikes, 5 St Davids Square (Mon–Sat 9am–5.30pm, Sun

11am–4pm; 📞 01792 464640, 🌐 actionbikesswansea .co.uk; £12/half day, £18/day); they do repairs too.
Tourist information The TIC is on Plymouth Street, next to the bus station (Mon–Sat 9.30am–5.30pm; June–Sept also Sun 10am–4pm; 📞 01792 468321, 🌐 visitswanseabay .com); there's stacks of material here on both the city and Gower, and you also can pick up the comprehensive bi-monthly magazine *What's On*. The staff here can also book accommodation.

ACTIVITIES

Swimming Swansea has two excellent swimming facilities; the Wales National Pool (📞 01792 513513, 🌐 walesnational poolswansea.co.uk) on Sketty Lane near the university, and the waterpark at the LC leisure complex on Oystermouth Road (📞 01792 484672, 🌐 thelcswansea.co.uk).

Watersports 360 Beach and Watersports, just down from Victoria Park on Mumbles Road (📞 01792 655844, 🌐 360swansea.co.uk), offers kayaking, paddleboarding, kitesurfing and lots more.

1

ACCOMMODATION

For a reasonably large city, Swansea is not exactly endowed with a surfeit of great **accommodation**. That said, there are some inexpensive hotels and B&Bs lining the seafront Oystermouth Road, and it's just a stone's throw to Gower, where there are further, albeit slightly pricier, options. There are no hostels in Swansea, and the nearest campsite is west of the city towards Mumbles (see p.128).

Crescent 132 Eaton Crescent, Uplands ☎ 01792 465782, ⓦ crescentguesthouse.co.uk. Large, sky-blue Edwardian guesthouse with pretty, pastel-shaded en-suite rooms, half of which have superb views over the city and the bay. **£65**

Dragon Kingsway Circle ☎ 01792 657100, ⓦ dragon -hotel.co.uk. Despite its officious-looking facade, this landmark central hotel is an elegant and modern establishment with plush, a/c rooms coloured vivid red; the luxury amenities include a gym, indoor pool and beauty salon, plus a lounge and piano bar, and restaurant. Breakfast is extra. **£75**

Grand Hotel Ivey Place, High St ☎ 01792 645898, ⓦ thegrandhotelswansea.co.uk. Accomplished yet pleasingly informal hotel opposite the train station with softly coloured, a/c rooms with flat-screen TV/DVD player, and sparkling bathrooms with fantastic showers. Convivial café/sports bar downstairs. Breakfast is extra. **£75**

★**Mirador** 14 Mirador Crescent ☎ 01792 466976, ⓦ themirador.co.uk. Swansea's most inspirational accommodation, a family-run town house in the Uplands area with seven fun rooms, each themed on a particular country and furnished accordingly (African, Oriental, Egyptian, Roman and so on). **£69**

Morgans Somerset Place ☎ 01792 484848, ⓦ morganshotel.co.uk. Swansea's showpiece boutique hotel, split between the sumptuously converted old Port Authority HQ and the beautiful Regency terrace town house opposite. The superbly appointed rooms boast hardwood flooring, polished wood fittings and Egyptian cotton bed linen and goosedown duvets. **£65**

Windsor Lodge Mount Pleasant ☎ 01792 642158, ⓦ windsor-lodge.co.uk. This 200-year-old house has nicely decorated, if slightly dated, rooms, and the bathrooms are a little poky, but it's in a good location and provides fair value for money. **£70**

EATING AND DRINKING

Swansea is no gastronomic paradise, but it does boast a select core of worthwhile **restaurants**. On the other hand, there's no shortage of nightlife in the city, with a proliferation of **bars** and **clubs** to the fore; while most of the action is overwhelmingly centred on Wind Street– not a place for the faint-hearted at the weekend – the Uplands area is far more enjoyable, bursting with a number of independently minded pubs and live music venues. The city's theatrical and high **cultural** life is also robust and varied.

CAFÉS AND RESTAURANTS

Gallini's 3 Fishmarket Quay ☎ 01792 456285, ⓦ gallinisrestaurant.co.uk. This somewhat ordinary-looking but cheery Italian restaurant offers some terrific flavour combinations such as prawns in chilli and lime jam. The downstairs coffee shop is a relaxing spot to kick back with a fresh cup of coffee and take in the view across the marina. Restaurant daily noon–2.30pm & 6pm–midnight; coffee shop 10am–5pm.

Govinda's 8 Craddock St ☎ 01792 468469. Simple and

clean vegetarian restaurant in the Hare Krishna tradition, selling wholesome light bites like chapati wraps and *subji* for as little as £4, as well as freshly pressed juices. Mon–Sat noon–5pm.

Joe's 85 St Helen's Rd ☎ 01792 653880. This perennially popular outlet has been doling out some of the country's finest ice cream since 1922. All the classic flavours are here, as well as many specialist creations, such as raspberry crumble, hazelnut fudge and lemon meringue. Daily 11am–9pm.

SWANSEA FESTIVALS

The **Swansea Bay Summer Festival** (ⓦ swanseabayfestival.co.uk) features intermittent events (music, theatre and outdoor concerts) between May and September, culminating with **Proms in the Park** in Singleton Park. In mid-June, various venues around the Maritime Quarter (principally the Dylan Thomas Centre) play host to the terrific **Swansea International Jazz Festival** (ⓦ sijf.co.uk). The highbrow **Swansea Festival of Music and the Arts** (ⓦ swanseafestival.org) lasts throughout October with concerts in the Brangwyn Hall and several other venues, while the two-week long **Dylan Thomas Festival** (ⓦ dylanthomas.com /festival) in November celebrates the city's favourite son with various events at the Dylan Thomas Centre.

★**Mosaic** 218 High St ☎01792 655225, ⓦmosaicswansea.com. Modern industrial design and understated cool mark this café-cum-restaurant out as something a little different from most places in Swansea; the daytime food menu comprises scrummy light bites like king prawn chowder, and grilled bacon with peanut butter and sweet chilli in a folded flatbread (£7.95), while on Friday and Saturday evenings, tapas and meze dishes are served – a great accompaniment to the live music. Tues–Sat noon–4pm, plus Fri & Sat 6.30pm–late.

Rose Indienne 73–74 St Helen's Rd ☎01792 467000, ⓦrose-indienne.co.uk. Comfortably the best of Swansea's many Indian restaurants, the beautifully appointed *Rose Indienne* offers some exciting and unusual dishes, such as Goan duck curry, and salmon marinated in masala with mint chutney (£11.95), in addition to a dozen or so lentil- and vegetable-based dishes. It's charmingly staffed too. Mon–Sat noon–2.30pm & 5.30–midnight, Sun noon–midnight.

★**Slice** 73–75 Everley Rd ☎01792 290929, ⓦsliceswansea.co.uk. Located out in the Sketty area, the diminutive *Slice* – so named because of the quirkily shaped building – offers a level of cuisine unmatched anywhere in the city, with confident contemporary dishes such as roast cod, potato and chorizo terrine. Three courses £35. With just a handful of tables, booking is essential. Wed & Thurs noon–2pm, Fri–Sun noon–2pm & 6.30–10pm.

NIGHTLIFE

The Chattery 59 Uplands Crescent ☎01792 473276. Although nominally a restaurant, this longstanding venue is also well regarded for the quality of its musical guests (both local and touring UK/US acts), with gigs typically taking place on two or three Saturdays a month. Mon 10am–3pm, Tues–Sat 10am–5pm, plus gig nights 7.30pm–midnight.

★**The Garage** 47 Uplands Crescent ☎01792 475147, ⓦwhitez.co.uk. Cracking Uplands venue that has firmly established itself as the city's premier live music venue, by virtue of its quality (and wonderfully varied) acts and understatedly cool atmosphere; rock'n'roll is to the fore, but there's much else besides. Tricky to find, the entrance is through Whitez pool club. Mon, Tues & Sun 8.30am–8pm, Wed–Sat till 11pm.

Monkey Café 13 Castle St ☎01792 480822. Groovy, inexpensive, mosaic-floored café with a relaxed atmosphere that draws a pretty diverse crowd.

ENTERTAINMENT

Brangwyn Hall The Guildhall, Guildhall Rd South ☎01792 635432. Vastly impressive music hall in the Art Deco civic centre which hosts regular concerts by the BBC National Orchestra of Wales and others.

Dylan Thomas Theatre Dylan Thomas Square,

BARS AND PUBS

Cross Keys Inn 12 St Mary St ☎01792 630921. Dating from the 1700s, Swansea's oldest hostelry is a deceptively large affair, offering good ales, a sunny beer garden (BBQs in summer) and a loyal band of rugby followers. Mon–Sat 11am–11pm, Sun noon–10.30pm.

Eli Jenkins Ale House 24 Oxford St ☎01792 641067. Named after the Dylan Thomas character in *Under Milk Wood*, this pleasant, popular locals' pub sits surprisingly well amid the surrounding shopping precincts, and the beer is pretty good too. Mon–Thurs 8am–11pm, Fri & Sat 8am–midnight, Sun 11am–11pm.

Noah's Yard 38 Uplands Crescent ☎01792 447360. Classy wine bar with big bay windows, bare brick walls and Art Deco lighting, Chesterfield sofas and trunks for tables, as well as lots of post-modern artwork including a piece by Banksy, the infamous street artist. Live jazz every Monday at 8.30pm (£3). Daily 2pm–midnight.

No Sign Bar 56 Wind St ☎01792 465300. If you deign/ dare to visit one place on Wind St, make it *No Sign*, one of the oldest hostelries in town. A narrow frontage leads into a long, warm pub interior with bare brick walls, pale wood flooring and squishy sofas, while down in the vaulted cellar you'll catch live music most weekends. The meaning of the name is explained in depth in the window. Mon–Sat 11am–1am, Sun noon–11pm.

Happenings almost daily, including live music, DJs, burlesque, tango and salsa classes, and even cookery classes. Art exhibitions are regularly held here too. On a good night, it's the best place in town. Daily 11am–2am, Fri & Sat till 4.30am.

Sin City 14–16 Dillwyn St ☎01792 468892, ⓦsincityclub.co.uk. Another of the city's superb live music venues, though the emphasis here is firmly on indie and heavy rock, notably the Friday-night Monsters rock/ metal shindig. Riotous club nights too, including Sink (drum'n'bass/dubstep) on Saturday. Thurs–Sat 10pm–late.

Uplands Tavern 42 Uplands Crescent ☎01792 458242. Next to *Noah's Yard*, this former haunt of Dylan Thomas – the walls of the Dylan snug corner are plastered with some fabulous photos – is today a bastion of local live music, especially rock and blues, usually Thursdays to Saturdays. Daily 11am–11pm, Fri & Sat till midnight.

Maritime Quarter ☎01792 473238, ⓦdylanthomastheatre.org.uk. Thriving community operation staging reruns of Thomas's classics, alongside modern works, in the Little Theatre.

Grand Theatre Singleton St ☎01792 475715,

1

ⓦswanseagrand.co.uk. One of Britain's best provincial theatres, with a wide-ranging diet of visiting high culture, comedy, panto, farce and music.

Taliesin Arts Centre Swansea University

ⓣ01792 602060, ⓦtaliesinartscentre.co.uk. Welsh, English and international visiting theatre, film, dance and music (jazz, world), including offbeat and alternative fare.

DIRECTORY

Hospital Singleton Hospital, Sketty Park Lane, Singleton, West Swansea (ⓣ01792 205666).

Internet Swansea Central Library, Civic Centre,

Oystermouth Road (Tues–Fri 8.30am–8pm, Sat & Sun 10am–4pm; ⓣ01792 636464).

Police The main station is on Grove Place (ⓣ01792 456999).

Gower

Thrusting into the Bristol Channel west of Swansea, the nineteen-mile **GOWER** (Gŵyr) peninsula is fringed by sweeping yellow bays and precipitous cliffs, caves and blowholes to the south, and wide, flat marshes and cockle beds to the north. Brackened heaths with prehistoric remains and tiny villages lie between, interspersed with castle ruins, curious churches and the scent of wild garlic.

Gower starts in Swansea's western suburbs, along the coast of Swansea Bay, which curves round to a point in the charmingly old-fashioned and increasingly swish resort of **Mumbles** and Mumbles Head, marking the boundary between the sandy sweep of Swansea Bay and the rocky inlets along the southern Gower's serrated coastline. This southern coast is punctuated by sites exploited for their defensive capacities, best seen in the eerie isolation of the sandbound **Pennard Castle**, high above **Three Cliffs Bay**. West, the wide sands of **Oxwich Bay** sit next to inland reedy marshes, beyond which is the picturesque village of **Port Eynon**. West again, the coast becomes a wild, frilly series of inlets and cliffs, capped by a five-mile path that stretches all the way to the peninsula's glorious westernmost point, **Worms Head**.

Rhossili Bay, a breathtaking four-mile span of sand backed by the village of Rhossili, occupies the entire western end of Gower from Worms Head to the islet of **Burry Holms**, and, when conditions are right, provides some of the best **surfing** in Wales. The northern coast merges into the tidal flats of the estuary, running past the salted marsh of **Llanrhidian**, overlooked by the gaunt ruins of **Weobley Castle**, and on to the famous cockle beds at **Penclawdd**. Mumbles aside, there's not an abundance of **accommodation** on Gower, so you'd do well to make reservations in advance, including for campsites.

GETTING AROUND   GOWER

By bus There are no train services on Gower, but with its proximity to urban Swansea, bus transport is reasonably comprehensive. Buses (services #115 to 118) run regularly from Swansea's bus station to Rhossili, Port Eynon, Parkmill and Oxwich in South Gower; and through North Gower to Llanrhidian, Llangennith and Llanmadoc. A Swansea Bay day pass costs £4.70.

By car Traffic at the height of the summer can be heavy, so take care when driving, especially when rounding blind corners on the narrow – often single-lane – twisting roads. Most car parks charge a one-off fee of around £3.

On foot and by bike Cycling and walking are ideal ways to tour the area, as the peninsula's attractions are all within a short distance of each other and, in many cases, well off-road.

Mumbles

At the westernmost end of Swansea Bay on the cusp of Gower, the lively, upmarket seaside town of **MUMBLES** (Mwmbwls) takes its name from French sailors who dubbed the twin islets off the end of Mumbles Head *mamelles* (French for "breasts"). Today, the name "Mumbles" also refers interchangeably to the entire loose sprawl of **Oystermouth** (Ystumllwynarth), the area between Swansea and Mumbles.

Once known as the "Mumbles Mile", thanks to the stags and hens that used to trawl the pubs here, the seafront is now an uninterrupted curve of stylish hotels and B&Bs,

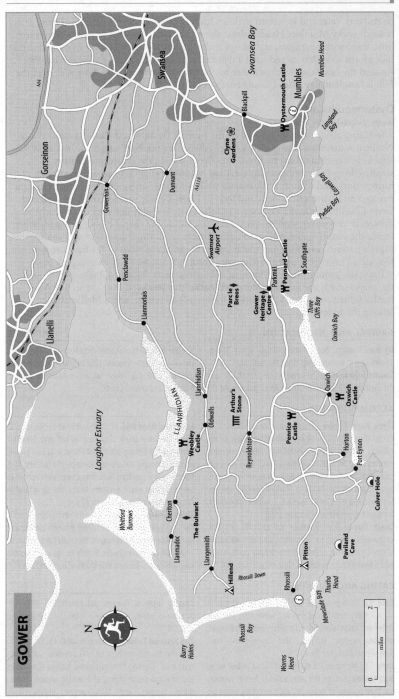

GOWER

Swansea

Swansea Bay

Mumbles Head

Oystermouth Castle
Mumbles
Blackpill
Langland Bay

Clyne Gardens

Gorseinon

M4

Dunvant

A4118

Caswell Bay

Pwlldu Bay

Gowerton

Swansea Airport

Southgate

Penclawdd

Parc le Breos

Pennard Castle
Parkmill

Gower Heritage Centre

Llanmorlais

Three Cliffs Bay

Oxwich Bay

Llanelli

Llanrhidian

Oxwich
Oxwich Castle

Loughor Estuary

LLANRHIDIAN

Oldwalls

Arthur's Stone

Penrice Castle

Weobley Castle

Reynoldston

Horton

Port Eynon

Whitford Burrows

Cheriton

The Bulwark

Culver Hole

Llanmadoc

Llangennith

Hillend

Rhossili Down

Paviland Cave

Pitton

Rhossili Bay

Burry Holms

Rhossili

Mewslade Bay

Thurba Head

Worms Head

N

0   2
miles

1

restaurants, cafés and ice-cream parlours leading down to the old-fashioned **pier**, towards rocky Mumbles Head. Behind the promenade, a warren of streets climbs the hills, lined with boutiques, craft shops and galleries and further places to eat and drink; indeed, the town has earned itself a reputation as something of a foodie destination. Around the headland, reached either by the longer coast road or a short walk over the hill, is **Langland Bay**, with a sandy beach popular with **surfers**.

Oystermouth Castle

Newton Rd • April–Sept daily 11am–5pm • £2.50

The hilltop above town is crowned by the ruins of **Oystermouth Castle**. Founded as a Norman watchtower, the castle was strengthened by the Normans to withstand Welsh attacks before being converted into a residence during the fourteenth century. A sensitive long-term restoration project has restored the castle to something like its former glory, and with its thick curtain walls, turreted battlements and warren of dank passages and staircases, it looks and feels just how a castle should. The keep, hall and Great Chamber form the earliest part of the castle (roughly late twelfth and early thirteenth centuries), with the remainder (including the chapel block) later additions. Inside the chapel, stairs lead up to a glass bridge platform, from where you can see the superb traceried east window, which frames magnificent views of the bay. The ramparts, too, afford lush vistas over the Mumbles headland, Swansea and its sweeping bay.

The castle grounds stage an array of colourful events throughout summer, though the major one is the four-day **Mumbles Marvellous Weekend** over the second May Bank Holiday, with jazz and classical music, a food festival and a Medieval fayre among the happenings.

ARRIVAL AND INFORMATION

MUMBLES

By bus Frequent buses from Swansea (every 10min; 15min) stop at various points along the seafront.

Tourist information The small but very helpful TIC is in the Methodist church on Mumbles Road, just beyond the

Newton Road junction (Easter–Sept Mon–Sat 10am–5pm; Oct–Easter 10am–4pm; ☎ 01792 361302, ✆ mumblesinfo .org.uk). Staff can advise on accommodation both in Mumbles and around Gower.

ACCOMMODATION

Clyne Farm Centre Westport Ave ☎ 01792 403333, ✆ clynefarm.com. Eco-minded farm with a variety of self-catering accommodation, including cottages sleeping between four and eight people, as well as a campsite (minimum two-night booking during summer weekends). Located just off the A4118 in Blackpill, roughly midway between Mumbles and Swansea. Camping **£6**/person, cottages for a weekend in summer **£450**

Coast House 708 Mumbles Rd ☎ 01792 368702, ✆ thecoasthouse.co.uk. Welcoming and very affordable seafront guesthouse with four fresh-looking rooms, two of which have glorious sea views. Closed Dec & Jan. **£70**

Langland Road B&B 17 Langland Rd ☎ 01792 361170, ✆ langlandroad.co.uk. Gay-friendly bed and breakfast providing five cleverly turned out rooms with DVD players and iPod docking stations and some playful touches; then there's a super breakfast (including a vegetarian option) to see you on your way. To get there, head to the top of Newton Road and turn left by the church. **£75**

Tides Reach 388 Mumbles Rd ☎ 01792 404877, ✆ tidesreachguesthouse.com. There are seven spacious and immaculate rooms in this elegant, cheerfully run guesthouse, where you can also enjoy the homely lounge and delightful courtyard garden bursting with roses and honeysuckle. **£75**

EATING AND DRINKING

Café 93 93 Newton Rd ☎ 01792 368793, ✆ cafe93 .com. Cheery, two-floored pink and white café, with tea, coffee and cakes, alongside crisp pizzas and juicy burgers, including veggie burgers. Mon 9am–5pm, Tues 9am–8pm, Wed–Sat 9am–11pm.

Joe's 524 Mumbles Rd ☎ 01792 368212. A few paces from the tourist office, this sister outlet to *Joe's* in Swansea has been making ice cream for nearly a century, offering a

dizzying array of flavours and concoctions. Mon–Sat 9.30am–5.30pm, Sun 11am–6.30pm, hatch open until 7.30pm.

The Kitchen Table 626 Mumbles Rd ☎ 01792 367616, ✆ thekitchentablecafe.co.uk. Comforting café-cum-restaurant, sporting formica-covered kitchen-style tables and mix-and-match chairs, and serving organic, home-made burgers and tasty veggie dishes. Daily

1

9.30am–4.30pm, plus 6–11pm Wed–Sat.

★**Munch** 650 Mumbles Rd ☎01792 362244, ⓦmunchofmumbles.com. The inconspicuous frontage conceals a similarly plain interior, but the food here is first-rate; the fixed-price three-course lunch and dinner menus (£19–27) invariably incorporate ingredients from Gower, resulting in dishes like Welsh lamb and rosemary pie with marsh samphire. Bring-your-own bottle. Wed–Sat noon–2.30pm & 6.30–10pm, Sun noon–2.30pm.

★**P.A.'s Wine Bar** 95 Newton Rd ☎01792 367723, ⓦpaswinebar.co.uk. Mumbles' most rewarding restaurant, whose myriad seafood possibilities (£18) and other meaty treats (marinated wild boar in Bramley apple and cider) perfectly complement its outstanding repertoire of wines. There's a gut-busting Sunday lunch too. The vine-covered terrace is a fine spot to eat in warmer weather. Mon–Sat noon–2.30pm & 6–11pm, Sun noon–2.30pm.

Verdi's Knab Rock ☎01792 369135. Overlooking the sea near the pier, this Welsh–Italian institution is well regarded for its superb pizzas and ice creams, sorbets and sundaes; the coffee's not half bad either. April–Oct daily 10am–9pm; Nov–March Fri–Sun 10am–6pm.

The south and west Gower coasts

From Mumbles Head, the limestone crags of the **southern Gower coast** twist and delve the fifteen miles or so to Worms Head, at the bottom of Rhossili Bay. Many of the sandy bays between the cliffs are easily accessible by car, so they tend to be extremely crowded in peak season.

Mumbles Head to Three Cliffs Bay

The first few miles of the southern Gower coast are highly developed, including the popular **surf beach** of **Langland Bay**, between two headlands. The narrow, golden-sanded **Caswell Bay** comes next, from where you can follow the cliff path to the tiny and remote former smugglers' haunt of **Brandy Cove**, or pebbly **Pwlldu Bay**. Brandy Cove and Pwlldu Bay are inaccessible by car; park in Bishopston village and walk the last mile or so.

Three miles along, huge **Three Cliffs Bay** is one of Gower's finest beaches, at the end of a silent valley fringed by dunes and the eerie ruins of **Pennard Castle**. The best approach is from the car park at **Southgate**, from where you hike a mile or so west along clifftops to Three Cliffs Bay, where you turn inland and follow the boundary of the golf course to the castle.

Gower Heritage Centre

On the main A4118 in Parkmill • Daily 10am–5pm • £6.45 • ☎01792 371206, ⓦgowerheritagecentre.co.uk

You can also reach Three Cliffs Bay from the **Gower Heritage Centre** in the village of **Parkmill**. A large crafts and rural life museum, it's arranged around the area's last remaining water mill, whose magnificent wheel is still operating at full tilt. At one time there were around fifty mills in Gower, as well as a similarly robust spinning and weaving industry, whose history is also relayed in the woollen mill, where demonstrations are given.

There are plentiful attractions for kids, too, including a puppet theatre with a classic Punch and Judy show, adventure play area, and a farm with geese, goats, sheep and so on; they can also participate in pottery, glassblowing and woodturning activities. Take a peek, too, inside La Charrette, a disused railway carriage that was converted into Wales' smallest cinema, seating just 23 people – today, it just shows a film on Gower. At reception you can pick up several useful leaflets outlining local walks, such as the one to Three Cliffs Bay.

Parc le Breos

A mile north of Parkmill (reachable via the lane that heads past the Heritage Centre) is the Neolithic burial chamber (3000–1900 BC) known, in honour of the thirteenth-century lords of Oystermouth Castle, as **Parc le Breos**. Although over-restored, the roofless chamber is impressive for its age and sheer size – 70ft long and divided into four separate chambers. In 1869, the skeletons of two dozen people were found inside. Just beyond the chamber and to the right, a deep fissure in a limestone outcrop marks the position of the dank and musty **Cathole Rock Cave**, in which flint tools, dating back over twelve thousand years, have been found.

1

Oxwich

One of the most curious landscapes in Gower is the reedy **nature reserve** around **Oxwich Burrows**, a flatland of salt and freshwater marshes reached via the lane that forks left off the A4118 at the ruined gatehouse of the privately owned Penrice Castle. Close by on the coast, the scattered village of **OXWICH** is grouped next to the gaping sands of Oxwich Bay. The sands and sea around here regularly receive awards, including the coveted blue flag.

Oxwich Castle

Above Oxwich beach • April–Oct Wed–Sun 10am–5pm • £3; CADW • ☎ 01792 390359

Crowning a headland above the beach, **Oxwich Castle** is a fine example of early sixteenth-century house gentrification by Sir Rice Mansel, member of a powerful Welsh dynasty. His son Edward added the many-windowed eastern range, a pile of rooms with a highly fashionable long gallery that fell into ruin shortly afterwards. Standing just outside the walls is the substantial ruin of the dovecote, whose nesting holes would have been used for the storage of eggs, meat and other provisions.

Port Eynon and around

The rocky cliffs from Oxwich Point fade into wide stony bays towards **PORT EYNON** and its deep, sweeping bay, its name allegedly taken from the tenth-century prince, Einion ab Owain. During World War I, the bay was a key training site for American troops in preparation for the D-Day landings.

The village's sands and dunes are sheltered by a prominent headland, easily reached by a series of paths that wind their way along the shore from the car park above the bleak ruins of the old shoreline salt house near Port Eynon Point. As well as being a place for salt extraction, the sixteenth-century salt house (now inaccessible) would probably also have been used as a smugglers' retreat. Now owned by the National Trust, the lichen-spattered limestone headland is a wild and windy spot, where tufted grass gives way to sharp limestone crags. There's exceptional flora and fauna along this stretch, with bloody cranesbill, evening primrose and purple orchids regulars, and along the coast it's not uncommon to see grey seals, porpoise and short-beaked common dolphins.

A natural cave at the tip can be seen from above, a great dome-shaped chasm that plunges into the hillside. Around the headland to the west is the remarkable, but fairly hard to find, **Culver Hole**, built into the cliffs. A man-made cave, it may originally have been a stronghold for the long-gone Port Eynon castle, though more prosaically it would certainly have served as a dovecote – given that culver comes from the word "culfre", meaning dove or pigeon.

The **coastal path** west from here is the most spectacular walk on Gower, veering along crags above thundering waves for five miles. The only real beach along this stretch is the secluded **Mewslade Bay**, just short of Rhossili and accessible by the path from Pitton. Along the coast walk, about midway between the two villages, is **Paviland Cave**, the site of an astonishing find in 1823, when the skeleton of a Stone Age hunter, at least 26,000 years old, was unearthed (see p.83). At **Thurba Head**, on the eastern side of Mewslade Bay, there are a few scant remains of an Iron Age hillfort sited magnificently a few hundred feet above the waves.

Rhossili and around

Heading west, Gower saves the best for last. The sublimely sited village of **RHOSSILI** (Rhosili) has wraparound views up into the hills and out to sea. It's a great place for coastal walking, particularly out to **Worms Head**, an isolated string of rocks with the spectacular appearance of a basking Welsh dragon, accessible for only five hours around low tide. Take care in this area: the **tidal currents** are extremely dangerous and people have lost their lives here. If you do get cut off, don't attempt to wade back – wait on the promontory until the tide recedes.

Below the village, a great curve of white sand stretches away into the distance, a dazzling coastline vast enough to absorb the crowds, especially if you are prepared to head a little

1

way north towards **Burry Holms**, an islet three miles distant that is cut off at high tide. These coastal waters were notorious for **shipwrecks** in the nineteenth century, and towards the Rhossili end of the beach you can see (at low tide) the black ribs of the hull of the *Helvetia*, which foundered here in 1887. The northern end of the beach can also be reached along the small lane from Reynoldston, in the middle of the peninsula, to **Llangennith**, on the other side of the towering sandstone **Rhossili Down**, rising up to 633ft.

Church of St Mary

Rhossili • Easter–Oct daily 8am–6pm

Standing in the heart of the village, the thirteenth-century **church of St Mary** is a typical Gower church, a thick-set stone construction with a distinctive saddleback tower. The church manifests some delightful detail, notably the late Norman carved door archway, to the left of which you can just about detect a scratch sundial, suggesting that, at one time, the door would have been open to the sky. Inside, take a look at the wall-mounted tablet dedicated to Rhossili son, Edgar Evans, who was the first member of Scott's Antarctic team to die.

INFORMATION	THE SOUTH AND WEST GOWER COASTS

Tourist information The National Trust Centre, at the head of the road beyond Rhossili village, stocks plenty of literature, some excellent local walking maps and a tide timetable (Jan & Feb Tues–Sun 10.30am–4pm, March–Dec daily 10.30am–4.30pm, June–Aug till 5pm; ☎01792 390707).

ACCOMMODATION

MUMBLES HEAD TO THREE CLIFFS BAY

Parc-le-Breos House A mile up a lane beside the Heritage Centre ☎01792 371636, ⊛parc-le-breos .co.uk. This old shooting lodge was one of the original Gower manor houses, but is now a grand B&B offering tidy, Victorian-era furnished rooms. **£90**

Three Cliffs Caravan Park North Hills Farm ☎01792 371218, ⊛threecliffsbay.com. Spectacularly positioned over Three Cliffs Bay between Parkmill and Penmaen, this is a small but well-equipped site with kitchen and laundry facilities, and a farm shop. Closed Oct–March. **£13**/pitch

OXWICH

Oxwich Bay Hotel Above Oxwich beach ☎01792 390329, ⊛oxwichbayhotel.co.uk. Set in splendid isolation just above the sands, this strangely plain-looking hotel has well-turned-out rooms, in addition to rooms in cottages a short walk away. The mirrored restaurant serves some tasty dishes (rabbit with creamed potato and plum and port sauce), but not as appealing as the grassy terrace overlooking the beach, an alluring spot for a beer on a warm day. **£75**

Oxwich Camping Park Penrice road over a mile back from the beach ☎01792 390777. A large but low-key site with modern washing facilities, a laundry and a small outdoor pool. Closed Oct–March. **£8**/pitch

PORT EYNON

Carreglwyd Camping and Caravan Park Above the YHA hostel ☎01792 390795, ⊛porteynon.com. Backing onto the beach and surrounded by cliffs, this large and picturesque site comprises five hedged-off fields and

good facilities (modern showers, laundry, shop). **£20**/pitch

Culver House Behind the sand dunes ☎01792 720300, ⊛culverhousehotel.co.uk. Nineteenth-century dwelling nicely tucked away, offering eight apartment-style suites, each one comprising one or two bedrooms and an open-plan kitchen/lounge area. All have sea-facing balconies. To find it, turn left at the sign for Borfa House, just before the beachfront. From **£80**

YHA Port Eynon By the beach ☎0845 371 9135, ⊛yha.org.uk. Occupying a tremendous beachside location, this Victorian-era lifeboat station has been converted into a super hostel, with four- to eight-bedded dorms as well as double rooms. Shared shower facilities, self-catering kitchen and lounge. Between November and March it is available to groups only. Dorms **£18**

RHOSSILI AND AROUND

Hillend Through Llangennith, just beyond the hamlet of Hillend ☎01792 386204, ⊛hillendcamping,com. Large, fabulously sited campsite behind the dunes and with direct access to the glorious beach. Two of the four fields are set aside for families and couples. Shop and on-site cafe/bar. Closed Sept–March. **£20**/pitch

King's Head Llangennith ☎01792 386212, ⊛kingsheadgower.co.uk. The most prominent accommodation in the village is in this sixteenth-century pub, offering rooms of a fairly high standard (some with sea views), both in the pub annexe and, better still, in the newer stone building across the car park. **£85**

★**Pitton Cross Caravan and Camping** Rhossili ☎01792 390593, ⊛pittoncross.co.uk. The only campsite

1

in the vicinity of Rhossili is an excellent, compact site with segregated paddocks and magnificent sea views; in fact you can walk directly down to the beach. The four- and five-berth shepherd's huts are superb. There's a great kite shop here too. Camping £11/pitch, huts £100

Rhossili Bunkhouse A mile or so back out of Rhossili, near the village of Middleton ☎01792 391509, ⓦrhossilibunkhouse.com. This bunkhouse, attached to the village hall, offers clean and simple two-, three- and four-bedded rooms. There's a kitchen for self-catering use. Note, though, that a minimum two-person, two-night stay is required. £76

★**Western House** Llangennith, on the lane towards the beach ☎01792 386620, ⓦwesternhousebandb .co.uk. There are three wildly colourful and wonderfully oddball rooms in this red limewashed B&B, whose remarkably chilled-out proprietors will ensure nothing less than a totally relaxing stay. £65

Worm's Head On the clifftop ☎01792 390512, ⓦthewormshead.co.uk. Spectacularly sited on the clifftop, this small, welcoming hotel has fairly ordinary rooms, but essentially you are paying for the views, which are nothing short of sensational. Even if you're not staying here, take a coffee on the terrace. £80

EATING AND DRINKING

Bay Bistro Rhossili ☎01792 390519. Easy-going café serving light meals, including terrific burgers and home-made cakes; park yourself inside on one of the sunken

armchairs or out on the windy terrace, although the coastal views are not as good as those from *Worm's Head* next door. Daily 10am–5.30pm, plus 7–9pm June–Sept.

Mid- and north Gower

The great sweep of land that rises to the north of the main Gower road does not attract anything like the number of visitors that the south and west do, due to the lack of comparable coastline. Gower's northern fringe comprises a flattened series of marshes and mud flats merging indistinguishably with the sands of the Loughor estuary. Wading birds, gulls and bedded cockles, as well as herds of cattle and wild horses, are all found among the flats, dunes and inlets burrowing into the land from the estuary.

The central plateau is a pleasant patchwork of pastoral farmland. Its backbone, the 500ft-high sandstone ridge Cefn Bryn, stretches across the centre of the peninsula, with wiry peat and grass dotted with hardy sheep, ancient stone cairns and holy wells. The best views over the peninsula are from the road brushing over its roof.

Reynoldston

The **Cefn Bryn** ridge makes a sublime walk, most easily explored from the quiet village of **REYNOLDSTON**, grouped around a sheep-filled village green and *King Arthur Hotel*. From Reynoldston, a dramatic road rises up the slope of Cefn Bryn before skating across its summit in a perfect, straight line. Several tracks lead off from the road giving clear views to both Gower coasts, but you might be best off stopping at the small car

---

SURFING AND SAILING ON GOWER

Gower has some of the finest surf in Britain, and its profile is certainly on the rise. The best surf is to be had around the bays and beaches of Langland, Caswell, Oxwich and Rhossili, though the most consistent is at Llangennith, which is also suitable for beginners. The website ⓦgowerlive.com has live webcams and tide times.

COURSES AND EQUIPMENT RENTAL

Euphoria Sailing ☎01792 448988, ⓦeuphoria sailing.com. Tuition and rental for sailing, waterskiing and wakeboarding.

PJ's Surfshop Llangennith ☎01792 386669, ⓦpjsurfshop.co.uk. The best place for equipment rental, with a wide range of rental surfboards (£11/day), boogie boards (£6/day) and wetsuits (£11/day). Daily 9am–5.30pm.

Sam's Surf Shack Rhossili ☎01792 390519, ⓦTrhossilileisure@hotmail.com. Both equipment hire and lessons (£20/hr).

Welsh Surfing Federation's Surf School At the Hillend campsite ☎01792 386426, ⓦwsfsurfschool .co.uk. The Welsh Surfing Federation's Surf School runs half-day surfing courses costing £25 for the first lesson and £20 for subsequent lessons.

1

ARTHUR'S STONE

Gower is littered with more dolmens, standing stones and other prehistoric remains than any other landscape in Wales. The most celebrated of all is **Arthur's Stone** (near Reynoldston and sometimes referred to as King Arthur's Stone), a massive burial chamber topped by a quartz capstone weighing over 25 tons. The dolmen is thought to be anything up to six thousand years old, while the ruptured capstone (which, before it split sometime around 1693, rested on six supporting stones) is mentioned, often as *Maen Ceti*, in documents dating back a thousand years.

Some believe that it's part of an astronomical alignment along with Lady's Well, a spring deemed holy and now enclosed in a hut, across the road; and Penmaen's ruined chapel and Neolithic burial chamber, some three miles southeast. This alignment is allegedly charged with a special energy that has, in fact, shown up in some curious photographs with streaks and dots in otherwise clear skies. Whatever the case, the views from up here are extraordinary.

park about a mile east of Reynoldston; from here, a path leads about half a mile across the boggy moor to **Arthur's Stone** (see box above).

Weobley Castle
A mile and a half west of Llanrhidian • Daily: April–Oct 9.30am–6pm; Nov–March 9.30am–5pm • £2.80; CADW • ☎ 01792 390012

The small village of **LLANRHIDIAN** sits above the largely inaccessible marsh of the same name, which is virtually indistinguishable from the sands of the Loughor estuary. Standing gaunt against the backdrop of the marsh and the estuary, **Weobley Castle** was built as a fortified manor in the latter part of the thirteenth century. Its first residents were the de la Bere family, who remained here until the fifteenth century, after which time it was variously lived in by a succession of wealthy landowners, such as Rhys Thomas and the Mansels, the latter owners of Oxwich Castle. The most intact parts of the complex are the north and west portions, formerly the hall, kitchen and accommodation block. The views across the marshes and mud flats are wonderful.

Llanmadoc
West of the village of **Cheriton**, with its charming thirteenth-century church, is **LLANMADOC**, where you can park and venture onto the land spit of **Whitford Burrows**, a soft patch of dunes now open as a nature reserve, with the only sea-washed cast-iron lighthouse in the UK. Steep paths lead from Llanmadoc village up **Llanmadoc Hill** to the south. **The Bulwark**, a lonely and windy hillfort, can be seen at the eastern end of Llanmadoc Hill's summit ridge.

ACCOMMODATION AND EATING   MID- AND NORTH GOWER

Dolphin Inn Llanrhidian ☎ 01792 391069. Warmly run eighteenth-century pub with a cosy interior, some fine real ales and a half-decent menu. The garden is a great place to kick back, and has a children's play area. Mon–Sat 1–11pm, Sun noon–11.30pm.

King Arthur Hotel Reynoldston ☎ 01792 390775, ⊛ kingarthurhotel.co.uk. The village's convivial pub has half a dozen comfortable en-suite rooms, though the annexe offers larger, more attractive rooms, with French windows and cast-iron beds. Dining-wise, the restaurant is fine, but better is the lovely bar, where you can chomp on some succulent Welsh rump washed down with one of the superb guest ales; in fine weather, though, most locals head out to the green and drink among the sheep. **£75**

Tallizmand Guesthouse Llanmadoc ☎ 01792 386373, ⊛ tallizmand.co.uk. The main accommodation option along Llanmadoc's main road is *Tallizmand Guesthouse*, with three en-suite rooms and a cosy communal lounge warmed by an open fire. **£65**

Southwest Wales

TENBY

Southwest Wales

The most westerly outpost of Wales, the counties of Carmarthenshire and, in particular, Pembrokeshire harbour fabulous scenery: bucolic and magical inland, where Carmarthenshire follows the Tywi Valley into the heart of the country; rocky, indented and spectacular around the Pembrokeshire Coast National Park and its 186-mile path. Industrial south Wales peters out at Llanelli, before the undistinguished county town of Carmarthen. A glorious road winds along the Tywi Valley, past ruined hilltop forts and the National Botanic Garden of Wales on the way to Llandeilo and Wales' most impressively positioned castle, Carreg Cennen, high up on a dizzy plug of Black Mountain rock. Further inland, the sparsely populated countryside of remote hills and tiny valleys is broken only by endearing small market towns such as Llandovery, the gloomy ruins of Talley Abbey and the Roman gold mines at Dolaucothi.

The wide sands of southern Carmarthenshire, just beyond Dylan Thomas' adopted home town of **Laugharne**, merge into the popular south Pembrokeshire seaside resorts of **Tenby** and **Saundersfoot**, sitting at the entrance to the south Pembrokeshire peninsula. The peninsula's turbulent, rocky coast is ruptured by some remote historical sites, including the Norman baronial castle at **Manorbier** and the tiny **St Govan's chapel**, wedged into a rocky cliff near Bosherston. At the neck of the peninsula is the old county town of **Pembroke**, dominated by its fearsome castle; to the north, beyond the **Milford Haven estuary**, is the market town and transport hub of **Haverfordwest**, dull but hard to avoid. St Bride's Bay is one of the most glorious parts of the coastal walk, leading north towards the village-sized city of **St Davids**, its exquisite cathedral sheltering in a protective hollow. Close by are opportunities for spectacular coast and hill walks, hair-raising boat crossings to islands, surf galore and numerous other outdoor activities.

The coast turns towards the north at St Davids, becoming the southern stretch of Cardigan Bay. The northernmost section of the Coast Path, from the pretty ferry port of **Fishguard** past the delightful little town of **Newport** to the outskirts of Cardigan, is the most dramatic and remote. Inland are the eerie **Mynydd Preseli**, relic-spattered mountains overlooking windswept plateaux of heathland and isolated villages – none more remote than the leafy valley of **Cwm Gwaun**.

GETTING AROUND

Despite the remoteness of much of southwest Wales, public transport is surprisingly efficient and comprehensive, though you'll have to plan carefully, even in summer. Bus and train **timetables** are widely available locally, and online at ⓦ pembrokeshiregreenways.co.uk and ⓦ carmarthenshire.gov.uk.

ST GOVAN'S CHAPEL, PEMBROKESHIRE

Highlights

❶ **The Tywi Valley** Castles, follies and the National Botanic Garden set among one of Wales' lushest and most atmospheric valleys. **See p.146**

❷ **Carreg Cennen Castle** The region's most dramatically sited fortress, perched on a vertiginous plug of rock and framed by green hills and glowering mountains. **See p.149**

❸ **Laugharne** A must for all Dylan Thomas devotees, but much more than that, this quirky place is the quintessential small Welsh coastal town. **See p.153**

❹ **St Govan's chapel** This tiny grey chapel is wedged into a fissure in the cliffs, just above the churning sea: a phenomenal statement of faith. **See p.172**

❺ **Skomer, Skokholm and Grassholm** Rough and rugged islands, where squawking colonies of birds rule the roost. **See p.178**

❻ **St Davids** The jewel of Pembrokeshire, Britain's smallest city is surrounded by fabulous scenery and fosters a burgeoning surf scene with superb après-surf. **See p.181**

❼ **Carn Ingli** One of Wales' holiest mountains, with great views over the mysterious Mynydd Preseli and the charming little seaside town of Newport. **See p.191**

HIGHLIGHTS ARE MARKED ON THE MAP ON PP.140–141

By train Direct trains connect Cardiff and Swansea with Llanelli, Carmarthen, Tenby, Pembroke, Haverfordwest, Milford Haven and Fishguard, while the Heart of Wales line shuffles out of Swansea and Llanelli to Llandeilo and Llandovery before delving into Powys. A West Wales Day Ranger ticket (£8.80; valid after 8.45am Mon–Fri, any time weekends) gives free travel west of Carmarthen.

By bus Bus services out to the smaller towns and villages are regular and dependable, especially in high summer, when most coastal villages have a fairly regular service. Carmarthen and Haverfordwest are the main hubs, with

some services from Tenby, Pembroke and Fishguard. The Pembrokeshire coast is well catered for, with various winsomely titled services – the Coastal Cruiser, the Puffin Shuttle, the Poppit Rocket – operating year-round under the banner of Pembrokeshire Coastal Bus Service (ⓦ pembrokeshire.gov.uk/coastbus). A West Wales Rover ticket (£7.50/day, £28/week) gives unlimited travel on most buses in Carmarthenshire and Pembrokeshire.

By boat Most of the offshore islands are reached by regular (seasonal) boat services, although few of these allow for overnight stops. Details are given in the chapter.

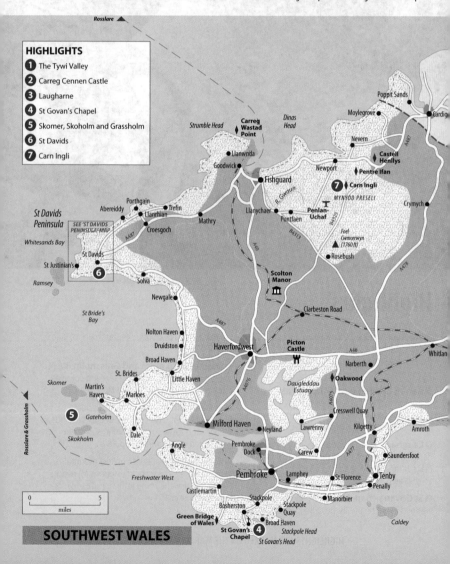

HIGHLIGHTS

1 The Tywi Valley
2 Carreg Cennen Castle
3 Laugharne
4 St Govan's Chapel
5 Skomer, Skoholm and Grassholm
6 St Davids
7 Carn Ingli

SOUTHWEST WALES

Llanelli and around

LLANELLI marks the border between anglicized southeast Wales and the *bro*, Welsh Wales, where the native language is part of everyday life. Once a major industrial hub, the town's steelworks have almost all been cleared and replaced with massive retail developments, sucking out what life was left in the town centre. Today, rugby very much remains a local passion, focused on the **Scarlets**, one of Wales' four regional teams. In addition to the central sights, **Llanelli Wetland Centre** makes a rewarding excursion.

2

Parc Howard Museum

Off the A476 Felinfoel road, half a mile north of the centre • April–Sept Tues–Fri 10am–1pm & 2–5pm, Sat 1–5pm; Oct–March Tues–Fri 11am–1pm & 2–4pm, Sat 2–4pm • Free • ☎ 01554 772029, ⓦ parchoward.org.uk

To learn something of Llanelli's metalworking days, when the town was known as Tinopolis, visit the **Parc Howard Museum** in its lovely park. Housed in an Italianate mansion, the museum provides good coverage of the town's industrial boom, from 1800, when its population was three thousand, to 1891, when it reached 33,464. It also displays samples of the famous Llanelli pottery.

Llanelly House

Cnr of Vaughan St and Bridge St • Mon–Sat 10am–5pm • Great Hall free; upstairs accessed by tours (£6) • ☎ 01544 772857, ⓦ llanelly-house.org.uk

By the parish church in the centre of town, historic **Llanelly House** is a Jacobean house rebuilt in 1714, with free access to the ground-floor café and Great Hall (housing an armorial dinner service, imported from China in 1762). Upstairs tours through the family and servants' rooms finish in the attic where an interactive inquest room reveals the truth (or not) behind their resident ghost.

Llanelli Wetland Centre

2 miles east of town off the A484 • Daily 9.30am–5pm; grounds open till 6pm in summer • £8.95 • ☎ 01544 741087, ⓦ wwt.org.uk

The **Llanelli Wetland Centre** overlooks an extensive area of salt marsh dotted with bird hides and landscaped walkways. Uneconomic farmland has been "returned" to nature, with "natural" ponds created around existing hedgerows. Important populations of lapwing, redshank and over-wintering pintail, wigeon and teal draw birders, but the centre caters just as well to kids and the curious – there are even sixty Caribbean flamingos here. The wilder western section is best explored by canoe safaris or on bikes (both free, daily mid-July to early Sept noon–4pm).

Millennium Coastal Park

Open access • Free

The wetland centre is linked to Burry Port and Pembrey via the Llanelli waterfront and the eight-mile-long Cefn Sidan beach by the **Millennium Coastal Park**, formerly industrial land along the Loughor estuary incorporating National Cycle Route 4, from London to St Davids, and the three-hundred-mile Celtic Trail (see p.43).

ARRIVAL AND DEPARTURE
LLANELLI

By train The train station is a mile south of the town centre.
Destinations Cardiff (20 daily; 1hr 20min); Carmarthen (25 daily; 30min); Llandeilo (5 daily; 40min); Llandovery (5 daily; 1hr); Llandrindod Wells (4 daily; 2hr); Shrewsbury

(4 daily; 3hr 30min); Swansea (29 daily; 20min).
By bus Buses from and to Carmarthen (2 hourly; 1hr), Kidwelly (2 hourly; 30min) and Swansea (4 hourly; 1hr) arrive at and depart from Island Place, immediately east of the centre.

INFORMATION

Tourist office The TIC (daily: mid-May to Sept 10am–8pm; Oct to mid-May 10am–5pm; ☎ 01554 777744) is in the Discovery Centre at North Dock, half a

mile southwest of the town centre beside the Coast Path.
Bike hire Available at the tourist office.

ACCOMMODATION AND EATING

Coastal Park 86 Queen Victoria Rd ☎ 01554 755357, ⓦ coastalpark.co.uk. Not actually on the coast but not far west from the train station, this fairly ordinary B&B also has

an evening grill-bar. £60
Langostinos 1 Murray St ☎ 01554 773711, ⓦ langostinosllanelli.co.uk. A relaxed, unassuming place

serving classy tapas, pasta (£14), steaks and fish dishes (£18–22) and a three-course dinner for £22. Daily 9am–3pm plus Tues–Sat 6–11pm.

Llwyn Hall Llwynhendy, 2 miles east of Llanelli off the B4297 ☎01554 777754, ⓦllwynhall.com. The best of the town's guesthouses, this has very welcoming staff and a good restaurant; there's also a cottage for groups. **£85**

Sheesh Mahal 53 Stepney St ☎01554 773773, ⓦsheeshmahal.net. Offers some of south Wales' finest curries with fast and friendly service; starters £2.50–5, mains £5.50–10, baltis £7–8. Sun–Thurs 5.30–11pm, Fri & Sat 5.30pm–midnight.

Kidwelly

KIDWELLY (Cydweli) is a sleepy little town dominated by an imposing **castle**, strategically sited above the River Gwendraeth and a vast tract of coast.

The castle

Just north of the town centre • March–June, Sept & Oct daily 9.30am–5pm; July & Aug daily 9.30am–6pm; Nov–Feb Mon–Sat 10am–4pm, Sun 11am–4pm • £4; CADW • ☎01554 890104

A wooden castle was built here around 1106, rebuilt in stone in the 1270s and extended in the fourteenth century. Entering through the massive **gatehouse**, you can still see portcullis slots and murder holes, through which noxious substances could be tipped onto intruders. The gatehouse forms the centrepiece of the impressively intact semicircular **outer ward walls**, which date from around 1275. Views from the musty solar and hall, packed into the easternmost wall of the inner ward, show the castle's defensive position at its best, with the river directly below. Although the whole castle is long since roofless, the remains are among the most intact of any medieval Welsh castle that has not been extensively restored. A fourteenth-century town **gate** shields the castle approach from Castle Street, which is the main road through Kidwelly.

Kidwelly Industrial Museum

1 mile north of town (up Priory St and beyond the bypass) • Easter, May public hols & June–Sept Tues, Thurs & Sat 10am–5pm • Free • ☎01554 891078, ⓦkidwellyindustrialmuseum.co.uk

A 167ft brick chimney marks the modest but informative **Kidwelly Industrial Museum**, housed in a former tinplate works. Many of the works' old features have been preserved, including the rolling mills, where blocks of tin were rolled and spun into wafer-thin slices.

Carmarthen and around

The ancient capital of its region and county town of Carmarthenshire, **CARMARTHEN** (Caerfyrddin) is a lively market town with fifteen thousand inhabitants, but does not entirely live up to the promise of its status. Unlike Llanelli, new shopping developments have been built right in the centre, but there's still little reason to stay – fortunately, with so many beautiful and interesting places nearby, there's little need to. It's the first major town in west Wales where the native language is widely heard, and was once – in the early eighteenth century – the largest town in all Wales, thanks to its position at the tidal limit of the River Tywi. Two miles east of central Carmarthen, **Abergwili** is of interest for the Carmarthen County Museum, and its role as Merlin's resting place.

Brief history

Founded as a Roman fort, **CARMARTHEN**'s greatest moment of mythological fame dates from the Dark Ages and the supposed birth of the wizard **Merlin** just outside the town (see box, p.145) – its Roman name, Moridunum, may have given him his Welsh name, Myrddin. The Normans built a castle in 1095, and in 1313 Carmarthen was granted its first charter by Edward I, helping the town flourish as a centre of the wool trade. The town grew in importance, attracting trade and new commerce, industrial works and a key port.

Shire Hall

The Mount • Roughly 8am–5.30pm • Free

Across the river from the train station, the stern facade of the 1930s **Shire Hall** stands within the uninspiring remains of the **castle**, Edward I's reworking of a Norman fortress destroyed by Owain Glyndŵr in 1405. It can be entered from **Nott Square**, beneath which spreads the most picturesque eighteenth- and nineteenth-century part of town, around King Street.

Lammas Street and the market

From Nott Square, the broad, sloping Darkgate leads down to **Lammas Street**, a wide Georgian thoroughfare flanked by coaching inns. To the north, the St Catherine's Walk shopping precinct leads to the striking new **market** (Mon 9.30am–4.30pm, Tues–Sat 9.30am–5pm), a great centre for local produce, secondhand books, antiques and endearingly useless tat. On the main market days – Wednesday and Saturday – stalls spill outside.

Carmarthen County Museum

Abergwili, 2 miles east of Carmarthen • Tues–Sat 10am–4.30pm • Free • ☎ 01267 228696, Ⓦ carmarthenmuseum.org.uk • Served by Carmarthen–Llandeilo buses (6 daily; 12min from Carmarthen)

The severe grey Bishop's Palace at Abergwili was the seat of the Bishop of St Davids between 1542 and 1974, and now houses the **Carmarthen County Museum**, a spirited amble through the area's history. Pottery, archeological finds, wooden dressers and a lively history of local castles are well presented, along with material on crime and policing, geology, education, coracles and Carmarthen's role in the development of the eisteddfod tradition. There's a surprisingly interesting display on the first Welsh translation of the New Testament, produced here in 1567. Upstairs there's an art display plus the bishop's chapel and a re-created schoolroom and farmhouse interior.

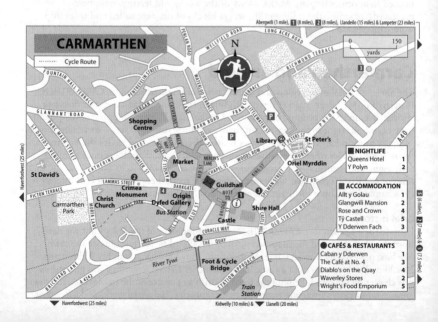

MERLIN

Merlin (Myrddin) is a difficult character to pin down. A mythic figure throughout Europe's Celtic fringe, he is variously described as a wizard and prophet, though over the centuries he has also been called a half-demon and Antichrist, as well as being credited with building Stonehenge. His most common association is with **King Arthur** (see box, p.74) to whom he was tutor, wizard and advisor. It was Merlin who arranged Arthur's rise to the throne through the sword-in-the-stone contest, Merlin who founded the Round Table, and Merlin who accompanied Arthur to the Isle of Avalon at the end of his life.

This interpretation dates back to the writings of **Geoffrey of Monmouth** who, in his *Historia Regum Britanniae* of 1134, drew on all sorts of tales and folklore (plus a fair bit of fabrication) to create the Merlin we know today. He is even credited with inventing the Latinized "Merlin" form to avoid his character being associated with "merde", the French for excrement.

According to Geoffrey and, half a century later, Giraldus Cambrensis (see box, p.377), Merlin was born in Carmarthen. Geoffrey built on stories of very different Merlins under different names – Myrddin Wyllt (Merlin the wild), Merlin Caledonensis (Scottish Merlin), and the most Welsh, Myrddin Emrys (Merlin Ambrosius) – perhaps separate people whose stories have blended, or the same person whose stories diverged over centuries of telling.

Local legend has it that Merlin sleeps under **Merlin's Hill**, where he will remain until the country is in great danger and King Arthur and his men rise up. Another story tells of Merlin predicting that "when Merlin's tree shall tumble down, then shall fall Carmarthen town". The oak, which once stood in the town centre, died a few years back, but Carmarthen remains. A piece of the tree can be seen in the Carmarthen County Museum.

Today Carmarthen celebrates its legendary connection with the **Gŵyl Myrddyn** (Merlin Festival; ⓦcarmarthenshire.gov.uk) in mid-August, with a funfair, coracle racing, medieval village, fortune tellers and wizards.

2

The Gwili Railway

Services from Bronwydd Arms train station, 3 miles north of Carmarthen • Easter, July & Aug daily; May & Oct Wed–Sun; June & Sept Tues–Sun; Santa Steamings Dec weekends • All-day ticket £11 • ☎ 01267 238213, ⓦ gwili-railway.co.uk • Buses #460 (Mon–Sat) and #215 (Mon–Fri) to Bronwydd Arms

South Wales' only standard-gauge tourist railway, with a mixture of steam and diesel haulage, the **Gwili Railway** gives a delightful trundle through ten miles of bucolic riverside, having been extended to Abergwili Junction on the edge of Carmarthen in 2014. Trains run from Bronwydd Arms, where there's a small museum, shop and tearoom.

ARRIVAL AND DEPARTURE CARMARTHEN AND AROUND

Frequencies given below are for Mon–Sat services; on Sun there are very few buses, and 4–6 trains on most lines, though the main line east from Carmarthen is served more frequently.

By train Trains between Swansea and Pembrokeshire stop at the station across the river from the town centre.

Destinations Cardiff (20 daily; 1hr 45min–2hr 10min); Fishguard Harbour (4 daily; 1hr); Haverfordwest (11 daily; 40min); Kidwelly (15 daily; 15min); Llanelli (28 daily; 25min); Milford Haven (11 daily; 1hr); Narberth (9 daily; 25min); Pembroke (9 daily; 1hr 10min); Swansea (26 daily; 50min); Tenby (9 daily; 50min).

By bus Carmarthen's bus station is on Blue Street, north of the river.

Destinations Aberaeron (hourly; 1hr 45min); Aberystwyth (hourly; 2hr 20min); Brechfa (2 daily; 30min); Cardigan (hourly; 1hr 25min); Cenarth (hourly; 1hr 10min); Haverfordwest (3 daily; 1hr); Kidwelly (every 30min; 25min); Lampeter (hourly; 1hr); Laugharne (5 daily; 30min); Llandeilo (10 daily; 40min); Llandovery (8 daily; 1hr 20min); Llanelli (every 30min; 1hr); Llansteffan (7 daily; 20min); London (2 daily; 6hr); Narberth (3 daily; 50min); National Botanic Garden of Wales (Mon–Thurs & Sat 1 daily; 25min); Swansea (every 30min; 1hr 20min); Tenby (1 daily; 1hr 10min).

INFORMATION AND TOURS

Tourist office The TIC (April–Nov Mon–Sat 9.30am–4.30pm; Dec–March Mon & Wed–Sat same hours; ☎ 01267 231557, ⓔ carmarthentic@carmarthenshire.gov.uk) is in the Old County Lockup, Castle House, between the castle's ring walls. There's an authentic re-creation of the police station and cells that were here from 1860.

Internet There's free wi-fi at the TIC, or for free internet access visit the library (Mon–Sat 9am–5pm) on King Street opposite St Peter's church.

Walking tours The TIC does free Town Tours on Weds in summer and Eerie Walkabouts also in summer.

ACCOMMODATION

The range of **accommodation** in Carmarthen is limited, and few places are truly notable, so we also list a selection of places in the nearby Tywi Valley.

Allt y Golau Felingwm Uchaf, 8 miles northeast of Carmarthen ☎01267 290455, ⌨alltygolau.com. Superb sustainability-minded B&B in a renovated 1812 farmhouse with three tastefully decorated rooms and sumptuous breakfasts. Close to the Botanic Garden. **£70**

Glangwili Mansion Llandllawdog, 7 miles northeast of Carmarthen ☎01267 253735, ⌨glangwilimansion .co.uk. A beautiful designer guesthouse, with lots of bright abstract art, hens, alpacas and an eagle owl; it's near Brechfa Forest, for hiking or biking. **£115**

Rose and Crown Lammas St ☎01267 232050, ⌨roseandcrowncarmarthen.co.uk. Ancient coaching inn in central Carmarthen, well refurbished with chic rooms, free wi-fi, DVD players and full Welsh breakfasts in the bar downstairs. **£65**

Tŷ Castell Station Rd, Nantgaredig, 6 miles east of Carmarthen along the A40 ☎01267 290034, ⌨ty -castell.co.uk. Wonderful outdoors-oriented farmhouse B&B by the Towy, with evening meals available. **£72**

Y Dderwen Fach 98 Priory St ☎01267 234193, ⌨ydderwenfach.co.uk. The best of the central budget B&Bs, in a simple seventeenth-century house. Some rooms have bathtubs. **£48**

EATING AND DRINKING

Caban y Dderwen 11 Mansel St ☎01267 238989. The best spot in town for snacks and light lunches, including pan-fried laver bread with cockles (£6). Named after the famous oak tree that once stood outside. Mon–Wed & Sat 9am–5pm, Thurs 9am–3.30pm, Sun noon–2.30pm.

The Café at No. 4 4 Queen St ☎01267 220461, ⌨cafeno4.com. Established as a stylish café, this now only opens for dinner three nights a week with a three-course set menu (£25) that might start with chèvre and mascarpone mousse or carpaccio of beetroot, pomegranate and hazelnuts, followed by beef daube, Welsh lamb or mushroom, spinach and ricotta gnocchi, and good desserts. Unlicensed – bring your own wine. Thurs–Sat 6–9pm.

Diablo's on the Quay Coracle Way ☎01267 223000, ⌨diablos.co. Cosy gastropub by the river that's ideal for the express lunch (£8.50) or starters such as crispy pork cheek or goat's cheese pannacotta and beetroot salad (£5–6), mains such as the vegetarian pie of the week, ham hock or pan-roasted trout (£10–14), and desserts such as Eton mess (£5–8). There's also an outside deck for cocktails. Daily noon–late; food served noon–3pm (Sun to 4pm) & 6–9pm.

Queens Hotel 10 Queen St ☎01267 231800, ⌨thequeenscarmarthen.co.uk. The best beer in town, in a wood-panelled coaching inn (with beer garden) that also offers pub grub, notably cawl (Welsh broth) as well as sandwiches and jacket potatoes (all around £5).

Mon–Thurs 10am–11.30pm, Fri & Sat 10am–midnight, Sun 10.30am–8pm; food served daily noon–2.30pm, plus 6–9pm Tues–Sat.

Waverley Stores 23 Lammas St ☎01267 236521. A large health-food shop with a vegetarian café and tea garden, also serving tasty lunch dishes for around £5. Mon–Sat 10am–3pm (lunch 11.30am–2pm).

★**Wright's Food Emporium** Llanarthne ☎01558 668929, ⌨wrightsfood.co.uk. This former pub is now a wonderful café-deli, run by food writer Simon Wright. It sells local cheese, meat, beer and cider as well as olive oil and wine (by the glass or bottle or in bulk), its own bread and cakes, and sophisticated versions of simple dishes such as Welsh rarebit, bruschetta or poached sewin tartine. It still feels pubby, with its open fire, and has six en-suite rooms upstairs. Mon & Tues 11am–7pm, Wed & Thurs 9am–7pm, Fri & Sat 9am–10pm (specials), Sun 11am–5pm.

★**Y Polyn** Capel Dewi, Nantgaredig, on the B4310 2 miles north of National Botanic Garden ☎01267 290000, ⌨ypolyn.co.uk. A country pub offering some of the area's best food. The modern British cuisine makes superb use of local ingredients and everything is served with relaxed panache. Set dinners cost £24 for two courses, £30 for three. Tues–Thurs noon–2pm & 7–9pm, Fri noon–2pm & 6.30–9.30pm, Sat noon–2.30pm & 6.30–9.30pm, Sun noon–2.30pm.

The Tywi Valley

The **River Tywi** curves and darts its way east from Carmarthen through some of the most spellbinding scenery in south Wales. It's not hard to see why the Merlin legend has taken such a hold in these parts – the landscape does seem infused with a kind of eerie magic. The thirty-mile trip from Carmarthen to **Llandovery** is punctuated by gentle, impossibly green hills topped with ruined castles, notably the wonderful **Carreg Cennen** near the appealing town of Llandeilo. Two fine gardens have sprung up here in recent years: one completely new in the form of the **National Botanic Garden of Wales**; the other a faithful restoration of the original walled gardens around the long-abandoned house of **Aberglasney**.

Brechfa Forest

Ten miles northeast of Carmarthen in the lovely Cothi valley, **Brechfa Forest** is becoming increasingly renowned for its **mountain-biking** trails, but it's a beautiful area for **walking** too. Quiet narrow lanes cut through the sixteen thousand acres of mixed ancient forest and recent plantations, emerging near Talley and Dolaucothi.

ARRIVAL AND DEPARTURE	BRECHFA FOREST

By bus There are services from/to Carmarthen (Mon–Sat 2 daily; 30min), Abergorlech and Llandeilo (2 weekly, 1hr).

ACCOMMODATION AND EATING

Black Lion Abergorlech, 5 miles northeast of Brechfa ☎ 01558 685271, ⓦ blion.co.uk. A fine old inn close to the start of the main mountain bike trails, with a flagstone bar, riverside beer garden, restaurant extension and bike washing facilities. Mains are around £8–14. April–Oct Mon–Fri noon–3pm & 7–10pm, Sat & Sun noon–11pm; Nov–March Tues & Wed 7–11pm, Thurs & Fri noon–3pm & 7–11pm, Sat & Sun noon–11pm; food generally served noon–2pm & 7–9pm.

Gilfach-Wen Barn Half a mile south of Brechfa ☎ 07970 629726, ⓦ brechfa-bunkhouse.com. Useful, well appointed and pleasantly sited self-catering bunkhouse accommodation. £15/person

Ty Mawr Country Hotel Brechfa ☎ 01267 202332, ⓦ wales-country-hotel.co.uk. Upmarket accommodation (with two more accessible ground-floor rooms) that's winning a reputation for its menu of (partly organic) seasonal local food that changes daily. £115

The National Botanic Garden of Wales

1 mile north of the A48 and 7 miles east of Carmarthen • Daily: April–Sept 10am–6pm; Oct–March 10am–4.30pm • £8.50, Nov–Feb £5; half-price for those arriving by bike or bus • ☎ 01558 668768, ⓦ gardenofwales.org.uk • Bus #279 runs daily from Carmarthen (25min)

Though only opened in 2000, the great glass "eye" of the **National Botanic Garden of Wales** has quickly become the Tywi Valley's centrepiece. It occupies what's left of the vast estate of the nineteenth-century banker William Paxton, whose house, Middleton Hall, burnt down in 1931. A central walkway leads past sculptures and lakes (drained in 1939 and restored in the 1990s), with walks down towards planted areas and different wood and wetland habitats. These continue through the **Waun Las National Nature Reserve** all the way to the three-cornered **Paxton's Tower** (built to honour Nelson in 1809) on a hilltop two miles northeast.

Paxton's **double-walled garden** now provides vegetables for the café-restaurant), and has been enhanced by the addition of a small but exquisite Japanese garden, a tropical house, and a bee garden housing a million bees.

The glasshouse and Millennium Square

At the top of the hill is the garden's most audacious feature: the vast oval **glasshouse**, a stunning piece of architecture by Norman Foster. It houses endangered plants from regions with a Mediterranean climate in South Africa, Australia, Chile and California, as well as the Mediterranean itself.

The stableyard houses a restaurant and an excellent exhibition on medicinal plants and the dynasty of Welsh herbalists known as the Physicians of Myddfai (Meddygon Myddfai, supposedly descended from the Lady of the Lake), abutting **Millennium Square**, a venue for open-air performances. The entire garden is sustainably managed:

the glasshouses are heated by burning wood coppiced on the grounds; wastewater is purified through a series of reed beds; rainwater is used for irrigation; and a large tract of surrounding land is being turned over to organic farming using Welsh breeds of cattle and sheep.

Aberglasney

5 miles northeast of the Botanic Garden, half a mile south of the A40 near Broad Oak • Daily: April–Sept 10am–6pm; Oct–March 10.30am–4pm • £8 • ☎ 01558 668998, ⓦ aberglasney.org

A natural twin to the Botanic Garden lies nearby at **Aberglasney**. The decaying and abandoned manor house supposedly had protected status, but it was only in 1994, when the grand double portico (added in 1830) came up for auction, that the authorities took notice. The portico was withdrawn from sale and reattached to the house as part of a major restoration undertaken by the Aberglasney Trust from 1998, although the house's stabilized shell is destined to play second fiddle to its remarkable **gardens**. Much smaller and more intimate than the National Botanic Garden, they are being steadily re-created as living historical documents.

The walled gardens

Once massively overgrown, these mostly sixteenth- to eighteenth-century **walled gardens** have regained much of their original formal splendour. Especially noteworthy are the replanted **kitchen garden** and what is thought to be Britain's only secular **cloister garden**, dating from the late sixteenth century. Above, a walkway gives access to a set of birdless Victorian aviaries, and great views over the Jacobean Pool Garden to mature woodlands beyond. On the lawn near the gatehouse (c1600, but long thought to be a Victorian folly) is a line of five yews planted three centuries ago, and trained over to root on the far side, a feature unique in Britain.

The courtyard garden

In 2005, the house's central **courtyard** was glassed in to form an atrium populated with subtropical plants – tree ferns, cycads, orchids and more. Dubbed a Ninfarium (after gardens at Ninfa, near Rome), it makes a beautiful counterpoint to the outdoor gardens. You'll also find a video history of the estate and arts and crafts displays in the entrance hall. Leave time for tea and cakes from the tempting **café** built into the wall of the Pool Garden.

Llandeilo and around

Beautifully set below the magnificent Black Mountain, **LLANDEILO** is in transition. Still a quiet market town, it is becoming known as an upmarket rural retreat for the aspirational of Swansea, Cardiff and beyond, with a couple of boutique hotels, some fancy shops and galleries on King St, and a handful of delis, cafés and restaurants. It also hosts an up-and-coming music festival in mid-July (ⓦllandeilomusicfestival.org.uk). Llandeilo makes an excellent base for exploring the area, particularly Dinefwr and Carreg Cennen.

Church of St Teilo

Rhosmaen St • Llandeilo Fawr Gospels display: Easter–Oct Tues–Sat 11am–4pm

Spend a few minutes in the parish **church of St Teilo** (rebuilt from 1848 by George Gilbert Scott), home to a pair of eighth-century Celtic crosses. The base of the tower houses an interactive display on the **Llandeilo Fawr Gospels**, an eighth-century parchment manuscript which contains the earliest-known example of written Welsh. The book itself is in Lichfield Cathedral in England, but you can browse its digitized text and learn something of both these gospels and the closely related (and more famous) Lindisfarne Gospels.

Dinefwr Castle

Dinefwr Park, 1 mile west of Llandeilo • Open access • Free (£6 to park at Newton House, 10am–4pm)

The strategic importance of the Tywi Valley is underlined by the tumbledown ruins of **Dinefwr Castle**, set high on a wooded bluff above the river. The castle was built in 877 by Rhodri Mawr, King of Wales, and became the seat of the rulers of Deheubarth. It was rebuilt in stone from 1165 by the Lord Rhys (Rhys ap Gruffudd), who united the warring Welsh princes against the Normans, and then strengthened by Edward I after 1282. It was never lost by the English until the seventeenth century, after which it was allowed to fall into "Romantic" ruin.

There's free access by public footpaths through the park, and you can climb to the highest point of the largely thirteenth-century ruins for stunning views across the valley and, in the other direction, to Newton House. With a car, it's easiest to park at Newton House and follow the well-marked half-mile walk from there.

Newton House

1 mile west of Llandeilo • April–Oct daily 11am–6pm; Nov–March Fri–Sun 10am–4pm • £4.40; NT • ☎ 01558 668998

By Tudor times Dinefwr Castle had become ill-suited to the needs of the Lord Rhys' descendants, who built a new residence half a mile away. Now named **Newton House**, it was much transformed over the centuries, being rebuilt in the 1660s and given corner towers in the 1750s and a new "Venetian Gothic" facade in the 1860s; it then fell into disrepair before being saved in the 1990s. It isn't the most distinguished of stately homes, but the basement and ground floor have been imaginatively set up as though it were a Sunday in 1912. Below stairs you can try your hand at brushing a top hat or correctly folding a shirt before progressing upstairs, where a formal lunch is laid out and a gramophone plays in the drawing room. Up the splendid staircase there are interesting displays on the Rhys family genealogy, the estate's heritage and the impact of World War II. The lovely **park**, mostly landscaped in the 1770s following suggestions by Capability Brown, now contains rare White Park cattle and fallow deer.

Carreg Cennen Castle

4 miles southeast of Llandeilo • Daily: April–Oct 9.30am–6.30pm; Nov–March 9.30am–4pm • £4; CADW • ☎ 01558 822291, Ⓦ carregcennencastle.com

Isolated in the rural hinterland southeast of Llandeilo is the most magnificently sited castle in Wales. **Carreg Cennen Castle** was constructed on its fearsome outcrop in 1248 (though Sir Urien, one of King Arthur's knights, is said to have built a fortress here earlier), but fell to Edward I in 1277. It remained in use until 1462, when it was partly destroyed by the Earl of Pembroke for being a rebel base.

The castle's most striking aspect is its vertiginous location, three hundred feet above a sheer drop into the green valley of the Cennen River. From the car park and **farm**, with rare breeds of cows and sheep, a path climbs sharply upwards, with astounding **views** towards the severe purple lines of the Black Mountain, in utter contrast to the velvet greenery of the Tywi and Cennen valleys. The castle seems impenetrable, its crumbling walls merging with the limestone on which it defiantly sits. The highlights of a visit are the views down into the valley and the long, damp descent into a pitch-black **cave** that served as a shelter in prehistoric times. Torches (which can be rented for £1.50 from the excellent tearoom near the car park) are essential; continue as far as possible and then turn them off to experience absolute darkness.

ARRIVAL AND DEPARTURE   LLANDEILO AND AROUND

By train The train station, on the eastern edge of town, is on the scenic Heart of Wales railway, running from Swansea and Llanelli to Llandovery and Shrewsbury. Destinations Llandovery (4 daily; 20min); Llandrindod Wells (4 daily; 1hr 20min); Llanelli (4 daily; 40min); Shrewsbury (4 daily; 2hr 50min); Swansea (5 daily; 1hr 10min).

By bus Buses from/to Carmarthen (8 daily; 40min), Llandovery (8 daily; 40min) and Swansea (6 daily; 90min) stop on New Road. Buses along the A40 between Carmarthen and Llandeilo give access to Aberglasney.

ACCOMMODATION

Abermarlais Caravan Park A40, 6 miles east of Llandeilo ☎01550 777868, ⓦabermarlaiscaravanpark .co.uk. Spacious rural campsite that's perfect for families. Closed Nov–March. **£12**/pitch

The Cawdor 70 Rhosmaen St ☎01558 823500, ⓦthecawdor.com. Llandeilo's focal point, this former coaching inn has been given a postmodern makeover with delightful, simply decorated rooms (all different) and stunning attic suites. **£65**

★**Fronlas** 7 Thomas St ☎01558 824733, ⓦfronlas .com. This large terraced house has been creatively transformed into a modern three-room B&B, all bare boards, funky lighting, wild wallpapers and minimalist design. Breakfasts are largely organic and of local ingredients. The lounge has an honesty bar and good DVDs. **£60**

EATING AND DRINKING

★**Angel Hotel** 62 Rhosmaen St ☎01558 822765, ⓦangelbistro.co.uk. Convivial pub serving real ales and superb bar meals featuring daily specials, with a slightly more formal restaurant at the rear (mains £11–15). Mon–Wed you'll pay £10 for two courses or £12 for three, or £12/14 on Fri and Sat; Thurs is an internationally themed buffet. Mon–Sat 11.30am–11pm, Sun 11am–11pm; food served Mon–Sat 11.30am–3pm & 6–11pm.

The Cawdor 70 Rhosmaen St ☎01558 823500, ⓦthecawdor.com. Excellent semi-formal restaurant serving sumptuous two- or three-course lunches (£13/16) and dinners (£15/20), which might include grilled duck breast with sautéed celeriac and a red wine sauce. Good wine, guest ales and deep leather sofas also attract a broad clientele for bar snacks, cream teas or just a drink. Restaurant Wed–Sun noon–2pm & 7–9pm (Sun till 8pm); bar snacks daily 11am–8pm.

Heavenly 60 Rhosmaen St ☎01558 822800, ⓦheavenlychoc.co.uk. Great organic ice cream and hand-made chocolates that are, well, heavenly. Mon–Thurs 9.30am–5pm, Fri & Sat 9.30am–5.30pm, Sun 11.30am–3pm.

Plough Inn Rhosmaen ☎01558 823431, ⓦploughrhosmaen.com. Just a mile north of town, this famed pub/restaurant uses the best local ingredients to offer a set lunch (Mon–Sat £10–19 for 1–3 courses; Sun £17/19 for 2–3 courses) and dinner (Sun–Thurs £18–23 for 2–3 courses), as well as an à la carte menu (Fri & Sat eve) that's less exciting, apart from the curry of the day. Daily 11.30am–2.30pm & 5.30–9.30pm.

Rosetta 139 Rhosmaen St ☎01558 823444. A great deli (for fine Welsh cheeses and organic bread) and health-food shop, with seating upstairs to savour the coffee. Mon–Fri 9.30am–5.30pm, Sat 9.45am–5pm.

Llandovery and around

Twelve miles northeast of Llandeilo, the former cattle drovers' town of **LLANDOVERY** (Llanymddyfri) makes a natural base for exploring the Tywi Valley and the breathtaking countryside around Llyn Brianne and Dolaucothi to the north and west. The town's architecture and layout have changed little for centuries, the main Broad Street lined with solid early nineteenth-century town houses and older inns, much as it was when itinerant writer George Borrow visited in 1854, remembering it as the "pleasantest little town in which I have halted in the course of my wanderings". The market hall, built in 1840, was new then, and is now the Dinefwr Crafts Centre (daily 10am–5pm), housing a café and stalls selling crafts such as wicker furniture, love spoons and raku pottery.

The castle ruins

South side of Broad St • Open access • Free

Spread over a grassy mound, the scant ruins of a twelfth-century **castle** give fine views over Llandovery's huddled grey buildings and the Bran River. The real draw, though, is a ridiculously shiny stainless-steel **sculpture** of local lord Llywelyn ap Gruffydd Fychan, the "Welsh Braveheart", raised on the six-hundredth anniversary of his execution in the Market Square in front of the English king Henry IV, for helping the rebel Owain Glyndŵr escape in 1401.

Local History Exhibition

Castle Hotel, Kings Rd • Easter–Sept daily 9.30am–5pm; Oct–Easter Mon–Sat 10.30am–12.30pm, Sun 2–4pm • Donation appreciated

The community-run **Local History Exhibition** contains interesting displays on the legend of the Lady of the Lake from Llyn y Fan Fach; sixteenth-century outlaw Twm Sion

Cati, the "Welsh Robin Hood"; seventeenth-century vicar Rhys Prichard, author of *Canwyll y Cymry* ("The Welshmen's Candle"); the Physicians of Myddfai (see p.177); and the cattle drovers and their Black Ox bank, now part of LloydsTSB. A second room mainly houses temporary exhibitions.

The Dolaucothi Gold Mine

Pumsaint, 10 miles northwest of Llandovery off the A482 • Mid-March to June, Sept & Oct daily 11am–5pm, July & Aug daily 10am–6pm • £7.70; NT • ☎ 01558 650177

West of Llandovery the countryside is blissfully quiet, with a web of lanes that see little traffic. The principal route is the A482, which heads six miles from the A40 between Llandeilo and Llandovery to the **Dolaucothi Gold Mine**.

This is the only place in Britain where we can be sure the Romans mined gold, using remarkably advanced systems to extract the precious metal from the rock; an opencast mine and a few water channels can still be seen. The mine lay abandoned from around 350 AD until 1872, when new shafts were sunk and sporadically exploited until 1938. The site appears much as it was in the 1930s, and there are good displays, but you'll get a much better appreciation by joining one of the hard-hat underground tours.

Near the entrance to the mine is a stone used by the Romans for crushing gold ore; it's marked with indentations supposedly left by five saints who slept here one night, an event which gives its name to the adjacent village of **Pumsaint** (Five Saints).

Talley

Nine miles west of Llandovery on the B4302, the crumbling twelfth-century tower of Wales' only Premonstratensian **abbey** (daily 10am–4pm; free; CADW) dominates the village of **TALLEY**, also home to the serene lakeside **church of St Michael**, rebuilt in 1773 (largely from the stones of the abbey) and still including its original box pews. Talley's more recent claim to fame is as the home of Wales' famous **Tipi Valley**, a hippy encampment set up in the 1970s just south near Cwmdu. Controversy has dogged the place ever since, but there now seems to be a stoic truce between the locals and the tepee dwellers. The National Trust owns the village's characterful community-run pub.

Dinas Nature Reserve

11 miles north of Llandovery • Open access to the trail • Parking £1

Four miles beyond the village of Rhandirmwyn, at the Ystradffin chapel, there's a car park for the RSPB's **Dinas Nature Reserve**, deep within which is the reputed hideout cave of Twm Sion Cati (see opposite). You're discouraged from seeking out the bandit's lair lest you disturb the woodpeckers, nuthatches, dippers, redstarts and pipits, but a spectacular **trail** loops through the gorge and ancient woodland.

Llyn Brianne

12km north of Llandovery

The **Llyn Brianne** reservoir, built in the 1970s (to supply Swansea), fits well into the region's hilly contours and offers peaceful shoreline walks. The land to the north is remote and spectacular, with walks following the Tywi valley into the Elenydd hills and to the Dolgoch hostel.

ARRIVAL AND DEPARTURE   LLANDOVERY AND AROUND

By train Llandovery's train station is on the main A40 just west of town.

Destinations Llandeilo (4 daily; 20min); Llandrindod Wells (4 daily; 1hr); Llanelli (4 daily; 1hr 10min); Shrewsbury (4 daily; 2hr 30min); Swansea (5 daily; 1hr 30min).

By bus Buses leave from the car park by the castle and also call at the train station.

Destinations Brecon (3 daily; 40min); Carmarthen (8 daily; 1hr 20min); Dolaucothi (6 weekly; 25min); Lampeter (8 weekly; 45min); Llandeilo (8 daily; 40min).

2

INFORMATION

Tourist office On Kings Road, by the central car park, the joint TIC and Brecon Beacons National Park visitor centre (Easter–Sept daily 9.30am–5pm; ☎01550 720693, ✉ llandovery.ic@breconbeacons.org) is well stocked with leaflets on local walks and natural history, and has an interpretive centre on the Black Mountain.

ACCOMMODATION

Cwmgwyn Farm Llangadog Rd, A4069, 2 miles southwest of Llandovery ☎01550 720410, ✇ cwmgwyn-holidays.co.uk. Charming farmhouse B&B with spacious rooms, tasty breakfasts and a wood-beamed lounge complete with inglenook fireplace. **£68**

Cynyll Farm A4069, 5 miles southwest of Llandovery ☎01550 777316, ✇ cynyllfarm.co.uk. Great-value, long-standing B&B in a seventeenth-century farmhouse and nearby barn and bungalow, just northeast of Llangadog, where there are some great pubs. **£56**

The Drovers 9 Market Square ☎01550 721115, ✇ droversllandovery.co.uk. Six elegantly individual rooms and a huge lounge with books and board games, in an eighteenth-century town house; very welcoming owners serve superb locally sourced breakfasts. **£78**

Henllys Estate 2 miles northwest of Llandovery ☎01550 721332, ✇ henllysestate.co.uk. The best-value of the rural B&Bs hereabouts, in converted barns with lovely oak-floored en-suite bedrooms, digital TV and good breakfasts. There's also access to their woodland reserve. **£70**

The Level Crossing A40, opposite the station ☎01550 721155, ✇ thelevelcrossing.co.uk. This new hostel has dorm beds and en-suite family rooms, plus a bistro with pizza and tapas on Fri nights, and occasional live music. Dorms **£19**; doubles **£42**

New White Lion 43 Stone St ☎01550 720685, ✇ newwhitelion.co.uk. An understated exterior hides Llandovery's finest accommodation, combining modern style and selected antiques, plus an honesty bar featuring speciality gins. Excellent breakfasts and dinners available. **£120**

Royal Oak Inn Rhandirmwyn, 7 miles north of Llandovery ☎01550 760201, ✇ theroyaloakinn.co.uk. Tucked away on quiet lanes, this popular pub's five rooms make a perfect base for walking, mountain-biking or just enjoying rural peace. **£78**

CAMPING

Erwlon 1 mile east of Llandovery off A40 ☎01550 720332, ✇ erwlon.co.uk. The nearest campsite to town (300yd from a supermarket), with caravan sites and camping; freezer space available plus wi-fi across the site. **£13**/pitch

Gellifechan 7 miles north of Llandovery, 2 miles beyond Rhandirmwyn ☎01550 760397. A basic tap-in-a-field and portaloo campsite, but in an idyllic dark-skies site by the Iron Bridge (1913) and associated pub. **£6**/pitch

EATING AND DRINKING

Castle Hotel Kings Rd ☎01550 720343, ✇ castle -hotel-llandovery.co.uk. The town's leading hotel has been given a cool makeover and is now also its classiest place to eat. There are plenty of leather sofas where you can enjoy coffee, cakes and sandwiches, plus bar areas with open fires and a more formal restaurant. Highlights of the menu include good tapas and mezze platters (£13), Welsh lamb confit (£13) and steaks (£13–19), and a fish of the day. Restaurant Mon–Thurs noon–3pm & 6–9.30pm, Fri & Sat noon–3pm & 6–10pm, Sun noon–3pm & 6–8.30pm; café daily 11am–6pm.

Indian Lounge 34 High St ☎01550 720022. Great curry restaurant with a standard selection of north Indian curries plus unusual specialities such as grilled halibut or pan-fried seabass with coconut cream and garlic (both £10). Daily noon–2.30pm & 5.30–11pm.

Just So Scrumptious 4 Kings Rd ☎01550 720824, ✇ justsoscrumptious.co.uk. This award-winning deli and café is renowned for its home-made fudge and cookies, as well as filling pasties and sausage rolls; it's also busy at lunchtime serving sandwiches, salads and soups. Mon–Sat 9am–5pm, Sun 10am–4pm.

King's Head Inn 1 Market Square ☎01550 720393, ✇ kingsheadcoachinginn.co.uk. Come to this former drovers' inn for traditional bar meals (£8–10), rack of lamb (£16) or duck breast in plum sauce (£17). Daily 10am–11pm; food served noon–2.30pm & 6–9.30pm (8.30pm Sun).

Royal Oak Inn Rhandirmwyn, 7 miles north of Llandovery ☎01550 760201, ✇ theroyaloakinn .co.uk. Country pub that's well worth the trip for its beer – it's been CAMRA's Carmarthenshire pub of the year four times already in the twenty-first century – and for its imaginative menu, ranging from laverbread and potato cake (£4) or cawl (£6.50) to Welsh cheese and creamed leek strudel or Welsh lamb pie (both £9). Mon–Sat noon–2pm & 6–11pm, Sun noon–2pm & 7–10.30pm; food served noon–2pm & 6.30–9.30pm.

Southern Carmarthenshire

Frequently overlooked in the stampede towards the Pembrokeshire resorts, **southern Carmarthenshire** is a quiet part of the world, its coastline broken by the triple estuary of the Tywi, Taf and Gwendreath rivers. **Llansteffan** huddles below its ruined castle alongside the Tywi, while the Taf estuary is home to lovely **Laugharne**, not just a place of pilgrimage for Dylan Thomas lovers.

Llansteffan

The pretty village of **LLANSTEFFAN**, on the Tywi estuary ten miles southeast of Carmarthen, is overshadowed by a dramatic ruined **castle** (unrestricted access). This prime example of Norman fortifications was built between the eleventh and thirteenth centuries; long before the present castle, an Iron Age fort was occupied by 600 BC. The entrance used today is not the original gatehouse, which was converted into living quarters in the fourteenth century. In both gatehouses, however, the portcullis and murder holes can still be seen. Atop the towers, it's easy to appreciate the site's defensive position, with far-reaching **views** in all directions. Returning from the castle to where the path doubles back to the right near a house, continue ahead (west) for half a mile then left down the lane towards the **beach**. The door in the wall on the right conceals **St Anthony's Well** (Bwthyn Sant Antwn), which can supposedly heal lovesickness. At anything but high tide you can return via the beach.

ARRIVAL AND DEPARTURE
LLANSTEFFAN

By bus There are regular buses between Llansteffan and Carmarthen (Mon–Sat 6 daily; 20 min).

ACCOMMODATION AND EATING

Ger-y-Berllan B4312 ☎01267 241052, ⓦger-y -berllan.co.uk. In a modern house overlooking the village as you arrive from Carmarthen, this friendly B&B has four rooms for between one and four people, and excellent Welsh breakfasts. **£60**

Pant-yr-Athro Country Inn 2 miles towards Carmarthen ☎01267 241014, ⓦbackpackershostelwales.co.uk. Slightly pokey hostel-style accommodation plus one double room, with a bar serving Mexican food (the adjoining hotel also serves food). Dorms **£14**; double **£30**

The Village Store High St ☎01267 241888. The post office shop houses an off-beat little café serving breakfasts, light lunches (and a full Sunday lunch), sandwiches, coffee and home-baked cakes; also themed evenings such as tapas or Chinese food. April–Oct Mon–Fri 9am–5pm, Sat & Sun 9am–1pm; Nov–March Mon, Tues, Thurs & Fri 9am–4pm, Wed & Sun 9am–1pm.

★Yr Hen Dafarn High St ☎01267 241656. A superb restaurant that's a real labour of love. The menu is seasonal, specializing in fish and game (and malt whisky), and portions are large. It's open just two evenings a week, with unfixed hours; booking is essential. Fri & Sat eve.

Laugharne

When quiet, the village of **LAUGHARNE** (Talacharn) is a delightful spot, with a ragged castle looming over the reeds and tidal flats and narrow lanes snuggling in behind. However, it has increasingly been taken over by the legend of Dylan Thomas, the nearest Wales has to a national poet, making it hard to value the place for its own sake.

Dylan Thomas Boathouse

Dylan's Walk • Daily: May–Oct & Easter 10am–5.30pm; Nov–April 10.30am–3.30pm • £4 • ☎01994 427420, ⓦ dylanthomasboathouse.com

Down an exceedingly narrow lane (unsuitable for cars) beside the estuary you'll reach the **Dylan Thomas Boathouse**, the simple home of Thomas, his wife Caitlin and their three children from 1949 until 1953 when he died on a lecture tour in New York. His death was attributed to "a massive insult to the brain" (spurred by numerous whiskies), but it's possible he was a victim of pneumonia or diabetes and incompetent doctors. It's an enchanting museum with a feeling of inspirational peace above the ever-changing water. In the bedrooms upstairs are a video on Thomas' life and a selection of local artists' views of the estuary and the village. Downstairs, the family parlour has been preserved intact, with the rich tones of the man himself reading his work via a period wireless set. A small tearoom (free entry) and outdoor terrace look over the water.

Back along the lane, you can peer into the green garage where Thomas wrote: a wood-burning stove, curling photographs of literary heroes, pen collection and numerous scrunched-up balls of paper under the cheap desk suggest that he could return at any minute. Thomas is buried with Caitlin, who died in 1994, in the graveyard of the parish church at the northern end of the village, marked by simple white crosses. Inside the church door is a painting by Benjamin West (the Anglo-American second president of the Royal Academy), plus a tenth-century Celtic cross in the south transept.

Tin Shed Experience

Clifton St · May–Oct 10am–5.30pm · £3 · ⓦ tinshedexperience.co.uk

Just north of the village centre (note the doorways of the fine Georgian town houses), the **Tin Shed Experience** is literally a tin garage housing mementoes of the World Wars; it's a key venue for The Laugharne Weekend (ⓦthelaugharneweekend.com), a popular and relaxed arts festival in mid-April that's beginning to attract big names.

Laugharne Castle

Wogan St · April–Oct daily 10am–5pm · £3.80; CADW · ☎ 01994 427906

Laugharne's main street courses down to the imposing ruins of **Laugharne Castle**. Built in the twelfth and thirteenth centuries, most of the original buildings were obliterated

in Tudor times when Sir John Perrot (possibly the illegitimate son of Henry VIII) transformed it into a splendid mansion. The "castle brown as owls" (Dylan Thomas) was largely destroyed in the Civil War. The mix of medieval might and Tudor finery is intriguing, especially in the **Inner Ward**, dominated by two towers, the domed roof of one giving sublime views over the huddled town. This is now surrounded by an attractive formal garden with fine mature trees; a gazebo contains an explanatory panel on another Welsh writer, Richard Hughes, best known for his novel *A High Wind in Jamaica*, who rented the adjoining Castle House from 1934 to 1942 and first brought Thomas to Laugharne.

Town hall

The tiny toytown **town hall** is the seat of Laugharne's unique Corporation, which has run the town since c1290, with citizens electing a portreeve (mayor) and jury (council). The building is topped by a whitewashed Italianate bell tower, which once served as a single-cell prison.

DYLAN THOMAS

Dylan Thomas (1914–53) was the quintessential Celt – fiery, verbose, richly talented and habitually drunk. Born into a snugly middle-class family in Swansea, Dylan's first glimmers of literary greatness came when he was posted, as a young reporter, on the *South Wales Evening Post* in Swansea; some of the most popular tales in his *Portrait of the Artist as a Young Dog* were inspired by his time working on the newspaper.

Rejecting the provincialism of Swansea and Welsh life, Thomas arrived in London as a broke 20-year-old in 1934, weeks before the appearance of his first volume of **poetry**. Another volume soon followed, cementing the engaging young Welshman's reputation. Married in 1937, he and his wife Caitlin returned to Wales, settling in the backwater of Laugharne, before moving to New Quay in Cardiganshire for part of World War II. **Short stories** – crackling with rich and melancholy humour – tumbled out as swiftly as poems, widening his base of admirers, although they remained few until well after his death. Despite his evident hedonism and his long days boozing in *Brown's Hotel*, Thomas was a self-disciplined writer, honing some of the most instantly recognizable poetry of the twentieth century. Perhaps better than anyone, he wrote in an identifiably Celtic, rhythmic wallow. Although Thomas knew little Welsh – he grew up when the native language was stridently discouraged – his English usage is definitively Welsh in its cadence and bold use of words.

Thomas, especially in public, liked to adopt the persona of an archetypal stage Welshman: sonorously loquacious, romantic and fond of a stiff tipple. This role was particularly popular in the **United States**, where he made lucrative lecture tours, and where he died in 1953. Just one month earlier, he had put the finishing touches to what many regard as his masterpiece: **Under Milk Wood**, the "play for voices". Describing the dreams, thoughts and lives of a Welsh seaside community over 24 hours, the play has never dipped out of fashion and has lured Wales' greatest stars, including Richard Burton and Anthony Hopkins, to the narrator's role. The small town of Llareggub (spelt Llaregyb by the BBC, which wouldn't allow the use of the expression "bugger all" backwards) is loosely based on Laugharne, New Quay, and a vast dose of Thomas' own imagination.

ARRIVAL AND INFORMATION

LAUGHARNE

By bus Buses run from Carmarthen to Pendine via Laugharne (Mon–Sat 5 daily; 30min).

Tourist information At Corran Books, opposite *Brown's Hotel* on King Street (Mon–Sat 10am–5pm; ☎01994 427444).

ACCOMMODATION

Ants Hill Caravan Park 1 mile north of Laugharne on A4066 ☎01944 427293, ⊛antshill.co.uk. The closest camping and caravan park to town, with laundry and games rooms and a swimming pool. Closed Nov–Feb. **£20**/pitch

Boat House 1 Gosport St ☎01994 427263, ⊛theboathousebnb.co.uk. Stylish, comfortable four-room B&B, full of local art, and right in the centre. Great breakfasts might include vanilla waffles or smoked salmon. **£80**

Brown's Hotel King St ☎01994 427688, ⊛browns-hotel.co.uk. Dylan's old boozing hole, built in 1752, reopened as a "bar-with-rooms" in 2012 – the "genuine" Dylan Thomas dartboard has been reinstated. Rooms are in a retro 1950s style, but with modern gadgets. **£95**

★**Coedllys Country House** Llangynin, 7 miles north of Laugharne ☎01994 231455, ⊛coedllyscountryhouse.co.uk. Wonderful, thoughtfully run farmhouse accommodation comprising three rooms, each with antique furniture, classy bedding and a comfy sofa. Visit the farm animal sanctuary or the fitness centre, which has an exercise pool, spa and sauna. **£90**

The Corran East Marsh ☎01994 427417, ⊛thecorran.com. Formerly *Hurst House*, beloved of the Soho set, this has reopened and been extended, with twenty more rooms, a lovely skylit restaurant and a spa, and is even more stylish than before. **£150**

The Cors Newbridge Rd ☎01994 427219, ⊛thecors.co.uk. A small, gracious country house that's now a classy restaurant with three "shabby-chic" but comfortable rooms and an eclectic blend of artworks as well as lovely gardens. **£80**

Keeper's Cottage A4066 ☎01994 427404, ⊛keepers-cottage.com. At the north end of the village, this friendly B&B has three good-sized rooms and offers a full breakfast featuring scrambled eggs with smoked salmon. **£80**

2

Café Culture 6 Grist Square ☎01994 427422, ⓦcafecultureuk.com. This lively Medtierranean-style licensed café serves breakfasts till noon, then a range of pastas and other Italian dishes (£10–17) as well as Greek mussaka and Welsh cawl. Mon–Fri 8am–6pm, Sat & Sun 8am–10pm.

★**The Cors** Newbridge Rd ☎01994 427219, ⓦthecors .co.uk. Excellent modern Welsh cuisine, served by candlelight, might include smoked haddock crème brûlée or grilled sewin (sea trout), with mains for around £20. The gardens are delightful. Booking essential. Thurs–Sat from 7pm.

New Three Mariners High St ☎01994 427426, ⓦnewthreemarinersinn.co.uk. Cheery pub that offers the best drinking in town as well as bar meals and pizzas. Mon–Fri 4–11pm, Sat & Sun noon–midnight.

Narberth and the Landsker Borderlands

Edging west into Pembrokeshire, the first town of any significance is **Narberth**, a cheerful little place with a burgeoning reputation for its upmarket shopping. It's also the "capital" of the **Landsker Borderlands**, a quiet, charming region dotted with some beautiful but little-visited villages. *Landsker* is a Norse word meaning "frontier", referring to the division between Cymric north Pembrokeshire and the anglicized south. The division goes back to the Norman colonization of the south of the county, though the name has only been used since the 1930s. The area is also home to Europe's largest wooden roller coasters at the **Oakwood** theme park, as well as the wonderful Celtic cross, castle and tidal mill at **Carew**.

Narberth

According to *The Mabinogion*, a collection of ancient Celtic folk tales and legends, **NARBERTH** (Arberth) was the court of Pwyll, and its **castle** was probably home to the Welsh princes. Today, though, it has a growing reputation as Pembrokeshire's prime boutique **shopping** destination, with a dozen or so delis, galleries and clothing and homeware shops along High Street, and a lively farmer's market on Thursday afternoons in the Queen's Hall (see opposite). You'll certainly notice the curious, spiky **town hall**, midway down High Street, built in the 1830s with a clock tower added in 1881, and now housing a gift shop. Outside, a plaque marks the cell where the leaders of the Rebecca Riots (see p.233) were imprisoned.

Narberth Museum

Church St • Tues–Sat plus spring & summer public hols 10am–5pm • £3.50 • ☎01834 860500, ⓦnarberthmuseum.co.uk

Water Street, with views to the castle ruins, leads down from the town hall to Church Street, where you'll find the fine new **Narberth Museum** in the former Bonded Stores, where whisky, brandy, port and sherry were diluted and bottled. Upstairs, displays include house interiors, items from old shops and businesses, especially brewing and bottling, as well as nineteenth- and twentieth-century fans, costumes and military uniforms, and a geared penny-farthing bicycle, one of only six in the world.

ARRIVAL AND GETTING AROUND   **NARBERTH**

By train The train station is on the edge of the town a mile east from High Street; bus #381 (every hour or so) will take you to the centre in 4min.
Destinations Carmarthen (every 2hr; 30min); Pembroke (every 2hr; 45min); Swansea (every 2hr; 1hr 25min); Tenby (every 2hr; 30min).
By bus Buses stop at the top of High Street.
Destinations Cardigan (3 daily; 1hr); Carmarthen (3 daily;

40min); Haverfordwest (hourly; 20min); Tenby (hourly; 45min).
Bike rental Pembrokeshire Bikes, 1 Rushacre Enterprise Park, Redstone Road, half a mile north of Narberth on the B4313 (☎01834 682755, ⓦpembrokeshirebikes.co.uk). Hybrid bikes can be rented from £15/day, here or in Croesgoch (on the A487 south of Porthgain), or with delivery by arrangement.

LITTLE ENGLAND BEYOND WALES

Ever since the Normans stormed their way through Wales, securing their rule with castles, Pembrokeshire has been effectively divided. But its colonization began even earlier, when seaborne Viking raiders seized the best land – the sandy southern coast and the fertile pasture of the Daugleddau estuary – and the Normans only continued an established practice by intermingling with the Vikings (to produce a very English racial mix) and restricting the Celtic Britons (the Welsh) to the northern part of the country.

Today, the racial divide of the past is still evident, delineated by what has become known as the **Landsker Line**, a vestigial boundary through the heart of Pembrokeshire. Along the line are some sixteen castles or castle mounds (such as Roche, Haverfordwest, Llawhaden and Narberth), while on either side of it village names are either demonstrably Welsh or anglicized. This historical partition explains why the area south of the line, dubbed **"Little England Beyond Wales"**, has appealed to English migrants and tourists, while the north tends to attract Celts and other Europeans. Whereas the Tenby and Pembroke area has inclined towards the most Unionist of UK parties, the Conservatives (who hold very little sway in the rest of Wales), the north dallies between the old Liberal tradition and modern Welsh nationalism in the shape of Plaid Cymru.

ACCOMMODATION

Canaston Oaks On the A4075, just north of Oakwood ☎01437 541254, ⓦcanastonoaks.co.uk. A luxury B&B in converted farm buildings featuring beautifully furnished rooms (all individual) with iPod docks plus a fabulous breakfast. **£90**

The Grove Molleston, 2 miles southwest of Narberth ☎01834 860915, ⓦthegrove-narberth.co.uk. Derelict in 2007, this Georgian mansion has been restored as one of Wales' finest country-house restaurants with rooms. Rooms are spacious, as are the bathrooms, and plushly furnished. **£170**

Highland Grange Farm Robeston Wathen, 2 miles west of Narberth on A40 ☎01834 860952, ⓦhighlandgrange.co.uk. Reliable guesthouse on a working farm with Shetland ponies; well placed for walking or cycling in Canaston Woods and beyond. **£52**

Plas Hyfryd Country Hotel Moorfield Rd, north end of town ☎01834 869006, ⓦplashyfrydhotel.com. Comfortable hotel in a former rectory with fourteen rooms (including family and executive suites), bar and restaurant, with terrace dining. **£95**

EATING AND DRINKING

The Angel 43 High St ☎01834 860579. The best spot in town for pub food such as breaded plaice (£7) or lasagne (£9), and there's also a beer garden. Daily 11am–11pm; food served 11am–9pm.

The Grove Molleston, 2 miles southwest of Narberth ☎01834 860915, ⓦthegrove-narberth.co.uk. The restaurant at this restored country house (see above) offers superb Modern British choices for vegetarians and carnivores, with dinner at £49 for three courses or £78 for seven, with a wine flight at £45. Daily noon–2pm & 6–9.30pm.

Jabajak Banc y Llain, Llanboidy Rd, 3 miles north of Whitland ☎01994 448786, ⓦjabajak.co.uk. Bare-boards and rock-walled restaurant with rooms where you might follow half a dozen pan-fried local scallops (£9) with Welsh lamb with a citrus and cranberry sauce (£24.50). The wine list is very good, and includes their own white wine.

Advance reservations only. Mon–Sat eve.

Kirkland Arms St James St ☎01834 860423. Cheery memorabilia-filled pub at the top of town that's great for a beer or a game of pool; there's also basic food. Daily 11am–11pm.

Sospan Fach 44 High St ☎01834 862767. Modern café-restaurant in The Queen's Hall serving tasty daytime snacks, soups, salads, mussels (£9), pasta (£8) or a Mediterranean platter (£8). Mon & Wed 9.30am–5pm, Tues & Thurs 11.30am–5pm, Fri & Sat 9.30am–8pm.

★**Ultracomida** 7 High St ☎01834 861491, ⓦultracomida.co.uk. Perfect for lunch, this little slice of Spain tucked in behind a fabulous deli has hams hanging from the ceiling, large shared tables and a menu featuring delicious authentic tapas (£5) or larger *raciones* (£9), washed down with Iberian wines. Mon–Sat deli, drinks and takeaways 10am–6pm; restaurant 10am–5pm.

ENTERTAINMENT

The Queen's Hall 44 High St ☎01834 861212, ⓦthequeenshall.org.uk. One of Pembrokeshire's best

emerging venues, hosting concerts, comedy, theatre and art exhibitions in the Oriel Q gallery. Wed–Sat 10am–5pm.

Oakwood

5 miles southeast of Narberth on the A4075 • April to mid-July daily 10am–5pm; mid-July to Aug daily 10am–6pm (Wed to 10pm); Sept–Oct weekends 10am–5pm • £21 • ☎ 01834 891376, ⊛ oakwoodthemepark.co.uk

Oakwood, Wales' largest theme park, makes for an exciting day out. Its forte is roller coasters, including Megafobia, the largest wooden roller coaster in Europe, and the stomach-churning Vertigo. There's also tobogganing, boating, go-karting and numerous smaller rides such as the self-explanatory Speed and Treetops.

Blue Lagoon

Near Oakwood (see above) on the A4075 • Daily 10am–6pm except (in school terms): Wed to 7pm, Thurs to 7.30pm, Fri to 9pm • £6–10/3hr, combined ticket with Adventure Centre £9–16; rope course £20 • ☎ 01834 862410, ⊛ bluelagoonwales.com

Near Oakwood is the **Blue Lagoon** water park, with a wave pool, flumes and Lazy River; from 6pm most evenings during school holidays there's a "beach party" with music, light effects and water fun getting steadily wilder. There's also the indoor **Adventure Centre** with soft play, climbing wall, mini-golf, Wii gaming, Lego Room and the Techniquest interactive science centre, plus a **ropes course**.

The Eastern Cleddau

West of Narberth, quiet lanes wind down towards the muddy banks of the Cleddau estuary amid a charming landscape with inconsequential little settlements and some great, if occasionally overgrown, walking following the waymarked **Knight's Way** and **Landsker Borderlands Trail**.

Lawrenny

Pretty **LAWRENNY** village, eight miles southwest of Narberth, is dominated by the magnificent twelfth-century **St Caradoc's church**. Half a mile away, the Cresswell and Carew rivers meet at **Lawrenny Quay** from where a lovely **loop walk** (3 miles; 1–2hr; 200ft ascent) weaves through the ancient oaks of Lawrenny Wood, giving fine views of the privately owned **Benton Castle** across the estuary. The waymarked Landsker Borderlands Trail and South of the Landsker Trail also pass through Lawrenny Quay.

ACCOMMODATION AND EATING   **LAWRENNY**

Knowles Farm 1 mile north of Lawrenny village ☎ 01834 891221, ⊛ lawrenny.org.uk. A great farmhouse B&B, serving organic breakfasts and handy for some wonderful walks (there's even a slipway if you bring your own boat). £70

Millennium Youth Hostel Lawrenny village, 300yd beyond the church ☎ 01646 651270, ⊛ lawrenny village.co.uk/hostel. A community-owned hostel in a Victorian schoolhouse, with dorms and family rooms plus a

kitchen and lounge with books and games. Dorms £16; family rooms £50

Quayside Lawrenny Quay ☎ 01646 651574, ⊛ quaysidelawrenny.co.uk. The staff here really care about their food: super-fresh panini compete with Welsh rarebit or crab sandwiches (£8), served either in the airy pine interior or outside, where you can look out to yachts moored midstream. Easter–Sept daily 11am–5pm.

Carew

The pretty village of **CAREW** (Caeriw), on the banks of the Cleddau estuary four miles east of Pembroke, is famed for its 13ft **Celtic cross**, by the road just south of the river crossing. Erected as a memorial to Maredydd, ruler of Deheubarth, who died in 1035, the gracefully tapering shaft is covered in fine tracery of ancient Welsh designs.

Carew Castle and Tidal Mill

In the centre of the village (opposite the pub) • April–Oct daily 10am–5pm; Nov–March Mon–Fri 11am–3pm • April–Oct £4.75; Nov–March £4 (castle only) • W carewcastle.com

An Elizabethan walled garden houses the ticket office for **Carew Castle and Tidal Mill**. Here you can pick up an explanatory leaflet and audioguide (free) for the castle, a hybrid of defensive necessity (c1100) and Elizabethan whimsy. It offers an excellent example of the organic nature by which castles grew, from the Norman tower (probably the original gatehouse) and thirteenth-century battlements to the Tudor gatehouse and Elizabethan mansion grafted onto them.

Carew Tidal Mill

A few hundred yards west of the castle is the **Carew Tidal Mill**, probably established in the sixteenth century, rebuilt around 1800 and last used in 1937. The impressive exterior of the only restored tidal mill in Wales belies the pedestrian exhibitions and moderately interesting audiovisual displays of the milling process inside.

ARRIVAL AND DEPARTURE   CAREW

By bus Carew is served by buses from/to to Tenby (9 daily;   30min) and Pembroke (4 daily;10min).

ACCOMMODATION AND EATING

Carew Inn Opposite the castle ☎01646 651267, W carewinn.co.uk. A fine traditional inn for real ale and pub grub; the pleasant garden hosts a barbecue and live music on Thurs & Sun, with more music on alternate Saturdays. Daily 11am–11pm ; food served noon–2pm

& 6–9pm.

Cresswell House Cresswell Quay ☎01646 651435, W cresswellhouse.co.uk. In an idyllic waterfront setting across the bridge from the pub, this large Georgian house has just two stylish rooms, with excellent breakfasts. £85

South Pembrokeshire coast

The southern zigzag of coast on either side of **Tenby** is a strange mix of caravan parks and Ministry of Defence shooting ranges above some spectacularly beautiful bays and gull-covered cliffs. For walkers, the coast is constantly beguiling, as it nips and tucks past some excellent, comparatively quiet beaches, many also accessible by car.

Northeast of Tenby, **Saundersfoot** and **Amroth** have popular beaches, separated by cliffs topped by caravan parks. West of Tenby, worthwhile destinations include **Manorbier**, with its dramatic castle above a small bay, and quintessentially pretty **St Florence**. You can stroll along the beautiful sandy **Barafundle Bay** and past the Bosherston lily ponds at the National Trust's **Stackpole Estate**, then cross MOD land to the ancient **St Govan's chapel**, squeezed into a rock cleft above the crashing waves. The limestone sea arch known as the **Green Bridge of Wales** is the pick of the area's dramatic scenery, which gradually softens towards the village of **Angle**, facing the petrochemical installations across the actual harbour of Milford Haven.

Amroth

Six miles northeast of Tenby, the tiny beach village of **AMROTH** marks the eastern end of the 186-mile **Pembrokeshire Coast Path**, winding around every cove and cliff in the county. The **Carmarthen Bay Coast Walk** starts half a mile to the east with a surprisingly rugged five-mile hike to the tatty seaside resort of Pendine via Marros Beach.

Colby Woodland Gardens

1 mile inland from Amroth • Daily: mid-Feb to mid-Nov 10am–5pm; mid-Nov to mid-Feb 10am–3pm • £5.40; NT • ☎ 01834 811885

The attractive **Colby Woodland Gardens** are wedged into a wooded valley in an area that was extensively mined for anthracite and iron ore until the nineteenth century.

Highlights include the sloping walled garden and gazebo and, in May and June, the explosion of colour in the numerous rhododendron bushes. Between April and October there are art and craft galleries and a useful tearoom.

Saundersfoot

The cliffs between Amroth and Tenby are lined with caravan parks, although the Coast Path and cycle route pass below them from Wiseman's Bridge to Saundersfoot through former tramway tunnels. The only break is the picturesque harbour of **SAUNDERSFOOT**, built in the 1830s for the export of coal and anthracite. The industry has long since folded and the predictable clutch of cafés, tacky shops and boisterous pubs make the town a popular, good-natured place to hang out beside the wide yawn of sand.

ARRIVAL AND INFORMATION   SAUNDERSFOOT

By train Saundersfoot is served by trains running between Swansea and Pembroke Dock; the station is over a mile northwest up The Ridgeway from the harbour. Services run every 2hr from/to Carmarthen (40min), Narberth (12min), Pembroke (35min), Swansea (90min) and Tenby (8min).

By bus Buses from/to Tenby (roughly hourly; 15min) stop in the centre of the village.

Tourist office The TIC (Easter–Oct daily 10am–4pm; ☎01834 813672, ⓦvisit-saundersfoot.com) is on the harbourfront.

THE PEMBROKESHIRE NATIONAL PARK AND COAST PATH

Of Britain's fifteen national parks, the **Pembrokeshire Coast National Park** is the only largely sea-based one, hugging the rippled coast of southwestern Wales. Established in 1952, the park is a set of occasionally unconnected patches of coast and inland scenery. Starting from the southeast, the first segment clings to the coast from Amroth through to the Milford Haven waterway, an area of sweeping limestone cliffs and some fabulous beaches. The second (and much the quietest) part covers the pastoral Daugleddau estuary, plunging deep into Pembrokeshire's rural heart southeast of Haverfordwest. The third section includes the scenic cliffs and beaches of St Bride's Bay, a great chunk scooped out of Wales' westernmost land. Finally, beyond Fishguard to the north, the park boundary runs far inland to encompass the Mynydd Preseli, a barren but invigoratingly beautiful range of hills dotted with ancient relics.

Following almost every wriggle of the coast, the **Pembrokeshire Coast Path** winds 186 miles from Amroth in the southeast to its northernmost point at St Dogmael's near Cardigan. Mostly it clings to the clifftops, overlooking seal-studded rocks, craggy islands, unexpected gashes of sand and shrieking clouds of sea birds. Only on the southwestern end of the Castlemartin peninsula, occupied by army training camps and firing ranges, does the path veer substantially inland; it also ducks briefly inland along the Milford Haven estuary, where the huge expanse of hill-backed water lined by oil refineries provides one of the route's many surprises.

The Coast Path's most ruggedly inspiring segments are around St Davids Head and the Marloes peninsula, either side of St Bride's Bay; the stretch from the castle at Manorbier to the tiny cliff chapel at Bosherston along the southern coast; and the undulating contours, massive cliffs and tiny coves along the northern coast, either side of Fishguard. These offer miles of windswept walking among flashes of gorse and heather, with close-up views of thousands of sea birds. Basking seals frequent some of the more inaccessible beaches, particularly in autumn when their pups are born.

Spring is perhaps the finest season for walking: the crowds have yet to arrive and the clifftop flora is at its most vivid. The national park's excellent free newspaper *Coast to Coast*, detailing special walks, boat trips and other events, is published every spring and can be picked up from visitor centres across the area. The best **websites** are the park's general site ⓦpembrokeshire coast.org.uk, and ⓦnt.pcnpa.org.uk, with more practical trip-planning advice.

For those with walking difficulties, the *Easy Access Routes* booklet (£3) details flatter sections, many remodelled with gates rather than stiles.

ACCOMMODATION AND EATING

Cliff House Wogan Terrace ☎01834 813931, ⓦcliffhousebbsaundersfoot.co.uk. A lovely former ship-owner's home, this has great sea views from some rooms and the sitting-room balcony, plus excellent breakfasts. **£65**

Mulberry Brewery Terrace ☎01834 811313, ⓦmulberry-restaurant.co.uk. Near the harbour, this lively bistro serves fish, steak and good three-course set menus (£17 lunch/£20 dinner), plus vegetarian pasta (£14). There's a splendid Sunday lunch, with tapas at weekday lunchtimes. Mon–Sat noon–2.30pm & 6–9pm, Sun noon–2.30pm.

Royal Oak Inn Corner of High St and Wogan Terrace ☎01834 812546. A homely freehouse for good food and beer

in the centre of the village. Daily noon–11pm; food served Mon–Fri noon–2.30pm & 6–9pm, Sat & Sun noon–9pm.

St Brides Spa Hotel St Brides Hill ☎01834 812304, ⓦstbridesspahotel.com. High on the hill overlooking the beach, this is one of Pembrokeshire's finer hotels, with contemporary style, an elegant restaurant and a spa with an infinity hydrotherapy pool. **£150**

Wiseman's Bridge Inn 1.5 miles north of Saundersfoot ☎01834 813236, ⓦwisemansbridgeinn.co.uk. This thoroughly enjoyable beachside pub is good for a drink or a meal. Daily 11am–11pm; food served noon–1.30pm & 6–9pm.

Tenby

Beguilingly old-fashioned **TENBY** (Dinbych-y-Pysgod) is everything a seaside resort should be, wedged on a promontory between two sweeping beaches fronting an island-studded seascape. Narrow streets wind downhill from the medieval centre to the harbour, past miniature gardens fashioned to catch the afternoon sun. Steps down the steeper slopes give magical views of the dockside arches, while rows of brightly painted houses and hotels are strung along the clifftops. Simply walking around the streets and along the beaches at low tide is a delight, but Tenby is best visited during quiet times such as May or late September – in busy months, you'll be fighting for space with hordes of fellow holiday-makers.

Tenby is also one of the major stopping-off points along the **Pembrokeshire Coast Path**, providing walkers with a welcome interlude of glitter and excitement amid mile upon mile of undulating cliff scenery. A few miles offshore from Tenby, the monastic **Caldey Island** makes for a pleasant day-trip.

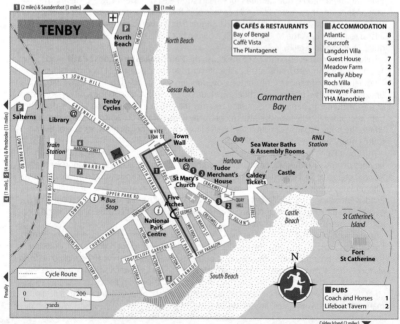

Brief history

Tenby's pedigree is long. First mentioned in a ninth-century bardic poem, the town grew under the Normans, who erected a **castle** on the headland. The town was sacked by the Welsh three times in the twelfth and thirteenth centuries; the last time, in 1260, by Prince Llewelyn himself. In response, the castle was refortified and the stout town walls were built.

Tenby prospered as a **port** between the fourteenth and sixteenth centuries, and although decline followed, the arrival of the railway brought renewed prosperity as the town became a fashionable **resort**. Now firmly middle-market, it caters to both retirees and more rumbustious fun-seekers – although the town is now trying to quell its popularity with hen and stag parties.

The old town walls

Tenby's old centre is triangular, with two sides meeting at the castle and the third following the remaining **town walls**, built in the late thirteenth century and massively strengthened in 1457 by Jasper Tudor, Earl of Pembroke and uncle of Henry VII. Tenby was further fortified in the 1580s, when it was seen as a likely target for the Spanish Armada. The only town gate still standing is the **Five Arches** (roughly halfway along the wall), a semicircular barbican with hidden lookouts and acute angles to surprise invaders, now busy with oblivious pedestrians. The wall continues south to the Esplanade, with a line of snooty hotels facing out over South Beach.

St Mary's church

Between Tudor Square and St George's St

The town centre's focal point is the 152ft spire of the largely fifteenth-century **St Mary's church**. Its light triple-naved interior shows off the chancel's elaborate ceiling bosses, while fifteenth-century tombs attest to Tenby's mercantile tradition. On the church's western side runs Upper Frog Street, replete with craft shops and an arcaded indoor market.

Tudor Merchant's House

Quay Hill • 11am–5pm: April–July & Oct daily except Tues; Feb half-term & Aug daily; March & Nov Sat & Sun • £3; NT • ☎ 01834 842279

Quay Hill runs down towards the harbour past some of Tenby's oldest dwellings, including a **Tudor Merchant's House**, built in the late fifteenth century when Tenby was second only to Bristol as a west-coast port. The compact house with its Flemish-style chimneypieces is on three floors, and has been filled with reproduction Tudor furniture that you are welcome to sit on. The rear herb garden gives a good view of the huge Flemish chimney.

The harbour and Castle Hill

When it's not too crowded, the **harbour** can look idyllic. Sheltered by the curving headland and fringed by pastel-hued Georgian and Victorian houses, it's ideal for an evening stroll. By day, it's the departure point for numerous excursion boats, especially the short trip to Caldey Island. Above the harbour is the headland of **Castle Hill**, its grassy slopes rife with Victoriana in the form of huge flowerbeds (including an indigenous small daffodil in springtime), benches, a bandstand and a pompous memorial to Prince Albert – upstaging the ruins of the Norman **castle**, notable for the all-round view from its windswept tower. On the north side of the headland, the modern RNLI **lifeboat station** (daily 8.30am–5.30pm; donations) has photos of wrecked ships, videos, a viewing gallery and a schedule of launch exercises, plus a souvenir shop.

Sea Water Baths and Assembly Rooms

Harbour Square • No general access

Returning to the harbour from Castle Hill, you'll pass the **Sea Water Baths and Assembly Rooms**, built in 1806 and 1811 by Sir William Paxton; having made money in India, and built Middleton Hall, now the National Botanic Garden of Wales (see p.147), he then invested heavily in reviving Tenby as a bathing resort, and left it set for Victorian prosperity even after the end of the Napoleonic Wars reopened access to the continental spas and resorts.

South Beach

Castle Hill offers great views over the quieter **South Beach**, where the sea recedes so far at low tide that tiny St Catherine's Island (no access) becomes fully beached. It's topped by the remains of the 1869 St Catherine's Fort, one of Palmerston's Follies (see box, p.170).

Tenby Museum & Art Gallery

Castle Hill • Easter–Oct daily 10am–5pm; Nov–Easter Tues–Sat 10am–5pm • £4 • ☎ 01834 842809, ⓦ tenbymuseum.org.uk

The **Tenby Museum & Art Gallery** presents a broad history of the town and harbour since the tenth century with a scale model showing Tenby in 1586, before it burst the town walls. The geology section includes ancient axes and a skull dating from around 1300 BC, and there are books written in the 1550s by locally born mathematician Robert Recorde, who was the first to use the "equals" symbol. The real attraction, though, is the **art collection**, featuring work by Tenby-born Augustus John and Nina Hamnet, as well as John Piper and Augustus' sister Gwen.

Caldey Island

3 miles offshore • Boats leave Tenby Harbour (or Castle Beach when the tide is out) every 20min (10am–5pm: Easter–Oct Mon–Fri plus Sat May–Sept; 20min each way; £11 return; ☎ 01834 844453, ⓦ caldey-island.co.uk); tickets sold at the kiosk at the harbour

Caldey Island (Ynys Pyr) was settled by Celtic monks in the sixth century, perhaps as an offshoot of St Illtud's monastery at Llantwit Major. This community may have been wiped out in Viking raids, but in 1136 the island was given to the Benedictine monks of St Dogmael's at Cardigan, who founded a priory here. After the dissolution of the monasteries in 1536, the island changed hands willy-nilly until 1906, when it was again sold to a Benedictine order, and subsequently to Reformed Cistercians. The island has been a **monastic home** almost constantly ever since, with fifteen monks currently in residence.

Caldey Village

A short woodland walk from the island's jetty leads to its main settlement: a tiny post office, the popular tea gardens and a **perfume shop** selling the herbal fragrances distilled by the monks from Caldey's abundant flora. The narrow road to the left leads past the abbey to the heavily restored **chapel of St David**, whose most impressive feature is the round-arched Norman door.

The old priory

A lane leads south from the village to the old **priory**, abandoned in 1536 and restored at the beginning of the twentieth century. Its centrepiece is the twelfth-century **St Illtud's church**, distinguished by its curiously blunt (and leaning) steeple, and by the presence of one of the most significant pre-Norman finds in Wales. The sandstone **Ogham Stone**, with an inscription from the sixth century (added to, in Latin, during the ninth), was discovered under the stained-glass window on the south side of the nave. The church's rough sixth-century flooring consists largely of pebbles from the island's beaches. From here, the lane continues south, climbing up to the gleaming white island lighthouse, built in 1828 – views from here are memorable.

ARRIVAL AND GETTING AROUND   TENBY

By train The train station is just west of the town centre, at the bottom of Warren Street.

Destinations Carmarthen (9 daily; 50min); Lamphey (9 daily; 20min); London (1 daily; 5hr); Narberth (9 daily;

TENBY GHOST WALKS AND MORE

A nice way to explore Tenby is to join Marion Davies for her **Ghost Walk of Tenby** (mid-June to mid-Sept Mon–Sat; £5; reservations recommended on ☎01834 845841 or ☎07970 420734, Ⓦguidedtourswales.co.uk), which leaves from the Lifeboat Tavern in Tudor Square at 8pm and spends an hour and a half exploring the town's past and its inhabitants. She also leads other themed walks and offers out-of-season specials – see the notices at the tourist office or contact her directly.

2

20min); Pembroke (9 daily; 20min); Pembroke Dock (9 daily; 30min); Saundersfoot (9 daily; 10min); Swansea (8 daily; 1hr 45min); Whitland (9 daily; 30min).

By bus Local buses stop on South Parade at the top of Trafalgar Road and on Upper Park Road; National Express coaches call on Upper Park Road.

Destinations Amroth (8 daily; 40min); Carew/Cresswell (4 daily; 40min); Carmarthen (1 daily; 1hr); Haverfordwest (hourly; 1hr); Manorbier (hourly; 20min); Narberth (hourly; 45min); Pembroke (hourly; 45min); Saundersfoot (every

30min; 15min).

By car Note that cars are banned in central Tenby between 11am and 5pm from mid-July to early Sept. Free shuttle buses (daily 10am–6pm) run from the Salterns and North Beach car parks (both pay-and-display), to the west and north of the town centre, respectively.

By taxi Call Tenby Taxis on ☎01834 842371.

Bike rental Tenby Cycles, 16a The Norton (☎01834 845573, Ⓦtenbycycles.co.uk), rents out hybrids (£12/day) as well as tag-a-longs and trailers.

INFORMATION

Tourist office The TIC (Easter–Oct Mon–Fri 9.30am–5pm, Sat & Sun 10am–4pm; Nov–Easter Mon–Sat 10am–4pm; ☎01834 842402, Ⓔtenby.tic@pembrokeshire.gov.uk) is just along from the bus shelter on Upper Park Road.

National Park Centre South Parade (April–Sept daily

9.30am–5pm; Oct–March Mon–Thurs 10.30am–3.30pm, Fri & Sat 10.30am–4pm; ☎01834 845040, Ⓔtenbycentre @pembrokeshirecoast.org.uk). Interesting child-friendly displays on the Pembrokeshire coast and around.

ACCOMMODATION

Atlantic The Esplanade ☎01834 842881, Ⓦatlantic -hotel.uk.com. The South Beach's best hotel, with fine rooms (some with sea views), a good restaurant and a pool and spa. Breakfast included. **£110**

Fourcroft North Beach ☎01834 842886, Ⓦfourcroft -hotel.co.uk. Decent three-star hotel with forty rooms, sun terraces, an outdoor pool (April–Oct), spa pool and sauna all year, plus an adequate restaurant. **£110**

Langdon Villa Guest House 3 Warren St ☎01834 849467, Ⓦlangdonguesthousetenby.co.uk. Handy for the station, this four-star B&B has a range of double and twin rooms and a hearty breakfast. **£55**

Penally Abbey 1 mile west of Tenby, close to Penally station ☎01834 843033, Ⓦpenally-abbey.com. Luxurious country-house hotel on the site of a sixth-century abbey, with great sea views. Standards are very high, but the atmosphere is relaxed and the food unpretentious. **£145**

Roch Villa 1 Harding Villas ☎01834 843096, Ⓦrochvillabandb.com. Budget accommodation with three rooms with shared bathrooms and video or DVD

player. Limited parking but close to the station. No meals; bed only. **£40**

YHA Manorbier Skrinkle Haven ☎0845 371 9031, Ⓔmanorbier@yha.org.uk. Modern hostel in an old MOD building overlooking the cliffs 5 miles west of Tenby, near the Manorbier bus route. Meals, private rooms and camping facilities available. Closed Nov–Feb. Dorms **£19**; private rooms from **£54**

CAMPING

Meadow Farm Northcliffe ☎01834 844829, Ⓦmeadowfarmtenby.co.uk. Under a mile north of town on the Coast Path, this dog-free campsite in a grassy field has only limited facilities but long views over the town towards Caldey Island – a great alternative to the family-fun-park-style places. Closed Nov–March. **£8**/person

Trevayne Farm Monkstone, 2 miles north off A478 ☎01834 813402, Ⓦtrevaynefarm.co.uk. Family-oriented caravan and campsite with superb views over Saundersfoot and the sandy arc sweeping round to Amroth and Pendine. Closed Nov–March. **£12**/pitch

EATING AND DRINKING

Bay of Bengal 1 Crackwell St ☎01834 843331, Ⓦbayofbengaltenby.com. Reliable curry restaurant; no licence so bring your own alcohol. Ask for a seat downstairs,

for great bay views. Service can be variable. Daily 5/5.30–11pm.

Caffè Vista 3 Crackwell St ☎01834 849636. Great little

2

TENBY FESTIVALS

The week-long **Tenby Arts Festival** (ⓦ tenbyartsfest.co.uk) in mid-Sept is fairly highbrow but has a rowdy and lively Fringe. The three-day **Tenby Blues Festival** (ⓦ tenbyblues.co.uk) in mid-Nov is gaining in profile.

Greek–Australian-run café with excellent panini, pies, espresso and cakes, plus a small selection of dishes such as beef or butterbean stew. Great harbour views from the small terrace, free wi-fi and it's licensed. Daily 9am–5pm, Thurs–Sat to 10.30pm in summer school hols.

Coach and Horses Upper Frog St ☎ 01834 842704. Animated, wooden-beamed pub (said to be the oldest in Tenby) with good beer, well-prepared bar meals and some tasty Thai dishes. Daily noon–midnight; food served noon–3pm & 6–9pm.

Lifeboat Tavern St Julian's St ☎ 01834 844948. Popular and enjoyable pub, with a youthful clientele and family-friendly food such as steaks, fish and chips,

and burgers; live music Tues & Sun. Daily noon–midnight; food served Mon–Fri noon–9pm, Sat & Sun noon–7pm.

★ **The Plantagenet** Quay Hill ☎ 01834 842350. This cosy and thoroughly enjoyable restaurant makes optimum use of local produce. It's in one of Tenby's oldest houses – ask for a table inside the massive tenth-century Flemish chimney. Dinner mains go for £21–27 (£16 for vegetarian), but lunch is cheaper (£8–13), or just have a drink in the intimate bar. April to late Oct & Christmas/New Year daily noon–2.30pm & 5–10pm; late Oct to March Fri 5–10pm, Sat noon–2.30pm & 5–10pm, Sun noon–2.30pm.

DIRECTORY

Banks The main banks are on Tudor Square and have ATMs and currency-changing facilities.

Hospital Gas Lane ☎ 01834 845400 (minor injuries).

Internet Free access at the library on Greenhill Road (Mon–Fri 9.30am–5pm, Sat 9.30am–12.30pm); paid-for

at *Café No.25*, 25 High Street. There's also free wi-fi at *Caffe Vista* (see p.165).

Police Warren Street ☎ 0845 330 2000.

Post office Warren Street.

Lydstep Haven

Three miles southwest of Tenby the Coast Path reaches the glorious, privately owned beach of **Lydstep Haven**; it's a beautiful spot, with limestone caverns to explore in the craggy Lydstep Point, and worth the small fee. Although some of the caverns are only accessible at low tide, the **Smugglers' Cave** is safe at all times.

ARRIVAL AND DEPARTURE LYDSTEP HAVEN

By bus You can get to Lydstep Haven by bus from Tenby (8min), Manorbier (12min) or Pembroke (30min) on the hourly Tenby–Haverfordwest service.

Manorbier

As it proceeds west, the Coast Path veers inland to avoid the artillery range on Old Castle Head, then leads into the quaint village of **MANORBIER** (Maenorbŷr; pronounced "manner-beer"). Giraldus Cambrensis, or "Gerald of Wales" (see p.377), was born in the castle here in 1146, which he later described as "excellently well defended by turrets and bulwarks, and … situated on the summit of a hill extending on the western side towards the sea".

Manorbier Castle

Daily April–Sept plus Feb & Oct half-terms 10am–5pm • £5 • ☎ 01834 871394, ⓦ manorbiercastle.co.uk

Founded in the early twelfth century as a baronial residence and little changed since, the **castle** sits above the village and its beach on a hill of wild gorse. The Norman walls are very well preserved, surrounding walled gardens and a grass courtyard in which the extensive remains of the castle's chapel and staterooms jostle for position with the nineteenth-century domestic residence. Views from the ramparts are wonderful, taking in the corrugated coastline, bushy dunes, deep-green fields and the village's smoking chimneys. There's a warren of dark passageways to explore, occasionally opening out into little cells populated by lacklustre wax figures, including Gerald himself.

St James' church

Church Lane • Easter–Sept daily 9am–6pm

The lane below the castle leads to the **church of St James the Great**, a Norman structure whose curious, elongated tower has been rendered with a "buttermilk limewash" to mimic how the whole church would apparently once have looked. It's a striking sight but not universally popular.

2

The beaches

From the car park between church and castle, a path leads via a sandy break in the red sandstone cliffs to Manorbier's shell-shaped **cove**. For more secluded bathing, follow the path on the left of the beach (as you face the sea) over the headland called the Priest's Nose, past a Neolithic cromlech (burial chamber) known as the **King's Quoit**, and round for just over half a mile to the steep steps down to often-deserted **Presipe Beach**. High tides can cover the whole beach, so check times. Alternatively, follow the Coast Path two-and-a-half miles right (west) to **Swanlake Bay**, known for its stunning rock pools and formations.

ARRIVAL AND DEPARTURE

MANORBIER

By train Trains run every 2hr from/to Carmarthen (1hr), Narberth (30min), Pembroke (10min), Swansea (1hr 50min) and Tenby (12min).

By bus There are hourly buses from/to Haverfordwest (1hr 15min), Lamphey (15min), Pembroke (20min) and Tenby (20min).

St Florence

The village is served by buses from/to Tenby (4 daily; 15min)

Three miles north of Manorbier is the delightful little village of **ST FLORENCE**, whose whitewashed stone cottages, many with their original medieval "Flemish" chimneystacks, huddle around tiny lanes. St Florence was a port until the river was dammed in 1820, leaving a lovely walk down to Penally (on the edge of Tenby, three miles southeast) beside the usually dry bed of the Ritec stream.

Mid-Pembrokeshire

Central Pembrokeshire is generally ignored by visitors intent on reaching the more obvious coastal pleasures to the south and west. None of the towns is especially interesting, but they're the county's largest settlements.

Historically, the most significant is **Pembroke**, the old county town with its formidable **castle**, plus the nearby ruins of the Bishop's Palace at **Lamphey**. Just north is **Pembroke Dock**, on the southern banks of the magnificent Daugleddau River estuary, from where ferries leave for Ireland. Across the massive Milford Haven waterway, described by Nelson as the greatest natural harbour in the world, American Quakers founded the town of **Milford Haven**, which has a dramatic setting and a good museum but probably won't detain you long.

Seven miles to the north, the region's chief town, **Haverfordwest**, is an important market and transport centre. Despite some handsome architecture, it remains rather soulless, though it's made more palatable by its proximity to **Scolton Manor**, housing the county museum, and **Picton Castle**.

Pembroke and beyond

The old county town of **PEMBROKE** (Penfro) grew up solely to serve its **castle**, the mightiest link in the chain of Norman strongholds across southern Wales and the base for the invasion of Ireland in 1171. Stretched along a ridge, the walled town flourished as a port shipping local goods to all parts of Britain, as well as Ireland, France and Spain. Though it chose the winning side during the Wars of the Roses, Pembroke was less fortunate in the Civil War, being besieged and captured by Cromwell.

A centre for leather-making, weaving, dyeing and tailoring, Pembroke was a prosperous port in the eighteenth century, when many of its simple Georgian houses were built; however it was in grave decline by the twentieth century, its port long since overtaken by nearby rivals. Happily this means that central Pembroke was spared postwar redevelopment, although the town's fringes are largely modern and bland.

History buffs shouldn't pass up a trip out to the ruined Bishop's Palace in **Lamphey**, though unless you're off to Ireland you might skip **Pembroke Dock**.

The town's sole thoroughfare, **Main Street** stretches from the train station (as Station Rd) in the east to the mighty walls of the castle. From the thirteenth-century **St Mary's church** (open daily; free), just before the castle, Northgate Street drops to the bridge and the lovely **Mill Pond**, now a nature reserve (unrestricted access) and home to swans and otters. A pondside promenade leads past the most impressive remnants of the thirteenth-century town **walls** to the ruined **Barnard's Tower** and a path back up to the east end of Main Street.

The castle

Westgate Hill • Daily: April–Aug 9.30am–5.30pm; March, Sept & Oct 10am–5pm; Nov–Feb 10am–4pm • £5.50 • ☎ 01646 684585, ⓦ pembrokecastle.co.uk

After the Norman Conquest, Rhys ap Tewdwr, ruler of Deheubarth (west Wales), held off the Normans for a while, but after his death in battle in 1093, Lord Roger de Montgomery invaded and raised a castle, rebuilt in stone after 1189. Surrounded by water on three sides, **Pembroke Castle** proved impregnable for the next four centuries. In 1452 Henry VI granted it to Jasper Tudor, whose nephew Harri was born here, later becoming the Lancastrian claimant to the throne, and, in 1485, King Henry VII. During the Civil War, Pembroke was a Parliamentarian stronghold until switching to the Royalist side in 1648. Cromwell's 48-day siege of the town only succeeded after he cut off its water supply. There's a new café, gift shop and a brass-rubbing centre here, very handy on a rainy day.

The gatehouse

Despite Cromwell's battering and centuries of subsequent neglect, the castle's sheer, bloody-minded bulk still inspires awe, even if it's largely due to extensive restoration over the last century. You enter through the soaring **gatehouse**, home to some excellent displays on the history of the castle, the Tudor empire and the Civil War. The intact walls and towers contain many walkways and dark passages that give ample chance to chase around spiral stairways into great oak-beamed halls. Eventually you'll descend into the large, grassy courtyard, enclosed by battlements and punctuated by hulking towers where the town walls formerly joined the fortress.

The keep

In the inner ward, the 75ft-high Norman **keep** has walls 18ft thick and a high domed interior; it's the largest and most impressive thirteenth-century keep in Britain. Alongside, you can peer down into the gloomy cell below the Dungeon Tower, housing a model of its last prisoner.

Wogan Cavern

Steps beside the Dungeon Tower lead far down into **Wogan Cavern**, a huge natural cavern, dank and slimy, where light beams in through a barred hole in the wall facing out over the waterside path. Inhabited at least twelve thousand years ago, the cavern was fortified by the Normans, who built the spiral staircase by which you enter.

ARRIVAL AND DEPARTURE

PEMBROKE

By train The train station is off Upper Lamphey Road, east of the town centre.

Destinations Lamphey (9 daily; 3min); Manorbier (9 daily; 12min); Pembroke Dock (9 daily; 10min); Swansea (8 daily; 2hr 10min); Tenby (9 daily; 20min); Whitland (9 daily; 50min).

By bus Buses stop near the castle on Main Street.

Destinations Angle (May–Sept 4 daily; Oct–April Mon, Thurs & Sat 2 daily; 30min–1hr 25min); Bosherston (May–Sept 6 daily; Oct–April Mon, Thurs & Sat 4 daily; 35min–1hr); Carew/Cresswell (4 daily; 20min); Castlemartin (May–Sept 6 daily; Oct–April Mon, Thurs & Sat 4 daily; 40min–1hr 10min); Haverfordwest (hourly; 55min); Manorbier (hourly; 20min); Milford Haven (hourly; 50min); Pembroke Dock (every 20min; 10min); Stackpole (May–Sept 6 daily; Oct–April Mon, Thurs & Sat 4 daily; 30min–1hr 15min); Tenby (hourly; 40min).

INFORMATION

Tourist office The TIC (Easter–Oct Mon–Fri 10am–4pm, Sat 10am–1pm; Nov–Easter Tues–Sat 10am–1pm; ☎01646 776499, ✉pembroke.tic@pembrokeshire.gov .uk) on Commons Road, parallel to Main Street, can provide a useful free town guide and information on the Pembrokeshire National Park and Coast Path.

Internet access The library, in the same building as the TIC, offers free internet access.

ACCOMMODATION AND EATING

Cornstore Café North Quay ☎01646 684290, ⊛thecornstore.com/cafe. Down by the river, this place serves good espresso, light meals and fantastic home-made cakes. It's attached to an eclectic furnishings shop. Mon–Sat 10am–5pm.

Food at Williams 18 Main St ☎01646 689990, ⊛foodatwilliams.co.uk. A stylish licensed café, serving fine coffee and cakes and (from noon) sandwiches, light lunches such as Glamorgan sausages or mackerel paté (£7.50) and daily specials. Mon–Fri 9am–5.30pm, Sat 9am–4.30pm, Sun 10am–3.30pm.

Old King's Arms 13 Main St ☎01646 683611, ⊛oldkingsarmshotel.co.uk. This pub serves good bar meals and more substantial restaurant dishes; there's also an evening tapas menu. Daily 11am–11pm; food served noon–2.15pm & 6.30–10pm.

Penfro 111 Main St ☎01646 682753, ⊛pembroke -bed-and-breakfast.co.uk. Three large rooms in a fine Georgian town house, some without bathroom or TV; there's a lovely and spacious garden at the rear. **£70**

Poyerston Farm Off the A477, 3 miles northeast of Pembroke ☎01646 651347, ⊛poyerstonfarm.co.uk. Open all year, this is a top-quality farmhouse B&B; Aga-cooked breakfasts are served in a conservatory looking over the lush gardens. **£70**

Tregenna 7 Upper Lamphey Rd ☎01646 621525, ⊛tregennapembroke.co.uk. Some 900yd beyond the train station, this B&B offers four en-suite rooms plus covered bike storage and a drying room. **£60**

Pembroke Dock

Workaday **PEMBROKE DOCK** (Doc Penfro), three miles north of Pembroke, is principally of interest for its ferries to Rosslare in Ireland and its naval dockyard, active from 1814 to 1926 and now slowly awakening from suspended animation. The end of shipbuilding was swiftly followed by "PD" becoming the world's largest flying boat base during World War II, as recalled by the informative panels, models and relics from sunken planes in the **Fleets to Flying Boats Centre**, 1 The Terrace (Tues–Sat 10am–4pm; free; ☎01646 684220, ⊛sunderlandtrust.org.uk), in the old dockyard gatehouse near the ferry port. This is to move to the newly restored Garrison Chapel, just east on Meyrick Owen Way, the only Neoclassical Georgian church in Wales, as part of a new Welsh Military Heritage Centre. At the **Flying Boat Centre Workshop** at the western end of the docks (Gate 4, Fort Rd; Tues–Sat 10am–4pm; free; ☎01646 684220) you can talk to enthusiasts restoring Pegasus engines and discuss their hopes of ultimately restoring a Sunderland, and view flying boat models, photos, medals and uniforms.

The Gun Tower

Front St • Easter–Oct Sun–Fri 10am–4pm • £2.50 • ☎ 01646 622246, ⓦ guntowermuseum.org.uk

The harbourside **Gun Tower**, one of Palmerston's Follies (see box below), was built in 1851 and now houses a few moderately diverting exhibits on the history of the town and dockyard. There's a smaller "Martello" tower (not open) at the western end of Fort Road, just beyond the Flying Boat Centre.

ARRIVAL AND DEPARTURE   PEMBROKE DOCK

By train Pembroke Dock's train station is in the centre of town, half a mile east of the ferry terminal. **Destinations** Carmarthen (every 2hr; 1hr 20min); Pembroke (every 2hr; 8min); Swansea (every 2hr; 2hr 15min); Tenby (every 2hr; 30min).
By bus Buses stop on Laws Street, just west of the train station.

Destinations Carew (4 daily; 15min); Haverfordwest (hourly; 40min); Milford Haven (hourly; 30min); Pembroke (3 hourly; 10min); Tenby (hourly; 1hr).
By ferry Irish Ferries (☎ 08705 329543, ⓦ irishferries .com) sail to Rosslare, currently departing at 2.45am and 2.45pm; the crossing takes 4hr.

ACCOMMODATION

Cleddau Bridge Hotel Essex Rd ☎ 01646 685961, ⓦ cleddauhotel.co.uk. Fairly utilitarian and not that close to the ferry port, but it's the best there is. There's an adequate restaurant plus bar food. **£70**

Lamphey

The pleasant village of **LAMPHEY** (Llandyfai), two miles east of Pembroke, is best known for the ruined **Bishop's Palace**, off a quiet lane to the north of the village.

The Bishop's Palace

Off the A4139 • Daily April–Oct 10am–5pm; Nov–March 10am–4pm • April–Oct 3.50; Nov–March free; CADW • ☎ 01646 672224

Dating from at least the thirteenth century and abandoned at the Reformation in the mid-sixteenth century, Lamphey's **palace** was built as a country retreat for the bishops of St Davids. Stout walls surround the scattered ruins, and many of the palace buildings are long lost under the grassy banks. Most impressive are the remains of the **Great Hall** at the complex's eastern end, topped by the fourteenth-century Bishop Gower's hallmark arcaded parapets, similar to those of the Bishop's Palace of St Davids. Lit only by narrow slits, the gloomy undercroft below the Great Hall has the feeling of a crypt.

ARRIVAL AND DEPARTURE   LAMPHEY

By train Trains run every 2hr from/to Carmarthen (1hr 10min), Pembroke (5min), Pembroke Dock (15min), Swansea (2hr) and Tenby (20min). The station is on the A4139 in the centre of the village.

PALMERSTON'S FOLLIES

The coast of southern Britain, and particularly that of south Pembrokeshire, is littered with what are known as **Palmerston's Follies**, nineteenth-century naval defences that never saw action. As Prime Minister in 1860, Lord Palmerston felt that Britain was ill-prepared to withstand an attack by Napoleon III, who was newly equipped with iron-clad battleships. Britain's navy had barely been upgraded since Nelson's victory at Trafalgar half a century earlier, so a Royal Commission recommended building a series of forts to protect naval dockyards while the navy modernized.

Palmerston wholeheartedly backed the recommendation and had forts built right along the south coast of England and around Milford Haven and Pembroke. By the time they were completed in the 1880s, Anglo–French relations had improved, and the forts were never attacked. Arguably, the forts had been an effective deterrent, but in the public eye they became known as Palmerston's Follies. Most remain inaccessible to the public, though you can visit the Gun Tower at Pembroke Dock (see above).

The best examples around Pembrokeshire are at Tenby, West Angle Bay, West Blockhouse Point and Milford Haven.

> ### CLEDDAU BRIDGE
>
> One of the most impressive sights in this part of Wales is the view from the 1970s **Cleddau Bridge** (car toll 75p) between Pembroke Dock and Neyland on the north bank; it's open to pedestrians and cyclists, with National Cycle Network route 4 continuing to Haverfordwest on the traffic-free Brunel Trail. The views are magical, especially at sunset, with the masts of boats far below and the full skies reflected in the clear water. Even the refineries look attractive from this far up.

By bus Buses stop at the church, between the train station and the lane to the Bishop's Palace; services run hourly from/to Haverfordwest (1hr), Pembroke (8min) and Tenby (40min).

ACCOMMODATION

Lamphey Court Hotel & Spa Half a mile north of the village ☎01646 672273, ⓦlampheycourt.co.uk. This small mansion in a lovely park, opposite the palace ruins, offers grand if slightly over-the-top accommodation, with a spa and decent restaurant. **£99**

Lamphey Park About a mile northeast of the train station ☎01646 672906, ⓦlampheypark.co.uk. A characterful and very welcoming Georgian farmhouse, with three bedrooms (with good modern bathrooms) and some outbuildings converted into self-catering cottages. **£60**

Portclew House Freshwater East, 2 miles south of Lamphey ☎01646 672800, ⓦportclewhouse.co.uk. Half a mile from the superb beach of Freshwater East, this Grade II-listed Georgian house offers seven spacious rooms, plus self-catering units. **£60**

The Stackpole Estate

One of the best starting points for breathtaking clifftop walks is the National Trust's **Stackpole Estate**, encompasssing spectacular coast and beautiful inland waterways and woods. The old mansion is long gone, but there's a new **exhibition** on the estate's history in the former dairy, brewery and game larder, and you can visit the adjacent **walled gardens** and **Lodge Park**. Just across the river from here, pretty **Stackpole Village** consists of little more than a fine pub and a few houses.

Stackpole Quay and Barafundle Bay

Road access to the coast is at two main points on either side of Stackpole Village, the more easterly being the gorgeous harbour of **Stackpole Quay**. It's one of the tiniest harbours you'll find anywhere, with barely room for four boats between its slabs of stratified limestone. A half-mile walk south brings you to **Barafundle Bay**, inaccessible by car and one of Britain's finest beaches, with clear water and a soft sand fringed by wooded cliffs pierced by three arches.

Stackpole Head

South of Barafundle Bay, a spectacular stretch of the Coast Path leads to **Stackpole Head**, a tufted plateau on craggy arches jutting into the sea. The Stackpole estate is home to around twenty pairs of choughs, about five percent of the British population.

Broadhaven South

The Coast Path continues through the dunes of **Stackpole Warren** to **Broadhaven South** – the next spot on the coast accessible by car – where a nice small beach overlooks several rocky islets owned by the National Trust.

Bosherton Lily Ponds

Just inland from Broadhaven South, by the village of **Bosherston**, are the **Bosherston Lily Ponds**, three reed-fringed fingers of water created in the late eighteenth century for coarse fishing, and now beautifully landscaped, though lilies no longer carpet its surface as they once did. The westernmost lake remains the prettiest, especially in June and

2

July, when the flowers are in full bloom. You can still fish here (except March–June), though you'll need a permit (£10/day), available from the National Trust estate office (see below) or *Ye Olde Worlde Café* in Bosherston.

St Govan's chapel
1 mile south of Bosherston • Always open • Free

From Bosherston it's a mile to the coast across the **army training grounds**, by a road that is usually open at weekends but frequently closed Monday to Friday (firing orders are posted at the Bosherston car park and outside *Ye Olde Worlde Café* or call ☎01646 662367 after 4.30pm for the next day's programme). Follow the lane through the MOD checkpoint to a spot overlooking the cliffs where **St Govan's chapel** is wedged. This tiny grey structure is at least eight (and possibly as much as fourteen) centuries old. Legend has it that when St Govan was attacked here by pirates in the sixth century, the cliffs opened up and folded gently around him, saving him from certain death; he later chose to be buried here. Steps descend into the sandy-floored chapel, with its simple stone altar, and thence to a small cell hewn from the rock, containing the fissure that reputedly sheltered Govan. The steps continue all the way down to the spume-flecked sea for a magnificent close-up view of the precarious crags, caves and arches.

ARRIVAL AND INFORMATION

By bus The #387 and #388 coastal cruiser makes a loop from Pembroke (around 30min), calling 3 times daily at Bosherston and Stackpole Village and twice at St Govan's and Stackpole Quay (Thurs & Sat only in winter).

By car The Stackpole Estate is off the B4319 south of Pembroke. There are NT car parks at Bosherston Lily Ponds, Stackpole Village, Broadhaven South and Lodge Park (for

THE STACKPOLE ESTATE

the estate office and exhibition); all charge £5/day, £2 after 2pm (NT members free) and tickets are transferable between car parks.

Information The estate office by Lodge Park car park can give out maps, walking leaflets and other information (Mon–Fri 10am–5pm; ☎01646 661359, ⓦ nationaltrust .org.uk/stackpole).

ACCOMMODATION AND EATING

Boathouse Tearoom Stackpole Quay ☎01646 661359. Tasty lunches (of local crab and produce from the Stackpole estate) and teas are served in a sheltered, sunny courtyard by the quay. Mid-Feb to March & Nov Fri–Sun noon–3pm; April–Oct daily 10am–5pm.

Stackpole Inn Jason's Corner, Stackpole village ☎01646 672324, ⓦ stackpoleinn.co.uk. Real ales and superb pub

meals with straightforward lunches (mains £5–8) and more elaborate dinners (mains £13.50–20) such as pan-fried sea bass or Moroccan lamb cutlets. They also have spacious and pleasant nautically themed rooms. Mon–Fri noon–2.30pm & 6.30–11pm, Sat noon–11pm, Sun noon–3.30pm & 6.30–11pm; food served noon–2pm (Sun to 2.30pm) & 6.30–9pm (lunchtime only in winter); **£90**

The Castlemartin Ranges

The area west of Broad Haven is the MOD's **Castlemartin Ranges** and is entirely out of bounds except for a four-mile clifftop strip on which the Coast Path and bridleway lead past the striking cleft of **Huntsman's Leap** and two isolated beaches at **Bullslaughter** and **Flimston Bay**, to **Stack Rocks**. This area, known as Range East, is open to the public when firing is not taking place, ie at weekends, bank holidays, August, Christmas and New Year, and most evenings after about 4.30pm – call ☎01646 662367 for recorded information or ☎01646 662496 for the Range Office. National Park rangers lead occasional walks here and in the otherwise closed Range West (☎01834 845040; £4/evening, £8/day); despite the military activity, the ranges are rich in wildflowers, butterflies and choughs. An inland alternative is the trail from Bosherston to the army camp of **MERRION**, on the B4319. The only vehicle access to the coast is a lane (open only as above) from Merrion to Stack Rocks past the mournful little chapel at **FLIMSTON**, a hamlet forcibly abandoned to the army.

Stack Rocks jut out of the sea here like a series of tall, lichen-spattered stepping stones. A hundred yards further west (as far as you're allowed to go), a graceful limestone arch rises from a wave-flattened rock platform, known as the **Green Bridge**

of Wales. On a quiet day, your only company will be the shrieking gulls, guillemots and kittiwakes swooping to their perches on the limestone ledges.

Freshwater West

The Coast Path (and the Coastal Cruiser bus) follows the B4319 a couple of miles to **Freshwater West**, a beach that's great for **surfing**, though the currents can be too strong for swimming. Indeed, there's a memorial to the 73 men drowned here in 1943 while training for amphibious assaults. Behind the beach, desolate wind-battered dunes, recently used as locations for Robin Hood and Harry Potter films, make for interesting walking; there's also good birdwatching here.

Angle

The B4319 meets the B4320 from Pembroke near the **Devil's Quoit**, a Neolithic burial chamber topped by an impressive capstone. It continues down the final finger of the peninsula, to the remote village of **ANGLE** at the western end of a wide curve of mud known as **Angle Bay**, frequented by migrating waders such as redshank, curlew, whimbrel, dunlin and turnstone. Angle consists of one long street, bounded by old, coloured cottages. **West Angle Bay**, a secluded spot a mile to the west of the village, is better for swimming, and overlooks one of Lord Palmerston's forts (see p.170) on **Thorn Island**.

ARRIVAL AND DEPARTURE   ANGLE

By bus Angle can by reached on the Coastal Cruiser bus from Pembroke (30min), which runs twice a day from May to Sept and on Thurs & Sat only for the rest of the year.

EATING AND DRINKING

Old Point House ☎01646 641205. A delightful rustic inn (reached by walking behind the church and 10min east along the shore), whose fire is said to have burned continuously for over three hundred years until the mid-1990s, since when it has only been lit in winter. Quality meals come in large portions: the specials board usually includes several examples of the day's catch. March–Oct Mon–Fri noon–10pm, Sat noon–11pm, Sun noon–2.30pm; Nov–Feb Wed–Sun noon–3pm & 6–10pm; food served March–Oct daily 12.30–2.30pm & 6.30–8.15pm, Nov–Feb Fri & Sat 6.30–8.30pm, Sun 12.30–2.30pm.

Milford Haven

Taking its name from the waterway, the town of **MILFORD HAVEN** (Aberdaugleddau), four miles west of Neyland, was founded in 1790 by Quakers from Nantucket, brought here to work as whalers. Their grid pattern – principally three streets rising sharply parallel to the waterway – survives today, although the town stagnated until developing as a major fishing port from the 1880s. These days, despite a magnificent site and interesting heritage, the town centre hasn't got much going for it, but public funding has transformed the old **docks** into a lively café-lined marina.

The waterside

ⓦ milfordmarina.co.uk

The **waterside** is undeniably impressive, with ferries and tankers ploughing the glittering waters of the haven that stretch out below the pleasant public gardens. It's also the site of the interesting **Milford Haven Museum** (Easter–Oct Mon–Sat 10.30am–4pm, Sun during school hols & bank holiday weekends noon–5pm; £2; ☎01646 694496, ⓦ milfordhavenmuseum.co.uk), which occupies the old Customs House (1797), whose exhibits include photographs and mementos from the fishing trade, details of the town's Quaker origins, and some fascinating material on Milford Haven in wartime, when massive convoys formed here. Across the water, around the end of

2

the harbour, the **Waterfront Gallery** in The Old Sail Loft (Mon–Sat: April–Sept 10am–5pm; Oct–March 10.30am–4pm; ☎01646 695699, ⓦthewaterfrontgallery .co.uk; free) showcases contemporary works from artists in West Wales.

ARRIVAL AND DEPARTURE   MILFORD HAVEN

By train Milford Haven train station is below the Hakin road bridge, next to the docks.
Destinations Carmarthen (11 daily; 1hr); Haverfordwest (11 daily; 15min); Swansea (8 daily; 2hr 20min).
By bus Buses stop at Tesco near the train station and on

Charles Street (westbound) or Hamilton Terrace (north/eastbound).
Destinations Dale (3 daily; 30min); Haverfordwest (every 30min; 25min); Marloes (3 daily; 40min); Pembroke (hourly; 50min).

INFORMATION

Tourist office Limited information is available at the library at 19 Cedar Court, in the retail park just west of the train station (Mon–Wed & Fri 9.30am–5pm, Thurs

9.30am–8.30pm, Sat 9.30am–1pm; ☎01437 771888, ⓔmilford.tic@pembrokeshire.gov.uk).

ACCOMMODATION AND EATING

Belhaven House 29 Hamilton Terrace ☎01646 695983, ⓦwestwaleshotel.com. One of the nicer places in town, overlooking the gardens and haven, with very welcoming owners; rooms seem dated but are spacious and en suite. **£65**
Crows Nest Café Cleddau House, Milford Marina ☎01646 697147. This licensed coffee shop is renowned for its all-day breakfast, but also serves paninis, cakes, coffee and tea. Tues–Sun 8.30am–5pm.
Martha's Vineyard Cleddau House, Milford Marina ☎01646 697083. A good eating option with a balcony overlooking the marina, offering soups and sandwiches

(around £4), salads and lots of pasta choices (£11) as well as fish and sirloin (£17). Daily noon–2pm & 6–9.15pm.
Sandy Haven Near Herbrandston, 4 miles west of town ☎01646 698844, ⓦsandyhavencampingpark .co.uk. A quiet little site right by the water, with free boat parking available. Closed early Sept to Easter. **£10**/pitch
Upper Neeston Lodges Upper Neeston Farm, Dale Rd ☎01646 690750, ⓦpembrokeshirebunkhouse.co.uk. These comfy energy-efficient barn conversions, 2 miles west of the town centre, comprise two family-sized units and two for couples. **£16**/person.

Haverfordwest and around

Ancient but dull **HAVERFORDWEST** (Hwlffordd), seven miles north of Milford Haven, grew up around the castle that dominates the skyline to this day. Built in earth and timber by the Flemish Tancard around 1110, it was rebuilt in stone then refurbished by Queen Eleanor in 1289–90, and demolished after the Civil War. This was one of Wales' largest towns in Tudor times, prospering as a port and trading centre, but the Civil War and an outbreak of plague in 1651–52 put an end to that. Haverfordwest is once again the county town of Pembrokeshire, but despite a slew of fine architecture from its glory days, it's hardly a place in which to linger. The diminutive Castle Square forms the heart of the town. Beside *Castle Hotel*, a small alleyway ascends to the **castle**, which fails to live up to the expectations created by the views from below, since there's nothing to see but the bare shell of the thirteenth-century inner ward.

Haverfordwest Town Museum

Castle St • Easter–Oct Mon–Sat 10am–4pm • £1 • ☎01437 763087, ⓦhaverfordwest-town-museum.org.uk
In the imposing governor's house (1779) next to the castle is the **town museum**, a motley collection of fairly interesting local history exhibits, such as the first ballot paper used here, Nelson's freedom of the borough charter, and lots of good historical photos.

The lower town

Below the castle, the Riverside Shopping Centre follows the River Cleddau from Castle Square to the Old Bridge, by the bus terminus and tourist office. The more appealing parts of Haverfordwest lie up the handsome High Street, rising from Castle Square towards the thirteenth-century St Mary's church, the north arcade of which is one of the finest early Gothic works in Wales, with beautifully carved capitals.

Picton Castle

Rhos, 2 miles south of the A40 • April–Sept daily 10.30am–5pm; also Feb & Oct half-terms & pre-Christmas events (castle tours start 12.15pm, 1.15pm & 2.15pm) • £9.60 (grounds only £6.60, all year) • ☎ 01437 751326, ⓦ pictoncastle.co.uk

Three miles east of Haverfordwest on the main A40, signs lead two miles south to **Picton Castle**, a chunky mansion built between 1295 and 1308 and remodelled between 1790 and 1800. Set in glorious **grounds** with walled garden, maze and play area, the castle still has its original contents, notably wonderful marble fireplaces by Sir Henry Cheere, a circular library and long thin chapel, as well as family portraits (some by Graham Sutherland) plus a Renoir and the earliest-known fake Van Gogh (from the 1920s).

Scolton Manor

4 miles northeast of Haverfordwest via B4329 • **House/museum** April–Oct daily 10.30am–5.30pm • £3 • **Park** Daily: April–Oct 9am–6pm; Nov–March 9am–4.30pm; parking £1 • ☎ 01437 731328, ⓦ pembrokeshirevirtualmuseum.co.uk

A modest mansion completed in 1842, **Scolton Manor** is home to the Pembrokeshire County Museum. In the house itself you can appreciate the lifestyle of a rich Victorian family: the gilt, brocade and fine furnishings upstairs contrast with the servants' quarters below. Beside the house is an agreeable café specializing in cawl. Next head to the new glass-fronted building beyond the main car park at the bottom of the site, housing agricultural machines, corn dollies, a preserved shop and cottage interior, as well as a room of railway history and a display on the local impact of World War II. Finally, check out the surrounding **country park**, whose visitor centre stresses environmental awareness.

ARRIVAL AND DEPARTURE   HAVERFORDWEST AND AROUND

By train The train station is a 10min walk to the east. Destinations Cardiff (7 daily; 2hr 25min); Carmarthen (11 daily; 40min); Milford Haven (11 daily; 25min); Swansea (7 daily; 1hr 30min).

By bus The bus station is across the Old Bridge from the town centre, near the TIC. Destinations Broad Haven (6 daily; 20min); Cardigan (hourly; 1hr 20min); Carmarthen (3 daily; 1hr); Dale (3 daily; 55min); Fishguard (hourly; 40min); Manorbier (hourly; 1hr 10min); Milford Haven (every 30min; 25min); Narberth (hourly; 20min); Newgale (hourly; 25min); Newport, Pembrokeshire (hourly; 1hr); Pembroke (hourly; 55min); Rosebush (1 on Tues only; 45min); St Davids (hourly; 45min); Solva (hourly; 40min); Tenby (hourly; 1hr).

INFORMATION

Tourist office The TIC (Mon, Wed & Thurs 9.30am–5pm, Tues & Fri 9.30am–7pm, Sat 9.30am–1pm; ☎ 01437 775244, ✉ haverfordwestlendinglibrary@pembrokeshire .gov.uk) is on Dew Street, behind the library, where there is also wi-fi.

Bike rental Mike's Bikes, 17 Prendergast (☎ 01437 760068, ⓦ mikes-bikes.co.uk), 400yd northeast of the bus station, rents out mountain bikes and hybrid tourers (both £12/day) with panniers, lock and helmet, and tag-a-longs for kids.

ACCOMMODATION

Boulston Manor 3 miles southeast of Haverfordwest ☎ 01437 764600, ⓦ boulstonmanor.co.uk. Set in a stunning site overlooking the Western Cleddau, this top-end B&B has just three rooms, all furnished in Georgian style but with all modern comforts. **£80**

College Guest House 93 Hill St ☎ 01437 763710, ⓦ collegeguesthouse.com. One of several decent B&Bs at the top of Hill Street (plenty of free parking), this Georgian town house has rooms on three storeys. **£78**

Lower Haythog Farm Spittal ☎ 01437 731279, ⓦ lowerhaythogfarm.co.uk. Comfortable farmhouse B&B near Scolton Manor, with welcoming hosts and superb evening meals for £23. **£70**

Rising Sun Inn Pelcomb Bridge, St Davids Rd, 2 miles northwest of Haverfordwest on the A487 ☎ 01437 765171, ⓦ therisingsunwest.co.uk. This spacious campsite with all facilities sits behind a pub serving filling and family-friendly meals. **£12**/pitch

2

EATING AND DRINKING

★**Casa Maria** 2 Castle Square ☎01437 751346, ⓦcasamariadeli.co.uk. This classy deli sells Spanish, French and Welsh cheeses, meats and olives, with a café-bar serving tapas with wine. Probably moving soon to Picton Castle (see p.175). Daily 10am–5pm.

The George's 24 Market St ☎01437 766683, ⓦthegeorges.uk.com. A great option for lunch, taking a wholefood approach to delicious peasant dishes. You can eat in a lovely walled garden if the weather allows, or the cellar bistro if not. Tues–Sat 10am–5.30pm.

Hotel Mariners Mariners Square ☎01437 76335, ⓦhotelmariners.co.uk. Despite external appearances and the shoddy hotel itself, this is actually one of the most popular and reliable places to eat here. The menu contains few surprises, with specials such as lamb shank or duck breast costing around £15. Daily noon–2pm & 7–9pm.

Shire's Coffees 47 High St ☎01437 762291, ⓦshirescoffee.com. Ambitious restaurants come and go in the Old Shire Hall (1835), but the current survivor is this day-time café and wine bar, serving baguettes, jacket potatoes and tapas. Mon–Thurs 8am–6pm, Fri & Sat 8am–11pm.

St Bride's Bay

At the westernmost end of Wales, **St Bride's Bay** is one of the country's most enchanting areas, with rocky outcrops, islands and broad, sweeping beaches curving around between two headlands that sit like giant crab pincers facing out into the warm Gulf Stream. The southernmost of these, St Ann's Head, offers calm, east-facing sands at **Dale**, sunny expanses of south-facing beach at **Marloes** and wilder west-facing sands at **Musselwick**. From **Martin's Haven**, boats depart for the islands of **Skomer**, **Skokholm** and **Grassholm**.

The golden sands of the main scoop of St Bride's Bay are backed by popular holiday villages such as **Little Haven**, **Broad Haven** and **Newgale**. From here, the lacerated coast veers west as **St Davids peninsula**, the stunning cliffs interrupted only by occasional gashes of sand. Just north of **St Non's Bay**, the tiny cathedral city of **St Davids**, founded in the sixth century by Wales' patron saint, is a justified highlight. Rooks and crows circle above the impressive ruins of the huge **Bishop's Palace**, beside the more delicate bulk of the **cathedral**, the most impressive in Wales. The peninsula, more windswept and elemental than any other part of Pembrokeshire, tapers out just west of the city at the popular **Whitesands Bay** and the hamlet of **St Justinian's**, staring out over the crags of **Ramsey Island**.

Dale and around

The tiny but ancient village of **DALE**, fourteen miles west of Haverfordwest, huddles at the head of a huge bite out of the coast. Dale is blighted by views of oil refineries, but it's surprisingly sunny and its sheltered, east-facing beach makes it a popular yachting and **watersports** centre. The calm waters of Dale are deceptive, and as you head south towards **St Ann's Head** the wind gets wilder, with waves and tides to match. This was where the tanker *Sea Empress* was wrecked in 1966, though thankfully all visible reminders of the oil slick have now vanished.

Around the Dale peninsula

The area offers invigorating **walking**. The Coast Path sticks tight to the undulating coastline, passing tiny bays en route to St Ann's lighthouse. Tucked in the eastern lee of

---

WATER ACTIVITIES AROUND DALE

Water activities around Dale are focused on the beachside shack of West Wales Wind, Surf and Sailing (☎01646 636642, ⓦsurfdale.co.uk), which offers lessons (April–Oct; £35–65/half day) in **windsurfing**, **sailing** and **kayaking**. With adequate proficiency you can rent equipment: a basic windsurfer costs £35 a half day; a superior ensemble £45; and a kayak £20.

St Ann's Head is **Mill Bay**, where Henry VII landed in 1485, marching the breadth of his native Wales and gathering an army to face Richard III at Bosworth Field.

The coast turns and heads north from St Ann's Head to reach sandstone-backed **West Dale Bay**, less than a mile from Dale on the opposite side of the peninsula; the seven-mile walk around the peninsula is highly worthwhile, but swimming here is hazardous, due to currents and hidden rocks.

ARRIVAL AND DEPARTURE   DALE AND AROUND

By bus Dale is served by three daily buses from/to   Haverfordwest (55min) and Milford Haven (30min).

ACCOMMODATION

Allenbrook Castle Way ☎01646 636254, ⓦallenbrook -dale.co.uk. A luxurious, charming, richly furnished country house; all rooms have sea views across the lawns, and they also have a couple of self-catering cottages. **£80**

Richmond House Off South St ☎07974 925009, ⓦrichmond-house.com. A comfortable B&B next to the pub (which does decent bar meals) on the Dale waterfront; rooms (or "cabins") are small but snug. **£80**

Marloes and around

A mile north of Dale, the village of **MARLOES** backs the great sandy curve of **Marloes Sands**, known for its stunning cliffs of grey, gold and purple folds of rock, alternate layers of grey shale and old red sandstone. At **Three Chimneys**, two-thirds of the way along the beach, three vertical lines of hard Silurian sandstone and mudstone were formed horizontally and forced up by ancient earth movements.

Gateholm Island

Accessible at mid-tide and below; most easily reached from the YHA hostel (see p.178) 100yd beyond a National Trust car park

The beach at Marloes is crowned at its western end by **Gateholm Island**, where over 130 Iron Age hut circles, pottery and pieces of jewellery have been found on what is thought to have been an ancient monastic community. Today, Gateholm is powerfully atmospheric, though getting topside involves a tricky scramble: head around the left side as you look at the island.

Martin's Haven

The road west from Marloes ends at **Martin's Haven**, a basic jetty that is the main departure point for **boats** to the islands of Skomer, Skokholm and Grassholm (see p.178). Just above are a battered **Celtic ring cross** and the small **Skomer Marine Nature Reserve** information point (April–Oct 10am–6pm; ☎0845 1306229), with videos of underwater life. Covering the coast of the headland as well as the island, the reserve harbours soft coral, forty species of sea anemone and over seventy species of sponge, as well as octopus, crabs and lobster. A small gateway in the wall just beyond the car park gives access to the **Deer Park**, the sublime headland at the western tip of this peninsula (inexplicably bypassed by the Coast Path). It was never actually stocked with deer; the National Trust now grazes it with Welsh mountain ponies. Paths radiate across the headland, all with stunning views over St Bride's Bay and the islands, and the prospect of a glorious sunset.

Musselwick Sands and St Bride's Haven

Musselwick Sands, just north of Marloes, is a beautiful and unspoilt beach, though it vanishes at high tide. Further north along the peninsula is the narrow **St Bride's Haven**, a tiny, sheltered inlet with a small beach at the end of the lane that peters out by the tiny chapel of St Bridget (c1291) and the newly restored Pump House (built in 1904 to supply fresh water to the Victorian St Bride's Castle), in which you can see the gleaming pumps still in full working order. There are some good rock pools around the beach.

ARRIVAL AND DEPARTURE

By bus The Puffin Shuttle runs between St Davids and Marloes (1hr 30min) three times a day from May to Sept

MARLOES AND AROUND

(Oct–April Thurs & Sat only); it also stops at Martin's Haven (5min from Marloes).

ACCOMMODATION AND EATING

The Clock House Gay Lane ☎01646 636527, ⓦ clockhousemarloes.co.uk. There's not much to the village of Marloes, but you can stay centrally at *The Clock House*, which has six white and airy rooms with wi-fi. Breakfast is served in their quality *Clock House Café*, which specializes in crab – sandwiches, ciabatta, salad and so forth. Easter–Oct Tues–Sun 11.30am–5.30pm; £84

West Hook Farm ☎01646 636424, ⓦ westhookfarm -camping.co.uk. Spacious but simple site (coin-op showers, no electric hook-ups) usefully placed half a mile east of Martin's Haven and right beside the Coast Path. Closed Nov–Easter. **£5.50**/person

YHA Marloes Sands ☎0845 371 9333. Converted farm buildings owned by the National Trust, overlooking the northern end of Marloes Sands; a traditional simple hostel with dorms and family rooms, self-catering only. Closed Oct–April. Dorms **£19**

Skomer and the offshore islands

One of the highlights of this stretch of coast is a boat trip out around the **offshore islands**, though the only one day-trippers can land on is **Skomer**, a 722-acre flat-topped island that dominates the near horizon. It has the largest **sea bird** colonies in southern Britain, the remains of hundreds of ancient hut circles, a stone circle, collapsed defensive ramparts and settlement systems and a Bronze Age standing stone known as Harold's Stone, near the narrow neck where boats land. The stars of Skomer are the two hundred thousand-plus **Manx shearwaters**, which only leave their burrows at night, though there's a live video of one in a burrow for day visitors to see. There are also puffins (best May–July), gulls, guillemots, razorbills, storm petrels, cormorants, shags and kittiwakes. Land birds include buzzards, skylarks, jackdaws, chough, owls and peregrines. On Skomer's north side, facing out over the Garland Stone, there's a good chance of seeing grey seals, especially from late August to October. Risso's dolphins and harbour porpoise can be seen offshore, with whales further out. In spring and early summer, wild flowers carpet the island.

Skokholm

Two miles south of Skomer is the 240-acre island of **Skokholm**, whose warm red sandstone cliffs are a sharp contrast to Skomer's grey severity. Britain's first bird observatory was founded here in the 1930s (closed in 1976, it reopened in 2014),

---

BOAT TRIPS TO AND AROUND THE ISLANDS

Boats operate from April to October; the only company authorized to land on **Skomer** is Dale Sailing (☎01646 603109, ⓦ pembrokeshire-islands.co.uk), operating **from Martin's Haven** (Tues–Sun & bank hols 10am, 11am & noon, returning from 3pm; £21), giving you several hours to explore the island. The company also has hour-long, round-the-island cruises (daily 1pm; £12), a two-hour evening trip that's great for sea birds (May–July Tues, Wed & Fri 7pm; £16), and Sea Safari trips in fast, rigid-inflatables around Skomer and Skokholm (April–July daily 9.30am, 3.30pm & 6.30pm; 2hr 30min; £40).

Dale's trips around **Grassholm** are either on its Grassholm Gannetry Experience sea safari (April–July daily 12.30pm; 2hr 30min; £40) or the *Grassholm Cruise* (Mon at 1pm; 3hr; £35). Thousand Islands Expeditions (☎01437 721721, ⓦ thousandislands.co.uk) offers a day tour to Grassholm with an RSPB warden (April–Oct daily 9.30am **from St Justinian's**, near St Davids; £54) as well as a **whale- and dolphin-watching** trip to Grassholm and beyond (daily 9am, 3.15pm, 4.15pm; £60).

At present there are no day-trips landing on **Skokholm** but that may change – contact the Wildlife Trust of South and West Wales (☎01239 621600, ⓦ welshwildlife.org).

and the island is still rich in **birdlife**, above all puffins, Manx shearwaters and storm petrels.

Grassholm

Six miles west of Skomer, the tiny islet of **Grassholm** resembles a small iced cake: the "icing" is, in fact, a swarming mass of forty thousand **gannets**, one of the northern hemisphere's largest colonies, covering well over half the island.

ACCOMMODATION	SKOMER AND THE OFFSHORE ISLANDS
Wildlife Trust of South and West Wales bunkhouses ☎01239 621600, ⍾welshwildlife.org. Self-catering accommodation (April–Oct) in old farm buildings on Skomer and Skokholm; perfect for birders and those in	search of solitude. The boat to Skokholm costs £25 return (Mon & Fri only), while the boat to Skomer costs £11 return (9am daily). Skokholm bunkhouse £100–130/person for 3–4 nights; Skomer bunkhouse £30–60/person

Little Haven to Solva

The long, straight west-facing back of St Bride's Bay, with its sublime Atlantic surf, is flanked by dramatic stretches of cliffs from Little Haven to Druidston, and on either side of the miniature fiord of Solva.

Little Haven

Five miles north of Marloes, steep streets descend to the sheltered stony beach of **LITTLE HAVEN**, a picturesque old fishing village and former coal port that's extremely popular with divers and swimmers in summer. At low tide, walks along the shore towards Broad Haven are superb: you can explore caves and rock pools or just enjoy the full westerly skies. There's some striking geology between Little Haven and Broad Haven, with alternating bands of hard and soft rocks producing caves and blowholes.

Broad Haven

The Coast Path cuts inland from Little Haven for a mile to reach brash **BROAD HAVEN**, a dramatic contrast to its unassuming neighbour, especially in summer, with cars cruising its waterfront and holiday-makers spilling out of its pubs. Still, it has a wide beach fringed by fissured and shattered cliffs.

Druidston Haven

A couple of miles north of Broad Haven, the quiet sandy beach at **DRUIDSTON HAVEN** is hemmed in by steep cliffs and reached along small paths at the bottom of the sharply sloping lane from Broad Haven. The best access is from the unique *Druidstone Hotel* (see p.180).

Newgale

The next bay north of **Nolton Haven** (little more than a pub and a few houses and caravans around a sheltered shingle cove) is the vast, west-facing **Newgale Sands**, virtually untouched at its southern end, but popular with families and surfers around the uninspiring **NEWGALE**.

Immediately north, Brandy Brook disgorges onto the beach, marking the boundary of "Little England Beyond Wales" (see box, p.157) and the limit of Norman colonization of Pembrokeshire.

Solva

Beyond Newgale the coast turns west, rising abruptly to craggy cliffs that make this a wilder, more Celtic landscape than that of southern Pembrokeshire. The Coast Path from Newgale to **SOLVA**, three miles west, is marvellous, with easy clifftop walking,

2

magnificent coastal views and, in the lee of the Dinas Fach headland, a secluded sandy beach at **Porthmynawyd**. Solva itself is a touristy, picture-postcard village at the top of an inlet running down to **Gwadn beach**. Above this, the **Gribin Headland** between the valleys of the Solva and Gribin rivers gives memorable views and has an imposing Iron Age earthwork on its summit.

ARRIVAL AND DEPARTURE

By bus Buses from Haverfordwest to St Davids (11 daily

LITTLE HAVEN TO SOLVA

except Sun) pass through Newgale and Solva.

ACTIVITIES AND OPERATORS

Big Blue Experience Newgale ☎07816 169359, ⓦbigblueexperience.co.uk. Kitesurfing courses (£95/day) and land-based kiteboarding (£40/2hr) from April to Oct.
Haven Sports Marine Rd, Broad Haven, just behind the Galleon Inn ☎01437 781354, ⓦhavensports.co.uk. Rental of sit-on-top kayaks and bodyboards.

Newsurf Newgale ☎01437 721398, ⓦnewsurf.co.uk. Rental of kayaks and surfing gear, plus surfing lessons (£35/2.5hr); open year round.
Nolton Stables Just inland from Nolton Haven ☎01437 710360, ⓦnoltonstables.com. Fantastic beach riding, particularly the trip to Druidston (1hr 30min; £45).

ACCOMMODATION

BROAD HAVEN

Belmont Barn Long Lane ☎01437 781372, ⓦbelmontbarn.co.uk. A mile inland, this B&B has two rooms (sharing a shower), kitchenette and lounge with balcony, all upstairs and with big sea views. **£60**
Bower Farm Half a mile southeast of Broad Haven ☎01437 781554, ⓦbowerfarm.co.uk. A welcoming farmhouse B&B, reached by a narrow twisty road from Broad Haven. **£76**
YHA Broad Haven Northern end of the village ☎01437 781688 or 0845 371 9008, ⓔbroadhaven @yha.org.uk. Almost on the seafront, the modern, spacious hostel comes with bunks and a good-value café-bar. Closed Nov–Feb. Dorms **£15**; en-suite rooms **£70**

DRUIDSTON HAVEN

★**Druidstone Hotel** ☎01437 781221, ⓦdruidstone .co.uk. A rambling and easy-going place on the cliff with a quirky array of B&B rooms, some with superb sea views,

self-catering cottages, including an old circular croquet pavilion, and a cellar bar that spills out onto the clifftops. Under the stairs is the smallest bookshop in Wales. Rooms are frequently booked months in advance, especially at weekends. **£80**
Shortlands 200yd inland, in Druidston hamlet ☎01437 781234, ⓦshortlandsfarm.co.uk. This small and friendly campsite is on a rare-breeds organic farm with great views of St Bride's Bay. It also has a static caravan and a low-allergen self-catering cottage, both open all year and let by the week or for short breaks. Camping **£5**/person; caravan **£360**/week; cottage **£600**/week

NEWGALE

Newgale Camping Site ☎01437 710253, ⓦnewgalecampingsite.co.uk. Just across the road from the beach, so very popular with surfers; coin-op showers and a few electric hook-ups, but no fires and no dogs. Closed Oct to late March. **£7**/person

EATING AND DRINKING

LITTLE HAVEN

Ceri's Café at Captain Morgan's 2 St Bride's Rd ☎01437 781233. In the former post office, near the beach, this cheery place is open for breakfast, sandwiches, rolls, cakes and hot food including pizza. Easter–Oct daily 9am–9.30pm; Nov–Easter daily 9am–4pm.
The Swan Point Rd ☎01437 781880, ⓦtheswanlittlehaven.co.uk. This beachside gastropub offers quality bar meals at lunch (faggots or fish and chips for £11) and more refined evening dining featuring unusual fish such as sand sole or superb spider crab (£13.50) or perhaps belly pork (£15), followed by chocolate & ginger torte with poached pear (£5.50). Daily 10am–11pm; food served 10am–9pm.

DRUIDSTON HAVEN

Druidstone Hotel ☎01437 781221, ⓦdruidstone .co.uk. The dinner menu changes nightly, but expect anything from lamb kofte (£8) to sea bass with tapenade (£21). Tuesdays are feast nights, with a buffet of, say, Cajun or Jamaican food for £16.50 (vegetarian £14.50). There's a lighter lunch menu, and vegetarians are well catered for. Daily 12.30–2.30pm & 7–9.30pm (Fri until 10pm).

NEWGALE

Sands Café ☎01437 729222. A great place for baguettes, panini, espresso, ice creams and the likes of green pea and pesto soup (£5) and smoked mackerel pâté (£6.50). Daily 9.30am–4.30pm.

SOLVA

Lavender Café The Old Chapel, Main St ☎01437 721907. Run by a Cuban artist/musician and his photographer wife, this is a great place for a sandwich or a ploughman's; there's often live music too. April–Oct daily 10.30am–6pm; Nov, Dec & March Wed–Sun 11am–4pm.

St Davids

Perched at the very western point of Wales on a windswept, treeless peninsula, **ST DAVIDS** (Tyddewi) is a miniature city – really just a large village. It clusters around its cathedral, Wales' spiritual and ecclesiastical centre and formally independent of Canterbury.

St Davids High Street courses down to the triangular Cross Square, with its centrepiece **medieval cross**, and continues under the thirteenth-century **Tower Gate**, the entrance to the serene **Cathedral Close**. The cathedral lies down to the right, hidden for safety in a hollow by the River Alun. On the other side of the babbling Alun lie the ruins of the Bishop's Palace.

There are numerous small commercial **art galleries** and craft outlets throughout St Davids: some are tacky, but most reflect the quality of the many artists attracted to this spirited area by the unique quality of its light. The best by far is **Oriel y Parc**, a landscape gallery (daily 10am-4pm; free) at the National Park visitor centre (see p.183), which features works by Graham Sutherland and rotating loans from the National Museum of Wales.

The cathedral

The Close • Mon–Sat 8.30am–5.30pm, Sun 12.45–5.30pm; evensong Sun 6pm • £3 donation requested • Guided tours (Aug Mon 11.30am & Fri 2.30pm, other times by appointment; £4) are arranged at the bookshop in the nave • ☎01437 720202, ⓦ stdavidscathedral.org.uk

The gold-and-purple stone tower of the **cathedral** is approached down the Thirty-Nine Steps (traditionally named after the Thirty-Nine Articles, the key tenets of Anglicanism), descending from the medieval **Tower Gate**, which now houses a history exhibition (daily 10am–5pm; £1) above a tiny display of carved stones (free).

The nave

The tower has clocks on only three sides (the people living to the north couldn't raise enough money for one facing them), and is topped by pert pinnacles that seem to glow a different colour from the rest of the building. The most striking feature of the low twelfth-century **nave** is its intricate latticed oak roof, built to hide sixteenth-century emergency repairs. The support buttresses inserted in the northern aisle still look incongruously temporary and the floor has a clear slope.

The organ and choir stalls

At the crossing, an elaborate **rood screen** was constructed by fourteenth-century Bishop Henry Gower to incorporate his own tomb. Behind the screen and the organ, the choir sits directly under the tower's magnificently bold and bright lantern, also added by Gower. The Norman round arch over the organ contrasts with the other three supporting the tower, which are pointed and date from the 1220s. At the back of the right-hand choir stalls is a unique **monarch's stall**, complete with royal crest,

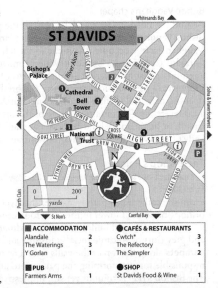

■ ACCOMMODATION		● CAFÉS & RESTAURANTS	
Alandale	2	Cwtch*	3
The Waterings	3	The Refectory	1
Y Gorlan	1	The Sampler	2
■ PUB		● SHOP	
Farmers Arms	1	St Davids Food & Wine	1

2

A PILGRIMAGE CITY

Founded by Wales' patron saint himself in 550, the shrine of **St David** has drawn **pilgrims** for a millennium and a half – William the Conqueror included – and in 1124 Pope Calixtus II decreed that two journeys to St Davids were spiritually equivalent to one pilgrimage to Rome. The cathedral was built from 1181, the settlement growing around it, and St Davids today still relies on the imported wealth of newcomers to the area, attracted by its savage beauty. St Davids was officially declared a **city** in 1995, despite having just 1600 inhabitants.

---

for, unlike any other British cathedral, the queen is an automatic member of the St Davids cathedral Chapter. The misericords under the choir seats display earthy medieval humour; there's one of a chaotic wild boar hunt and another of someone being seasick.

The Treasury

Off the north transept, the Treasury (free) recounts the cathedral's history through a small, well-presented display of its treasures. Also in the north transept is the tomb of St Caradog, with two pierced quatrefoils in which it is believed people would insert diseased limbs in the hope of a cure.

The presbytery

Separating the choir and the presbytery is an unusual **parclose screen** of finely traced woodwork; beyond this is the tomb of Edmund Tudor, father of King Henry VII. On the right/south side is a carved sedilla, a seat for the priest and deacon celebrating Mass, and the tombs of two thirteenth-century tombs of bishops. On the other side of the sanctuary is the disappointingly plain thirteenth-century tomb of St David, largely destroyed in the Reformation. The back wall of the **presbytery** was once the cathedral's eastern end, as shown by its windows. The upper row is intact, while the lower three were filled with delicate gold mosaics in the nineteenth century. The colourful fifteenth-century roof, with its deceptively simple medieval pattern, was restored by Sir George Gilbert Scott in the 1860s.

Bishop Vaughan's chapel

Behind the filled-in lancets at the back of the presbytery altar is the Perpendicular **Bishop Vaughan's chapel**, with an exquisite fan tracery roof completed in 1522. Bishop Vaughan's statue occupies the niche to the left of the altar. To the right is an effigy of Giraldus Cambrensis, Gerald of Wales, a mitre placed not on his head, but at his feet – a reminder that he never attained the status of bishop to which he evidently aspired. Opposite, a peephole looks west into the presbytery. The four crosses around the opening may well predate the Norman church: the bottom one is largely obscured by a casket, reputedly containing some of the intermingled bones of St David and his friend, St Justinian. Behind Bishop Vaughan's Chapel is the ambulatory and the simple **Lady Chapel** with its sentimental Edwardian stained glass.

The Bishop's Palace

The Close • March–June & Sept–Oct daily 9am–5pm; July & Aug daily 9am–6pm; Nov–March Mon–Sat 10am–4pm, Sun 11am–4pm • £3.50; CADW

From the cathedral, a path leads over the river to the splendid **Bishop's Palace**, built by bishops Beck and Gower in the early fourteenth century. A huge quadrangle is enclosed by an array of ruined buildings in extraordinarily rich colours: the green, red, purple and grey tints of volcanic rock, sandstone and many other types of stone. The **arched parapets** along the top of the walls were a favourite motif of Gower, who was largely responsible for transforming the palace into an architectural and political powerhouse. The **Bishop's Hall** is ruinous yet still impressive, while the enormous **Great Hall**, with its glorious rose window, overlays dank vaults housing an interesting exhibition on the palace and the indulgent lifestyles of its occupants. The palace's destruction was largely due to Bishop Barlow (1536–48), who supposedly stripped off the lead roofs to provide dowries for his five daughters' marriages to bishops.

ARRIVAL AND DEPARTURE ST DAVIDS

By bus From mid-April to Sept, the Celtic Coaster bus (#403) connects the Grove car park (by the tourist office) and the centre of St Davids with Whitesands Bay, St Justinian's and Porth Clais. Buses from/to Fishguard and Whitesands Bay stop on New Street (arriving) and Nun Street (leaving).

Destinations Broad Haven (3 daily; 45min); Fishguard (7 daily; 50min); Haverfordwest (hourly; 45min); Marloes (3 daily; 1hr 20min); Porthgain (3 daily; 30min); Solva (hourly; 10min); Whitesands Bay (mid-April to Sept hourly, late May to Aug every 30min; 30min).

INFORMATION

Oriel y Parc /National Park visitor centre Entering St Davids from Haverfordwest, the main A487 (here called the High St) passes the National Park's visitor centre (daily: March–Oct 9.30am–5pm; Nov–Feb 10am–4.30pm; ☎01437 720392, ⓦstdavids.co.uk), where you'll also find

an art gallery, café and toilets.
National Trust visitor centre In the Captain's House on Cross Square (Mon–Sat 10am–5pm, Sun 10am–4pm; ☎01437 720385).

ACCOMMODATION

There are numerous places to **stay** on and around St Davids peninsula, with prices fairly high in season at the larger hotels, but falling dramatically for the rest of the year. Campsites abound in and around the city.

Alandale 43 Nun St ☎01437 720404, ⓔalandale @tinyworld.co.uk; map p.181. Small, friendly, central guesthouse (built for coastguard officers in the 1880s) with a bike shed, lounge and five en-suite rooms, some with long views; healthy breakfasts. **£90**
★**Crug Glâs** Abereiddi, 4 miles northeast of St Davids off the A487 ☎01348 831302, ⓦcrug-glas.co.uk; map p.185. Luxurious country house on a working farm. The five large rooms are elaborately decorated with gold fittings, tasselled cushions and either half-tester or four-poster beds, plus there's a spacious attic suite. Breakfasts are excellent (great bacon) and dinners are very classy, with starters such as Abercastle crab cake and mains such as cannon of lamb, plus a good long wine list. **£115**

Ramsey House Lower Moor ☎01437 720321, ⓦramseyhouse.co.uk; map p.185. Quality B&B on the road to Porth Clais, with six boutique-style rooms and excellent breakfasts (with their own hen and duck eggs). They also do three-course dinners for £40 and have a bar. Closed Dec–Feb. **£100**
The Waterings Anchor Drive ☎01437 720876, ⓦwaterings.co.uk; map p.181. Very comfortable en-suite rooms and suites in a former marine research establishment, which retains a maritime theme. There are lovely grounds and you can play croquet on the lawn. **£75**
Y Gorlan 77 Nun St ☎01437 720837, ⓔmikebohlen @aol.com; map p.181. Guesthouse with en-suite rooms, in a Victorian house that's in the centre of town yet has

---

ACTIVITIES AROUND ST DAVIDS

Several local companies run **boat trips** to the outlying islands (see p.178). There are a number of other outdoor activities available, most run through TYF, 1 High St (☎01437 721611, ⓦtyf .com), which pioneered **coasteering**, an exhilarating multi-sport combo which involves scrambling over rocks, jumping off cliffs and swimming across the narrow bays of St Davids peninsula. This is possible for just about anyone (there are even itineraries for non-swimmers) and operates throughout the year, as do **surfing**, **kayaking** and **rock climbing** (all £58/half day, £99/full day; £62/105 in July/Aug); TYF can also organize multi-day sessions and longer courses. Preseli Venture, halfway to Fishguard near Mathry (☎01348 837709, ⓦpreseliventure .co.uk), also offers coasteering, sea kayaking, surfing, walking and biking; a half day costs £55 (£59 weekends May–Sept) and a full day £105 (£115), and also has superb hostel-style accommodation in its Eco Lodge (£39 B&B, £62 full board).

Ma Simes Surf Hut at 28 High St (☎01437 720433, ⓦmasimes.co.uk) is the place to rent **surfboards** (£12/day) or book a lesson (£35/half day). Next door the unsunghero Surf Shop (28a High St, ☎07799 626779, ⓦunsunghero surf.co.uk) makes its own boards and rents out surf and kayak gear.

2

REALLY WILD FESTIVALS

Held on the outskirts of St Davids in late May, **Really Wild** (ⓦreallywildfestival.co.uk) brings together local food producers, wild food gatherers and artisans such as instrument makers, spinners, weavers and feltmakers, to celebrate the delights of West Wales' food and crafts; there's more raucous fun in pig racing, welly-wanging and other events, and on the Verge (festival fringe). If the dates don't work, try the **Pembrokeshire Fish Festival** (ⓦpembrokeshirefishweek .co.uk) the first week of July or **Narberth Food Festival** (ⓦnarberthfoodfestival.com) the last weekend of September. On a different note, the cathedral is home to a superb annual **music festival** in late May/early June (ⓦstdavidscathedral.org.uk).

---

great views across towards Whitesands Bay. **£80**

YHA St Davids Llaethdy, 2 miles northwest of St Davids near Whitesands Bay ☏0845 371 9141, ✉stdavids @yha.org.uk; map opposite. Large, renovated hostel in a former farmhouse and outbuildings. Daytime lockout and 11pm curfew. Closed Nov–March. Dorms **£20.50**; private rooms from **£50**

CAMPING

Caerfai Farm Caerfai Bay, 1 mile south of St Davids ☏01437 720548, ⓦcawscaerfai.co.uk; map opposite. The best campsite around, on an organic dairy farm (and shop) with stunning coastal views. £2.50 discount if arriving on foot or by bike. Closed mid-Nov to Feb. **£14**/pitch

Glan-y-mor Caerfai Rd, half a mile south of town ☏01437 721788, ⓦglan-y-mor.co.uk; map opposite. The nearest campsite to town, with a pub and restaurant on site. No bookings – just turn up on spec. Closed Oct to mid-March. **£12**/pitch

Lleithyr Farm Just off the B4583, 1 mile northwest of St Davids ☏01437 720245, ⓦlleithyrfarm.co.uk; map opposite. High-standard campsite and caravan park half a mile from Whitesands Bay with heated shower rooms in winter. Closed Nov-Feb. **£5**/person

Rhoson St Justinian's ☏01437 721911, ⓦstdavids camping.co.uk; map opposite. Basic field campsite (tents only) with cold water and no showers but handy for the boats to Ramsey Island. Closed Nov–Easter. **£3**/person

EATING AND DRINKING

On the surface a bit of a backwater, St Davids is in fact a real magnet for surfers, outdoor types and musicians. In the summer, and over Christmas/New Year, parties can break out just about anywhere. It's also a good place to eat, with something for all tastes and budgets.

★**Cwtch*** 22 High St ☏01437 720491, ⓦcwtch restaurant.co.uk. Some of the finest dining in Pembrokeshire can be found at *Cwtch** (pronounced "cutsh"), an intimate and easy-going restaurant that's all slate and wood and blackboard menus. Top-quality local ingredients are sourced for unfussy dishes such as roasted red pepper and tomato soup, and hake with lime and anchovy butter. Dinner £26/30 for two/three courses; £22/26 within 45min of opening; booking recommended. Mid-Feb to Easter & Nov–Dec Wed–Sat 6–9.30pm (last orders), Sun noon–2.30pm; Feb half-term, Easter & Oct Mon–Sat 6–9.30pm, Sun noon–2.30pm; Easter–Sept daily 5/6pm–9.30pm.

Farmers Arms Goat St ☏01437 721666, ⓦfarmersstdavids.co.uk. Lively and very friendly pub, with a terrace overlooking the cathedral – especially enjoyable on a summer's evening. Good food available (summer only), such as panini, salads, jacket potatoes and mains for £7–12. Easter–Sept daily 11am–midnight;

Oct–Easter Mon–Thurs 4pm–midnight, Fri 3pm–midnight, Sat & Sun 11am–midnight.

The Refectory St Davids Cathedral ☏01437 721760. The beautiful St Mary's Hall is a great spot for tea and cakes, and also serves delicious meals at moderate prices. Free wi-fi. Daily: Nov–Easter 11am–4pm; Easter–Nov 10am–5pm.

St Davids Food & Wine High St ☏01437 721948, ⓦstdavidsfoodandwine.co.uk. A splendid deli, selling organic local cheeses and over thirty Welsh beers; the best place to pick up filled rolls or picnic makings. Mon–Sat 8.30am–5.30pm.

The Sampler 17 Nun St ☏01437 720757, ⓦsampler -tearoom.co.uk. Child-free coffee shop serving delicious clotted-cream teas. The walls are covered with an impressive collection of needlework samplers. Generally March–Nov and about 2 weeks over Christmas Mon–Thurs 10.30am–5pm (last orders), plus Sat in summer and Sun in Aug (same hours).

St Davids peninsula

Surrounded on three sides by inlets, coves and rocky stacks, St Davids is an easy base for excellent walking around the headland of the same name. A mile south, the popular

Caerfai Bay is a sandy gash (vanishing at high tide) in the purple-sandstone cliffs, from which masonry for the cathedral was quarried. Half a mile to the west is the craggy indentation of **St Non's Bay**, where, according to legend, St Non gave birth to St David during a tumultuous storm around 500 AD. A spring opened up between her feet, and despite the crashing thunder all around, an eerily calm light filtered down onto the scene.

St Non's Bay

This point on the coast south of St Davids received pilgrims for centuries, resulting in the foundation of a tiny Celtic chapel, whose successor's thirteenth-century ruins now lie in a field to the right of the car park, beyond the simple well and shrine where Wales' patron saint is said to have been born. The 1934 **chapel**, in front of the austere 1929 **Retreat House**, was built in simple Pembrokeshire style from the rocks of ruined houses, which, in turn, had been built from the stone of ancient,

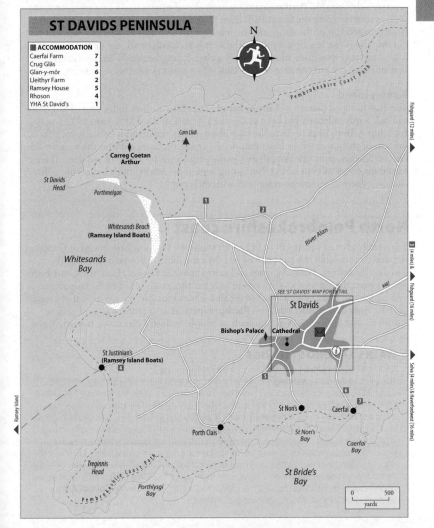

ST DAVIDS PENINSULA

ACCOMMODATION	
Caerfai Farm	7
Crug Glâs	3
Glan-y-môr	6
Lleithyr Farm	2
Ramsey House	5
Rhoson	4
YHA St David's	1

N

Carn Llidi

Carreg Coetan
Arthur

St Davids
Head

Porthmelgan

Whitesands Beach
(Ramsey Island Boats)

Whitesands
Bay

River Alan

Pembrokeshire Coast Path

SEE 'ST DAVIDS' MAP FOR DETAIL

St Davids

Bishop's Palace Cathedral

St Justinian's
(Ramsey Island Boats)

Ramsey Island

St Non's ● Caerfai

Porth Clais

St Non's
Bay

Caerfai
Bay

Treginnis
Head

Porthlysgi
Bay

Pembrokeshire Coast Path

St Bride's
Bay

Fishguard (12 miles) ▶

Fishguard (16 miles) ▶ A487 (4 miles) &

Solva (4 miles) & Haverfordwest (16 miles) ▶

0   500
yards

abandoned churches. Just to the west, **Porth Clais** was the city's main harbour from Roman times, the spruced-up remains of which can still be seen at the bottom of the turquoise river creek.

St Justinian's

Running due west out of St Davids, Goat Street ducks past the ruins of the Bishop's Palace and over the plateau for two miles to the harbour at **ST JUSTINIAN'S**, little more than a roofless chapel (no access), lifeboat station (open daily in summer 10am–4pm) and ticket hut for the frequent **boats** over to **Ramsey Island** (see below).

Whitesands Bay

Two miles to the north and reached via the B4583 off the Fishguard road, **Whitesands Bay** (Porth Mawr) faces west and offers good **surfing**, especially for intermediates. The spectacularly beautiful **Porthmelgan**, a narrow slip of cove reached by a fifteen-minute walk northwest along the Coast Path from Whitesands car park, is far less crowded, largely on account of the dangerous swimming. The thin spit of rock and cliff that juts out into the ocean less than a mile to the west is **St Davids Head**, site of an Iron Age coastal fortress, its outline most visible in spring. Rising behind Whitesands and Porthmelgan, the gnarled crag of **Carn Llidi** tops a pastoral patchwork of fields.

Ramsey Island

The dual-humped plateau of **Ramsey Island** (Ynys Dewi), three miles west of St Davids and half a mile offshore, has been under the able care of the RSPB since 1992 and is enchanting. Birds of prey circle the skies above it, but the island is better known for the tens of thousands of sea birds that noisily crowd the sheer cliffs on the western side. On the beaches, seals laze sloppily below the paths worn by a herd of red deer. There's something to see all year round, but spring is great for nesting birds (especially puffins and shearwaters), and autumn for seals with their pups.

North Pembrokeshire coast

The stretch of coast just north of St Davids forms the very southern sweep of Cardigan Bay and is noticeably less commercialized than the touristy littoral of south and mid-Pembrokeshire. From the crags and cairns above St Davids Head, the Coast Path perches precariously on the cliffs, where only the thousands of sea birds have access.

Although the area's major source of income is now tourism, the remains of old mines, quarries and ports at **Abereiddi** and **Porthgain** bear witness to the slate and granite industries that once employed hundreds of people. Industry dies down towards **Trefin**

WALKS AROUND ST DAVIDS

OS 1:25,000 Explorer map OL35 (North Pembrokeshire) is advised.

There's some fabulous **walking** around St Davids, largely on the coast path, while the Celtic Coaster bus service means that you won't need to retrace your steps. The National Park visitor centre (see p.183) stocks a number of leaflets (50p), each detailing a short coastal walk. One good and relatively leisurely **day walk** is from Caerfai Bay, past Porth Clais and round Treginnis Head to St Justinian's. At half tide the waters between here and Ramsey Island churn up into an impressive maelstrom. Another good day walk makes a loop from Whitesands Beach around St Davids Head, one of the most mysterious and magical places in Wales. Evidence of ancient civilization is everywhere, and many mystics have pinpointed the area as a focus of the earth's natural energies. Highlights include the rocky summit of **Carn Llidi** (595ft), approached on the south side past two cromlechs (capped burial stones), and **Carreg Coetan Arthur** (Arthur's Quoit), a six thousand-year-old burial chamber.

2

CRUISES TO RAMSEY ISLAND

Several operators run trips to Ramsey either from St Justinian's or Whitesands Beach.

Thousand Islands Expeditions Cross Square in St Davids ☎ 01437 721721, ⚏ thousandislands.co.uk; (April–Oct daily). The only operator allowed to land you on the island. Boats depart from St Justinian's at 10am and noon, returning at noon and 4pm (£17); you can come back on either boat, allowing you up to six hours of exploration, or you can take a guided walk with an RSPB warden (£23). Perhaps the best deal is their combined Landing & Around trip (April–Oct 10am; £37), which gives you a good look at the wildlife all around. There's also the evening Puffin & Shearwater trip (6pm; £30) and the Whale & Dolphin

experience (9am, 3.15pm, 4.15pm; £60).

Venture Jet From Whitesands Bay (☎ 01348 837764, ⚏ venturejet.co.uk). Operates jet boats to Ramsey and Grassholm, from £25 for an hour to £65 for 3hr 30min.

Voyages of Discovery 1 High St (☎ 01437 721911, ⚏ ramseyisland.co.uk) and **Ramsey Island Cruises** New St (☎ 01437 721423, ☎ 0800 028 6212, ⚏ ramseyislandcruises.co.uk). Both have similar offerings (bar landing on the island) and charge from roughly £25 for an hour to £60 for a 2hr 30min trip to Grassholm.

and up to the more remote beaches and inlets that punctuate the coast as it climbs up to the splendid knuckle of **Strumble Head**. To the east is **Carregwastad Point**, the site of the last invasion of Britain in 1797. The event is also remembered in the port town of **Fishguard**, where the invading French surrendered at the *Royal Oak Inn*.

Abereiddi to Abercastle

The fantastic stretch of coast northeast of St Davids combines rugged cliffs and birdlife with remnants of long-closed industry and even more ancient cultures.

Abereiddi

Five miles north of St Davids, a small lane tumbles down into the bleak hamlet of **ABEREIDDI**, where you can find tiny fossilized animals in the shale of the black-sand beach. At the back of the beach are remains of workers' huts and a tramway that once climbed over the hill to Porthgain, all part of the slate quarry that closed in 1904. The quarry itself was dynamited for safety reasons, producing a "blue lagoon" due to the minerals suspended in the seawater.

Porthgain

The lane parallel to the coast passes the hamlet of Cwmwdig Water and leads to tiny **LLANRHIAN**, where a left turn takes you a mile down to the rambling village green of **PORTHGAIN**. This fascinating little port grew up from 1850 below its slate works, the stumpy remains of which huddle around the tiny quay, together with an old brickworks, lime kiln and eerie ruins of workers' cottages. It also has WCs, a couple of small art galleries and the eighteenth-century *Sloop Inn* (see p.188). There's a superb circular walk (4 miles; 2 hr) back to Abereiddi, which is largely level after the steep climb out of Porthgain, returning inland or by the Strumble Shuttle bus.

Abercastle

The coastal lane continues east across a ford then climbs steeply to **ABERCASTLE**, past the 4500-year-old **Carreg Samson** cromlech (burial chamber) at Longhouse, precariously topped by a 16ft capstone. If walking, continue past the cromlech and down to the Coast Path to the attractive and popular harbour of Abercastle, once used for the export of limestone and coal. From there, one of the most scenic parts of the Coast Path zigzags east along the wild, vertiginous cliffs to the point at **Trwyn Llwynog**, about two miles away.

2

By bus From May to Sept the Strumble Shuttle (bus #404) connects St Davids with Fishguard via coastal villages such as Abereiddi, Porthgain and Trefin 3 times daily; from Oct to April it runs twice daily on Thurs & Sat only. Bus #413 (Mon–Sat 6 daily) runs from St Davids to Fishguard via Trefin.

ACCOMMODATION AND EATING

★ **Caerhafod Lodge** Porthgain, half a mile north of Llanrhian ☎ 01348 837859, ⓦ caerhafod.co.uk. Within walking distance of Porthgain, this is a brilliant independent hostel with a tranquil atmosphere, good views and helpful hosts. They offer self-catering facilities and mostly four-bedded rooms (sheets supplied). **£17**/person

Old School Hostel Ffordd-yr-afon, Trefin ☎ 01348 831800, ⓦ theoldschoolhostel.co.uk. A mile or so east of Porthgain, ecologically minded *The Old School Hostel* is a former YHA hostel that has been revamped and rejuvenated. It offers bunks and ultra-cheap private rooms, as well as light breakfasts and packed lunches. **£14**/person

The Shed Porthgain ☎ 01348 831518, ⓦ theshedporthgain.co.uk. As well as a tearoom and a fresh fish and cheese deli, this is a classy fish and chips bistro (from £10), with most of the produce caught locally. Shop and tearoom daily 10am–5pm, bistro Mon & Wed–Sat 5.30–9pm (open daily in school hols).

Sloop Inn Porthgain ☎ 01348 831449, ⓦ sloop.co.uk. This charming pub has numerous photographs of the port in its sepia heyday and a perfect terrace to while away the evening, as well as good bar food and a Sunday roast. Mon–Fri 9.30am–10pm, Sat & Sun 9.30am–11pm; food served 9.30–11.30am, noon–2.30pm & 6–9.30pm.

Strumble Head

The headland – known as **Pen Caer** – that rises to the north of Abercastle, peaking at **STRUMBLE HEAD**, is delightful: tiny hedge-backed lanes bump around between rocky cairns, with fields of wild flowers and sudden glimpses of the shimmering sea. From this remote and spectacular section of the Coast Path there's access to the sandy stretch of **Aber Mawr**, smaller **Aber Bach**, and the west-facing gash of **Pwllcochran**.

Nearly two miles further north, there's the simple but fabulously sited *Pwll Deri* YHA **hostel**. Looming large on the inland side of the hostel are the three crags of **Garn Fawr** (699ft): by following a path from the car park at their eastern edge, on the lane up to Strumble Head, you can explore the vestiges of Iron Age ditches, ramparts and hut circles.

Strumble Head itself, just over a mile north of Garn Fawr, is reached either by the rugged Coast Path – with astounding views over the two-mile-long "wall" of cliffs to the south – or along a floral country lane. At the headland, the 1908 **lighthouse** is perched atop **Ynys Meicel**, connected to the mainland by a metal footbridge that's closed to the public. It's a peaceful yet invigorating spot that's perhaps the best in Wales for **sea bird spotting**, with gannets, fulmars, kittiwakes, Manx shearwaters, guillemots and fulmars, and four other types of shearwaters, as well as porpoises. On land you may see stonechats, linnets, choughs, peregrines, buzzards and ravens.

Almost three miles on, the hamlet of **LLANWNDA** merits a historical footnote as the site of the **last invasion of Britain** (see box opposite). The **church of St Gwyndaf** is also well worth a visit for its charming setting, an ancient history which winds back beyond the eighth century, and the collection of pre-Norman carved stones embedded in its walls.

YHA Pwll Deri Castell Mawr, Trefasser ☎ 0845 371 9536, ⓔ pwllderi@yha.org.uk. Splendidly sited self-catering cottage (almost 5 miles from Fishguard and the nearest shops), with en-suite dorms and a couple of private double rooms. Closed Oct–March. Dorms **£18**; doubles **£49**

Carregwastad Point

The 1.5-mile **walk** from Llanwnda to **Carregwastad Point** is fabulous, coasting gently down fields and across the top of a craggy cwm. Start by crossing the stile up the track from the church entrance. At the coast turn left to reach Carregwastad Point and the plaque

THE LAST INVASION OF BRITAIN

In 1797, while Napoleon was absent fighting in Italy, a newly formed Franco–Irish revolutionary command was trying to make its mark in Paris. Believing that the oppressed countryfolk of Britain would sympathize with their revolutionary views and join their cause, a motley band of "liberators" – some just out of prison and still shackled – launched a madcap plan to invade Britain. Winds blew their ships from their planned landing at Bristol and they ended up at **Carregwastad Point**, just south of Fishguard, now marked with a memorial stone. The disorganized army of 1400 made its base at Trehowel Farm, midway between Strumble Head and Llanwnda, which was stocked with food and drink for an imminent family wedding. Indeed most local farms were full of contraband liquor plundered from a recent Portuguese shipwreck. The would-be conquerors set to with gusto, swiftly becoming too drunk to do anything except loot the silver plate in Llanwnda's church.

After two days the invasion had collapsed and the invaders surrendered on February 24 to a local militia at the **Royal Oak** in Fishguard, claiming they had seen "troops of the line to the number of several thousand". No such army was in the vicinity and some say the bleary-eyed French mistook several hundred local women clad in stovepipe hats and red flannel shawls for British Redcoats. While that may not be true, it's a fact that fourteen soldiers were rounded up with a pitchfork by a 47-year-old cobbler's wife, Jemima Nicholas – dubbed ever since the "Welsh Heroine".

commemorating the invasion (see box above), or right to **Aber Felin**, a bay often littered with grey seals.

Fishguard

FISHGUARD (Abergwaun) occupies a lofty headland between the pretty Lower Town and the port of **Goodwick** (Wdig), just under a mile northwest. Though often seen only as somewhere from which to catch a ferry to Ireland, it's an enjoyably arty place, with fine views from the easy coastal walks around town.

In the centre of town, the **Royal Oak Inn** was the scene of the surrender of the "last invasion of Britain" in 1797. The episode's heroine, Jemima Nicholas (see box above), is buried beside the Victorian **parish church** behind the pub.

Last Invasion Gallery

Main St • Mon–Sat 9.30am–5pm, Thurs until 6.30pm; Oct–March closes 1pm on Sat; Sun school holidays & bank holiday weekends 10am–4pm • Free

Inside the town hall, the **Last Invasion Gallery** contains the 100ft-long **Fishguard Tapestry**, inspired by the famous Bayeux model and made to mark the event's bicentenary in 1997. The tapestry offers a wonderful depiction of the invasion, including debauched French soldiers, with one unfortunate thief shown on the lower border with his throat cut. A video tells the story of the local artists and embroiderers who made it all happen, and the bicentenary re-enactment.

Lower Town

Main Street winds northeast, then plummets down to **Lower Town** (Y Cwm), a cluster of old-fashioned cottages around a muddy, thriving, herring-fishing and pleasure-boat port. Views from above Lower Fishguard over the town headland and out to the breakwater are superb. Lower Fishguard's moment of glory came in 1971, when Richard Burton and Elizabeth Taylor filmed Dylan Thomas' *Under Milk Wood* here.

ARRIVAL AND GETTING AROUND   FISHGUARD

By train Trains call at Fishguard & Goodwick station on Station Hill in Goodwick (where occasional buses to Fishguard stop across the road, except Sun) and terminate at Fishguard Harbour on Quay Road in Goodwick.

Destinations Cardiff (6 daily; 2hr 45min); Carmarthen (7 daily; 50min); Swansea (7 daily; 1hr 45min).

By bus Buses stop by the town hall in the central Market Square, right outside Fishguard's tourist office, and on The Parrog in Goodwick.

Destinations Cardigan (hourly; 40min); Haverfordwest (hourly; 40min); Newport, Pembrokeshire (hourly; 15min); Rosebush (1 on Tues only; 25min); St Davids (6–8 daily;

45min); Trefin (6–8 daily; 30min).

By ferry Fishguard harbour, for ferries to Rosslare, Ireland (2 daily; 3hr 30min), is on Quay Road in Goodwick. Most buses stop half a mile away at Station Hill. A taxi (☎01348 873075, 875129, 870288) into Fishguard costs about £4 from the harbour.

By car Cars can be rented from Hertz on Wern Road, Goodwick (☎01348 874701, ⊛hertz.co.uk).

INFORMATION

Fishguard tourist office The TIC (Mon–Fri 9am–5pm plus Sat 10am–4pm June–Aug; ☎01347 776636, ℮fishguard .tic@pembrokeshire.gov.uk) is in the town hall on the central Market Square. It has free internet access (15min maximum, or for longer sessions visit the library upstairs; Mon–Sat 9.30am–5pm, Thurs until 6.30pm).

Goodwick tourist office On the Parrog on the Goodwick

foreshore (daily: Easter to late July & early Sept to Oct 9.30am–5pm; late July to early Sept 9.30am–6pm; Nov–Easter 10am–3.45pm; ☎01348 874737, ℮fishguard harbour.tic@pembrokeshire.gov.uk); it's in the Ocean Lab, an education centre with an exhibition on marine life (£2) and detailed information on the Coast Path, as well as a coffee shop with wi-fi.

ACCOMMODATION

★**Cefn-y-Dre** 1 mile south along Hamilton St ☎01348 875663, ⊛cefnydre.co.uk. There's a relaxed and understated elegance to this lovely country house, partly dating from the early sixteenth century. Just three rooms, attractive grounds, tasty breakfasts, and superb home-cooked meals (£26.50; reserve in advance) prepared by wonderful hosts. £79

Gwaun Vale Caravan Park 1.5 miles southeast of Fishguard on the B4313 ☎01348 874698, ⊛gwaunvale.co.uk. Well-appointed site on the fringes of Cwm Gwaun that is relatively wind-free even when the Coast Path is getting battered. £16/pitch

Hamilton Lodge 21–23 Hamilton St ☎01348 874797,

⊛hamiltonbackpackers.co.uk. Cosy, very central and well-set-up hostel with dorms, doubles, triples and family rooms, and a free light breakfast. Bedding is provided. Dorms £17; doubles £45

Plain Dealings Tower Hill ☎01348 873655, ⊛plaindealings.co.uk. Peaceful and attractive top-quality B&B half a mile east of the centre, with views of the Lower Town. Closed Nov–Feb. £80

YHA Pwll Deri 4 miles west of Fishguard ☎0845 371 9536, ℮pwllderi@yha.org.uk. Recently revamped, this is a superbly sited clifftop hostel, with dorms and a couple of private double rooms. Dorms £18; doubles £44

EATING AND DRINKING

The Lounge at No.3 3 Main St ☎01348 871845, ⊛theloungerestaurant.co.uk. A rather draughty Georgian town house is home to this lively new bistro, serving pasta, pizza and other Italian-based dishes, with plenty of vegetarian and non-allergenic options. Wed–Sat 11am–2.30pm & 6–10pm (plus Tues June–Sept).

Pepper's aka Café Celf 16 West St ☎01348 873867, ⊛westwalesartscentre.com. Arty café that's great for a restful cake and espresso or a lunch platter with smoked salmon, salami or roast vegetables (£7–11). Mon–Sat 10am–10.30pm.

Royal Oak Market Square ☎01348 873355, ⊛theroyaloakfishguard.co.uk. Historic pub with real ales and a separate area for good pub lunches. There's also a long-established folk night on Tues – participants very welcome. Mon–Thurs & Sun noon–11pm; Fri & Sat noon–1.30am; food served daily noon–4pm.

Ship Inn Lower Town ☎01348 874033. Eccentric, unmissable pub with lots of interesting clutter all over the walls and ceiling, including black-and-white photos of the filming of *Under Milk Wood* and *Moby Dick*. There's often live music on Fri nights. Daily noon–11pm.

FISHGUARD'S FESTIVALS

The increasingly popular **Fishguard Folk Festival** (⊛pembrokeshire-folk-music.co.uk) takes place over the bank holiday weekend at the end of May, while there's also the **Fishguard International Music Festival** (⊛fishguardmusicfestival.co.uk) in late July, combining classical, choral, jazz and blues; the **Aberjazz Festival** in late August (⊛aberjazz.com); and **Fishguard's Autumn Festival** (⊛fishguardsautumnfestival.co.uk) around the first weekend of November. **Theatr Gwaun** on West St (☎01348 873421, ⊛its4u.org.uk) mainly shows films but also has the occasional music or drama event.

Mynydd Preseli

In a county famed for its magnificent coastal scenery, Pembrokeshire's interior is frequently overlooked. The **Mynydd Preseli** (Preseli Mountains) occupy a triangle of land in the north of the county, flecked with prehistoric remains and roughly bounded by the coast in the north, the B4313 to the west and the A478 to the east.

The main A487 coast road is the area's only major **bus** route, cruising from Fishguard to Cardigan through delightful **Newport**, handy for the historic peak of **Carn Ingli**, the bucolic church at **Nevern** with its "bleeding" yew, and the reconstructed Iron Age settlement at **Castell Henllys**. This is also the final (or initial) stretch of the Pembrokeshire Coast Path and the cognoscenti's favourite, with awesome solitude, abundant natural life and stunning cliff formations.

Inland from Fishguard, the **Gwaun River** wriggles southeast through its green cwm, with tiny villages and remote churches seemingly untouched by modernity. Formed around two hundred thousand years ago, this is Europe's oldest glacial meltwater valley and the subject of many a geology field trip. The brooding mountains hereabouts shelter innumerable standing stones, stone circles, hillforts, cairns and earthworks, several linked by a hike along the **Golden Road**.

Newport

The A487 winds through **NEWPORT** (Trefdraeth), an ancient, proud and wealthy little town that is without doubt the best base in north Pembrokeshire. Set on a gentle slope coursing down to the estuary of the Afon Nyfer, it is a quietly enjoyable place, with superb accommodation, food and drink, welcoming inhabitants and a selection of fine coastal and hill walks on its doorstep. Newport still appoints a mayor annually, a legacy of its days as the seat of the Norman Marcher Lordship of Cemaes. One visible manifestation of this heritage is the annual custom, on the third Friday of August, of "Beating of the Bounds", when the mayor marks out the town's boundaries. The town's **festival**, Ffair Gurig, is held the week of June 27, with a carnival on its last Saturday.

South of the main thoroughfare, **Bridge Street**, a number of pretty lanes rise up to the intriguing **castle** (private), a nineteenth-century residence fashioned out of the thirteenth-century gatehouse. The other obvious landmark, just to the west, is **St Mary's church**, with a Norman font and a massive fifteenth-century tower, and a history display in the north transept.

The Nyfer estuary and beaches

Long Street and Lower St Mary Street head down to the **Nyfer estuary**, over which squawking gulls circle and skim the water's edge. A path hugs its southern shore – turn east (or take Parrog Road if you're driving) for a gentle stroll to the **Parrog**, Newport's nearest beach, mostly shingle but with sandy stretches at low tide. A better beach is the vast dune-backed **Traethmawr**, on the north side of the estuary, reached over the Iron Bridge down Feidr Pen-y-Bont – note the pilgrims' stepping stones upstream from the bridge. The footpath that follows the river either side of the bridge is marked as the Pilgrims' Way, and makes a delightful riverbank stroll to Nevern (see p.193), a couple of miles east. Just short of the bridge, on the town side, **Carreg Coetan Arthur**, a well-preserved capped burial chamber, can be seen behind holiday bungalows.

Carn Ingli

Follow Church Street past St Mary's for the relatively easy two-hour ascent of **Carn Ingli** (Hill of Angels), once the core of an active volcano and one of Wales' holiest mountains. It gets its name from St Brynach who lived here in quiet contemplation, supposedly with angels as his companions. More certainly, stone embankments of the

Iron Age hillfort and the nearby Bronze Age hut circles prove that the hill once had a sizeable community.

ARRIVAL AND INFORMATION NEWPORT

By bus Buses stop on Bridge Street in the centre of town. The Poppit Rocket (May–Sept 3 daily; Oct–April Thurs & Sat 3 daily) runs to the Parrog and Trefdraeth beaches as well as Poppit Sands.

Destinations Cardigan (hourly; 20min); Fishguard (hourly; 15min); Haverfordwest (hourly; 1hr).

Tourist office The National Park tourist office (☎ 01239 820912, ✉ newportTIC@pembrokeshirecoast.org.uk; April–Oct

Mon–Sat 10am–5.30pm; Nov–March Mon, Wed & Fri 10.30am–1pm & 1.30–3.30pm, Sat 10.30am–1.30pm) is on Long Street and offers paid internet access.

Bike rental Carn Ingli Bike Hire, at the Carningli Centre, East Street (opposite Newport Wholefoods; ☎ 01239 820724, ⓦ carningli.co.uk), has bikes for £15/day and tagalongs for kids for £10.

ACCOMMODATION

Cnapan East St ☎ 01239 820575, ⓦ cnapan.co.uk. Five comfortable rooms and an old-fashioned friendly welcome are the hallmarks of this long-standing favourite above a great restaurant. Closed Jan–March. **£95**

The Globe Upper St Mary St ☎ 01239 820296, ⓦ theglobebedandbreakfast.co.uk. About the cheapest place around, a former pub with two rooms, shared bathroom and a pleasant garden, with continental breakfast included. **£73**

★**Llys Meddyg** East St ☎ 01239 820008, ⓦ llysmeddyg .com. Comfy-chic restaurant with rooms fashioned from a Georgian coaching inn, displaying fine local art. All rooms have great bedding, classy toiletries and individual decor. **£100**

Morawelon The Parrog ☎ 01239 820565,

ⓦ campsite-pembrokeshire.co.uk. Seaside campsite 300yd from town, nicely set in pleasant gardens and with its own café overlooking the beach, and coin-op showers. Closed Nov–Feb. **£6**/person

Y Bryn Fishguard Rd, 200yd west of town ☎ 01239 820288, ⓦ brynbedandbreakfast.co.uk. Great-value B&B with four unfussy rooms, all with private bathroom (three also have sea views); the spacious attic room is particularly appealing. A full breakfast is served and there's off-street parking. **£75**

YHA Newport Lower St Mary St ☎ 0845 371 9543, ✉ reservations@yha.org.uk. This classy conversion of an old school has dorms and a couple of private rooms. April to early Oct; self-catering only. Dorms **£15**; doubles **£75**

EATING AND DRINKING

★**Cnapan** East St ☎ 01239 820575, ⓦ cnapan.co.uk. Fresh local produce is key at this classic dinner-only restaurant, where spicy mussel chowder might be followed by guinea fowl with gooseberry and elderflower sauce. £26/32 for two/three courses. Booking essential. Mid-March to Dec daily except Tues 6.15–8.45pm (last orders).

Golden Lion East St ☎ 01239 820321, ⓦ goldenlion pembrokeshire.co.uk. Bare stone and timber-beamed pub with real ales and a superb menu of carefully prepared pub meals (£10) and fancier restaurant-style dishes (£11–21), both served either in the bar or more formally out the back. Daily noon–midnight; food served noon–2pm & 6–9pm.

Llys Meddyg East St ☎ 01239 820008, ⓦ llysmeddyg .com. A Georgian dining room, the cellar bar or the partly

walled kitchen garden (July & Aug) provide the settings for exquisite dinners, which might start with local baby crab cakes with papaya mustard (£7) then wild bass with a sweet-and-sour mushroom broth (£18). Lunches are no less appealing. April–Sept Tues–Sat noon–3pm & 6.30–9pm, Sun noon–3pm; Oct–March Wed–Sat same hours.

LouLou's Organic Café Market St ☎ 01239 820777. A handy place for excellent coffees, cakes or lunch, to eat in or take away (baguettes £5.50, flan £7.50, felafel £7); evening meals can be ordered to take home. Mon–Sat 9.30am–5pm.

Morawelon The Parrog. Waterfront café specializing in seafood, with crab and prawn sandwiches (£5–6.65) and baked crab (£16), as well as vegetable tagine (£9.50), waffles (£5) and cream teas (£4.10). April–Sept daily 9am–5pm; Oct & Dec–March Wed–Sun 10am–4pm.

Around Newport

Either side of Newport, the Coast Path runs through some sublime scenery. To the **west**, the trail edges around the protuberant Dinas Head, en route to Fishguard. Two miles west of Newport's Parrog beach, a very narrow road leads to the popular strand at **Cwm-yr-Eglwys**, where the scant seafront ruins of the twelfth-century **St Brynach's church** are all that survived a huge storm on the night of October 25, 1859, when the rest of the church and some 114 ships at sea were wrecked.

Along the coast

The three-mile walk around Dinas Head offers splendid views over the huge cliffs, where thousands of sea birds nest between May and mid-July. On the western side of the headland, accessible by car off the A487, is the grey-sand beach of **Pwllgwaelod**.

The stretch of path running **east from Newport** to the fringes of Cardigan at St Dogmael's is perhaps the wildest and toughest of the whole Coast Path: it plummets and climbs, passing rocky outcrops, blowholes, caves, natural arches, ancient defensive sites and thousands of sea birds. The only access by car is at the spectacularly folded cliffs of **Ceibwr Bay**, eight miles from Newport near the pretty pastel village of **MOYLEGROVE** (Trewyddel).

Nevern

Just over a mile east of Newport by road, but about double that by the pleasant riverside walk, the straggling village of **NEVERN** (Nanhyfer) is darkly atmospheric, with a couple of intriguing sights.

The church of St Brynach

On the B4582, in the centre of the village

The brooding bulk of the **church of St Brynach**, founded in the sixth century and with an intact Norman tower, has many features of interest. The churchyard's ancient yews give it a dank, dark presence. Note the second tree on the right, the famous "**bleeding yew**", so called for the brown-red sap that oozes mysteriously from its bark. Legend has it that it will continue to bleed until a Welsh lord of the manor is reinstated in the village castle – unlikely in the foreseeable future, given its tumbledown state. Also outside the church, just by the south transept, is the stunning **Great Cross**, an inscribed tenth-century Celtic masterpiece standing some 13ft high. Inside, two ancient inscribed stones have been built into the south transept's windowsills: the **Maglocunus Stone**, with Latin and Ogham inscriptions from about the fifth century AD, and the **Cross Stone**, marked with a very early Celtic cross.

Nevern Castle

On the north side of the village • Open access • Free

High on a bluff above the village, the ruins of the Norman **castle**, built in 1108 and abandoned in 1195, are being excavated and restored a bit; visitors are welcomed at the dig in June or July. A circular walk starts by the church gate, crosses the stream and climbs to the large motte, on top of which is the circular base of a stone keep raised in the mid-twelfth century by Rhys ap Gruffudd, who ended up imprisoned here by his own sons before the castle was burnt by them to prevent its falling into Anglo–Norman hands.

Pentre Ifan

2 miles south of Nevern • Open access • Free

The well-signposted cromlech at **Pentre Ifan** is a vast burial stone – the largest in Wales – with its 16-tonne arrowhead top-stone precariously balanced on three stone legs, and dating back over four thousand years. The views are superb, situated as it is on the cusp of the stark, eerie Mynydd Preseli with the pastoral rolls of the countryside to the east.

Castell Henllys

2 miles east of Nevern • Easter–Oct daily 10am–5pm; Nov–Easter Mon–Fri 11am–3pm • Easter–Oct £4.75 ; Nov–Easter £4 • Guided tours (1hr; free) April–Oct 11.30am & 2.30pm • ☎ 01239 891319, ⓦ castellhenllys.com

Signposted off the A487, excavations of the Iron Age hillfort of **Castell Henllys** are turning up more and more of its past. Four roundhouses and a granary, complete with thatch, have been reconstructed on their two thousand-year-old foundations, and throughout the summer the National Park lays on opportunities to watch ancient skills and learn what Iron Age life was like here. Children's activities during school holidays (£2.50 for 1hr 30min; book ahead) give kids a chance to try wool dyeing and basket making or train as a warrior. A sculpture trail through the woods and river valley brings to life the tales of *The Mabinogion*, and further trails lead into the ancient oak woodlands of the adjacent Pengelli Forest. Guided tours come with a strong environmental message, looking at land usage, wood management and conservation.

2 Cwm Gwaun and the inland hills

Cwm Gwaun, the valley of the burbling River Gwaun, is one of the great surprises of Pembrokeshire – a bucolic vale of impossibly narrow lanes, surrounded by the bleak shoulders of bare mountains. It is a timeless place whose residents retain an attachment to the pre-1752 Julian calendar, celebrating New Year on January 13.

Llanychaer

The B4313 heads two miles southeast from Fishguard to tiny **LLANYCHAER** where, opposite the *Bridge End Inn*, a lane runs almost half a mile steeply uphill to the **church** and "**cursing**" **well** of the lost settlement of **Llanllawer**. The well had a pre-Christian reputation for cementing curses and ill omens if you left a bent pin, although most pilgrims sought miraculous cures, particularly for eye conditions. The lane running east opposite the well and church leads to seven large standing stones – the longest megalithic alignment in Wales – in **Parc y Merw** (the Field of the Dead), just short of Trellwyn Farm.

Back on the B4313, nearly a mile beyond Llanychaer, a lane branches left and drops down into Cwm Gwaun, soon crossing the river near a picnic site from where there are some good walks up into the old oak forests lining the valley.

Pontfaen

Three miles off the B4313 you reach the scattered settlement of **PONTFAEN**, complete with its time-warped pub, the rustic and remote *Dyffryn Arms* (see below). By turning sharp right before the pub and following the lane across the river and up a sharp hill for a quarter of a mile, you'll reach Pontfaen's exquisitely restored **church** (open daily), dedicated, like so many round here, to St Brynach. The circular graveyard indicates pre-Christian origins before the church was founded, according to tradition, by the wandering Breton saint in 540 AD. In the graveyard are two impressive but very worn stone crosses, dating from between the sixth and ninth centuries.

Gerddi Penlan-Uchaf

2 miles northeast of Pontfaen • March–Nov daily 9am–dusk • £3 • ☎ 01348 881388, ⓦ penlan-uchaf.co.uk

Well tucked away, the delightful **Gerddi Penlan-Uchaf** is a set of hillside **gardens** cut through by a stream with wonderful views over the valley. They contain thousands of miniature flowering and alpine plants, and acres of herbs and wild flowers together with some impressive dwarf conifers. You can also buy their Carn Edward lamb and longhorn beef.

ACCOMMODATION AND DRINKING   CWM GWAUN AND THE INLAND HILLS

★**Dyffryn Arms** Pontfaen ☎ 01348 881305. Known as *Bessie's* after its aged proprietor, you can enjoy good company here in an old-fashioned living room. There's a small beer garden, or you can take your drinks into the riverside field across the road. No fixed hours, but usually open all day.

Erw-Lon Farm B4313 between Pontfaen and Rosebush ☎ 01348 881297, ⓦ erwlonfarm.co.uk. Welcoming B&B in an area where accommodation is limited; three

comfortable en-suite rooms, lounge, and a garden with huge views. **£70**

Gwaun Valley Brewery Kilkiffieth Farm, Pontfaen, on the B4313 5 miles from Fishguard ☎ 01348 881304, ⓦ gwaunvalleybrewery.co.uk. Friendly microbrewery with a simple all-year campsite. Daily: March–Oct 10am–6pm; Nov–Feb noon–4pm; evenings on request, acoustic music sessions Sat 7–10pm; **£5**/pitch

Rosebush

As you head east, the brooding nature of the Mynydd Preseli makes itself most apparent. This is bleak, invigorating countryside, the wild, open hills scattered with the relics of ancient civilizations. The characteristic **Preseli bluestone**, which was used between 2000 and 1500 BC to construct Stonehenge, some 140 miles away, came from these slopes.

Slate is also found hereabouts, and was quarried until 1905 near the weird little village of **ROSEBUSH**, just off the B4313 around ten miles southeast of Fishguard. The Klondike atmosphere of the place is partially explained by the fact that it was built quickly as a would-be resort following the arrival of the railway in 1876.

Foel Cwmcerwyn

A good hike leads from Rosebush along the eastern edge of the coniferous Pantmaenog Forest to the 1760ft summit of **Foel Cwmcerwyn** (4 miles return; 2hr; 800ft ascent), the highest point in Pembrokeshire. Topped by a Bronze Age cairn, the rounded hill sits above **Craig y Cwm**, the most recently glaciated valley (c8000 BC) in the area.

ARRIVAL AND DEPARTURE	ROSEBUSH
By bus Services are sparse here: bus #344 runs from Fishguard to Haverfordwest on Tues; the #345 runs from Crymych to Fishguard on Thurs; and the #432 runs from	Crymych to Haverfordwest on Fri (passing through Maenclochog, just south of Rosebush), all heading in to town in the morning and returning in the afternoon.

ACCOMMODATION AND EATING	
Rosebush Caravan Park Y Bwthyn ☎ 01437 532206. This well-maintained, adults-only lakeside site welcomes campers, caravans and motorhomes. Closed Nov to mid-March. **£10**/pitch	ⓦ tafarnsinc.co.uk. A large red corrugated-iron shack houses the wood-panelled bar, a good spot for a pint and a meal (£8–11) in the garden on a fine day. Tues–Sun noon–11pm; food served Tues–Sat noon–2pm & 6–9pm, Sun noon–2pm.
Tafarn Sinc ("Zinc Tavern") Y Bwthyn ☎ 01437 532214,	

The Golden Road

The main range of the Preselis lies just northeast of the village, crossed by an ancient track, in use for at least 3500 years, known as the **Golden Road**. A hike (8 miles one way; 4–5hr; 1000ft ascent) taking in the best section runs due north out of Rosebush past the old slate quarries through Pantmaenog Forest and up onto the Golden Road.

Turn right to reach many of the Preselis' cairns and ancient sites, such as **Beddarthur**, an eerie stone circle that is supposed to be the great king's burial place, **Carn Menyn**, probably the quarry from which most of the Stonehenge bluestones were cut, and **Foeldrygarn** ("the Hill of Three Cairns"), with its hugely impressive Iron Age ramparts and hut circles. Public transport is of little use, so plan for a full day out and hike both ways: the perspective is quite different on the way back.

The Brecon Beacons and Powys

SUGAR LOAF, NEAR ABERGAVENNY

The Brecon Beacons and Powys

The vast inland county of Powys takes up a full quarter of Wales. Often traversed quickly en route to the coast, it's well worth exploring in its own right. The most popular area is the Brecon Beacons National Park at the county's southern end, an area of moody heights, wild, rambling moors and thundering waterfalls. The main centres within the Beacons are Wales' culinary capital, Abergavenny, in the far southeast, and Brecon. The bleaker part of the Beacons lies to the west, around the raw peaks of the Black Mountain (Mynydd Ddu) and Fforest Fawr geopark, and includes the immense Dan-yr-ogof caves and the mighty waterfalls around Ystradfellte. Architecturally charming towns such as Crickhowell and Talgarth, set in quiet river valleys, also make good bases for walkers. At the northern corner of the national park, the border town of Hay-on-Wye is famous for its dozens of secondhand bookshops and attracts thousands to its annual literary festival.

3

Northwest of Hay lie the old spa towns of Radnorshire and Brecknockshire, namely **Llanwrtyd Wells**, **Llandrindod Wells** and the largest, **Builth Wells**. Crossed by spectacular mountain roads such as the **Abergwesyn Pass** from Llanwrtyd, the countryside to the north is supremely beautiful, dotted with ancient churches and remote hill-farming hamlets, from the lively border communities of **Presteigne** and **Knighton** to inland centres like **Rhayader**, the nearest centre of population for the grandiose reservoirs of the **Elan Valley**.

The northern portion of Powys, **Montgomeryshire**, is as sparsely populated and remote as its two southern siblings. In common with most of mid-Wales, country towns here, such as **Llanidloes**, have a sizeable stock of New Age health-food shops, healing groups and arts activity. To the west, the inhospitable mountain of **Plynlimon** is flecked with boggy heathland and gloomy reservoirs, beyond which the hearty town of Machynlleth (covered in Chapter 4) sits out on a limb of Powys. The eastern side of Montgomeryshire is home to the anglicized old county town, **Montgomery**, between the robust towns of **Welshpool** and **Newtown**. The northern segment of the county is even quieter, with the only crowds being found along the banks of **Lake Vyrnwy**, a flooded-valley reservoir.

BOOK SHOPPING AT HAY-ON-WYE

Highlights

❶ Brecon Beacons There are some terrific hikes to be had through these frequently glorious mountains, while the park itself is now an acclaimed stargazing site. **See p.201**

❷ Ystradfellte waterfalls Explore the trio of great waterfalls in the limestone country around Ystradfellte. **See p.204**

❸ Glasbury Canoe downstream along the tranquil River Wye to Hay. **See p.213**

❹ Abergavenny Enjoy locally sourced Welsh cuisine from some of the country's finest chefs at Abergavenny's restaurants or dine at its prestigious food festival. **See p.218**

❺ Hay-on-Wye Browse millions of secondhand books at over thirty bookshops in this bibliophile's paradise or just dive into the world-famous festival itself. **See p.223**

❻ Llanwrtyd Wells Get your festival fix at the home of Welsh wacky events, such as the Man versus Horse Marathon or the Real Ale Wobble. **See p.225**

❼ Offa's Dyke A walk along this massive earthwork, through the ever-changing borderlands, is one of Wales' most rewarding. **See p.239**

❽ Powis Castle While undoubtedly one of the country's most sumptuous castles, the real glory of Powis is its stunning gardens. **See p.248**

HIGHLIGHTS ARE MARKED ON THE MAP ON P.200

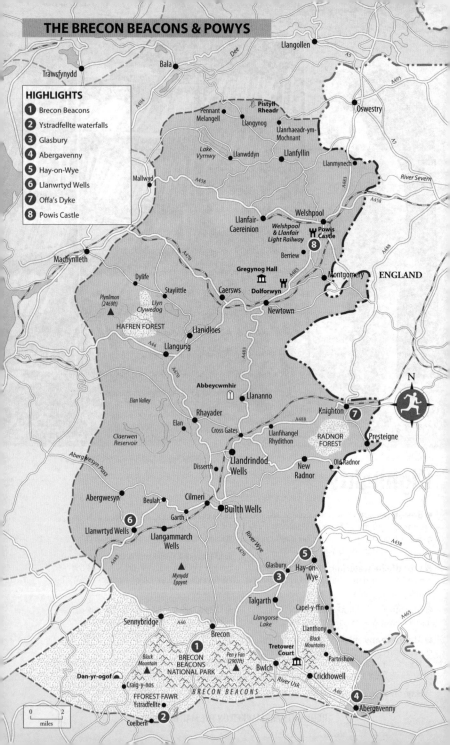

By train Services are restricted to the Heart of Wales line from Shropshire to Swansea via Knighton, Llandrindod Wells, Llanwrtyd Wells and smaller stops in between, and the Shrewsbury–Machynlleth route through Welshpool and Newtown.

By bus Many larger centres such as Brecon, Llanidloes, Rhayader, Builth Wells and Hay-on-Wye rely on sporadic bus services, although most places can be reached via a handful of daily services. One of the most useful long-distance buses is the T4, which runs from Cardiff up to Newtown, calling in at Brecon, Builth Wells, Llandrindod on the way up, though there's no service on Sundays.

Brecon Beacons National Park

With the lowest profile of Wales's three national parks, the **Brecon Beacons** are refreshingly uncrowded, primarily attracting local urban walkers. Spongy hills of grass and rock tumble and climb around river valleys peppered with glass-like lakes and villages that seem to have been hewn from one rock. Known for the vivid quality of their light, the hills of the Beacons disappear and re-emerge from hazy blankets of cloud, with shafts of sun sharpening the lush green patchwork of fields.

Covering 520 square miles, the national park straddles southern Powys and northern Monmouthshire from west to east. The most remote parts are around the **Black Mountain** peaks to the west, with miles of tufted moorland and bleak, often dangerous, summits, plummeting to the porous limestone country in the southwestern section, a rocky terrain of rivers, deep caves and spluttering waterfalls. To the northeast, the lonely **Black Mountains** (not to be confused with the entirely separate Black Mountain to the west) are separated from the Beacons themselves by the Monmouthshire and **Brecon Canal**, which forges a passage along the Usk Valley. Built around the beginning of the nineteenth century to support coal mining, iron ore and limestone quarrying, the canal is an impressive feat of engineering, successfully steering a 25-mile lock-free stretch (Britain's longest) through some of the most mountainous terrain in Wales.

In 2013, the park was granted **International Dark Sky Reserve** status, the first in Wales and one of only seven in the world. The park has become a major destination for stargazers, while regular events are organized by the park authorities.

By train Abergavenny is the only town with a train station, though Merthyr Tydfil, on the southern flank of the park, is well connected by rail to Cardiff.

By bus With relatively frequent services (often 4–6 daily) along the major routes, buses are a much better bet than trains; a smattering of services only run on certain days. The main routes are from Brecon to Crickhowell and Abergavenny (#X43); Brecon to Talgarth, Hay-on-Wye and Hereford (#39); and Brecon to Swansea via Sennybridge, the Dan-yr-ogof Showcaves, Craig-y-nos and Ystradgynlais (#X63). On Sundays (and bank holidays) between the end of May until the end of September, there's a bike bus (#B1), which runs from Cardiff to Brecon, enabling you to bus it here (£5), explore some of the park and then cycle back down the Taff Trail (p.208).

By bike The relatively compact nature of the region, the profusion of narrow lanes and the many opportunities to get off-road make this a great place to travel by bike: rental locations include Brecon, Abergavenny and Hay-on-Wye.

By car If you don't have your own car – which is by far the best way to get the most out of this part of Wales – then you might consider an innovative new scheme run by Eco Travel Network (🆆 ecotravelnetwork.co.uk), which offers

---

ACCOMMODATION IN THE BRECON BEACONS

The Brecon Beacons offers plenty of diffuse **accommodation**, including low-budget options; 🆆 breconbeacons.org/stay covers all kinds of accommodation, including B&Bs, hostels, bunkhouses and campsites, while there's a comprehensive list of bunkhouses at 🆆 brecon-beacon.com/bunkhouses – most charge £10–15 a night. If you're interested in self-catering accommodation, the best companies locally are Brecon Beacons Holiday Cottages (🆆 breconcottages.com) and the Abergavenny Farm Holidays Group (🆆 afhg.co.uk).

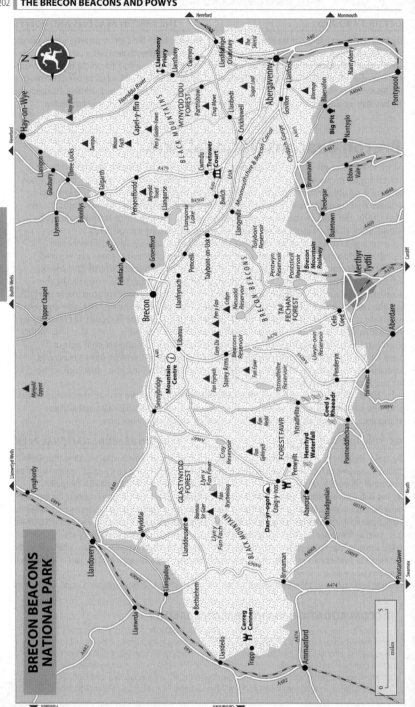

BRECON BEACONS NATIONAL PARK

two-seater, electric "Twizy" cars, which you can rent for between one day and a week from seven locations in the Brecon Beacons.

By horse Horseriding here is also extremely popular and well organized; see the listings throughout this chapter or visit ⓦ horseridingbreconbeacons.com.

The western Beacons

The **western Beacons** comprises the bleak uplands of Black Mountain and Fforest Fawr, and the sparsely populated valleys in between. It is evident everywhere that this is limestone country: caves, sinkholes and waterfalls dot the map. From the valleys, invigorating walks or bike rides thread up to the lonely moors for sweeping views across the mountains.

Black Mountain

The most westerly expanse of upland in the national park is known as the **Black Mountain** (Mynydd Ddu). Despite being named in the singular (as distinct from the Black Mountains further east), the "mountain" actually covers an unpopulated range of barren, smooth-humped peaks that break suddenly at rocky escarpments towering over quiet streams and glacial lakes.

The area provides the most challenging and exhilarating walking in south Wales. Paths cross the wet, wild landscape from Dan-yr-ogof in the east, and from the soaring ruins of Carreg Cennen Castle, just short of Llandeilo in the west. Other good starting points for forays into the open Black Mountain uplands are Tyhwnt, near Ystradgynlais, in the south and, in the north, the hamlet of Llanddeusant, seven miles south of Llandovery.

ACCOMMODATION   **BLACK MOUNTAIN**

YHA Llanddeusant ⓣ 0845 371 9750, ⓦ yha.org.uk. A cosy hostel in the former village pub, with four-, six- and eight-bed dorms as well as family rooms. You can camp here too (Easter–Sept), with full access to all the hostel's facilities. Closed Nov–Jan. Camping **£10**/pitch, dorms **£17**

Fforest Fawr

Covering a vast expanse of hilly landscape between the Black Mountain and the central Beacons southwest of Brecon, **Fforest Fawr** (Great Forest) seems something of a misnomer for an area of largely unforested sandstone hills dropping down to a porous limestone belt in the south. The "forest" tag refers more to the old definition of a forest as land used as a hunting ground. In 2005, Fforest Fawr was recognized – and is now subsequently administered – by UNESCO as a geopark, becoming part of the Europe-wide network of other geoparks.

The hills rise up to the south of the A40 west of Brecon, with the dramatic A4067 Sennybridge–Ystradgynlais road scoring the western side of the range and the A470 Brecon–Merthyr road defining the Fforest's eastern limit.

A WALK AROUND LLANDDEUSANT

The OS Explorer 1:25,000 Explorer map OL12 (Brecon Beacons – Western & Central Area) is recommended.

Passing both Llyn y Fan Fach and Llyn y Fan Fawr, this bleak and lonely ascent weaves through classic post-glacial scenery: valleys slashed with tumbling streams cut between purple hills, while occasional mounds and moraines of rock debris indicate the force of the ice that pushed through the valleys. Such heaps sometimes grew to a size large enough to form a natural dam, building up lakes, such as Llyn y Fan Fach, in their wake.

The walk (12 miles; 4–5hr; 1400ft ascent) starts in Llanddeusant and climbs steeply to Llyn y Fan Fach, from where a precarious path leads around the top of the escarpment, following the ridge to **Fan Brycheiniog** (2630ft), above the glassy black waters of Llyn y Fan Fawr. Return the same way.

Dan-yr-ogof Showcaves

Just west of A4067 • April–Oct daily 10am–3.30pm • £13.75 • ☎ 01639 730284, ⓦ showcaves.co.uk

The upper reaches of the Afon Tawe, Swansea's river, mark the limestone belt, as seen in the hamlet of **GLYNTAWE** at the **Dan-yr-ogof Showcaves**. Discovered by two local farmers in 1912, and opened to the public in 1939, it's claimed the caves form the largest system of subterranean caverns in northern Europe.

In a self-guided tour, with commentary resonating from loudspeakers, the path first leads you into the **Dan-yr-ogof** cave, the longest showcave in Britain, and a warren of caverns framed by stalactites and frothy limestone deposits. Although the whole cave is known to be around ten miles long, you'll be steered around a circular route of about a mile and a half. Back outside, you pass a re-created Iron Age "village" and walk past some of the many life-size fibreglass dinosaurs sprinkled around the site to reach **Cathedral Cave**, a succession of spookily lit caverns leading into the "cathedral" itself, a hugely impressive 150ft-long, 70ft-high cave inside of which are two 20m high waterfalls.

Reachable via a precarious path behind the dinosaur park is **Bone Cave**, the third and final cavern, known to have been inhabited by Bronze Age tribes, with some 42 human (and many animal) skeletons found here. There's plenty more to see and do here, especially for kids, including a museum, shire horse centre, playground and farm.

Craig-y-nos Castle

400yd south of Dan-yr-ogof Showcaves • ☎ 01639 730205, ⓦ craigynoscastle.com • Free self-guided tour of ground floor; historian led-tours £10 (on request, but book in advance)

The nineteenth-century **Craig-y-nos Castle** is a grand folly built in 1842 and fancifully extended from 1878, when it was bought by Adelina Patti, the celebrated Italian–American opera singer. In her forty years of residence, she turned the place into a diva-esque castle, even adding a scaled-down version of the Drury Lane opera house for performances. After Patti's reign, Craig-y-nos suffered decades of chronic neglect, until it was bought in the mid-1990s, renovated and turned into an oddball **hotel** and entertainment venue. The Grade I listed opera house, which was once used as a hospital, still stages the occasional concert.

Some 44 acres of the castle's grounds form part of the Brecon Beacons National Park and operate as **Craig-y-nos Country Park** (unrestricted access). From the car park, there are signposted walks around a landscaped site along the banks of the young River Tawe.

Ystradfellte

A wonderful, twisting mountain road between Pontneddfechan to the south and the A4067 crosses the Fforest Fawr and drops down into the valley of the Afon Llia and the limestone crags around the hamlet of **YSTRADFELLTE**. Little more than a handful of houses, a church and a pub, this is, nonetheless, a phenomenally popular centre for walking, as a result of the dazzling countryside on its doorstep. Lush, deep ravines – a total contrast to the barren mountains immediately to the north – carve through the limestone ridge south of the village, with great pavements of bone-white rock littering fields next to cradling potholes, disappearing rivers and thundering waterfalls.

The River Mellte waterfalls

A mile south of Ystradfellte, the River Mellte tumbles into the dark and icy mouth of the **Porth-yr-ogof** cave, emerging into daylight a few hundred yards further south. A signposted path heads south from the Porth-yr-ogof car park and into the green gorge of the River Mellte. Continue for little more than a mile to the first of its three great waterfalls, **Sgwd Clun-Gwyn** (White Meadow Fall), where the river crashes 50ft over two huge, angular steps of rock before hurtling down course for a few hundred yards to the other two falls, the graceful **Sgwd Isaf Clun-Gwyn** (Lower White Meadow Fall) and, a little further on, the mighty **Sgwd y Pannwr** (Fall of the Fuller).

The path continues through the foliage to the confluence of the rivers Mellte and Hepste, half a mile further on. A quarter of a mile along the Hepste is arguably the most impressive of the area's falls, the **Sgwd yr Eira** (Fall of Snow), where the rock below the main tumble has eroded back 6ft, allowing people to walk directly behind a dramatic 20ft curtain of water – particularly dazzling in afternoon or evening light.

Pontneddfechan waterfalls

Just off the A465 along the forested valley of the River Nedd (or Neath), near the village of **PONTNEDDFECHAN**, are some spectacular waterfalls. The most famous of these is the **Sgwd Gwladus** (The Lady Falls), an easyish mile's walk along the river from Pontneddfechan, which, like Sgwd yr Eira, overhangs enough to allow you to walk behind. A few hundred yards further, though accessible only via stepping stones and a bit of a scramble that can be tricky after heavy rain, is perhaps the best of all, the sublime **Sgwd Einion Gam** (The Fall of Crooked Einion).

Penderyn Welsh Whisky Distillery

Pontpren • Daily 9.30am–5pm • Tours £6, pre-booking advised • ☎ 01685 813300, ⓦ welsh-whisky.co.uk

Four miles east of Pontneddfechan in the village of **PENDERYN** is the **Penderyn Welsh Whisky Distillery**. When it opened in 2000, Penderyn became Wales's first working distillery for more than one hundred years, and today it produces three single malt whiskies, matured in bourbon barrels and finished in Madeira wine casks. Hour-long **guided tours** of the centre take in an exhibition on the working of the distillery, an explanation of the distillation and bottling processes, and, of course, a little taster at the end. Uniquely, the process here at Penderyn involves the use of a single copper pot still – as opposed to the conventional two or three – before the whisky is matured for between four and seven years. The distillery also produces a Brecon gin, vodka and cream liqueur.

INFORMATION	FFOREST FAWR
Tourist information The Waterfalls Centre in the centre of Pontneddfechan (Easter–Sept daily 9.30am–1pm, 1.30–5pm; Oct–Easter Sat & Sun 9.30am–3pm;	☎ 01639 721795) can provide lots of good information on walks to the many falls. There's also an exhibition on the Fforest Fawr geopark.

ACCOMMODATION AND EATING

Changing Seasons Above the car park next to Craig-y-nos Castle ☎ 07535 488009. This lovely tea room and restaurant keeps local walkers satisfied with its selection of home-made pies and pasties, cakes and ice cream. There's lots of seasonal and organic produce to buy, too. Mon–Thurs & Sun 10am–6pm, Fri & Sat 10am–10.30pm.	**Craig-y-nos Castle** 400yd south of Dan-yr-ogof Showcaves ☎ 01639 730284, ⓦ craigynoscastle.com. Various blocks and rooms within the castle have been converted into a whole range of high-class rooms and apartments sleeping two to four people, with quite a few family rooms. **£125**

The central Beacons

The **central Brecon Beacons** – after which the whole national park is named – are well set up for walking and pony trekking. The area, to the immediate south of Brecon town, centres on the two highest peaks in south Wales, **Pen y Fan** (2907ft) and **Corn Du** (2863ft), half a mile to the west. Although neither reaches 3000ft, the terrain is unmistakably and dramatically mountainous: classic old red sandstone country with sweeping peaks rising out of glacially carved land.

The combined ascent of **Pen y Fan** and **Corn Du** is the most popular walk in the park. The most direct route up is the well-trampled red-mud path that starts from Pont ar Daf, half a mile south of Storey Arms on the A470, midway between Brecon and Merthyr Tydfil. The ascent is a comparatively easy five-mile round trip, gradually climbing up the southern flank of the two peaks. A longer and generally quieter

---

A CIRCULAR WALK AROUND CORN DU AND PEN Y FAN

The OS Explorer 1:25,000 Explorer map OL12 (Brecon Beacons West & Central) is recommended.
Few walkers visiting the Brecon Beacons for the first time can resist making an ascent of the two highest peaks: Corn Du and Pen y Fan. Most take one of the shorter routes from the A470 south of Brecon, but connoisseurs prefer this longer and infinitely more rewarding circular "**Gap**" **route** (8 miles; 4–5hr; 1400ft ascent) that makes an anticlockwise circuit around a ridge-top horseshoe of the Beacons.

The hike starts at the car park by the late Victorian Neuadd reservoirs and crosses the dam of the lower, smaller reservoir, then climbs westwards up the hill in front. Head right (north) along a well-defined path along the ridge top including Graig Fan Ddu. Follow the obvious path that strikes up the sandstone ridge to the first summit, then down to a shallow saddle and up again to the peak of Pen y Fan, the highest point in south Wales. Either carry on to the next summit, Cribyn, and then descend to the Gap, or turn right by the stream in the valley between Pen y Fan and Cribyn, around the base of Cribyn and then back to the Neuadd reservoirs.

3

route leads up to the two peaks from the "Gap" route (see box above) – the pre-nineteenth-century (and possibly Roman) main road winding north from the Neuadd reservoirs through the only natural break in the central Beacons' sandstone ridge to the bottom of the lane. The route eventually joins the main street in the Brecon suburb of Llanfaes as Bailihelig Road. Although the old road is no longer accessible for cars, car parks at either end open out onto the track for an eight-mile round-trip ascent up Pen y Fan and Corn Du from the east.

Brecon and around

The handsome Georgian buildings of **BRECON** (Aberhonddu) stand at the northern edge of the Beacons, bearing testimony to the town's past importance. A Roman fort was built near here, but the town only started to grow with the building of a Norman castle and Benedictine monastery, founded in 1093 on the banks of the Honddu River, which gives the town its Welsh name. To the dual strands of military and ecclesiastical importance was added the status of regional market centre and cloth-weaving town. In the seventeenth-century Civil War, the townsfolk demonstrated their neutrality between the forces of Parliament and the Crown by demolishing most of the castle and large sections of the town walls, dissipating the appeal for either side of seizing their town. Today, it's a lively base for walkers and less active visitors alike, with good accommodation, and plenty of places to eat and drink.

Brecon's imposing central square, at the western end of **The Bulwark**, is flanked by the solid, red sixteenth-century tower of **St Mary's church**, an assortment of old-fashioned shop frontages and the elegant Georgian portico of the **Wellington Hotel**. The grid of streets north and west of The Bulwark is packed with some delightful Georgian and Victorian buildings. Northwest, at the crossroads of High Street Inferior, Ship Street descends down to the **River Usk**, the bridge crossing the Usk next to the point where the smaller Honddu River flows in from the north.

Brecknock Museum

Captain's Walk • Mon–Fri 10am–5pm, Sat 10am–1pm & 2–5pm • £1 • ☎ 01874 624121

At the junction of The Bulwark and Glamorgan Street is the neo-Grecian frontage of the **Brecknock Museum**, though it's currently closed pending major renovation works and is not expected to open before 2016 at the earliest. When it does re-open, expect to see comprehensive galleries on town and rural life, an archeology section featuring inscribed stones dating back to the fifth century and a selection of painstakingly carved Welsh love spoons – some over four hundred years old – that were betrothal gifts for courting Welsh lovers. The prize exhibit, however, is a remarkably well-preserved,

15ft-long *crannog* (log boat or dug-out canoe), dredged up from Llangorse Lake in 1925 and reckoned to date from around 760 AD. There's also a nineteenth-century assize court, last used in 1971 and preserved in all its ponderous splendour, overseen by the high judge's throne.

Regimental Museum

The Watton • Easter–Sept Mon–Fri 10am–5pm, Sat 10am–4pm, plus certain Sun's; Oct–March Mon–Fri 10am–5pm • £5 • ☎ 01874 613310, ⓦ rrw.org.uk

Beyond the foreboding frontage of the South Wales Borderers' **barracks** is its **Regimental Museum**, packed with mementos from the regiment's three-hundred-year existence. As well as an extraordinary stache of guns and medals, there's coverage of campaigns in Burma, the Napoleonic and Boer Wars, both World Wars and more recent wars in Iraq and Afghanistan. Most absorbing, though, are the tales of the 1879 Zulu War when 140 Welsh soldiers faced an attack by four thousand Zulu warriors at Rorke's Drift; more Victoria Crosses (eleven) were awarded in the aftermath of that one battle, the most ever received in a single action by one regiment, before or since. There's even a piece of the Berlin Wall here.

Brecon Cathedral

Cathedral Close, Priory Hill • Daily 8.30am–6pm • Free • ☎ 01874 623857, ⓦ breconcathedral.org.uk

Over the rushing waters of the Honddu, Priory Hill climbs up to the stark grey buildings of the monastery settlement, centred on the **cathedral**, or Priory Church of St John the Baptist. Its surprisingly lofty interior, framed by a magnificent timber roof, is graced with a few Norman features intact from the eleventh-century priory that was built here on the site of a probable earlier Celtic church. The hulking Norman font sits at the western end of the nave, near the entrance, as does the

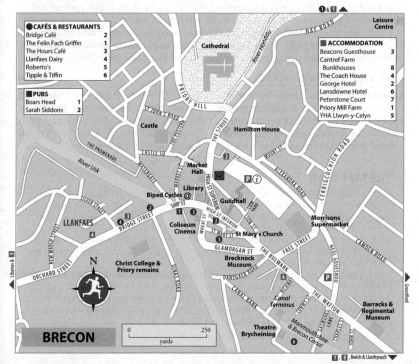

unusual **Cresset Stone**, a large boulder indented with thirty scoops in which to place oil or wax candles; it's thought to be the last remaining one in the country. From here the south aisle runs down to the most interesting of the many family memorials, the **Games monument** (1555), made up from three oak beds and depicting an unknown woman whose hands remain intact in prayer, but whose arms and nose have been unceremoniously hacked off.

Architecturally, the most impressive aspect of the cathedral is the Early English-style **chancel**, distinguished by three long, high windows extending up to the superb vaulted ceiling; no less striking is the relatively modern, stone carved reredos (1936), depicting the Crucifixion, other biblical scenes and Welsh saints. Lunchtime recitals take place each Monday at 1pm.

Heritage Centre

Cathedral Close, opposite the cathedral • Daily: April–Oct 10.30am–4.30pm; Nov–March Mon–Sat noon–4pm • Free • 🕿 01874 625222

A converted seventeenth-century tithe barn houses the cathedral's **heritage centre**, holding a small and intermittently interesting collection of gilded vestments, Bibles, crucifixes and the like. The star piece, though, is an oversized chair believed to have been used by King Charles I when he stayed at Priory House in 1645. The attached *Pilgrims* tearoom is extremely popular.

Brecon Beacons Mountain Centre

6 miles southwest of Brecon, off A470 (turn off at Libanus) • Daily: March–June & Sept–Oct 9.30am–5pm; July & Aug 9.30am–5.30pm; Nov–Feb 9.30am–4.30pm • Free • 🕿 01874 623366, 🌐 breconbeacons.org • The T4 bus from Brecon stops in Libanus, from where it's a 25min uphill walk (follow the signs) along the lane to the centre

Scenically placed outside town is the National Park Visitor Centre, also known as the **Brecon Beacons Mountain Centre**. It's chiefly useful for its well-stocked shop of maps, books and guides. There are also interesting displays on the flora, fauna, geology and history of the area, as well as an excellent café serving hot meals. You can walk straight out from the door onto Mynydd Illtud Common, laced with gentle paths looking across to some major peaks. Staff here can give experienced hikers details of walks tackling the more challenging peaks of Corn Du and Pen y Fan (see p.206).

ARRIVAL AND GETTING AROUND   BRECON

By bus Buses stop above the car park on Heol Gouesnou. Destinations Aberdulais (6 daily; 1hr 15min); Abergavenny (hourly Mon–Sat; 40min–1hr); Builth Wells (7 daily Mon–Sat; 45min); Cardiff (6 daily; 1hr 40min); Craig-y-nos/Dan-yr-ogof (7 daily; 40min); Crickhowell (hourly Mon–Sat; 25–45min); Hay-on-Wye (6 daily; 45min); Libanus (every 30–60min; 15min); Llandrindod Wells (7 daily Mon–Sat; 1hr); Merthyr Tydfil (hourly; 40min); Sennybridge (9 daily; 15min); Swansea (5 daily; 1hr 40min); Talgarth (7 daily; 25min); Talybont (7 daily Mon–Sat; 20min).

THE TAFF TRAIL

Running from Brecon to Cardiff Bay, the 55-mile **Taff Trail** (🌐 tafftrail.org) passes through a spectacular cross section of south Wales scenery: the Usk Valley, the Brecon Beacons uplands, the former coal-mining Taff Valley and urban parkland. Most of the route – which is open to hikers and bikers – is on forest trails, designated pathways and country lanes and is seldom steep. Pubs and restaurants along the way are marked on the free Taff Trail map, available from tourist offices and park information centres, which also shows the location of train stations and the occasional trail-side campsite.

Perhaps the best way to tackle the whole trail is to start in Brecon (where there's bike rental), ride to Cardiff – downhill much of the way – then catch a train back to Merthyr Tydfil and ride the fifteen miles back over the hills to Brecon. Keen riders could do this in a day, though you might prefer to break the journey in Pontypridd or Cardiff. You can also take the Beacons Bus Cardiff bike service to Cardiff and ride back (see p.201).

By bike Bikes for all ages and levels can be rented for around £20 a day at Bikes & Hikes, Lion Yard (daily 9am–5pm; ☎ 01874 610071, ⓦ bikesandhikes.co.uk) and Biped Cycles, 10 Ship Street (Mon–Sat 9am–5.30pm; ☎ 01874 622296, ⓦ bipedcycles.co.uk).

INFORMATION AND TOURS

Tourist information The TIC is in the large car park off Lion Street (Mon–Fri 9.30am–5.30pm, Sat & Sun 10am–4pm; ☎ 01874 622485, ⓦ breconbeacons.org). Its vast stock of material includes a comprehensive range of walking maps for the Brecons.

Internet At the TIC (£1 for 15min) and free at the town library on Ship Street (Mon & Wed–Fri 9.30am–5pm, Tues 9.30am–7pm, Sat 9.30am–1pm).

Canal cruises A series of colourful terraced streets runs down to the town's theatre and the northern terminus of the Monmouthshire and Brecon Canal, where afternoon cruises aboard the *Dragonfly* (March–Oct daily 12pm, plus 3pm July & Aug; £7.50; ☎ 07831 685222, ⓦ dragonfly-cruises.co.uk) ease their way out of town for enjoyably relaxed two-and-a-half-hour trips. Inside the old tollhouse at the same spot, Beacon Park Day Boats (canoe £20/half day, boat £40/half day; ☎ 0800 612 2890, ⓦ beaconparkdayboats.co.uk) has six- and eight-seat boats and three-seat canoes to rent.

ACCOMMODATION

Ample accommodation to suit all pockets exists in Brecon's compact town centre, while the suburb of **Llanfaes**, across the river from the main town, has a handful of smaller hotels and B&Bs on its main street. There's also a decent stock of hostel-style accommodation around the fringes of town. Places get booked up months in advance for the August **jazz festival**.

HOTELS AND GUESTHOUSES

Beacons Guesthouse 16 Bridge St, Llanfaes ☎ 01874 623339, ⓦ thebreconbeacons.co.uk. Converted town house concealing a large number of pinky-beige coloured rooms (some with shared showers), all leading off a central spiral staircase. Pleasant guest lounge and a dinky cellar bar with just two tables. **£60**

The Coach House 12/13 Orchard St, Llanfaes ☎ 01874 620043, ⓦ coachhousebrecon.com. High-class and very hospitable guesthouse with up-to-the-mark rooms painted in smooth creams and browns and furnished with designer lamps, mirrors and suchlike. Delicious Welsh breakfasts including vegetarian options. Staff can organize transport for walkers. **£80**

George Hotel George St ☎ 01874 623421, ⓦ george -hotel.com. The building itself is the most appealing thing about this centrally located seventeenth-century hotel, though the rooms (some with four-poster) are perfectly acceptable, if somewhat dowdily furnished. **£80**

Lansdowne Hotel 39 The Watton ☎ 01874 623321, ⓦ lansdownehotel.co.uk. Pleasantly old-fashioned hotel in a handsome Georgian corner house, offering nine smallish en-suite rooms, including some for families, but they are pretty much the cheapest in town. **£65**

Peterstone Court Llanhamlach, 3.3 miles east of Brecon ☎ 01874 665387, ⓦ peterstone-court.com. Historic country manor set in lush countryside, blending antique and contemporary furnishings. The rooms in the annexed stables are even more lavish and big enough to swing an elephant. There are also spa facilities, a swimming pool and a good restaurant. **£145**

HOSTEL, BUNKHOUSE AND CAMPING

Cantref Farm Bunkhouses Cantref Pony Trekking Centre, four miles southeast of Brecon off A40 ☎ 01874 665223, ⓦ cantref.com. Dormitory-style accommodation with rooms in two large stone farm buildings, both with kitchen, lounge and showers; minimum two-night stay on weekends. There's camping space too, with a separate shower block. Dorms **£15**; **£10**/person

Priory Mill Farm Hay Rd ☎ 01874 611609, ⓦ priorymillfarm.co.uk. Lovely, low-key riverside campsite, with wooden cabins for showers and trays for log fires. With some lovely wildlife hereabouts, there's a good chance of seeing herons and kingfishers on the river. It's on the northern edge of town, reached by a 10min walk along the riverbank. Open March–Oct. Pitches **£8**

YHA Llwyn-y-Celyn 7 miles southwest of Brecon, near Libanus ☎ 0845 371 9029, ⓦ yha.org.uk. Traditional farmhouse hostel surrounded by woodlands and overlooking the River Tarell, just off the A470 and main bus route to Merthyr. Good facilities, as well as home-cooked food and Brecon Brewery ale on tap. Nov–Feb weekends only. Dorms **£15**; doubles **£48**

EATING AND DRINKING

Brecon has a select number of decent places **to eat**, though the **drinking** options are fairly low-key and not quite so inviting. While here, be sure to try real ales from the local **Brecon Brewery** company, which you'll find on tap in many local pubs.

3

CAFÉS AND RESTAURANTS

Bridge Café 7 Bridge St ☎01874 622024, ⓦbridgecafe
.co.uk. Good-looking café/bistro by the bridge featuring a homespun interior with oak flooring, kitchen-style tables and chairs and fireside sofas. The menu changes monthly but expect a range of interesting dishes like Greek style casserole in red wine with new potatoes (£12). The only letdown is its very limited opening hours. Thurs–Sat 6.30–11pm, Sun 9–11am. Closed Nov–Feb.

★**The Felin Fach Griffin** Felinfach, A470 3 miles northwest ☎01874 620111, ⓦeatdrinksleepltd.uk. High-end restaurant with rooms serving some of the finest modern Welsh cuisine anywhere in the region; the menu is short and seasonal, with meat sourced locally (Bwlch venison with artichoke), fish delivered from Cornwall (monkfish tail with pancetta and parsley butter; £17.95), and veggies and fruit hand-picked from the kitchen garden. Daily 11.30am–11pm.

The Hours Café 15 Ship St ☎01874 622800, ⓦthe
-hours.co.uk. Cheerful daytime café-cum-bookshop, with sloping floors and black timber beams, where you can enjoy warm salads and toasted sandwiches, hearty soups, cakes and a good range of free-trade coffees. Tues–Sat 10am–5pm.

Llanfaes Dairy 19 Bridge St ☎01874 625892. Colourful ice-cream parlour in a slightly odd location just across the river, but venturing to for its scrumptious and exotic home-made flavours like apple and cinnamon, and roasted almond. Daily 10.30am–5.30pm.

Roberto's St Mary's St ☎01874 611880. Diminutive place occupying the town's former post office, offering a little slice of Italy, with Italian/Welsh classics like tagliatelle with king prawns, rocket and chilli (£11.95), as well as scrummy pizzas, including gluten-free possibilities. Mon–Sat 11am–3pm & 5.30–10pm.

Tipple & Tiffin Theatr Brycheiniog, Canal Wharf ☎01874 611866. A fetching waterside setting and easy-going atmosphere mark this place out as Brecon's most inviting restaurant; tapas-style dishes designed for sharing (deep fried cockles, crispy dug leg; £8), along with a few more substantial options chalked up daily on a blackboard. Largely frequented by the pre-theatre crowd, but a terrific place to come any time. Tues–Sat 10am–10pm, Sun noon–4pm.

PUBS

Boars Head Ship St ☎01874 622856. Two very different bars: the front is basic and frequented mainly by locals, whereas the back bar is younger and louder; there's also a not all together convincing stone terrace overlooking the water. Daily noon–midnight, Fri & Sat till 2am.

Sarah Siddons 47 High St Inferior ☎01874 610666. Named after the famous actress, born here in 1755 when the pub was then known as the *Shoulder of Mutton*. It's a small, fairly ordinary-looking boozer, but it's extremely popular, especially with off-duty soldiers. Daily 11am–midnight, Fri & Sat till 1.30am.

ENTERTAINMENT

Coliseum Cinema Wheat St, near the central crossroads ☎01874 622501, ⓦcoliseumbrecon.co.uk. The old-fashioned Coliseum cinema offers an agreeable mix of both mainstream and independent film.

Theatr Brycheiniog At the canal basin ☎01874 611622, ⓦbrycheiniog.co.uk. Offers a rich programme of music, comedy, theatre and dance.

The Usk Valley

Home to the majority of the national park's residents, and hence the greatest concentration of facilities for visitors, the wide, fertile **Usk Valley** leads southeast from Brecon, running parallel to the Monmouthshire and Brecon Canal and effectively dividing the Brecon Beacons proper from the Black Mountains to the northeast. The A40 connects Brecon and Bwlch with Tretower, Crickhowell and Abergavenny, providing a backbone for dozens of minor lanes that twist south over the Brecon Beacons or north into the bucolic headwaters of some of the Usk's tributaries.

BRECON JAZZ FESTIVAL

Held over the second or third weekend of August, the **Brecon Jazz Festival** (ⓦbreconjazz
.com) is one of Britain's most prestigious music gatherings, with more than thirty years under its belt. The line-up is invariably outstanding, with artists of the calibre of Burt Bacharach, Femi Kuti and Zoe Rahman playing venues as diverse as Brecon Cathedral, Christ's College and the Market Hall. Running concurrently, the Brecon Fringe Festival (ⓦbreconfringe.co.uk) encompasses alternative, predominantly local, bands playing cafés, pubs and galleries.

A CIRCULAR WALK AROUND THE EASTERN BEACONS

The OS 1:25,000 Explorer map OL11 (Brecon Beacons Central Area) is recommended.
A very rewarding objective around the **eastern Brecon Beacons** (but requiring careful map-reading) is Craig y Fan Ddu and the path skirting the top of the moorland rim beyond it, around the Caerfanell valley. By starting at the Blaen-y-glyn car park (grid reference SO 064169), on the lane between Talybont and Pontsticill/Merthyr Tydfil, you begin the ascent through forest. The walk starts across the road, follows the River Caerfanell, crosses a concrete bridge and forks left uphill, first along the edge of the forest, then through the forest itself, then left at the Torpantau car park entrance, and up the steep bank. You later face a hard climb up to the ridge of Craig y Fan Ddu, then carry on north a mile to Bwlch y Ddwyallt, where five paths converge. Bear southeast, past a monument, lying between two heaps of twisted metal, marking the spot of a wartime RAF plane crash. Climb to the top of the ridge and then walk southeast along the rim. After half a mile, at a spur of land, head straight on, down the steep grassy slope, later following a fence, down into the valley, then alongside the river on a path past some little waterfalls towards the starting point.

3

Talybont-on-Usk and around

Six miles southeast of Brecon, **TALYBONT-ON-USK** is idyllically situated for walks, bike rides or canal trips. The lane heading south of the village over the canal heads towards a number of **reservoirs**, starting with the 323-acre **Talybont Reservoir**. It then wiggles up onto the rocky hillsides, past the waterfalls on the Nant Bwrefwr and beyond to the isolated and hauntingly beautiful Neuadd (or Beacons) reservoirs to the north, a good starting point for walks to the summits of Pen y Fan and Corn Du along the old "Gap" route; or, to the south, the more popular (and hence busier) **Pentwyn** and **Pontsticill** (aka Taf Fechan) **reservoirs**. Two eastbound paths at either end of the Pontsticill Reservoir enable escape from fellow walkers in favour of a fairly steep climb up the rocky slopes for wonderful views over the lakes.

Brecon Mountain Railway

Jan–March 3 trains Sat & Sun, April–Sept 4 trains daily, Oct 3 trains daily · £12 return trip · ☎ 01685 722988, ⓦ breconmountainrailway .co.uk

From Pant station, just below Pontsticill, the tiny **Brecon Mountain Railway** shuttles passengers along a five-mile section of track on the eastern bank of the reservoir up to Torpantau (1313ft) before the return trip, stopping (for twenty minutes) at Pontsticill station on the way; here you'll find a sweet little steam museum, snack bar, picnic site and play area. If you want to look around Pontsticill, you can always wait for the next train to take you back to Pant. Visitor facilities at Pant include a restaurant. The round trip takes around ninety minutes.

ARRIVAL AND DEPARTURE   TALYBONT-ON-USK

By bus Regular Brecon–Crickhowell buses stop at Talybont.

ACCOMMODATION

Usk Inn Station Rd ☎ 01874 676251, ⓦ uskinn.co.uk. Upmarket village pub transformed into a country restaurant, with ten polished and fragrant-smelling rooms named after birds you'll spot along the River Usk. **£80**

White Hart Inn ☎ 01874 676227, ⓦ breconbunkhouse .co.uk. Pressed up hard against the canal, this big pub has an upstairs bunkhouse with four- and six-bed rooms and shared shower facilities, as well as a communal kitchen, drying room and bike storage facilities – hence its popularity with walkers and cyclists. Cooked breakfast included. Dorms **£25**

YHA Danywenallt ☎ 0845 371 9548, ⓦ yha.org.uk. Around a mile south of Talybont, at the northern end of the reservoir, this converted farmhouse offers small, bright dorms, a warming woodstove and meals by request (though no self-catering facilities). Dorms **£16**, doubles **£52**

EATING AND DRINKING

Star Inn ☎ 01874 676635. The most convivial of the village pubs, which stands out for its lengthy list of real ales, regular beer festivals and lively music nights. Daily 11am–11pm.

The Travellers ☎ 01874 676233, ⓦ travellersrestinn .com. A homely spot with a roaring fire and good-looking restaurant, and a lovely menu featuring the likes of Lemon sole and Parma ham roll with citrus butter sauce (£16.95). Wed–Sat 7–10pm, Sun 12.30–2.30pm & 7–10pm.

Llangorse

North of Talybont and Bwlch, the B4560 threads its way four miles through rolling countryside to **LLANGORSE** (Llangors), sheltered in the western lee of the Black Mountains. The village is a mile northeast of the reed-shored **Llangorse Lake** (Llyn Syfaddan), which is notorious in medieval times for its supernatural properties (blood-red water, eerie sounds and a mythical lost city). Its *crannog* (artificial lake island), the only one of its kind in Wales, is thought to have been a ninth-century seat of the royal house of Brycheiniog. Today, a reconstructed *crannog* at the water's edge has information panels interpreting the lake's history and legends.

Llangorse Multi Activity Centre

Gilfach Farm, 1 mile southeast of Llangorse • Mon–Sat 9.30am–10pm, Sun 9.30am–5pm • ☎ 01874 658272, ⓦ activityuk.com

Experienced climbers can rent gear cheaply here, and for beginners there are Learn to Climb sessions (£16/1hr; £30/2hr). Multi-activity indoor sessions (climbing, abseiling, scrambling) cost £26 for half a day and £47 for a full day, while there are many more outdoor pursuits available. The Sky Trek zipwire has fourteen connected lines zipping through the trees at heights of up to 22m. The centre also offers off-road horseriding for beginners and intermediates (£14.50/1hr, £33/half day) and hacking for the experienced (£45/half day).

ACCOMMODATION
LLANGORSE

Lakeside Caravan and Camping Llangorse Lake ☎ 01874 658226, ⓦ llangorselake.co.uk. Well-equipped site with modern shower blocks, laundry, play area, shop, bar and restaurant. Also has rowing boats, kayaks, canoes and bikes for hire. Electric hook-up £4.25 extra. Closed Nov to early March. £7.50/person

Llangorse Riding & Ropes Centre Gilfach Farm, on the east side of the lake ☎ 0333 600 2020, ⓦ activityuk .com. There are a couple of bunkhouses on site, and although preference is generally given to groups using the centre, it's worth asking; there's also a small but neat campsite overlooking the lake. Camping £5.50/person, dorms £15

Pen-y-Bryn House Llangorse ☎ 01874 658606. A mile up the road in Llangorse itself, there's top-quality B&B on offer at this delightful farmhouse. There's also a self-catering unit in the gardens that sleeps four. Doubles £65, self-catering £140

Talgarth

Five miles north of Llangorse, **TALGARTH** is a spirited and friendly village built around its unusual town hall and the hulking **St Gwendoline's church** tower, constructed in the fourteenth century but harking back to Talgarth's position as a defence centre against the Norman invasion.

Talgarth Mill

The Square • April–Sept daily 10am–4pm; Oct–March Tues–Sun 11am–4pm • £3.50 • ☎ 01874 711352, ⓦ talgarthmill.com

Originating from the mid-eighteenth century, **Talgarth Mill** ceased functioning in the 1940s as the milling industry fell into decline. Thereafter, the site variously functioned as a dentist, butcher's and builders yard, before being abandoned. An almost total rebuild was required in order to bring it back to anything like the condition it was before, and today it once again harnesses the local waters to grind the corn to produce flour for the on-site bakery, which in turn supplies the adjoining *Baker's Table* café with a delicious array of breads and cakes. Perched over the river, it's a lovely spot to rest before a tempting riverside walk along the banks of the River Ennig. Free guided tours of the mill are offered, as and when visitors turn up.

ARRIVAL AND INFORMATION

TALGARTH

By bus The #39 bus between Brecon and Hereford stops on the main square.

Tourist information The village's independently run and very well stocked TIC is inside the Tower Shop on the main

square (April–Oct Mon–Sat 10am–4pm, Sun 10am–1pm; Nov–March Mon–Sat 10.30am–3.30pm, Sun 10.30am–1pm; ☎ 01874 712226, ⊚ talgarthcentre.org.uk).

ACCOMMODATION, EATING AND DRINKING

Castle Hotel Bronllys Rd ☎ 07789 682335, ⊚ talgarthhotel.co.uk. Heading out of town in the direction of Bronllys, this roadside hotel/pub has five smart-looking rooms with snazzily designed bathrooms. They also own the cracking little fish and chip shop next door. **£60**

Strand Café Regent St ☎ 01874 711195. Part café, part secondhand bookshop, this quaint little establishment offers a gamut of snacky-style meals, from pies and salads

to pizzas and puddings. Mon 11am–2pm, Thurs–Sat 11am–9pm, Sun 11am–4pm.

Tower Hotel The Square ☎ 01874 711253, ⊚ towerhoteltalgarth.co.uk. The *Tower* has five perfectly adequate rooms, as well as a bunkhouse with four- and five-bed dorms and shared bathroom facilities. The downstairs pub is nothing special to look at, though it does brew some superb real ales and ciders. Mon–Fri 4–11pm, Sat & Sun noon–11pm. Dorms **£21**, doubles **£60**

Bronllys and around

Between Talgarth and the neighbouring village of **BRONLLYS** is **Bronllys Castle**, of which only a large twelfth-century cylindrical tower remains – climb to the top for stunning views up the Llynfi River valley and beyond to the light-washed peaks of the Black Mountains. There are some sparkling little places to **eat** and **sleep** around here.

Wye Valley Canoes

The Boat House, Glasbury • April–Oct • ☎ 01497 847213, ⊚ wyevalleycanoes.co.uk

Four miles northeast of Bronllys, just off the A438 on the B4350, the riverside village of **GLASBURY** is home to **Wye Valley Canoes**, where you can rent a kayak (single, double or Canadian canoe) to paddle the gentle currents of the River Wye. Rental for a five-mile trip downstream to Hay-on-Wye (around two and a half to three hours) costs £20 including minibus pick-up at the other end; longer trips, including multi-day rentals, are also possible. Bike hire is also available (£17.50/half day).

ACCOMMODATION

BRONLLYS AND AROUND

Llangoed Hall A couple of miles north of Llyswen on the A470 ☎ 01874 754525, ⊚ llangoedhall.co.uk. This luxurious pile is actually an ancient castle remodelled in the early twentieth century by Portmeirion's Clough Williams-Ellis. The large, decadent rooms are furnished in fabrics by Elanbach (the on-site textile printing company founded by Bernard Ashley, former husband of Laura) and adorned with some lovely touches such as antique mirrors and old-fashioned wireless radios. **£225**

River Café At Wye Valley Canoes in Glasbury ☎ 01497 847007, ⊚ therivercafeglasbury.co.uk. Four bright and refreshingly simple en-suite rooms above the restaurant (see

below), with splendid views across to the river; a few paces away, on the water's edge, the River Room comprises four single beds and minimal furnishings, and is ideally suited to walkers or canoeists. The neighbouring chapel has been converted into a quite brilliant bunkhouse, but this is almost always reserved for large groups. Dorms **£30**, River Room **£70**

Wye Knot Stop Llyswen ☎ 01874 754247, ⊚ wyeknotstop.co.uk. This village café possesses two spacious and uncluttered en-suite rooms, the upstairs one sleeping up to three people, and the downstairs (wheelchair-friendly) one sleeping up to four. Pleasantly restful place to stop over. **£65**

EATING AND DRINKING

Honey Café Just north of Bronllys on the main road, ☎ 01497 711904. A fixture since 1933, this striking red- and orange-painted café/restaurant remains hugely popular for its home-made cakes and desserts, though the

real pull is its spicy Tex-Mex evening menu. Summer daily 9am–10pm; winter Mon, Tues & Sun 9am–6pm, Wed–Sat 9am–10pm; closed Jan.

River Café At Wye Valley Canoes in Glasbury

☎ 01497 847007. Very fine restaurant right by the river, whose fresh, Mediterranean-influenced fish and pasta menu might include peppered squid and fennel, or crab pappardelle (£13.95) – alternatively, stop by for a heart-starting coffee and a home-baked treat out on the terrace. May–Sept Mon–Sat 9am–11.30pm, Sun 9am–5pm;

Oct–April Wed–Sat 9am–11pm, Sun 9am–5pm.

Wye Knot Stop Llyswen ☎ 01874 754247, ⓦ wyeknotstop.co.uk. Breezy daytime café serving the best coffee for miles around, alongside cream teas, a scrummy selection of cakes and pastries, and a belter of a breakfast (£5.50). Thurs–Tues 10am–4pm; closed Jan.

Tretower castle and court

Three miles northwest of Crickhowell • April–Oct daily 10am–5pm; Nov–March Fri & Sat 10am–4pm, Sun 11am–4pm • £4.75; CADW • ☎ 01874 730279

Rising from the valley floor twelve miles south of Talgarth, the solid round tower of the **castle and court** at **TRETOWER** (Tre-twr) was built to guard the valley pass, and still dominates the skyline from both the A40 and A479. Having replaced an earlier Norman fortification, the high, circular thirteenth-century tower is pretty much all that remains of the castle building, alongside a few sections of wall adjoining a farm. More impressive is the late fourteenth-century manor house, whose downstairs rooms contain a mock-up kitchen, pantry and buttery. The upstairs rooms, which can be viewed from an upper-level walkway, are now mostly stripped bare, but still retain a certain faded grandeur.

Crickhowell

One of the gems of the Brecon Beacons, **CRICKHOWELL** (Crucywel; locally referred to as "Crick") lies on the northern shore of the wide and shallow Usk. Many a local myth has been spawned by its grand seventeenth-century **bridge** with thirteen arches visible from the eastern end but only twelve from the west. Bridge Street rises from the river and up to the uninspiring mound of the ruined **castle** and the wide **High Street**, which is lined with many coloured, rough-hewn tenements, handsome-looking shops and several old-fashioned butchers. New Road runs parallel to Bridge Street from the river, passing the steeple of the town's fourteenth-century **church of St Edmund**.

Table Mountain

Crickhowell's spectacular northern backdrop is **Table Mountain** (1481ft), whose brown cone presides over the rolling green fields below. The most scenic route up it is along the path that goes off by the electricity substation past The Wern off Llanbedr Road. At the summit are remains of the 2500-year-old hillfort (*crug*) of Hywel, from which Crickhowell takes its name. A steeper, and far shorter, route to Table Mountain starts from the village of **LLANBEDR**, some two miles north of Crickhowell, and heads up alongside the stream behind the *Perth-y-pia* bunkhouse. The views are among the best in the area. Many walkers follow the route to the north from Table Mountain, climbing two miles up to the plateau-topped limestone hump of **Pen Cerrig-calch** (2302ft).

ARRIVAL AND DEPARTURE | **CRICKHOWELL**

By bus Buses set down on the main square at the top of the High Street.

Destinations Abergavenny (Mon–Sat hourly; 20min); Brecon (Mon–Sat hourly; 25–45min).

ⓘ CRICKHOWELL'S FESTIVALS

Crickhowell stages two superb annual festivals. The big one is the **Green Man Festival** (ⓦ greenman.net), a three-day music jamboree in mid-August embracing some of the biggest names in folk, indie and Americana. In addition, there are drum workshops, literary events, a cinema tent, kids' activities, performance art, comedy and a "healing field". At the beginning of March, Crickhowell hosts a popular nine-day **Walking Festival** (ⓦ crickhowellfestival.com) with guided walks ranging from tough all-day treks to easy strolls, costing £5–6.50 per walk, per person. A range of special-interest walks and talks is also part of the programme.

INFORMATION AND ACTIVITIES

Tourist office The Crickhowell Resource and Information Centre on Beaufort Street (daily 10am–5pm; ☎01873 811970, ⍵crickhowellinfo.org.uk) also incorporates a café, internet (£1.50/30min) and an upstairs gallery selling quality local art.

Activities Crickhowell Adventure Gear shop, opposite the market cross at 1 High Street (Mon–Sat 9am–1pm & 2–5.30pm, Sun 10am–4pm; ☎01873 810020) sells caving and walking paraphernalia, while Mountain and Water (☎01873 831825, ⍵mountainandwater.co.uk) has kayaks and two- and three-seater canoes for hire (£45/day); usefully, they also have camping sets for hire.

ACCOMMODATION

Bear Hotel Beaufort St ☎01873 810408, ⍵bearhotel .co.uk. A grand old coaching inn whose architectural quirks have lent themselves to some highly idiosyncratic rooms. Those in the hotel itself possess more character, while those in the old courtyard stables are a touch more polished. **£99**

Dragon High St ☎01873 810362, ⍵dragoninncrick howell.com. Salmon-pink building at the quieter, far end of the High Street, with sharply furnished rooms sporting violet and burgundy coloured trimmings, wall length mirrors, and

bits of Welsh art. Relaxing and friendly option. **£70**

★**Ty Gwyn** Brecon Rd ☎01873 811625, ⍵tygwyn .com. Impressive eighteenth-century stone gatehouse a 5min walk north of town, offering three warm and sunny rooms, each one conceived on a Welsh literary theme and stocked accordingly (Dylan room, Cordell room, Vaughan room). Breakfast is taken in the delightful conservatory dining room and there are extensive gardens for rambling. Superb value. **£72**

EATING AND DRINKING

Bear Hotel Beaufort St ☎01873 810408. Romantic candlelit restaurant that is ideally suited to winter dining, while the outdoors garden is just the job for a summertime splurge of game or fish. The hotel's low-beamed pub is pretty much the town's social hub, sporting bags of charm and serving terrific beer. Daily noon–2pm & 6–11pm.

Bridge End Inn Bridge St ☎01873 810338. Comprising part of the town's former tollhouse, this is a truly old-fashioned pub with flagstone flooring, a stone fireplace and brass, copper pots hanging from the walls and ceilings, and a sweet riverside garden. Daily 11am–11.30pm.

Nantyffin Cider Mill Brecon Rd ☎01873 810775, ⍵cidermill.co.uk. Housed in a great stone barn a mile or

so along the A40 towards Brecon, the old mill (with the cider press still intact) is now a tip-top restaurant where it'd be remiss not to try one of the gut-busting steaks (£16) straight out of the Inka (charcoal) oven. There's a serious wine list here too and a choice of ciders, while the Thursday "Pie and Pints" night is good fun. Bar open all day; food served Wed–Sun noon–3pm & 6–11pm.

Number 18 18 High St ☎01873 810337. Smart, glassed-in artisan coffee shop with basement, street-level and mezzanine seating, that'll tempt you in for its wicked selection of hot drinks and cakes, or something a little more substantial if you prefer (honey glazed sausages with onion mash; £6.95). Daily 9am–6pm.

Abergavenny and around

Six miles southeast of Crickhowell, Wales's culinary mecca, **ABERGAVENNY** (Y Fenni), is a vibrant, confident town, though its history is somewhat more chequered. Today, Abergavenny's combination of urban amenities and countrified setting makes it an ideal jumping-off point for forays into the central and eastern sections of the Brecon Beacons.

Brief history

The first main settlement was around the Norman castle, which was built by the English king Henry I's local appointee, Hameline de Ballon, with the express aim of securing enough power to evict local Welsh tribes from the area, an important through route into Wales. Hostility to the Welsh reached its peak at Christmas 1175, when William de Braose, then lord of the town, invited Gwent chieftains to the castle, only to murder them all. The town was shaken badly by the Black Death (1341–51) and a routing by Owain Glyndŵr in 1404, but continued to grow, thanks largely to the weaving and tanning trades that developed from the sixteenth century. The industries prospered alongside Abergavenny's flourishing **market**, still the focal point for a wide area (see box p.216).

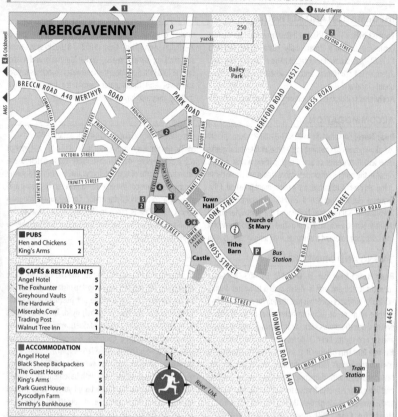

ABERGAVENNY

PUBS
| Hen and Chickens | 1 |
| King's Arms | 2 |

CAFÉS & RESTAURANTS
Angel Hotel	5
The Foxhunter	7
Greyhound Vaults	3
The Hardwick	6
Miserable Cow	2
Trading Post	4
Walnut Tree Inn	1

ACCOMMODATION
Angel Hotel	6
Black Sheep Backpackers	7
The Guest House	2
King's Arms	5
Park Guest House	3
Pyscodlyn Farm	4
Smithy's Bunkhouse	1

The castle

Any street heading south off Cross or High streets leads to Castle Street, where the dark, fragmented remains of Abergavenny's medieval **castle** (free access) languish serenely above the River Usk. Entrance to the eleventh-century castle is through the sturdy, though now roofless, gatehouse, to the right of which stands an extensive portion of the curtain wall. The castle's keep, meanwhile, was remodelled in the nineteenth century, and sits in the middle of the forsaken ruins like an incongruous Lego model. Glorious views aside, the grounds are a lovely spot for a picnic.

Town museum

Castle grounds • March–Oct Mon–Sat 11am–1pm & 2–5pm, Sun 2–5pm; Nov–Feb Mon–Sat 11am–1pm & 2–4pm • Free •
☎ 01873 854282, ⓦ abergavennymuseum.co.uk
While in the castle grounds it's worth visiting the quirky **town museum**, where displays cover the town's history, using photographs and billboards, and re-created interiors

ABERGAVENNY MARKET

Next to the turreted Victorian Gothic town hall on the High Street, you'll find the wonderful covered **market**, which sells produce on Tuesdays, Fridays and Saturdays. On Wednesdays, there's a flea market, with regular weekend antiques fairs, and there's a farmers' market on the fourth Thursday of every month.

including a saddlery, a sanitized Border farmhouse kitchen of 1890 and Basil Jones's grocery shop, once on Main Street. After the death of Jones's son in 1989, the contents of the shop were transported to the museum lock, stock and biscuit barrel. Some of it is recent, but much of it dates from the 1930s and 1940s. One of the more unexpected exhibits is a Red Cross parcel sent to Rudolf Hess whilst he was imprisoned in the town's mental asylum after his plane crash-landed in Scotland in 1941; there's also a lager mat with his signature on it.

Church of St Mary

Monk St • Free • ☎ 01873 858787, ⓦ stmarys-priory.org

Abergavenny's parish **church of St Mary**, on Monk Street, contains effigies and tombs spanning the entire medieval period. Originally built as the chapel of a small twelfth-century Benedictine priory, the existing building goes back only as far as the fourteenth century, although some of the monuments within predate the building itself. The interior manifests a wealth of outstanding detail, not least the **Jesse Tree**, one of the finest late medieval sculptures anywhere in Britain; a recumbent, twice-life-size statue of King David's father, it would once have formed part of an altarpiece tracing the family lineage from Jesse to Jesus.

There are effigies of Sir John de Hastings, who contributed greatly to the rebuilding of the priory, as well as members of the de Braose family, in addition to a host of marble and stone-cut tombs. Take a look, too, at the finely crafted fifteenth-century choir stalls, complete with (relatively) contemporary eighteenth-century graffiti.

Tithe Barn

Monk Street • Mon–Fri 9am–5pm, Sat 9am–4pm; Food Hall Café same times • Free • ☎ 01873 858787, ⓦ stmarys-priory.org

Adjacent to the church is the splendidly restored fourteenth-century **Tithe Barn**, which in times past has variously functioned as a coach house, a theatre for travelling actors and even a disco. It's now a heritage centre, with a well-put-together exhibition on the history of the town, though this is somewhat overshadowed by the **Abergavenny Tapestry**, an expansive, brightly coloured visual record of the town's past. Completed just in time for the millennium, it was stitched by over fifty devoted volunteers and took around four years. The ground floor is occupied by the town's tourist office and the bright *Food Hall Café*, which is an agreeable spot for some refreshments after absorbing the church.

Court Cupboard Craft Gallery

New Court Farm, Llantilio Pertholey, off the A465 2 miles northeast of Abergavenny • Daily 10.30am–5pm; Jan & Feb till 4pm • Free • ☎ 01873 852011, ⓦ courtcupboardgallery.co.uk

Housed within a five hundred-year-old farm, and occupying the old stables, piggery, and milking parlour, the **Court Cupboard Gallery** is a superbly conceived artist's enclave of workshops, selling anything and everything, from leather crafts (including beautiful handmade bags), ceramics and glass, to jewellery, pottery and watercolour paintings. You can often chat with the artists as they work, and the gallery also mounts regular exhibitions as well as art and craft courses, like basketry and spinning.

ARRIVAL AND DEPARTURE

ABERGAVENNY AND AROUND

By train Abergavenny's train station is half a mile southeast of the centre.

Destinations Cardiff (every 30–60min; 45min); Hereford (every 45–60min; 25min); Newport (every 30–60min; 30min).

By bus Buses depart from Swan Meadows bus station, at the bottom of town on Cross Street.

Destinations Brecon (hourly; 40min–1hr); Cardiff (hourly; 2hr 20min); Clydach (hourly; 40min); Crickhowell (hourly Mon–Sat; 20min); Llanfihangel Crucorney (7 daily; 15min); Merthyr Tydfil (hourly; 1hr 30min); Monmouth (6 daily; 45min); Newport (hourly; 1hr 10min); Raglan (6 daily; 25min).

GETTING AROUND AND INFORMATION

By bike Hopyard Cycles in Govilon, a couple of miles west of town (T 01873 830219, W hopyardcycles.co.uk; mountain bikes from £15/day), can deliver bikes (for a small charge) throughout the area.

By boat To explore the Monmouthshire and Brecon Canal, you can rent narrowboats (and day-rental motorboats, as well as canoes) from Beacon Park Boats at Llanfoist (T 01873 858277, W beaconparkboats.com), a mile south of town.

Tourist office The TIC is inside the Tithe Barn on Monk Street (daily: April–Oct 10am–5pm; Nov–March 10am–4pm; T 01873 853254, W visitabergavenny.co.uk) and nominally functions as the Brecon Beacons National Park office too.

ACCOMMODATION

HOTELS AND GUESTHOUSES

Angel Hotel 15 Cross St T 01873 857121, W angelhotelabergavenny.com. Occupying an old coaching inn, Abergavenny's premier central hotel is a warren of corridors with a range of very classy rooms, fitted out in soft beige tones, with plush carpets, big comfy beds and large bathrooms replete with posh toiletries. £101

The Guest House 2 Oxford St T 01873 854823, W theguesthouseabergavenny.co.uk. Fun, popular guesthouse with six sunny rooms, each named after local peaks. Guest lounge with Sky Sports and a Wii console, the resident parrot (Alfie) in the dining room and a backyard petting area with chickens; hence fresh eggs daily. No credit cards. £80

King's Arms 29 Neville St T 01873 855074, W kingsarmsabergavenny.co.uk. Limewash beams, bare, sloping wood floors and low, crooked doorways are all identifiably quirky features of this pleasing, sixteenth-century coaching inn. The neatly conceived pod-like bathrooms, meanwhile, variously feature roll-top or jacuzzi baths. £85

Park Guest House 36 Hereford Rd T 01873 853715, W parkguesthouse.co.uk. Exceptionally good-value B&B in a beautiful Georgian town house a short walk north of the centre. Six low-key rooms, three of which are en suite, offering a simple mix of styles and colours. £58

HOSTEL, BUNKHOUSE AND CAMPING

Black Sheep Backpackers 24 Station Rd T 01873 859125, W blacksheepbackpackers.com. A few paces down from the station, this converted railway hotel has accommodation in six- to ten-bed dorms (with shared showers), as well as en-suite doubles. There are self-catering facilities and a launderette across the road. Continental breakfast included. Dorms £16, doubles £60

Pyscodlyn Farm Llanwenarth Citra, 2 miles west of town off A40 T 01873 853271, W pyscodlyncaravanpark.com. Primarily a caravan site, but there is one sheltered field for campers. Good access as all Brecon or Crickhowell buses pass by. Also sells day fishing licences. £14/pitch

Smithy's Bunkhouse Lower House Farm, Pantygelli T 01873 853432, W smithysbunkhouse.com. Self-catering dormitory accommodation under the slopes of the Sugar Loaf a couple of miles north of town. Comprehensive facilities including a well-equipped kitchen, common room with wood-burning stove, and drying room. Dorms £15

EATING AND DRINKING

Abergavenny's reputation as Wales's culinary hotbed is more than justified, boasting as it does the finest concentration of **restaurants** anywhere in the country. The best of these, though, are outside town, which will necessitate having your own wheels.

CAFÉS AND RESTAURANTS

Angel Hotel 15 Cross St T 01873 857121, W angelhotelabergavenny.com. High tea within the hotel's gracious Wedgewood dining room (or courtyard terrace) is a good enough reason alone to come to Abergavenny; the lavish spread includes a selection of

ABERGAVENNY'S FESTIVALS

Abergavenny's annual **Food Festival** (W abergavennyfoodfestival.co.uk) in mid-September is one of the most prestigious in Britain, two bumper days of markets, master classes, tastings and talks, and pretty much any other take on food you can think of. The festival also has several spin-off events throughout the year, full details of which are on the main website. The town's other key annual event is the week-long **Festival of Cycling** (W abergavennyfestivalofcycling.co.uk) at the end of June. Wales's most important two-wheeled gathering draws some of the biggest names in the sport for various time trial and town centre races, though there's plenty going on for non-elite riders and children, including tandem and hand cycle races through town, cyclocross and film nights.

sandwiches, scones with jam and cream, pastries, and tea or coffee, and costs £19.80 per person. Mon–Fri 3–5pm, Sat & Sun 2–5pm.

The Foxhunter Nantyderry, 7 miles southeast of town ☎01873 881101, ⓦthefoxhunter.com. Modern British cuisine by chef Matt Tebbutt, served in a lovingly restored former stationmaster's house and named after a locally bred, 1952 Olympic Games gold-medal winning horse. In addition to mouthwatering offerings like duck breast with roasted black figs and honey and thyme (£22), there's a fantastic wild food menu available (£40), or you can partake in a specially tailored foraging trip. Tues–Sat noon–3pm & 7–10pm, Sun noon–3pm.

Greyhound Vaults Market St ☎01873 858549. Don't be fooled by the dull, pub-like exterior and earthy interior, this place serves a wide range of tasty, moderately priced Welsh and English specialities, such as Welsh Black steak with leeks, and topside of beef with Yorkshire pudding. Tues–Thurs 12–2.30pm, Fri & Sat 12–2.30pm & 7–9.30pm, Sun 12–2.30pm.

The Hardwick Old Raglan Rd ☎01873 854220, ⓦthehardwick.co.uk. Headed up by chef Stephen Terry, this fabulous-looking pub, two miles east of town, offers a choice of brilliantly simple but fantastically presented dishes such as free range chicken breast with chargrilled sweetcorn and barbequed beans (£22). The Sunday three-course set lunch is superb value at £26. Bar daily 11am–11pm; food served daily noon–3pm & 6.30–10pm.

Miserable Cow Cibi Walk Precinct ☎07910 460548. There's nothing miserable about this cheery open-air café, complete with formica-covered tables and separate smoking/no smoking sections. Serves fine Fairtrade coffee alongside sweet and savoury treats. Mon–Sat 7.30am–6pm, Sun 9am–4pm.

Trading Post 14 Neville St ☎01873 855448. The former eighteenth-century *Cow Inn* – cast your eyes up to the row of cows' heads on the front of the building – is now a sprightly coffee house and bistro, and an ideal spot for poring over one of the papers while sipping a cappuccino or tucking into some Welsh rarebit. Mon–Sat 9am–5pm.

★**Walnut Tree Inn** B4521 at Llanddewi Skirrid, 2 miles north of town ☎01873 852797, ⓦthewalnuttreeinn .com. Highly regarded foodies' paradise under the helm of Shaun Hill, its one Michelin star drawing diners from afar for its Mediterranean-accented British cuisine like turbot with octopus, chorizo and paprika sauce (£27), and gooseberry parfait with elderflower sauce; the menu changes daily. Tues–Sat noon–3pm & 7–11pm.

PUBS

Hen and Chickens Flannel St, off High St ☎01873 853613. Timeless, traditional pub popular with locals and visitors alike, serving some of the best beer in town and staging regular live music, including jazz most Sunday evenings. Daily 10.30am–11pm.

Kings Arms 29 Neville St ☎01873 855074. Handsome pub combining old (stone fireplace and wonderful curving beams on the low ceiling) and new (neat modern furnishings) to smart effect. Good local beer from the Wye Valley and very creditable food in the restaurant section, for example, belly of pork with black pudding mash and spiced apple gravy (£13.75). Mon–Thurs & Sun 11am–11pm, Fri & Sat 11am–1am; food served daily noon–3pm & 6–9.30pm.

The Black Mountains

Appearing only partly tamed by human habitation, the northeastern-most section of the Brecon Beacons National Park, known as the **Black Mountains** (plural, as distinct from the Black Mountain forty miles west) is made up of a series of high, finger-like ridges enclosing, remote, secretive valleys dotted with tiny villages. The wide valley of the River Usk divides the Beacons heartland from the Black Mountains, whose sandstone range rises to more clearly defined individual peaks than those in the western end of the park.

The **Vale of Ewyas** stretches along the extreme eastern boundary of the Brecon Beacons National Park, making one of the most enchanting and reclusive regions in Wales, most memorably seen by car on the narrow road past Llanthony Priory, over the Gospel Pass and on to Hay-on-Wye.

The most rewarding areas to **walk** are around Llanthony and the hilltops above, Hay Bluff and along the southern band of peaks, notably Pen Cerrig-calch, Table Mountain and the Sugar Loaf. The mass of rippling hills in the centre and to the north is less easy to reach, although a couple of good paths follow the contours around them.

Llanfihangel Crucorney

Some six miles north of Abergavenny, on the main village street of **LLANFIHANGEL CRUCORNEY** (Llanfihangel Crucornau; the "Sacred Enclosure of Michael at the Corner of the Rock"), are a fifteenth-century **church** and the reputedly haunted *Skirrid Mountain Inn* (see below).

EATING AND DRINKING   LLANFIHANGEL CRUCORNEY

Skirrid Mountain Inn Llanfihangel Crucorney ☎01873 890258. First mentioned in 1110 and thus thought to be the oldest pub in Wales. During the seventeenth century, some 180 people are believed to have been hanged here – you can still see the beam inside the inn, which bears the scorch marks of the rope. It's an atmospheric spot for a drink, particularly in winter when the fireplaces roar into life. Tues–Fri 11.30am–2.30pm & 5.30–11pm, Sat 11am–11pm, Sun noon–5pm.

Partrishow church

From Llanfihangel Crucorney, the main road through the valley heads north into the Vale of Ewyas. After a mile, a lane heads west towards the enchanting valley of the **Grwyne Fawr**, lost deep in the middle of quiet hills. The road is well worth following to the hamlet of **PARTRISHOW**, where a bubbling tributary of the Grwyne Fawr trickles past the delightful **church** and **well** of St Issui – you'll need to confirm opening times with the Abergavenny tourist office (see p.218).

First founded in the eleventh century, the tiny church features a lacy fifteenth-century **rood screen**, carved out of solid Irish oak and adorned with crude symbols of good and evil, most notably in the corner, where an evil dragon consumes a vine, a symbol of hope and well-being – the rest of the whitewashed church breathes simplicity by comparison.

Of special note are the **wall texts** painted over the apocalyptic picture of a skeleton and scythe. Before the Reformation, such images were widely used with the intent of teaching an illiterate population about the scriptures; however, King James I ordered it to be whitewashed over and repainted with scripture texts. Here, the ghostly grim reaper is once again seeping through the whitewash. Encased in glass by the pulpit is a rare example of a 1620 Bible in Welsh.

BLACK MOUNTAINS SUMMITS

Blorenge (1834ft) The simplest way up is from the road that strikes off the B4246 a mile short of Blaenafon: the open road climbs the shale- and sheep-covered slopes to the car parks near the radio masts. An easy walk from here leads across boggy heathland to a long cairn at the summit, from which there are some glorious views. There is a steeper ascent of the Blorenge from Llanfoist, a mile southwest of Abergavenny, which cuts past the church and under the canal before zigzagging up the mountain.

Sugar Loaf (1955ft) The broad and smooth cone of Sugar Loaf commands the Black Mountains foothills to the northwest of Abergavenny. The easiest ascent is from the south, taking the right fork of Pentre Lane off the A40, half a mile west of Abergavenny, and following the road that climbs Mynydd Llanwenarth.

The Skirrid (1595ft) Shooting up from the Gavenny Valley, three miles northeast of Abergavenny, the Skirrid (Ysgyryd Fawr) is the most eye-catching mountain in the area. The Skirrid has long been held to be a holy mountain; the almighty chasm that splits the peak is said to have been caused by the force of God's will on the death of Christ, a theory that drew St Michael and legions of other pilgrims to this bleak but breathtaking spot. Another theory claims that Noah's Ark clipped it as it passed by. The best path, although it's still a steep ascent, leads from the lay-by on the B4521 just short of the *Walnut Tree Inn*. At the summit, a few leaning boulders are all that remains of a clandestine chapel built by persecuted Catholics.

Hay Bluff (2220ft) Giving terrific views from its often windy summit, this is easily climbed from the top of the road at the Gospel Pass south of Hay-on-Wye. A prominent track runs up to the summit cairn, from which you can continue southeast around the rim of the hill until turning left down the Offa's Dyke Path, which drops steadily to the road to make a magnificent three-mile circuit.

Cwmyoy

If you're prepared for some adventurous driving, take the little lane that peels off the the Vale of Ewyas road, as it dips down over the river and into the village of **CWMYOY** and its wonky **parish church of St Martin**, which has subsided substantially due to geological twists in the underlying rock. Nothing squares up: the tower leans at a severe angle from the bulging body of the church and the view inside from the back of the nave towards the sloping altar, askew roof and straining windows is unforgettable; a wry smile is guaranteed. No less stunning are the views back down through the valley.

Downey Barn Gallery

Cwmyoy • Visit by appointment only • ☎ 01873 890993, ⊕ properdragontales.co.uk

A few yards below Cwmyoy church, the **Downey Barn Gallery** occupies a timber barn adjacent to the home of artist and children's author Caroline Downey. Her artwork largely takes the form of shadowy, moonlit landscapes, which complement the enchanting series of illustrated tales set in the Black Mountains, entitled *Proper Dragon Tales*; you may also get to meet her ginger cat, Merlin, who features in her books. Although you could just pitch up in the hope that the gallery is open, it's best to make an appointment.

Llanthony Priory

Llanthony • Daily 10am–4pm • Free; CADW

In the heart of the Vale of Ewyas is the secluded hamlet of **LLANTHONY**, where a handful of houses, an inn and a few farms cluster around the remains of **Llanthony Priory**, whose ruins retain a real sense of spirituality and peace, set against an inspiring backdrop of river and mountain. It's believed the priory was founded on the site of a ruined chapel around 1100 by Norman knight William de Lacy, who was allegedly so captivated by the site that he renounced worldly life and founded a hermitage, attracting like-minded recluses and forming Wales's first Augustine priory. The church and outbuildings still standing today were constructed in the latter half of the twelfth century. Roving episcopal envoy Giraldus Cambrensis visited the emerging priory church in 1188, noting that "here the monks, sitting in their cloisters, enjoying the fresh air, when they happen to look up at the horizon behold the tops of mountains, as it were touching the heavens". A track behind the ruins winds up to the Offa's Dyke Path, which runs along a lofty, windy ridge.

ACCOMMODATION AND EATING | LLANTHONY PRIORY

Court Farm Just behind the priory ☎01873 890359, ⊕ llanthony.co.uk. *Court Farm* offers superb self-catering units (sleeping five) in the farmhouse, together with a lovely bunkhouse in an old stone barn called The Wain House (usually taken by groups, so minimum charges may apply). There's also a field for camping, the only facility being toilets. Camping **£3**/pitch, dorms **£14**, self-catering **£370**/week

Llanthony Priory Hotel ☎01873 890487, ⊕ llanthonyprioryhotel.co.uk. Fashioned out of part of the tumbledown priory, the hotel was built in the eighteenth century as a hunting lodge. Even the most easily accessed of the four antique-laden rooms (with shared bathrooms) involves scaling a narrow spiral staircase and the tower rooms are several steep flights up. Minimum two-night stay at weekends. Tucked away down beneath the medieval arches, the hotel's restaurant and cellar bar has bags of charm. Opening hours are convoluted – check the website. **£80**

Capel-y-ffin

From Llanthony, the road climbs alongside the narrowing Honddu River before coasting by ruined farmhouses for four miles to the isolated hamlet of **CAPEL-Y-FFIN**. Locked in the middle of sheer hills, it has a devotional feel, because the village is made up of little more than two tiny chapels (one accommodating a congregation of just twenty) and a curious ruined monastery. A lane forks off by the phone box, leading up to the ruins of the privately owned (and confusingly named) **Llanthony Monastery**, founded in 1870 by the Reverend Joseph Lyne. The religious order failed to survive his death in 1908, but the place later became a self-sufficient outpost of the art world when, in 1924, it was bought by English sculptor, typeface designer and eccentric Eric Gill, whose commune, a motley collection of artists and their families, drew much of their creative inspiration from the area.

Gospel Pass

From Capel-y-ffin, the hedge-lined road narrows further still as it weaves a tortuous route up into the **Gospel Pass** and out onto the glorious roof of the Black Mountains. A howling, windy moor by **Hay Bluff**, five miles up from Capel-y-ffin, gives panoramic views and terrific walking over springy hills. The road drops just as suddenly as it climbs, descending five miles into Hay-on-Wye.

ACCOMMODATION AND EATING   **CAPEL-Y-FFIN**

The Grange Capel-y-Ffin ☎01873 890215, ⓦgrangetrekking.co.uk. A comfortable, friendly B&B with three en-suite rooms, as well as extensive gardens in which you can pitch a tent; campers are free to use the showers. You can also get well-priced evening meals here, and staff can organize pony trekking (£18/hr). Closed Nov–Easter. Doubles £74, camping £6/pitch

Hay-on-Wye

The quaint border town of **HAY-ON-WYE** (Y Gelli), at the northern tip of the Brecon Beacons, is synonymous with secondhand books. Since the first bookshop opened here in the 1960s, just about every spare inch of space has been given over

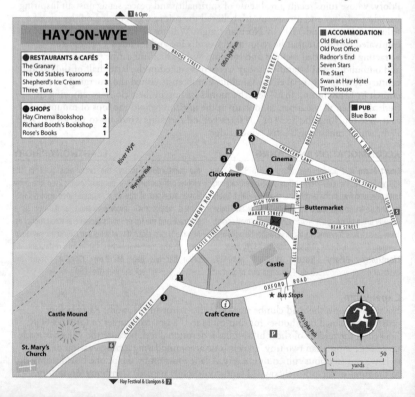

HAY-ON-WYE

● RESTAURANTS & CAFÉS
The Granary 2
The Old Stables Tearooms 4
Shepherd's Ice Cream 3
Three Tuns 1

● SHOPS
Hay Cinema Bookshop 3
Richard Booth's Bookshop 2
Rose's Books 1

■ ACCOMMODATION
Old Black Lion 5
Old Post Office 7
Radnor's End 1
Seven Stars 3
The Start 2
Swan at Hay Hotel 6
Tinto House 4

■ PUB
Blue Boar 1

RICHARD BOOTH AND THE HAY BOOK BUSINESS

Richard Booth, whose family originates in the area, opened the first of his Hay-on-Wye **secondhand bookshop** in 1961. Since then, he has built an astonishing empire and attracted other booksellers to the town, turning it into the greatest market of used books in the world.

Whereas so many mid-Welsh and border towns have seen populations ebb away over the past half-century, Hay is booming on the strength of its bibliophilic connections. Booth views this transformation of a hitherto ordinary little market town as a prototype for reviving rural economies, based on local initiatives and unusual specialisms. This, coupled with Hay's geographical location slap-bang on the Wales–England border and Booth's own self-promotional skills, led him to declare Hay independent of the UK in 1977, with himself, naturally, as king. He appoints his own ministers and offers "official" government scrolls, passports and car stickers to visitors. Although such a proclamation carries no weight officially, most of the people of Hay seem to have rallied behind King Richard and are delighted with the publicity – and visitors – that the town's continuing high profile attracts.

Booth's avant-garde ideas and the events surrounding the 1977 declaration are laid out in his entertaining autobiography, *My Kingdom of Books*.

to the trade, including the old cinema, houses and most shops. There are now well over thirty bookshops in town, most of which cluster on and around Castle Street. Many of the bookshops are highly specialized, including ones dedicated solely to travel, poetry, children, and even "murder and mayhem". You can pick up the annually revised leaflet *Hay-on-Wye Booksellers, Printsellers & Bookbinders* (free), detailing all the town's booksellers and literary happenings, from the tourist office. Sprouting up alongside are an increasing number of antique shops, galleries and fine-food haunts.

The written word is the chief concern of this small market town, and the ideal place to start sampling the wares is up the track towards the castle, a fire-damaged Jacobean mansion built into the walls of a thirteenth-century fortress and owned, until recently, by Hay's ruling "monarch", Richard Booth. Under new ownership, the castle is currently undergoing extensive renovation.

ARRIVAL AND GETTING AROUND   HAY-ON-WYE

By bus Buses from Brecon and Hereford stop by the Oxford Road car park, next to the tourist office.
Destinations Brecon (6 daily; 45min); Hereford (5 daily; 1hr); Talgarth (6 daily; 20min).

Bike rental Drover Cycles, Forest Road (£17.50/half day, £27.50/full day; ☏ 01497 822419, ⓦ drovercycles.co.uk) has a superb range of bikes, does servicing and repairs, and can deliver (free of charge).

INFORMATION

Tourist information The TIC is housed in the craft centre on Oxford Road (daily: Easter–Oct 10am–1pm & 2–5pm; Nov–Easter 11am–1pm & 2–4pm; ☏ 01497 820144,

ⓦ hay-on-wye.co.uk). Staff can advise on and make reservations for local accommodation and there's internet access here too.

HAY FESTIVAL

Hay positively bursts at the seams in the last week of May, when fashionable London and international literati decamp here for the **Telegraph Hay Festival** (ⓦ hayfestival.com), Britain's leading literary gathering, bar none. Dubbed the "Woodstock of the mind" by former festival attendee, Bill Clinton, the festival incorporates a raft of high-profile keynote readings alongside top-rank music and comedy, while there are loads of events for children of all ages. Running concurrently, the innovative **HowTheLightGetsIn Festival** (ⓦ howthelightgetsin.org) gathers together some of the world's leading thinkers in music and philosophy.

3

ACCOMMODATION

As a major tourist venue, Hay is well served for accommodation, although prices are a little higher here than in other places nearby, and there are no hostels. Just about everywhere gets booked up months in advance during the **Hay Festival**.

HOTELS AND GUESTHOUSES

★**Old Black Lion** Lion St ☎01497 820841, ⓦoldblacklion.co.uk. Very well-regarded thirteenth-century inn which has charming en-suite rooms both above the pub and in the neighbouring annexe, though those in the annexe are slightly more appealing. **£99**

Old Post Office Llanigon, 2 miles south of Hay ☎01497 820008, ⓦoldpost-office.co.uk. A wonderful seventeenth-century vegetarian B&B, with good-looking rooms leading off a spiral oak staircase. Well placed for local walks, including the Offa's Dyke Path. Two-night minimum stay at weekends. **£80**

Seven Stars 11 Broad St ☎01497 820886, ⓦtheseven-stars.co.uk. Former town pub near the clock tower, with eight modestly sized but cosy rooms, some with original oak beams and window frames. There's also an indoor swimming pool and sauna. **£84**

The Start Hay Bridge ☎01497 821391, ⓦthe-start.net. Neatly renovated Georgian house on the riverbank, with three rooms boasting antique furnishings and linen,

and handmade quilts. The vegetable garden provides many of the ingredients for breakfast, including scrummy Glamorgan sausages and organic porridge. **£75**

Swan at Hay Church St ☎01497 821188, ⓦswanathay.co.uk. The town's most prominent hotel, with spotless and attractively furnished rooms, some of which sport period features and garden views. **£99**

★**Tinto House** 13 Broad St ☎01497 821556, ⓦtinto-house.co.uk. The splendid Regency frontage of this charming old house conceals three large and sumptuous rooms, each a different style and colour, in addition to a self-contained unit in the old stable block that has fabulous garden views. **£90**

CAMPING

Radnors End 10min walk from town across the Wye bridge on the road to Clyro ☎01497 820780, ⓦhay-on-wye.co.uk/radnorsend. Small, neat field in a beautiful setting overlooking Hay, with on-site showers, laundry facilities and a kids play area. Closed Nov–Feb. **£5**/pitch

EATING AND DRINKING

CAFÉS AND RESTAURANTS

The Granary Broad St ☎01497 820790. White rough-hewn walls and simple wooden tables and chairs mark this thoroughly unpretentious café and bistro out as one of the most enjoyable venues in town. There's a wide range of excellent vegetarian and meat-based meals (£10), many made from local produce. Save space for the wonderful desserts and good espresso. Daily 9am–5.30pm; school holidays till 9pm.

The Old Stables Tearooms Bear St ☎07796 484766. Barely half a dozen tables are crammed into this delightful eatery, with boards chalked up all over the place offering superb Welsh produce, including a fantastic array of speciality teas and home-made tarts. On a warm day, the flower-filled yard is a lovely spot to come and eat. Tues–Fri 10.30am–3pm, Sat 10.30am–4.30pm.

Shepherd's Ice Cream 9 High Town ☎01497 821898. Popular Georgian-style café/ice-cream parlour doling out local

ice cream made from sheep's milk, often in offbeat flavours like raspberry cheesecake and banana toffee crunch; the less calorie conscious might want to try the waffle topped with ice cream and whipped cream. Mon–Fri 9.30am–5.30pm, Sat 9.30am–6pm, Sun 10.30am–5.30pm.

★**Three Tuns** Broad St ☎01497 821855, ⓦthree-tuns.com. Set in Hay's second-oldest building (after the castle), the ancient stonework, outdoor terrace and crackling open fires make for an atmospheric dining spot. Food includes creations such as seared scallops with truffle cauliflower puree and fennel dressing (£15). Daily 11am–11pm.

PUB

Blue Boar Castle St ☎01497 820884. Tasteful, wood-panelled real ale pub centred around a gently curving bar and two stone fireplaces, with a separate dining area to one side. Daily 9am–11pm; food served 11.30am–2pm & 6am–9.30pm.

SHOPPING

Hay Cinema Bookshop In the old town cinema, Castle St ☎01497 820071, ⓦhaycinemabookshop.co.uk. Great for new remaindered editions at low prices. Mon–Sat 9am–9pm, Sun noon–8pm.

Richard Booth's Bookshop Just off the top of Castle St ☎01497 820322, ⓦboothbooks.co.uk. The largest bookshop in Hay is Richard Booth's Bookshop which, although no longer owned by Booth, still trades under his

name. Once you're done browsing this superb emporium, pop into the bright café for a drink or bite to eat. Incorporated into the rear of Richard Booth's Bookshop, the little Bookshop Cinema screens arthouse movies at weekends. As you enter the bookshop itself, take a look at the beautiful glazed tiles on the facade, painted with agricultural motifs. Mon–Sat 9.30am–5.30pm, Sun 10.30am–5.30pm.

Rose's Books Opposite the Clock Tower at 14 Broad St ☎ 01497 820013. Another worthwhile bookshop, with a wonderful stock of rare and collectable children's and illustrated books. Mon–Fri 10am–1.30pm, Sat & Sun 9.30am–5.30pm.

Radnorshire and Montgomeryshire

Even quieter than the quiet Brecon Beacons, the northern tranche of Powys – comprising the old counties of Radnorshire and Montgomeryshire – is a hugely rewarding area to explore. This is farming country, where urban life comes no bigger than a few small market towns. Between the towns, the contours of the impossibly green, sheep-flecked farmland are shaped by the glassy lakes and lively rivers that run down from the open moorland of the Cambrian Mountains, which form Wales's spine. Despite the area's remoteness, the quality and pace of life here has proved irresistible to "alternative" lifestylers over the years, resulting in wholefood cafés and quirky festivals.

In the south of **Radnorshire** and in bordering Brecknockshire, four distinctly different communities jointly form the **Wells towns** (spa towns), each of which grew up around a reputedly health-giving spring. There's more water in the **Elan Valley**, to the west, centred around four interlocking reservoirs and graced by an abundance of red kites. To the east, close to the English border, **Presteigne** is a charmingly villagey town with a great museum, while for walkers, **Knighton** is ideally situated at the start of **Glyndŵr's Way**, as well as midway along the eighth-century **Offa's Dyke**.

The northernmost section of Powys is mellow **Montgomeryshire**. Good bases include the cheerily offbeat little town of **Llanidloes**, the laid-back northern outpost of **Llanfyllin**, the stately old county town of **Montgomery** and its much larger and more bustling replacement, **Welshpool**.

The Wells towns

Straddling the old border of Brecknockshire and Radnorshire, around fifteen miles north of Brecon, mid-Wales's four former spa towns are strung out along the Heart of Wales rail line and the main A483. All were obscure villages up until the eighteenth century, until royalty and nobility spearheaded the fashion for taking a cure. Once the railway arrived, the four Welsh spas became much more egalitarian, each developing its own distinct clientele and atmosphere.

The westernmost spa of **Llanwrtyd Wells**, hunkered down beneath the hills, is best known for its weird array of offbeat festivals and unusual events. Both **Builth Wells** and

---

WACKY EVENTS

Belying its appearance as a sleepy kind of place, Llanwrtyd Wells has its distinctly zany moments. Although a host of events take place here throughout the year, three in particular take precedent. In mid-June, the **Man Versus Horse Marathon** is a punishing 22-mile endurance test between man and beast over various types of terrain. Then, at the end of August, it's the turn of the **World Bog-Snorkelling Championships**, in which competitors must complete two lengths of a water-filled trench cut through a peat bog – the current world record, posted here in 2010, is one minute thirty seconds. Then in November there's the wonderfully named **Real Ale Wobble**, two days of combined mountain biking and beer drinking, an event for the somewhat less serious-minded cyclist. Visit ⓦ green-events.co.uk for full event listings.

A fourth major event takes place bi-annually (every even-numbered year); in the wake of the 2012 Olympic Games in London, organizers here decided to set up their own **World Alternative Games** (ⓦ worldalternativegames.co.uk), two weeks of weird and wonderful events (over sixty in total) such as worm charming, belly flopping and wife carrying!

Llandrindod Wells are worth a stop, the latter having retained some exceptional Victorian-era architecture, though both places are struggling economically these days.

Llanwrtyd Wells and around

Around twenty miles northwest of Brecon, **LLANWRTYD WELLS** was the spa to which the Welsh – farmers of Dyfed alongside the Nonconformist middle classes from Glamorgan – came to great eisteddfodau in the valley of the Irfon. One of the smallest towns in Britain, these days it's more well known for being the Welsh capital of wacky events. Moreover, along with Abergavenny, it boasts the finest coterie of restaurants in mid-Wales.

Main Street runs through the centre of town, crossing the Irfon River just below the main square, **Y Sgwar**, which is framed by an assortment of boldly coloured buildings and dominated by a striking sculpture of a red kite by Sandy O'Connor. Although the sulphurous aroma had been apparent in the area for centuries, it was "discovered" in 1732 by the local priest, Theophilus Evans, who drank from a vile-smelling spring after seeing a healthy frog pop out of it. The spring, named **Ffynnon Drewllyd** (Stinking Well), bubbles up among the dilapidated spa buildings on Dolecoed Road.

Mynydd Eppynt

To the south of Llanwrtyd Wells, the remote **Crychan Forest** and the rippling mountains of the **Mynydd Eppynt** make up the northern outcrops of the Brecon Beacons, best seen from the roads that snake across the moors from the towns of Garth and Builth. The bulk of the Eppynt, however, has been appropriated by the British Army, as evidenced by the many red flags flying stiffly, warning you not to stop or touch anything.

Coed Trallwm Mountain Bike Centre

Abergwesyn • July–Sept daily noon–4pm; call for opening times during the rest of the year • Free • ☎ 01591 610229,
Ⓦ coedtrallwm.co.uk

Five miles north of Llanwrtyd, the lane from Llanwrtyd meets another road from Beulah at the riverside hamlet of **ABERGWESYN**, home to the **Coed Trallwm Mountain Bike Centre**, from where four graded trails fan out, one of which is just under a mile long, with the other three between two and three miles. You'll need to bring your own bike, however, as there's no rental here. The centre's visitor centre occupies a log cabin with an organic café.

The Abergwesyn Pass

A magnificent winding road twists up from Beulah to the **Abergwesyn Pass**, threading its way up through dense conifer forests to wide, gorse- and heather-strewn valleys bereft of any sign of human habitation, framed by craggy peaks and waterfalls. At the little bridge over the tiny Tywi River, a track heads south past the wonderfully isolated, gaslit *Elenydd Wilderness Hostel* at **Dolgoch**.

On the other side of the river, a new road channels past the thick forest on to Llyn Brianne (see p.151), a couple of miles further on. This is as remote a walking holiday as can be had in Wales – paths lead from Dolgoch, through the forests and hillsides to the exquisitely isolated chapel at **Soar-y-Mynydd** and beyond, over the mountains to the next *Elenydd Wilderness Hostel*, Ty'n Cornel (also spelt Tyncornel), five strenuous miles from Dolgoch.

From Dolgoch, the road continues over expansive terrain before dropping down along the rounded valley of the Berwyn River and into Tregaron. Although the entire Llanwrtyd–Tregaron route is less than twenty miles in length, it takes a good hour for

drivers to negotiate the twisting, narrow road safely. The old drovers, driving their cattle to Shrewsbury or Hereford, would have taken at least a day or two over the same stretch.

ARRIVAL AND DEPARTURE — LLANWRTYD WELLS

By train The train station is a 5min walk east of town on Station Road.

Destinations Builth Wells (4 daily; 20min); Knighton (4 daily; 1hr 10min); Llandrindod Wells (4 daily; 30min); Shrewsbury (4 daily; 2hr); Swansea (4 daily; 2hr).

By bus Buses serve Builth Wells (5 daily; 25min).

INFORMATION AND ACTIVITIES

Tourist information There's no tourist office in town, but you can get (very) limited information from the Neuadd Arms on the main square.

Pony trekking The area around Llanwrytd is great

trekking terrain. If you fancy saddling up, Llanwrtyd Wells Riding and Trekking (☎07833 963537, ⓦridingand trekking.co.uk) offers pony trekking (£25/hr, £70/full day), as well as hacking and riding lessons.

ACCOMMODATION

★**Ardwyn House** Station Rd ☎01591 610768, ⓦardwynhouse.co.uk. Stunning turn-of-the-twentieth-century period piece with three, richly detailed en-suite rooms, including roll-top baths, cast-iron fireplaces and antique light fittings, while downstairs, guests can avail themselves of a marvellous book-lined billiards room and honesty bar. **£80**

Carlton Riverside Irfon Crescent ☎01591 610248, ⓦcarltonriverside.com. Striking stone building nestled alongside the river, offering four differently sized, individually designed rooms, with glass and leather furnishings and wall prints. Two rooms overlook the river, one of which is a very small, but cheaper, double. **£75**

The Drover's Rest The Square ☎01591 610264, ⓦfood-food-food.co.uk. On the opposite side of the bridge from the Carlton, the Drover's offers four sweet, cottage-like rooms (including one single) tastefully furnished in beautiful fabrics and with splashes of artwork on the walls. It also has accommodation a few minutes' walk away in *High View House* and a riverside restaurant (see below). **£60**

Elenydd Wilderness Hostel Dolgoch and Ty'n Cornel ☎01974 298680 or ☎01440 730226, ⓦelenydd-hostels.co.uk. Two converted farmhouses with nice, clean dorms (four-, six- and ten-bed dorms at Dolgoch and two eight-bed dorms at Ty'n Cornel), and there's also space for camping at both. Advance bookings for both hostels is essential in winter. Camping **£6**/person, dorms **£12**

Lasswade Station Rd ☎01591 610515, ⓦlasswade hotel.co.uk. A few paces down from Ardwyn House, this is a lovely Edwardian residence overlooking lush fields with eight tranquil, florally decorated rooms. There's a five percent discount for those arriving by train. **£75**

Stonecroft Lodge Dolecoed Rd ☎01591 610332, ⓦstonecroft.co.uk. This self-catering guesthouse, adjoining the pub (see opposite), looks fairly grubby from the outside, but it has a perfectly acceptable selection of triple- quad- and six-bed rooms, though all are with shared shower facilities. There's also a lounge and fully equipped kitchen for use. Dorms **£16**

EATING AND DRINKING

★**Carlton Riverside** Irfon Crescent ☎01591 610248, ⓦcarltonriverside.com. The food at this well-regarded place run by Mary Ann Gilchrist is traditional Welsh, prepared with supreme flair and imagination – such as slow braised beef in Welsh ale with punchnep (root vegetables) and buttered cabbage (£22) – and with a wine list to match. The restaurant itself has just half a dozen

well-spaced, crisply laid tables offering river views. There's also a cool little cellar bar serving home-baked pizza. Mon–Sat 7–11pm; cellar bar Thurs–Sat 7–11pm.

★**Drover's Rest Riverside Restaurant** ☎01591 610264, ⓦfood-food-food.co.uk. Bric-a-brac and other accoutrements fill this warm, cottagey-like restaurant, where wholesome traditional Welsh dishes are the order of

---

ROYAL WELSH SHOWGROUND

On the other side of the river is Builth's major modern source of prosperity, the **Royal Welsh Showground** (☎01982 553683, ⓦrwas.co.uk), which hosts numerous agricultural events, together with monthly flea markets and occasional specialized collectors' fairs. The undoubted highlight on its calendar is the animated **Royal Welsh Show**, Europe's largest agricultural fair, which takes place over four days in mid- to late July, attracting over one hundred thousand visitors; even if you haven't got an interest in all things agricultural, this is quite some event.

the day; Brecon venison in red wine, Celtic pork tenderloin, as well as some delicious cheese-based vegetarian dishes. Cookery and art classes are also run here. Reservations essential. Tues & Thurs–Sun 10.30am–3.30pm & 7.30–10pm.

★**Lasswade Hotel** Station Rd ☎01591 610515, ⓦlasswadehotel.co.uk. Run by Wales's Organic Champion Chef, this consummate restaurant is highly regarded for its sustainable food policy, not surprising given that most of the food is sourced from the hotel's kitchen and cottage gardens. The menu, which changes daily, is wonderfully ambitious, featuring the likes of Elan Valley mutton with a soufflé of leeks and roasted root vegetables in Madeira wine. Three-course meal £34.

Booking required. Daily 7.30–9pm.

Neuadd Arms The Square ☎01591 610236. Lively place and home to the Heart of Wales Brewery, which currently produces seven fabulous ales (including Welsh Black, a delicious stout) that you can soak up with good bar food, including some great curries. Note the memorial top hat on the exterior wall, in honour of Screaming Lord Sutch, who performed here on several occasions. Daily 11am–midnight; food served noon–2pm & 6–9.30pm.

Stonecroft Inn Dolecoed Rd ☎01591 610332. The riverside beer garden at this superb pub is a particularly idyllic spot to down a pint of one of the locally brewed real ales and there's occasional live music to boot. Mon–Thurs 5pm– late, Fri–Sun noon–late.

Builth Wells

3

Once the spa of the Welsh working classes, **BUILTH WELLS** (Llanfair ym Muallt) still has a vibrant, welcoming feel, as well as good amenities and transport links. The town stretches along the Wye below its architecturally jumbled High Street, a narrow, winding thoroughfare lined with a hardy array of time-worn shops, an old-fashioned butcher's and the odd café and pub. This becomes Broad Street as it descends to the town bridge, where you'll find an eye-catching mural of Prince Llywelyn.

ARRIVAL AND INFORMATION

BUILTH WELLS

By train Builth Road train station is nearly three miles north of the town and inaccessible by public transport – a taxi (☎01982 551159 or 553210) costs about £5.
Destinations Knighton (4 daily; 55min); Llandrindod Wells (4 daily; 15min); Llanwrtyd Wells (4 daily; 20min).
By bus Buses depart from the car park by the river bridge.
Destinations Brecon (7 daily; 45min); Llandrindod Wells

(hourly Mon–Sat; 20min); Llanwrtyd Wells (4 daily Mon–Sat; 30min).
Tourist information There's no tourist office here, but the library on the High Street (Mon–Tues & Thurs–Fri 9.30–1pm & 2–5pm, Sat 9.30am–12.30pm) can furnish you with basic information on the town and its surrounds.

ACCOMMODATION

Bron Wye 5 Church St ☎01982 553587, ⓦbronwye .co.uk. Backing onto parkland by the River Wye, this family-run, nineteenth-century residence offers the best-value accommodation in town: five pleasant charcoal-grey coloured rooms, a homely guest lounge and a filling breakfast in the park-facing dining room. **£65**
Greyhound Hotel Garth Rd ☎01982 553255, ⓦthegreyhoundhotel.co.uk. The grey-brick exterior of this establishment, located a few minutes west of the centre, is far from enticing, but the rooms are thoroughly modern and nicely sized. The restaurant/bar is well rated locally, too. **£75**
★**Trericket Mill** Erwood ☎01982 560312, ⓦtrericket .co.uk. Just beyond the village of Erwood, some 9 miles

south of Builth on the A470, Trericket has a variety of terrific accommodation picturesquely set between a cool, rushing brook and lush sloping lawns with free-roaming ducks and chickens. It includes five camping pitches with covered outdoor kitchen (March–Nov), an eco-cabin sleeping up to five, and a cosy, three-roomed guesthouse (includes breakfast), with a two-bed bunkhouse room attached. Camping **£8**/person, bunkhouse **£34**, doubles **£69**
White House Campsite Hay Rd ☎01982 552255, ⓦwhitehousecampsite.co.uk. Located right by the River Wye, a 5min walk south of the centre on the A470, this level field site is particularly popular with caravanners. Its modern, but limited, amenities include a shower block. **£10**/person

EATING AND ENTERTAINMENT

Builth Male Voice Choir ☎01982 553397, ⓦbuilthmalechoir.org.uk. This is one of the finest choirs in mid-Wales, so if you fancy catching a rehearsal, pop along to the Greyhound Hotel (see above) at 8pm on Monday evenings.
Fountain Inn 7 Broad St ☎01982 553888. Restored

fourteenth-century inn that's still predominantly a pub, though there's also an adjoining café, both with oversized TVs. Popular with townsfolk, so if you want local info, this is the place to come. Pub daily 9am–midnight; café Mon–Thurs 9am–5pm, Fri–Sun till 8pm.

The Strand 2 Groe St ☎ 01982 552652. Genteel two-floored café specializing in home-made treats, especially cakes and puddings, as well as all-day breakfasts (£6.95), toasted sandwiches and pies. Mon–Sat 9am–5pm.

Wyeside Arts Centre ☎ 01982 553683, ⓦ wyeside.co.uk.

Superb multi-purpose centre converted out of the town's Victorian Assembly Rooms, and venue for all manner of excellent cultural happenings, including film, comedy, music (of all genres), theatre and dance, and visual arts.

Llandrindod Wells

Following the 1864 arrival of the railway, **LLANDRINDOD WELLS** (Llandrindod; locally referred to as "Llandod" or simply "Dod") was once Wales's most elegant spa resort. Its Victorian heyday is long since over, however, although many of the fine buildings from the era still stand, and it's well worth a stop to admire the faded glamour of its ornate architecture. Moreover, there are a couple of very worthwhile museums, as well as a fantastic Victorian park in which to while away an hour so in.

Local **walks** from Llandrindod include routes to the Iron Age hillfort on Cefnllys, taking in the witch's-hat spire of the thirteenth-century **St Michael's church** and **Bailey Einon Wood** nature reserve.

The signal box

Llandrindod station • June–Aug Fri & Sat 11am–3pm • Free • ☎ 01597 823116

On the station platform is an old London North Western Railway **signal box**, dating from 1865, but actually moved here in 1986 from the level crossing a little further up

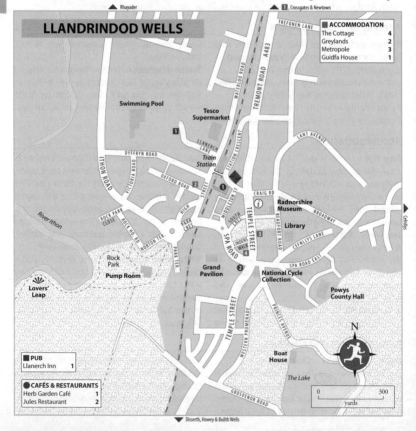

LLANDRINDOD WELLS

▲ Rhayader   ▲ 🚂 Crossgates & Newtown

■ ACCOMMODATION	
The Cottage	**4**
Greylands	**2**
Metropole	**3**
Guidfa House	**1**

Swimming Pool
Tesco Supermarket
TREFONEN LANE
WATERLOO ROAD
TREMONT ROAD
A483
LANT AVENUE
LLANERCH LANE
DYFFRYN ROAD
STATION CRESCENT
Train Station
OXFORD ROAD
CRAIG RD
ITHON ROAD
VICTORIA ROAD
HIGH STREET
MIDDLETON ST
SOUTH CREST
Radnorshire Museum
BROADWAY
River Ithon
ROCK PARK CLOSE
ROCK RD / RD
NORTON TER.
PARK CRES
PARK TER.
SPA ROAD
LINDEN WALK
BEAUFORT ROAD
TEMPLE STREET
Library
CEFNLLIS LANE
Rock Park
SPA ROAD EAST
Grand Pavilion
National Cycle Collection
Pump Room
Lovers' Leap
Powys County Hall
TEMPLE STREET
WESTERN PROMENADE
PRINCES AVENUE
N
Boat House
The Lake
GROSVENOR ROAD
Cefnllys

■ PUB	
Llanerch Inn	**1**

● CAFÉS & RESTAURANTS	
Herb Garden Café	**1**
Jules Restaurant	**2**

0 ——— 300
yards

▼ Disserth, Howey & Builth Wells

the tracks. Still with its original fixtures and fittings, it now houses an interesting little display about the railway and its spirited survival in the face of repeated plans for closure over the last fifty years.

Radnorshire Museum

Temple St • April–Sept Tues–Fri 10am–4pm, Sat 10am–4pm; Oct–March Tues–Fri 10am–4pm, Sat 10am–1pm • £1 • ☎ 01597 824513

The small but hugely entertaining **Radnorshire Museum** evokes the area's history with exhibits ranging from archeological finds to items from Victorian spa days. Among the pick of these is a Sheela-na-gig, a typically crude, though remarkably well-preserved, carved relief of a vulva, found in the local parish church, and a log-boat dredged up from the Ifor River in 1929 and thought to date from around 1200 AD. Elsewhere, look out for the original clock from the station signal box, and an elegant needle shower of the kind used at the old pump room.

In between the museum and the tourist office, take a look at the unusual and extraordinary tufa (calcite) rock wall – still partly covered by a glass roof – this being all that remains of a conservatory that stood here until it was demolished in the 1970s.

National Cycle Collection

Temple St • May–Oct Mon–Fri 10am–4pm; Nov–April Tues, Thurs & Fri 10am–4pm • £4 • ☎ 01597 825531, ⓦ cyclemuseum.org.uk

Down Temple Street the marvellous **National Cycle Collection**, a nostalgic collection of some 240 velocipedes, including ordinaries (aka penny-farthings), trikes, racers and an 8ft-high "Eiffel Tower" advertising bike from 1899. The museum holds some notable machinery, not least a bike belonging to the prolific, but little-known about, George Nightingale, the first man to ride 25 miles in under an hour (in 1938). There are also bikes belonging to another serial record-breaking time trialist, Eileen Sheridan, and 1992 Olympic gold medallist Chris Boardman (with his racing skin). Look out, too, for the Pneumatic Tyred Racer dating from 1890, its front wheel larger than the rear, which, some experts believe, may have been used in the first modern Olympics, in 1896.

Rock Park

Quietly tucked away on the southwest side of town, and accessed via several paths, **Rock Park** is a delightful spot for a leisurely ramble. Part Victorian arboretum (including Douglas Fir, Japanese Red Cedar), part native woodland, and bisected by the frothing Arlais Brook, it's also the site of numerous mineral-rich springs, such as the Chalybeate spring, consisting of an ornate pink marble fountain and drinking basin. At the heart of the park, the once-lavish **spa pump room** is now, somewhat more prosaically, a conference centre, though the iron and glass-framed pavilion, connecting the pump room and old treatment centre, still resonates. From here, a path leads to "**Lovers' Leap**", a Victorian fake cliff overlooking the river. Next door to the pump room, the tiny café is an unlikely spot to grab the best coffee in town. There's also a 1.5km-long Tree Trail through the park; pick up a leaflet from the spa building reception.

ARRIVAL AND INFORMATION	**LLANDRINDOD WELLS**
By train The train station is in the heart of town between the High Street and Station Crescent.	Destinations Builth Wells (4 daily; 15min); Knighton (4 daily; 40min); Llanwrtyd Wells (4 daily; 30min);

VICTORIAN FESTIVAL

Llandrindod Wells' town's strong Victorian heritage is celebrated each August in the vibrant, week-long **Victorian Festival** (ⓦ victorianfestival.co.uk), with concerts, plays, guided walks, food and craft tents, a Victorian fayre and circus, and, of course, Victorian costume parades; the week culminates with a fireworks display over the lake.

Shrewsbury (4 daily; 1hr 40min); Swansea (4 daily; 2hr 30min).

By bus Buses leave from outside the train station. Destinations Aberystwyth (1 daily; 1hr 40min); Brecon (7 daily Mon–Sat; 1hr); Builth Wells (hourly; 20min);

Newtown (6 daily; 50min); Rhayader (7 daily; 25min).

Tourist information The TIC is in front of the Radnorshire Museum on Temple Street (Easter–Oct Mon–Fri 10am–4pm, Sat 10am–1pm; Nov–Easter Mon–Sat 10am–1pm; ☏ 01597 822600, ⊛ llandrindod.co.uk).

ACCOMMODATION

The Cottage Spa Rd ☏ 01597 825435, ⊛ thecottagebandb.co.uk. Handsome Edwardian property fronted by a pretty, tree-filled garden, with seven differently configured rooms, all laden with period-style furnishings. No TVs in the rooms but guests are welcome to use the lounge. Exceptional value. **£65**

Greylands High St ☏ 01597 822253, ⊛ greylands guesthouse.co.uk. Tall Victorian red-brick house in the town centre, near the station, with seven comfortable, good-value rooms, comprising singles, twins, doubles and family options. **£60**

Guidfa House Crossgates, 3 miles north on A44 ☏ 01597 851241, ⊛ guidfa-house.co.uk. This relaxing

Georgian guesthouse set in deep countryside has six pretty rooms, each one thoughtfully designed and neatly presented. There's also an elegant sitting room with log fire, and the hosts can also provide simple, snack-type meals made from local produce. **£95**

Metropole Temple St ☏ 01597 823700, ⊛ metropole .co.uk. Fronted by a splendid Art Nouveau canopy, this imposing, deep-green-coloured hotel has been a prominent fixture in town since 1896. Despite its size, and obvious business/group oriented approach, the personal touch remains (it is privately owned) and the rooms are spot on. There's also a spa centre, as well as a very decent bar/brasserie and restaurant. **£126**

EATING AND DRINKING

Herb Garden Café 5 Spa Centre ☏ 01597 823082. Fresh, organically produced salads and platters (£7.50), juicy house burgers and a stack of sweet treats at this attractive, friendly diner/gallery. The big windows and squashy sofas make this a great venue to kick back. Mon–Sat 9.30am–5pm.

Jules Restaurant Temple St ☏ 01597 824642, ⊛ julesrestaurant.blogspot.co.uk. Brashly coloured restaurant and wine bar offering a menu of great variety (stuffed cherry peppers, Kerala fish curry) including some tempting vegetarian options (spicy pumpkin tagine,

cottage cheese and pepper curry). The Light Bite menu (£10) is good value. Tues–Sat 11.30am–2pm & 5.30–11pm, Sun noon–2pm.

Llanerch Inn Llanerch Lane ☏ 01597 822234. Directly opposite the train station, this sixteenth-century hostelry is central Llandrindod's only pub, and predates most of the surrounding town by quite some time. A pint in front of the stone fireplace or a well-cooked, classic pub meal are two good reasons to come here. Daily 11am–11pm.; food served noon–2.30pm & 6–9.30pm.

North and east Radnorshire

Before the reorganization of British counties in 1974, Radnorshire was the most sparsely populated county in either Wales or England, and it's still a remote area, especially to the north and east. In the northwest, **Rhayader** is the only settlement of any real size. Most people base themselves here to explore the wild countryside to the west of the town, a hilly patchwork of waterfalls, bogland, bare peaks and the four interlocking reservoirs of the **Elan Valley**, built at the beginning of the twentieth century and displaying a grandiose Edwardian solidity.

The countryside to the northeast of Rhayader is slightly tamer, with lanes and bridlepaths delving in and around the woods and farms, occasionally brushing through minute settlements like the village of **Abbeycwmhir**, named for the scant ruins of the Cistercian abbey in the dank, eerie valley of the Clywedog Brook. From here, the hills roll eastwards towards the English border and some of the most intact parts of **Offa's Dyke**, the eighth-century King of Mercia's border with the Welsh princes. The handsome border town of **Knighton** is well geared-up for walkers and cyclists. Seven miles south and inches from England, the dignified town of **Presteigne** contains some intriguing reminders of its former role as the county capital. The River Lugg flows through Presteigne from the Radnorshire hills, passing the isolated church at **Pilleth**, where Owain Glyndŵr captured Sir Edmund Mortimer, agent of the English king, in 1402.

Rhayader

Ten miles west of Llandrindod Wells lies the small, bustling town of **RHAYADER** (Rhaeder Gwy, literally "waterfall on the Wye"). Although the waterfall invoked by the town's name virtually disappeared when the town bridge was built in 1780, the Wye still frames the town centre, running in a loop around the western and southern sides. Rhayader was a centre of the mid-nineteenth-century "**Rebecca Riots**", when local farmers disguised themselves in women's clothing in order to tear down tollgates that were prohibitively expensive for travellers and local workers. Rhayader's four main streets – named North, South, East and West – meet at a small clock tower in the centre of town.

Gilfach Farm Nature Reserve

Three miles north of Rhayader, just off the A470 • Visitor & exhibition centre: April–Sept Sat & Sun 10.30am–5pm • Free • ☎ 01597 870301 or ☎ 823298, ⓦ rwtwales.org

The peaceful **Gilfach Farm Nature Reserve** is the showpiece of the Radnorshire Wildlife Trust. Within the 418 acres are meadows, oak forest, moorland, an old railway tunnel that's home to some bats, and river habitats supporting a huge variety of wildlife and flora. The restored longhouse barn has now been kitted out as a **visitor and exhibition centre**, showing live video footage from four birds' nests around the reserve.

Gigrin Farm Red Kite Feeding Station

Off South Road (the A470 from Builth) on the outskirts of Rhayader • Daily: summer 1–5pm, winter 1–4pm • £5 • ☎ 01597 810243, ⓦ gigrin.co.uk

One of the best places anywhere in Europe to watch **red kites feeding** is at **Gigrin Farm**. Each day at 3pm (2pm in winter), these magnificent birds are lured here (ravens and buzzards join in the frenzy too), with as many as five hundred descending at any one time – it's a fantastic sight. A handful of hides are used for viewing, including some specialized photography/filming hides, though a fee is payable for the use of these and they must be pre-booked. There's also a scenic one-and-a-half-mile-long nature trail here as well as a small visitor centre.

ARRIVAL AND GETTING AROUND   RHAYADER

By bus Buses stop in the main Dark Lane car park behind the leisure centre and serve Builth Wells (hourly; 20min) andLlandrindod Wells (7 daily; 25min).

By bike Bike rental is available from Clive Powell Bikes on West Street, on the road out towards the Elan Valley (daily 9am–5.30pm; £6/hr, £24/day; ☎ 01597 811343, ⓦ clivepowell-mtb.co.uk) which also does servicing and repairs.

ACCOMMODATION

Beili Neuadd 2 miles northeast of town off the B4518 ☎ 01597 810211, ⓦ belineuadd.co.uk. A laid-back farmhouse B&B, this also has a sixteenth-century stone barn bunkhouse containing three rooms, each with bathroom, kitchen and lounge. Walkers and cyclists are particularly welcome. Dorms **£18**, doubles **£80**

Elan Hotel West St ☎ 01597 810109, ⓦ elanhotel .co.uk. Ten well insulated rooms above a pub, each one furnished in simple pinewood, with wall-mounted TVs and decent enough bathrooms. **£67**

Ty Morgans East St ☎ 01597 811666, ⓦ tymorgans .com. Superb building housing nine effortlessly cool rooms, most of which still feature their original red or grey bare brick walls and oak-beamed ceilings. Thick carpets, low-slung beds and numerous mod cons round things off in great style. **£80**

CAMPING

Gigrin Farm Off South Road (the A470 from Builth) ☎ 01597 810243, ⓦ gigrin.co.uk. A quiet, very basic option (flush toilets, hot water but no showers) at the red kite feeding station (see above). **£5**/pitch

Wyeside Immediately north of town off the A470 ☎ 01597 810183, ⓦ wyesidecamping.co.uk. On the banks of the Wye, this is a smart site with separate camping and caravan areas and clean, modern amenities. Closed Nov–Feb. **£17**/pitch

EATING AND DRINKING

Crown Inn North St ☎ 01597 811099. Most agreeable of the town's several boozers, with lots of small, dark wooden tables gathered around a large stone fireplace and Brains beer. Daily noon–11pm.

Old Swan Corner of West and South sts ☎01597 811060. Tuck into chunky pasties and lots of home-made sugary treats (baklava, carrot cake, cream scones) in this agreeably old-fashioned daytime tearoom with faded Formica tablecloths and plenty of clutter. Mon–Sat 9am–5pm, Sun 11am–5pm.

Ty Morgans East St ☎01597 811666. The pick of what

few places there are to eat in town, this buzzy bar/bistro offers a mouthwatering burger menu (including a pork, honey and mustard burger) in addition to more sophisticated fare (pan-seared duck breast with braised red cabbage, £12.99). The bistro leads through to the bustling Strand coffee house and deli. Bistro daily 8am–10pm; coffee house daily 8am–5pm.

Elan Valley

Until the last decade of the nineteenth century, the untamed countryside west of Rhayader received few visitors, although the poet Shelley did holiday here. Shelley's honeymoon retreat at Nantgwyllt was among the couple of dozen buildings submerged by the waters of the **Elan Valley** reservoirs, a nine-mile-long string of four lakes created between 1892 and 1903 to supply water to the rapidly growing industrial city of Birmingham, 75 miles away; in the 1950s, a supplementary reservoir at Claerwen, to the immediate west, was opened. Although the lakes enhance an already beautiful and idyllic part of the world, the colonialist way in which Welsh valleys, villages and farmsteads were seized and flooded to provide water for England is something tourist promotions prefer to gloss over.

The "appeal" of the Elan Valley is, nonetheless, extremely strong, not only for the landscape but for the profusion of rare plants and birds in the area. **Red kites** are especially cherished – in the 1930s, when numbers were down to just a couple of breeding pairs, the Elan Valley looked set to enter the history books as their last outpost in Britain. Loss of habitat, along with nest robbing by collectors and poisoning at the hands of farmers, was largely to blame, but conservation work undertaken by a few dedicated individuals saved the day. Since then, these birds of prey have staged an impressive recovery, becoming so common they've started repopulating surrounding areas. There is also a healthy population of kestrels, peregrines, merlins, buzzards, goshawks and sparrowhawks.

Claerwen Reservoir

From the Elan Valley visitor centre, a road tucks in along the bank of Caban Coch to the **Garreg Ddu** viaduct, from where you can follow the bank for four spectacular miles to the vast 1952 dam on **Claerwen Reservoir**. More remote and less popular than the Elan lakes, Claerwen is a good base for the more determined walker with paths for eight to ten miles across the harsh terrain to the abbey of Strata Florida or the lonely **Teifi Pools**.

Pen-y-garreg

From the Garreg Ddu viaduct, a more popular road continues north along the long, glassy finger of **Garreg Ddu Reservoir**, before doubling back on itself just below the awesome **Pen-y-garreg** dam and reservoir; if the dam is overflowing, the vast wall of foaming water is mesmerizing. At the top of Pen-y-garreg lake, it's possible to drive over the dam at **Craig Goch** for a close-up view of its gracious curve, elegant Edwardian arches and green cupola. The lake beyond it is fed by the Elan River, which the road crosses just short of a junction. A bleak, invigorating moorland pass heads west from here before dropping into the eerie moonscape of Cwmystwyth, while the eastbound road funnels into a beautiful valley back to Rhayader. On the way back, fork off the Elan Valley Road in Rhayader onto the smaller Aberystwyth Road.

INFORMATION

ELAN VALLEY

Elan Valley visitor centre Just below the dam of the first reservoir, Caban Coch (daily 10am–4.30pm; ☎01597 810898,

ⓦ elanvalley.org.uk), the centre has stacks of info on the valley (including a series of leaflets on local walks), an

exhibition about the history and ecology of the area, bike hire (£5/1hr, £20/day) and a tearoom. Look out, too, for the superb ranger-led events (such as botanical and birdwatching safaris), some of which are free to attend.

ACCOMMODATION AND EATING

Elan Valley Hotel Elan Valley ☎01597 810448, ⓦ elanvalleyhotel.co.uk. Delightful, privately run country house on the Rhayader side of Elan village, which offers eleven subtly decorated, individually styled rooms, good food in its well-regarded restaurant and a lively bar. Restaurant daily 6.30–9pm; bar daily 11am–11pm, food served 12.30–2.30pm & 6.30–8.30pm. **£85**

Penbont House Tea Room Pen-y-Garreg Dam ☎01597 811515. Hospitable two-roomed B&B with shared shower facilities, located just below the Pen-y-Garreg Dam. It's warm tearoom is equally inviting after a long walk; light meals, cakes, coffee and afternoon teas are on offer. Tearoom daily 11am–5pm. **£85**

Abbeycwmhir

ABBEYCWMHIR (Abaty Cwm Hir), seven miles northeast of Rhayader, takes its name from the abbey whose meagre ruins (open access; free) lie beneath the village. Cistercian monks founded the abbey in 1146, planning one of the largest churches in Britain, whose 242ft nave has only ever been exceeded in length by the cathedrals of Durham, York and Winchester. Destruction by Henry III's troops in 1231 scuppered plans to continue the building, however. The sparse remains of what they did build – a rocky outline of the floorplan – lie in a conifer-carpeted valley alongside a gloomy green lake, lending weight, if only by atmosphere, to the site's melancholic associations. Llywelyn ap Gruffydd's body, after his head had been carted off to London, was rumoured to have been brought here from Cilmeri (near Builth Wells) in 1282, and a new granite slab, carved with a Celtic sword, lies on the altar to commemorate this last native prince of Wales. It should look incongruous, but somehow it only adds to the eerie presence of the ruins and the village.

The Hall at Abbeycwmhir

Tours daily 10.30am & 2pm; advance booking essential • Tours £15, gardens only £5 • ☎01597 851727, ⓦ abbeycwmhir.com

Presiding over the ruins at Abbeycwmhir is the resplendent, privately owned manor house **The Hall at Abbeycwmhir**, set in twelve acres of flower-filled gardens and woodlands. Built in 1834 by Thomas Wilson, this Gothic Victorian pile possesses 52 rooms – mostly restored in the late 1990s – each and every one of which can be viewed on a guided tour conducted by one of the family members. Among the highlights is the beautifully tiled entrance hall with its decorative plasterwork, the magnificent snooker room complete with stained-glass ceiling, and variously themed bedrooms and bathrooms (castles, trains and the seaside to name but three). Afterwards, have a wander around the gardens and grounds, comprising silky lawns and terraces, woodland, a lake and waterfall.

Presteigne

Twenty miles east of Llandrindod Wells, the charming town of **PRESTEIGNE** (Llanandras) has attracted refugees from the rat race ever since the 1960s, which partly accounts for the craft, antique and book shops, and laid-back cafés occupying the town's gracious and old-fashioned buildings. The town tucks in between the B4362 town bypass and the River Lugg, the border with England, which flows under the seventeenth-century bridge at the bottom of Broad Street. Just before the bridge, the solid parish **church of St Andrew** contains Saxon and Norman fragments, as well as a sixteenth-century Flemish tapestry.

The end of the High Street is the site of the town's most impressive building, the Jacobean **Radnorshire Arms**, built as a private home for Sir Christopher Hatton, Lord Chancellor of England and, allegedly, lover of Queen Elizabeth I, who owned neighbouring property.

PRESTEIGNE FESTIVAL

During the last week of August, Presteigne stages the prestigious **Presteigne Festival** (ⓦpresteignefestival.com), a classical music arts event, with concerts held in venues such as St Andrew's church, the Assembly Rooms and other churches in nearby villages.

Judge's Lodging

Broad St • March–Oct Tues–Sun 10am–5pm; Nov Wed–Sun 10am–4pm; Dec 1–22 Sat & Sun 10am–4pm • £7.50 • ☎01544 260650, ⓦ judgeslodging.org.uk

Presteigne's standout attraction is the **Judge's Lodging**, a fabulously interpreted trawl through the rooms where circuit judges stayed while presiding over the local assizes. Before entering the lodging properly, take a peek at the old holding cells, which replaced the original underground cells located beneath the dock in 1900. The evocative wall mounted photos recall the history of the Radnorshire Constabulary, formed in 1847 (and at the time the smallest force in the country) but which then merged with Brecknockshire in 1948 to become the Mid-Wales constabulary. Its most recent incarnation came in 1968 when it joined several other regional forces to become the Dyfed-Powys police force, the second largest in Britain.

Armed with a good old-fashioned Walkman, your audio guide introduces you to various characters along the way, though this does ramble on somewhat and you'll probably end up fast-forwarding certain sections. Nothing is roped off or hidden behind screens, and it feels more like visiting a private home than a museum, while the oil lamps that light the upper floors and the gas-flame lighting in the servants' quarters provide a whiff of authenticity. Finally you emerge in the courtroom, where an alleged thief that you've "met" in the cells is being tried for allegedly stealing ducks and poultry.

ARRIVAL AND INFORMATION   PRESTEIGNE

By bus Buses from Knighton, Kington and Leominster stop outside the *Radnorshire Arms* or at the coach park on the bypass.

Tourist information The TIC is housed within the Judge's Lodging (March–Oct Tues–Sun 10am–5pm; Nov Wed–Sun 10am–4pm; Dec 1–22 Sat & Sun 10am–4pm; ☎01544 260650, ⓦpresteigne.org.uk).

ACCOMMODATION AND EATING

Gumma Farm Nearly 2 miles west on the road to Discoed ☎01547 560243. Homely charms abound at *Gumma Farm*, which has one double en suite, and a twin and single sharing a bathroom; you can also camp here. Double **£60**; camping **£3**/person

Hat Shop Restaurant 7 High St ☎01544 260017, ⓦthehatshoprestaurant.co.uk. This perky, two-floored eatery sporting bright orange and sunflower-yellow painted wood-panelled walls is a delightful spot to try out the Welsh/Italian accented food. Look out too for various themed food nights. Mon–Sat 10am–3pm & 6.30–10pm.

No. 46 Wine Bar 46 High St ☎01544 267675. A fun time is almost certainly guaranteed at this cosmopolitan wine bar, laid out with stripped wood flooring and creative, colourful furnishings. Wine and wine tastings aside, there's also a terrific selection of Trappist beers and tapas dishes, as well as a regular programme of events including live music and poetry readings. Daily 11am–2pm & 5pm–late.

Old Vicarage Norton 2 miles north on the road to Knighton ☎01544 260038, ⓦoldvicarage-nortonrads .co.uk. Sumptuous Victorian country house designed by Sir George Gilbert Scott with three gorgeous, antique-furnished rooms (no TVs but vintage radios), each with fine views across the Marches and a wonderful garden. Minimum two-night stay at weekends between March to October. **£112**

Radnorshire Arms High St ☎01544 267406, ⓦradnorshirearmshotel.com. The "Rad" is a lovely, historic boozer boasting oak-panelled walls, an open fire and a superb choice of real ales; weekly happenings include Jam night on Monday, and pool (free) on Wednesday. The pub's warm restaurant is a good spot to chow down on one of the house burgers or steaks, as is the family-friendly tented beer garden. There are distinguished-looking period guestrooms (thick, plush carpets and oak wood panelling) in the main building, in addition to a modern set of rooms in the surprisingly cosy garden lodge to the rear. Breakfast is extra. Daily 11am–11pm; food served noon–2.15pm & 6.30–9pm. **£115**

> ## GLYNDŴR'S WAY
>
> The fabulous **Glyndŵr's Way** (ⓦnationaltrail.co.uk/glyndwrsway) weaves for 135 miles through the solitary rural landscapes of Montgomeryshire and northern Radnorshire, from Knighton to Welshpool. Well signposted all the way, though depending rather a lot on lane and road walking, Glyndŵr's Way is far quieter than the Offa's Dyke Path, both in the number of settlements en route and the number of hikers on the trail. Varied scenery includes barren bog, exhilarating uplands, reservoirs, undulating farmland and sections of river-valley walking. You can pick up an official route guide for £12.99 from tourist offices in the region or order it online at ⓦpowystrails.org.uk.

Old Radnor

Just off the A44 six miles southwest of Presteigne, **OLD RADNOR** was once the home of King Harold, killed at the Battle of Hastings by William the Conqueror's troops. The site of his vanished castle is down the lane running southeast from the large, very English-looking **church of St Stephen**, looking across to Radnor Forest. Inside, beyond the elaborately carved 15th-century rood screen and dating from the 16th century, is Britain's oldest organ case (though the organ is newer), and there's a chunky pre-Norman font on four stone feet.

ACCOMMODATION AND EATING   OLD RADNOR

Harp Inn Old Radnor ⓣ01544 350655, ⓦharpinn radnor.co.uk. In a rambling, fifteenth-century former farm building, the *Harp Inn* serves delicious Welsh meals like bacon-wrapped wild rabbit in mustard and cream, plus a few Mediterranean excursions and hard-to-find real ales. It also has atmospheric rooms, some with four-poster or wrought-iron beds. Bar & restaurant Tues–Fri 6–11pm, Sat & Sun noon–3pm & 6–11pm. **£75**

Radnor Forest

North of New Radnor, the deep ravines and wooded hillsides of **Radnor Forest** offer some memorable high-level walking and birdwatching. A good starting point is the village of **New Radnor** from where a lane called Mutton Dingle gives access to a couple of routes around the isolated summit of **The Whimble** and above spectacularly deep Harley Dingle towards the prominent mast on Black Mixen. Further west, just off the A44, a track signposted from the car park leads into a thick forest and to the rushing cascade of the **Water-break-its-neck waterfall**, at its icicle-adorned best in winter.

Knighton

Lively, attractive **KNIGHTON** (Tref-y-clawdd, "the town on the dyke"), six miles north of Presteigne, straddles King Offa's eighth-century border and the modern Wales–England divide, and has come into its own as a base for those walking the **Offa's Dyke Path** and the **Glyndŵr's Way** footpath (see box above).

So close is Knighton to the border that the town's **train station** is actually in England. From here, Station Road crosses the River Teme into Wales and climbs a couple of hundred yards into the town, joining the pretty Broad Street at Brookside Square. Further up the hill is the town's Victorian clock tower, where Broad Street becomes West Street and the steep High Street soars off up to the left, past rickety Tudor buildings and up to the mound of the old **castle**.

ARRIVAL AND DEPARTURE   KNIGHTON

By train The train station is at the bottom of Station Road, a few minutes' walk from the centre.
Destinations Llandrindod Wells (4 daily; 40min); Llanwrtyd Wells (4 daily; 1hr 10min); Shrewsbury (4 daily; 1hr); Swansea (4 daily; 3hr 10min).
By bus Buses serve Ludlow (4 daily; 1hr) and Presteigne (5 daily; 20min).

GETTING AROUND AND INFORMATION

By bike The nearest bike rental firm, Wheely Wonderful (☎01568 770755, ⊛wheelywonderfulcycling.co.uk), is over the border in Shropshire at Petchfield Farm, Elton, near Ludlow, but will deliver to Knighton. £20 full day/£15 half day.

Tourist information The Offa's Dyke Centre on West Street (Easter–Oct daily 10am–5pm; Nov–Easter Mon–Sat 10am–4pm; ☎01547 528753, ⊛offasdyke.demon.co.uk or ⊛visitknighton.co.uk) has all the information you need, both on the town and the Dyke itself; there is an informative exhibition on the latter here.

ACCOMMODATION AND EATING

Barclay's Coffee House 7 Broad St ☎01547 520950. The freshly roasted coffee at this laid-back café is the best in town, an experience made all the more enjoyable thanks to the haphazardly arranged shelving piled high with secondhand books. Mon–Sat 9am–5pm.

Fleece House Market St ☎01547 520168, ⊛fleecehouse.co.uk. A converted eighteenth-century coaching inn that's now a low-key little guesthouse with just two twin-bedded rooms decked out with slate-tiled walls and home-made wooden furnishings. **£80**

Horse and Jockey Wylcwm Place ☎01547 520062, ⊛thehorseandjockeyinn.co.uk. The town's main hostelry is this fourteenth-century coaching inn, whose warming snug is a lovely spot to hunker down in with a pint. The restaurant features a lip-smacking menu of sizzling steaks as well as the usual pub standards. Daily noon–11pm; food served noon–2pm & 6–9pm.

Knighton Hotel Broad St ☎01547 520530, ⊛theknighton.com. This smart hotel offers sixteen beautifully appointed rooms positioned around a gorgeous double staircase. The Spa Suite, incorporating steam room, sauna and jacuzzi, rounds things off nicely, if expensively. **£130**

★**Offa Dyke House** 4 High St ☎01547 528886, ⊛offadykehouse.com. Homely, very accommodating guesthouse whose proprietor is an author – hence the prevailingly bookish atmosphere; the three rooms (two have bathrooms in the corridor) are appealingly furnished with writing desks, handsome beds and some thoughtful little touches like fresh fruit and flowers. It's tricky to find; the entrance is by the little gate opposite the Clock Tower. **£75**

Panpwnton Farm Panpwnton ☎01547 528597. Cheap camping in a field over the river and half a mile up the lane that forks left at the station. **£3.50/person**

Montgomeryshire

The northern part of Powys is made up of the old county of **Montgomeryshire**, an area of enormously varying landscapes and few inhabitants. The best base for the spartan and mountainous southwest of the county is the spirited little town of **Llanidloes** ten miles north of Rhayader on the River Severn (Afon Hafren), which arrives in the town after rising nearby in the dense **Hafren Forest** on the bleak slopes of **Plynlimon**.

From Llanidloes, one of Wales's most dramatic roads rises past the chilly shores of the **Llyn Clywedog Reservoir**, squeezed into sharp hillsides, and up through the remote hamlet of **Dylife**. East of here, **Newtown** serves as a good transport interchange and will interest followers of **Robert Owen**; close by lie the dank hilltop remains of **Dolforwyn Castle**.

OFFA'S DYKE

George Borrow, in his classic book *Wild Wales*, noted that it was once "customary for the English to cut off the ears of every Welshman who was found to the east of the dyke, and for the Welsh to hang every Englishman whom they found to the west of it". Certainly, **Offa's Dyke** has provided a potent symbol of Welsh–English antipathy ever since it was created in the eighth century as a demarcation line by King Offa of Mercia, ruler of the whole of central England. It appears that the dyke was an attempt to thwart Welsh expansionism.

Up to 20ft high and 60ft wide, the earthwork made use of natural boundaries such as rivers in its run north to south, and is best seen in the sections near Knighton in Radnorshire and Montgomery. Today's England–Wales border crosses the dyke many times, although the basic boundary has changed little since Offa's day. The glorious **long-distance footpath** (⊛nationaltrail.co.uk), opened in 1971, runs from Prestatyn on the north Clwyd coast for 177 miles to Sedbury Cliffs, just outside Chepstow, and is one of the most rewarding walks in Britain – neither too popular to be unpleasantly crowded, nor too monotonous in its landscapes.

This stark, uplifting scenery contrasts with the gentler, greener contours that characterize the east of the county, where the muted old county town of **Montgomery**, with its fine Georgian architecture, perches above the border and Offa's Dyke. In the north of the county, **Welshpool** is the only major settlement, packed in above the wide flood plain of the Severn and linked by an impossibly cute toy rail line to **Llanfair Caereinion**. On the southern side of Welshpool is Montgomeryshire's one unmissable sight, the sumptuous **Powis Castle** and its exquisite terraced gardens. The very north of the county is pastoral, deserted and beautiful, particularly around **Lake Vyrnwy**.

Llanidloes and around

Transforming itself from rural village to weaving town and, more recently, into a centre for artists and craftspeople, **LLANIDLOES** (pronounced Thlann-idd-loiss) has managed to avoid the decline of so many other small market towns. It's a charming little place which receives few visitors, but is well worth a detour.

The town centres on four main streets, which all meet at the market hall – the main thoroughfare is Great Oak Street, a wide, handsome road framed by well-proportioned, two- and three-storey buildings variously accommodating shops, restaurants and tenements. Running in the opposite direction, west of the market hall, is Short Bridge Street, a line of fine buildings running down to the River Severn, past two imposing

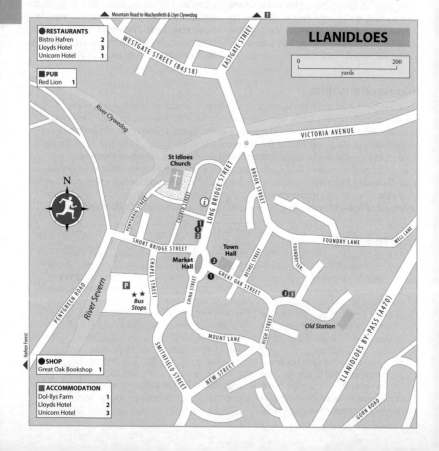

nineteenth-century chapels – one Zionist, one Baptist – staring across the road at each other. North and south of the market hall are China Street and Long Bridge Street – the latter is good for interesting little shops.

The Market Hall and exhibition centre

Great Oak St • Late May–Sept Tues–Sun 11am–4pm • Free • ☎ 01686 412388

At the junction of the town's four mains streets is the superb black-and-white **market hall**, built on timber stilts around 1600, allowing the market – now long since moved – to take place on the cobbles underneath. The only surviving timber-framed market hall in Wales, it's also known as the Booth Hall, and remained a popular trading place until the early twentieth century, as well as functioning, at one time or other, as a law court, a meeting place for the Quakers, a flannel store, and the local Working Men's Institute.

Today it houses an **exhibition centre** with a fascinating display on other similarly timbered buildings in Llanidloes and further afield. You can pick up a free trail leaflet outlining the town's many timbered buildings.

St Idloes church

Church St, off Bridge St • Daily 10.30am–3.30pm • Call ☎ 01686 412370 to confirm opening hours

The glory of the **church of St Idloes** is its impressive fifteenth-century hammerbeam roof (also known as the "Angel Roof"), originally thought to have been poached from Abbeycwmhir; however, recent tree-ring dating (a sample of which forms part of the market hall exhibition) suggests that this was most probably not the case. The pillars and arches, though, were most certainly taken from the abbey following its dissolution in 1536. The adjoining mid-fourteenth-century tower, meanwhile, is typical of those found in the county, a massive square block crowned by a wooden belfry and pyramidal roof.

The Town Hall and Museum

Great Oak St • Museum Tues, Thurs & Fri 11am–1pm & 2–4pm, Sat 11am–2pm • £1 • ☎ 01686 413777

At the centre of Great Oak Street is the **town hall**, originally built as a temperance hotel to challenge the boozy **Trewythen Arms** opposite. A plaque on the closed hotel commemorates Llanidloes as an unlikely-seeming place of industrial and political unrest, when, in April 1839, Chartists stormed the building, dragging out and beating up special constables who had been dispatched to the town in a futile attempt to suppress the political fervour of the local flannel weavers. Free guided town walks set off from the town hall between June and September from Tuesday through to Saturday at 10.30am.

Back across the road in the town hall complex, the eclectic **museum** offers a diverting collection, ranging from old local prints and mementos, including pictures of boomtown Dylife, to a stuffed two-headed lamb, born locally in 1914.

Llyn Clywedog

Four miles northwest of Llanidloes, the beautiful **Llyn Clywedog Reservoir** was built as recently as the 1960s and has settled well into the folds of the Clywedog Valley. At its southern end, the modern concrete dam is Britain's tallest (237ft), towering menacingly over the remnants of the **Bryntail lead mine**, through which a signposted path runs. The roads along the southern shores of Clywedog wind around into the dense plantation of **Hafren Forest**, the only real sign of life and vegetation on the bleak, sodden slopes of **Plynlimon** (Pumlumon Fawr, 2469ft). There's a car park at **RHYD-Y-BENWCH**, in the heart of the forest, from where **walking paths** fan out, the most popular being a six-mile round trip following the River Severn up through the trees, past a waterfall and out to its source, a saturated peat bog in some of the harshest terrain in Wales.

Dylife

Nine miles northwest of Llanidloes, old mine workings herald the approach to **DYLIFE** (pronounced Duh-levah), a lead-mining community of almost two thousand people in the mid-nineteenth century, with a reputation as a lawless and licentious gambling pit. The mine closed in 1896, and the population has since dwindled to around just twenty (it features on the excellent historical website, Abandoned Communities, at ⓦabandonedcommunities.co.uk).

Good walks from Dylife include that up to Pen-y-crocbren, the mine-pocked slope that rises to the south of the village, and west to **Glaslyn**, or "blue lake", and the reedy shores of **Bugeilyn**. The scenically varied **Glyndŵr's Way** footpath (see box, p.238) crosses this patch on its way to Machynlleth. A popular viewpoint on the road two miles west of Dylife has been furnished with a cheery memorial to broadcaster and author **Wynford Vaughan-Thomas** (1908–87), whose outstretched slate hand points out to the dozens of rippling peaks and verdant valleys.

ARRIVAL AND INFORMATION

LLANIDLOES

By bus China Street curves down to the car park from where all bus services operate.

Destinations Aberystwyth (3 daily; 1hr); Newtown (7 daily; 30min); Ponterwyd (3 daily; 40min); Shrewsbury (6 daily; 2hr); Welshpool (6 daily; 1hr 10min).

Tourist information There's no tourist office in town, but the Llani Leisure shop, at 16 Long Bridge Street (daily 9am–5.30pm, closed Sun Oct–March; ☎01686 414893, ⓦllanidloes.com), stock lots of literature on the town and surrounds.

ACCOMMODATION AND EATING

Bistro Hafren 2 Great Oak St ☎01686 414936. Simple unfussy restaurant with little about it by way of decor, but which has a broad range of dishes (medallions of pork with cider and cream sauce, pan-fried lambs liver) as well as good-value set menus, such as the three-course dinner menu for £13. Mon & Wed–Sat 9am–2pm & 6–11pm, Sun noon–2pm.

Dol-llys Farm Trefeglwys Rd ☎01686 412694, ⓦdolllyscaravancampsite.co.uk. Large site around a 15min walk north of town, where you can choose from a pitch on the level field near the facilities, or a more secluded spot down by the river, where campfires are permitted. There are also some excellent play areas, and free fishing is available on site. Closed Nov–Easter. **£7**/person

★**Lloyds Hotel** Cambrian Place ☎01686 412284, ⓦlloydshotel.co.uk. Superbly run, highly idiosyncratic hotel possessing seven beautifully conceived rooms, each one awash with colour and character. Lots of lovely personal touches, right down to the wall-mounted sepia prints and watercolours. *Lloyds* is also the place for a unique dining

experience; pre-dinner drinks are served at 7.30pm followed by a surprise four-course menu (£35), and ending with teas and coffees – contact the hosts in advance if there is anything you don't eat. Advance booking is essential, as sittings are not every day and vary from week to week. **£86**

Red Lion 8 Long Bridge St ☎01686 412270. The most agreeable of the town's pubs; the main lounge bar has comfy leather seating huddled around an imposing stone fireplace festooned with brass, while the noisier other room is principally for bar games. Daily 11am–midnight.

Unicorn Hotel 4 Long Bridge St ☎01686 411171, ⓦunicornllanidloes.co.uk. A small hotel of considerable charm and quality, hosting six crisp, generously sized and impeccably clean rooms. There's a substantial breakfast to look forward to as well. The fabulous daytime bistro/ evening restaurant offers some deliciously sauced dishes (such as pork belly with a hoi-sin glaze, spring onions and plum sauce) alongside some fishy treats (pan fried sea bass with garlic and saffron £16). Tues–Sat 10.30am–2.30pm & 6.30–10pm. **£70**

SHOPPING

Great Oak Bookshop 35 Great Oak St. Worth popping into is the Great Oak bookshop, with loads of Celtic and Welsh-interest stuff and a barn full of good new and secondhand fiction. Mon–Sat 9am–5pm, Sun till 4pm.

Newtown and around

Despite its name, **NEWTOWN** (Y Drenewydd), thirteen miles northeast of Llanidloes, was founded in the thirteenth century, growing steadily until experiencing a massive population explosion in the nineteenth century as a centre for weaving and textiles – the town once boasted fifty pubs and six breweries. Today, its activity is much reduced and it's hardly awash with great amenities, but its compact town centre, straddling the River Severn, has a certain appeal. The main thoroughfare is Broad Street, which intersects with High Street by the nineteenth-century red terracotta **clock tower**. A few paces down High Street, it's worth popping into the **W.H. Smith** shop, which opened in 1927. It was decided, amid the company's modernization programme in the 1970s, to restore this particular branch to its original state, hence the marvellous oak shelving and other 1920s fixtures and fittings. Take a look, too, at the original tiling on the frontage.

Robert Owen Memorial Museum

The Cross, Broad St • Mon–Fri 11am–3pm, plus Sat July & Aug • Free • ☎ 01686 625544, ⓦ robert-owen-museum.org.uk

Back up near the clock tower, a plaque on the wall of Barclays Bank denotes the birthplace (the original house has long since gone) of early socialist **Robert Owen** (see box, p.244). His remarkable life is celebrated in the **Memorial Museum** directly opposite, its visitors' book indicating just how much of a shrine the place has become, with a roll call of socialist politicians and trade unionists scrawling their thanks for Owen's work in its pages. Among the many personal effects are some of his furnishings, many letters, his funeral procession card and a lock of hair. A two-minute walk down the road, on the outside wall of St Mary's church, is Owen's tomb, enclosed by a high black railing.

Textile Museum

5–7 Commercial St • June–Aug Mon, Tues & Thurs–Sat 2–5pm • £1 • ☎ 01938 622024

Over the river from the town centre, the **Textile Museum** sits above six cramped old weavers' cottages. Exhibits show the dramatic ebb and flow of the town's staple trade, from the flannel and handloom factories of the 1790s, through the social unrest and industrial decline of the 1830s and 1840s (Wales' first Chartist demonstration took place here in 1838), the revival of trade thanks to local entrepreneur Pryce Jones' world-first mail-order service, and its subsequent dwindling to nothing by 1935.

Oriel Davies Gallery

The Park • Mon–Sat 10am–5pm • Free • ☎ 01686 625041, ⓦ orieldavies.org

Adjacent to the car park and bus station, the **Oriel Davies Gallery** is a contemporary arts and crafts gallery comprising three separate spaces hosting imaginative temporary exhibitions, ranging from multimedia to ceramics and experimental artworks. There's a decent café here too.

Gregynog Hall

Gardens daily 8am–8pm • £3 • ☎ 01686 650224, ⓦ gregynog.org

Five miles north of Newtown, the mock-Tudor **Gregynog Hall** was the home from 1920 of Gwendoline and Margaret Davies, aesthete sisters who inherited a vast fortune from their port-building father and spent much of it on a world-class art collection, most of which now resides in Cardiff's National Museum of Wales. Gregynog became the headquarters for their artistic revival, including the establishment of a world-famous small press, which is up and running once more. It's now a tertiary institution, offering public courses in Welsh language and culture, but is perhaps best known for hosting the prestigious **Gregynog Music Festival** in late June, a high class feast of classical music.

The hall is not generally open to the public but the Grade 1 listed **gardens** are bursting with rhododendrons and azaleas, and there are some delightful woodland walks; once done there, you can replenish with a light lunch, and even a tipple, in the sunny courtyard café.

ARRIVAL AND DEPARTURE   **NEWTOWN AND AROUND**

By train Newtown's train station is on the southern edge of the town centre.

Destinations Aberystwyth (8 daily; 1hr 20min); Machynlleth (8 daily; 50min); Welshpool (8 daily; 15min).
By bus A path heads past the Victorian parish church of St David and up Back Lane to the bus station.

Destinations Llandrindod Wells (6 daily; 50min); Llanidloes (7 daily; 30min); Machynlleth (6 daily; 50min); Montgomery (8 daily; 20–40min); Welshpool (hourly; 40min).

ACCOMMODATION

Maesmawr Caersws ☎01686 688369, ⓦmidwales arts.org.uk. Some six miles west of Newtown, on the main road just beyond the village of Caersws, the vibrant Mid Wales Arts Centre (see below) also has delightful farmhouse accommodation. There are four rooms, each with wonderful views and containing original pieces of

artwork, some of which is for sale. **£80**

Yesterdays Severn Square ☎01686 622644, ⓦyesterdayshotel.com. Located in the square behind the clock tower, this sweetly old-fashioned B&B offers a mix of single, double and triple rooms and locally sourced Welsh breakfasts. **£70**

EATING, DRINKING AND ENTERTAINMENT

Maesmawr Caersws, six miles west of Newtown ☎01686 688369, ⓦmidwalesarts.org.uk. This lively, privately run arts centre often stages events and exhibitions worth looking out for.
Oriel Café Oriel Gallery ☎01686 625041. The location, next to the bus station, is far from glorious, but the funky-coloured, atrium-like interior is a fun place to try one of the imaginative (typically vegetarian) daily specials, like roast nut burger in a garlic and herb bun. Mon–Sat 10am–4pm.
Parker's Café 1 Short Bridge St ☎01686 626095.

Smart, civilized, daytime café next to the clock tower that is equally good for a sandwich or a slice of quiche, as it is a lunchtime glass of wine. A fuller evening menu is available later in the week. Mon–Sat 9am–5pm, plus 6–9pm Thurs–Sat, Sun 10am–3pm.
The Sportsman 17 Severn St ☎01686 623978. The town's one standout pub has a rough-hewn red-brick frontage hiding a clean, good-looking interior where you can avail yourself of one of the many fine ales from the local Monty's brewery. Tues–Sun noon–11pm.

Montgomery and around

Eight miles northeast of Newtown, the tiny, anglicized town of **MONTGOMERY** (Trefaldwyn) lies at the base of a dilapidated **castle** on the Welsh side of Offa's Dyke and the present-day border. Construction of the castle began in 1233 under the English king, Henry III, and today's remains are not on their own worth the steep climb up the lane at the back of the town hall, although the view over the lofty

ROBERT OWEN, PIONEER SOCIALIST

Born in Montgomeryshire in the late eighteenth century, **Robert Owen** (1771–1858) left Wales to enter the Manchester cotton trade at the age of 18 and swiftly rose to the position of mill manager. His business acumen was matched by a strong streak of philanthropy towards his subordinates. Fundamentally, he believed in social equality between the classes and was firmly against the concept of competition between individuals. Poverty, he believed, could be eradicated by cooperative methods. Owen recognized the potential of building a model workers' community around the New Lanark mills in Scotland and joined the operation in 1798, swiftly setting up the world's first infant school, an Institution for the Formation of Character and a model welfare state for its people.

Owen's ideas on cooperative living prompted him to build up the model community of New Harmony in Indiana, USA, which he had established between 1824 and 1828, before handing the still-struggling project over to his sons. Before long, and without the wisdom of its founder, the idealistic tenets of New Harmony collapsed under the weight of greed, ambition and too many vested interests. Undeterred, Owen, by now back in Britain, was encouraging the formation of the early trade unions and cooperative societies, as well as leading action against the 1834 deportation of the **Tolpuddle Martyrs**, a group of Dorset farm labourers who withdrew their labour in their call for a wage increase. Owen's later years were dogged by controversy, as he lost the support of the few sympathetic sections of the British establishment in his persistent criticism of organized religion. He gained many followers, however, whose generic name gradually changed from Owenites to "socialists" – the first usage of the term. Owen returned to Newtown in his later years, and died there in 1858.

church tower, handsome Georgian streets and the gargantuan green bowl of hills around the town is stunning.

Montgomery is near one of the best-preserved sections of **Offa's Dyke**, which the long-distance footpath shadows either side of the B4386 a mile east of the town. Ditches almost 20ft high give one of the best indications of the dyke's original look, twelve hundred years after it was built.

Old Bell Museum

Arthur St • April–Sept Wed–Fri & Sun 1.30–5pm (daily in Aug), Sat 10.30am–5pm • £1 • ☎ 01686 668313, ⓦ oldbellmuseum.org.uk

The symmetrical main thoroughfare, Broad Street, swoops up to the red-brick **town hall**, crowned by a trim clock tower. A few paces further along is the **Old Bell Museum**, formerly a temperance house and butcher's, but now an unusually enjoyable local history collection. Crammed into every nook and cranny of this marvellous little building are artefacts from excavations, scale models of local castles, mementos from Montgomery civic life and displays on the region's various trades, with due prominence given to the likes of clogmakers, clockmakers, carpenters and tanners.

Church of St Nicholas

The Rectory, Lion Bank • Daily 8am–6pm; Free

At the other end of Broad Street from the Old Bell Museum, the rebuilt tower of Montgomery's parish **church of St Nicholas** dominates the diminutive buildings around it. Largely thirteenth-century, the highlights of its spacious interior include the 1600 canopied tomb of local landowner, Sir Richard Herbert, his wife, Magdalen, and their eight children (including Elizabethan poet George Herbert). The two medieval effigies on the floor at the end of the tomb are of uncertain origin, although the farther one is thought to be of Sir Edmund Mortimer ("revolted Mortimer", as Shakespeare had him), son-in-law of Owain Glyndŵr, brother-in-law of Hotspur and once Constable of Montgomery Castle. Equally impressive are the elaborately carved fifteenth-century double screen and accompanying loft, believed to have been built from sections removed from a priory over the border in Cherbury.

Dolforwyn Castle

Off to A483 • Daily 10am–4pm • Free; CADW

Four miles southwest of Montgomery, a small left turn off the A483 leads up to the gaunt remains of **Dolforwyn Castle**. Described by Jan Morris as "the saddest of all the Welsh castles", this was the last fortress to be built by a native Welsh prince on his own soil – Llywelyn ap Gruffydd in 1273 – as a direct snub to the English king, Edward I, who had forbidden the project. Llywelyn built his fortress and started to construct a small adjoining town as a Welsh fiefdom to rival heavily anglicized Welshpool, just up the valley. Dolforwyn only survived for four years in Welsh hands before being overwhelmed after a nine-day siege by the English, and the castle was left slowly to rot. In the past twenty years, the remains have been excavated and significant portions of the fragile old castle have emerged on the wind-blown hilltop, with astounding views over the Severn Valley, 400ft below. Note that, if driving, you must park in the car park, from where it's a stiff fifteen-minute uphill climb to the castle.

Glansevern Hall Gardens

Berriew • April–Oct Tues–Sat 10.30am–5pm • £7 • ☎ 01686 640644, ⓦ glansevern.co.uk

Just over three miles northwest of Montgomery, you'll find **Glansevern Hall Gardens**, spreading around a stately Georgian mansion. Sited on the banks of the River Severn, there's much to enjoy among the 25 acres of land, including a walled garden (within which are several themed gardens), a folly garden, Georgian orangery and Victorian grotto. The lakeside walk and wildflower meadow are particularly lovely, and once you're done with all that, you can take some alfresco refreshments in *The Potted Shed Café*.

ARRIVAL AND INFORMATION

By bus Buses pick up and drop off in front of the Town Hall at the bottom of Broad Street.

Destinations Newtown (8 daily; 30min); Shrewsbury (4 daily; 50min); Welshpool (8 daily; 25min).

ACCOMMODATION

Brynwylfa 4 Bishops Castle St ☎01686 668555, ⓦ brynwylfa.co.uk. Just off the main square, there are just two rooms in this beautiful Georgian town house: a twin-bedded room with exposed brick walls and a double room with a gorgeous roll-top bath. Breakfast is taken in the garden-facing conservatory. **£70**

★**The Checkers** Broad St ☎01686 669822, ⓦ thecheckersmontgomery.co.uk. The five understatedly elegant rooms of this erstwhile coaching inn are characterized by higgledy-piggledy beams and low ceilings

EATING AND DRINKING

Castle Kitchen 8 Broad St ☎01686 668795. Sociable café/deli with an open kitchen doling out both savoury

MONTGOMERY AND AROUND

Tourist information There's no tourist office in Montgomery, but the grey telephone box, located on a grassy triangle as you enter the town on the Welshpool road, has leaflets and information on local events.

and doorways. Free-standing baths and wet rooms (with posh toiletries), Egyptian cotton sheets and duck down duvets are all standard, with further thoughtful touches like freshly ground coffee with home-made shortbread. **£125**

Dragon Hotel Market Square ☎01686 668359, ⓦ dragonhotel.com. Next to the town hall, the rambling, seventeenth-century black-and-white *Dragon Hotel* has a good complement of rooms at a range of prices (mostly according to size), and some have four-poster beds. There is also an indoor pool. **£59**

(soups, quiches and tarts) and sweet (cakes and pastries) delights. The busy downstairs area extends to a vine-covered

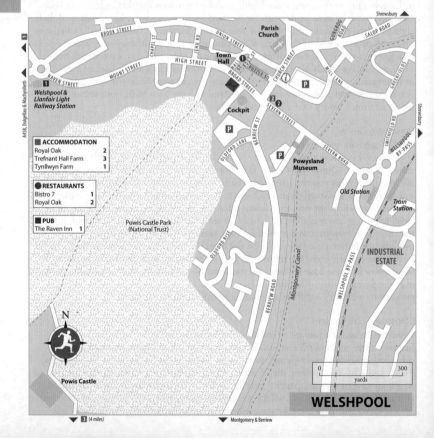

ACCOMMODATION

Royal Oak	2
Trefnant Hall Farm	3
Tynllwyn Farm	1

RESTAURANTS

| Bistro 7 | 1 |
| Royal Oak | 2 |

PUB

| The Raven Inn | 1 |

WELSHPOOL

terrace, and upstairs is all wonky flooring and stripey walls. Mon–Sat 9.30am–4.30pm, Sun 11am–4pm.

★**The Checkers** Broad St ☎01686 669822, ⓦthecheckersmontgomery.co.uk. Outstanding, pleasingly informal Michelin-starred restaurant, whose nicely spaced out, stripped down wooden tables make for an inviting setting. From the canapes served before your meal, to the classically French seasonal menus featuring the likes of smoked Blaenavon cheese souffle with apple and almond

salad, and assiette of guinea fowl with puy lentils and Monbazillac sauce, you're in for a genuinely special evening. Booking essential. Tues–Thurs 6–10pm, Fri & Sat noon–2pm & 6–10pm.

Ivy House Church Bank ☎01686 668746. Sweet, two-floored florally decorated tearoom serving veggie snacks, teas and cakes, as well as foodstuffs to take away. Head to the cosy upstairs dining room for lovely views of the main square. Daily 9am–5pm.

Welshpool

Three miles from the English border and five miles north of Berriew, eastern Montgomeryshire's chief town, **WELSHPOOL** (Y Trallwng), was formerly known merely as Pool, acquiring its prefix in 1835 to distinguish it from the English seaside town of Poole in Dorset. The town's well-proportioned roads are lined with some Tudor and many good Georgian and Victorian buildings, but it's sumptuous **Powis Castle**, one of the greatest Welsh fortresses, that puts Welshpool on most people's agenda.

Powysland Museum

Canal Wharf • Mon, Tues, Thurs & Fri 11am–1pm & 2–5pm; June–Aug also Sat & Sun 10am–1pm & 2–5pm; Oct–April also Sat 11am–2pm • Free • ☎01938 554656

This large wharfside warehouse has been carefully restored as the **Powysland Museum**, an impressively wide collection covering the history of the local area. The entrance is heralded by Andrew Logan's spangly blue outsized handbag, beyond which displays include archeological finds from a local Neolithic timber circle and Roman remains through to exhibits showing the changing patterns of domestic and civic life, as well as surprises like an intricate model of a guillotine carved from mutton bones, left behind by prisoners of the Napoleonic Wars, and a slice of wallpaper that was allegedly taken from Napoleon's residence on St Helena. There's also a nostalgic look at the Welshpool & Llanfair Railway, with a ceremonial spade, bugle and the like.

Broad Street

Broad Street is the most architecturally interesting of the streets leading off from the town's central crossroads, with the ponderous Victorian town hall and its dominating clock tower overlooking Tudor and Jacobean town houses.

The Cockpit

New Street • Generally Tues & Fri 11am–2pm; at other times, contact the town council • Free • ☎01938 553142

On New Street, behind the NatWest bank, you can wander around an early eighteenth-century circular **cockpit**, where cockfights were held until 1849, after which time the practice was made illegal.

Welshpool & Llanfair Railway

Raven Square • Generally 2–4 trains on operating days: April to early July & Sept Tues–Thurs, Sat & Sun; mid-July to Aug daily; Oct holidays & weekends only • £13 return • ☎01938 810441, ⓦwllr.org.uk

Broad Street changes name five times as it rises up the hill towards the tiny Raven Square terminus station of the **Welshpool & Llanfair Railway**, half a mile beyond the town hall. The eight-mile narrow-gauge line originally operated for less than thirty years, closing in 1931 – these days, scaled-down engines once more chuff along the equally small-scale valleys of the Sylfaen Brook and Banwy River to the quiet village of **LLANFAIR CAEREINION**; the round journey takes two hours.

Powis Castle

1 mile southwest of town up Park Lane • Daily: March & Oct castle 12.30–4pm, gardens 11am–4pm; April–Sept castle 12.30–5pm, gardens 10am–6pm; Nov & Dec castle noon–4pm, gardens 11am–4pm • Castle and gardens £13, gardens only £9.60; NT • ☎ 01938 551944

Located on the site of an earlier Norman fort, work on the outstanding **Powis Castle** was started in the reign of Edward I by the Gwenwynwyn family; to qualify for the site and the barony of De la Pole, they had to renounce all claims to Welsh princedom. In 1587, Sir Edward Herbert bought the castle and began to transform it into the Elizabethan palace you see today.

After purchasing your ticket from the **Old Coach House**, take a look at the stagecoach that once belonged to the third Earl of Powis, complete with a magnificent silver-plate harness and buttercup yellow silk lining. In the castle itself, the sumptuous period rooms are undoubtedly impressive, from the vast and kitsch frescoes by Lanscroon above the balustraded staircase to the mahogany bed, brass and enamel toilets and decorative wall hangings of the state bedroom; the bed itself is set within its own alcove behind an ostentatious balustrade, said to be modelled on the one in Versailles and the only one of its kind in the country. Many rooms throughout the castle were remodelled in the Jacobean style in the early 1900s on the orders of the fourth earl, George Herbert, hence the proliferation of oak panelling and elaborate plasterwork ceilings. There are some notable paintings, too, including one of Henrietta Herbert (wife of Edward Clive, see below) by Joshua Reynolds, and another, in the Oak Drawing Room, entitled *Little Boy* by Gainsborough.

The former ballroom houses the **Clive Museum** – named after the diplomat Robert Clive (aka Clive of India on account of his political and military deeds in the country during the mid-eighteenth century), and his son Edward, who married into the family in 1784; it's a remarkable collection, providing a lively account of the British in India through diaries, notes, letters, paintings, tapestries, weapons and jewels. No less impressive is part of the campaign tent belonging to Tipu Sultan, ruler of the Kingdom of Mysore.

Designed by Welsh architect William Winde, the **gardens** are spectacular in their own right. Dropping down from the castle in four huge stepped terraces, the design has barely changed since the seventeenth century, with a charmingly precise orangery and topiary. Summertime outdoor concerts, frequently with firework finales, take place in the gardens.

ARRIVAL AND INFORMATION WELSHPOOL

By train The train station is at the bottom of Severn St, with the neo-Gothic turrets of the old Victorian station (now with shops and a restaurant) just in front of it.
Destinations Aberystwyth (8 daily; 1hr 30min); Birmingham (8 daily; 1hr 30min); Machynlleth (8 daily; 1hr); Newtown (8 daily; 15min); Pwllheli (2 daily; 3hr 30min); Shrewsbury (8 daily; 25min).
By bus Buses depart from the Old Station on Severn Road. Destinations Llanfyllin (4 daily Mon–Sat; 30min); Llanidloes (6 daily; 1hr 20min); Llanymynech (5 daily;

30min); Montgomery (7 daily Mon–Sat; 25min); Newtown (9 daily; 35min); Oswestry (4 daily; 45min); Shrewsbury (6 daily; 45min).

Tourist information The TIC, just off Church Street in the Vicarage Gardens car park (Mon–Sat 9.30am–5pm, Sun 10am–4pm; ☎ 01938 552043, ⊛ welshpool.org), is one of the few tourist offices within the region, and you can get stacks of information here, while the staff can also advise on, and book, accommodation.

ACCOMMODATION AND EATING

Bistro 7 7 Hall St ☎ 01938 552879, ⊛ bistroseven .co.uk. By some distance the best place to eat in Welshpool. The menu – chalked up above the bar – is noticeable for its big strong flavours, like roast loin of cod in a leek cider sauce, and paprika and garlic pork chops with a chorizo hash. The fun interior has vintage ads dispersed around the walls. Mon–Sat 11am–10pm.

The Raven Inn Raven Square ☎ 01938 553070. The perky *Raven* has a great reputation for its menu, featuring carnivorous treats such as steak and pepper grilled kebabs, and fillet steak with blue stilton and spinach, as well as home-made burgers (£12). Tues–Sun noon–11pm.
Royal Oak The Cross ☎ 01938 552217, ⊛ royaloakhotel .info. Traditional Georgian coaching inn and former home of

the Earl of Powis, the Oak offers a range of crisply presented rooms, which come in three categories; standard, the marginally more polished contemporary rooms, and superior classic rooms, with Laura Ashley furnishings. The hotel's comfortable restaurant/bar serves a mix of classic (braised beef in ale with triple-cooked chips) and contemporary dishes (pan fried pork loin with tiger prawns; £11). The adjoining bar is a relaxing spot to kick back with an early-morning coffee or early-evening glass of wine. Restaurant daily noon–3pm & 6–10pm; café/bar 9am–11pm. **£89**

Trefnant Hall Farm 4 miles southwest of Welshpool,

beyond Powis Castle 𝕋 01686 640262, 𝕎 trefnanthall .co.uk. You'll need wheels to get to this isolated Georgian farmhouse, whose three florally decorated rooms have delightful head-on views towards green sloping fields. Guests are free to use the lounge with its gorgeous fireplace. **£60**

Tynllwyn Farm Groes-Pluen, 1 mile west of town on A490 𝕋 01938 553175, 𝕎 tynllwynfarm.co.uk. Warmly run B&B offering good-sized, homely rooms, a fabulous breakfast and extremely generous hospitality. There are also a couple of self-catering cottages. **£60**

Llanfyllin

The hills and plains of northern Montgomeryshire conceal a maze of deserted lanes and farms as the land rises towards the foothills of Denbighshire's Berwyn Mountains. The only real settlement of any size is **LLANFYLLIN**, a handsome and friendly hillside town, ten miles northwest of Welshpool in the valley of the River Cain. The High Street is busy with bright pubs, cafés, shops and a weekly Thursday market, while the square-cut, red-brick parish church is a rare example of eighteenth-century church building in Wales.

ARRIVAL AND DEPARTURE   LLANFYLLIN

By bus Bus destinations include: Llanrhaeadr-ym-Mochnant (3 daily Mon–Sat; 20min); Oswestry (4 daily

Mon–Sat; 35min); Welshpool (5 daily Mon–Sat; 35min).

ACCOMMODATION AND EATING

Cyfie Farm South of Llanfihangel-yng-Ngwynfa, towards the village of Dolanog 𝕋 01691 648451, 𝕎 cyfiefarm.co.uk. The tranquil, ivy-draped seventeenth-century *Cyfie Farm* has a combination of luxury B&B suites and self-catering cottages (all sleeping between two and four), each with glorious countryside views. It also serves four-course evening meals (£27.50), while the terraced gardens are something of an attraction themselves. **£120**

Seeds 5 Penybryn Cottages, High St 𝕋 01691 648604. Sixteenth-century seed merchant's house (it also hosted Napoleonic War prisoners) that now boasts a superb restaurant. Take your place at one of the six small tables in front of the log burner and enjoy warm black pudding salad with blackcurrant, or pan-fried lamb's kidneys with seed-grain mustard and sherry sauce; there's a serious wine list to boot. Three courses £27.95. Wed–Sat noon–2pm & 7–11pm.

The Tanat and Rhaeadr valleys

Parallel to the valley of the River Cain, north of Llanfyllin, are the lush valleys of the **Afon Tanat** and its tributary, the **Afon Rhaeadr** – a beguiling and sparsely populated backwater, set against the looming Berwyn Mountains.

Llanrhaeadr and Pistyll Rhaeadr

The small, low-roofed village of **LLANRHAEADR-YM-MOCHNANT**, six miles north of Llanfyllin, is best remembered as the parish of Bishop William Morgan, who translated the Bible into Welsh in 1588, a pivotal act that ensured the survival of the old tongue.

Llanrhaeadr lies at the foot of the wild walking country of the southern Berwyn Mountains. From the middle of the village, Waterfall Street becomes a lane that courses northwest for four miles to a dead end at the enchanting **Pistyll Rhaeadr**, Wales's highest waterfall at 240ft. The river tumbles down the crags in two stages, flowing under a natural stone arch known as the Fairy Bridge. It's well worth walking the twenty or so minutes to the top of the falls for the dizzying views down the valley, as well as the chance to follow further paths leading up into the remote and moody Berwyns; little explored, these mountains were once a major centre for lead-mining, and have always has strong links to spiritualism. Pistyll Rhaeadr is rich in legend, which you can absorb at the riverside café *Tan-y-Pistyll* (see p.250).

ACCOMMODATION AND EATING   LLANRHAEADR

Bron Heulog Waterfall St ☏01691 780521, ⑩bronheulog.co.uk. Grand Victorian house with three beautifully decorated rooms, each themed around a different type of flower, namely bluebell, sunflower and orchid. **£70**

Plough Inn ☏01691 780654, ⑩ploughcountryinn .com. There are just two rooms (a twin and double, both en suite) in this delightful country pub, which itself is a great spot for a pint or a bite to eat. Mon–Fri 4–11pm, Sat &

Sun noon–11pm. **£55**

Tan-y-Pistyll Café Pistyll Rhaeadr ☏01691 780392, ⑩pistyllrhaeadr.co.uk. Easy-going café with two en-suite rooms, a cottage sleeping five and a lovely campsite in the back field, where there's a shower block and fires are allowed. Staff also operate various spiritual retreats. Café summer 9.30am–6pm; winter 10am–4pm. Camping **£6.50**/person, doubles **£85**, cottage **£140**

Sycarth

East from Llanrhaeadr, the B4396 runs along the Tanat Valley and through the village of **LLANGEDWYN**. A mile or so after the village, few visitors make it up one of the left turns leading to **SYCARTH**, only a mile from the English border, but one of the most Welsh of all shrines: a grass mound marks the site of Owain Glyndŵr's ancestral court, reputedly a palace of nine grand halls. Bard Iolo Goch immortalized this Welsh Shangri-la as a place of "no want, no hunger, no shame/No-one is ever thirsty at Sycarth".

Just east of Sycarth, the English–Welsh border tightly encircles the 740ft limestone crag of **Llanymynech Rocks** (now a nature reserve), before cutting down to run right through the middle of the village of **LLANYMYNECH**.

Llangynog

Heading northwest from Llanrhaeadr, the B4391 hugs the river as far as the sleepy former mining village of **LLANGYNOG**, where it heads north into the Berwyn Mountains and Denbighshire. A lane by the bridge leads to a stunning four-mile hike over the top of Y Clogydd and down to the elfin charms of Pistyll Rhaeadr.

Pennant Melangell

You can walk (or, less strenuously still, drive) two miles further up the Tanat Valley from Llangynog to the hamlet of **PENNANT MELANGELL**, sitting low in a quiet, sheer-sided valley of sparkling brooks, and the site of one of Wales's most enduring sites of pilgrimage. Legend has it that the eighth-century saint Melangell was praying in the valley when a hare being chased by a hunt pack led by Prince Brochwel took refuge in her skirts. The hounds drew to a sudden stop before her and fled howling. The prince drew his horn to his lips to call them, only to find himself unable to remove it. The prince was so moved by Melangell's gentle humanity that he granted her the valley, in which she built a religious community.

The little **church** here dates from the eighth century; inside, a twelfth-century shrine and supposed effigy of St Melangell lie beneath an exquisite barrel roof. Melangell's grave is in the semicircular *cell y bedd* at the back of the church. Intact Norman features include a window in the main church, the south door porch and the font.

Lake Vyrnwy

A few miles south of Pennant Melangell, the magnificent **Lake Vyrnwy** (Llyn Efyrnwy) combines its functional role as a water supply for Liverpool with Victorian self-aggrandizement in the shape of the huge nineteenth-century dam and Disneyesque turreted straining tower. Constructed during the 1880s, Vyrnwy was the first of the massive reservoirs of mid-Wales. The village of **Llanwddyn** was flattened and rebuilt at the eastern end, its people receiving only meagre compensation for the loss of their homes.

The lake also makes a terrific base for **birdwatching**, with three hides for the more enthusiastic twitcher; up at the northern end of the lake, some five miles distant from the visitor centre, the Centenary and Lakeside hides are dedicated to spotting peregrines, typically between April and July, as well as buzzards, kestrels, redstarts and spotted flycatchers. In the small Coed-y-Capel hide across the road from the RSPB Visitor Centre, you can sit and watch forest birds attacking the feeders outside the windows. The lake is well stocked with fish, particularly brown trout; fishing in boats is permitted and these can be rented from *Lake Vyrnwy Hotel* (see below).

For walkers, half a dozen coloured **trails** fan out around the lake, ranging from a gentle one-mile circular walk through woodland, to a couple of five miles treks along the lakeside and up into the forest – you can pick up a leaflet from the visitor centre.

INFORMATION AND ACTIVITIES

LAKE VYRNWY

Tourist information On the western side of the dam, the RSPB Visitor Centre (daily 10.30am–4pm; ☎ 01691 870278, ⓦ rspb.org.uk/lakevyrnwy) is really just a shop, but the knowledgeable staff here can advise on the best places to birdwatch, and they also offer free guided walks of the lake and environs (phone for details).

Bike rental Just below the RSPB centre, the *Artisans Coffee Shop* (£5/hr, minimum two hours; ☎ 01691 870317) rents out bikes.

Fishing Between mid-March and mid-October, fishing permits can be obtained from *Lake Vyrnwy Hotel* (£40/boat/day).

ACCOMMODATION

Fronheulog At the top of the hairpin bends two miles from the lake on the road to Llanfyllin ☎ 01691 870662, ⓦ fronheulog-caravan-park.co.uk. There are a handful of pitches at this decent site. Closed Nov–March. **£3**/person

Lake Vyrnwy Hotel Above the southeastern shore ☎ 01691 870692, ⓦ lakevyrnwy.com. The most prominent accommodation hereabouts is this lavish spa

retreat overlooking the waters above the southeastern shore. Top-notch rooms have either hill or (more expensive) lake views. **£130**

The Oaks Just beyond the visitor centre ☎ 01691 870250, ⓦ vyrnwyaccommodation.co.uk. An old-fashioned but very pleasant B&B offering three pastel-coloured rooms, two of which share a bathroom. Small TV and tea-making facilities in each room. **£70**

EATING AND DRINKING

Artisans Coffee Shop The Old Sawmill ☎ 01691 870317. Large and well-stocked café serving teas, coffees, cakes and snacks. Daily 9.30am–4.30pm.

Lakeview Tearoom On the lakeside road some two miles beyond the Lake Vyrnwy Hotel ☎ 01691 870286.

Daytime snacks and full evening meals are available at this sweet, mildly quirky tearoom (and evening restaurant; booking required). Fantastic views over the lake. Tearoom Mon–Fri noon–3pm, Sat & Sun 11.30am–4.30pm; restaurant daily 7.30–10pm.

3

The Cambrian coast

THE COAST NEAR ABERYSTWYTH

The Cambrian coast

Cardigan Bay (Bae Ceredigion) takes a huge bite out of Wales' west coast, bordered by the Pembrokeshire peninsula in the south and the Llŷn in the north. Between these two rugged projections lies the Cambrian coast, which starts where the rugged seashore of Pembrokeshire ends, continuing in much the same vein of great cliffs, isolated beaches and swirling sea birds, punctuated with sarnau, stony offshore reefs largely exposed at low tide. This coast is split by tumbling rivers, while the bulwark of the Cambrian Mountains lies to the east. Before the nineteenth-century construction of the railway and improved roads, these served to isolate this stretch of coast from the rest of Wales, with only narrow passes and cattle-droving routes pushing through the rugged terrain to the markets in England. Today, development is still low-key, with large sand-fringed sections sprinkled with enchanting coastal resorts.

North of the charismatic town of **Cardigan**, the coast breaks at some popular seaside resorts – the best being **Llangrannog** and **New Quay** – before the tiny Georgian harbour town of **Aberaeron**, with its concentration of good places to stay and eat.

A bucolic **inland** alternative to the coastal resorts follows the **River Teifi**, which meets the sea at Cardigan and meanders eastwards through lush meadows past a clutch of small towns: the stalwart market centre of **Newcastle Emlyn**, the pint-sized university town of **Lampeter** and the charmingly old-fashioned community of **Tregaron**.

The coastal and inland routes connect at the cosmopolitan "capital" of mid-Wales, **Aberystwyth**, built on the estuary of the **Rheidol**, a fast-flowing river with dramatic ravines that make for great walking country. A narrow-gauge railway, an attraction in itself, climbs out of Aberystwyth to **Devil's Bridge**, where three bridges, one on top of the other, span a plunging chasm of cascading waterfalls.

Machynlleth, at the head of the Dyfi estuary, was once the seat of Owain Glyndŵr's putative fifteenth-century Welsh parliament and is still a thriving market centre. Just outside the town is the **Centre for Alternative Technology**, Britain's renowned showpiece for sustainable living and renewable energy.

The train line and narrow coastal road then skirt west around **Cadair Idris**, the monumental mountain that dominates the southern third of **Snowdonia National Park**. Each of the mountain's crag-fringed faces invites exploration, but it is best approached from the south, where the narrow-gauge **Talyllyn** rail line reaches the tiny settlement of **Abergynolwyn**, a great base for the unhurried delights of the **Dysynni Valley**. Cadair Idris' northern flank slopes down to the market town of **Dolgellau**, the best base for

CADAIR IDRIS

Highlights

❶ New Quay Follow Dylan Thomas' footsteps through the salty seaside town that inspired *Under Milk Wood* and provided much of the backdrop for film *The Edge of Love*. **See p.261**

❷ Aberaeron Make a beeline for Aberaeron's Seafood Festival, or simply stroll around its colourful Georgian harbour, lined with great places to eat and sleep. **See p.264**

❸ Aberystwyth Hang out in this lively seaside university town rooted firmly in Welsh culture and language. **See p.271**

❹ Bwlch Nant yr Arian Visit mid-afternoon for the impressive sight of dozens of red kites

squabbling over a heap of beef and lamb. Combine that with some of the best single-track mountain biking in Wales. **See p.278**

❺ Devil's Bridge Ride the scenic narrow-gauge, steam-powered Vale of Rheidol Railway from Aberystwyth to this towering triplet of bridges and series of cascades. **See p.279**

❻ Machynlleth Learn about ways to reduce your impact on the planet at the cutting-edge Centre for Alternative Technology. **See p.285**

❼ Cadair Idris Hike up southern Snowdonia's highest peak for swooping views and the chance to become a poet … or go mad. **See p.291**

HIGHLIGHTS ARE MARKED ON THE MAP ON P.256

visiting the superb running and mountain biking trails at **Coed-y-Brenin**. Dolgellau is at the head of the scenic Mawddach estuary and linked by waterside path to the likeable resort of **Barmouth**. The coastal strip then broadens out with complex dune systems protecting the approaches to **Harlech** and its virtually intact castle, the southernmost link in Edward I's chain of thirteenth-century fortresses, perched high on its rocky promontory.

THE CAMBRIAN COAST

HIGHLIGHTS

1. New Quay
2. Aberaeron
3. Aberystwyth
4. Bwlch Nant yr Arian
5. Devil's Bridge
6. Machynlleth
7. Cadair Idris

GETTING AROUND THE CAMBRIAN COAST

By train The most relaxing way to get fairly swiftly to, and along, the Cambrian coast is on the Cambrian Line (⊛thecambrianline.co.uk) from Shrewsbury in England through Welshpool and Newtown to Machynlleth. At Machynlleth, the line splits: one branch runs south to Aberystwyth, from where you can pick up the Vale of Rheidol line to Devil's Bridge; the other swings north, calling at 25 stations in under sixty miles before terminating at Pwllheli on the Llŷn. The Day Ranger ticket (see p.31) offers flexible travel at moderate prices.

By bus All towns and many villages in the region can be reached by bus. The most useful routes are:
X32 Aberystwyth–Machynlleth–Dolgellau–Porthmadog–Caernarfon.
X40 Swansea–Carmarthen–Lampeter–Aberaeron–Aberystwyth.
X50 Cardigan–Aberaeron–Aberystwyth.
There's also the Cardi Bach bus (April–Oct daily except Wed; Nov–March Mon, Thurs & Sat), which connects all the villages and coves between Cardigan and New Quay.

From Cardigan to Aberaeron

The southern section of the Ceredigion coastline has Wales' highest sea-cliffs, safe, sheltered beaches, great coastal walking, and a resident pod of bottlenose dolphins. Many of the coast's settlements retain a timeless, salty charm: the one-time smuggler's port of **New Quay** uncoils down the hair-raisingly steep hillside to the craggy coastline, while smaller places like **Llangrannog**, **Penbryn**, **Mwnt** and **Tresaith** juxtapose rolling pastoral countryside and wide, sweeping beaches, and brightly painted cottages huddle around the boat-filled harbour at **Aberaeron**. Just inland, at the mouth of the Teifi, is the pretty and cheerful old county town of **Cardigan**.

4

Cardigan and around

Until the River Teifi silted up in the nineteenth century, **CARDIGAN** (Aberteifi) was one of the greatest sea ports in Britain, although these days there's little evidence of its former status. It is, however, a sprightly little town, with some great diversions and a relaxed ambience.

The main focus of town, and just a stone's throw from Cardigan's **medieval bridge**, is the modest **castle** (⊛cardigancastle.com), gradually being rescued from dereliction and due to reopen in 2015. Founded by the Norman lord Roger de Montgomery in 1093, it was the site of the first Welsh eisteddfod in 1176. From here, the picturesque High Street leads up to the spiky turrets of the **Guildhall** and the town's bustling **covered market** (daily except Wed & Sun), an eclectic mix of locally produced food and plenty of browsable oddities. Leading off the High Street, narrow thoroughfares come crammed with Georgian and Victorian buildings.

There's more pleasure in visiting the surroundings, particularly the delightful **Teifi Marshes** and a rugged section of coast centred on the ancient church at **Mwnt**.

CEREDIGION COAST PATH

Cardigan is the start and end of both the Pembrokeshire Coast Path and the **Ceredigion Coast Path** (⊛ceredigioncoastpath.org.uk), which follows the coast for some 60 wind-blown miles from Cardigan to Ynyslas on the edge of the Dyfi estuary; both parts form part of the Wales Coast Path.

You can walk the whole thing over several days making use of the Cab-a-bag service with local taxis delivering your luggage to your next stop for £1.50 a mile. Alternatively, just walk short sections using the Cardi Bach buses (see above) to loop back to your starting point. Tourist offices sell leaflets detailing short sections of the route, or you can download descriptions from the website.

There is no shortage of wonderful walking, but some of the most dramatic sections are from Llangrannog north to New Quay.

Teifi Marshes Nature Reserve

The extensive **Teifi Marshes Nature Reserve** hugs the banks of the Teifi right on the fringes of Cardigan. It encompasses several important habitats – reed beds, meadows, marshes and untouched oak woodland – for otters, badgers, butterflies and birds, including Wales' largest resident group of Cetti's warblers. A herd of **buffalo**, brought in to control invasive bulrushes, wanders incongruously among the native inhabitants and can be seen from the various trails which access viewing hides.

You can drive from Cardigan (a very roundabout route of about four miles), but the best approach is to simply walk (or cycle) from the town's river bridge along the bed of an old railway. It is an inviting route past reed beds and a couple of bird hides, and in fifteen minutes you'll be at the Welsh Wildlife Centre.

Welsh Wildlife Centre

Teifi Marshes • Daily: mid-Feb to March, Nov & Dec 10am–4pm; April–Oct 10am–5pm • Free; parking £3 • ☎ 01239 621600, Ⓦ welshwildlife.org

The elegant, modern timber-and-glass structure in the centre of the Teifi Marshes is the **Welsh Wildlife Centre**, home to informative displays and an airy café with expansive views over the reserve and an adventure playground to keep kids entertained. You can easily spend half a day here exploring the four themed trails, the shortest of which is an easy ten-minute walk around the meadow, and the longest a 45 minute trail through the wetlands. There are also seven observation hides (including an otter hide) dotted around the reserve, with binocular hire available. This area is best explored, however, on **kayak** or **canoe trips** run by Cardigan Bay Active (see opposite).

4

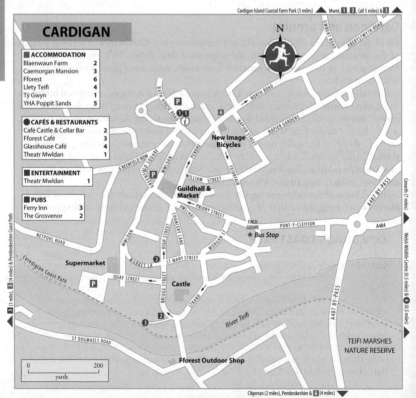

Cardigan Island Coastal Farm Park

Gwbert, 3 miles north of Cardigan · April–Oct daily 10am–6pm · £3.90 · ☎ 01239 623637, ⓦ cardiganisland.com

The B4548 follows the Teifi Estuary north to the straggling seaside village of **GWBERT**, a peaceful spot with good sea views best enjoyed from the **Cardigan Island Coastal Farm Park**, a great place for kids, offering the chance to spot dolphins and fur seals on a coastal walk. The farm itself has a curious mixture of animals, including llamas, pigs, emus and wallabies, as well as more traditional British stock – ponies, chickens, ducks and a donkey.

Mwnt

Five miles north of Cardigan, tiny lanes bump down to the isolated little hamlet of **MWNT**, where the exquisite sandy beach and cliffs are under the custodianship of the National Trust. Set in windswept solitude above the cliffs, the tiny, whitewashed church is the oldest in Ceredigion – its foundation dates back to the sixth century, although most of today's thickset building dates from the thirteenth century. Mwnt's finest hour came in 1155, when invading Flemings landed here, only to be routed by the Welsh. The occasion, which became known as *Sul Coch y Mwnt*, the Bloody Sunday of Mwnt, has been periodically remembered through the whole skeletons and other human bones that have been unearthed en masse in the vicinity.

ARRIVAL AND DEPARTURE   CARDIGAN

By bus Buses stop on Finch Square.
Destinations Aberaeron (hourly; 1hr); Aberystwyth (hourly; 1hr 45min); Carmarthen (hourly; 1hr 30min);

Cenarth (hourly; 15min); Cilgerran (5 daily; 5min); Llangrannog (2 daily; 50min); Newcastle Emlyn (hourly; 20min); New Quay (hourly; 50min).

INFORMATION AND ACTIVITIES

Tourist information The TIC is inside Theatr Mwldan on Bath House Road (July–Aug Mon–Sat 10am–5pm, Sun noon–5pm; Sept–June Mon–Sat 10am–5pm; ☎ 01239 613230, ⓦ visitcardigan.com).
Bike rental New Image Bicycles, 29 Pendre (☎ 01239 621275, ⓦ bikebikebike.co.uk), charges £20 a day for a standard MTB or hybrid; it also does repairs and maintenance.

Canoeing and kayaking Cardigan Bay Active, whose main office is down on the quay (☎ 01239 612133, ⓦ cardiganbayactive.co.uk), but which also has a centre at the Teifi marshes (☎ 01239 613961), runs gentle, guided canoeing trips along the Teifi (£35), and more adventurous kayaking trips (£40) bumping over a few rapids. It offers a host of other land and sea-based adventure activities.

ACCOMMODATION

Blaenwaun Farm Mwnt, 5 miles north of Cardigan ☎ 01239 613456, ⓦ blaenwaunfarm.com. Well-equipped family-run caravan site a walk up through the wooded ravine from the Mwnt church. There's a modern amenities block with showers, washing and laundry facilities, kids' play area, and a well-stocked shop. Campfires allowed. March–Oct. Pitches **£15**
★Caemorgan Mansion Caemorgan Rd, one mile northeast of town just off the A487 ☎ 01239 613297, ⓦ caemorgan.com. An outstanding level of comfort and hospitality awaits at this marvellous guesthouse, whose five rooms have been appointed to the highest order, and include, among other things, luxury Egyptian cotton linen, underfloor heating, and smart drinks stations with fresh milk; and you'll not find better cooked Welsh breakfasts anywhere. **£120**
Fforest Cwmplysgog, Cilgerran just off A478 at Pen y Bryn, 2 miles south of Cardigan ☎ 01239 623633,

ⓦ coldatnight.co.uk. Luxury goes outdoors at this wonderful farmland site beside the Teifi Marshes. They provide the tents (all sleeping at least four) – geodesic dome, tepee, bell etc – all with their own fully equipped cooking area. There's loads of privacy but also an on-site "pub", sauna and occasional meals. Closed Nov–March. Tents **£130**
Llety Teifi Pendre ☎ 01239 615566, ⓦ lletyteifi -guesthouse.co.uk. A raspberry-pink boutique guest house with ten contemporary rooms in a Victorian town house with its own restaurant/bar. Breakfast is taken in the wonderful conservatory. **£75**
Tŷ Gwyn Mwnt, 5 miles north of Cardigan ☎ 01239 614518, ⓦ campingatmwnt.co.uk. 200yds beyond the Mwnt church, and with wonderful sea views, this otherwise basic campsite has few facilities beyond showers. Come supplied, as there are no shops nearby. Pitches **£14**
YHA Poppit Sands Poppit, 4 miles northwest of Cardigan ☎ 0845 371 9037, ⓔ poppit@yha.org.uk.

4

Remote hostel at the northern end of the Pembrokeshire Coast Path, whose dorms offer great views across the water, and there's also a self-catering kitchen. Get there on the Poppit Rocket bus service (May to late Sept 3 daily; late Sept to April 3 per week); the year-round #407 stops within half a mile. Camping is allowed in the hostel grounds. Closed Nov–Feb. Pitches £5.30, dorm £18, double £45

EATING AND ENTERTAINMENT

Castle Café & Cellar Bar 25–26 Quay St ☎01239 621882. The home-made cawl at this café is wonderfully warming on a chilly day, but a better reason to visit is the music – with lunchtime acoustic happenings, open mic on Thursday, and all sorts on Friday and Saturday. Daily 9am–6pm.

Ferry Inn St Dogmael's, just over a mile west of Cardigan ☎01239 615172, ⓦferry-inn.com. A great spot with loads of seating beside the Teifi, great beer and range of wonderfully tasty meals in hearty portions at moderate prices (mains from £11). Daily noon–11.30pm.

Fforest Café Cambrian Quay ☎01239 615286. The main reason to visit this easy-going waterside café, run by the folks who operate Cardigan Bay Active, is to sample one of the wood-fired pizzas (£7) under the ingeniously conceived pizza tepee – and there's live music on Saturday evenings too. June–Sept Tues–Sat 10am–9.30pm.

Glasshouse Café Welsh Wildlife Centre ☎01239 621212. With 360 degree views of the Teifi Marshes through its all-glass surrounds, this restful café is a wonderful spot to tuck into a Welsh cheese ploughman's or some Homity Pie (£7.75), perhaps followed by a slice of polenta lemon cake. Daily 10am–5pm.

The Grosvenor Bridge St ☎01239 613792. Well-kept ales, better than average bar meals and outdoor seating overlooking the river comfortably make this the most worthwhile pub in town. Mains from £10. Mon–Thurs 11am–10pm, Fri & Sat 11am–11pm, Sun noon–10pm.

Theatr Mwldan Bath House Rd ☎01239 621200, ⓦmwldan.co.uk. Cardigan's main cultural centre offers much more than a town of this size should reasonably expect, including a full programme of theatre, dance, comedy, music and film. The café's a decent spot to rest too. Café Tues–Sat 10am–8pm, Sun noon–4pm.

Tresaith, Llangrannog and around

Between Cardigan and New Quay, the coast is a mass of impossibly narrow, hedgerow-hemmed lanes leading down to gorgeous little bays – especially **Tresaith**, **Penbryn** and **Llangrannog** – that aren't much more than clefts in the rugged cliffs.

Tresaith

At the scenic hamlet of **TRESAITH**, eight miles northeast of Cardigan, there's a great little beach, a kiosk renting wetsuits and aquatic playthings, and the *Ship Inn*. Fifty yards around the rocks to the east, a sandy cove has its own natural after-sea shower – a **waterfall** crashing down from the River Saith above. There's often good **surf** (heed the signs if you're swimming), as well as **dinghy races** on calmer summer Sundays.

Penbryn

The wide, sandy, National Trust beach at **PENBRYN**, a mile northeast of Tresaith, is accessed by yet more impossibly narrow lanes (and by the clifftop Ceredigion Coast Path). Almost a mile in length, its unspoilt shallow waters make it ideal for children. Parking is 400yds back from the beach beside the small café.

Llangrannog

Three miles northeast of Penbryn, **LLANGRANNOG** is the most attractive village on the Ceredigion coast, wedged in between hills covered with bracken and gorse. The very narrow streets wind their way to the tiny seafront, catering for visitors with a couple of cafés and pubs and assorted sporting activities. The beach can become congested in midsummer, though the madness is easily escaped on a clifftop walk.

ARRIVAL AND DEPARTURE	TRESAITH AND LLANGRANNOG

By bus The Cardi Bach bus (see p.257) departs from Cardigan at 9am and 2pm every day except Wednesday, calling at both Tresaith and Llangrannog.

ACCOMMODATION AND EATING

Ffynnon Fendigaid Rhydlewis, 3 miles south of Llangrannog ☎01239 851361, ⦿ffynnonf.co.uk. This eclectically decorated rural B&B in an eighteenth-century farmhouse in extensive semi-wild grounds has two guest rooms (very good breakfasts) plus a self-catering cottage for four; walkers and cyclists are particularly welcome, with pick-ups and drop-offs possible. **£75**

Llety Caravan Park Tresaith ☎01239 810354, ⦿lletycaravanpark.co.uk. Amid the static caravans there's a wonderful (if significantly sloping) clifftop field for tents and tourers with a pretty footpath that descends straight to the beach. Good toilets and showers. Pitches **£16**

The Penrallt Off B4333, Aberporth ☎01239 810227, ⦿thepenrallt.co.uk. Classy 26-room hotel in a sixteenth-century mansion peacefully set in 42 acres. Rooms are modern and beautiful, and both the casual *Terrace* and the Modern British *Bay Restaurant* are among the finest places to eat in these parts. Mains from £16. Terrace: daily noon–9.30pm; Bay Restaurant: Wed–Sat 6.30–9.30pm, Sun noon–3pm. **£150**

The Ship Llangrannog ☎01239 654510. Gentrified pub with a patio for summer relaxing and a fire in winter. Good food (mains from £10), a decent range of wines and a changing roster of real ales. Daily 11am–11pm.

Ship Inn Tresaith ☎01239 811816, ⦿shiptresaith .com. Although a typically ordinary Brains brewery pub, Tresaith's only hostelry is still worth visiting for its low-cost food (mains from £9), good beer (supped on the terrace on a sunny day) and four comfy rooms all with fantastic sea views. Daily 8am–11pm. **£70**

New Quay

NEW QUAY (Cei Newydd) lays claim to being the original Llareggub in **Dylan Thomas'** *Under Milk Wood*. Certainly, it has the little tumbling streets, pastel-painted Victorian terraces, cobbled harbour and dreamy isolation that Thomas evoked so successfully in his "play for voices", as well, perhaps, as the darkly eccentric characters he describes.

New Quay's main road cuts through the upper, residential part of town, past **Uplands Square**, from where acutely inclined streets plunge down to a pretty harbour, formed by its sturdy stone quay, and with a small, curving main beach. Back from the sand, the

4

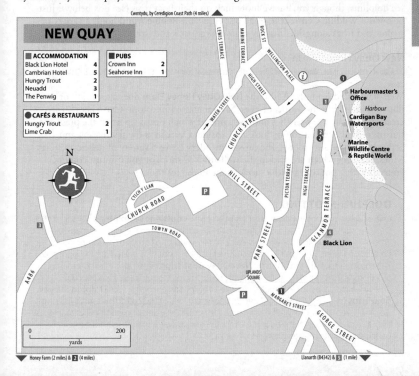

DYLAN THOMAS IN NEW QUAY

Dylan Thomas and his young family lived in New Quay during the last half of World War II, and his experiences here showed him the odder side of human nature. Thomas' metropolitan ways and poetic demeanour did not go down too well in such a close-knit little town, particularly so with an ex-commando officer, fresh home from the war, with whom he had a row in the *Black Lion* pub. The soldier, convinced that his wife was in a *ménage à trois* with Thomas and his wife Caitlin, followed the writer home and shot at his rented bungalow, the Majoda, with a machine gun, while the family was inside. The officer was charged with attempted murder in June 1945, and acquitted. Dylan Thomas and family left the area soon afterwards. The story forms the centrepiece of the 2008 film *The Edge of Love*, much of which was filmed in the area.

Two free leaflets from the tourist office highlight places where the poet spent time: *Dylan Thomas' Ceredigion*, which guides you through local villages, and *Dylan Thomas' New Quay* **walking trail**, concentrating on places he lived and his favourite pubs; one of these was the *The Black Lion*, on Glanmor Terrace, where you'll find lots of photos of Thomas lining the walls.

higgledy-piggledy lines of multicoloured shops and houses comprise the lower town, the more traditionally seaside part of New Quay, full of standard-issue cafés, pubs and beach shops.

Cardigan Bay Marine Wildlife Centre (CBMWC) and Reptile World

Glanmor Terrace • **Marine Wildlife Centre** April–Oct daily 9am–4pm • Free • ☎ 01545 560032, Ⓦ cbmwc.org • **Reptile World** April–Oct daily 9am–4pm • £2 • ☎ 07958 339149, Ⓦ nqreptileworld.co.uk

Tucked away down the slipway above the main harbour beach, the **Cardigan Bay Marine Wildlife Centre** contains some interesting exhibits on the dolphins, sea birds and seals that inhabit Cardigan Bay. Staff will point you to the best spots on land from which to see dolphins, though you'll have more luck on their boat trips (see box below). Just below the Wildlife Centre, the small but enjoyable **Reptile World** holds a variety of snakes and frogs alongside brightly coloured iguanas and lizards.

New Quay Honey Farm

Off A486 at Cross Inn, 2 miles inland from New Quay • Easter–Oct Tues–Sat 10am–5pm • £3.75 • ☎ 01545 560822, Ⓦ thehoneyfarm .co.uk

Well-signposted from the A486, the **New Quay Honey Farm** does a great job of illustrating the life and works of bees. Several glassed-in colonies have bees busily creating hives in tree branches and logs, one of which opens up upon the press of a button to show what a colony looks like inside. Don't miss the fascinating and very active leaf-cutter ant colony. The on-site meadery farms a variety of delicious honey wines, many of which are sold in the well-stocked shop, or you can just content yourself with a pot of tea and a slice of cake in the tea room.

DOLPHIN-SPOTTING

One of only two pods in Britain, the Cambrian coast's **bottlenose dolphins** are one of New Quay's major attractions, and can often be seen frolicking by the harbour wall, particularly when the tide is full and the weather calm. A mile-wide strip of the coastal waters forms the Ceredigion Marine Heritage Coast, in summer plied by boat trips geared around sightings. The cheapest trips are those run by **New Quay Boat Trips**, based at the harbourmaster's office on the harbour wall (April–Oct daily; £8 for 1hr, or £15 for 2hr; ☎ 1545 560800, Ⓦ newquayboattrips.co.uk), though chances of a sighting are better with **Dolphin Survey Boat Trips** (part of the CBMWC; April–Oct daily; ☎ 01545 560032, Ⓦ dolphinsurveyboattrips .co.uk; £12 for 1hr, or £18 for 2hr), which go further offshore and up along the heritage coast; they also do four- and eight-hour trips. Your fee goes towards marine mammal research, partly done by the on-board ranger.

WALKING THE COAST PATH: NEW QUAY TO LLANGRANNOG

It's easy to escape New Quay's bustle (such as it is) using one of the most spectacular sections of the Ceredigion Coast Path, easily broken into two very manageable sections. The terrain is fairly undulating the whole way; explanatory leaflets are available at local TICs. The Cardi Bach bus service (see p.257) usually provides access to Cwmtydu and Llangrannog.

New Quay to Cwmtydu (4 miles; 2–3hr). Start around the rocky promontory of New Quay Head, where an invigorating path steers along the top of the sheer drops to Bird Rock, aptly named for the profusion of razorbills and guillemots nesting here. There's a good chance of seeing dolphins too. Continue past Cwm Soden, an area of interesting folded geology, and on to Cwmtydu.

Cwmtydu to Llangrannog (6 miles; 3–4hr). A wonderful section of path, often cut into the coastal slopes high above the water with long views both ways. It also runs through the National Trust lands of **Ynys Lochtyn** and can be turned into a loop walk using an alternative route through a wooded valley.

Cwmtydu

One of the highlights of the coast is the glorious cave-walled beach at **CWMTYDU**, two miles southwest of New Quay (though almost five miles by road). Approached along tiny lanes winding steeply down from above, Cwmtydu was once a smugglers' cove and is often visited by dolphins and seals; the mainly shingle beach makes a relatively safe spot for water sports.

ARRIVAL, INFORMATION & ACTIVITIES   NEW QUAY   4

By bus Buses stop at the top of Church Street.
Destinations Aberaeron (hourly; 20min); Aberystwyth (hourly; 1hr); Cardigan (hourly; 50min).
Tourist information The TIC is at the corner of Church Street and Wellington Place (April–Oct Mon–Sat 10am–5pm; ☎ 01545 560865, ✉ newquaytic@ceredigion.gov.uk).

Watersports Cardigan Bay Watersports, Main Beach (☎ 01545 561257, ⊛ cardiganbaywatersports.org.uk; April–Oct), has various equipment to hire, including windsurfs (£16), sailing dinghies (from £14), and single and double kayaks (£12–16), the latter perfect for exploring the rocky coast to the south; they also offer various watersports courses.

ACCOMMODATION

The Black Lion Glanmor Terrace ☎ 01545 561144, ⊛ blacklionnewquay.co.uk. Thomas's favourite New Quay watering hole has been smartened up considerably in recent times, with nine rooms (five with superlative sea views) characterized by high ceilings, sash windows and stripy, boldly coloured curtains. £70

Cambrian Hotel New Rd, 1 mile southeast of New Quay along B4342, towards Gilfachreda ☎ 01545 560295, ⊛ cambrianhotel-newquay.co.uk. Clean, well-presented and friendly landmark hotel with beautiful, understated rooms and original features like stained-glass leadlight windows. Good restaurant too. £75

Hungry Trout 2 South John St ☎ 01545 560680,

⊛ thehungrytrout.co.uk. A couple of delightful rooms, both with sea views but only one with en suite (£110), set above a seafood restaurant, where breakfast is served. £95

Neuadd Behind the Penrhiwllan Inn at the top of the hill on A486 to Synod Inn ☎ 01545 560709, ⊛ neuaddcaravanpark.com. The nearest campsite to town with tent pitches on a grassy site overlooking the rooftops and the sea. 50p tokens for showers. Pitches £11

The Penwig South John St ☎ 01545 560910, ⊛ penwig .co.uk. For a Brains pub, the seven rooms here are surprisingly accomplished, and three have fabulous sea views; moreover, it's not nearly as noisy as you might expect, given that it's right above one of the town's busiest bars. £70

EATING AND DRINKING

New Quay has some fine places to eat and drink, though pubs around the area greatly enhance the selection. Fuelled by a huddle of pubs and a transient young population, summer nights can be boisterously good-natured. New Year's Eve here is legendary, when virtually the whole town gets kitted out in fancy dress and spends most of the night locked in the pubs or dancing out in the streets.

Crown Inn Llwyndafydd, 4 miles south of New Quay ⊛ thecrowninnandrestaurant.co.uk. Excellent pub that's

well regarded for its straightforward food in hearty portions and the Sunday carvery lunches (noon–2pm; £8). Real ales and a kids' menu and play area. Daily noon–midnight.

Hungry Trout 2 South John St ☎01545 560680, ⓦ thehungrytrout.co.uk. Don't expect to find a seat easily at New Quay's finest seafood restaurant, especially on the cramped balcony terrace. Dishes are rustled up according to the day's catch, but expect the likes of crayfish tails with avocado salad, and poached sea trout in a white wine parsley cream (£15). Daily 8am–10pm.

The Lime Crab South John St ☎01545 561400. Eye-catching, lime-coloured fish and chip shop that offers a

slightly more refined take on your average chippie, with the likes of scallops, salt 'n' pepper squid, and mackerel goujons, all for around £7 each. Moreover, they've got gluten-free fish and chips. Daily 11.30am–8pm.

Seahorse Inn Margaret St. This fine, traditional local, a world away from the holiday bustle down the street, is little more than one room with exposed stonework, fake beams, pool and a limited range of good ales. It was known to Dylan Thomas as the *Commercial* and was the model for the *Sailor's Arms* in *Under Milk Wood*. Daily 11am–11.30pm.

Aberaeron and around

In complete contrast to the precipitous, zigzagging streets of New Quay, **ABERAERON**, seven miles up the coast, faces away from the ocean, its brightly coloured Georgian houses and level streets clustered instead around the town's internal harbour. It is a beguiling sight which, combined with a handful of superb places to stay and eat, has helped make Aberaeron *the* weekend getaway of the Cambrian Coast. The well heeled of Cardiff, Swansea and even London descend for a few days of good eating and breezy walks along the coast path.

Aberaeron's harmonious maritime appearance results from its being built en masse after the 1807 Harbour Act paved the way for port development. Reverend Alban Gywnne spent his wife's inheritance dredging the Aeron estuary as a new port for mid-Wales and constructing a formally planned town around it – reputedly from a design by John Nash. Georgian planning is most evident around the central **Alban Square**, with graceful, small-scale terraces of quoin-edged buildings and the odd pedimented porch.

From the square, a grid of narrow streets stretches away to the sea at **Quay Parade**, a neatly ordered line of colourful houses on the seafront. The southern end of Aberaeron's stony **beach** is marginally better than its northern extent, but the most agreeable activity is simply ambling around the waterfront and grazing in the cafés and pubs.

ARRIVAL AND INFORMATION

ABERAERON

By bus The main bus stop is on the north side of Alban Square, from where it's a walk across the road down towards the harbour area.

Destinations Aberystwyth (every 30min; 40min); Cardigan (hourly; 1hr); Carmarthen (hourly; 1hr 30min); Lampeter (hourly; 30min); New Quay (hourly; 20min).

Tourist information The TIC, down by the harbour at

3 Pen Cei (July–Sept daily 10am–5pm; Oct–June Mon–Sat 10am–5pm; ☎01545 570602, ⓔ aberaerontic@ceredigion .gov.uk), can book local accommodation.

Bike rental Cyclemart, Cilcennin, 6 miles east (Tues–Sat 10am–6pm; ☎01570 470079, ⓦ cyclemart.co.uk); a wide range of bikes from £10 a day.

ACCOMMODATION

★**3 Pen Cei** 3 Pen Cei ☎01545 571147, ⓦ pen-cei -guest-house.co.uk. The deep navy-blue exterior of this

former harbourmaster's headquarters conceals five dashing rooms, variously painted in shades of pink and

---

FESTIVALS IN ABERAERON

The town is positively hopping during its fun-filled **festivals**, notably the annual **Seafood Festival** (ⓦ aberaeronfishfest.com) held on the second or third Sunday in July, with lots of big name chefs rustling up free food alongside loads of great live entertainment. Other festivities include the **Cob Fair** (mid-Aug; ⓦ aberaeronfestival.co.uk), with horses and local art and crafts taking over the streets; and the **Aberaeron Carnival** (August Bank Holiday Monday), when the town swings to live jazz. One other event not to be missed if you're in the area at the beginning of August is a mass **Tug of War** across the harbour, with the losers getting a serious dunking.

mauve, with oak panelled walls and marble and glass topped dressing tables. Breakfast can be taken in the garden. **£105**

Drefnewydd Farm A487, 400yd north of town ☎ 07971 402201, ⓦ campingonthefarm.co.uk. Laidback, family-run campsite in a plum spot right on the shoreline; facilities are limited, but there are clean toilets and hot showers. April–Sept. Pitches **£18**

★ **Harbourmaster Hotel** 1 Pen Cei ☎ 01545 570755, ⓦ harbour-master.com. Wonderful hotel that originally put the Aberaeron hospitality scene on the map, with thirteen ultramodern rooms spread across three buildings, seven of which are located in the Grade II listed harbourmaster house itself; exposed stone walls, brown and red leather armchairs, and vintage Welsh blankets all

feature prominently, and there are splendid views to boot. **£135**

Llys Aeron Lampeter Rd, 1 mile south of town ☎ 01545 570276, ⓦ llysaeron.co.uk. You'll get fresh flowers in your spacious room, a warm welcome and a top-rate breakfast at this upscale B&B on the outskirts of town. Coast Path walkers might fancy the hot tub in the back garden (£4/head) and there's also self-catering for four available (£130/night; min 2 nights). **£85**

The Monachty Market St ☎ 01545 570389, ⓦ monachtyaberaeron.co.uk. A reasonable budget option in a town full of otherwise pricey establishments, the seven light-filled rooms here come with big dollops of colour, and despite being above a pub, are well insulated. **£60**

EATING AND DRINKING

Cadwgan 10 Market St ☎ 01545 570149. Great, unpretentious local that provides a wonderful antidote to Aberaeron's gentrification. It's like walking into someone's living room – someone who serves a rotating roster of real ales and a few bar snacks, that is. Daily 11am–10pm or later.

Harbourmaster Hotel 1 Pen Cei ☎ 01545 570755, ⓦ harbour-master.com. Two places in one. The wonderfully convivial bistro/bar is perfect for sinking into a sofa with one of their excellent Welsh ales or something from the extensive list of wines by the glass. There's no attempt to be flash, but the cooking is done with aplomb; the restaurant (£25 for two courses) serves the likes of Cardigan Bay lobster with Thai butter and Asian slaw, or you might plump for some salt and pepper squid with chilli jam in the bistro, which also serves breakfast until 11.45am. Bistro daily 8am–10pm; restaurant daily noon–2.30pm & 6.30–9pm.

★ **The Hive** Cadwgan Place ☎ 01545 570599, ⓦ thehiveaberaeron.com. Terrific, buzzy waterside café

and bar/grill with several seating areas, the best of which is the sunny gravelled terrace with brightly painted tables and benches. With an adjoining fishmonger's, the seafood menu is strong, but there's plenty more besides, such as rack ribs and the house Hive Burger. Treat yourself, too, to some wonderful honey-sweetened ice cream sold from the kiosk outside. Live music Friday evenings. Mon, Tues & Sun 10am–4pm, Wed–Sat 10am–late; ice-cream kiosk daily 10.30am–6pm.

Naturally Scrumptious 18 Market St ☎ 01545 574733, ⓦ naturallyscrumptious.co.uk. Excellent deli groaning with Welsh cheese, pies, posh sausages and panini. The cakes are best eaten with a coffee or one of their fine teas in the hot-pink painted café to the rear. Mon–Sat 10am–4.30pm.

New Celtic 8 Market St ☎ 01545 570369. The best fish and chips around, to take away or eat in on their restaurant terrace; breakfasts, coffees and cakes, and an ice-cream parlour too. Daily 8am–9pm.

Llanerchaeron

Ciliau Aeron, A482, 3 miles east of Aberaeron • April–Oct daily 10.30am–5.30pm; reduced hours in winter • £7.10 • **Parkland** Daily dawn–dusk • Free • ☎ 01545 570200 • NT

Llanerchaeron is the substantially restored remains of a late eighteenth-century Welsh country estate that was bequeathed to the National Trust in 1989. It is a remarkable example of a type of holding once common in these parts. Over the last decade or so, a century of decline has been arrested and partially reversed, leaving the Nash-designed main house in pristine shape. The original, mostly Edwardian set-piece rooms only hint at the fact that this was someone's home little more than two decades ago. This is much more apparent in the servants' quarters and the serviced courtyard which acted as laundry, dairy, salting room and home brewery. Today, the estate is a working organic farm with a considerable vegetable- and fruit-growing enterprise in the **walled garden**, a time capsule of horticultural history, featuring early greenhouses and hotbeds with underground heating styled on Roman hypocausts.

By bus The #X40 bus from Aberaeron to Lampeter passes within half a mile of the site.

By bike You might find it just as easy to ride (or walk) the two and a half miles along the cycle path connecting

Aberaeron with Llanerchaeron. Apart from a small hill in town, the route is flat, as it follows the old railway line; access is off South Road in Aberaeron.

The Teifi Valley

The meandering Teifi is one of Wales' most eulogized rivers for its spawning fish, otter population and the coracles that were a regular feature from pre-Roman times. The river flows through undulating, vivid-green countryside to the river's estuary at Cardigan, dotted with a string of pleasant little market towns with a strong Welsh ambience. To foodies it is the centre of Welsh cheesemaking (ⓦ teifivalleycheeseproducers.com), and you'll often find the good stuff on restaurant cheese platters.

The river is tidal almost as far up as the massive ramparts of **Cilgerran Castle**, though it narrows appreciably by the time it reaches the rapids at **Cenarth**. Further upstream, it swirls around three sides of another fortress at **Newcastle Emlyn**, and also takes in the tiny university town of **Lampeter**. Beyond here, the river passes through harsher landscapes to **Tregaron**, a good base for nearby **Llanddewi Brefi**, with some spectacular walks up into the Abergwesyn Pass and the reedy bogland of **Cors Caron**. The river's infancy can be seen in the solid village of **Pontrhydfendigaid**, famed for its annual eisteddfod, and the nearby ruins of **Strata Florida Abbey**, beyond which the river emerges from the dark and remote **Teifi Pools**.

Cilgerran Castle

Cilgerran • Daily: April–Oct 10am–5pm; Nov–March 10am–4pm • April–Oct £3.20; Nov–March free; NT • ☎ 01239 621339

Just a couple of miles up the Teifi from Cardigan (four miles by road) is the commandingly situated village of **Cilgerran**. Park considerately on the wide main street to visit the massive ramparts of **Cilgerran Castle** that rise on a high wooded bluff above the river, which was still navigable for seagoing ships during the castle's construction in 1100. A few years later, in 1109, Nest (the "Welsh Helen of Troy") was abducted here by a lovestruck Prince Owain of Powys. Nest's husband, Gerald of Pembroke, escaped by slithering down a toilet waste chute through the castle walls.

The massive dual entry towers still dominate the castle, and the outer walls are some 4ft thicker than those facing the inner courtyard. Walkways high on the battlements – not for vertigo-sufferers – connect the other towers. The outer ward is a good example of the evolution of the keepless castle throughout the thirteenth century. Any potential attackers would be waylaid instead by the still-evident ditch and the outer walls and gatehouse, of which only fragmentary remains can be seen. Another ditch and drawbridge pit protect the inner ward underneath the two entry towers.

Cenarth

A lure for tourists since the nineteenth century, tiny **CENARTH**, six miles upstream from Cilgerran, is still chock-full of tearooms and gift shops thanks to its pretty (albeit rather tame) **rapids**, caused by the Teifi tumbling and churning its way over the craggy limestone.

National Coracle Centre

Easter–Sept Mon–Fri & Sun 10.30am–5.30pm; other times by appointment • £3.50 • ☎ 01239 710980, ⓦ coraclemuseum.co.uk

By the river is the **National Coracle Centre**, a delightful small museum with intriguing displays of original coracles from all over the world, many of of them from Wales. There are some fascinating stories to be told here, not least one bamboo coracle from Vietnam that

was used to transport a handful of refugees hundreds of miles across the South China Sea to Hong Kong. The heyday of the coracle fishing industry in Wales was the early twentieth century, when some two hundred vessels would ply the waters hereabouts. Commercial practices started to wane around thirty years ago, though between April and August, you may still see people fishing for salmon from these traditional boats, which the fishermen strap to their backs to haul upstream. Your best bet, though, if you want to see coracles in action, is to attend Cilgerran's fun annual **coracle races**, which take place in mid-August.

Newcastle Emlyn and around

An ancient farming and droving centre, **NEWCASTLE EMLYN** (Castell Newydd Emlyn) still retains an earthy agricultural feel, particularly during the busy and bellowing Thursday market. The swooping meander of the Teifi River made the site a natural defensive position, first built on by the Normans. The "new" **castle** – of which only a few stone stacks and an archway survive – replaced this original fortress in the mid-thirteenth century. Although the ruins aren't impressive, the river setting, surrounded by grazing sheep and rugby fields, is quintessentially Welsh. The castle is tucked away at the bottom of dead-end Castle Terrace, which peels off the main street by a squat little stone **market hall**. That's about it for sights, but there are some great pubs and decent enough places to eat, along with a strong sense of community, an eclectic range of shops and an unhurried charm.

National Wool Museum

Dre-fach Felindre, 3 miles southeast of Newcastle Emlyn • Daily: April–Sept 10am–5pm; Oct–March Tues–Sat 10am–5pm • Free • ☎ 01559 370929, ⓦ museumwales.ac.uk

At the beginning of the twentieth century, the village of Dre-fach Felindre was at the heart of the Welsh wool trade, with 43 working mills in and around the village; today there are twelve fully operational mills remaining in Wales. One of these, the Cambrian Mills, has been turned into the marvellous **National Wool Museum**, which recalls the lower Teifi's prolific past as a weaving centre. Its history is told through excellent exhibits spanning the entire process – from the different wools produced by Wales' eleven million sheep, through demonstrations of working presses and looms to stunning examples of the finished flannels, shawls and blankets. Don't miss the "Mighty Mule", which, with its four hundred spindles spinning the wool into yarn, is quite a sight when operating at full throttle. Throughout, video footage and informative wall displays put the industry into its social and cultural contexts.

ARRIVAL AND DEPARTURE   NEWCASTLE EMLYN

By bus The #460, which stops on New Road, serves Cardigan (hourly; 25min) and Carmarthen (hourly; 1hr).

ACCOMMODATION AND EATING

★ **The Daffodil** A475, 4.5 miles east at Penrhiwllan ☎ 01559 370343, ⓦ daffodilinn.co.uk. This large village inn has been stylishly revamped and now comprises a handsome, olive green restaurant with skylight, cosy bar and, best of all, a raised wooden decking area with fabulous views across the valley. Dishes might include pan-fried duck breast with star anise and port sauce (£17.50), though it'd be remiss not to try something from the dessert menu, with summery tempters like elderflower crème brulee with pomegranate to round things off. Book ahead for the two-course Sunday roast (£14.95). Mon–Sat noon–2.30pm & 6–10pm, Sun noon–2.30pm.

Emlyn Hotel Bridge St ☎ 01239 710317, ⓦ gwestyremlynhotel.co.uk. Nicely refurbished old coaching inn with stylish, modern rooms, plus gym, sauna and spa pool. The hotel is easily the best place to eat in town, too, thanks to its smart *Bwyty'r Bont* restaurant (mains from £12), or there are two more informal bars where you can grab a light meal and a pint or glass of wine. Restaurant daily noon–2.30pm & 6–9pm. **£120**

La Calabria Ffostrasol, 6 miles northeast of Newcastle Emlyn ☎ 01239 851101, ⓦ la-calabria.co.uk. Run by a Welsh–Italian, Tony, in the converted cowshed of a farm, the food here is rustic southern Italian – *pollo marsala*, *saltimbocca* (sirloin stuffed with parma ham with ratatouille, £15.95), as well as pasta and pizza – with kids well catered for too. Be sure to try the ice cream made with milk from the owner's herd. Tues–Sat noon–2.30pm & 6–10.30pm.

Maes-y Derw 0.5 mile towards Cardigan on A484 ☎ 01239 710860, ⓦ maes-y-derw.co.uk. Classy B&B with spacious rooms in a beautifully restored house on the edge of town. Great breakfasts, evening meals by arrangement and there's a self-catering cottage. **£80**

Lampeter

The old-fashioned town of **LAMPETER** (Llanbedr Pont Steffan), twenty miles east of Newcastle Emlyn, is best known as a remote outpost of the British university system, known as Trinity St David. It was founded in 1822 by the Bishop of St Davids to aid Welsh theological students unable to travel to England for their education. Though the town has fewer than three thousand residents, it's a lively place, with frequent gigs and theatre performances and an eclectic population of current students, graduates who forgot to leave, hippies and farmers. At the end of July, the considerable grounds of St Davids are taken over by the hugely enjoyable **Lampeter Food Festival**.

The town's three main streets – High, Bridge and College – meet at **Harford Square**, named after the local landowning family responsible for the construction of the early nineteenth-century **Falcondale Hall**, now an opulent hotel on the northern approach to Lampeter.

St Davids Building and Lampeter Museum

Lampeter Museum College St • Tues, Thurs & Sat 10am–4pm • Free • ☎ 01570 422769, ⓦ hanesllambed.org.uk

Off College Street are the main university buildings, which include C.B. Cockerell's **St Davids Building**, the original stuccoed quadrangle dating from 1827 and modelled along the lines of an Oxbridge college. Tucked right underneath the main buildings, the motte of Lampeter's long-vanished **castle** forms an incongruous mound amid such order. The history of St Davids, featuring some delightful etchings, can be viewed inside the nearby **Lampeter Museum** – possibly the country's smallest museum – which also features an exhibition on the town during World War I.

ARRIVAL AND INFORMATION

LAMPETER

By bus Most buses stop outside the NatWest Bank on the High Street.
Destinations Aberaeron (hourly; 30min); Aberystwyth (every 30min–1hr; 1hr 15min); Carmarthen (hourly; 1hr); Llanddewi Brefi (6 daily; 25min); Tregaron (9 daily; 25–35min).

Information There's no tourist office in town, but staff at the Lampeter Museum should be able to furnish you with local information.

ACCOMMODATION

Falcondale Mansion Hotel Falcondale Drive ☎ 01570 422910, ⓦ falcondalehotel.com. Italianate Victorian mansion in spacious parkland, 600yds west along High Street then twice that along its stately drive. Rooms (which vary enormously) are beautifully opulent, and the meals are wonderful (set dinner £40). Even if you're just passing through, consider afternoon tea (3–4.30pm; book ahead; £15) or the excellent Sunday lunch (£17). Restaurant daily noon–2.30pm, 3–5pm & 6.30–10pm. **£140**

Haulfan Guest House 6 Station Terrace ☎ 01570 422718, ⓦ haulfanguesthouse.co.uk. The only worthwhile option in the centre of town, this quiet, family-run B&B has four rooms (one without bathroom), the pick of which is the one just below street level. **£65**

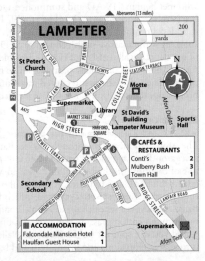

4

EATING AND DRINKING

Conti's 5 Harford Sqyare ☎ 01570 422223. Venerable, Italian run café whose rich, home-made, organic ice creams have been pulling in the punters for the best part of seventy years; if it's too cold for that, try some hot fudge cake and a cup of freshly roasted coffee. Mon–Sat 9am–5.30pm.

Mulberry Bush 2 Bridge St ☎ 01570 423317. Airy café above a long-standing wholefood shop, serving a tasty range of mostly vegetarian-inspired dishes like vegan lasagne and cashew nut risotto (£7.50). Breakfasts are also available between 9 and 11am. Occasional music nights. Mon–Sat 9am–6pm.

Town Hall High St ☎ 01570 421599. Smart, light-filled café and deli in the Town Hall with a short menu of cheeses, cold meats, olives and salads served up in tasty sandwiches and platters (£5–6). Good coffee and cakes, and heaps of foodie books to browse. Mon–Sat 9am–4pm.

Tregaron and around

On the cusp of the verdant Teifi Valley and the desolate moors rising above it, the small town of **TREGARON**, ten miles northeast of Lampeter, was for long seemingly untouched by the modern world, but is now gradually being drawn into the twenty-first century.

All roads to Tregaron lead into the spruced-up market square, hemmed in by solid eighteenth- and nineteenth-century buildings. The **statue** in the centre of the square is of Tregaron-born Henry Richard (1812–88), the founder of the Peace Union, forerunner of the League of Nations and, subsequently, the United Nations.

Rhiannon Welsh Gold Centre

Cnr Dewi Rd & Market Square • Mon–Sat: March–Dec 10am–5pm; Jan & Feb 11am–4pm • ☎ 01974 298415, ⓦ rhiannon.co.uk

Tregaron born Rhiannon Evans has been designing Celtic-inspired jewellery for the best part of thirty years, and there's every chance that you'll get to see her at work in the classy **Rhiannon Welsh Gold Centre**. Most of the items on display are fashioned from Welsh gold, though a number of pieces are cultivated from silver and other materials. These displays are backed up with galleries of painting, glassware, woollen throws and assorted knick-knacks, plus a good café.

Llanddewi Brefi

Through the mid-2000s the single shop in the village of **LLANDDEWI BREFI**, three miles south of Tregaron, did a roaring trade in souvenir T-shirts commemorating the fictitious home of Dafydd, the "only gay in the village" from the BBC comedy *Little Britain*.

Llanddewi Brefi's previous claim to fame was the legend of 118 Welsh churchmen who met here in 519 AD and summoned Dewi Sant (St David). On appearing, Dewi began to speak to the men, but had trouble being heard, until the ground beneath him shuddered ominously and suddenly rose, giving him a natural platform to continue speaking – the massive **parish church** of St David sits on the mound to this day. Part of the church wall consists of two discernible stones inscribed with fragments of Latin script. These were originally part of a single memorial that dated from within a century of David's death – the first recorded mention of the Welsh patron saint – but they were broken up, reportedly, by an illiterate eighteenth- or nineteenth-century mason.

Cors Caron

B4343, 2 miles north of Tregaron • Open access • Free • ⓦ ccw.gov.uk

The Afon Teifi meanders through a wide, flat valley into the eerie wetland of **Cors Caron** (Tregaron Bog), a national nature reserve of peatland that was once cut for fuel. It is one of the most prodigious wildlife areas in Wales, home to rare marsh grasses, black adders, buzzards and red kites. A couple of walks lead off from a parking area beside the **Tregaron–Aberystwyth cycle trail**, which follows an old railway line along the bog's flanks. Easiest is a wheelchair-accessible **boardwalk** (2-mile loop; 1hr; flat) that weaves out through cotton grass, bog mosses and birch to a hide with huge windows. Part way round you can spur off on the **Riverside Walk** (4 miles; 2–3hr; uneven), which extends into a large loop along the infant Teifi and back along the disused railway.

Strata Florida

6 miles north of Tregaron and 1 mile east of Pontrhydfendigaid • Daily: April–Oct 10am–5pm; Nov–March 10am–4pm • April–Oct £3.50; Nov–March free; CADW • ☎ 01974 831261

In glorious rural solitude against wide-open skies and sheep-flecked hills stand the atmospheric ruins of **Strata Florida Abbey**, originally located in Ystrad Fflur, "the valley of the flowers", two miles away, but relocated in its early years to this equally fertile spot. Founded in 1164, the Cistercian abbey swiftly grew into a centre for milling, farming and weaving, and became important political centre for Wales. In 1238, a dying Llywelyn the Great, fearful that his work of unifying Wales under one ruler would disintegrate, summoned the lesser Welsh princes here to command them to pay homage to his son, Dafydd.

Although very little survived Henry VIII's dissolution of the monasteries, the huge, Norman west doorway gives some idea of the church's vast dimensions. Fragments of side chapels include beautifully tiled medieval floors, and there's also a serene cemetery. A yew tree in the neighbouring graveyard shades the spot where Dafydd ap Gwilym, fourteenth-century bard and contemporary of Chaucer, is said to be buried.

ARRIVAL AND DEPARTURE
TREGARON

By bus Buses arrive at the market square and serve: Aberystwyth (10 daily; 1hr); Lampeter (9 daily; 25–35min); Llanddewi Brefi (6 daily; 10min).

ACCOMMODATION AND EATING

Llew Du Pontrhydfendigaid ☎ 01974 831624, ⊛ blacklionhotel.co.uk. The *Llew Du* (Black Lion) is a great local pub. It is particularly welcoming to cyclists and walkers, and has a roaring fire when the temperature drops. Bar meals are unsophisticated but well made, and there are comfortable rooms. Daily 11am–11pm. **£70**

★**Talbot Hotel** Market Square ☎ 01974 298208, ⊛ ytalbot.com. Dominating the main square, this classically symmetrical old drovers' inn has been given a smooth contemporary gloss, its thirteen rooms stylishly spare and well appointed. The classy Modern British restaurant does a fine Sunday lunch (two courses for £16, three for £20), but more fun is the old bar, which retains its low timber beams, slate flooring and a fabulous inglenook fireplace; the Welsh ales and ciders are terrific. Bar daily 11am–11pm, restaurant daily noon–2.30pm & 6–9pm. **£80**

Aberystwyth

Midway along the Cambrian coast, spirited **ABERYSTWYTH** (or "Aber", as it's known locally) is a blast of fresh sea air. Two long bays skirted by pebbly beaches curve between twin rocky heads: Constitution Hill to the north, and Pen Dinas to the south above the town harbour's marina, where both the Rheidol and Ystwyth rivers empty into the sea. East of the town centre, the district of Penglais is home to the graceful Portland stone buildings of the National Library and the modernist blocks of Aberystwyth University, one of the UK's most prestigious educational institutions (the Prince of Wales, Prince Charles, studied here). The presence here of Wales' National Library makes the city home – it's claimed – to more books per capita than anywhere else in the world. There are plenty of other cultural and other diversions in town too, as well as an array of Victorian and Edwardian seaside trappings, including a cliff railway.

Aberystwyth's anti-establishment past and anarchic soul manifest in diverse ways. Pubs – and there are loads – stay open late, the political scene is green-tinged, and the town overall is emphatically Welsh – making it an easy-going and enjoyable place to gain an insight into the national psyche. The *Cymdeithas yr Iaith* (Welsh Language Society) was founded in Aberystwyth in 1963 and is still located in the town.

The precursor of Aberystwyth is the inland village of **Llanbadarn Fawr**, the seat of Wales' oldest bishopric between the sixth and eighth centuries, whose massive parish church still reeks of past power. Aberystwyth and Llanbadarn grew together around the church and the seafront thirteenth-century castle, minting its own coins and headquartering Owain Glyndŵr's revolutionaries in the Middle Ages.

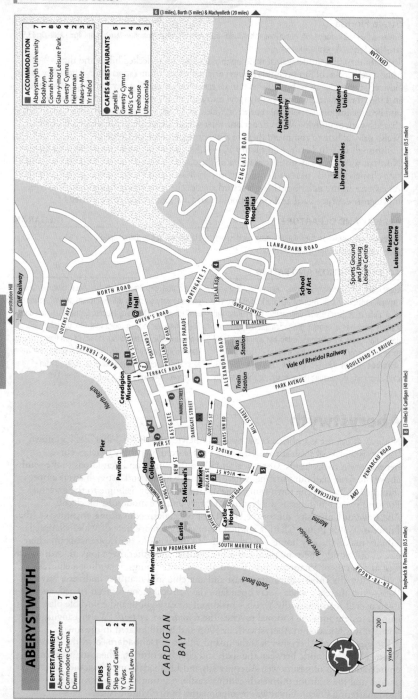

ABERYSTWYTH

ENTERTAINMENT

Aberystwyth Arts Centre	7
Commodore Cinema	1
Drwm	6

PUBS

Rummers	5
Ship and Castle	2
Y Cŵps	4
Yr Hen Lew Du	3

ACCOMMODATION

Aberystwyth University	7
Bodalwyn	1
Conrah Hotel	8
Glan-y-mor Leisure Park	6
Gwesty Cymru	4
Helmsman	2
Maes-y-Môr	3
Yr Hafod	5

CAFÉS & RESTAURANTS

Agnelli's	5
Gwesty Cymru	4
MG's Café	1
Treehouse	3
Ultracomida	2

Constitution Hill and the cliff railway

Railway April–June, Sept & Oct daily 10am–5pm; July & Aug daily 10am–6pm; Nov–March Wed–Sun 10.30am–4pm • £4 return •
☎ 01970 617642, Ⓦ aberystwythcliffrailway.co.uk

The 430ft-high **Constitution Hill** (Y Graig Glais) rises sharply from the rocky beach at the long Promenade's northern end. It's accessible on foot, though if you don't fancy the invigorating but stiff walk up, you can take the clanking 1896 **cliff railway**, which creeps up the crooked tracks at scarcely more than walking pace from the grand terminus building at the top of Queen's Road, behind the Promenade. Originally employing a water balance system, it was electrified in 1921, and remains Britain's longest electric funicular railway. On a clear day, the views of Cardigan Bay are fantastic.

Camera Obscura

April–Oct daily 11am–5pm • £1 • ☎ 01970 617642, Ⓦ aberystwythcliffrailway.co.uk

At the top of Constitution Hill you'll find a café, picnic area, telescopes and an octagonal **camera obscura**, a device popular in the pre-TV era using a mirror and hefty lens to project close-up and long-shot views over the town, the surrounding mountains and bays, plus a vista of the hordes of caravans to the north, resembling legions of tanks poised for battle. The existing structure was built in 1985 on the ground plan of the Victorian original, but with its scale expanded to make it the largest of its type in the world.

The seafront

From the bottom of Constitution Hill, the **Promenade** – officially Marine Terrace – arcs away to the south, past ornate benches decorated with snakes, a continuous wall of hotels and guesthouses, a prim bandstand and a shingle beach.

Ceredigion Museum

Terrace Rd • Mon–Sat: Easter–Oct 10am–5pm; Nov–Easter noon–4.30pm • Free • ☎ 01970 633088, Ⓦ ceredigion.gov.uk

The **Ceredigion Museum** is atmospherically housed over three floors in the ornate Edwardian Coliseum music hall, which last functioned as a cinema in 1977. Mementos of the building as a theatre and cinema give a sense of place to an otherwise wonderfully disparate collection, the most fascinating of which charts the seafaring exploits in the Bay, where, during the course of the eighteenth and nineteenth centuries, over a thousand ships were built. Among the many intriguing exhibits is the barometer designed by Robert Fitzroy, captain of HMS *Beagle* during Darwin's voyage to Tierra del Fuego. There's much more besides, including a surprisingly interesting look at the history of time-keeping – to this end, note, as you exit, the pendulum from the Old Town clock (taken down in 1956) swinging in the window.

Old College

New Promenade

West of Marine Terrace and the spindly **pier**, the seafront is dominated by the dazzling, John Nash-designed, turreted villa known as the **Old College**. Dating from 1790, the villa was massively extended in the 1860s, as a hotel designed to soak up the anticipated masses arriving on the new rail line. The venture failed, and in 1872 it was sold to the fledgling university, whose property it remains; indeed, it was the focus of most university activity until the 1960s, when work began to develop the Penglais campus (see p.274).

The castle and around

Open access • Free

At the southern end of the Promenade, a rocky headland is occupied by the **castle** ruins, which stare blankly out to sea. Built by Edward I as part of his conquest of Wales, the thirteenth-century fortress is more notable for its breezy position than for the buildings themselves, of which the two outer gates are the most impressive remains.

4

While in the area, wander past the Art Nouveau **Castle Hotel**, 37 SouthRoad, built in the style of an ornate Edwardian gin palace, and still with etched glass windows designating "Public Bar", "Lounge Bar" and "Luncheon Bar".

The harbour and Pen Dinas

South of the castle is the quiet, sandy beach along South Marine Terrace, which peters out by the wide **harbour**, the mouth of the Rheidol and Ystwyth rivers. The quietest beach is further south still, across the other side of the rivers' mouth, at **Tanybwlch**. High above the shingle strand is the Iron Age hillfort of **Pen Dinas** (413ft), crowned with what looks like a chimney – actually an 1853 memorial to the Duke of Wellington. Paths lead to the top from the car park at Tanybwlch.

The University and around

Aberystwyth's cultural heart beats strongest around the hillside suburb of Penglais, home to the **National Library of Wales** and the **Aberystwyth Arts Centre**. At the foot of the hill the **School of Art Gallery & Museum** deserves a short visit, perhaps on your way out to see the ancient **church of St Padarn** at Llanbadarn Fawr.

School of Art Gallery & Museum

Buarth Mawr • Mon–Fri 10am–5pm • Free • ☎ 01970 622460, ⊛ aber.ac.uk/en/art

A hundred yards north of the station, Stanley Road leads to the splendid **School of Art**, housed inside the Edward Davies building. Originally bequeathed to the university by the Davies sisters of Gregynog Hall (see p.243), this impressive Edwardian building, topped with a distinctive cupola, has been the home of the art department since 1995. The public galleries on the ground floor mount both touring exhibitions and rotating exhibitions from the university's extensive permanent collection, with an emphasis on Welsh art.

National Library of Wales

Penglais Rd • Mon–Fri 9.30am–6pm, Sat 9.30–5pm • Free; free 1hr guided tours Mon 11am & Wed 2.15pm • ☎ 01970 632800, ⊛ llgc.org.uk • Bus 03 (every 20min, Sat & Sun hourly) from the bus station

Housed in a massive white stone Edwardian building overlooking the town, the **National Library of Wales** was established in 1907 and possesses fine manuscripts including the oldest extant Welsh text, the twelfth-century *Black Book of Carmarthen*, and the earliest manuscript of *The Mabinogion*. Occasionally these form part of the typically excellent temporary exhibitions held in the corridors near the entrance, the upstairs Gregynog Gallery and the downstairs Peniarth Gallery. Displays from the library's permanent collection of books, manuscripts and papers include the **World of the Book**, which looks at the history of the written word and publishing in Wales.

As one of the UK's copyright repositories, the library holds copies of every new book published in Britain. If you're tracing family history you'll want access to the **Reading Rooms**, for which you'll need two forms of ID, including one that shows your current address. Otherwise, all manner of (often free) events are held here, including films, exhibitions, live performances and lectures – and with a good café to boot – you can easily spend a few hours here.

Aberystwyth Arts Centre

Penglais Rd • ☎ 01970 623232, ⊛ aberystwytharts centre.co.uk

The excellent **Aberystwyth Arts Centre**, a quarter of a mile uphill from the National Library, sits in the middle of the university's main campus. A curious mix of 1960s brutalism and postmodern elegance, the Arts Centre is a great place to while away an hour or two, taking in the various temporary art and photographic exhibitions, browsing the designer crafts and bookshops, catching a film or enjoying a drink in the café, which affords sublime views over the town and bay.

Church of St Padarn

At Llanbadarn Fawr, just off A44, 1 mile southeast of Aberystwyth • Generally daily 10am–4pm

The suburb of **Llanbadarn Fawr** is the original settlement from which Aberystwyth grew but warrants little attention except for the stunning sight of the massive, thirteenth-century **church of St Padarn**. The site's religious association goes back to the Breton St Padarn who established a monastic settlement here in the second half of the sixth century, decades before even St Augustine's mission to the English of 597 AD.

Inside the church, opposite the main door, hangs an enlargement of a page from *Rhygyfarch's Psalter* of 1079, one example of the beautifully decorated texts for which the monks of Llanbadarn became renowned. In the south transept, there's a fascinating exhibition on St Padarn's monastic foundation and the area's history that includes two fine tenth-century crosses, moved inside from the churchyard in 1916. The taller one, about 8ft high, is woven with exquisite Celtic tracery. Perhaps the most entertaining part of the exhibition deals with poet **Dafydd ap Gwilym** (c.1320–70) and his upbringing in Llanbadarn parish. His poem *Merched Llanbadarn* ("Women of Llanbadarn") tells of his frustration at sitting in the church watching the beautiful parish girls:

Plygu rhag llid yr ydwyf,	*Passion doubles me over,*
Pla ar holl ferched y plwyf!	*Plague take all the parish girls!*
Am na chefais, drais drawsgoed,	*Because, frustrated trysting,*
Onaddun'yr un erioed,	*I've had not a single one.*
Na morwyn fwyn ofynaig,	*No lovely, longed-for virgin,*
Na merch fach, na gwrach, na gwraig.	*Not a wench nor witch nor wife.*

ARRIVAL AND DEPARTURE

ABERYSTWYTH

By train Main line and Vale of Rheidol trains use the same train station on Alexandra Road, a 10min walk from the seafront.
Destinations Borth (10 daily; 12min); Machynlleth (10 daily; 30min).
By bus The main bus station is adjacent to the train station on Alexandra Road.

Destinations Aberaeron (every 30min; 40min); Borth (hourly; 20min); Cardigan (hourly; 1hr 45min); Carmarthen (hourly; 2hr 20min); Lampeter (hourly; 1hr 15min); Machynlleth (hourly; 40min); New Quay (hourly; 1hr); Pontrhydfendigaid (3 daily; 45min); Tregaron (10 daily; 1hr); Ynyslas (hourly; 30min).

INFORMATION AND ACTIVITIES

Tourist information The TIC is just off the seafront on Terrace Road (July & Aug daily 10am–5pm; Sept–June Mon–Sat 10am–5pm; ☎01970 612125, ✉aberystwythtic @ceredigion.gov.uk). Staff can help with accommodation and sell tickets for local events.
Internet Free at the library inside the Town Hall on Queens Road (Mon–Fri 9.30am–6pm, Sat 9.30am–5pm).

Horseriding Rheidol Riding Centre, off A44, 5 miles east of Aberystwyth ☎01970 880863, ⊛rheidol-riding-centre .co.uk. Offers a variety of lessons and leisure rides for all standards in farmland in the Vale of Rheidol.
Swimming Plascrug Leisure Centre, off Llanbadarn Road ☎01970 624579. Has two indoor pools, a sauna and solarium, squash and tennis courts, and a multi-gym.

ACCOMMODATION

Accommodation is generally reasonably priced and easy to find, though everywhere fills up to the gills during graduation week (usually the second or third week of July), when prices invariably jump. Guesthouses and B&Bs predominate; anywhere on the seafront is likely to charge a premium.

HOTELS AND GUESTHOUSES
Bodalwyn Queens Ave ☎01970 612578, ⊛bodalwyn .co.uk. Quiet and roomy guesthouse blending contemporary furnishings with original features, such as decorative fireplaces. All eight rooms have well-appointed en-suite bathrooms, and breakfast is served in a sunny conservatory. **£76**
Conrah Hotel A487, 4 miles south ☎01970 617941,

⊛conrah.co.uk. This stately Georgian hotel has a bit of a businessy feel, but the rooms – each one different – are very comfortable and the restaurant and lounges have great views over the spacious grounds; you'll also see red kites nesting in the grounds. **£95**
★**Gwesty Cymru** 19 Marine Terrace ☎01970 6122252, ⊛gwestycymru.com. The town's most appealing place to stay by far, this classy guesthouse offers eight

4

colour-themed, artfully designed rooms (four with sea view), each with handcrafted oak furnishings inlaid with slate, crisp white cotton sheets, and applestone-tiled bathrooms; the feel is most definitely modern Welsh. Breakfast is served in the half-basement restaurant. **£100**

Helmsman 43 Marine Terrace ☎01970 624132, ⓦhelmsmanguesthouse.co.uk. Traditional seafront guesthouse with fairly drab public areas but tidy rooms, which are either garden- or sea-facing, though there's no premium for the latter. Closed Dec–Feb. **£70**

Yr Hafod 1 South Marine Terrace ☎01970 617579, ⓦyrhafod.co.uk. Good-value seafront accommodation, with six spacious, well-maintained, though plainly furnished rooms (some en suite and several with sea views), appealingly situated south of the castle. **£70**

HOSTELS, CAMPING AND SELF-CATERING

Aberystwyth University Penglais ☎01970 621960, ⓦaber.ac.uk/en/visitors. During the university's summer recess (mid-June to August) the university offers some single-bed accommodation in self-contained flats with bed linen, full cooking facilities and access to the university facilities, including two sports halls and a heated pool. Pre-booking required. Per person **£33**

Glan-y-mor Leisure Park Clarach Bay, 3 miles north of Aberystwyth ☎01970 828900, ⓦsunbourne.co.uk. Situated on the other side of Constitution Hill, with a variety of options including on-site caravans and tent pitches, plus a superb range of leisure facilities including (for an extra fee) a heated indoor pool and gym. Pitches **£20s**

Maes-y-Môr 25 Bath St ☎01970 639270, ⓦmaesymor .co.uk. Brightly painted and very central hostel-cum-guesthouse with nine rooms (seven twins, a double and a family room), though bathrooms are shared; there's a kitchen for use by guests, as well as laundry facilities. Breakfast not included. **£50**

EATING AND DRINKING

Aberystwyth's cultural and gastronomic life is a cosmopolitan, year-round affair, thriving on students in term time and visitors in the summer. As well as a varied range of **pubs** and **restaurants**, the town is a good place to hear Welsh **music** and a lively centre for theatre and cinema. Daytime **café** culture is booming, and the Arts Centre is home to two fabulous cafés and two bars.

RESTAURANTS AND CAFÉS

★**Agnelli's** 3 Bridge St ☎07969 959466. You'll find the best espresso for miles around at this warm and welcoming Italian-run deli/café, which goes down a treat with a slice of Sicilian cannoli with vanilla; there's more substantial fare too, such as grilled Tuscan sausages with Pancetta, and baked aubergines in a Parmesan crust. Mon & Tues 10am–7pm, Wed–Fri till 8pm, Sat 9am–6pm.

★**Gwesty Cymru** 19 Marine Terrace ☎01970 6122252, ⓦgwestycymru.com. Accomplished slate-floored half-basement restaurant with an exciting, thoroughly modern Welsh menu featuring the likes of gingerbread-crusted rack of lamb with buttered leeks in Welsh cider sauce (£18.75), and blueberry and Brecon Gin Bakewell. The seaview terrace out front makes an ideal spot for a pre-dinner drink on a warm summer's evening. Mon–Sat noon–2.30pm & 6–9pm, Sun noon–2.30pm.

MG's Café 6 Chalybeate St ☎01970 625624. Comfy sofas, newspapers, super espresso, and a range of savoury dishes (£5–6) and tasty cakes (many gluten-free) make this one of the most tempting places in town to hang out on a grotty day. Mon–Fri 8am–6pm, Sat 8.30am–6pm, Sat 10am–4pm.

Treehouse 14 Baker St ☎01970 615791, ⓦtreehousewales.co.uk. Upbeat café situated above a bustling little organic shop. While the lunchtime menu is largely of a vegetarian bent, there is usually one meat-based special each day, and there are gluten-free options too (mains £7.50); it's no less enjoyable a spot for coffee and cake, which are all home-made. Mon–Fri 10am–5pm, Sat 9am–5pm.

★**Ultracomida** 31 Pier St ☎01970 630686, ⓦultracomida.co.uk. Spain comes to Aber in this fabulous deli, its wall lined with Iberian wines, meats and olives, alongside Welsh cheeses and all manner of other goodies. Meanwhile, you can sample tapas, like chorizo in Welsh cider, or salt cod salad (£2.50–3.50 each), in the casual restaurant/bar through to the rear, which is also a cool spot to kick back with a coffee. Deli Mon–Sat 10am–6pm, Sun noon–5pm; restaurant Mon 10am–5pm, Tues–Sat 10am–9pm, Sun noon–4pm.

PUBS

Rummers Bridge St. Studenty, late-closing pub with slate floors, outside seating by the river and live music most weekends. It calls itself a wine bar but you're better sticking to beer and spirits. Daily 11am–11pm.

Ship and Castle Corner of Vulcan and High sts ☎01970 612334. Much smarter inside than out, this nicely refurbished pub offers a pool table and a great jukebox, and takes considerable pride in having the best selection of real ales in town. Daily 2pm–midnight.

Y Cŵps (Coopers Arms) ☎01970 624 050 Llanbadarn Rd. Fun and friendly Welsh local much-frequented by students, with regular folk and jazz nights and jam sessions. Daily 11am–11pm.

Yr Hen Lew Du (The Old Black Lion) 14 Bridge St ☎01970 615378. Boisterous, very Welsh and hugely enjoyable pub that's easily the best place in Aberystwyth to catch an international match on the big screen – there are six of them. Daily noon–midnight.

ENTERTAINMENT

Aberystwyth Arts Centre The University, Penglais ☎ 01970 623232, ⓦ aberystwythartscentre.co.uk. The town's main venue for art-house cinema, touring theatre, classes, events and wide-ranging temporary exhibitions (see p.274). Look out, too, for the Aberystwyth Musicfest held here in late July, which features mostly classical and jazz.

Commodore Cinema Bath St ☎ 01970 612421. Screens mainstream current releases.

Côr Meibion Aberystwyth ☎ 01970 202980, ⓦ aberchoir.co.uk. Visitors are welcome to attend rehearsals of the Male Voice Choir, which take place at the Aberystwyth Rugby Cub on Plascrug Avenue (Thurs 7–8.30pm).

Drwm National Library, Penglais ☎ 01970 632800, ⓦ drwm.llgc.org.uk. Hip centre for film, lectures and concerts.

Around Aberystwyth

Immediately inland of Aberystwyth lies the **Vale of Rheidol**, a region of forested glades and remote villages easily accessed by road. A more enjoyable approach is on the narrow-gauge steam train that terminates at the spectacular **Devil's Bridge**. Further exploration takes you into the **Vale of Ystwyth**.

The coast north of Aberystwyth draws sunseekers to the beach at **Borth** and the dunes close to the mouth of the Dyfi estuary. Birdwatchers will prefer to head further northeast to the RSPB's **Ynys-Hir Nature Reserve**, with its complex series of habitats.

The Vale of Rheidol

The River Rheidol winds its way down to Aberystwyth through a secluded, wooded valley, where occasional old industrial workings have moulded themselves into the contours, past waterfalls and minute villages. Devil's Bridge is easily accessed by the Vale of Rheidol Railway (see below) and the Rheidol Cycle Trail (see box below) and by car. For a **day out**, drivers can head straight for Devil's Bridge (along the A4120), then get to the lead mines in time for the kite feeding at Bwlch Nant yr Arian. If you've stayed for the kite feeding you're probably too late for side trips to the Cwm Rheidol Reservoir and the butterfly house on the same day.

Vale of Rheidol Railway

April–Oct 2–4 trains most days • £18 return • ☎ 01970 625819, ⓦ rheidolrailway.co.uk

The glorious Vale of Rheidol is best seen from the 23.5in-gauge **Vale of Rheidol Railway**, a narrow-gauge steam train which huffs and puffs along twelve miles of steep hillsides, climbing over 600ft in the process. It was built in 1902, ostensibly for the valley's lead mines but with a canny eye on its tourist potential. For many years it operated as part of British Rail's network, running steam trains until 1989 (over twenty years after steam locos had ceased operating elsewhere). It was then sold to the private group which now operates it using authentic Rheidol rolling stock. The trip takes one hour each way, and is most enjoyable from the comfortable first-class observation carriage (£2.50 extra each way) or the open-sided "summer car". There's also an excellent GPS-triggered audio guide to the line and valley for just £2 extra.

CYCLING THE VALE OF RHEIDOL AND THE YSTWYTH TRAIL

You can explore the valley by bike using the **Rheidol Cycle Trail**, a combination of designated cycle paths and quiet country lanes which runs eighteen miles from Aberystwyth to Devil's Bridge: the tourist office in Aberystwyth has a free leaflet outlining the route. Unfortunately, bikes can't be taken on the Vale of Rheidol Railway.

The twenty-mile **Ystwyth Trail** from Aberystwyth to Tregaron is another winner, partly following the trackbed of the Manchester & Milford Railway across Cors Caron (see p.271).

Cwm Rheidol Reservoir

On a side road 4 miles east of Capel Bangor Visitor centre Easter & May–Sept 10.15am–4.15pm; Free Power station tours 11am–3.30pm • Free • ☎ 01970 880667

Midway along the valley, the Rheidol is dammed at the **Cwm Rheidol Reservoir**, the final element in a small, showpiece hydroelectric scheme that starts high in the headwaters at the Nant-y-moch Reservoir. It is all explained at the visitor centre, where you can join a free 45-minute tour of the **power station**, where impressive sluices and channels funnel the water according to need.

Magic of Life Butterfly House

Behind the Cwm Rheidol Reservoir visitor centre, on a side road 4 miles east of Capel Bangor • Daily: April–Sept 10am–5pm; Oct 10am–4pm • £6.50 • ☎ 01970 880928, ⓦ magicoflife.org

The **Magic of Life Butterfly House** houses dozens of beautiful butterflies and moths – including the lovely blue morpho – in a wild garden and tropically heated polytunnel. Visitors are encouraged to interact with the butterflies, which are at their most active in the mornings, making this the best time of day to visit.

Bwlch Nant yr Arian

A44, 9 miles east of Aberystwyth • Visitor centre daily: Easter–Sept 10am–5pm; Oct–Easter generally 10.30am to dusk • Free; parking £1.50 • ☎ 01970 890453, ⓦ forestry.gov.uk/bwlchnantyrarian • Buses #47 and #525 from Aberystwyth stop right outside the entrance.

In recent years, **Bwlch Nant yr Arian** has become famous for its red kites, easy walks and varied mountain biking. From the visitor centre, which has a decent café with a pleasant deck, three well-marked walking trails (30min, 1hr & 2hr) head out into the evergreen forest and among the abandoned detritus of lead mining.

The easiest trail (which is wheelchair accessible) loops around a lake past the kite hide, a superb spot for watching the daily **red kite feeding** (3pm during daylight saving, 2pm in winter) when some 20lb of beef and lamb are placed on a grassy patch by the lake. When this practice first started, fewer than a dozen birds would come, but now it isn't uncommon to see two hundred kites all squabbling over the pickings.

The woods also offer top-class **mountain biking**, with three dedicated trails; two red (9km and 16km) and one black, the latter some 35km long and taking around four to five hours to complete; pick up a bike trail map from the shop, though there's no bike hire here – the nearest rentals are in Cardigan (see p.259), and near Aberaeron (see p.264).

Silver Mountain Experience

A44, 1 mile east of Bwlch Nant yr Arian • April to mid-July daily 10am–4pm, mid-July to Sept daily 10am–5pm, Oct Sat & Sun 10am–4pm • £3.95 or £7.95 to include one tour • ☎ 01970 890620, ⓦ silvermountainexperience.co.uk

Bwlch Nant yr Arian forest's lush foliage makes it difficult to imagine how stark the valley once looked. A truer picture unfolds in the impressively barren scenery around the old **Llywernog Silver Mine**, which opened in the 1740s before closing in the early twentieth century; it reopened as a museum in the early 1970s, since which time the site has expanded in an appropriately rustic manner.

Recently recast as the **Silver Mountain Experience**, visitors now have a choice of taking one of three character-led tours, each 45 minutes long; there's the straightforward, heritage-based "Miner's Life" guided tour, though most visitors plump for "The Black Chasm", a fantasy-based tour led by actors of a somewhat spookier disposition; "A Dragon's Tale", meanwhile, is suited to younger visitors. Topside, you can pan for "fool's gold", build a dam, or dowse for veins of galena, a silver-rich mineral once mined locally – the remains of waste tips scarring hillsides and shafts pockmarking former sites are now mostly hidden among the evergreens of the Rheidol Forest; in the latter half of the 1800s, the whole of northern Ceredigion lured galena speculators and opportunists by the trainful.

Devil's Bridge

Folk legend, incredible scenery and travellers' lore combine at **DEVIL'S BRIDGE** (Pontarfynach), a tiny settlement twelve miles east of Aberystwyth – reached by road (A4120) or the Vale of Rheidol Railway – built largely for the long-established visitor trade. To avoid the congestion, visit at the beginning or end of the day, or out of season.

The main attraction is the Devil's Bridge itself, where three roads (the A4120, the B4343 and the B4574) converge and cross the churning River Mynach yards above its confluence with the Rheidol to form three bridges, one on top of the other. The bridge in front of the alpine *Hafod Arms* hotel (see below) is the most recently built of the three, dating from 1901. Immediately below it and wedged between the rock faces are the stone bridge from 1753, and, at the bottom, the original bridge, dating from the eleventh century and reputedly built by the monks of Strata Florida Abbey (see p.271).

The Punch Bowl

£1 coin in the turnstile

The classic view of the **three stacked bridges** is from the Punch Bowl path. Standing by the modern road bridge with your back to the hotel, take the right-hand turnstile for a ten-minute loop.

Slippery steps lead down to the deep cleft in the rock, where the water pounds and hurtles through the gap crowned by the bridges. The Punch Bowl is the name given to a series of rock bowls scooped by the sheer power of the thundering river, which rushes through past bright-green mossy rocks and saturated lichen.

Mynach Falls

Pay at the ticket office by the entrance to the walks • Easter–Oct daily 9.45am–5.30pm • £3.75; outside these times plus Nov–Easter, pay £2 in the turnstile

There are more extensive trails and many more steep steps across the road from the Punch Bowl. A path leads down into the valley and ultimately to the crashing **Mynach Falls**. The scenery here is magnificent: sharp, wooded slopes rising away from the frothing river, with distant mountain peaks surfacing on the horizon. A platform overlooks the series of falls, from where a steep flight of steps takes you further down to a footbridge dramatically spanning the river at the bottom.

ACCOMMODATION AND EATING   **DEVIL'S BRIDGE**

Hafod Hotel A4120, Devil's Bridge ☎ 01970 890232, ⊛ thehafodhotel.co.uk. Right at the head of the falls, the *Hafod* is the social hub of this scattered community, and though mainly frequented for its restaurant, bar and tearoom, it does have comfortable, if expensive, rooms, most of which overlook the gorge. Daily 9am–10pm. **£100**

Woodlands Caravan Park A4120, Devil's Bridge ☎ 01970 890233, ⊛ woodlandsdevilsbridge.co.uk. Reasonably priced camping with a few static caravans and spacious and picturesque touring sites, plus showers, a kids' playground, camp store and tearooms. Pitches **£16**

The Vale of Ystwyth

The Ystwyth River runs pretty much parallel to the Rheidol, a couple of miles to the south. Four miles south of Devil's Bridge is the quiet village of **PONTRHYDYGROES**, the former centre of local lead-mining activity. The B4574 climbs out of the village and past the country estate of **Hafod**, once the seat of a great house belonging to the wealthy Johnes family. Their last mansion was demolished in 1958 as an unsafe ruin, and all that remains is the beautiful estate Thomas Johnes landscaped and forested two hundred years ago. The church, off the B4574, is the best place to embark on the waymarked **trails** that lead through the estate, past its trickling streams, monumental relics and planted glades, down to the river. A bridge spans the river, where paths fan out along its banks and up through the tiny valley of the Nant Gau.

North from Aberystwyth

The A487 runs north from Aberystwyth towards Machynlleth, slicing between the mountains to the east and the flat lands bordering the vast Dyfi estuary. The seaward plain is essentially a raised bog, **Cors Fochno**, visible from the main road but better viewed from the railway line or the coastal B4353. This road sneaks through **Borth**, stretching for nearly two miles along the seafront, to the **nature reserve** at **Ynyslas**, the best place to explore the sand dunes, flanking a supremely scenic **beach** looking across the Dyfi estuary.

Inland, the eighteenth-century iron foundry at **Furnace** heralds **Ynys-hir**, an RSPB nature reserve with an impressive range of bird habitats, and **Cors Dyfi**, where ospreys can be viewed for most of the summer.

Borth

Hemmed in by the sea on one side and a vast peat bog on the other, **BORTH**, five miles north of Aberystwyth, is an old fishing village that gradually adapted to caravan park tourism. The village is strung out along ruler-straight High Street, which regularly gets battered by weather fronts from the Atlantic. Its three-mile-long shallow **beach** is excellent: swimming is fine as long as you don't go too far up towards the mouth of the Dyfi.

ARRIVAL AND DEPARTURE   BORTH

By train The train station is on Cambrian Terrace, midway along the High Street. Destinations Aberystwyth (10 daily; 12min); Machynlleth (10 daily; 18min).

By bus Bus #512 to Aberystwyth (hourly; 25min) departs from the train station.

ACCOMMODATION AND EATING

Tir a Mor High St ☎ 01970 871042. Cheery two-floored café-cum-gallery with squidgy sofas in the loft, where you can grab a pair of binoculars and gaze out across the Cors Fochno; terrific ice-cream parlour too. Mon–Fri 9am–5pm, Sat & Sun 9am–6pm.

YHA Borth High St ☎ 0845 371 9724 or ☎ 01970 871498, ✉ borth@yha.org.uk. Edwardian YHA hostel at the northern end of town, with dorm beds and some family rooms, as well as a kitchen, lounge and licensed bar. Easter–Oct. Dorms **£17**

Ynyslas Nature Reserve

Just off B4353, 3 miles north of Borth • Open access • Visitor centre Easter–Sept daily 9.30am–5.30pm • Free • ☎ 01970 872901

Northwards from Borth, the flat landscape meets the formidable sand dunes that line the southern side of the Dyfi estuary. The road follows the coast a couple of miles to the dramatic estuary-side **Ynyslas nature reserve**. In winter, wading and sea birds feed among the dunes and mud flats, while in summer, butterflies flit among vibrant sand plants growing in the grass. The views here stretch inland to the mountains, along the estuary and coast, and over the river to the colourful huddle of Aberdyfi.

The reserve's **visitor centre** is the starting point for guided walks and tours most summer weekends. Walk half a mile along the beach to a **fossilized forest** where, at low tides, the sands near the water's edge are studded with the petrified stumps of a dozen or so five thousand-year-old trees, a reminder that the coast was some twelve miles away when these trees were in their prime. A more romantic explanation is the Welsh legend that tells of a drowned land known as Cantre'r Gwaelod which was protected by sea walls and floodgates. Their keeper, Seithenyn, happened to get drunk the night of an almighty storm and the sea burst through, drowning a thousand people and fourteen settlements.

Dyfi Furnace

A487, 11 miles north of Aberystwyth • Open access • Free; CADW

During the latter half of the eighteenth-century, the barn-like **Dyfi Furnace** was the centre of the silver and iron smelting activities in Wales; charcoal, limestone and iron ore were brought here from Cumbria, before being cast into pig iron and then shipped across to the forges in the Midlands. The power of the Einion River was harnessed using an immense water wheel driving the bellows, and with the recent installation of a generator this magnificent water wheel is once again producing power. Take two minutes to stroll around the back to a picturesque waterfall that feeds the water wheel.

Cwm Einion

A narrow lane from Dyfi Furnace follows the river through a forest and out into the idyllic **Cwm Einion**, known as "Artists' Valley" because of its popularity with nineteenth-century landscape painters. A parking area about a mile and a half along the lane gives access to footpaths which head up into the deserted foothills of Plynlimon, across the spongy moors and through dark conifer forests to the remote glacial lakes of **Llyn Conach** and **Llyn Dwfn**, three miles away. It is a landscape which may soon be massively changed by the installation of huge wind turbines.

Ynys-hir Nature Reserve

A487, 0.5 mile north of Dyfi Furnace • **Reserve** daily 9am–9pm or dusk if earlier • £5 **Visitor centre** daily: April–Oct 9am–5pm, Nov–March 10am–4pm • ☎ 01654 700222, ⓦ rspb.org.uk/wales • Bus #X28 stops in the village of Eglwys-fach, from where it's a fifteen-minute walk to the visitor centre

The two-thousand-plus-acres of **Ynys-hir Nature Reserve** comprise five distinct habitats. Redstarts, pied flycatchers and warblers flit about the ancient hanging oak woodland so typical of mid-Wales, while cormorants flock to the estuarine salt marshes, and red-breasted mergansers and elusive otters inhabit the freshwater streams and pools. The remnant peat bogs are a riot of wild flowers in spring; winter brings water rails to the reed beds to join the herons. The attractions are obvious to the birders who return time and again to the network of hides and viewing points, but there's enough along the three one- and two-hour designated trails to interest anyone.

Cors Dyfi and the Osprey Project

A487, 5 miles north of Dyfi Furnace • **Cors Dyfi** Daily 10am–6pm • Free **Osprey Project** April–Sept daily 10am–6pm • £2.50 • ☎ 01654 781414, ⓦ dyfiospreyproject.co.uk

At **Cors Dyfi**, a short wheelchair-accessible boardwalk leads out among the reeds, ponds and bog plants inhabited by water buffalo that have been brought in to manage the invasive birch and willow that would otherwise turn the place into a forest. The best reason to visit the reserve is the opportunity to see **ospreys** nesting on the top of a pole, some 200m away from the newly built observatory, which affords wonderful views of the Dyfi Valley and the Snowdonian mountains. There are currently four breeding pairs of ospreys in Wales, including the pair here at Cors Dyfi, though, surprisingly, it wasn't until 2004 that these magnificent birds were first officially recorded in the country. In the visitor centre itself, CCTV cameras give you fabulous close-ups of the nest: in May you might see the chicks hatch, while they typically fledge in August. There's also a live stream of the nest on the website.

Southern Cadair Idris and the Dyfi and Talyllyn valleys

The southern coastal reaches of Snowdonia National Park are almost entirely dominated by **Cadair Idris** (2930ft), a five-peaked massif standing defiant in its isolation. Tennyson claimed never to have seen "anything more awful than the great veil of rain drawn straight over Cader Idris", but catch it on a good day, and the views from the top – occasionally stretching as far as Ireland – are phenomenal. During the last Ice Age, the heads of glaciers scalloped out two huge cwms from Cadair Idris' distinctive dome, leaving 1000ft cliffs dropping away on all sides to cool, clear lakes. The largest of these amphitheatres is Cwm Gadair, the **Chair of Idris**, which takes its name from a giant warrior poet of Welsh legend, although some prefer the notion that Idris' Chair refers to a seat-like rock formation on the summit ridge, where anyone spending the night (specifically New Year's Eve, some say) will become a poet, go mad or die.

Cadair Idris' southern limits are lapped by the broad expanse of the Dyfi estuary, which in turn bleeds into the grand, green scenery of the **Dyfi Valley**. The valley's focal point is the engaging town of **Machynlleth**, which lies just south of the renowned **Centre for Alternative Technology**.

There's pleasure in staying at small-scale coastal resorts such as **Aberdyfi**, a good base for exploring the inland cormorant colony at **Craig yr Aderyn**, the brooding thirteenth-century **Castell-y-Bere** and the quaint narrow-gauge **Talyllyn Railway**, which runs seven miles up the **Talyllyn Valley** to **Abergynolwyn** at the foot of Cadair Idris.

Machynlleth and around

MACHYNLLETH (pronounced Mah-hun-cthleth, and referred to locally as Mac) is Wales' "alternative" capital in more ways than one. Shortlisted as a possible capital of Wales in the 1950s and site of Owain Glyndŵr's totemic fifteenth-century Welsh parliament, it retains some handsome architecture, while the town's excellent facilities, lively atmosphere and proximity to the coast make it an ideal jumping-off point for exploring the area. It also boasts a long tradition of progressive and environmentally conscious thinking and innovation, long before such concerns became universally fashionable.

The wide main street is **Heol Maengwyn**, busiest on Wednesdays, when a lively **market** swings into action. Heol Maengwyn comes to an end at a fanciful **clock tower**,

4

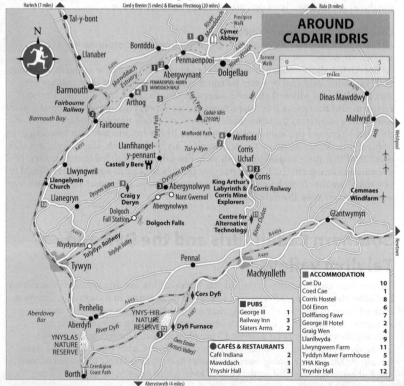

AROUND CADAIR IDRIS

ACCOMMODATION

Cae Du	10
Coed Cae	1
Corris Hostel	8
Dôl Einon	6
Dolffanog Fawr	7
George III Hotel	2
Graig Wen	4
Llanllwyda	9
Llwyngwern Farm	11
Tyddyn Mawr Farmhouse	5
YHA Kings	3
Ynyshir Hall	12

PUBS

George III	1
Railway Inn	3
Slaters Arms	2

CAFÉS & RESTAURANTS

Café Indiana	2
Mawddach	1
Ynyshir Hall	3

built in 1873 by local landowner, the Marquess of Londonderry, to commemorate his son and heir's coming of age.

Owain Glyndŵr Centre

Heol Maengwyn • March–Dec daily 11am–3pm (closed Sun & Mon during term-time) • £2.50 • ☎ 01654 702932, ⌨ canolfanglyndwr.org

Glyndŵr's partly fifteenth-century **Parliament House** is a modest-looking black-and-white-fronted building concealing a large interior and is now home to the **Owain Glyndŵr Centre**. Displays chart the course of Owain Glyndŵr's life, his military campaigns, his downfall, and the 1404 parliament in the town, when he controlled almost all of what is now known as Wales and even negotiated international recognition of the sovereign state (see box below). The sorriest tales are from 1405 onwards, when tactical errors and the sheer brute force of the English forced an ignominious end to the great Welsh uprising. The most important exhibit is a reproduction of the "Pennal Letter", sent by Glyndŵr

---

OWAIN GLYNDŴR, WELSH HERO

No name is so frequently invoked in Wales as that of **Owain Glyndŵr** (c1349–1416), a potent figurehead of Welsh nationalism ever since he rose up against the occupying English in the first few years of the fifteenth century.

Little is known about the man described in Shakespeare's *Henry IV, Part I* as "not in the roll of common men". There seems little doubt that the charismatic Owain fulfilled many of the mystical medieval prophecies about the rising up of the red dragon. He was of aristocratic stock – descended from the princes of Powys and Cyfeiliog – and had a conventional upbringing, part of it in England, of all places. He studied in London and became a distinguished soldier of the English king before returning to Wales and marrying a local woman.

Wales in the late fourteenth century was a turbulent place. The brutal savaging a century earlier of Llywelyn the Last and Edward I's stringent policies of subordinating Wales had left a discontented, cowed nation where any signs of rebellion were sure to attract support. Glyndŵr became the focus of the rebellion when his neighbour, the English Lord of Ruthin, seized some of his land. When the courts failed to back him, Glyndŵr took matters into his own hands. With four thousand supporters and a new declaration that he was "Prince of Wales", he attacked Ruthin, and then Denbigh, Rhuddlan, Flint, Hawarden and Oswestry, before encountering an English resistance at Welshpool. As Glyndŵr consolidated his position in north Wales, English king Henry IV imposed punitive laws on Welsh land ownership, even outlawing Welsh-language bards and singers. Glyndŵr's support swelled enough for him to take the castles at Conwy, Harlech and Aberystwyth. By the end of 1403, he controlled most of Wales.

In 1404, Glyndŵr assembled a parliament of four men from every *commot* (community) in Wales at Machynlleth, drawing up mutual recognition treaties with France and Spain. He also had himself crowned ruler of a free Wales. A second parliament in Harlech took place a year later, with Glyndŵr making plans to carve up England and Wales into three as part of an alliance against the English king: Glyndŵr would rule Wales and the Marches of England. He then demanded independence for the Welsh Church from Canterbury and set about securing alliances with English noblemen who had grievances with Henry IV. This last, ambitious move heralded Glyndŵr's downfall.

The English army concentrated with increased vigour on destroying the Welsh uprising, and the Tripartite Indenture was never realized. From then on, Glyndŵr lost battles, ground and castles and was forced into hiding – dying, it is thought, in Herefordshire.

Anti-Welsh laws stayed in place until the accession to the English throne of Henry VII, a Welshman, in 1485. Wales became subsumed into English custom and law, and Glyndŵr's uprising became an increasingly powerful symbol of frustrated Welsh independence. In modern times, the shadowy organization that surfaced in the early 1980s to burn the holiday homes of English people and English estate agents dealing in Welsh property took the name Meibion (the sons of) Glyndŵr.

The figure of Glyndŵr, his trademark double-pointed beard to the fore, can often be seen gracing Welsh pub signs of inns called the Prince of Wales – as distinct from those who, by dint of being the first-born son of the reigning British monarch, have occupied the title ever since.

4

to King Charles of France in 1406, in which he lays out his plans for an autonomous Welsh nation whilst simultaneously pledging his support for the idea of a French pope – the original letter resides in Paris.

Plas Machynlleth

Gallery Mon–Wed & Fri–Sat 10am–5pm, Sun 11am–4pm • Free • ☎ 01654, ⓦ dyfiartsguild.org.uk

Opposite the Owain Glyndŵr Centre, a path leads into the landscaped grounds of **Plas Machynlleth**, the elegant seventeenth-century mansion of the Marquess of Londonderry. Its solitude is entirely intentional: in the 1840s the Marquess bought up all the surrounding buildings and had them demolished, and rerouted the main road away from his grounds. Today, the house accommodates the bright Dyfi Arts Guild gallery and shop, where visitors can view and buy a wide range of works of art; there's a super café here too.

Museum of Modern Art, Wales

Heol Penrallt, towards the station • Mon–Sat 10am–4pm • Free • ☎ 01654 703355, ⓦ momawales.org.uk

The **Museum of Modern Art, Wales** (MOMA Cymru) is housed in Y Tabernacl, a beautifully serene old chapel that hosts an ongoing programme of temporary exhibitions, including some from its own growing collection. It is also the place to go for theatre, comedy, concerts, good coffee and the highbrow Gŵyl Machynlleth festival (last week in August; ⓦ machynllethfestival.co.uk), which combines classical and some folk music with theatre and debate.

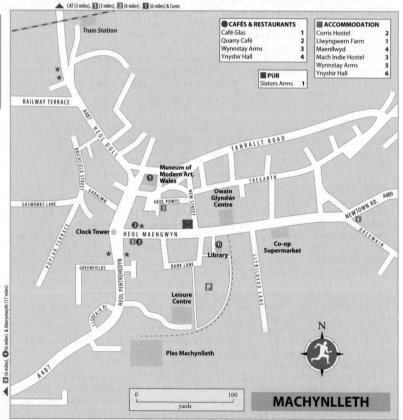

Centre for Alternative Technology

A487, 3 miles north of Machynlleth • Easter–Oct daily 10am–5pm • £8.50, £1 off for walkers, cyclists and bus users, fifty percent off for train arrivals • ☎ 01654 705950, ⊕ cat.org.uk • Bus #34 (Mon–Sat hourly, Sun 4) from Machynlleth

After the inception of the **Centre for Alternative Technology** (CAT or *Canolfan y Dechnoleg Amgen*) during the oil crisis of 1974, seven acres of a once-derelict slate quarry were turned into an almost entirely sustainable community. At one stage, eighty percent of the power was generated from wind, sun and water, but this is no back-to-the-land hippie commune. Right from the start, the idea was to embrace technology – much of the on-site equipment was developed and built here, reflecting the centre's achievements in this field. With the general rise of eco-consciousness in the twenty-first century the emphasis has shifted more towards promoting its application in urban situations. With this in mind, they've used low-carbon-footprint techniques – timber construction with lime and hemp cladding etc – in building the Wales Institute for Sustainable Education (WISE); its 22ft rammed-earth wall is the highest in Britain.

CAT's water-balanced **cliff railway** (Easter–Oct only) whisks visitors 200ft up from the car park to the main site, sensitively landscaped using local slate and wood, and you can easily spend half a day sauntering around. There's plenty for kids to do, including a **children's theatre** (mainly mid-July to Aug), while the wholefood **restaurant** turns out delicious food and the excellent **shop** stocks a wide range of alternative literature, along with crafts and intriguing toys.

Corris

The #34 bus (Mon–Sat 8 daily; 15min) from Machynlleth serves Corris, and the #X27 from Machynlleth to Dolgellau (hourly; 15min) serves the Craft Centre.

Three miles higher up the valley from Machynlleth, **CORRIS** is a small former slate-quarrying settlement in the middle of the Dyfi Forest. Half a mile further up the valley, the **Corris Craft Centre** occupies a former slate mine, and houses half a dozen or so craft shops, café, children's playground, and two of the area's main attractions.

Corris Railway and Museum

Corris village • Generally six services on weekends and Bank Holidays May–Sept, plus Mondays and Tuesdays in August • £6 return • ☎ 01654 761303, ⊕ corris.co.uk

Built in 1859 as a horse-hauled tramroad, and subsequently used to transport passengers until 1930, the sweet little **Corris Railway** today shuttles passengers along a half-mile stretch of the 27in-gauge line that linked the slate quarries of the Dulas Valley with the main line at Machynlleth. There are plans to restore a further two miles, but for the moment, it's a short fifty-minute return trip; the entrance fee also includes a look around the engine sheds and workshop, and a small museum.

King Arthur's Labyrinth

A487 • April–Oct daily 10am–5pm, call for winter hours • Labyrinth £9.35, Lost Legends £4.95, combined ticket £11.80 • ☎ 01654 761584, ⊕ kingarthurslabyrinth.com

Based deep within the flooded tunnels of a former slate mine, **King Arthur's Labyrinth** is a fun subterranean jaunt through the legend that is the mythical king. Following a short DVD presentation, you are led (complete with hard hat) into the mine proper by a guide dressed as a monk; a boat then carries you into the heart of the atmospherically lit mountain, where you proceed through several caverns complete with son et lumière tableaux illustrating various Welsh legends.

Up above ground, the cleverly conceived **Lost Legends of the Stone Circle** outdoor floral maze reveals "mystical stories echoing across the ages" by way of various iconic sculptural figures from Welsh folklore, alongside druid ruins and the stone circle itself; it's is a great way to help ensure these Welsh stories are retained by younger generations.

"MAC" MOUNTAIN BIKING

Machynlleth has become one of the country's most important mountain biking centres, with a number of excellent purpose-built tracks in the vicinity. The most impressive of these is located a few miles miles southwest of Machynlleth in Derwenlas, where there's the Mach 1 trail (16km; moderate), while, in Corris, there's the Cli-machx trail (15km; difficult to severe). There's currently nowhere in town that offers cycle rental, but the best place for information – as well as repairs and maintenance – is JP's (☎ 07789 062981) adjoining the *Mach Indie Hostel*.

Corris Mine Explorers

A487 • Tours all year on demand, book ahead • 1hr Taster £11, 2hr Explorer £22, 4hr Expedition £42 • ☎ 01654 761244,
Ⓦ corrismineexplorers.co.uk

With **Corris Mine Explorers** you head into different levels of the same old slate mine that houses King Arthur's Labyrinth, though the experience could hardly be more different. Sporting a climbing harness and miner's helmet, you'll ideally spend at least a couple of hours in the cool, dark tunnels that have been barely touched since the miners downed tools for the last time back in 1970. Ancient tallow candles are stuck to the walls, hand drills lie scattered along the passageways and winch flywheels still spin at the slightest touch. There's no production-line feel about these trips: all are tailored to the fitness of the group. You'll also hear some fascinating stories about the lives of the miners, while adventurous parties could find themselves clipped into safety wires as they sidle along the steeply shelving walls of a vast slate cavern. Wear something warm and prepare to have fun.

ARRIVAL AND DEPARTURE
MACHYNLLETH

By train Trains stop at the station, a 5min walk up Heol Penrallt from the town's central clock tower.
Destinations Aberdyfi (8 daily; 20min); Aberystwyth (9 daily; 30min); Barmouth (8 daily; 55min); Birmingham (7 daily; 2hr 15min); Harlech (8 daily; 1hr 20min); Porthmadog (8 daily; 1hr 50min); Shrewsbury (7 daily; 1hr 20min).

By bus Buses stop close to the town's central clock tower, and many also call at the train station.
Destinations Aberdyfi (8 daily; 20min); Aberystwyth (hourly; 45min); Corris (hourly; 15min); Dolgellau (mostly hourly; 30min); Tywyn (8 daily; 35min).

INFORMATION

Tourist information There is no TIC, but staff at Dyfi Crafts, next to Parliament House on Heol Maengwyn, are tremendously helpful.

Internet Free at the library, Heol Maengwyn (Mon & Fri 9.30am–1pm & 2–7pm, Tues & Wed 9.30am–1pm & 2–5pm, Sat 9.30am–1pm).

ACCOMMODATION

HOTELS AND B&BS

Maenllwyd Newtown Rd ☎ 01654 702928, Ⓦ maenllwyd.co.uk. Comfortable eight-room B&B in a former manse. All is clean and well maintained, the family room has a DVD player and there's a large garden plus off-street parking. £65

Wynnstay Arms Heol Maengwyn ☎ 01654 702941, Ⓦ wynnstay-hotel.com. You'll want to shop around as there's considerable variation in the twenty-odd smartened-up rooms at this 1800 former coaching inn. Some have heavy beams, creaky floors and a four-poster, others are relatively modern. The hotel is effectively the heart of the town's social life and there are cosy guest lounges where you can curl up with a book. £90

★**Ynyshir Hall** A487, 6 miles southwest of Machynlleth, beside the Ynys-hir Nature Reserve ☎ 01654 781209, Ⓦ ynyshirhall.co.uk. Sublime

country-house hotel in expansive manicured grounds that is gracious without being the slightest bit stuffy. The ten rooms, each named after a famous artist, are as opulent as they come, but at the same time, surprisingly playful; from the four-poster bed Hogarth room to the extraordinary, dazzling-pink Matisse room complete with grand brass bedstead. In-room spa treatments are available, but overall, the service is discreet. £205

HOSTELS AND CAMPING

★**Corris Hostel** Old Rd, Corris ☎ 01654 761686, Ⓦ corrishostel.co.uk. There's a strong ethical philosophy and a spiritual tenor to this low-key hostel, which occupies a wonderful old school building on a steep road just up from the centre of the village. Accommodation is in two large single-sex dorms, doubles and several family rooms, and there are excellent self-catering facilities, though home-cooked (mostly vegetarian) meals are available. The garden, with a firepit, backs out onto thick woods. Dorm £16, doubles £35

Llwyngwern Farm Pantperthog, 3 miles north of Machynlleth, near the Centre for Alternative Technology ☎01654 702492. Machynlleth's closest camping in a grassy field beside oaks and the burbling Afon Dulas. Fairly basic toilets and hot showers. April–Sept.

Pitches £12.50

Mach Indie Hostel Off Heol Powys ☎07788 747074, ⓦmachhostel.co.uk. Easy-going, walker- and cyclist-friendly hostel in the heart of town with a mix of dorm and family rooms, as well as camping in their grassy yard; there's also a self-catering kitchen, drying room, bike storage shed and bike wash facility. Dorms £17.50, camping £5

EATING AND DRINKING

Café Glas Inside MOMA Cymru, Heol Penrallt. The antithesis of the *Quarry Café* (see below): delicate cakes and excellent coffee in peaceful, arty surrounds. Mon–Fri 10am–3pm.

Quarry Café Heol Maengwyn ☎01654 702624. This popular, veggie wholefood café run by the Centre for Alternative Technology is like stepping back into the 1980s with its menu of cheesy vegetable bakes and the "Big Mach" burger (lentil patty, soya mayonnaise and a wholesome salad; £7.50). The walls come lined with noticeboards listing info about healing workshops and so on. Mon–Fri 9am–4pm, Sat 10am–3pm.

Slaters Arms Corris ☎01654 761324, ⓦtheslatersarms.com. Welcoming old village pub that is Corris' social centre with straightforward bar meals, pool table, dominoes and some fine, locally brewed ales from the Celt Experience; on Mondays, you get free cheese with your ale. Mon–Fri 5pm–midnight, Sat noon–1am, Sun noon–11.30pm.

Wynnstay Arms Heol Maengwyn ☎01654 702941, ⓦwynnstay-hotel.com. While the classic slate-floored restaurant itself is justifiably popular (loin of venison with red cabbage and root vegetable sauce, £16.95), it's the superb pizzeria in an adjoining building to the rear that most people come here for. The bar is a fine place for a beer. Bar daily 11am–11pm; restaurant daily noon–2pm & 6.30–9pm; pizzeria Tues–Sat 4.30–9.30pm.

★**Ynyshir Hall** A487, 6 miles southwest of Machynlleth ☎01654 781209, ⓦynyshirhall.co.uk. As elegant as the hotel it's housed in, this refined restaurant is headed by chef Gareth Ward, who creates consistently sublime Modern British dishes using seafood from the Dyfi estuary, river fish and local game, as well as ingredients plucked from the kitchen garden and surrounding woods; hence dishes like mackerel with elderflower, cucumber and wild green strawberry, and sheep's yoghurt with olive oil and wood sorrel; the five-course à la carte lunch menu (£29.50) is great value, or, alternatively, pop over for the full afternoon tea (£19.50), served in the grounds or any of the delightful public rooms. Daily noon–2pm, 3–5pm & 7–10pm.

Aberdyfi

The proud maritime heritage of **ABERDYFI** (sometimes anglicized to Aberdovey) has largely been replaced by the life of a well-heeled resort. With its south-facing aspect across the Dyfi estuary backed by lush mountains, Aberdyfi has one of the highest proportions of holiday homes anywhere on this coast. There's no watercraft rental available, nor much else in the way of activities, but the deep, golden beach is fabulous and swimming is possible. Tidal currents make it potentially hazardous in town, so head about a mile and a half north to the safer waters of **Cemetery Beach**. It also makes a great base for exploring the delights of the Talyllyn and Dysynni valleys to the north.

In the mid-nineteenth century, the town, with its seamlessly joined eastern neighbour, **Penhelig**, built shallow-draught coastal traders for the inshore fleet, a past remembered in the small historic and **maritime display** in the tourist office. Otherwise, take a look under the jetty, where you may chance upon Aberdovey's **Time and Tide Bell**, said to be linked to the legend of a submerged lost kingdom somewhere beneath Cardigan Bay, and which you can hear ringing at high tide.

ARRIVAL AND DEPARTURE · ABERDYFI

By train Aberdyfi is served by two train stations: the request-only Penhelig, 0.5 mile east (the most convenient for the centre of town), and Aberdyfi, 0.5 mile west of the tourist office.
Destinations Barmouth (8 daily; 45min); Machynlleth

(9 daily; 20min); Porthmadog (8 daily; 1hr 30min); Tywyn (8 daily; 15min).
By bus The #28 & #X29 stop close to the TIC.
Destinations Machynlleth (8 daily; 20min); Tywyn (8 daily; 10min).

INFORMATION

Tourist information The TIC is in Wharf Gardens (Easter–Oct daily 9.30am–5pm; ☎01654 767321,

✉ tic.aberdyfi@eryri-npa.gov.uk).

ACCOMMODATION

Cartref Guest House Penrhos, near Aberdyfi train station ☎01654 767273, 🖰 cartref-aberdovey.co.uk. Quality B&B in a large Edwardian house just a few steps from the station. The five rooms are all done in muted tones with crisp white linen, and breakfasts are excellent. **£80**

Llety Bodfor 1 Bodfor Terrace ☎01654 767475, 🖰 lletybodfor.co.uk. The fairly typical frontage of this Aberdyfi town house does little to suggest that within lies the town's swankiest accommodation: three dashing rooms,

each on its own floor and all with sea views. The guest lounge, meanwhile, is equipped with a piano, games, DVDs and a stack of old vinyl. Breakfast costs extra. **£125**

The Vanner Seaview Terrace ☎01654 767274, 🖰 thevanner.co.uk. This may be one of the cheapest places around but standards are still high. The two quiet rooms (both at the back of the house) share a guest lounge with great sea views. Full breakfast includes home-made bread and jam. **£65**

EATING AND DRINKING

Britannia Inn 13 Seaview Terrace ☎01654 767426, 🖰 britannia-aberdovey.co.uk. There is usually a lively atmosphere at this town-centre pub, especially when the sun comes out and everyone piles onto the deck for the sunset with a pint of real ale. Meals are a significant cut above the usual pub standard and might include Aberdyfi crab (£12.95). Mon–Wed 11am–midnight, Thurs–Sat

11am–1am, Sun noon–midnight.

Y Bwtri Blasus 7 Seaview Terrace ☎01654 767470. Great little deli and café that makes a fine place to hang out over a coffee and a slice of cake, or stock up on picnic essentials. The bread and quiches (£5.95) are freshly made locally and they'll whip up a sandwich with whatever you desire. Daily 9am–5pm.

The Talyllyn Valley

Around four miles north of Aberdyfi, two connected valleys – the Talyllyn and Dysynni – spur northeast from the coast towards Cadair Idris. The scenery hereabouts is monumentally beautiful, and there's superb lowland and mountain walking, particularly on Cadair Idris itself.

The **Talyllyn Valley** starts at the faded resort town of Tywyn and is initially traced by the delightful Talyllyn Railway, the first of Wales' restored narrow-gauge lines. There are several diversions along the course of the line, not least the lovely Dolgoch Falls, beyond which there are trails at both Abergynolwyn and Nant Gwernol; the valley ends at the placid waters of Tal-y-Llyn.

Talyllyn Railway

Station Rd, Tywyn • April–Oct 2–7 trains daily, plus some winter weekends • £14.50 unlimited one-day travel • ☎01654 710472, 🖰 talyllyn.co.uk

An excellent way to experience the lower Talyllyn Valley is aboard the cute 27in-gauge **Talyllyn Railway**, the inspiration for Thomas the Tank Engine. The railway tootles seven miles inland from Tywyn through the delightful wooded valley to the old slate quarries at Nant Gwernol. From 1865 to 1946, the rail line hauled slate to Tywyn Wharf station. Five years after the quarry's closure, rail enthusiasts took over the running of services, making this the world's first volunteer-run railway. The round trip (at a maximum 15mph) takes around two and half hours (with a pause), but you can get on and off as frequently as the schedule allows, taking in some fine broadleaf **forest walks**, best at Dolgoch Falls. At the end of the line, more woodland walks take you around the site of the old slate quarries. In mid-August each year, the schedule is disrupted by the "Race the Train" event, when runners attempt to beat the train on its fourteen-mile trip to Abergynolwyn and back. Some do. Of the original Talyllyn rolling stock, two steam engines and all five of the oak and mahogany passenger carriages still run up to Nant Gwernol. Look out, too, for the many fabulous themed trains and special events run here.

Narrow-Gauge Railway Museum

April–Oct daily 10am–4.30pm • Free • ☎ 01654 710472, ⓦ ngrm.org.uk

Leave half an hour to peruse the superb **Narrow-Gauge Railway Museum** at Tywyn Wharf station. Along with the history of the railway and a re-created study of Thomas the Tank Engine inventor, the Revd W. Awdry, the museum holds some fine rolling stock from the Talyllyn and other narrow-gauge lines around the British Isles, including a Guinness shunter.

Dolgoch Falls, Abergynolwyn and Nant Gwernol

Five miles northeast of Tywyn, reachable via the B4405 and Talyllyn Railway, are the lovely **Dolgoch Falls**, where three trails (maximum 1hr) lead off through oak woods to the lower, mid and upper cascades. Pied flycatchers and redstarts can often be seen flitting about.

The Dysynni Valley joins the Talyllyn two miles northeast of Dolgoch Falls at the twin valleys' only real settlement, **Abergynolwyn**. Here, a few dozen quarry workers' houses crowd around a small visitor centre, a café, a pub and the Talyllyn Railway station. It is a short stroll up from here to the Talyllyn Railway's **Nant Gwernol** station, from where you can start the Quarryman's Trail (4 miles; 2–3hr; 800ft ascent), an excellent loop through quarry remains and a couple of waterfalls. Beyond Nant Gwernol and the placid Tal-y-Llyn lake, the B4405 meets the A487 right by the start of the Minffordd Path (see box opposite).

ARRIVAL AND DEPARTURE   THE TALYLLYN VALLEY

Your own vehicle gives maximum flexibility, but it is possible to explore the Talyllyn Valley using the **Talyllyn Railway** and **bus** #30 (4 daily) which runs from Tywyn to Abergynolwyn and continues to Minffordd (where you can catch #32 or #X32 to Dolgellau or Machynlleth).

ACCOMMODATION AND EATING

Dôl Einion B4405 at Minffordd, just before A487 junction ☎ 01654 761312. Excellent three-acre campsite at the foot of the Minffordd Path up Cadair Idris. There are toilets, showers and electric hookups. Per person **£6**
Dolffanog Fawr B4405 at the north end of Tal-y-Llyn lake ☎ 01654 761247, ⓦ dolffanogfawr.co.uk. This charmingly run B&B makes for a great getaway, with four rooms offering mountain views, plus a big lounge, outdoor

hot tub, and inviting grounds. Three-course evening meals (£25) are also available, along with a very good wine selection. **£100**
Railway Inn B4405 in Abergynolwyn ☎ 01654 782279. Great little pub that serves the best range of real ales for miles, together with some great food. There's a cosy interior and outdoor seating with idyllic valley views. Book for dinner (mains from £9) and Sunday lunch. Daily 11am–11pm.

The Dysynni Valley and around

Running almost parallel to the Talyllyn Valley, the idyllic **Dysynni Valley** meets the A493 near the church at Llanegryn. From there you can head upstream past the birds at Craig y Deryn then either turn southeast to join the Talyllyn Valley at Abergynolwyn or continue up the Dysynni to the ruins of Castell-y-Bere and the church of St Michael at Llanfihangel-y-Pennant. A few miles north up the coast, Llangelynin is worth a brief stop for its time-warped church.

Llanegryn church and Craig-y-Dern

Just off A493 • Generally open daytime

Half a mile northwest of the village of Llanegryn, the little hilltop **Llanegryn church** has an unexpectedly beautiful rood screen, probably carved in the fifteenth century, which is said to have been carried overnight from Dolgellau's Cymer Abbey after its dissolution.

Three miles northeast of Llanegryn at **Craig y Deryn** (Birds' Rock), around thirty breeding pairs of cormorants colonize a stunning 760ft-high cliff some four miles from the coast. As the sea has gradually withdrawn from the valley, the birds have remained loyal to their home, making this Europe's only inland cormorant nesting site. It's reachable via a signposted path (2 miles; 1hr; 750ft ascent).

CADAIR IDRIS: THE MINFFORDD PATH

The OS Explorer 1:25,000 map OL23 "Cadair Idris & Llyn Tegid" is recommended.

The most dramatic ascent of Cadair Idris follows the **Minffordd Path** (6 miles; 5hr; 2900ft ascent), a justifiably popular route which makes a full circuit around the rim of **Cwm Cau**, probably the country's most impressive mountain cirque.

The path starts just west of the *Minffordd Hotel* at the junction of the A487 and the B4405. From the car park, follow the signs along an avenue of horse chestnuts until you come to the **Visitor Centre**, with an exhibition on the various stages of the climb up the mountain, as well as a live feed of the Lesser Horseshoe Bat roost ensconced in the attic.

From the visitor centre, continue up through the woods, heading north. At a fork, take the left path, which wheels around the end of Craig Lwyd into Cwm Cau. Before you reach the lake, fork left and climb onto the rim of Cwm Cau, following it round to **Penygadair** (2930ft), the highest point on the massif. Here, there's a circular shelter and a tin-roofed hut originally built for dispensing refreshments to thirsty Victorians, and now affording none-too-comfortable protection from wind and rain.

The shortest descent follows the summit plateau northeast, then down to a grassy ridge before ascending gradually to **Mynydd Moel** (2831ft), from which you get a magnificent view down into a valley and Llyn Arran, the smallest of Cadair's lakes. The descent starts beside the fence which you cross just before the summit – follow the fence south all the way to the fork below Cwm Cau.

Castell-y-Bere and Church of St Michael

Castell-y-Bere Llanfihangel-y-Pennant, 5 miles northeast of Llanegryn • Open access • Free; CADW

With large slabs of the main towers still standing, there's plenty of opportunity to poke around at **Castell-y-Bere**, a native Welsh fortress built by Llywelyn ap Iorwerth (Llywelyn the Great) in 1221 to protect the mountain passes. After being besieged twice in the thirteenth century, this – one of the most massive of the Welsh castles – was consigned to seven centuries of obscurity and decay. Castell-y-Bere seems to rise almost imperceptibly out of the rock on which it was built – it is a great place just to sit or picnic, with good views to Cadair Idris and Craig y Deryn.

On the dead-end lane a few hundred yards beyond Castle-y-Bere is Llanfihangel-y-Pennant and its stocky little **church of St Michael**, which has a couple of interesting exhibits in its vestry, including a fabulous 3-D map of the valley, some 14ft long and built to a scale of one foot to one mile from patchwork and cloth. There are also some exhibits centred on **Mary Jones** – famed for her 1800 Bible-buying walk to Bala (see p.322) – whose ruined cottage, **Tŷn-y-ddôl**, is just up the lane and marked with a monument.

Llangelynin church

A493, 7 miles north of Tywyn • Generally daily 9am–5pm

Half a mile short of the hamlet of **Llangelynin**, a track descends seawards off the main road to another ancient **church**: a mainly eleventh-century building on the foundations of an eighth-century structure, and bare but for a few basic pews and a bier which was carried by horses. Look out for the ancient board inscribed with the Ten Commandments in Welsh, and the skeletal **figure of death** wall painting with his scythe. Probably painted in the seventeenth century, it was only discovered during plaster removal in 2003. Just outside the porch is the grave of Abram Wood, patriarch of Y Teulu Wood, a clan of Romanies who settled in Wales at the beginning of the eighteenth century.

ARRIVAL AND DEPARTURE   THE DYSYNNI VALLEY

There is no public transport in the Dysynni Valley, so your best bet is to make your way by train or bus to Tywyn and go from there.

ACCOMMODATION

Cae Du A493 at Llangelynin, just over 2 miles west of Llanegryn ☎ 01654 711234. Wonderfully dramatic clifftop site that's pretty simple but has hot showers, access down to a beach and allows campfires. The slope means you'll need to pick your site carefully, and it is pretty exposed when the wind gets up. Easter–Oct. Pitches £15

Llanllwyda ☎ 01654 782627. Well-equipped caravan and campsite in grassy fields on a working farm near the start of the path to Craig y Deryn; campfires allowed too. Pitches £12

Northern Cadair Idris and the Mawddach Estuary

Gouging their way deep into the heart of the mid-Wales mountains, the Mawddach Estuary's broad tidal flats create dramatic backdrops from every angle. With the sun low in the sky and the tide ebbing, the constantly changing course of the river trickles silver through the golden sands. That colour isn't just an illusion: the sands actually do contain gold, albeit in tiny amounts, as the abandoned mines littering the hills around testify. Spasmodic gold fever still occasionally hits the region's main town, **Dolgellau**, but most people come here for excellent walking up Cadair Idris and along the estuary, the mountain biking at Coed-y-Brenin to the north, or to hit the beaches, particularly at **Barmouth**, the area's main resort.

Fairbourne

The blink-and-you'll-miss-it settlement of **FAIRBOURNE**, on the southern side of the Mawddach Estuary, was developed in the late nineteenth century as the country estate of the chairman of the McDougall's flour company. There's a decent beach and sublime views along the coast and across the estuary, but otherwise the only attraction is the steam-hauled railway.

Fairbourne Railway

April–Oct 4–8 trains most days • £9 day rover • ☎ 01341 250362, ⓦ fairbournerailway.com

Travelling between Fairbourne and Barmouth is easy on the mainline train which crosses the Mawddach Rail Bridge. More fun, however, is the tiny, 12in-gauge **Fairbourne Railway**, which runs along the seafront for just a mile between Fairbourne and the Barmouth Ferry Station; here, connecting passenger ferries (£3 return) cross the estuary mouth to Barmouth itself. Midway along, a halt on the line boasts the name Gorsafawddacha'idraigodanhedddogleddollônpenrhynareurdraethceredigion ("The station on the Mawddach with dragon's teeth on the north Penrhyn Drive on the golden Cardigan sands"). The "dragon's teeth" are, alas, a set of grim concrete defences left over from World War II. Before you depart, spend a few moments looking around the museum inside the terminal at Fairbourne, which has some lovely model railways.

ARRIVAL AND DEPARTURE | FAIRBOURNE

By train Fairbourne is well served by trains, and the train station is right in the centre of town, just off Beach Road. Destinations Aberdyfi (8 daily; 30min); Barmouth (8 daily; 10min); Machynlleth (9 daily; 50min); Tywyn (9 daily; 20min).

EATING

Café Indiana 3 Beach Rd ☎ 01341 250891, ⓦ indianacuisine.co.uk. There may be a curry restaurant in every British town but few rate as highly as this simply decorated place, run by Noorie, the wife of Bollywood superstar Mayur Verma (Raj). The North Indian cuisine is all cooked fresh, and the execution of dishes is way above the norm. Mains from £8.25. Mon & Wed–Sat 6–10pm, Sun 1–3pm & 6–10pm.

Dolgellau and around

The old county town of Meirionethshire, **DOLGELLAU** still maintains an air of unhurried importance, never more so than when all the area's farmers roll up for market day every Thursday morning. Its dark buildings gleam forebodingly in the frequent downpours, but in fine weather, the lofty crags of Cadair Idris perfectly frame the stone squares and streets.

There's little to see or do in town itself these days, but it's the most convenient access point to the southern reaches of Snowdonia National Park. The local **walks** are superb, the **Mawddach Trail** offers some of the finest easy cycling around, and nearby Coed-y-Brenin has become a major centre for **mountain bikers**.

Brief history

Dolgellau is a much older town than appearances suggest, lying at the junction of three Roman roads that converged on a now vanished military outpost. It was here that Owain Glyndŵr assembled the last Welsh parliament in 1404, and later signed an alliance with Charles VI of France for providing troops to fight against Henry IV of England (see box, p.283). Seventeenth-century Quakers sought freedom from persecution here, and in the 1860s Dolgellau became the focus of numerous **gold rushes**, drawing waves of prospectors to pan the estuary or blast levels into Clogau shale or mudstone sediment under the Coed-y-Brenin Forest. The quartz veins yielded some gold, but in quantities too small to make much money.

Cymer Abbey

2 miles north of Dolgellau, signposted off A470 • Open access • Free; CADW

Gold frenzy first hit Dolgellau when the Romans found flecks glinting in the Mawddach silt. Later, the thirteenth-century Cistercian monks based at **Cymer Abbey** were given "the right in digging or carrying away metals and treasures free from all secular exaction". The fine location at the head of the Mawddach Estuary is typical of

4

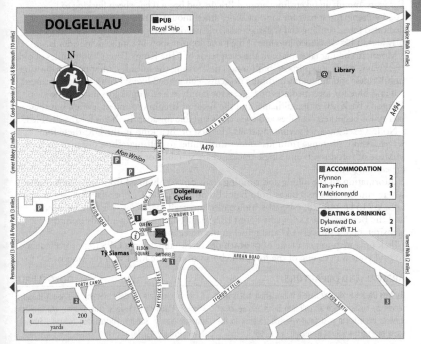

DOLGELLAU

■PUB
Royal Ship 1

N

@ Library

Precipice Walk (2 miles)

A494

BALA ROAD

BONT FAWR

Coed-y-Brenin (7 miles) & Barmouth (10 miles)

Cymer Abbey (2 miles),

Afon Wnion

A470

■ ACCOMMODATION
Ffynnon 2
Tan-y-Fron 3
Y Meirionnydd 1

SMITHFIELD ST

BRIDGE ST

Dolgellau Cycles

MARIAN ROAD

Pennmaenpool (3 miles) & Pony Path (3 miles)

LION ST

GLWNDWR ST

●EATING & DRINKING
Dylanwad Da 2
Siop Coffi T.H. 1

QUEENS SQUARE

Ty Siamas

ELDON SQUARE

SMITHFIELD SQ

ARRAN ROAD

Torrent Walk (2 miles)

PORTH CANOL

WELLS ST

SPRINGFIELD ST

MEYRICK STREET

FFORDD Y FELIN

FRON SERTH

2

3

0   200
      yards

WALKS AND RIDES AROUND DOLGELLAU

Cadair Idris: Pony Path (9 miles; 4–5hr; 2800ft ascent). If the weather is fine, don't miss this classic and enjoyable ascent of Cadair Idris which starts from the car park at Tŷ Nant, 3 miles southwest of Dolgellau along Cadair Road (no buses). Early views to the craggy flanks of the massif are tremendous, but they disappear as you climb steeply to the col, where you turn left on a rocky path to the summit shelter on **Penygadair** (2930ft). Take the 1:25,000 Explorer OL23 map ("*Cadair Idris & Llyn Tegid*").

Mawddach Trail (10 miles from Dolgellau to Barmouth; flat). Follow this beautiful combined walking and cycle route beside the Mawddach Estuary's broad sands along a disused rail line. Walkers seeking the most interesting section should start from Penmaenpool (catch bus #28), 2 miles west. Highlights include the wooden toll bridge and *Hotel George III* (see opposite) at Penmaenpool, an RSPB wetland walk at Arthog, and the Barmouth bridge.

Precipice Walk (3–4 miles; 2hr; negligible ascent). Though the path is narrow in places and there are some steep banks, there is little precipitous on this easy-going loop with great views to the 1000ft ramparts of Cadair Idris and along the Mawddach Estuary – best in late afternoon or early morning sun. Starts 3 miles north of Dolgellau off the road to Llanfachreth.

Torrent Walk (2 miles; 1hr; 100ft ascent). Attractive lowland stroll following the cascading, bedrock-carved Clywedog River through some gnarled old woodland that drips with antiquity. Starts on the B4416, just off the A470, 3 miles east (bus #32/X32).

this austere order, but unfortunately the surrounding caravan site mars the effect of the remaining Gothic slabs. A path beside the abbey makes an alternative approach to the Precipice Walk (see box above).

Coed-y-Brenin

A470, 7 miles north of Dolgellau • **Forest** Open access • Free • **Visitor Centre** April–Oct daily 9.30am–5pm; Nov–March Mon–Fri 9.30am–4.30pm, Sat & Sun 9am–5pm • Parking £5 all day • ☎01341 440747, ⓦ forestry.gov.uk/coedybrenin

For years, mountain bikers from around Britain and beyond have been flocking to **Coed-y-Brenin** forest park for some of Wales' finest **mountain biking**. With the addition of dedicated forest running and walking trails, orienteering and geocaching courses and a kids' play area, it has developed into one of the most popular spots in southern Snowdonia.

Mountain biking takes place in the evergreens of "The King's Forest", with miles of old trackways, roads and purpose-built trails crisscrossing the hillsides, offering lung-busting uphill rides, and adrenalin-pumping descents – all graded like ski runs: black for experts, red and blue for intermediates and green for family riders. Highlights include the Dragon's Back (20 miles; difficult) and the Beast of Brenin (25 miles; severe), but there's plenty for beginners, families and even trails suitable for adaptive bikes for the disabled.

No less exciting are the **running trails**, the first of their kind in the UK; these four waymarked trails range from just under three miles to half-marathon distance on a mixture of forest roads and single tracks, so are suitable for both novices and more experienced runners.

Information all the biking and running trails can be obtained from the **visitor centre**, where you can also **rent bikes** from Beics Brenin (hardtails £25 per day, full suspension £45; ☎01341 440728, ⓦbeicsbrenin.co.uk), buy trail maps covering Coed-y-Brenin and the Betws-y-Coed's Gwydir Forest (£2.50; also free map downloads from the website), take a shower (£1) and refuel in the excellent café.

Pick up a map to get a taste of **geocaching**, essentially using a GPS (rent for £5 a day) to find your way to one of the four little boxes of treasure hidden in the woods.

ARRIVAL AND DEPARTURE   DOLGELLAU

By bus Dolgellau doesn't have a train station, but is well served by buses, which all pull into Eldon Square. Most services head north past Coed-y-Brenin. To stick to the coast, pick up the train at Barmouth (see p.296).

Destinations Bala (8 daily; 35min); Barmouth (hourly; 25min); Llangollen (8 daily; 1hr 30min); Machynlleth (mostly hourly; 30min); Porthmadog (6 daily; 50min); Tywyn (6 daily; 55min).

INFORMATION

Tourist information The TIC is on Eldon Square (daily 9.30am–12.30pm & 1–5pm; ☎ 01341 422888, ⓦ discoverdolgellau.com).

Bike rental Dolgellau Cycles on Smithfield St (Easter–Oct daily 9.30am–5pm; ☎ 01341 423332, ⓦ dolgellaucycles .co.uk) rents out bikes suitable for the Mawddach Trail (£13 half day, £20 full day) and also does repairs and servicing.

Internet Free at the library, Ffordd y Bala, on the northeastern edge of town (Mon & Fri 9.30am–7pm, Tues & Thurs 9.30am–5pm, Wed 9.30am–1pm, Sat 9.30am–noon).

ACCOMMODATION

While there's commendable accommodation in Dolgellau itself (some catering to the legions of mountain bikers frequenting Coed-y-Brenin), there are more appealing options scattered around the district, some so close to Cadair Idris that you can start your hike at the back door.

HOTELS AND GUESTHOUSES

Coed Cae A496 at Taicynhaeaf, 4 miles west of Dolgellau ☎ 01341 430628, ⓦ coedcae.co.uk; map p.282. Sustainability and appreciation of the outdoors are the watchwords at this three-room B&B handily sited for the Mawddach Trail (bike rental £20 a day), just across the toll bridge. Guests are free to avail themselves of the lounge with its superb log burner, while locally sourced meals and packed lunches are available on request. <u>£80</u>

Ffynnon Love Lane ☎ 01341 421 774, ⓦ ffynnontownhouse.com; map p.293. Six impeccable rooms in this large house, variously furnished with mahogany beds, slipper baths and French chandeliers, but all with separate sitting areas and great views. Rates include afternoon tea on arrival and daily newspapers. Two-night minimum stay at weekends. <u>£150</u>

George III Hotel A493, Penmaenpool, 2 miles west of Dolgellau ☎ 01341 422525, ⓦ georgethethird.co.uk; map p.282. Handsome seventeenth-century hotel superbly sited at the head of the Mawddach Estuary (bus #28), with six rooms in the main hotel building itself, and five smartly updated ground-level rooms in the Lodge, the former train station buildings. <u>£100</u>

Tan-y-Fron Arran Rd ☎ 01341 422638, ⓦ tanyfron .co.uk; map p.293. Cosy, slightly old-fashioned B&B with three rooms in the house and a couple of separate cottages. All come with a small fridge and a full cooked breakfast, although the cottages gets breakfast requisites delivered. <u>£70</u>

Tyddyn Mawr Farmhouse Islawrdref, 3 miles southwest of Dolgellau ☎ 01341 422331, ⓦ wales -guesthouse.co.uk; map p.282. Eighteenth-century farmhouse on the slopes of Cadair Idris at the foot of the Pony Path accommodating one ground floor room with its own patio, and a first floor room with balcony. Complimentary tea and cakes on arrival. Check ahead for winter closures. <u>£80</u>

★**Y Meirionnydd** Smithfield Square ☎ 01341 422554, ⓦ themeirionnydd.com; map p.293. This solid stone Georgian town house has been re-fashioned as a chic five-roomed hotel with light tones and blond woods offset by feature cushions and curtains; the retro Roberts radios are a great addition too. The smart little bar leads through to a distinguished little restaurant where the cracking breakfast is served. <u>£85</u>

HOSTELS AND CAMPING

★**Graig Wen** A493, 5 miles west of Dolgellau near Arthog ☎ 01341 250482, ⓦ graigwen.co.uk; map p.282. Access is steep but the Mawddach Estuary views make it all worthwhile at this wonderfully tranquil campsite with B&B. There's camping in both the upper and lower (car-free) fields, the latter offering a wilder camping experience with compost toilets and campfires. There's plenty of comfort available too, courtesy of a couple of yurts, a bell tent, and a "Caban" timber pavilion; the *Slate Shed B&B* is yet another step up in the comfort stakes. Bike hire available too. Closed Jan & Feb. Per person <u>£7</u>, B&B <u>£110</u>, yurt <u>£220</u>

YHA Kings Penmaenpool, 4.5 miles west of Dolgellau ☎ 0845 371 9327, ✉ kings@yha.org.uk; map p.282. Large country house a mile up a delightful wooded valley off the #28 Tywyn bus route (last bus around 6pm), with six-bed dorm rooms and a self-catering kitchen but no TV or even mobile reception. An ideal base for the Pony Path up Cadair Idris. Reception 8–10am & 5–10.30pm. <u>£14</u>

EATING, DRINKING AND ENTERTAINMENT

Dolgellau and the surrounding area are blessed with some good eating options. Evening life focuses on the numerous pubs, together with odd concerts and performances – see local noticeboards. Look out, too, for happenings at Ty Siamas (☎ 01341 421800, ⓦ tysiamas.com), the National Centre for Welsh Folk Music, located on Eldon Square.

THE BIG SESSION

Dolgellau's Sesiwn Fawr (ⓦ sesiwnfawr.co) or "Big Session" was once huge, but has now returned to its smaller Celtic folk roots. It takes place in the meadows west of the river bridge in mid-July and features much of the best of Welsh and wider Celtic folk.

★Dylanwad Da 2 Smithfield St **☎**01341 422870, ⓦdylanwad.co.uk; map p.293. Part wine bar, part café, this charmingly run establishment is a great place to visit any time of day, be it for a glass of red wine with some cheese, or a cup of coffee and a slice of cake. It's slated to move to nearby premises in 2015. Tues–Thurs 10am–4pm, Fri & Sat 10am–4pm & 7–9pm.

George III A493, Penmaenpool, 2 miles west of Dolgellau **☎**01341 422525, ⓦgeorgethethird.co.uk; map p.282. Superb spot for a pub meal overlooking the Mawddach Estuary or a sunset drink in the dark-wood bar. Meals might include lamb shank, fish and chips or bacon-wrapped chicken. Daily 11am–10.30pm.

★Mawddach A496, 2 miles northwest **☎**01341 421752, ⓦmawddach.com; map p.282. Dark and slate-floored downstairs, airy with bare boards and exposed beams upstairs, this contemporary restaurant occupies a converted barn with views of Cadair Idris. The menu, meanwhile, comprises simply prepared and beautifully cooked dishes such as Welsh black beef and red wine with leek and potato pie and anise-glazed carrots (£15.50). Wed–Sat noon–2.30pm & 6.30–9.30pm; Sun noon–2.30pm.

Royal Ship Queen's Square **☎**01341 422209; map p.293. Large and cheerful old coaching inn, with good beer, outside seating and a range of fairly standard bar meals at moderate prices (mains £10). Daily 11am–10.30pm.

★Siop Coffi T.H. Glyndŵr St; map p.293. This large, perennially busy café was once the town's ironmongers, as the old fixtures and fittings testify: a long, raised wooden table where folk tap away on laptops (free wi-fi), and the former glassed-in office, which is now a snug. Freshly made baguettes and panini, sumptuous cakes and freshly roasted coffee. Mon–Sat 9am–5pm, Sun 10am–4pm.

Barmouth and around

Cluttered with shops selling takeaway food, buckets and spades, and pleasure-beach sideshow attractions, lively **BARMOUTH** (Abermaw) tucks in beneath steep cliffs, lapped by both estuary and sea. It was popularized by nineteenth-century English Midlands sea-bathers who mostly arrived over the 2253ft-long **Barmouth Bridge**, which traverses 113 spindly wooden spans across the Mawddach Estuary south of town.

Barmouth was once a shipbuilding centre, and a maritime air lingers around the quay at the south end of town, departure point for a **passenger ferry** to Fairbourne and the miniature railway (see p.292).

The Last Haul
Corner of The Quay and Church St

The most famous of many shipwrecks along this coast was that of the 700-ton Genoese galleon known locally as the *Bronze Bell*. It sank in 1709 complete with its cargo of finest Carrara marble. Forty or so two-ton blocks of marble still lie on the sea bed but one piece was raised in the 1980s, and fashioned by local sculptor Frank Cocksey into "**The Last Haul**". Three centuries under the sea have left the surface fabulously pockmarked, though the quality of marble comes through in the carved section which depicts three fishing generations working together to haul in a catch.

Tŷ Gwyn Museum and Tŷ Crwn Roundhouse
Ty Gwyn Museum The Quay • June–Sept daily 1–4.30pm • Free • **The Roundhouse** • Daily 10.30am–5pm • Free

A medieval tower house where Henry VII's uncle, Jasper Tudor, is said to have plotted Richard III's downfall now houses **Tŷ Gwyn Museum**. The house was thought to have been destroyed until renovations in the 1980s revealed its identity. It now contains explanatory panels on local shipwrecks plus a few artefacts including the 1677 bronze bell that gave the nameless galleon its local moniker.

A few paces away, the **Tŷ Crwn Roundhouse** acted as a lockup for drunken sailors in the nineteenth century. The circular design, with two cells on opposite sides, was reputedly conceived to prevent the Devil lurking in any corners and further tempting the incarcerated mariners.

ARRIVAL AND DEPARTURE   **BARMOUTH**

By train The train station is on Station Road right in the centre of town.

Destinations Aberdyfi (8 daily; 35min); Harlech (8 daily; 25min); Machynlleth (8 daily; 55min); Porthmadog

THREE PEAKS YACHT RACE

In late June each year, the highly competitive **Three Peaks Yacht Race** (wthreepeaks yachtrace.co.uk) starts in Barmouth, a two- to three-day amateur monohull yachting event entailing navigation to Caernarfon, the English Lake District and Fort William in Scotland, and a run up the highest peak in each country. The current record, set in 2002, is two days, fourteen hours and four minutes.

(8 daily; 50min).

By bus Buses to Dolgellau (hourly; 25min) and Harlech (hourly; 30min) stop on Jubilee Road, near the train station.

By ferry A number of passenger ferries run from the harbour to Fairbourne (Easter–Oct; as frequently as custom demands; £3 return).

INFORMATION

Tourist information The TIC is inside the train station building on Station Road (Easter–Oct daily 10am–5pm; Nov–Easter Mon–Sat 10am–3.30pm; ☎01341 280787, wbarmouth-wales.co.uk).

Bike rental Birmingham Garage on Church Street (☎01341 280644) rents out basic machines that are ideal for the Mawddach Trail (£13/day).

ACCOMMODATION

Bae Abermaw Hotel Panorama Hill ☎01341 280550, wbaeabermaw.co.uk. Very un-Barmouth, this former Victorian hotel is now contemporary, with minimalist white-on-white rooms, an elegant bare-boards lounge and a pricey but sublime restaurant, almost all with unfurling views over Cardigan Bay. **£100**

Hendre Mynach Llanaber Rd, 1 mile north of town ☎01341 280262, whendremynach.co.uk. Barmouth's closest campsite, a large level site just off the beach with comprehensive facilities including modern shower blocks, launderette, shop and a cool kids' play area. Closed Jan & Feb. Pitches **£20**

Llwyndû Farmhouse Hotel Llanaber, 2 miles north of Barmouth ☎01341 280144, wllwyndu-farmhouse .co.uk. A gem of a B&B with en-suite rooms in the seventeenth-century farmhouse building (complete with mullioned windows and inglenook fireplace), the adjacent converted barn or the granary. **£100**

Sandpiper 7 Marine Parade ☎01341 280318, wthesandpiperguesthouse.co.uk. Just a few steps from the train station, this is just one of many B&Bs along the seafront, a well-presented guesthouse with a mix of singles, doubles and family rooms, many with sea views. March–Oct. **£60**

EATING AND DRINKING

Bae Abermaw Panorama Hill ☎01341 280550, wbaeabermaw.co.uk. Comfy chairs, wooden floors, white walls and a wintertime fire all enhance the best of Modern British cuisine served here – such as fillet of black bream with tomato and olive couscous (£14.95), and fig, plum and pistachio tart for dessert. Tues–Sat 6.30– 10pm, Sun noon–2.30pm.

Last Inn Church St ☎01341 280530, wlastinn -barmouth.co.uk. Locals and tourists alike mingle happily in this flower bedecked former cobbler's shop, where you

can also get good pub meals such as beer-battered cod and chips. The outdoor tables catch the afternoon sun. Live music on Tuesdays. Daily noon–11pm.

Llwyndû Farmhouse Hotel Llanaber, 2 miles north of Barmouth ☎01341 280144, wllwyndu-farmhouse .co.uk. Delicious evening meals served in the romantic dining room with candles flickering on the tables. Meals (two courses for £25, three for £28) offer three or four choices per course (one vegetarian) and local ingredients are the order of the day. Mon–Sat 7–10pm.

Ardudwy

North of Barmouth, the coast opens out to a narrow coastal plain running a dozen miles towards Snowdonia and flanked by the heather-covered slopes of the Rhinog mountains, five miles inland. This is **Ardudwy**, a fertile land used as a fattening ground for black Welsh cattle on their way to the English markets, and now tamed by caravan sites and golf courses.

No modern road crosses the Rhinogs to the east, but until the early nineteenth-century building of coach roads, the existence of two mountain passes made this a

WALKS FROM BARMOUTH

Barmouth–Fairbourne loop (5 miles; 2–3hr; 300ft ascent). A rewarding low-level coastal circuit, this easily managed walk around Barmouth and Fairbourne gives superb mountain, estuarine and coastal views all the way. You cross the rail bridge (90p return toll; £1.50 with a bike) to Morfa Mawddach station, then follow the lane to the main road, cross it onto a footpath that rises around the back of a small wooded hill to Pant Einion Hall, then follow another lane back to the main road near Fairbourne. Turn north then left down the main street of Fairbourne to the sea; from here you can return to Barmouth either by taking the Fairbourne Railway, or by walking north along the beach and catching the ferry.

Panorama Walk and Dinas Oleu (3 miles; 2hr; 400ft ascent). A bracing walk taking in a fine viewpoint over town and estuary plus Dinas Oleu (Fortress of Light), the cliffs immediately above Barmouth, which became the National Trust's first property in 1895. Essentially the route follows Gloddfa Road off High Street onto the exposed clifftops, where there is a map of the reserve. Go through the metal gate and follow the path past Frenchman's Grave to a road where you turn left to the Panorama Viewpoint. Return by the same route.

strategic and populous area, as the numerous minor Neolithic burial chambers testify. Further up the coast, the town of **Harlech** was built as one link in Edward I's chain of magnificent fortresses. It is the only real town in the region, followed in importance by **Llanbedr**, from where a road runs west to the dune-backed camping resort on **Shell Island**, and another rises east, splitting into two delightfully remote valleys.

Llanbedr and around

LLANBEDR, seven miles north of Barmouth, isn't much in itself, but is central to a diverse bunch of scattered sites from Neolithic burial chambers and wild dunes to a disused slate quarry and a pair of gorgeous valleys from where hikes lead up into the wild **Rhinog** range.

Morfa Dyffryn National Nature Reserve

Off A496, 2 miles southwest of Llanbedr • Open access • Free

The constantly changing coastal dunes of **Morfa Dyffryn National Nature Reserve** stretch from Llandwyne four miles north to the edge of Shell Island (see below). Notable for its flora, particularly the marsh helleborine, this is a fragile zone and large areas are fenced off, but there's beach access across a boardwalk. Follow the path from Dyffryn Ardudwy station through the caravan parks and the dunes to the splendid, vast **beach**. A section of shore a few hundred yards to the north serves as Wales' only official **naturist beach** (well, when it's warm enough).

Dyffryn Ardudwy Burial Chambers

Signposted behind the school in Dyffryn Ardudwy off A496, 3 miles south • Open access • Free; CADW

Dyffryn Ardudwy Burial Chambers comprise two supported capstones lying among a bed of small boulders, the base stones of a mound thought to have been 100ft long; the site dates from around 3500 BC. Finds from a dig here in the 1960s – including pottery, finely polished stone plaques and bones – are on display at the National Museum in Cardiff.

Shell Island

2 miles west of Llanbedr • Road toll £5 per vehicle; no access at high tide • ⓦ shellisland.co.uk

A lane from Llanbedr snakes its way alongside the babbling Afon Artro, past the train station and redundant airfield to **Shell Island**, or Mochras. A peninsula at anything other than high tide, the island is reached by a tidal causeway and offers the chance to swim, sail, look for wild flowers or scour the beach for some of the two hundred varieties of shell found here. At low tide you can see a line of rocks in the sea leading out towards Ireland, known as Sarn Badrig (St Patrick's Causeway) and traditionally thought to be the road to a flooded land known as the Cantre'r Gwaelod ("The Low Hundreds").

Llyn Cwm Bychan

A narrow road dives six miles northeast of Llanbedr through gorgeous woods as it follows the Afon Artro to the waters of **Llyn Cwm Bychan**, deep in the heather and angular rocks of the Rhinog range. Pay the farmer to park on the property here to take the path up to the **Roman Steps** – most likely a medieval packhorse route, made of flat slabs cutting through the range – onto Rhinog Fawr (see box below). Branching off the Cwm Bychan road a mile out of Llanbedr, another delightful road leads to **Cwm Nantcol**, the next valley south. Two hundred yards up the lane, **Capel Salem** is a Baptist chapel immortalized by Sidney Curnow Vosper's 1908 painting of the same name – a copy hangs inside.

ARRIVAL AND DEPARTURE

LLANBEDR

By bus Bus #38 services the coast from Barmouth to Harlech, then inland to Blaenau Ffestiniog.

By train Llanbedr is on the Cambrian coast line, and the

station is in the centre of the village.
Destinations Barmouth (8 daily; 15min); Harlech (8 daily; 10min); Porthmadog (8 daily; 30min).

ACCOMMODATION AND EATING

★ **Nantcol Waterfalls** 2 miles east of Llanbedr ☎ 01341 241209, ⊛ nantcolwaterfalls.co.uk. Fairly simple but blissfully secluded tent and caravan site at the base of the

Rhinogs and beside a burbling river. Facilities include a shower block, laundry and basic shop, while campfires are allowed (though you'll need to bring your own firewood or purchase).

4

WALKS ON THE RHINOGS

The northern **Rhinogs** offer some surprisingly tough walking. At under 2500ft, they're hardly giants, but the typically large, rough, gritstone rocks hidden in thick heather make anything but the most well-worn paths hard-going. The rewards for your efforts are long views across Cardigan Bay, a good chance of stumbling across a herd of feral goats and a strong sense of achievement. The two walks described here start at the head of different valleys (see p.288 & p.290), but share a common summit, that of Rhinog Fawr. Take the OS 1:25,000 Explorer #OL18 map "Harlech, Porthmadog & Bala".

RHINOG FAWR AND THE ROMAN STEPS FROM CWM BYCHAN

For this walk (5 miles return; 3–4hr; 1900ft ascent), start at the car park in **Cwm Bychan** (see above) and follow signs up through a small wood onto the open moor. The **Roman Steps** (most likely a medieval packhorse route) guide you up to a pass, Bwlch Tyddiad, giving views east to Bala and beyond. The terrain then becomes steeper and the path less well defined. You may have to use your hands to finally reach Rhinog Fawr (2362ft). Return by the same route.

RHINOG FAWR AND RHINOG FACH FROM CWM NANTCOL

This demanding walk (6–7 miles return; 5–6hr; 2900ft ascent) begins by the Maes-y-Garnedd farmhouse at the head of Cwm Nantcol for a fairly rugged circuit over Rhinog Fawr and Rhinog Fach. Follow the track north from the car park to the house, into the fields and over the stile, then turn northeast and walk gradually towards the base of the rocky southwest ridge, following the white marker posts. Eventually, the path turns north to a cairn on the skyline, then east following more cairns up the ridge to the summit trig point of **Rhinog Fawr**.

After an arduous descent into Bwlch Drws Ardudwy (The Pass of the Door of Ardudwy), cross the stone wall and start on a fairly clear line up Rhinog Fach (2236ft). Explore the summit ridge to get the best views of Cwm Nantcol then descend to Cwm Nantcol by first walking to a rocky ledge overlooking Llyn Hywel to the south. From here you should be able to see a scrappy path running very steeply down to the lake on the right-hand edge of the ledge. You'll have to use your hands at times, and there are sections of scree, but you're soon on a clear path that skirts north around the base of Rhinog Fach towards Bwlch Drws Ardudwy and back to Cwm Nantcol.

Best of all, there are some lovely woodland and riverside walks leading off from the site. March–Oct. Per person **£9**

Shell Island campsite ☎ 01341 241453, ⓦ shellisland .co.uk. Massive 300-acre tent and motorhome campsite (no caravans) that spreads along the beach from the harbour down to the vast dunes of Morfa Dyffryn. It is Europe's biggest, and although it can get crowded during the holiday season, campers must pitch tents a minimum of 20yd from each other (unless agreed with your neighbours), guaranteeing relative solitude amid spectacular scenery, with some of the best sunsets in north Wales. No walk-ins; you must have a vehicle. March–Oct. Per person **£7.50**

Shell Island restaurant and tavern ☎ 01341 241453, ⓦ shellisland.co.uk. People come from miles around for the Sunday lunches here (£14.50). There are good meals at other times too and the adjacent tavern sells the excellent Purple Moose ales from Porthmadog just up the coast. March–Oct daily noon–10pm.

Victoria Inn Llanbedr ☎ 01341 241213, ⓦ vic-inn .co.uk. Stone-built village pub that's a winner for its beer garden and à la carte meals made from produce from its own market garden. The five rooms are well above average for your typical pub. Bar open Mon–Thurs & Sun 11am–11pm, Fri & Sat 11am–midnight. **£80**

Harlech

HARLECH, three miles north of Llanbedr, is one of the highlights of the Cambrian coast and makes a dramatic first impression. Its commanding castle clings to a rocky outcrop, while the charming township cloaking the hill behind takes in one of Wales' finest views: over the Morfa Harlech dunes across Cardigan Bay to the Llŷn, and north to the jagged peaks of Snowdonia.

HARLECH

Harlech's **sand dunes** and **beach** are among the finest on this coast and are reached via Beach Road, which shoots off the main road through town, directly below the castle. On the way to the sands, you'll swing by the exclusive **Royal St Davids golf course**, venue of many championships. There's a handful of inviting places to eat (though relatively few places to stay) in the town's steep and narrow streets, plus wonderful walking country and further superb beaches on the doorstep.

Harlech Castle

March–June, Sept & Oct daily 9.30am–5pm; July & Aug daily 9.30am–6pm; Nov–Feb Mon–Sat 10am–4pm, Sun 11am–4pm · £4.25; CADW · ☎ 01766 780552

Harlech's showpiece is its substantially intact **castle**, rising mightily on its 200ft bluff. Intended as one of Edward I's Iron Ring of monumental fortresses (see box, p.404), construction of Harlech castle began in 1283, just six months after the death of Llywelyn the Last. It was built of a hard Cambrian rock, known as Harlech grit, hewn from the moat. One side of the fortress was originally protected by the sea – the waters have now receded, though, leaving the castle dominating a stretch of duned coastline.

■ ACCOMMODATION		● CAFÉS & RESTAURANTS			
Castle Cottage	2	Castle Cottage	1	Soul Food	4
Pen-y-Garth	3	Cemlyn Tea Shop	3		
Tremeifion	1	Hufenfa'r Castell	2		

The castle has seen a lot of action in its time: it withheld a siege in 1295, was taken by Owain Glyndŵr in 1404, and the youthful, future Henry VII – the first Welsh king of England and Wales – withstood a seven-year siege here at the hands of the Yorkists from 1461 to 1468, until the castle was again taken. It subsequently fell into ruin, but was put back into service for the king during the Civil War, and in March 1647 it became the last Royalist castle to fall.

The first defensive line comprised the three successive pairs of gates and portcullises built between the two massive half-round towers of the **gatehouse**, where an exhibition now outlines the castle's history. Much of the outermost ring has been destroyed, leaving only the 12ft-thick curtain walls rising up 40ft to the exposed battlements, and only the towering gatehouse prevents you walking the full circuit. Otherwise, the views stretching away over the golf course towards Snowdonia and the Llŷn Peninsula are magnificent.

ARRIVAL AND DEPARTURE HARLECH

By train Trains stop by the A496 below the castle. Destinations Barmouth (8 daily; 25min); Machynlleth (8 daily; 1hr 20min); Porthmadog (8 daily; 20min).

By bus Buses to Barmouth (hourly; 30min) and Blaenau Ffestiniog (3 daily; 35min) generally call both at the train station and at the southern end of High Street.

INFORMATION

Tourist information The TIC (Easter–Oct daily 9.30am–12.30pm & 1–5.30pm; ☎01766 780658, ✉ticharlech@eryri-npa.gov.uk) is currently on High Street, though its future is in doubt; information in future is likely to be available from the new castle interpretive centre, due to open 2015 or 2016.

ACCOMMODATION

★**Castle Cottage** Y Llech ☎01766 780479, ⓦcastlecottageharlech.co.uk. Established restaurant with rooms with a contemporary yet cosily informal feel. The seven rooms (including three fabulous suites) are natural-toned and very well appointed (big TVs, high-flow showers, leather sofa etc) but otherwise totally different, many with massive weathered beams and slate floors. Residents get a discount on dinner and on green fees at the local golf course. **£130**

Pen-y-Garth Old Llanfair Rd ☎01766 781352, ⓦpen-y-garth.co.uk. High-standard B&B in a former YHA with three, mostly all-white, rooms, each with a view of either the castle or coast. Cyclists, walkers and vegetarians are particularly welcome – they can also provide packed lunches. **£70**

Tremeifion A496 at Talsarnau, 4 miles north of Harlech ☎01766 770491, ⓦtremeifionvegetarianhotel.co.uk. Long-standing vegetarian and vegan hotel with three rooms of the highest order, each with views across the Dwyryd estuary to Portmeirion. There's no TV but plenty of places to read or play games, and three acres of grounds to explore. Rates include an imaginatively prepared three-course dinner, with many ingredients grown on site. Staff will pick up from the train station, a 10min walk away. **£175**

EATING AND DRINKING

★**Castle Cottage** Y Llech ☎01766 780479, ⓦcastlecottageharlech.co.uk. People travel from miles around for the wonderful food at this unpretentious Modern British restaurant with Welsh art on the walls. Choose from either a two- (£35) or three-course (£40) menu, for which you get canapés followed by the likes of lobster and prawn soup with cognac, and roasted porchetta with Dauphinoise potatoes and calvados jus. Daily 7–10pm.

★**Cemlyn Tea Shop** Stryd Fawr ☎01766 780425, ⓦcemlynteashop.co.uk. Upmarket café serving the best loose-leaf teas and espresso coffees around, plus home-made gluten and dairy free cakes, and afternoon tea (£6). If you can, grab a table on the sunny terrace where you can soak up the marvellous coastal views. Mid-March to Dec Wed–Sun 10am–5pm.

Hufenfa'r Castell Castle Square ☎07810 164547, ⓦhufenfa.co.uk. The "Castle Creamery" serves up the best ice cream for miles around, made on the premises and producing flavours like honeycomb, Welsh fudge and chocolate cherry truffle; there are some delicious sorbets too, notably beetroot. April–Oct daily 9.30am–5pm.

Soul Food Stryd Fawr ☎01766 780416, ⓦcaribbean crabharlech.com. Harlech seems an unlikely place to find a restaurant specializing in contemporary Caribbean cuisine, though it makes a welcome change. Creole-influenced dishes are the mainstay of a deliciously spicy menu, featuring the likes of caramelized lime chicken (£14.50) and saltfish buljol, with onion, tomatoes and sweet and chilli peppers. March–Oct Tues–Thurs 6.30–10.30pm, Fri & Sat 6.30–11pm, Sun 6.30–10pm.

4

The Dee Valley and around

VALLE CRUCIS

5

The Dee Valley and around

The Dee Valley and its immediate environs is a region with something of a split identity, encompassing both industrialized flatlands that spill over the border from England and attractive folds of green hill country that are as Welsh as anywhere. There's plenty to see here, but few of the region's sights top most people's list, and visitors often travel through with their minds set firmly on the more obvious destinations further west. The two main routes through the region – the Dee Valley and the Vale of Clwyd – both start in the English border country known as the Marches, an area long contested by the Welsh and English. Llangollen is the valley's undoubted highlight, with the International Eisteddfod folk music festival each July and a broad selection of ruins, rides and rambles to tempt visitors throughout the rest of the year.

At its heart is the region's largest conurbation, **Wrexham**, where the light industrial hinterland is leavened by the mining and smelting heritage along the **Clywedog Valley**. The only surviving Marcher fortress of note is **Chirk Castle**, a potent reminder of the centuries after the Norman conquest of England, when powerful barons fought the Welsh princes for control of these fertile lands. The castle makes a fine introduction to the **Dee Valley**, running between the Welsh borders and the rugged mountains of Snowdonia. The Dee Valley remains more firmly Welsh than the Marches, and three hundred years after the arrival of the Normans the area was the site of the first big revolt against them. From his base near **Corwen**, Wales' greatest hero, Owain Glyndŵr, attacked the property of a nearby English landowner, sparking a fourteen-year campaign which, at its height, saw Glyndŵr ruling most of Wales. Little remains to commemorate the era, and most people drive through oblivious of its heritage, making straight for **Bala** with its lake, watersports and cascading rapids.

The bucolic lands to the north reward a leisurely approach. The historic but dull market town of **Mold** is the gateway to the bald tops of the **Clwydian Range**, easy walking country overlooking the pastoral **Vale of Clwyd**. Its sights include the appealing town of **Ruthin** with its fine medieval buildings and jail tour, and **Denbigh**, surmounted by its craggy castle.

GETTING AROUND

THE DEE VALLEY AND AROUND

By train Chirk and Wrexham are served by the Shrewsbury–Chester rail line.

By bus The upper Dee Valley is accessed by the X94 from Wrexham to Barmouth via Llangollen, Bala and Dolgellau.

There is no easy connection between Llangollen and Betws-y-Coed: if you're making for the immediate vicinity of Snowdon, head along the north coast to Llandudno Junction or Bangor and change there.

PONTCYSYLLTE AQUEDUCT AT FRONCYSYLLTE

Highlights

❶ **Erddig** Amble around the most interesting stately home in Wales, complete with finely preserved servants' quarters, outbuildings and gardens. **See p.309**

❷ **Llanarmon Dyffryn Ceiriog** Enjoy great accommodation and food in a tiny village on the edge of bleak moors. **See p.310**

❸ **Plas Newydd, Llangollen** An elegant monument to romantic friendship, Plas Newydd always inspires. **See p.314**

❹ **Castell Dinas Brân, Llangollen** Hike up to this ragged ruin of a Welsh castle for a breath of air and fantastic views. **See p.315**

❺ **Pontcysyllte Aqueduct, Llangollen** Cruise over Thomas Telford's wonderful aqueduct, part of the Llangollen Canal, one of the great late-Georgian feats of engineering. **See p.316**

❻ **Rug Chapel and Llangar Church, Corwen** Buy one ticket to visit two small churches, and a finer pair you couldn't hope to find. **See p.320**

❼ **Ruthin** This compact hilltop town offers a cluster of diverting sights and easy access to gentle walks on the Clwydian hills. **See p.325**

HIGHLIGHTS ARE MARKED ON THE MAP ON P.306

5

Wrexham and around

While not a classically pretty place, **WREXHAM** (Wrecsam), the largest town in North Wales, has a boisterous charm and some fine older buildings amid the identikit chain stores. Having long looked more to the industrial northwest of England than its own Welsh hinterland, Wrexham's Welshness is obvious only when the Welsh football team plays at the town's Racecourse Ground.

A marketplace in medieval times for the fertile lands all around, the discovery of iron ore, coal and lead nearby propelled Wrexham into the industrial age. The legacy of these times is best seen to the south and west of town in the Clywedog Valley and at the splendidly evocative stately home Erddig.

St Giles' Church

Church St • Daily 10am–4pm • ⓦ wrexhamparish.org.uk

Built at the end of the fifteenth century, **St Giles' Church** was topped off with a so-called steeple, its five tiers and four hexagonal pinnacles replicated at America's Yale University in homage to the ancestral home of the college's benefactor, Elihu Yale, whose tomb faces the tower. The engraved stone in the tower wall nearby came from the university, replacing

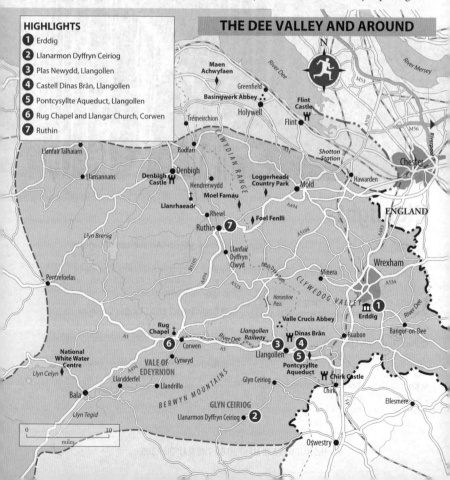

HIGHLIGHTS

1. Erddig
2. Llanarmon Dyffryn Ceiriog
3. Plas Newydd, Llangollen
4. Castell Dinas Brân, Llangollen
5. Pontcysyllte Aqueduct, Llangollen
6. Rug Chapel and Llangar Church, Corwen
7. Ruthin

THE DEE VALLEY AND AROUND

one that now holds up a replica tower there. The interior boasts the remains of a mural of the Last Judgement (c1500) above the entrance to the chancel, and an abundance of Victorian and contemporary stained glass. The church is approached through wrought-iron gates installed in 1718–24 by famed ironworkers Robert and John Davies of Bersham, also responsible for the gates at Chirk Castle and St Peter's church in Ruthin.

Wrexham County Borough Museum

Regent St • Mon–Fri 10am–5pm, Sat 10.30am–3pm • Free • ☎ 01978 297460, ⓦ wrexham.gov.uk/heritage

The small but engaging **Wrexham County Borough Museum** exhibits a miscellany from the town's nineteenth-century boom years, alongside Roman nuggets and the remarkable remains of the Bronze Age **Brymbo Man**, unearthed from a local sandstone burial cist complete with his pottery beaker and flint knife. Along with the reconstruction of the grave, look out for the exhibits commemorating the 266 miners who lost their lives in the 1934 Gresford Mine Disaster not far from here.

ARRIVAL AND DEPARTURE
WREXHAM

By train Trains from Bidston (connecting from Liverpool) via Shotton (for the North Wales coast) arrive at Wrexham Central, calling first at Wrexham General (a 10min walk northwest on Mold Rd) to connect with trains from Shrewsbury (for mid/south Wales) to Chester.
Destinations Bidston (hourly; 1hr); Chester (hourly; 20min); Chirk (hourly; 15min); Shrewsbury (hourly; 40min).

By bus The bus station on King Street is served by frequent local buses plus some National Express coach services (buy tickets online or from the TIC).
Destinations Bala (8 daily; 90min); Birmingham (1 daily; 2hr 40min); Chester (every 15min; 40min); Chirk (roughly hourly; 40min); Llangollen (every 15min; 35min); London (1 daily; 6hr); Manchester (1 daily; 1hr 40min); Mold (every 20min; 40min–1hr).

INFORMATION

Tourist office The TIC is on Lambpit Street (April to mid-Oct Mon–Sat 10am–5pm; mid-Oct to March Mon–Sat 10am–4pm; ☎ 01978 292015, ⓔ tic@wrexham.gov.uk).

Internet Free at the library/art gallery on Rhosddu Road (closed Sun), and pay facilities at Arrow (Mon–Sat 9am–5pm) at 1 Vicarage Hill.

ACCOMMODATION

★**The Lemon Tree** 29 Rhosddu Rd ☎ 01978 261211, ⓦ lemon-tree-hotel-wrexham.com. Modernized hotel converted from a Victorian Gothic villa, with small and simple yet tasteful en-suite rooms (some with canopy beds and DVD players), and a good restaurant. **£70**

Woodhey 9 Sontley Rd ☎ 01978 262555, ⓦ woodhey -guesthouse.com. The best of the low-cost central B&Bs, with seven rooms in a Victorian house, plus a pleasant lounge and garden and filling breakfasts. Very good value. **£55**

EATING

Anise 1 Smithfield Rd ☎ 01978 261273, ⓦ anise wrexham.co.uk. Easily the best curry house in these parts, serving all the usual suspects (£9–12) with aplomb. Sun–Thurs 5.30–10.30pm, Fri & Sat 5.30–11.30pm.
Bwtri At the museum on Regent St ☎ 01978 290302. Conservatory café offering the town's best light lunches – panini, jacket potatoes and tapas, all celebrating local producers and seasonal fare. Mon–Fri 10am–5pm, Sat 10.30am–3pm.
The Lemon Tree 29 Rhosddu Rd ☎ 01978 261211,

ⓦ lemon-tree-hotel-wrexham.com. Bustling, brightly decorated restaurant with an extensive menu of Modern British food (starters £5–6, mains £13–18, desserts £5–8). Daily 7am–10pm or later.
Sleepy Panda Farndon St ☎ 01978 310700, ⓦ sleepypanda.org. Upmarket Cantonese restaurant (also featuring Szechuan and Beijing dishes) on the edge of the centre opposite the Tesco supermarket (mains £8–9, menus £12.50–20). Daily 5.30–11.30pm.

NIGHTLIFE AND ENTERTAINMENT

At weekends, you'll find a handful of lively **nightclubs** in the area around the junction of Brook Street and Vicarage Hill. **Male voice choirs** practise in local halls (all year except Aug on Mon, Wed, Thurs & Sun): call the TIC for details.

Central Station Hill St ☎ 01978 358780, ⓦ central stationvenue.com. The town's best venue for live bands

(around £12) and club nights; Sat nights feature chart/ indie/alternative music. Wed–Sun 7pm–2am.

5

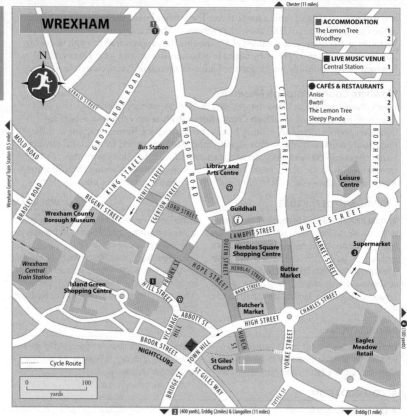

The Clywedog Valley

Forming an arc around the western and southern suburbs of Wrexham, the **Clywedog Valley** was the crucible of industrial development in the northern Welsh borders during the eighteenth century. Iron production boomed here, thanks to an abundance of ore deposits and cheap water power. As the Industrial Revolution forged ahead, coal became a more important energy source than water and factories moved away, closer to their raw materials, leaving the valley in peace.

Clywedog Valley Trail

The long-abandoned industrial ruins here – principally a mine, a mill and an ironworks – have been partly restored and are now waypoints on the nine-mile-long **Clywedog Valley Trail**, easily visited in one long, varied day.

Minera Lead Mines

Minera, 4 miles west of Wrexham • Visitor Centre April to mid-July Sat & Sun noon–5pm; Easter & mid-July to Aug Mon & Thurs–Sun noon–5pm • Free • ☎ 01978 318970

The surface workings of the **Minera Lead Mines** have largely vanished, and the area is now a country park, but the **engine house** and a pithead derrick have been rebuilt, together with some ore-processing machinery by the small **museum** in the former ore house. For a better impression of the layout, walk up onto the hill behind – a heather-clad moor on the fringe of an area called **World's End** – and look back on the valley. In the eighteenth century this was full of mines extracting galena, a silver-and-zinc-rich lead ore, from shafts over 1200ft deep.

Nant Mill

Near Coedpoeth, 3 miles west of Wrexham • Easter–Oct daily 10.30am–4.30pm; Nov–Easter Sat & Sun 10.30am–4.30pm • Free • ☎ 01978 752772

The Clywedog Valley Trail leads a mile and a half east along the river from Minera Lead Mines to the child-oriented **Nant Mill** visitor centre, where you can pick up leaflets for nature trails leading to a very visible section of **Offa's Dyke** in the nearby Pas Power Woods.

Bersham Ironworks and Heritage Centre

Bersham Rd • April to mid-July Sat & Sun noon–5pm; mid-July to Aug Mon & Thurs–Sun noon–5pm • Free • ☎ 01978 318970

The Clywedog Valley Trail runs through woodland to the seventeenth-century **Bersham Ironworks**, expanded by Cumbrian ironmaster John "Iron-Mad" Wilkinson who, in 1775, patented a method for horizontally boring out cylinders. This produced the first truly circular smooth-bore iron, perfect for highly accurate cannons – hundreds were made here for the Napoleonic and American Civil Wars – and the production of fine-tolerance steam cylinders. Engineer James Watt was a big customer, producing steam engines that made water-powered sites unprofitable and eventually put Bersham out of business.

The old **foundry** survives largely intact, and around it the ironworks' remains are now being unearthed after nearly two centuries of neglect, revealing a broad area of knee-high foundations.

A ten-minute walk east (but run as the same site), the **Bersham Heritage Centre** has a room dedicated to Wilkinson and outdoor displays of equipment from the agricultural revolution and Bersham Coal Mine.

Erddig House

2 miles southwest of Wrexham • Early March to Oct daily 12.30–4.30pm; Nov to early March daily 11am–3.30pm (kitchens, outbuildings, garden, shop and restaurant only) • Early March to Oct £7.40, £11.50 with house; Oct to early March £5; NT • ☎ 01978 355314

Erddig House, built in the 1680s, is one of the most fascinating stately homes in Wales. Ever since the Yorke family – all seemingly called Simon or Philip – took over in 1733, they took a hands-off attitude, especially the fourth Simon Yorke, who inherited in 1922. He failed to install electricity, running water, gas or a phone, and ignored the chronic damp that had the Chinese hand-blocked paper peeling off the walls. The National Trust took charge in 1973, restoring the house to its 1922 appearance and returning the jungle of a garden to its formal eighteenth-century plan.

The servants' quarters

The house itself isn't especially distinguished, but, as nothing was ever thrown away, the collection of fine furniture and portraits – including a Gainsborough of the first Philip Yorke – is unusually complete. The real interest, however, lies below stairs, particularly in the **Servants' Hall**, where portraits of eighteenth- and early nineteenth-century staff members are accompanied by evocations in verse by a Yorke – an extraordinary display of benevolence. You can also see the smithy, stables, laundry, the still-used bake house and kitchen.

The walled garden

Keep some time for the **walled garden**, saved from the worst of the eighteenth-century landscaping craze despite the best efforts of William Emes, a contemporary of Capability Brown, who worked on the surrounding parkland. Manicured yew hedges delineate beds planted with pleached lime trees, the walls support some 150 species of ivy, and apple trees produce fruit celebrated during an apple festival in early October.

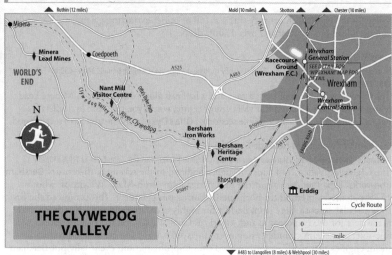

THE CLYWEDOG VALLEY

GETTING AROUND   **THE CLYWEDOG VALLEY**

On foot Aside from Minera and Nant Mill, all the sites lie within a couple of miles of Wrexham.
By bus To take in the whole valley in a day (a total of 9 miles walking), catch a #9 or #10 bus to Minera, follow the Clywedog Trail to Erddig, then wander the mile and a half back into Wrexham via the *Squire Yorke Inn*.

Chirk and around

The Normans founded **CHIRK** (Y Waun) almost a thousand years ago, their motte remaining as a small tree-covered mound at the southern end of this pleasant enough village with long views up the valley to the Berwyn hills. The attractive twin-aisled church, full of ornate memorials, is worth a look, as is the war memorial by Eric Gill (1920).

Chirk Castle guards the entrance to the **Glyn Ceiriog Valley**, which runs parallel to, and three miles south of, the Dee Valley. This blissfully quiet and beautiful area was for centuries an important route into the heart of Wales and over the Berwyns into Snowdonia. There are no compelling sights, but the area makes a perfect getaway.

The minor B4500 follows the river for six bucolic miles to Glyn Ceiriog, then past a rocky gorge and on a further five miles to the appealing **LLANARMON DYFFRYN CEIRIOG** (usually referred to as Llanarmon DC), nothing but a few houses, a church, the odd artist's studio and some excellent **accommodation** in a couple of high-quality country inns, both serving excellent **meals**.

Chirk Castle

2 miles west of Chirk • March, Oct & Nov 10am–4pm; April–Sept 10am–5pm; rest of year reduced access • £10.50 (winter £9.15); garden only £7.20 (winter £5.25); NT • ☏ 01691 777701

Having lured Llywelyn ap Gruffydd, last Prince of Wales, to his death, Roger Mortimer was rewarded by Edward I with the grant of Chirk and began the construction of massive drum-towered **Chirk Castle** in 1295.

The gatescreen

Access to this Marcher fortress is guarded by a magnificent Baroque **gatescreen**, the finest work of the Davies brothers of Bersham, who wrought it between 1712 and

1719. The ebullient floral designs are capped by the Myddleton coat of arms and a red hand, the family's crest and source of all the "Hand" hotels dotting the region. The gates are flanked by a pair of wolves, perhaps a memorial to one of the last wolves in Wales, said to have kept watch over the moat in the 1680s.

The castle

From the gates, an oak-lined avenue leads up to the **castle**, an austere-looking place softened only by its mullioned windows. The original plan was probably to mimic Beaumaris Castle, started just a couple of months earlier, but Chirk lacks Beaumaris's purity and symmetry. It seems the southern walls were never completed, perhaps because of the unstable slope, and attackers were able to enter here in 1322 and 1330; the present north gate and south wall were built c1400 against Owain Glyndŵr's forces.

The castle was bought in 1595 by Sir Thomas Myddelton, whose son found himself besieging his own home in the Civil War after it was seized by Royalist forces; then he became a Royalist and was besieged by the Parliamentarians. The Myddeltons added a **Long Gallery** and the grand eighteenth-century **state apartments**, leaving a legacy of sumptuous rooms reflecting sixteenth- to nineteenth-century tastes, many returned to their former states after some Victorian meddling by Pugin in the 1840s. The **east wing** has recently been opened up, including one of the last great Welsh family libraries, with volumes dating back to 1535. In winter only the Adam Tower (c1300) is open, furnished with wooden benches and a truckle bed; you can go up two flights and further down to the dungeon.

The gardens

After touring the house, leave time to explore the clipped yew hedges in the beautiful ornamental **gardens** or trace the section of Offa's Dyke that runs across the front of the house (though it was flattened in 1758 for use as a cart track).

ARRIVAL AND DEPARTURE   **CHIRK**

By train Trains stop at Chirk's station on Station Ave.
Destinations Chester (hourly; 30min); Shrewsbury (hourly; 25min); Wrexham (hourly; 15min).
By bus Buses stop in the town centre on Holyhead Road.

Destinations Llanarmon DC (7 daily, via the station; 30min); Llangollen (hourly; 20min); Wrexham (roughly hourly; 40min).

ACCOMMODATION AND EATING

Bridge End Inn Bridge St, Ruabon ☎01978 810881, ⓦmcgivernales.co.uk. This traditionally authentic and very friendly little place was CAMRA's real-ale pub of the year in 2011. They are happy to show visitors their brewery out the back and stock other fine beers and ciders too; food is limited to pies and Scotch eggs. Mon–Thurs 5–11pm, Fri 4–11pm, Sat & Sun noon–11pm.

Fron Frys Glyn Ceiriog ☎01691 718880, ⓦfronfrys .co.uk. Lovely farmhouse B&B about a mile down the

B4579 towards Oswestry; it's dog- and outdoor-activity-friendly, and there's a secluded family wing. __£60__

Hand Hotel Llanarmon DC ☎01691 600666, ⓦthehandhotel.co.uk. Converted sixteenth-century farmhouse with a convivial wood-beamed bar and relaxed dining room. The well-prepared pub grub ranges from steak and ale pie (£13) to Welsh rib-eye (£23); or you can enjoy the daily specials for lunch or dinner (£14.50/2 courses). Try to get one of the older, more atmospheric but

---

A SHORT WALK FROM CHIRK

On the way back from Chirk Castle deviate for a fun **short walk** (1.5 miles return; 30–45min; flat) along the **Shropshire Union Canal**, which takes in a canal tunnel, an aqueduct and the English border. About 50yd west of the railway station a short track leads down to the entrance to the 459yd **Chirk Tunnel**. Walk south through the tunnel (torch handy but not absolutely essential), to emerge at the start of **Chirk Aqueduct** over the River Ceiriog, and a parallel rail viaduct. You can walk to the far end where the canal enters England. Return the same way, or avoid the tunnel using Station Road, which runs above it.

5

less well-appointed rooms (£127) rather than those in the modern extension. Bar daily 11am–11pm (Sun from noon); food served noon–2.15pm & 6.30–8.45pm; **£90** **West Arms** Llanarmon DC ☎01691 600665, ⓦthewestarms.co.uk. Ancient farmhouse-turned-inn with stone-flagged floor and a gorgeous inglenook fireplace, plus a public bar and garden out back. There are a couple of cheaper, more modest rooms, but you'll really want one of the older rooms, full of character (£150). Enjoy sumptuous dinners (£28 for two courses, £33 for three) or affordable bar meals (mains £14–16). Daily noon–late; food served noon–2.30pm & 7–9pm. **£95**

The Dee Valley

The **Dee Valley** has long been the main transport route from the English Marches to Snowdonia, and it remains the most interesting route west. The course of the River Dee (Afon Dyfrdwy) is traced by Thomas Telford's A5 road between London and Holyhead which passes **Chirk**, with its fine Marcher castle, then **Llangollen** with its hilltop castle ruins, broken-down abbey and medieval bridge. Upstream, Owain Glyndŵr's stronghold, **Corwen**, deserves a stop to explore a couple of beautiful small churches.

Llangollen

Clasped tightly in the narrow Dee Valley between the shoulders of the Berwyn and Eglwyseg mountains, **LLANGOLLEN** is the embodiment of a Welsh town in both setting and character. The River Dee cuts a wide arc around the base of **Dinas Brân**, a conical tor surmounted by a ruined Welsh castle. At the apex of the bend, the Dee licks the angled buttresses of Llangollen's weighty Gothic bridge. On its south bank, half a dozen streets, harmoniously straggling up the rugged hillsides, form the core of the scattered settlement. With its wealth of historical sights, canal trips over a fine aqueduct, steam train rides and some highly worthwhile walks, Llangollen is very popular throughout the summer, particularly in early July when the town barely copes

THE LLANGOLLEN INTERNATIONAL EISTEDDFOD

Llangollen is heaving in summer, but never more so than during the first or second week of July, when for six days the town explodes into a frenzy of music, dance and poetry. Unlike the very Welsh National Eisteddfod, the **Llangollen International Eisteddfod** (tickets ☎01978 862001, ⓦinternational-eisteddfod.co.uk) draws around four thousand amateur performers from fifty countries, all competing for prizes in their chosen disciplines. Dances and choral performances take place at Plas Newydd, Valle Crucis and just about anywhere that people can congregate, though competitive performances are concentrated in the main venue, the **Royal International Pavilion**. When the day's competition is over, headlining stars often pack out the pavilion.

The first public eisteddfod was held in Corwen in 1789, and the international festival has been held in its present form since 1947, when it was started by one Harold Tudor to soothe the social wounds of World War II. Forty choirs from fourteen countries performed at the first (entirely choral) event, and it expanded, drawing praise quickly from Dylan Thomas, who declared that "the town sang and danced, as though it were right". Today this town of three thousand people is swamped by up to 150,000 visitors, but there is an irresistible *joie de vivre* as brightly costumed dancers walk the streets and fill the restaurants and fish and chip shops.

Tickets for all but the headlining shows can be obtained close to the time, often on the day itself. All-day access to the main site, with no guarantee of a seat, costs as little as £10 a day. Accommodation needs to be booked months in advance, so unless you are going specifically for the festivities, avoid trying to stay in Llangollen during the eisteddfod.

The eisteddfod is followed by the less frenetic **Llangollen Fringe** (☎0800 145 5779, ⓦllangollenfringe.co.uk), with a number of more "alternative" acts – music, dance, comedy and so on – performing in the town hall on Castle Street over the third week in July.

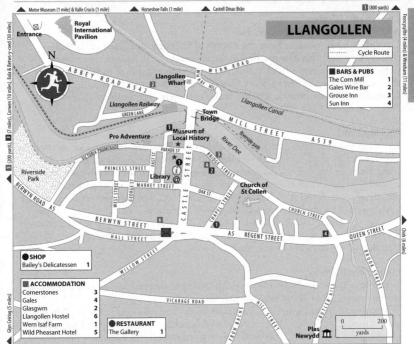

with the thousands of visitors to Wales' celebration of worldwide folk music, the **Llangollen International Eisteddfod** (see box opposite). This mostly takes place in the six-thousand-seat, white plastic **Royal International Pavilion**, raised in 1992 to evoke the shape of the traditional marquee formerly erected here each year, but looking more like some giant armoured reptile.

Brief history

As the only river crossing point for miles, Llangollen was an important town long before the early Romantics arrived at the end of the eighteenth century, when the Napoleonic Wars cut off their European Grand Tours. Turner came to paint the swollen river and the Cistercian ruin of **Valle Crucis**, a couple of miles up the valley; John Ruskin found the town "entirely lovely in its gentle wildness"; and George Borrow made Llangollen his base for the early part of his 1854 tour detailed in *Wild Wales* (see "Books", p.461). The rich and famous came not only for the scenery, but to visit the celebrated **Ladies of Llangollen**, an eccentric couple who became the toast of society from their house, **Plas Newydd** (see box, p.314). But some of the town's rural charm had already been eaten up by the works of one of the century's finest engineers, Thomas Telford (see box, p.316), who squeezed both his **London–Holyhead trunk road** and the **Llangollen Canal** alongside the river, spanning the valley with the majestic nineteen-span **Pontcysyllte Aqueduct**.

Town Bridge and Town Falls

Few visitors can resist admiring the view from the **town bridge** which, though widened and strengthened over the years, has spanned the river since 1345. Upstream, the Dee pours through the fingers of shale which make up the unimaginatively dubbed **Town Falls**. The bridge runs onto Castle Street, heading south past the TIC.

5

Church of St Collen

Church St, off Castle St • Late May to Sept Tues–Sat 2–6pm

Llangollen takes its name from the **Church of St Collen**, dedicated to its sixth-century founder. This boasts a fine sixteenth-century oak hammerbeam roof, said (wrongly) to have come from Valle Crucis. The graveyard is of equal interest for the triangular monument to Mary Carryll erected by her mistresses, the Ladies of Llangollen (see box below), who are also buried here and commemorated on the other two sides of her pillar.

Plas Newydd

Half a mile up Hill St from the southern end of Castle St • April–Oct daily except Tues 10am–5pm • £5.50; grounds free • ☎ 01978 862834

For almost fifty years, charming **Plas Newydd** was home to the famed **Ladies of Llangollen** (see box below). An excellent, self-guided audio tour (free) leads you around the house's half-dozen rooms, modest apart from the riot of dark wood panelling: a wonderful if slightly oppressive effect set off by assorted furniture similar to that owned by the ladies. As a counterpoint you can also visit the spartan attic room of their loyal housekeeper Mary Carryll. Outside, take time to wander through the twelve acres of formal **grounds**, including the **knot garden**, perfectly complementing the front of the house.

Llangollen Railway

Llangollen station, Abbey Rd • April–Sept Mon–Fri 3 services daily (usually steam), plus most Sat & Sun year-round up to 7 steam and diesel services daily • £12 return • ☎ 01978 860979, ⓦ llangollen-railway.co.uk

Wherever you are in Llangollen, the hills echo to the shrill cry of steam engines easing along the standard-gauge **Llangollen Railway**. Shoehorned into the north side of the valley, it runs west from Llangollen's time-warped station past Berwyn, near the Horseshoe Falls, to Corwen, ten miles up the valley. Using a restored section of the disused Ruabon–Barmouth line (pushed through Llangollen in 1865), belching steam engines (and diesels and railcars) rattle along the river bank, hauling ancient carriages sporting the liveries of their erstwhile owners.

Most visitors simply ride to the end of the line and back (2hr), but consider getting off partway along and walking back to town along the Dee Valley Way (see box, p.317), perhaps stopping for a pint in the riverside *Grouse Inn* at Carrog.

THE LADIES OF LLANGOLLEN

Lady Eleanor Butler and Sarah Ponsonby – better known as the **Ladies of Llangollen** – were Anglo-Irish aristocrats who twice failed to elope together, dressed in men's clothes. In 1778 they were grudgingly allowed to leave with an annual allowance of £280, enough to settle in Llangollen, where they became the country's most celebrated lesbians – though apparently they were affronted by the suggestion that their relationship was anything other than chaste. Regency society was captivated by their "model friendship" in what Simone de Beauvoir called "a peaceful Eden on the edge of the world".

Despite their desire for a "life of sweet and delicious retirement", they didn't seem to mind the constant stream of gentry who called on them. They found the Duke of Wellington a "charming young man, hansom, fashioned tall and elegant", and commemorated his visit in typically self-absorbed manner by engraving "E.B & S.P. 1814" over the mantelpiece in the Oak Room. Walter Scott was also well received, though he found them "a couple of hazy or crazy old sailors" in manner, and like "two respectable superannuated clergymen" in their mode of dress. Thomas de Quincey humoured the ladies, if only to earn forgiveness for his friend Wordsworth, who had displeased them by referring to their house as "a low roofed cot" in an inelegant poem composed in the grounds. Gothic oriel windows and porches were added by the Ladies to a simple farm cottage, but the mock-Tudor half-timbering was added after their time.

Castell Dinas Brân

Follow signs from Llangollen Wharf • Open access • Free

It's the view both ways along the valley that justifies a 45-minute slog up to **Castell Dinas Brân** (Crow's Fortress Castle), perched on a hill 750ft above the town. The lure certainly isn't the few sad but evocative vaulted stumps, a poor testament to what was once the district's largest and most important Welsh fortress. Prince Madog ap Gruffydd Maelor, ruler of northern Powys, raised the castle around 1260 on the site of an Iron Age hill fort. It was abandoned as soon as 1277, during Edward I's first campaign against Llywelyn ap Gruffydd, and left to decay, the antiquarian John Leland finding it "all in ruin" in 1540.

Although not much to look at, it's a great place to be when the sun is setting, imagining George Borrow sitting up here translating seventeenth-century bard Roger Cyffyn:

Gone, gone are thy gates, Dinas Brân on the height!
Thy warders are blood-crows and ravens, I trow;
Now no-one will wend from the field of the fight
To the fortress on high, save the raven and the crow.

Museum of Local History

Parade St • Daily except Wed 10am–4pm • Free • ☎ 01978 862862, ⓦ llangollenmuseum.org.uk

Housed in a Tardis-like structure, Llangollen's **Museum of Local History** occupies a ring of alcoves, centred on a replica of Eliseg's pillar, each covering a topic such as Valle Crucis, the eistedfoddau, the Ladies and the railway. There are lots of historic photos and documents, as well as an animatronic scribe.

Llangollen Motor Museum

A542, 1 mile west of Llangollen • March–Oct Tues–Sun 11am–5pm • £3.50 • ☎ 01970 860324, ⓦ llangollenmotormuseum.co.uk

An easy walk along the canal towpath leads to the **Llangollen Motor Museum**, a former slate-dressing shed that now smells evocatively of engine oil and old leather. Two dozen restored cars and three dozen British bikes from the glory years should please any vintage vehicle nut. Check out the 1957 three-wheeler "bubble car" and what is claimed to be Britain's oldest caravan, a tiny wooden affair.

Valle Crucis Abbey

A542, 2 miles west of Llangollen • Daily: April–Oct 10am–5pm; Nov–March 10am–4pm • April–Oct £3.50; Nov–March free; CADW • ☎ 01978 860326

The gaunt remains of **Valle Crucis Abbey** stand in Glyn y Groes, the "Valley of the Cross". In 1201, Madog ap Gruffydd Maelor chose this majestic pastoral setting for one of the last Cistercian foundations in Wales, as well as Britain's first Gothic abbey. Despite a devastating fire in its first century, and a complement of far from pious monks, it survived until the Dissolution in 1536. The church fell into disrepair, after which the monastic buildings, in particular the monks' dormitory, were employed as farm buildings. Later, Turner painted the abbey, imaginatively shifting it to sit immediately below Dinas Brân.

Valle Crucis greets you with its best side, the largely intact west wall of the church pierced by the frame of a rose window. Head through the mostly ruined cloister and past the weighty vaulting of the chapterhouse to reach the monks' dormitory, where a set of gravestones supposedly includes that of Owain Glyndŵr's resident bard, Iolo Goch. There are also displays on monastic life, and the small white cottage out the back contains an excellent exhibit conjuring up abbey life as it would have been around 1400.

Eliseg's Pillar

Beside A542, 400yd north of Valley Crucis Abbey • Open access • Free; CADW

The cross that gave Valley Crucis its name is the 8ft-tall **Eliseg's Pillar**, set on a Bronze Age cairn. Erected to a Prince of Powys in the early ninth century by his great-grandson,

5

it stood over 20ft high but was smashed during the Civil War of the 1640s. The stump remains, but you can now see only half of the full 31 lines glorifying the lineage of the Princes of Powys, translated from the remaining pieces in 1696.

The Llangollen Canal

When it opened in 1806, the **Llangollen Canal** was one of Britain's finest feats of canal engineering, designed both to transport slate from the quarries on the Horseshoe Pass and as a water supply for the Shropshire Union Canal. It starts at **Horseshoe Falls**, a crescent-shaped weir three miles west of Llangollen, which diverts water from the River Dee into the canal. In recognition of its significance, and its almost entirely intact state, the eleven miles from Horseshoe Falls across the Pontcysyllte Aqueduct and the Chirk Aqueduct (see box, p.311) to the English border are now a UNESCO World Heritage Site (w pontcysyllte-worldheritage.co.uk).

The Pontcysyllte Aqueduct

Off A542 4 miles west of Llangollen • 45min boat rides across the aqueduct and back offered by Jones the Boats (April–Oct daily at noon, 1pm, 2pm & 3pm; £5; T 01978 824166, W canaltrip.co.uk)

The Llangollen Canal avoids locks for its first fourteen miles, partly thanks to the thousand-foot-long **Pontcysyllte Aqueduct**, which spans the Dee at a maximum 127ft above the river. It was designed by the great engineer Thomas Telford (see box below), who supported long cast-iron troughs on nineteen great stone piers – a bold move for its time. You can take a vertiginous walk along the **towpath** to cross the aqueduct or take a leisurely **narrowboat ride** across and back.

ARRIVAL AND GETTING AROUND LLANGOLLEN

By car With your own vehicle, the most spectacular way to approach Llangollen is over the 1350ft Horseshoe Pass (A542) from Ruthin.

By train Trains stop 5 miles east at Ruabon, which is served by Llangollen–Wrexham buses.

By bus Buses stop on Parade Street, including a daily National Express coach from/to Birmingham and London; get tickets from the TIC. Note that it's difficult to access central Snowdonia from Llangollen: go via Denbigh and the north coast.

THOMAS TELFORD

The English poet Robert Southey dubbed **Thomas Telford** (1767–1834) the "Colossus of Roads" in recognition of his pre-eminence as the greatest road builder of his day, if not the greatest ever. Throughout the early years of the nineteenth century, he managed some of the most ambitious engineering projects yet attempted, and there was seldom a public work on which his opinion wasn't sought.

Born in Scotland, he was apprenticed to a stonemason in London where he taught himself engineering architecture, eventually earning himself a job with the Ellesmere Canal Company, which was planning a canal to link the Severn, Dee and Mersey rivers. His reputation was forged on the **Pontcysyllte Aqueduct**, part of the **Llangollen Canal**, hailed as innovative even before he had completed it.

Though lured away to build the Caledonian Canal in Scotland and St Katherine's Docks in London, he returned to Wales after the 1800 Act of Union between Britain and Ireland, when a good road was needed to hasten mail and to transport the new Irish MPs to and from parliament in London. What is now the A5 was wedged into the same valley as Telford's Llangollen Canal, then driven right through Snowdonia with its gradient never exceeding 1 in 20. The combination of its near-level route and the high quality of its well-drained surface cut hours off the journey time from 1815, but the Dublin ferries left from Holyhead on the island of Anglesey, separated from the mainland by the Menai Strait. Telford's solution and his greatest achievement was the 580ft-long **Menai Suspension Bridge**, strung 100ft above the strait to allow tall ships to pass under. Though the idea wasn't completely novel, the scale and the balance of grace and function won the plaudits of engineers and admiring visitors from around the world.

WALKS FROM LLANGOLLEN

Llangollen is a great place to explore **on foot**, perhaps using a narrowboat or steam train to shorten a loop. In addition, the Llangollen Lift **free minibus** run a handy service (see below) towards Horseshoe Pass and Plas Newydd. The Explorer **map** 225, "Llangollen & Berwyn", is useful for the following walks, each of which has an excellent free **leaflet** available from the TIC, pinpointing pubs and points of interest along the way.

Dee Valley Way This well-marked route along the north side of the Dee Valley between Llangollen and Corwen is fifteen miles long, but can be broken into smaller sections, or shortened by taking the Llangollen Railway to Glyndyfrdwy or Carrog then walking back. You can lunch well in *Grouse Inn* at Carrog (see p.318).

Llangollen History Trail–An easy-to-follow loop (6 miles; 3–6hr; 500ft ascent), initially tracing the canal towpath to Horseshoe Falls, then visiting Valle Crucis Abbey and Eliseg's Pillar before returning via Dinas Brân.

North Berwyn Way A wilder option flanking the south side of the Dee Valley between Llangollen and Corwen, along the wild moorland tops of the Berwyn hills and past an old slate quarry. The full walk is fifteen miles, but shorter versions are explained in the leaflet from the TIC (see above) and you can create a loop using parts of the Dee Valley Way.

Destinations Bala (8 daily; 1hr); Birmingham (1 daily; 4hr 30min); Chirk (hourly; 20min); Corwen (8 daily; 20min); Dolgellau (8 daily; 1hr 45min); Llanarmon DC (6 daily; 50min); London (1 daily; 7hr 30min); Wrexham (every 15min; 35min). **On foot** Buses are fairly infrequent, but you can easily walk most places: even Valle Crucis, the most distant sight, is only a mile and a half along the towpath.

The Llangollen Lift This free minibus (ⓦ clwydianrangeaonb.org.uk/llangollen-lift/) runs three times a day from Llangollen towards Horseshoe Pass (May–Nov weekends and bank hols) and to Plas Newydd (May–Sept weekends, plus Fri in Aug).
Bike rental Available from SK Cycles, 3 Berwyn Street ☎ 01978 869436.

INFORMATION

Tourist office The TIC (Easter–Oct daily 9.30am–5.30pm; Nov–Easter Mon–Sat 9.30am–5pm, Sun 9.30am–4pm; ☎ 01978 860828, ✉ llangollen@nwtic.com, ⓦ llangollen.org.uk) is in Y Capel on Castle Street.
Internet Free at the library, in the same building as the TIC (closed Sat afternoon and all day Thurs & Sun).

ACTIVITIES AND OPERATORS

NARROWBOAT TRIPS

Anglo Welsh Trevor Basin, Pontcysyllte Aqueduct ☎ 0117 304 1122, ⓦ anglowelsh.co.uk. Groups of up to ten can rent a self-steer narrowboat from £110/day. You can travel west as far as Llangollen and east across the aqueduct to Chirk; there are a couple of good pubs for lunch.
The Horse Drawn Boat Centre Llangollen Wharf, across the road from Llangollen train station ☎ 01978 860702, ⓦ horsedrawnboats.co.uk. Offers taster rides in a horse-drawn narrowboat (45min; £6.50), horse-drawn trips to Horseshoe Falls (2hr; £12) and four-mile motorized trips to cross the Pontcysyllte Aqueduct (2hr; £13.50). Trips run Easter–Oct daily, Nov & Dec weekends.
Jones the Boats Trevor Basin, Pontcysyllte Aqueduct ☎ 01978 824166, ⓦ canaltrip.co.uk. Daily 45 minute narrowboat trips across the aqueduct and back (see opposite).

RAFTING AND GORGE WALKING

ProAdventure The Weavers Shed, Parade St ☎ 01978 861912, ⓦ proadventure.co.uk. Runs all sorts of adventure activities including whitewater rafting, canoeing and kayaking, gorge walking and rock climbing (each £50/half-day); book in advance.
Safe and Sound Outdoors Regent St ☎ 01978 860471, ⓦ sasoutdoors.co.uk. Offers rafting (£59/3hr session), and gorge walking, climbing/abseiling, MTB, kayaking and canoeing (all £50/half day).
Ty Nant Outdoors Plas Ifa, Sun Bank ☎ 01978 869326, ⓦ tynantoutdoors.com. Charges £49 for a half-day of kayaking, canoeing, hill/gorge walking, climbing/abseiling or quadbiking, or £59 for whitewater tubing or rafting.
Whitewater Active Regent St ☎ 01978 860763, ⓦ whitewateractive.co.uk. Runs modest whitewater rafting trips (£55/2hr session) at Mile End Mill, a mile upstream along Berwyn Road. You get several runs down a half-mile bouncy but unmenacing section of the Dee.

5

ACCOMMODATION

Llangollen is a fine place to **stay**, with a hostel, handy campsites and an abundance of comfortable B&Bs. For upscale **country retreats** head for the Vale of Edeyrnion beyond Corwen. Finding rooms can be a chore in the middle of summer, especially during the eisteddfod (the week beginning the first or second Tues of July), though this is alleviated by people letting out one or two bedrooms in the peak period; bookings are made through the TIC.

Cornerstones 15–19 Bridge St ☎01978 861569, ⓦcornerstones-guesthouse.co.uk. The over-the-top exuberance of this luxury B&B can easily be excused when you see the river views from three of the six rooms spread across three sixteenth-century houses; there's also a self-catering flat (with breakfast included). **£80**

Gales 18 Bridge St ☎01978 860089, ⓦgalesof llangollen.co.uk. Large rooms in a very comfortable and central guesthouse above the restaurant of the same name, some with brass beds and oak beams. **£80**

★**Glasgwm** Abbey Rd ☎01978 861975, ⓦglasgwm -llangollen.co.uk. Very relaxed B&B where the relatively modest facilities are compensated by engaging hosts whose good taste is reflected in the decor of the doubles, twin and single (which has its own deep bath). There's a piano, books aplenty, and they do Offa's Dyke Path pick-ups and drop-offs as well as packed lunches and dinners. **£60**

★**Llangollen Hostel** Berwyn St ☎01978 861773, ⓦllangollenhostel.co.uk. Neat bunks in modernized rooms (mostly en suite with 4–6 bunks) in a Victorian town house plus a well-equipped kitchen, comfy lounge and free wi-fi – all the ingredients for an excellent town-centre hostel. Bunks **£18**; doubles **£45**

Wild Pheasant Hotel Berwyn Rd, A5 half a mile west of Llangollen ☎01978 860629, ⓦwildpheasanthotel.co.uk. Venerable hotel with an older wing of standard rooms and a luxurious, tastefully decorated new wing, plus spacious suites. Guests can use the modern spa pool, steam room and sauna (£10 day pass). Check website for frequent deals. **£75**

CAMPING

Wern Isaf Farm ☎01978 860632, ⓦwernisaf.co.uk. Simple but idyllic farmhouse campsite on the flanks of Dinas Brân just under a mile steeply up Wern Road (turn right over the canal on Wharf Hill). Some hookups. Closed Nov–March. **£14**/pitch

EATING AND DRINKING

Bailey's Delicatessen Castle St, next to the TIC ☎01978 860617. Come here for fine picnic ingredients, ranging from pies, pasties and cold meats to cakes and more. Mon–Sat 9am–6pm.

★**The Corn Mill** Dee Lane ☎01978 869555, ⓦbrunningandprice.co.uk/cornmill. Superb conversion of a town-centre mill, with a deck by the Falls that catches the afternoon sun. Good all day for coffee, fine ales and well-prepared café-bar food such as beef and horseradish sandwiches (£6) and mains (£11–19) like almond-crusted trout and braised beef with mushrooms and mash. Daily 11am–11pm (Sun to 10.30pm); food served noon–9.30pm (Sun to 9pm).

★**Gales Wine Bar** 18 Bridge St ☎01978 860089, ⓦgalesofllangollen.co.uk. Old church pews, wooden floors, a blackboard menu of delicious, bistro-style food (mains £11–18) and a good selection of wines from around the world make this chilled-out place a long-standing favourite. Mon–Sat noon–2pm & 6–9.30pm.

The Gallery 15 Chapel St ☎01978 860076, ⓦthegalleryrestaurantllangollen.co.uk. Friendly evening-only restaurant serving a good range of medium-priced pizza and pasta dishes (also to take away). Tues–Sun 6–10pm (winter Wed–Sun).

Grouse Inn just off A5, 8 miles west of Llangollen ☎01490 430272, ⓦthegrouseinncarrog.co.uk. Smart, modernized country pub with freshly cooked meals and outdoor seating overlooking the River Dee, a 5min walk from the Llangollen Railway's Carrog station. Daily from noon to around midnight; food served noon–10pm.

Sun Inn Regent St. Convivial slate-floored late-closing locals' pub with basic meals for a fiver, a wide range of beers and live bands (of just about any stripe) most nights. Daily 5pm–1am or later.

ENTERTAINMENT

Outside the eisteddfod and its fringe, there's not a great deal of **nightlife**, but local bands (and occasionally bigger acts) do play from time to time.

Acrefair School Hall Just off the A539, 5 miles east of Llangollen. Côr Meibion Froncysyllte (ⓦfronchoir .com), one of Wales' most exalted male voice choirs, rehearses here Mon & Thurs 7–9pm; directions are on their website.

Royal International Pavilion Abbey Rd ☎01978 860111, ⓦllangollenpavilion.co.uk. With a covered stage and smaller hall, the eisteddfod site serves as a year-round venue for anything from choral and classical concerts to comedy and rock gigs.

FROM TOP CASTELL DINAS BRÂN (P.315); MYDDLETON ARMS HOTEL, RUTHIN (P.326) >

5

Corwen and around

In the early fifteenth century local landowner and scourge of Henry IV, Owain Glyndŵr, set out from **CORWEN**, ten miles west of Llangollen, to wrest back Wales from the English barons. In his time cattle-droving routes from Anglesey and from Harlech met at Corwen for the final push to the English markets. Later a rail junction, the town declined steadily once the line closed. The extension of the Llangollen Railway to a new station behind the health centre may reverse this, as Corwen could make a handy base for visiting parking-challenged Llangollen. More enticingly, Corwen has two fine **churches** and the bucolic charms of the **Vale of Edeyrnion** on its doorstep.

In the centre of town, a modern equestrian **statue** of Owain Glyndŵr looks set to terrorize his persecutors once again, and he is further recalled in the south porch of the thirteenth-century church of St Mael and St Sulien, where a cross incised into a grey stone lintel is known as **Glyndŵr's Sword**. He is said to have cast it in anger at the townspeople from the hill behind, though it actually predates him by half a millennium. Just east of the centre, the imposing cruciform workhouse (built in 1840) now houses craft shops and a café.

Rug Chapel

A494, 1 mile west of Corwen • April–Oct Wed–Sun 10am–5pm • £3.80 (includes Llangar Old Parish Church); CADW • ☎ 01490 412025

Taking its name from the Welsh word for heather, **Rug Chapel** is one of Wales' best examples of an unaltered seventeenth-century church. It gives a charming insight into worship almost four hundred years ago, when Mass was a private clerical devotion, with the congregation kept behind the rood screen.

Much here is as it was built in 1637 by the former privateer and collaborator on William Morgan's Welsh Bible (see box, p.396), William Salusbury. The plain exterior gives no hint of the richly decorated interior: wooden angels support a roof patterned with stars and amoebic swirls, and a painted skeleton representing the transient nature of life and the inevitability of death. Informative displays in the ticket office give more details.

Llangar Old Parish Church

Just off the B4401, 1 mile south of Rug Chapel • April–Oct Wed–Sun 12.30–2.30pm • Obtain ticket first at Rug Chapel

Built in the fourteenth century, this church was made redundant by parish boundary changes in 1853, saving its extensive fifteenth-century wall paintings and seventeenth-century figure of death from obliteration. The interior woodwork is wonderful, from the beamed roof and minstrel's gallery down to the eighteenth-century box pews.

The Vale of Edeyrnion

South of Corwen, the B4401 heads towards Bala through the **Vale of Edeyrnion** past a couple of the area's best country hotels. None of the vale's peaceful villages (Cynwyd, Llandrillo and Llandderfel) is particularly interesting, but all make convenient bases for hikes on the largely undiscovered Berwyn Range to the east, where you can walk all day without seeing a soul. The rather easier Tegid Way links the three villages with Bala.

ARRIVAL AND DEPARTURE

By bus Wrexham–Barmouth buses call at the Interchange behind *The Eagles Inn*.
Destinations Bala (8 daily; 40min); Llandrillo (8 daily; 15min); Llangollen (hourly; 20min); Ruthin (hourly; 25min, connecting to Rhyl).

ACCOMMODATION AND EATING

Bron-y-Graig A5, on the east edge of Corwen ☎ 01490 413007, ⊚ north-wales-hotel.co.uk. Comfortable, authentically renovated Victorian rooms in a house built for the Sheriff of Denbigh. Most rooms have a sofa and either river or forest views, and there's a reasonable restaurant. Assorted dinner, B&B and multi-night deals plus self-catering cottages. **£60**

Rhug Grill A5, 2 miles west of Corwen ☎ 01490 411100, ⓦ rhug.co.uk. Next to the Rhug Estate organic farm shop, this excellent bistro serves up popular bison burgers, as well as soup (£5), sandwiches (£6–11.50), à la carte meals (£11–26) and Sunday roast; also offers takeaways. Mon–Thurs 8am–5pm, Fri–Sun 8am–5.30pm, also from 7pm on selected Sats.

★ **Tyddyn Llan Country House** B4401 at Llandrillo, 6 miles southwest of Corwen ☎ 01490 440264, ⓦ tyddynllan.co.uk. Luxuriate in this elegant "restaurant with rooms" (thirteen of them), where a sense of calm descends as you pass through the gate. The rooms are as comfortable as you need, but the emphasis is on Bryan Webb's Michelin-starred Modern British food (2 courses for £45, 3 for £55, 6-course tasting menu £70). The restaurant is open to non-guests for dinner daily and for lunch Fri–Sun (2 courses for £21.50, 3 for £29). Mon–Thurs 7–9pm, Fri & Sat 12.30–2pm & 7–9pm, Sun 1–2.30pm & 7–8.30pm. **£195**

Tyn-y-Fron Llandderfel, B4401, 7 miles southwest of Corwen ☎ 01490 440346, ⓦ tynyfrontipi.co.uk. Beautiful, never crowded camping spot overlooking the bucolic Vale of Edeyrnion with dispersed tent sites and a bell tent fitted with a double and two single futons (bring sleeping bags), a warming chiminea, gas cooking hob and exterior fire pits. Also a cabin and an attractive self-catering cottage. Camping **£10**/pitch; bell tent for up to four **£35**; cabin **£40**; cottage (open all year; one-week min in summer) from **£150**/weekend

Bala and around

The little town of **BALA** (Y Bala) sits at the northern end of Wales' largest natural lake, **Llyn Tegid** (Bala Lake). The four-mile-long body of water is perfect for **windsurfing**, with steady winds whipping from the coast up the Talyllyn Valley, between the Aran and Arenig mountains that flank the lake.

Bala's second lake, **Llyn Celyn**, five miles northwest, is very much an artificial affair created amid huge controversy in the 1960s, to supply water to Liverpool, in England. A lakeside chapel commemorates the valley-bottom village of Capel Celyn, flooded by the reservoir.

Tomen-y-Bala

On Heol y Domen off the northern end of High St • Generally open 9am–dusk • Free

Bala has a role in Welsh history that far outweighs its current modest status. The Romans built a fort at the southern end of the lake (not open to the public), then Roger Mortimer erected a motte in about 1310. This tree-covered **Tomen-y-Bala** gives a panoramic view over the rooftops.

Bala Lake Railway

The Station, Llanuwchllyn • April–Sept 4 trains most days • £9.50 return, £6.50 single • ☎ 01678 540666, ⓦ bala-lake-railway.co.uk

The 24-in-gauge **Bala Lake Railway** follows the level, lakeside course of the former Ruabon–Barmouth standard-gauge line, closed in 1963. Renovated north Wales slate quarry trains are put to use for a pretty, if hardly thrilling, five-mile run. Either walk around the head of the lake to the northeastern end of the line (10min), or drive six miles southwest to the main terminus at Llanuwchllyn where you can combine your train trip with a visit to the *The Eagles Inn* (see p.323).

BALA IN LEGEND

Bala sits slightly back from the edge of Llyn Tegid, perhaps to avoid the legendary catastrophe that **drowned** the old town, which stood where the lake is now. The story tells of the **prince Tegid Foel**, who was warned by a voice that because of his cruelty to his people "Vengeance will come". On the birth of his son, he held a banquet at which a hired harpist heard a voice saying "Vengeance has come". A bird led him away onto a hill where he slept, waking to find the town submerged beneath the lake which took the prince's name.

The lake also has a **legendary beast** lurking in its waters, but thankfully the tourist hype about "Tegi" hasn't done to Bala what the Nessie industry has done in Scotland. On the other hand, the lake really is home to a species of fish found nowhere else, the Gwyniad or whitefish.

5

ARRIVAL AND DEPARTURE

By car With your own vehicle, the best approach is the A4212 from Blaenau Ffestiniog over the wild open moorlands between the twin peaks of Arenig Fawr and Arenig Fach. Unfortunately, this can't be done by public transport.

GETTING AROUND AND INFORMATION

Bike rental Available from R.H. Roberts at 7 High Street (☎01678 520252; £13/day).

Tourist office The TIC (April–Sept daily except Wed &

BALA AND AROUND

By bus Bala's only bus, the #X94, stops on the High Street. It runs from Wrexham through the Vale of Edeyrnion to Barmouth.

Destinations Corwen (8 daily; 35min); Dolgellau (hourly; 35min); Llandrillo (8 daily; 25min); Llangollen (8 daily; 1hr).

Thurs 10am–5pm; ☎01678 521021, ✉bala.tic @gwynedd.gov.uk) is on the A494, half a mile south of Bala along High Street.

ACCOMMODATION

★**Abercelyn** A494, 1 mile south of Bala ☎01678 521109, ⒲abercelyn.co.uk. The pick of the local mid-range places, this fine country house occupies an eighteenth-century former rectory. Rooms (two with bathtub) are stylishly understated, and there are also three self-catering cottages. One-night stays incur a £10–14 supplement. **£80**

Bala Backpackers 32 Heol Tegid ☎01678 521700, ⒲bala-backpackers.co.uk. Extensively renovated hostel in a central Bala house offering beds (linen hire £3) in both small dorms and larger ones partitioned into smaller areas. There are also private twins (some en suite), most in an adjacent house. Cook for yourself or order breakfast in advance (£4.50). Closed Oct–April (except by prior reservation). Dorms **£21**; standard doubles **£49**; en-suite doubles **£59**

Bala Bunk House A494 at Tomen-y-Castell, 1.5 miles north of Bala ☎01678 520738, ⒲balabunkhouse .co.uk. Self-catering bunkhouse with small dorms, one self-contained unit sleeping six, and communal lounge and cooking areas, plus an inviting barbecue area in the woods

at the back. Use your own sleeping bag or rent a duvet (£2). Dorms **£16**

Bryniau Golau Llangower, off B4403 ☎01678 521782, ⒲bryniau-golau.co.uk. Set in extensive grounds across the lake from the town, this B&B has three very spacious rooms richly decorated in antique country style and an elegant guest lounge; walkers and cyclists are very welcome. **£100**

Bryn Tegid Llanycil, A494 1.5 miles south of Bala ☎01678 521645, ⒲bryntegid.co.uk. Attractive country house surrounded by lovely grounds and woodland with two of the three spacious rooms overlooking Llyn Tegid. **£80**

Monfa 6 Pensarn Rd, A494 at south end of town ☎01678 521388, ✉helen.hotson1@btinternet.com. The cheapest B&B in town still maintains high standards with one double and one twin room each with private (but not en-suite) bathroom. You get bathrobes, free wi-fi and good single rates (£40). **£55**

THOMAS CHARLES, MARY JONES AND MICHAEL D. JONES

During the seventeenth and eighteenth centuries, the religious needs of the Welsh were poorly met by the established Church. None of the bishops was Welsh, few were resident, and most regarded their positions as stepping stones to higher appointments. This allowed the rise of the new Nonconformist sects – Quakers, Baptists and, later, Calvinist and Wesleyan Methodists. Itinerant religious teachers improved literacy and the strident sermons of native Welsh-speakers fired their enthusiasm. **Thomas Charles**, the chief protagonist of Methodism in Wales, gave the movement a massive boost by founding the British and Foreign Bible Society, a group committed to distributing local-language Bibles worldwide. His statue stands outside the Presbyterian church on Tegid Street.

Charles had already reprinted Bishop Morgan's 1588 original Welsh translation, but was down to his last copy when 16-year-old **Mary Jones**, the daughter of a poor weaver from the far side of Cadair Idris, arrived on his doorstep. She had saved money for six years to buy a Bible from Thomas Charles and, in 1800, walked the 25 miles to Bala, barefoot some of the way, prompting Charles to found the society.

Many of the more pious converts sought greater religious freedom, and in 1865 reformist preacher **Michael D. Jones** recruited around Bala for the 153 Welsh settlers who established Y Wladfa, "The Colony", in Argentine Patagonia. The remains can still be found in the Chubut Valley. Jones stayed in Wales, setting up the Bala-Bangor Theological College and leading campaigns for Welsh causes, and many now regard him as "the father of modern Welsh nationalism".

5

RAFTING AND WATERSPORTS AROUND BALA

The only real **whitewater-rafting** in Wales takes place on the Afon Tryweryn at the **National White Water Centre**, 4 miles northwest of Bala on the A4212 (☎01678 521083, ⓦukrafting .co.uk). Water is released on around two hundred days a year, crashing down a mile and a half of Grade III rapids where competitions often take place on summer weekends. It's interesting enough to drop by and watch what's going on; alternatively book ahead to take part in activities. There are all sorts of rafting options including the Taster (40–60min; £32, wetsuit hire extra) involving two runs down the course. The 2hr session (£66) typically gives you four runs, or you can step up a notch to the Orca Adventure (half-day; £88), involving two runs down in a normal raft followed by a chance to tackle the rapids in a more challenging two-person inflatable. Proficient **kayakers** with their own gear can take to the water for a fee of £14, and **canyoning** trips (£48 for half a day) are also on offer. The centre is open Dec to mid-Oct daily 9am–dusk, and parking costs £3.

By the shores of Llyn Tegid, the **Bala Adventure and Watersports Centre** (☎01678 521059, ⓦbalawatersports.com) runs numerous aquatic courses and rents out kayaks (£12/hr), windsurfers (£18/hr), sailing dinghies (£28/hr) and more

CAMPING

Pen-y-Bont B4319, 1 mile southeast of Bala ☎01678 520549, ⓦpenybont-bala.co.uk. Well-tended campsite that's the nearest to town, by the outlet of the lake. Along with tent and caravan sites they have a gypsy caravan (bring your own bedding). Closed Nov to mid-March. **£16/** pitch; caravan **£50**

Tyn Cornel A4212 4 miles northwest of Bala ☎01678 520759, ⓦtyncornel.co.uk. Camping and caravan park next to the National White Water Centre (see above); usually packed with paddlers at weekends. Closed Nov–Feb. **£7.50**/pitch

EATING AND DRINKING

The Eagles Inn 5 miles southwest of Bala at Llanuwchllyn ☎01678 540278, ⓦtheeagleinn-bala .co.uk. Cosy local half a mile from the Lake Railway station serving Purple Moose beers and excellent bar meals in hearty portions (mostly £8–12) with several vegetarian options and a kids' menu. Also handy for the male voice choir rehearsals which take place in the village hall at 7.30pm on Thurs. Book at weekends. Mon–Fri 6–11pm, Sat 11am–midnight, Sun noon–3pm & 6–11pm; food served daily 6–9pm plus Sat & Sun noon–2pm.

Plas-yn-Dre 23 High St ☎01678 521256. Spacious bistro popular with locals for dishes such as chicken penne (£12), char-grilled rib-eye (£17) or four vegetarian options (£9.50). There's decent espresso at its café next door. Daily noon–10pm.

Y Cyfnod 48 High St ☎01678 521260. A local legend, this simple café was founded in 1885 and is still going strong for breakfasts, sandwiches, panini and cheap, filling lunches. Daily 9am–5pm.

Mold and the Vale of Clwyd

One of the least-travelled paths through northwest Wales leaves the English Marches at **Mold**, crosses the soft contours of the **Clwydian Range** – along whose tops runs a section of the long-distance **Offa's Dyke Path** – and approaches the north coast through the wide and fertile **Vale of Clwyd**. Lying between England and Snowdonia, and between Powys and Gwynedd, this was known as Perfeddwlad or the Middle Country and was the heart of Tudor Wales, when many churches were rebuilt in a characteristic double-naved style. Gerard Manley Hopkins eulogized the valley where he studied for the priesthood in the 1870s, celebrating its beauty in some of his best-loved poems, *The Windhover*, *In the Valley of the Elwy* and *Pied Beauty*. Linked by quiet roads through a patchwork of small farms, two attractive market towns of warm-hued stone sit on hillocks above the valley. **Ruthin** is the pick of the two, with its thirteenth-century castle, compact core of medieval buildings, intriguing jail and a host of good places to stay. Seven miles northwest is **Denbigh**, best known for its "hollow crown", the high-walled castle ruin that rings the hilltop behind the town.

5

Mold

The slow pace of **MOLD** (Yr Wyddgrug) is only disrupted by its Wednesday and Saturday **markets**, when stalls supplant cars along the High Street. Despite much interesting history tied to the town, there's not much reason to linger.

Mold was founded during the reign of William Rufus, though only a copse of beeches atop the mound of **Bailey Hill** marks the site of the motte-and-bailey fortifications at the top of High Street. Its commanding view over the River Alyn (Afon Alun) shows the strategic value of the site which alternated between Welsh and Anglo-Norman control until Edward I's clampdown on the region. In 1465, during the War of the Roses, local lord Rheinallt ap Gruffydd captured the Mayor of Chester, took him back to the Tower in Nercwys and presented him with a pie containing the rope that would hang him.

St Mary's church

High St • Usually open Wed morning and Sat mornings in summer, or obtain key from J.H. Jones shop at 53 High St • Free • ⓦ moldchurch.org

In gratitude for Henry VII's victory, his mother, Margaret Beaufort, commissioned the airy Perpendicular **St Mary's church**, set serenely on a grassy hillock. The north aisle retains its original oak roof carved with Tudor roses, and there's a quatrefoil and animal frieze outside beneath the small clerestory windows.

Among the Tudor stained glass, a Victorian window is Mold's meagre memorial to its most famous son (at least to English-speakers) and Wales' greatest painter, the eighteenth-century landscapist **Richard Wilson**, whose grave is by the church's north entrance. Although Wilson co-founded the Royal Academy in 1768 and was acclaimed by Ruskin, his work was undervalued and he died a pauper.

Mold Museum

Inside the library, Earl Rd • Mon, Tues, Thurs & Fri 9.30am–7pm, Wed 9.30am–5.30pm, Sat 9.30am–3pm • Free • ☎ 01352 754791

Local tailor and novelist **Daniel Owen** (1836-95) is commemorated by a statue outside the library. "Not for the wise and learned have I written but for the common people" is inscribed below, and it was his bluntly honest accounts of ordinary life that made him so unpopular with the Methodist leaders of the community. Writing only in Welsh, Owen became his country's most prominent writer. A little museum inside contains a small but effective display on the man, as well as a replica of the **Mold Cape**, an almost four-thousand-year-old beaten gold ceremonial garment discovered nearby in 1833. The original is in the British Museum.

Loggerheads Country Park

A494, 3 miles west of Mold • Park daily: Easter–Aug 8am–9pm; Sept–Easter 8am–6pm; Visitor Centre May–Oct daily 10am–5pm; Nov–April Sat & Sun 10am–4pm • ⓦ denbighshire.gov.uk

For peaceful walks beside the trickling River Alyn it's hard to beat family-oriented **Loggerheads Country Park**. Except for an old water channel and water wheel by the mile-long Industrial Trail, you'd barely know this was a busy lead-mining area in the nineteenth century.

ARRIVAL AND INFORMATION   MOLD

By bus Buses stop behind the cattle market on Hallfields, east of High Street.

Destinations Chester (every 30min; 50min); Flint (every 30min; 20min); Loggerheads (9 daily; 10min); Ruthin (hourly; 25–45min); Wrexham (every 20min; 40min–1hr).

Discover Flintshire Visitor Centre In the same building as the library and museum on Earl Road (Easter–Oct Mon–Fri 9.30am–5pm, Sat 9.30am–3pm; Nov–Easter Mon–Fri 9.30am–4pm; ☎ 01352 759331, ⓦ moldtouristinformationcentre.co.uk).

ACCOMMODATION

Beaufort Park Hotel Alltami Rd ☎ 01352 758646, ⓦ beaufortparkhotel.co.uk. A modern conference/ business hotel with serried ranks of spacious rooms in a rural setting plus a decent restaurant and coffee bar. Rooms

are heavily discounted when booked online (sometimes from as little as £51 a room). **£130**
Tower Nercwys Rd ☎ 0135 700220, ⊛ towerwales.co.uk

A mile south of Mold, this fortified manor, owned by the same family for five centuries, has just three plush rooms full of antique furniture and family portraits. **£80**

EATING AND DRINKING

Alexander's 52 High St ☎ 07912 159802. Facing the church, this is ideal for cooked breakfasts, tasty panini, salads and good espresso; the atmosphere is buzzing and it may be hard to find a table. Mon–Sat 9am–5pm.

Caffi Florence Loggerheads Country Park ☎ 01352 759225, ⊛ caffiflorence.co.uk. Extensive lawns outside Loggerheads' excellent café make a great spot for salads, sandwiches, hot lunches and afternoon teas, all made on site with love. Coffee is Fairtrade and they are dedicated to sourcing locally. Daily 10am–5pm.

Glasfryn Raikes Lane, 1 mile north of Mold off A5119

☎ 01352 750500, ⊛ brunningandprice.co.uk/glasfryn. Head here for high-class pub fare (mains £11–17) and an ever-changing range of real ales, best enjoyed on the terrace with views over the fields towards Mold. Mon–Sat 11am–11pm, Sun noon–10.30pm; food served daily noon–9.30pm.

Y Delyn 3 King St ☎ 01352 759642. Behind a plain red-brick Georgian facade, this cosy bar is renowned for its Belgian beers but also has a good choice of real ales and a fine wine list, and has recently started serving tapas (3 for £12). Tues–Sat 6pm–1am; food served 6.30–9pm.

The Clwydian Range

Mold is separated from the Vale of Clwyd by the wide-open spaces of the **Clwydian Range**, six miles west of town, easily accessed west of Loggerheads, where the B5429 branches right off the A494 following an old turnpike route between Mold and Ruthin. It climbs up to **Bwlch Penbarras**, a shallow pass where the road meets the **Offa's Dyke Path** (though not the Dyke itself), which follows the line of a Bronze Age trading route along these bald tops, passing the remains of six Iron Age hillforts. The highest point is the 1820ft **Moel Famau**, topped by a truncated **Jubilee Tower**. The subject of much disparaging comment when it was built in 1810 to celebrate George III's fifty-year reign, the 85ft-high obelisk collapsed in a storm in 1862 and was only partially repaired in 1970; in 2013 new stairs were built to a viewpoint atop the base. On a clear day views as far as Snowdon and Cadair Idris make a walk out here worthwhile (see box below). The relatively gentle terrain makes this a popular spot at weekends: stick to weekdays if possible.

ARRIVAL AND INFORMATION   THE CLWYDIAN RANGE

By bus The Clwydian Range is easily accessible on public transport, using buses #1 or #X1 between Mold and Ruthin; additionally, from mid-July to Aug a shuttle bus runs several

times a day between Loggerheads and Bwlch Penbarras.
Tourist information See ⊛ visitclwydianrange.co.uk and ⊛ clwydianrangeaonb.org.uk.

Ruthin

With its attractive knot of half-timbered buildings, a handful of sights and some of the finest food and lodging in the area, **RUTHIN** (Rhuthun), ten miles west of Mold, should not be missed. The town, built on a commanding rise in the Vale of Clwyd, is centred around **St Peter's Square**, the hub of the town's medieval street plan.

WALKS TO FOEL FENLLI AND MOEL FAMAU

From the car park at Bwlch Penbarras (small charge) you can make the steep climb southwards to the most impressive of the Clwydian hillfort sites on 1800ft **Foel Fenlli** (1 mile return; 40min; 500ft ascent). Excavations have uncovered 35 hut circles within earthworks three-quarters of a mile across. The height from ditch bottom to bank top reaches 35ft in places, with triple defences on the more vulnerable eastern flank.

From the same car park, a broad path leads a mile and a half north to **Moel Famau** (3 miles return; 1–2hr; 650ft ascent) and the Jubilee Tower.

For more **information**, pick up the leaflet *Clwydian Range* from Loggerheads.

5

Myddleton Arms
St Peter's Square

Ruthin's most photographed building is the **Myddleton Arms** (now part of the Castle Hotel), built in 1657 in Dutch style and topped by seven dormer windows known as "The Eyes of Ruthin", which overlook the square.

St Peter's church
St Peter's Square • Daily 9am–4pm or thereabouts • Free

St Peter's church is approached via a photogenic pair of iron gates wrought in 1727 by the Davies Brothers (who also made the gates of St Giles' church in Wrexham and Chirk Castle). The ceiling of its north aisle consists of 408 carved black oak panels with Tudor Rose bosses, brought from Basingwerk Abbey (see p.392) after its dissolution by Henry VIII. Get someone to turn the lights on for you if possible. One of the busts by the altar is of Gabriel Goodman who, in 1574, while Dean of Westminster, re-founded the **grammar school** that had been closed by Henry VIII forty years earlier; the building still stands behind the church, next to the Christ's Hospital Almshouses, also given to the town by Goodman in 1590.

Maen Huail
St Peter's Square

Outside Barclays Bank (aka Exmewe Hall) sits an unimpressive chunk of limestone known as **Maen Huail**. A less-than-convincing story has King Arthur and Huail, brother of a Welsh chieftain called Gildas, fighting over the attentions of a woman. Huail pierced Arthur's thigh, giving him a permanent limp, but promised never to mention Arthur's loss of face. Inevitably, though, Huail couldn't resist taunting him about it and an incensed Arthur had him beheaded on this stone.

The old courthouse and prison
St Peter's Square

One of the many timber-framed buildings around town is now the NatWest bank. Built in 1401 as a courthouse and prison, it still retains under the eaves the barely visible stump of a **gibbet**, last used in 1679 to hang a Franciscan priest.

Nantclwyd y Dre
Castle St, just off St Peter's Square • April–Sept Fri–Sun 10am–5pm, mid-July to Aug also Mon & Tues • £4 • ☎ 01824 709822, ⓦ nantclwyddydre.co.uk

The restored, timber-framed **Nantclwyd y Dre** partly dates from 1435, making this medieval hall-house the oldest in Wales. Restored from near dereliction using ancient techniques, it's a wonderfully higgledy-piggledy place, with wonky oak floors, interesting nooks and crannies and a general sense of nosing around someone's home. The house has been extended and updated over five centuries, and the major phases of its existence have been re-created in seven main rooms including Jacobean and Georgian bed chambers, a Stuart study, a Victorian schoolroom and an entrance hall of 1942, looking much as it did when the last family moved out in 1984. Outside there's a walled garden and a pretty little summerhouse.

Ruthin Gaol
Clwyd St, 300yds west of St Peter's Square • April–Sept Wed–Mon 10am–5pm • £4 • ☎ 01824 708281, ⓦ ruthingaol.co.uk

Ruthin Gaol has been a prison site since 1654, but the so-called "Gruelling Experience" focuses on the Victorian era and the four-storey cell block (1867) inspired by London's Pentonville. It was designed to improve living conditions and penal correction, with one prisoner per cell and the requirement to work while incarcerated. Most upper-floor cells now house the county archive, but you can poke around elsewhere, following the free audioguide which traces the prison life of a mythical "Will the Poacher". Informative panels in the lower cells and prison kitchen explain daily prison life and behind-the-scenes operations along with the real meaning of "screws" and "bobbies" and the source of the expression "money for old rope". One tale tells of John Jones, the "Welsh Houdini", who seemingly spent half his life escaping from prisons. He absconded from Ruthin in 1913 before being shot five days later.

Ruthin Craft Centre

Park Rd, 300yds northeast of St Peter's Square • Daily 10am–5.30pm • Free • ☎ 01824 704774, ⓦ ruthincraftcentre.org.uk

Save some time for the excellent **Ruthin Craft Centre**, Wales' centre for the applied arts, in a modern zinc-and-stone building housing three galleries, six artists' studios, workshops, a shop and excellent café. Exhibits are likely to include superb contemporary glass and ceramic wares as well as more traditional woodworking.

Ruthin Castle

Castle St • ☎ 01824 702664, ⓦ ruthincastle.co.uk

Hidden away in the trees on the southern edge of town lie the restored, red sandstone ruins of **Ruthin Castle**. It was built for Edward I in 1277 and by 1400 was owned by Lord de Grey of Ruthin, who used his influence with Henry IV to have Owain Glyndŵr declared a traitor and acquire his land. In response, Glyndŵr crowned himself Prince of Wales and stormed Ruthin on market day, plundering the goods being sold by the English and then razing the town. The castle went on to resist the Parliamentarians for eleven weeks during the Civil War, after which it was destroyed. A neo-Gothic mansion was built in 1856, with Italian and rose gardens landscaped around the ancient moat and crumbling ruins, and became a **hotel** in 1963. Strictly speaking, the grounds are open to residents and peacocks only, but you can wander around if eating or drinking here.

ARRIVAL AND INFORMATION   **RUTHIN**

By bus Buses stop at the corner of Market Street and Wynnstay Street.
Destinations Corwen (hourly; 25min); Denbigh (every 30min; 20min); Mold (hourly; 40min); Rhyl (hourly;

55min), Wrexham (hourly; 45min).
Tourist office 7 St Peter's Square ☎ 01824 702823, ⓔ hello@ruthintourism.co.uk, ⓦ visitruthin.com.
Internet Free access at the library on Record Street.

ACCOMMODATION

★**Firgrove** B5105, 1 mile southeast of Ruthin in Llanfwrog ☎ 01824 702677, ⓦ firgrovecountryhouse .co.uk. A large Georgian house with manicured gardens, offering B&B and one self-catering cottage. Everything is done with an understated elegance, and the three-course dinners (£30) are superb. **£80**

★**Manorhaus** 10 Well St ☎ 01824 704830, ⓦ manorhaus ruthin.com. Fluffy duvets, bright colours and bold artworks characterize this eight-room boutique hotel in a Georgian house, complete with a small gym, sauna, DVD/CD, book and

games library, and excellent restaurant and bar (see p.328). **£95**
Minffordd Campsite 2 miles north of Ruthin, just east of Rhewl ☎ 01824 707169. Simple tent- and campervan-only site: follow signs for Gellifor then turn right 150yds after a pair of stone bridges. Closed Oct–Easter. **£6**/pitch
Rhydonnen Llanychan, 3 miles north of Ruthin ☎ 01824 790258, ⓦ rhydonnen.co.uk. A well-appointed B&B in a fifteenth-century black-and-white farmhouse with oak beams and inglenooks aplenty; there's a pool table and fantastic home baking. **£60**

MOUNTAIN BIKING AT COED LLANDEGLA

Some of the best **mountain biking** in northeast Wales is in **Llandegla Forest** (late March to late Oct Mon–Thurs 9am–9pm, Fri–Sun 9am–6pm; late Oct to late March daily 9am–dusk), roughly 9 miles from Ruthin, Llangollen and Wrexham. Trails range from a gentle, family-friendly loop to technically challenging black runs and extreme freeriding options. There's a visitor centre (Tues–Sun 9am–5.30pm) with a café, workshop and bike rental (£22/half-day, £32/day; ☎ 01978 751656, ⓦ oneplanetadventure.com).

5

Sir John Trevor House 7 Castle St ☎01824 703176, ⓦsirjohntrevorhouse.co.uk. This half-timbered Elizabethan town house makes a delightful B&B in the heart of the town, with three spacious en-suite double rooms. **£75**

EATING AND DRINKING

★**Leonardo's Deli** 4 Well St ☎01824 707161. Great little deli/bakery where quality is paramount. Take away a superb stuffed baguette, a toothsome steak and red wine pie or a delectable tarte tatin. April–Oct Mon–Fri 8.30am–5pm, Sat 8.30am–4.30pm; Nov–March Mon–Thurs 9am–3.30pm, Fri 9am–4.30pm, Sat 9am–3pm.

★**Manorhaus** 10 Well St ☎01824 704830, ⓦmanorhausruthin.com. Stylish decor, subdued lighting and understated service make this a superb place for dinner (£25/30 for 2/3 courses), which might include smoked haddock rarebit or twice-cooked belly pork. Desserts are delicious and there's a good wine list. Wed–Sun 6.30–9pm.

On the Hill Restaurant 1 Upper Clwyd St ☎01824 707736, ⓦonthehillrestaurant.co.uk. This cosy wood-floored restaurant with oak beams is hard to beat for its bistro-style meals (mains £13–15.50) with personal service. Lunch comes as just a main (£11), two courses (£14) or three (£17). They do a great pudding sampler and have a well-thought-out wine list (£5/glass). Tues–Sat noon–2pm & 6.30–9pm, Sun 5–9pm.

Ruthin Castle Castle St ☎01824 702664, ⓦruthincastle.co.uk. Nip into this grand and extensively refurbished baronial castle for a bar meal or a drink in the panelled library bar. They also do ersatz Welsh medieval banquets (£42). Restaurant daily 6.30–9pm.

Ye Olde Cross Keys B5105, 1 mile southeast of Ruthin in Llanfwrog ☎01824 705281. Welcoming pub serving bar meals well above the normal standard but at modest prices. Daily noon–3pm & 6–10pm.

Denbigh and around

The castle ruins dominating the Vale of Clwyd eight miles north of Ruthin herald **DENBIGH** (Dinbych), in medieval times a fortified hill town, which still tumbles down towards its old centre where the Wednesday market takes place.

High Street is surrounded by a pleasing array of colonnaded medieval buildings which, thankfully, haven't been over-restored, helping retain the feel of a working town. From the eastern end of High Street several lanes run up past the crumbling **Burgess Gate**, the town's former northern entry, to the vast grassy ward of the ruined **Denbigh Castle**.

Brief history

For a long time, the River Clwyd formed the border of England and Wales, guarded here by a now vanished Welsh castle, which probably gave the town its name, meaning "small fort". The castle eventually fell to the English, enabling Edward I to fortify Rhuddlan and Ruthin, and entrust Denbigh to Henry de Lacy, Earl of Lincoln, who from 1282 employed Edward's experienced military architect, James of St George, to build a modern fortress. Much later, in 1841, Denbigh was the birthplace of Henry Morton "Dr Livingstone, I presume?" Stanley (then known as John Rowlands), commemorated by a new statue in front of the library.

Denbigh Castle

Castle Lane • April–Oct daily 10am–5pm; Nov–March daily 10am–4pm • April–Oct £3.50; Nov–March Mon–Thurs free, Fri & Sat £3.50; CADW • ☎01745 813385

Denbigh Castle's most imposing remnant is the **gatehouse**, with three octagonal towers enclosing an originally vaulted hall, making it one of the finest defensive structures of the era. You enter beneath a weathered statue of Edward I in a niche, flanked on the right by the Prison Tower (stained by five garderobes discharging into a common cesspit) and the Porter's Lodge Tower on the left. From here, you can walk atop the wall as far as the Great Kitchen Tower. On the far side, the Postern Tower was heavily strengthened after the Welsh revolt of 1294, as were the **town walls** that branched from the castle walls to form the outer ward. Continue along the short section of wall walk (key from the castle office, the library or the *Green Onion* café) down to the **Goblin Tower** from where in 1646 Sir William Salusbury threw the castle keys onto the heads of the all-conquering Roundheads, ending a six-month-long siege only after receiving the king's written order to surrender.

In 1563, Elizabeth I sold the castle to her favourite, Robert Dudley, Earl of Leicester, who in 1579 chose a site just below the castle for the Puritan church he hoped would supplant St Asaph cathedral, four miles north. It was never completed, but the shell still stands today as **Leicester's Folly**.

St Dyfnog's church

Just off the A525 at Llanrhaeadr, 3 miles south of Denbigh • Daily 10am–4pm or later • Free

St Dyfnog's church seems much too large for this tiny hamlet. In the sixth century St Dyfnog established a hermitage here on the site of a healing well, and donations from pilgrims funded the building of the present church in 1533. Typically for the area it has twin naves and, though heavily restored in 1880, drips with original features, including a glorious carved barrel roof with vine-leaf patterns and outstanding stained glass.

The **Jesse Window**, at the east end of the north aisle, depicts the descent of Jesus through the House of Israel from Jesse, the father of King David. One of the finest in Britain, it draws you in to the Virgin and Child, surrounded by 21 of their bearded, ermine-robed ancestors, their names recorded in medieval Latin. The window is believed to be contemporary with the church, though it was removed and stored in an oak chest during the Civil War, which is when its companion in the south aisle is thought to have been destroyed. In the nineteenth century fragments which may have belonged to it were found nearby and pieced together to form the west window.

ARRIVAL AND INFORMATION

By bus Buses stop centrally on High Street.
Destinations Rhyl (every 30min; 40min); Ruthin (every 30min; 20min); St Asaph (every 30min; 15min).
Tourist information The County Hall (built in 1572)

DENBIGH AND AROUND

contains the library (Mon 9.30am–7pm, Tues, Wed & Fri 9.30am–5pm, Thurs 1–5pm, Sat 9.30am–12.30pm), which has free internet access and a supply of tourist information leaflets. The website ⊛ visitdenbigh.co.uk is also useful.

ACCOMMODATION

Castle House Bull Lane ☎ 01745 816860, ⊛ castlehousebandb.co.uk. Three wonderfully luxurious rooms in one of Denbigh's finest houses – sharing the grounds of Leicester's Folly just below the castle – plus two separate cottages all with ornate furnishings and long views. Great guests' lounge and lovely grounds. **£140**
Cayo Guesthouse 74 Vale St ☎ 01745 812686, ✉ stay @cayo.co.uk. Long-standing Denbigh favourite in a homely Victorian house with large bedrooms, comfy beds and a great breakfast. Excellent value. **£60**
Guildhall Tavern Hall Square ☎ 01745 816533,

⊛ guildhalltavernhotel.co.uk. Classy modern reworking of a town-centre hotel, whose eleven rooms all sport chic design features while retaining plenty of character. There's a great bar and restaurant downstairs. **£79**
Station House Caravan Park A541, 4 miles northeast of Denbigh in Bodfari ☎ 01745 710372, ⊛ stationhouse caravanpark.co.uk. Denbigh's handiest campsite in a blissful rural setting close to the Offa's Dyke Path. A good range of facilities and a couple of pubs within an easy walk. Reached on bus #14. Closed mid-Oct to mid-March. **£12**/pitch

EATING AND DRINKING

Glass Onion 1 Back Row ☎ 01745 813125, ⊛ glassonioncafe.co.uk. Relaxed café good for inexpensive home-cooked daytime meals (including gluten-free and vegetarian options) plus free wi-fi, community information and local arts and crafts for sale. Mon–Fri 9am–4pm, Sat & Sun 10am–3pm.
Guildhall Tavern Hall Square ☎ 01745 816533, ⊛ guildhalltavernhotel.co.uk. A cosy but stylish renovation. Excellent ales, a good wine list and a modern take on quality pub fare (mains £8–17). Mon–Weds & Sun noon–10.30pm, Thurs–Sat noon–11.30pm; food served

Mon–Sat noon–2.30pm & 6–9pm, Sun noon–4pm.
★**White Horse Inn** 5 miles southeast of Denbigh at Hendrerwydd ☎ 01824 790218, ⊛ whitehorsere staurant.co.uk. Superb country gastropub in a sixteenth-century inn. They really care about their food and drink here, whether it be British tapas such as Menai mussels (£5), a pub classic such as fish, chips and peas (£12), or pork belly with caramelized apples and black pudding (£16). Monday curry night is excellent value. Mon 6–11pm, Wed–Sat 11am–11pm.

Snowdonia and the Llŷn

CWM IDWAL

Snowdonia and the Llŷn

The mountains of Snowdonia (Yr Eryri) are north Wales' defining feature, not just in their physical form but in the way they have shaped the communities within them. Huddled between the north-coast resorts and the thinly inhabited hills of mid-Wales, this mountainous kernel seemed to Henry VIII's antiquarian, John Leland, as "horrible with the sight of bare stones". The Romantics changed all that and the region is often acclaimed as the most inspiring in Wales – certainly by walkers and climbers. This is a compact land of sharp ridges and glacial valleys where sheer faces belie that the tallest peaks only just top three thousand feet. Little more than ten miles by ten, this tightly packed bundle of soaring cliffs, jagged peaks and plunging waterfalls has enough mountain paths to keep even the most jaded walking enthusiast happy for weeks. It's home to Wales's highest mountain, Snowdon (Eryri), where snows cling to 3000ft peaks well into April. Further to the west lies the Llŷn, a peninsula that juts into the Celtic Sea at a near right angle to the Cambrian coast. The Welsh castle at Criccieth, and the museum devoted to Lloyd George a couple of miles away, are good reasons to pause before Wales ends in a flourish of small coves around Abersoch and Aberdaron.

Snowdonia

With everything from woodland strolls to mountain scrambles, **SNOWDONIA** is fabulous walking country, and the small valley settlements make great bases or places to rest. Foremost among these is the Victorian resort town of **Betws-y-Coed**, very much a stop for the coach-tour brigade. The smaller walkers' hamlets of **Capel Curig** and **Pen-y-Pass** have a more robust atmosphere. The clear focus of the region is **Snowdon**,

WALKING IN SNOWDONIA

Highlights

❶ Tryfan Some of the finest hikes in Snowdonia converge on this craggy summit, where a leap between two monoliths crowns the day. **See p.346**

❷ National Slate Museum, Llanberis Learn about the lives and labours of those who worked the massive slate quarries hewn out of Llanberis's hillsides. **See p.351**

❸ Snowdon Scale Wales' highest mountain, the only one with half a dozen hiking paths and a cog railway converging on the summit-top café and bar. **See p.354**

❹ Caernarfon Castle Scramble around the walls of the mightiest link in Edward I's chain of Norman castles. **See p.356**

❺ Blaenau Ffestiniog Wales's slate capital – a tremendously atmospheric town, surrounded by mountains and rich in industrial heritage. **See p.364**

❻ Ffestiniog Railway The finest of Wales's narrow-gauge railways climbs 13 miles from the coast into the heart of the mountains. **See p.370**

❼ Portmeirion Spend the day at this surreal seaside "village", made from bits of rescued architecture and the setting for the cult TV series, *The Prisoner*. **See p.373**

❽ Ynys Enlli A point of Christian pilgrimage for centuries, this windswept sea-bird-strewn "Island of the Currents" is the destination for Wales' best offshore day-trip. **See p.383**

HIGHLIGHTS ARE MARKED ON THE MAP ON P.335

reached by superb hikes and a cog railway from **Llanberis**. Yet with the northern heimsphere's longest zipwire ride, a downhill mountain-bike descent and, by 2015, the world's first public surfing lake, the region is gunning for a reputation as the adrenaline capital of Britain. You're surprisingly close to the coast, too, specifically the stronghold of **Caernarfon**, where a mighty castle guards the entrance to the Menai Strait.

Close to Snowdon, other mountains are equally dramatic, often far less busy, and give unsurpassed views of Snowdon. The **Glyderau** and **Tryfan** are particular favourites, both best tackled from the **Ogwen Valley**. Elsewhere, most settlements tend to coincide with some enormous mine or quarry, notably at **Beddgelert**, where former copper mines are open to the public, and **Blaenau Ffestiniog**, the former "Slate Capital of north Wales", which is now leading the charge for white-knuckle rides by zipwire and mountain bike.

To the west, the mountain landscape bleeds into softer coastal contours around the harbour town of **Porthmadog**, linked to Snowdonia by the magnificent, narrow-gauge **Ffestiniog Railway** but more famous for the nearby Italianate dream village of **Portmeirion**.

Brief history

It was to this mountain fastness that Llywelyn ap Gruffydd, the last true Prince of Wales, retreated in 1277 after his first war with Edward I; it was also here that Owain Glyndŵr held on most tenaciously to his dream of regaining the title for the Welsh. Centuries later, the English came to remove the mountains; slate barons built huge fortunes from Welsh toil and reshaped the patterns of Snowdonian life forever, as men looking for steady work in the quarries fled the hills and became town dwellers.

From the late eighteenth century, Snowdonia became the focus for the first truly structured approach to **geological research**. The last Ice Age left a legacy of peaks ringed by cwms – huge hemispherical bites out of the mountainsides – while the ranges were left separated by steep-sided valleys, a challenge for even the most fly-footed climber. Scoured valley walls, scalloped mountainsides and hanging valleys became the first reliable evidence of the last Ice Age and its retreat ten thousand years ago. These pioneer geologists created the rock-type classifications familiar to any students of the discipline: Cambrian rock takes its name from the Roman name for Wales, Ordovician and Silurian rocks from the Celtic tribes, the Ordovices and the Silures.

Botanists found rare alpine flora, writers produced libraries full of purple prose, and Richard Wilson, Paul Sandby and J.M.W. Turner all came to **paint** the landscape, alerting the leisured classes to the area's beauty. Soon, those with the means began flocking here to marvel at the plunging waterfalls and walk the ever-widening mountain paths of Wales's first and largest national park (see box below).

SNOWDONIA NATIONAL PARK

In recognition of the region's scientific importance, as well as its scenic and recreational appeal, **Snowdonia National Park** (Parc Cenedlaethol Eryri; ⓦeryri-npa.gov.uk) was set out in 1951, becoming Wales's first, and still largest, national park. Covering 823 square miles of northwest Wales (more than the central part of Snowdonia covered in this chapter) it runs all the way from Conwy to Aberdyfi encompassing the Rhinogs, Cadair Idris and 23 miles of the Cambrian coast. Jagged mountains predominate, but the harsh lines come tempered by broadleaf lowland woods around calm glacial lakes, waterfalls tumbling from hanging valleys and complex coastal dune systems. You won't find total wilderness, however: sheep and cattle farming supports many of the 27,000 people who live in the park (some 65 percent of them Welsh-speakers) and another fourteen million people come here each year to tramp almost 2000 miles of designated paths. Most open areas are "access land" where you have freedom to roam anywhere. In apparent contradiction to its name, the national park is 75 percent privately owned by the Forestry Commission and National Trust. However, trespass isn't usually a problem as long as you keep to the ancient rights of way and access areas.

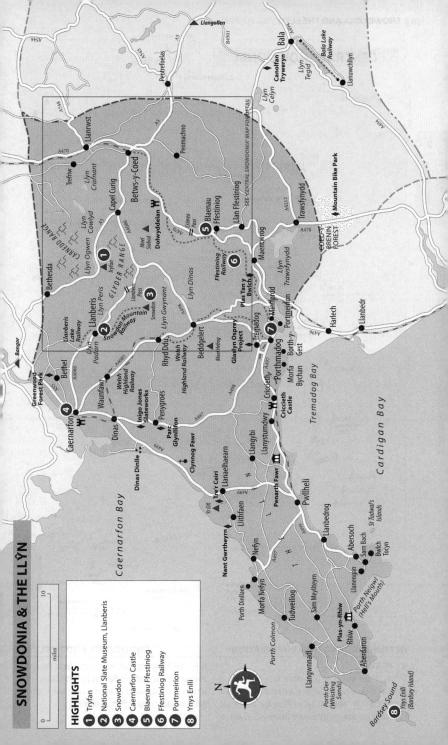

6

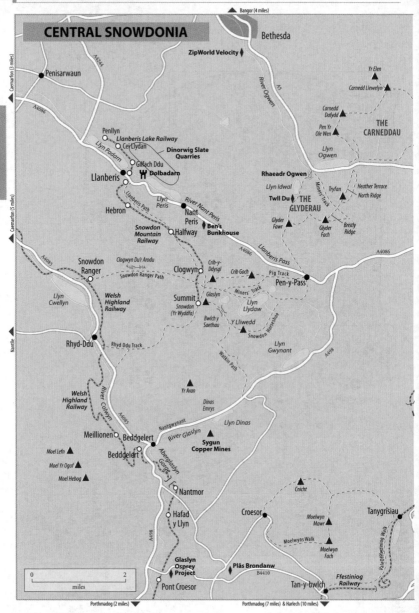

CENTRAL SNOWDONIA

GETTING AROUND AND INFORMATION

BY TRAIN

Getting to the fringes of Snowdonia from elsewhere in Wales is relatively easy: mainline trains run along the coast to nearby Bangor, while the Conwy Valley line branches at Llandudno Junction, penetrating to Betws-y-Coed and on

SNOWDONIA AND THE LLŶN

to Blaenau Ffestiniog. Here, you can transfer to the useful and highly scenic Ffestiniog Railway for Porthmadog – the latter is also a stop on the Cambrian Coast line, shuffling daily around the coast to Pwllheli on the Llŷn.

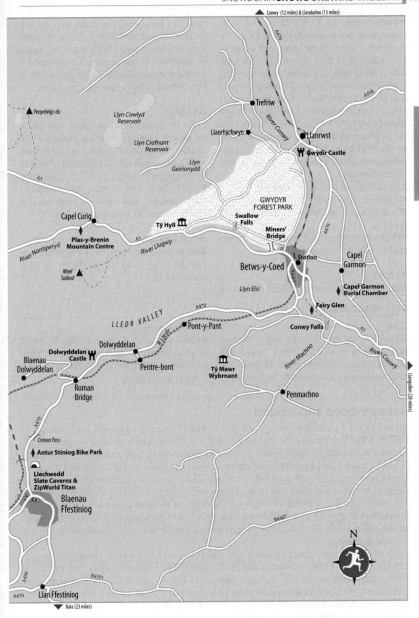

BY BUS

There are frequent bus services from Llandudno Junction (close to Llandudno and Conwy) up the Conwy Valley to Llanrwst (the area's bus hub) and Betws-y-Coed. From there, the Snowdon Sherpa services (see p.338) provide access to Llanberis, Beddgelert, Porthmadog, Bangor and Caernarfon. Pwllheli is the hub for transport on the Llŷn, with buses to most of the peninsula. Routes and times are detailed online via ⓦ gwynedd.co.uk or on leaflets from TICs and bus stations. Check Basics (see p.31) for discount fares and passes (some of which cover the region's narrow-gauge railways).

6

Snowdon Sherpa bus In central Snowdon, visitors are encouraged to park in surrounding towns and use the comprehensive Snowdon Sherpa bus system (timetables via ⓦgwynedd.co.uk) to access the mountains. This avoids finding trailhead parking (and the fees) and opens up hiking routes using buses to link the paths. The Snowdon Sherpa is a catch-all name for a handful of interconnecting bus services plying the roads between Betws-y-Coed, Bethesda, Llanberis, Caernarfon and Porthmadog. Most meet at Pen-y-Pass. That said, the service was in flux on our last visit after route provider operator Padarn Bus closed. Amateur wesbite ⓦswisstitalian paddlesteamers.com/snowdonsherpa is a good online source for current information.

Major routes through northern Snowdonia are:

#S1 Llanberis to Pen-y-Pass via Nant Peris

#S2 Betws-y-Coed to Llanberis via Capel Curig and Pen-y-Pass

#S4 Caernarfon to Pen-y-Pass via Waunfawr and Beddgelert

#S97 Pen-y-Pass to Porthmadog via Beddgelert

BY BIKE

Roads are well surfaced but well travelled, making cycle touring here less appealing than it might seem. That said, the views are great, parking isn't a problem and quieter roads on the Llŷn are perfect for relaxed pedalling. You can also explore the ever-expanding network of cycle tracks and get off-road at Blaenau Ffestiniog, as well as Coed-y-Brenin (see p.294) and the Gwydir Forest near Betws-y-Coed.

ON FOOT

If you're serious about doing some walking – and some of the walks described here *are* serious, especially in bad weather (Snowdon gets 200 inches of rain a year) – you need a good map, such as the OS 1:25,000 OL17 ("Snowdon & Conwy Valley") or the 1:50,000 115 ("Snowdon/Yr Wyddfa"). Always check mountain weather conditions before setting out: latest reports are usually posted in outdoor shops and TICs, or visit ⓦmetcheck.com.

INFORMATION

Website Most of this chapter falls within the county of Gwynedd – see ⓦdiscovergwynedd.com for more information.

ACCOMMODATION

Areas Accommodation is limited inside the Snowdonia National Park and most is on the fringes. The main exception is Betws-y-Coed, a resort packed with guesthouses that are all busy in summer. Elsewhere, B&Bs, hostels, bunkhouses and basic campsites are mostly geared towards walkers and climbers.

Hostels In all, there are six YHA hostels within five miles of Snowdon's summit and a further half-dozen other budget places, making walking from one to another possible with a medium-sized backpack.

Betws-y-Coed and around

Spread in a flat plain around the confluence of the Conwy, Llugwy and Lledr valleys, **BETWS-Y-COED** (pronounced "betoos-er-coyd") is almost totally devoted to the needs of visitors, particularly walkers. There is no good grocery shop and certainly no pharmacy. What Betws-y-Coed has is outdoor shops: at least seven, all stuffed with gadgets and clothing to entice the walking geek in the *sois-disant* "gateway to Snowdonia". Factor in the number of coach tours that pass through and it's been a while since Betws-y-Coed felt authentic. The riverside setting overlooked by the wooded slopes of the **Gwydyr Forest Park** is appealing, and there are more hotels and guesthouses than anywhere else in the region. Otherwise, an hour or so is all you'll need before you head out to surrounding sights.

No mountain trails start here, so if you're after high hills go west to the mountain centres of Capel Curig, Llanberis and the Ogwen Valley. Otherwise, there are some lovely strolls around the area, the most popular to the village's two principal scenic attractions, the **Conwy Falls** and **Swallow Falls** (see box, p.342). In recent years, Betws-y-Coed has become something of a magnet for **bikers** – both touring and mountain – the latter who ride in the Gwydyr Forest.

The quieter valleys in the vicinity can often be a lot more appealing than the village itself: places like handsome little **Llanrwst** five miles north (see p.343) and the **Lledr Valley** via **Dolwyddelan Castle**, to slate town turned adrenaline centre **Blaenau Ffestiniog** (see p.364). Yet there are sights here too, such as the house of William Morgan, who first translated the Bible into Welsh in **Penmachno**.

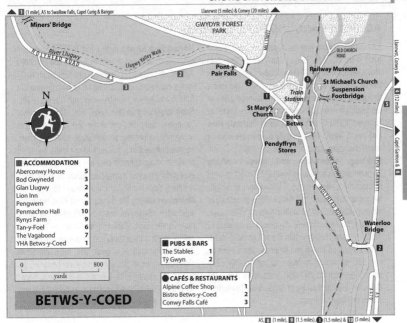

BETWS-Y-COED

Pont-y-Pair Falls

On sunny days the stone slabs around the low cataract of **Pont-y-Pair Falls** are full of people relaxing with an ice cream after a hard hour in an outdoors shop. The waters of the River Llugwy thunder over assorted boulders and funnel under the adjacent **Pont-y-Pair** ("Bridge of the Cauldron").

Conwy Valley Railway Museum

Train station, Station Rd • Daily 10am–5pm • £1.50; train £1.50, tram £1 • ☎ 01690 710568, ⓦ conwyrailwaymuseum.co.uk

Adjoining the train station, the **Conwy Valley Railway Museum** holds a collection of memorabilia and shiny engines, only slightly enlivened by a model of a Welsh slate quarry and the opportunity for kids to take a short ride on a miniature train or tram.

St Michael's church

Old Church Rd • Sun 10am–5pm; otherwise obtain key from Conwy Valley Railway Museum or TIC • Free

A lych gate and ancient yews frame the fourteenth-century **St Michael's church**. It's interesting for its whitewashed interior, specifically the thirteenth-century font and a carved effigy of an armoured knight, whose inscription identifies him as Gruffydd ap Dafydd Goch, the grandson of Llywelyn ap Gruffydd's brother, Prince Dafydd.

Fairy Glen

Signposted off the A470 towards Blaenau Ffestiniog • Car park £1, turnstile 50p • Access all hours

A mile or so southeast of the village, after negotiating a series of rapids, the waters of the Conwy river negotiate a staircase of drops and enter **Fairy Glen**, a lovely cleft in a small wood. It is named after the Welsh fairies, the Tylwyth Teg, once said to live hereabouts.

Conwy Falls

On the A5, 3 miles south of Betws-y-Coed • £1.50 • Access all hours via turnstile • Reached by the #64 bus

After Fairy Glen, the River Conwy plunges 50ft over the **Conwy Falls** into a deep pool. Slip your coins into the turnstile beside *Conwy Falls Café* and you can see the falls as

6

ACTIVITIES AROUND BETWS-Y-COED

Adventure centre Tree Top Adventure, A470, 1 mile east (daily: May–Sept 10am–6pm; Oct–April 10am–4pm; ☎ 01690 710914, ⓦ ttadventure.co.uk), lets you test your balance and nerve on a high-wire course through the forest canopy (£28). You're harnessed on – or jump safely from a 100ft-high platform on the Powerfan plummet (£20, £37 with ropes course). Obviously, older kids love it. There's also a long zip wire, an orienteering course and opportunities to try rock climbing.

Climbing, scrambling and gorge walking Serenventures, Vicarage Road (☎ 01690 710754, ⓦ seren ventures.com), offers a range of fun activities in the hills nearby: options include half-day climbing, scrambling or gorge walking (£45), or full multi-activity days (from £80).

Fishing There are salmon and sea trout on stretches of the Conwy and Llugwy within the village (mid-March to mid-Oct), and brown and American brook trout on Llyn Elsi, just south (late March to late Oct only). Buy rod licences from the post office and permits (fom £15/ day) plus a limited range of tackle from Pendyffryn Stores, on Holyhead Road.

Horseriding Gwydyr Riding and Trekking Stables, 4 miles south of Betws-y-Coed in Penmachno (☎ 01690 760248, ⓦ horse-riding-wales.co.uk), runs scenic hacks with views to Snowdon. Options range from an hour to a full day and include an entertaining pub ride (£22–70).

Mine exploring Go Below (☎ 01690 710108, ⓦ www .go-below.co.uk) runs one of the best half-day trips in Snowdonia, especially on wet days. With a harness, helmet and headlamp, you explore an old mine working and learn about its past in between zip lines, abseils and even paddling across a small lake (all can be bypasssed if required). Book in advance; minimum age 10; £49.

Mountain biking The Gwydyr Forest Park, north and west of the village, provides good trail riding. The classic route is the Marin Trail (78-mile loop; 2–4hr) with mostly forest track ascents and numerous single-track descents. The scenery is great, with mountain views along the higher sections. Other trails are laid in woods around the Conwy Falls. Bike rental is at Beics Betws (☎ 01690 710766, ⓦ bikewales.co.uk) behind the post office; staff offer hardtails (from £28/day).

well as a series of rock steps (actually a Victorian fish ladder cut in 1863). Clearly it wasn't too effective – there is now a fish tunnel cut through the rock on the far side.

Tŷ Mawr Wybrnant

Penmachno, off the A5, 5 miles south of Betws-y-Coed • Late April–Oct Thurs–Sun noon–5pm • £3; NT • ☎ 01690 760213

A useful sight to make a day of a trip south, the village of **Penmachno** lies a couple of miles upstream from the Conwy Falls. Nearly three beyond it stands **Tŷ Mawr Wybrnant**. In this isolated cottage, Bishop William Morgan, the man who first translated the Bible into Welsh (see p.396), was born in 1545 and lived until his teenage years, when he decamped to Gwydyr Castle to pursue his education. The original cottage has been restored to something like its sixteenth-century appearance: all bare stone and beams, with a gaping fireplace supporting a huge, sagging beam dating back to the thirteenth century. Its star attraction is the collection of Bibles and prayer books, including a Morgan original.

Capel Garmon Burial Chamber

0.5 miles south of Capel Garmon, 2 miles southeast of Betws-y-Coed • Open access • Free; CADW

Neolithic dwellers left their mark at the **Capel Garmon Burial Chamber**, a heavily reconstructed, multi-chambered burial site built between 2500 and 1900 BC. It's an atmospheric spot, comprising some rough stones lining a series of linked pits, with a central chamber covered by an enormous capstone. The site is a five-minute signposted walk across farmland from the road.

Swallow Falls

A5, 2 miles west of Betws-y-Coed • Open all times • £1.50

Easy access makes **Swallow Falls** (a mistranslation of *Rhaeadr Ewynnol*, or "foaming cataract") one of the region's most-visited sights, but it's really no more than a pretty waterfall enlivened by the occasional kamikazee kayaker. A path leads to a series of viewing platforms.

Tŷ Hyll

A5, 3 miles west of Betws-y-Coed • Early Feb–Easter & Nov Fri–Sun 10.30am–5pm; Easter–Oct daily 10.30am–5pm • ☎ 01492 643222, Ⓦ snowdonia-society.org.uk

As the A5 crosses the Llugwy river you can't miss **Tŷ Hyll**, known as the "Ugly House" for its construction of great stone hunks. Decked out with period furniture and surrounded by a cottage garden, wildlife pond and forest full of easy paths, it is now a historic cafe, *Pot Mêl*, owned by the environmental campaigning group Snowdonia Society, which sells the honeys produced by bees in its pretty cottage garden.

6

ARRIVAL AND DEPARTURE
BETWS-Y-COED

By train Trains on the Conwy Valley Railway (see box below) arrive at the central train station.

Destinations Blaenau Ffestiniog (5-6 daily; 30min); Llandudno (6 daily; 50min); Llandudno Junction (5 daily; 30min); Llanrwst (6 daily; 5min).

By bus Buses (including the Snowdon Sherpa) fan out from near the train station to: Blaenau Ffestiniog (Mon–Sat 8 daily; 20min); Capel Curig (5 daily; 10min); Idwal Cottage (3 daily; 20min); Llanberis (4 daily; 30min); Llandudno (6 daily; 50min); Llanrwst (every 2hr; 10min); Penmachno (6 daily; 10min); Pen-y-Pass (6 daily; 15min).

INFORMATION

Tourist information The TIC is in Royal Oak Stables off Station Road (daily: Easter to mid-Oct 9.30am–5pm; mid-Oct to Easter 9.30am–4pm; ☎ 01690 710426, ✉ tic .byc@eryri-npa.gov.uk), and has displays and a film giving a quick overview of Snowdonia.

Internet access There is free wi-fi at several cafés around the village.

ACCOMMODATION

Betws-y-Coed is stuffed with **B&Bs**, but has large numbers of visitors in summer, when it's worth reserving your bed rather than winging it. Since this is the regional hub, we've included several accommodation options in the surrounding area, including **Llanrwst**, three miles north.

B&BS AND HOTELS

Aberconwy House Lôn Muriau, Llanrwst Rd ☎ 01690 710202, Ⓦ aberconwy-house.co.uk. The best of several B&Bs grouped on the A470 just outside the centre, this has friendly young owners and has recently been refurbished to provide a stylish, relaxed stay with en-suite rooms and superb views from the front rooms. **£75**

★**Bod Gwynedd** A5, 0.5 mile towards Capel Curig ☎ 01690 710717, Ⓦ bodgwynedd.com. Smarter than the average B&B, this Victorian house on the edge of the village offers tasteful country-modern style and powerful showers in its en suites plus excellent breakfasts. One room has a four-poster. **£75**

Glan Llugwy A5 towards Capel Curig, 300yd beyond Pont-y-Pair ☎ 01690 710592, Ⓦ glanllugwy.co.uk. A traditional, well-maintained B&B that's one of the cheapest around; all rooms but one share facilities (the en suite costs £10 more). Helpful owners and good breakfasts. **£60**

Lion Inn B5384 at Gwytherin, 11 miles northeast ☎ 01745 860123, Ⓦ thelion-inn.co.uk. For peace (no TV, no internet, no mobile coverage) try this renovated pub deep in rolling hills. Expect chalky paint shades, wood furniture and traditional Welsh blankets, lazy meals for guests (reservation required) or snug nights in with a film from the DVD library. Bliss. No children under 7, minimum 2 nights. Closed Jan–Feb. **£83**

Pengwern Allt Dinas, 1.5 miles east on A5 ☎ 01690 710480, Ⓦ snowdoniaaccommodation.co.uk. Welcoming tastefully decorated country house set in two acres of woods, with guest lounge and just three rooms, two with valley views and one with a four-poster. There's also a separate self-catering cottage to let in summer. Doubles **£84**; cottage from **£370**/week

Penmachno Hall B4406 in Penmachno, 5 miles south

CONWY VALLEY RAILWAY

If you love train journeys, don't miss riding the **Conwy Valley Railway** (Ⓦ conwy.gov.uk/cvr), one of the more beautiful sections of the National Rail network. It is a gorgeous run from Llandudno Junction (near Conwy) through the pastures of the Conwy Valley to Betws-y-Coed, then through the twisting Lledr Valley. Deciduous and pine forests give way to the smooth, grassy slopes of the Moel Siabod before the route bores through over two miles of slate – the longest rail tunnel in Wales – to Blaenau Ffestiniog.

☎ 01690 760410, ⊛ penmachnohall.co.uk. Hide away in this hospitable country house in an 1862 former rectory, with three spacious bedrooms plus a sunny lounge (with log fire in winter) and an honesty bar. To save a trip into town they serve 2-course suppers (Tues–Fri; £18) and 5-course dinners on Sat (£38). **£90**

★**Tan-y-Foel** Capel Garmon (A470 towards Llanrwst, then turn right after 2 miles) ☎ 01690 710507, ⊛ tyfhotel.co.uk. Ultramodern public spaces and stylish, luxurious rooms in a sixteenth-century farmhouse make this one of the best small country hotels in the district, with sweeping views across eight acres of grounds to the Conwy Valley and outstanding three-course dinners for guests. **£130**

HOSTELS AND CAMPING

★**Rynys Farm** A5, 2 miles southeast near the Conwy Falls ☎ 01690 710218, ⊛ rynys-camping.co.uk. Pure rural bliss on a beautiful National Trust-listed farm campsite

with plenty of flat sites tucked behind trees or against dry-stone walls, great valley views, good facilities and eco-ethics. Charming owners, too. Also has a wonderful yurt and shepherd's hut plus a static caravan that sleeps four. Camping **£7.50**/person; yurt **£50**; hut **£45**; caravan **£40**

★**The Vagabond** Craiglan Rd ☎ 01690 710850, ⊛ thevagabond.co.uk. Excellent small independent hostel with four- to eight-bunk dorms, and good facilities including free wi-fi, secure bike lock-up and off-street parking. There's a self-catering kitchen but they also serve breakfasts (£5) and have an inexpensive bar. Bookings recommended at weekends when B&B is obligatory. Dorms **£15**

YHA Betws-y-Coed A5, 2 miles west of Betws-y-Coed ☎ 01690 710796, ⊛ swallowfallshotel.co.uk. Mostly four-bed dorms, but this hostel also has some smaller double rooms, including en suites. It's part of the *Swallow Falls Hotel* complex, with a bar, restaurant and sauna (£3), plus a campsite. Dorms **£18.50**; doubles **£40**; camping **£8**/person

EATING AND DRINKING

CAFÉS AND RESTAURANTS

Alpine Coffee Shop Betws-y-Coed train station ☎ 01690 710747. A bright daytime café with art on the walls and an appealing range of breakfasts and lunches including vegetarian dishes – expect home-made soups and quiche or the likes of cottage cheese, spinach and salmon croissants (£6) – as well as 45 speciality teas. Daily 8.30am–5.30pm.

Bistro Betws-y-Coed Holyhead Rd ☎ 01690 710328.

We've had good reports about this casual bistro since it was taken up by local star chef Gerwyn Williams. He retains its Welsh bias and emphasis on local produce. Lunches are light and dinners up the ante with dishes like local lamb marinated in Snowdonian honey (£14). March–Sept & Christmas period daily 11.30am–2.30pm & 6–9pm; Oct–Feb Wed–Fri 6–9pm, Sat–Sun 11.30am–2.30pm & 6–9pm.

★**Conwy Falls Café** A5, 2 miles south ☎ 01690 710696,

WALKS AROUND BETWS-Y-COED

These two lowland walks explore the valleys and waterfalls on the outskirts of the village. Neither is circular, so unless you plan to hitch back, consult local bus timetables first to avoid a long wait for the infrequent services.

Conwy Gorge walk (3 miles; 1hr 15min; descent only). An easy walk that links two of the district's best-known natural attractions, Fairy Glen (see p.339) and the Conwy Falls (see p.339), by way of a cool green lane (once the main road into Betws-y-Coed) giving glimpses of the river through the beech woods. Catch the #64 bus (8 daily) to *Conwy Falls Café*, then after having a look at the falls, walk 150yd back along the road towards Betws-y-Coed and follow a traffic-free lane (the original road into the village) parallel to the river through the trees. After about half an hour, you'll see the gate to Fairy Glen on your left. Returning to the main path, continue to the *Fairy Glen Hotel*, where you can cross the river by Beaver Bridge, turn right and follow a minor road a mile back to the village.

Llugwy Valley walk (6 miles; 2hr 30min; 600ft ascent). The car park on the north side of the Pont-y-Pair bridge marks the beginning of a forested path following the twisting river upstream to Capel Curig. With the A5 running parallel to the river all the way, there are several opportunities to cut the walk short and wait for the bus back to Betws-y-Coed. Less than a mile from Pont-y-Pair, you first reach a ford where the Roman road Sarn Helen crossed the river, then pass the steeply sloping Miners' Bridge, which linked miners' homes at Pentre Du on the south side of the river to the lead mines in the Gwydyr Forest. With its plunge pools and rocky diving platforms this is the place to take a dip. The path follows the river on your left for another mile to a slightly obscured view of Swallow Falls. Detailed maps available from the tourist office in Betws-y-Coed show numerous routes back through the Gwydyr Forest, or you can continue half a mile to the road bridge by Tŷ Hyll and follow the right bank to Capel Curig, passing the scant remains of the Caer Llugwy, a Roman fort, and a couple more treacherous rapids: The Mincer and Cobden's Falls.

ⓦ conwyfalls.com. Quality and provenance are watchwords at this friendly relaxed café in a Clough Williams-Ellis-designed building; most ingredients are sourced from local suppliers or overseas co-operatives. Cuisine is always fresh, wholesome and home-made, including everything from spinach and mushroom burgers, ploughman's lunches and stone-baked pizzas to tea and cake. Easter to mid-Oct Mon–Thurs & Sun 9am–4pm, Fri & Sat 9am–9pm; mid-Oct–Easter Fri & Sat 9am–9pm, Sun 9am–4pm.

PUB AND BAR
The Stables Royal Oak Hotel, High St ⓣ 01690 710219. Recently refurbished, the village's liveliest bar

provides good beer, outdoor seating, sports on the TV and occasional live jazz. Passable pub-grub such as home-made lasagne, local beef burgers, pies and fish and chips (mains average £9) is on the menu. Daily 11am–11pm.

★ **Tŷ Gwyn** A5, 0.5 mile southeast ⓣ 01690 710383, ⓦ tygwynhotel.co.uk. First choice for historic atmosphere is this beamed former coaching inn. Traditional British dishes such as local trout with prawns and crème fraiche (£15) or shepherd's pie made with 24hr-roast lamb (£18) are served in the intimate bar or slightly more formal restaurant. Reservations essential. Daily noon–2pm & 6.30–9pm (Jan closed Mon–Wed).

Llanrwst and around

The Conwy River heads north from Betws-y-Coed along a broad pastoral corridor to the sea. Five miles along the Conwy Valley, **LLANRWST** was once the largest wool market in north Wales. It had a spell as a centre for harp manufacture in the eighteenth century, too, and is still the most economically important town in the valley, retaining Wednesday and Friday livestock **markets**, and a general one each Tuesday on the central Ancaster Square. All this gives the feel of a proper, solid little market town – refreshing after the village resort of Betws-y-Coed.

St Gwrst Church and Llanrwst Almshouses

St Gwrst Church: Church St • Times vary • Free; £1 donation requested for south transept

St Gwrst Church contains an intricately carved rood screen thought to have come from Maenan Abbey, a few miles downstream, after it was dissolved by Henry VIII in 1536; look for the carved pigs. In the south transept (entered through a separate door) lies the thirteenth-century carved stone coffin (minus its lid) of Llywelyn the Great.

On the lane just before it are the **Llanrwst almshouses**, which date back to 1610 and were still in use until 1976. Previously two rooms in period style (1610 and 1850) were open as a municipal museum, however this was shut indefinitely on our last visit with no one sure whether it would be reopened.

Tu Hwnt i'r Bont and Pont Fawr

It sometimes seem like half of Llanrwst's visitors are photographing **Tu Hwnt i'r Bont**, a tearoom in a fifteenth-century former courthouse entirely smothered in Virginia creeper. It is approached over **Pont Fawr** (Big Bridge), a beautifully proportioned, humpback bridge designed by the seventeenth-century architect Inigo Jones; he is said to have spent his early years in Llanrwst. In summer, its single lane struggles to cope with the traffic across it.

Gwydir Castle

B5106, 0.5 mile west of Llanrwst • Apr–Oct Tues–Fri & Sun 10am–4pm • £3 • ⓣ 01492 641687, ⓦ gwydir-castle.co.uk

Most of the land around Betws-y-Coed and along the Conwy Valley was once part of the Gwydyr Estate owned by the Wynn family. Descended from the kings of Gwynedd, they were the most powerful dynasty in the region until the male line died out in 1678. A reminder of the family's might is **Gwydir Castle**, actually a low-slung manor house begun around 1490. Despite additions in the sixteenth and nineteenth centuries, with parts plundered from the post-dissolution Maenan Abbey, the building is a fabulous model of early Tudor architecture. Incidentally, it's also reputed to be among the most haunted houses in Wales.

Its core is a three-storey tower, whose windows relieve the gloom of the great halls, each with enormous fireplaces and stone-flagged or heavy timber floors. Most of the original fittings and Tudor furniture were sold in 1921, and much of the rest of the house was ruined in a fire a few months later. The subsequent restoration was kept simple – tapestries cover the solid stone walls, a few tables and chairs are scattered about and there's some fine painted glass. Some of the original furnishings have been tracked down, including the heavily carved oak panels, Baroque door-case and fireplace, and the gilded Spanish leather of the **dining room**. This was initially installed by Richard Wynn around 1642, and is attributed to Inigo Jones. The complete set was bought during the 1921 sell-off by American newspaper magnate William Randolph Hearst and shipped across the Atlantic. New York's Metropolitan Museum acquired it in 1956 and kept it boxed up for forty years until it was sold back to the castle in 1996 and re-installed.

Outside, the main attraction is the **Dutch Garden**, with its fountain, peacocks and cedars of Lebanon dating back to 1625. There's also excellent accommodation (see below).

Trefriw Woollen Mills

B5106 in Trefriw, 2 miles northwest of Llanrwst • **Mill:** Easter–Sept Mon–Fri 10am–1pm & 2–5pm; **shop:** daily April–Oct 9.30am–5.30pm, Nov–March 10am–5pm • Free • ☎ 01492 640462, ⓦ t-w-m.co.uk

The small village of Trefriw is home to the **Trefriw Woollen Mills**, where rugs, throws and bedspreads are made to traditional Welsh geometric designs using late nineteenth-century weaving methods, all driven by the power of Afon Crafnant, which flows right by the mill. The full fleece-to-fabric process is explained and you can often see old looms weaving away. Naturally, there's a big shop: double bedspreads start at around £200 but there are cheaper goods.

ARRIVAL AND INFORMATION

LLANRWST

By train/bus Trains on the Conwy Valley line and many of the region's buses stop close to Ancaster Square.

Internet access Free at the library (Mon & Wed–Fri 9.30am–5pm, Tues 3.30–7.30pm, Sat 10am–1pm) on Station Road just north of town.

ACCOMMODATION AND EATING

Caffi Contessa Ancaster Sq ☎ 01492 640754. A bright little café that's always busy, whether with workmen or locals chatting over coffee. The reason is its good reputation for outstanding breakfasts and fresh lunches like home-made soup or prawn and sweet chilli wrap (£5). Mon–Sat 9am–4pm.

★ **Gwydir Castle** 3 miles north of Llanwrst ☎ 01492 641687, ⓦ gwydir-castle.co.uk. A rare opportunity to stay in an authentic Tudor manor that still maintains the air of a family home. Two splendid bedrooms have been fitted out in baronial style with four-poster beds, deep baths and nicely eclectic decor. TVs are anathema. No children under 12. **£95**

Tu Hwnt i'r Bont Beside Pont Fawr bridge ☎ 01492 642322, ⓦ tuhwntirbont.co.uk. Classic, low-beamed tearoom "beyond the bridge" (as it translates from Welsh) that's great for daily soup and fresh sandwiches and essential for the excellent cream teas with sultana scones, good jam and leaf tea (£11.70). Visit the small gallery upstairs if only to experience the stone stairway. April–Sept daily 10.30am–5pm; March & Oct Tues–Sun 10.30am–5pm; Nov & Dec Fri–Sun 10.30am–5pm.

Y'Tanerdy (The Old Tannery) Willow St ☎ 01492 641655, ⓦ ytannerdy.co.uk. A loft bistro with a short menu of nicely presented light meals (mains around £11) – chef's recipe meatballs, lamb and leek sausages and mash, pan-fried duck or a speciality burger – in a relaxed setting or al fresco above the river. Mon–Thurs 10am–4pm, Fri–Sat 10am–4pm & 6–10pm, Sun 11am–4pm & 6–8.30pm.

Capel Curig

There's scarcely a building in tiny **Capel Curig** that isn't of some use to hikers, making it a perfect base for the walk up Moel Siabod (see box opposite) and for the two valleys that plunge westwards deep into the mountains. The A4086 follows Nant Gwryd southwest to the Snowdon massif, while the A5 prises apart the Carneddau and Glyder ranges to the northwest, forging through the Ogwen Valley.

HIKING MOEL SIABOD FROM CAPEL CURIG

5 miles; 4hr; 2200ft; OS maps: Landranger 115 or Explorer OL17

Despite Capel Curig's popularity among hikers, the only major **walk** from here is up the grassy-backed **Moel Siabod** (2861ft), a challenging ridge walk with views of the Snowdon Horseshoe. Start opposite the *Plas Curig* hostel, cross the concrete bridge and follow the right bank downstream past the falls by *Cobden's Hotel* to the Pont Cyfyng road bridge (30min), an alternative starting point for the walk. Take the road south and turn right on the second path signposted to Moel Siabod. You pass a disused slate quarry before the long scramble up the east ridge, which weaves around outcrops where a moment's inattention could be disastrous. Once you've admired the summit view of the Snowdon Horseshoe, turn northeast and follow the craggy summit ridge, which drops across grass to the moors below, soon rejoining your ascent route for the hike back to Pont Cyfyng.

6

Plas y Brenin: The National Mountain Centre

A4086, 400yd south of the centre • Daily: office hours 9am–5pm; climbing wall 10am–9pm • £6 • ☎ 01690 720214, ⓦ www.pyb.co.uk

Built around a former coaching inn, **Plas y Brenin** runs internationally renowned courses in hiking, mountaineering, kayaking, skiing and rock climbing (see p.52). Of more interest if you're just passing through, however, are its three-hour family-focused taster sessions in rock climbing, lake canoeing and geocaching held during the spring and summer school holidays (£25), while an 11m indoor climbing wall can be a godsend on rainy days. It also runs longer multi-activity full-day kids' adventure sessions (£40), where adults are welcome too, and rents basic hiking and climbing gear at reasonable prices.

ARRIVAL AND DEPARTURE
CAPEL CURIG

Buses Snowdon Sherpa buses (see p.338) serve: Betws-y-Coed (5 daily; 10min), Idwal Cottage (3 daily; 10min), Llanberis (4 daily; 30min) and Pen-y-Pass (8 daily; 10min).

ACCOMMODATION

Bron Eryri A5, 1 mile outside the village towards Betws-y-Coed ☎ 01690 720240, ⓦ www.eryriguesthouse .fsnet.co.uk. Four comfortable en suites, including one family room, are provided by a friendly walker/climber owner, who fills flasks and prepares lunchtime sandwiches. Communal breakfasts add to the relaxed vibe. Two-night minimum at summer weekends. **£65**

Bryn Tyrch Campsite A5, 600yd towards Betws-y-Coed ☎ 01690 720414. Basic grassy site (though not boggy in heavy rain) with token showers and very simple bunkhouses (bring everything). Dorms **£10**; camping **£4**/person

Bryn Tyrch Inn A5, 500yd towards Betws-y-Coed ☎ 01690 720223, ⓦ bryntyrchinn.co.uk. Sensitively modernized small inn with a relaxed informal style and tasteful rooms. Also has four-bunk rooms (minimum 3 in one room). Two-nights minimum at weekends; midweek and off-season discounts often available. Dorms **£25**/person; doubles **£79**

★**Plas Curig** A5, 500yd towards Betws-y-Coed ☎ 01690 720225, ⓦ snowdoniahostel.co.uk. Wales's only five-star hostel is a marvel for anyone who'd seen its former incarnation as a YHA. Public areas are beautiful with slate floors and reclaimed wood, and the dorms are splendid – custom-built pannelled bunks have privacy curtains, bed lights and lockable storage. It has four- and eight-bed dorms, doubles, twins and family rooms (no en suites). Check in 5–10pm. Closed Dec & Jan. Dorms **£25**; doubles **£55**

★**St Curig's Church** A5, by the junction in the heart of the village ☎ 01690 720469, ⓦ stcurigschurch.com. Great B&B fashioned from a former church, which retains a gilded mosaic of Christ in the pool and TV room. Though lacking the same wow factor, the six rooms are comfortable and include four-poster doubles. A recess off the lounge has a four-bed bunkroom, and everyone has access to a hot tub with views of the mountains. Dorms **£20**; doubles **£75**

EATING AND DRINKING

★**Bryn Tyrch Inn** A5, 0.3 miles towards Betws-y-Coed ☎ 01690 720223, ⓦ bryntyrchinn.co.uk. Offers real ales, garden seating and a view of Snowdon. Factor in high-quality honest meals and this lively inn is a winner after a

hard day in the hills. The seasonal menu might include roast pork belly with chorizo potatoes or Anglesey seabass with sugarsnap peas (mains £15–17). Bar mid-Jan to Easter & Oct to mid-Dec Fri–Sun noon–11pm;

WALKS FROM THE OGWEN VALLEY

Use the OS 1:25,000 OL17 Explorer map ("Snowdon & Conwy Valley") or the 1:50,000 115 Landranger map ("Snowdon/Yr Wyddfa"). For a general layout see our Snowdonia map.

Tourists hike up Snowdon, but mountain connoisseurs prefer the sharply angled peaks of the **Glyderau** with their challenging terrain, or **Tryfan** with its scary jump at the summit and fantastic views to Snowdon. We've outlined three walks on Tryfan and one on the Glyderau, but with a map you can plan all manner of variations.

The **Carneddau**, on the other side of the Ogwen Valley, could hardly be in greater contrast. The longest stretch of ground over three thousand feet in Wales, they form a rounded plateau stretching to the cliffs of Penmaenmawr on the north coast. The sound of a raven and perhaps a wild pony can often be your only company on inclement days, but in fine weather the easy walking and roof-of-the-world views make for a satisfying hike.

TRYFAN

Miners' Track (5 miles; 4–6hr; 2000ft ascent). The standard route up Tryfan, from the car park at Idwal Cottage. Take the path to Cwm Idwal then, as it bears sharply to the right, keep straight ahead and make for Bwlch Tryfan, the gap on the horizon between Tryfan and Glyder Fach. From there, the South Ridge of Tryfan climbs past the Far South Peak to the summit: this last section is an easy scramble, so you'll need to use your hands. Anyone who has seen pictures of people jumping the 5ft gap between Adam and Eve, two chunks of rhyolitic lava at the summit, will wonder what the fuss is about until they get there and see the mountain plummet on all sides. In theory the leap is trivial, but the consequences of overshooting would be disastrous. Return the way you came.

Tryfan via Heather Terrace (4 miles; 4–6hr; 2000ft ascent). You'll need a reasonable sense of adventure to enjoy the ascent via Heather Terrace, which follows a fault in the rock running diagonally across the east face. The route starts in the lay-by at the head of Idwal Lake and goes left across rising ground before finding its way onto the exposed "terrace". This ends at the col between South and the Far South peaks, where a right turn then starts your scramble for the summit. Descend the way you came or by the Miners' Track.

North Ridge of Tryfan (3–4 miles; 4–6hr; 2000ft ascent). If you've got the head for it this is one of the most rewarding scrambles in the country. It's not as precarious as Snowdon's Crib Goch, but you get a genuine mountaineering feel as the valley floor drops rapidly away and

---

Easter–Sept daily 11am–11pm; food served mid-Jan to Easter & Oct to mid-Dec Fri–Sun noon–9pm; Easter–Sept daily noon–9pm.

Snowdon Bar Plas y Brenin ☎ 01690 720214. Outdoor enthusiasts' bar in Plas y Brenin outdoors centre with a couple of its own brews. As well as serving budget bar meals like pea and ham soup (£4) it hosts talks and slide shows of recent international expeditions (usually Mon, Wed & Sat at 8pm; free). Bar Mon–Sat noon–2pm & 7–11pm, Sun noon–11pm; food served daily noon–2pm & 7–9pm.

The Ogwen Valley

Northwest of Capel Curig the gentle **Ogwen Valley** follows the Ogwen River towards Bethesda, home to one of the last slate quarries in Wales and the longest zip-wire ride in Europe. The reason most people come is the mist-shrouded Carnedd range to the north and the spiky Glyder range opposite, featuring the triple-peaked **Tryfan** (see box above), arguably Snowdonia's most demanding mountain. This forms a fractured spur out from the main range and blocks your view down the valley, the twin monoliths of Adam and Eve that crown Tryfan's summit picked out on the skyline. The courageous (or foolhardy) jump between them as a point of honour on every ascent.

West of Tryfan, the road follows a perfect U-shaped glacial valley, carved by rocks frozen into the undersides of the glaciers that creaked down **Nant Ffrancon** ten thousand years ago. In the middle of the valley is Llyn Ogwen, a post-glacial lake formed behind moraine left by the retreating ice. **IDWAL COTTAGE** is at its western end. But the only settlement in the valley is so small – just a new visitor centre with displays on geology and ecology, a basic snack bar and a YHA hostel – it isn't even named on

the views stretch further and further along it. The route starts in the lay-by at the head of Idwal Lake and goes left across rising ground, until you strike a path heading straight up following the crest of the ridge to the 3010ft summit. Return via Heather Terrace or the Miners' Track.

THE GLYDERAU

Glyder Traverse (6 miles; 5–8hr; 2500ft ascent). This day is a fairly rugged undertaking (with some moderate scrambling) but very rewarding. From Idwal Cottage, follow Tryfan's Miners' Track to Bwlch Tryfan where (by adding an extra hour) you can also tick off the summit of Tryfan. From Bwlch Tryfan, scramble up Bristly Ridge, which runs steeply south past some daunting-looking towers of rock. In good conditions it isn't difficult, but it should be avoided in winter unless you're suitably equipped. The ridge ends at the summit of Glyder Fach (3260ft), a chaotic jumble of grey slabs with a massive cantilevered rock.

From Glyder Fach, it is an easy stroll to Glyder Fawr (3280ft), reached by skirting round the rock formations of Castell y Gwynt (the Castle of the Winds), then following a path to the summit of frost-shattered slabs. The descent initially follows loose scree down to Llyn Cwn where you turn north, zigzagging down Twll Du (The Devil's Kitchen) to Llyn Idwal and back to Idwal Cottage.

THE CARNEDDAU

Carnedd Loop (9 miles; 5hr; 3500ft ascent). This fine day out, taking in the range's four mighty southern peaks, has less objective danger than the walks on Tryfan and the Glyderau but is just as exhausting. Start from the lay-by at the head of the lake near Tal y Llyn Ogwen farm and head right of the farm towards a small lake, Ffynnon Lloer, before turning left up the east ridge of Pen yr Ole Wen (3212ft), with its magnificent view down into Nant Ffrancon and back to Tryfan. In clear weather, you can see your route running north past Carnedd Fach, and what looks to be a huge artificial mound, to Carnedd Dafydd (3425ft). After a short easterly descent, the path skirts the steep Ysgolion Duon cliffs, then climbs over stones to the broad, arched top of Carnedd Llywelyn (3491ft), the highest of the Carneddau.

Descend towards Craig yr Ysfa, a sheer cliff that drops away into the vast amphitheatre of Cwm Eigiau to the north. Continuing with care, skirt around the north of Ffynnon Llugwy reservoir and climb to the grassy top of Penyrhelgi-du (2733ft), from where there's a steady broad-ridged descent to the road near Helyg. The mile-long trek back west to the starting point is best done on the old packhorse route running parallel to the A5.

most maps. Indeed the car park is larger. The main reason to come here is to tackle some of Wales's most challenging and rewarding hikes, or start the far easier walk to a magnificent glacial cirque, Cwm Idwal.

Cwm Idwal

Accessed from Idwal Cottage • Free; NT

The Idwal Cottage car park is the starting point of an easy well-maintained path to **Cwm Idwal** (1.5 miles return; 1hr; 200ft ascent), a shallow mountain bowl, which in 1954 became Wales's first **National Nature Reserve**. The evidence of glacial scouring is so clear here that you wonder why it took geologists so long to work out the process that created these hollowed faces and scored rocks. In 1842, Darwin recalled his visit with the geologist Adam Sedgewick eleven years earlier; they were so awed, he noted, "neither of us saw a trace of the wonderful glacial phenomena all around us". The cwm's scalloped floor traps **Llyn Idwal**, which reflects the precipitous grey cliffs behind and is accessed by a recently laid boardwalk around the lake. The rowan, bilberry and heather in a small but luxuriant fenced-off control area show how the area might look if the authorities ever succeed in keeping sheep out of the cwm – it's proving problematic.

Twll Du

The back of Cwm Idwal is marked by a dark chasm known as **Twll Du**, literally "black cleft", but dubbed the Devil's Kitchen by Victorian visitors. Down this channel, a fine watery haze runs off the flanks of **Glyder Fawr**, soaking the crevices where early botanists found rare arctic-alpine plants (see p.450). This is one of the few places where you can see the downfolded strata of what is known as the Snowdon syncline, evidence that the existing mountains sat between two much larger ranges some three hundred million years ago. To their left, the smooth inclines of the **Idwal Slabs** act as nursery slopes for budding rock climbers.

Rhaeadr Ogwen

A five-minute walk down the valley from Idwal Cottage car park, the road crosses a bridge over the top of **Rhaeadr Ogwen** (Ogwen Falls), which cascades down this step in the valley floor. Look under the road bridge and you'll see the simple mortar-free arch of a bridge that was on the original packhorse route through the valley before the road.

ZipWorld Velocity

Signposted off A5 south of Bethesda • Booking centre 9am–6pm • £50 • ☏ 01248 601444, ⓦ zipworld.co.uk

Who would have imagined that a disused quarry could be so much fun? Taking its cue from the mountain-bike trails in a former workings at Blaenau Ffestiniog (see p.365), Europe's longest zip wire was strung across a former slate quarry to provide a one-mile ride at speeds of up to 70mph. Reservations are essential and there are restrictions on weight, height and age. Note too that the weather can affect your ride and that ZipWorld offers rescheduling not refunds.

ARRIVAL AND INFORMATION   THE OGWEN VALLEY

By bus Five buses a day run along the valley between Bethesda and Capel Curig, with connections to Betws-y-Coed and Bangor.

On foot A footpath tracks the valley for five miles from Capel Curig to Idwal Cottage, although it runs parallel to the fast and often busy road.

Information centre At Cwm Idwal car park (daily 9am–5pm).

ACCOMMODATION AND EATING

★**Gwern Gôf Uchaf** A5, 4 miles west of Capel Curig ☏ 01690 720294, ⓦ tryfanwales.co.uk. Superbly sited campsite right at the base of Tryfan with a decent shower block, and a good fourteen-berth bunkhouse with a fully equipped kitchen and drying room; bring a sleeping bag and food. Dorms £10; camping £5/person

YHA Idwal Cottage A5, 5 miles west of Capel Curig ☏ 01629 592700, ⊜ idwal@yha.org.uk. Perfectly sited for walkers, this immaculate refurbished YHA in a former quarry manager's house has mostly four-bunk dorms, a double, a single, family rooms and an alcohol licence, but no meals. Opens 5pm for check-in. Closed all of Jan and weekdays in Nov, Dec & Feb. Dorms £18; doubles £48; camping £11/pitch

Llanberis and around

LLANBERIS is the nearest you'll get in Wales to an alpine climbing village. Its single main street is thronged with walkers and climbers in Gore-Tex, but it is otherwise a fairly dowdy town. The reason is **Snowdon**, to which it is inextricably linked, not least because of the five-mile umbilical cord of the **Snowdon Mountain Railway** to the summit.

Yet Llanberis is very much a Welsh rural community, albeit rather depleted now that slate is no longer being torn from the flanks of Elidir Fawr. For the best part of two centuries, the **quarries** employed up to three thousand men. They closed in 1969, leaving a vast staircase of 60ft-high terraced platforms and tiers of blue-grey rubble covering the mountainside. Yet it's an oddly compelling scene, especially when low cloud shrouds the workings and the hilltop **Dolbadarn Castle** looms from the murk like a lonely sentinel.

Soon after the quarries closed, proposals were tabled for a power station to be built over the former quarry sites on the fringes of the national park. Environmentalists were incensed. Not so the people of Llanberis, still reeling from the closure of the quarries. In the end both parties were pacified when the project went ahead underground as the **Dinorwig Power Station**.

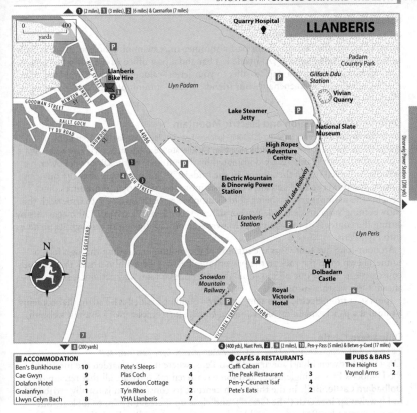

LLANBERIS

Quarry Hospital

Padarn Country Park

Gilfach Ddu Station

Vivian Quarry

Llyn Padarn

National Slate Museum

Lake Steamer Jetty

High Ropes Adventure Centre

Electric Mountain & Dinorwig Power Station

Llanberis Lake Railway

Llanberis Station

Llyn Peris

Dolbadarn Castle

Snowdon Mountain Railway

Royal Victoria Hotel

HIGH STREET · HENRY ST · NEWTON ST · GOODMAN STREET · BALLT GOCH · TY DU ROAD · SNOWDON ST · CAPEL GOCHROAD · VICTORIA TERRACE · A4086

Llanberis Bike Hire

0 — 400 yards

N

6

Dinorwig Power Station (200 yds)

▼ ❽ (200 yards)   ❹ (400 yds), Nant Peris, ❷, ❾ (2 miles), ❿, Pen-y-Pass (5 miles) & Betws-y-Coed (17 miles) ▼

■ ACCOMMODATION			
Ben's Bunkhouse	10	Pete's Sleeps	3
Cae Gwyn	9	Plas Coch	4
Dolafon Hotel	5	Snowdon Cottage	6
Graianfryn	1	Ty'n Rhos	2
Llwyn Celyn Bach	8	YHA Llanberis	7

● CAFÉS & RESTAURANTS	
Caffi Caban	1
The Peak Restaurant	3
Pen-y-Ceunant Isaf	4
Pete's Eats	2

■ PUBS & BARS	
The Heights	1
Vaynol Arms	2

When the sun breaks out, hiking competes with a choice of two **narrow-gauge railways** and myriad activities – from playing around in boats on the lake to scrambling and mountain biking.

Snowdon Mountain Railway

A4086, opposite the Royal Victoria Hotel • Mid-March to Nov 6–25 trains daily • Summit return £27, one-way £20; phone booking fee £3.50; £6 discount if reserving for 9am train by phone a day in advance • ☎ 0844 493 8120, ⓦ www.snowdonrailway.co.uk

The **Snowdon Mountain Railway** is Britain's only rack-and-pinion railway, completed in 1896. Trains (sometimes pushed by seventy-year-old steam locos) still climb to the summit in just under an hour along the most heavily maintained track in the country. The rails follow the shallowest approach to the top of Snowdon, struggling for five miles and three thousand feet up a mostly one-in-eight gradient.

Times and type of locomotive vary with demand and season, but whether steam or diesel, the full round trip takes two and a half hours, with half an hour on top. From mid-March to mid-May (and during high winds) services terminate three-quarters of the way up at **Clogwyn Station**, thirty minutes' walk from the summit. In summer (especially July, Aug and weekends in June and Sept) trains are often full, so book a day or so in advance. If you walk up by one of the routes detailed here (see p.354), you can still hope for a stand-by spot on a train down (round-trip passengers have priority).

Hafod Eryri summit café

Mid-May to Oct 10am until 20min before last train

From Llanberis the railway climbs past a summer-time swimming hole at Bishop's Falls to the **summit café** *Hafod Eryri*. Inside is a bar and a post office where, for a few pence, you can buy a "Railway Stamp" to affix to your letter – along with the Royal Mail one – thereby entitling you to enchant your friends with a "Summit of Snowdon – Copa'r Wyddfa" postmark.

Dinorwig Power Station and Electric Mountain

A4086 • **Underground tours** Hourly: Easter–Oct daily 10am–4pm; Nov–Easter Tues, Thurs & Sat–Sun 11am–3pm • £8.50 • ☎ 01286 870636, ⓦ electricmountain.co.uk • **Electric Mountain** Daily: June–Aug 9.30am–5.30pm; Sept–May 10am–4.30pm • Free

Views north from Llanberis are dominated by the entrance to the **Dinorwig Power Station**, hollowed out of the ground in the mid-1970s just five years after the quarries closed. The power station actually consumes more electricity than it produces, but benefits the national grid by being able to supply electricity instantly, to cope with the early evening surge in demand. Within sixteen seconds it can attain 1300 megawatts by letting the contents of the Marchlyn Mawr reservoir rapidly empty through its turbines into Llyn Peris.

An hour-long **bus tour** visits the innards of the mountain, heading through its tunnels hewn from the rock to the powerhouse below, where a film details the scheme's construction. This is one of Snowdonia's more popular rainy-day activities, so book ahead if the weather turns foul.

Tours start from **Electric Mountain**, actually a building beside Llyn Padarn that contains a café and a panel explaining Snowdon's microclimate (complete with summit webcam).

Dolbadarn Castle

Half a mile east of Llanberis centre, accessed from road to National Slate Museum • Open access • Free; CADW

On a rock between Llyn Padarn and Llyn Peris, where it once guarded the mouth of the Llanberis Pass, a single tower and some scattered masonry are all that remain of **Dolbadarn Castle**. Built in the thirteenth century, its construction is usually attributed to Llywelyn ap Iorwerth ("the Great"), and close up there's not a lot to look at. But viewed across Llyn Padarn, framed by the grey crags of the Pass behind, it is easy to see why Richard Wilson and Turner chose to paint it.

Llanberis Lake Railway

Gilfach Ddu • Mid-March to June, Sept & Oct 3–5 services daily; July & Aug 4–10 services daily • £7.80 return • ☎ 01286 870549, ⓦ lake-railway.co.uk

From 1843 to 1961, the original Padarn Railway transported slate and workers between the Dinorwig quarries and Port Dinorwig on the Menai Strait. When it closed it was sold for scrap, but enthusiasts subsequently relaid a two-mile stretch along the scenic shores of Lake Padarn as the family-oriented **Llanberis Lake Railway**. Tank engines that once pulled slate around the quarries now take an hour for the sedate round trip, which includes a stop halfway back at **Cei Llydan** station with a picnic spot by the lake.

Padarn Country Park

Gilfach Ddu • Open access • Free

At **Padarn Country Park** lake-side oak woods are gradually recolonizing the discarded workings of the defunct **Dinorwig Slate Quarries**, formerly one of the largest slate quarries in the world. Equipment and engines that once hauled materials up inclined tramways have been partly restored and punctuate the paths which link the levels chiselled out of the hillside. One of the most interesting spots is right near the parking area, where you can walk through a rock arch to the flooded **Vivian Quarry**, a dramatic spot and a popular destination for **scuba divers**.

National Slate Museum

Gilfach Ddu • Daily: Easter–Oct daily 10am–5pm; Nov–Easter 10am–4pm, closed Sat • Free • ☎ 01286 870630, ⓦ museumwales.ac.uk

In what looks more like a fort than former quarry's maintenance workshops, Wales' **National Slate Museum** houses a 50ft-diameter water wheel that once powered cutting machines through a cat's cradle of lineshafts and flapping belts still turns. Though most of the equipment dates back to the early part of the twentieth century, it was still in use until the quarries closed and is familiar to former quarry workers, some of whom may demonstrate their skills at turning an inch-thick slab of slate into six, even eight, perfectly smooth slivers. The slate was delivered to the slate-dressing sheds by means of a maze of tramways, cranes and rope lifts, all kept in good order in the fitting and repair shops. Using an iBeacon Bluetooth display (the world's first when installed, apparently), you'll learn about the scales used to calculate the price each rock cutter would be paid for his work, before the deductions for the rope and gunpowder he used to extract the slate, from mottled burgundy and bottle green to every shade of grey. You'll also discover the slate workers' cottages furnished in the style of 1861, 1901 and 1969. To keep everything in working order, the craftsmen here operate a foundry, producing pieces for branches of the National Museum of Wales, as well as repairing rolling stock on the **Llanberis Lake Railway**.

Quarry Hospital

500yd north of the Slate Museum • Easter & late May–Sept daily 11am–4.45pm; April and early May Sat & Sun 11am–4.45pm • Free

You can pick up leaflets of colour-coded **waymarked walking trails** from a kiosk near the slate museum, but it's easy enough just to meander around the old slate workings and through the ancient woodlands of Coed Dinorwig. At some point, go to the period-furnished **Quarry Hospital**, where the resident surgeon patched up quarrying injuries. Actually, tuberculosis was far more fatal to miners than gunpowder blasts or falling rock.

ARRIVAL AND DEPARTURE

LLANBERIS AND AROUND

By bus Buses, which stop along High Street, serve; Bangor (9 daily; 45min); Betws-y-Coed (6 daily; 30min); Caernarfon (hourly; 25min); Capel Curig (6 daily; 30min); Nant Peris (hourly or better; 10min); Pen-y-Pass (hourly or better; 15min).

INFORMATION

Tourist information The TIC is in Electric Mountain (manned Fri–Tues 10am–4pm, open with leaflets June–Aug daily 9.30am–5.30pm; Sept–May daily 10am–4.30pm; ☎ 01286 870765, ✉ llanberis.tic@gwynedd.gov.uk).

Internet Free wi-fi at both *Pete's Eats* and *Caffi Caban*.

ACCOMMODATION

HOTELS AND GUESTHOUSES

Dolafon Hotel High St ☎ 01286 870993, ⓦ dolafon .com. Appealing, well-priced B&B in a solid-granite Grade II-listed spacious house. Decor is traditional rather than exciting, but rooms are spacious and comfortable, especially larger front rooms (£85), the welcome warm and the price excellent value. **£65**

Graianfryn Penisarwaun, 3 miles northwest of Llanberis ☎ 01286 871007, ⓦ fastasleep.me.uk. An exclusively vegetarian and vegan wholefood B&B in a homely Victorian farmhouse; it's down a track, so look online or call for directions. Also offers three-course evening meals of home-grown produce on request. **£70**

★Plas Coch High St ☎ 01286 872122, ⓦ plas-coch .co.uk. New owners have done wonders to transform this B&B. Top to bottom refurbishment has produced seven hugely comfortable en-suite rooms, all chalky soft pastel shades, and added an extra bathroom with a slipper-tub for post-hike soaks as well as a drying room. A self-catering studio is promised. **£75**

Snowdon Cottage A4086, in front of Dolbadarn Castle 0.5 miles southeast of central Llanberis ☎ 01286 872015. B&B in a renovated eighteenth-century cottage with three shared-bath rooms, a cosy guest lounge and open fire that's perfect after a blustery day in the hills. Run by a walker who's always keen to help get you on the trail. Also a cute little two-bunk cabin in the garden rented out in summer for £40. **£56**

Ty'n Rhos Seion, nr Llanddeiniolen, 6 miles northwest of Llanberis ☎ 01248 670489, ⓦ tynrhos.co.uk. This country house is the most luxurious in the area, with plushly furnished rooms (some with mountain views) in cottage or more modern styles, plus a cosy lounge and conservatory, and an excellent in-house restaurant. **£115**

HOSTELS AND CAMPING

Ben's Bunkhouse, 1 mile southeast of Llanberis ☎ 07500 513765, ⓦ bensbunkhouse.co.uk. A good little bunkhouse that sleeps just 18 in three dorms (bring a sleeping bag), though it can be booked by groups. It also has a great kitchen with an urn of near-boiling water – perfect for a cuppa after the hills. A drying room is promised. **£15**

Cae Gwyn Nant Peris, 2 miles southeast of Llanberis ☎ 01286 870718. Climbers and bikers make up the bulk of the clientele in this field campsite and very primitive bunkhouse (bring everything) with £1 coin-op showers. It's almost opposite the pub *Vaynol Arms* and handy for the Pen-y-Pass park-and-ride. Camping per person **£6**, bunkhouse **£12**

Llwyn Celyn Bach 900yd uphill from town along Capel Coch Rd ☎ 01286 870923, ⓔ daviesllanberis@aol.com. The good news is that this is a lovely site spread over several fields with views over town to the slate quarries. The bad is that flat ground is in short supply – pick your site carefully. £1 coin showers. Per person **£6**, **£7** weekends July–Aug

Pete's Sleeps 40 High St ☎ 01286 872135, ⓦ petes -eats.co.uk. Super-central but fairly basic dorms above the café *Pete's Eats*, plus a couple of twin rooms (breakfast not included) with access to self-catering facilities. Can get booked by groups. Dorms **£16**, rooms **£37**

YHA Llanberis 700yd uphill from town along Capel Goch Rd ☎ 0845 371 9645, ⓔ llanberis@yha.org.uk. Hugely spacious and well-appointed older YHA hostel in an old quarrymaster's house, though looking rather tired on our last visit. Offers dorms, twin-bunk rooms and a couple of en-suite doubles plus meals (mains £8). Closed Dec & Jan. Dorms **£18**, doubles **£48**

EATING AND DRINKING

CAFÉS AND RESTAURANTS

★**Caffi Caban** Yr Hen Ysgol, Brynrefail, 2.3 miles northwest of Llanberis ☎ 01286 685500, ⓦ caban-cyf .org. Relaxed, bright licensed café which specializes in healthy meals made from organic, local or fair-trade ingredients, whether breakfasts (£4–7), sandwiches, baguettes or blackboard specials such as crab mousse with avocado or field mushrooms stuffed with bulghur and goat's cheese (£7.50). Delicious cakes and free wi-fi, too. Daily 9am–4pm.

The Peak Restaurant 86 High St ☎ 01286 872777, ⓦ peakrestaurant.co.uk. This unflashy open-kitchen restaurant serves easily the best food in Llanberis, all home made all fresh. Flavours are Modern British: bouillabasse with seabass, prawns and clams, Welsh lamb shank with redcurrant jus and mash or ribeye steak (average main £18). Booking advised. Wed–Sun 7–10pm.

Pen-y-Ceunant Isaf Snowdon Path ☎ 01286 872606, ⓦ snowdoncafe.com. Snug eighteenth-century cottage, 400-yd up the Llanberis Path, serving Welsh teas, coffee and snacks daily. There are no meals but you're welcome to eat yours here if you buy a cuppa. Visit if only to see the gallery of paintings and prints by Sir Kyffin Williams and other Welsh artists. Daily: April–Oct 9am–10pm; Nov–March 10am–6pm.

Pete's Eats 40 High St ☎ 01286 870117. A Llanberis legend for walkers, climbers and bikers with cheap caff food – full walker's breakfasts (£5), lamb burgers or fish and chips (£6) – in large portions. There are heaps of magazines and maps to browse and free wi-fi, so it's always busy when the weather turns bad. Summer daily 8am–8pm; winter Mon–Fri 9am–6.30pm, Sat–Sun 8am–8pm.

PUB AND BAR

The Heights 74 High St ☎ 01286 871179, ⓦ heightsllanberis.com. Stripped boards and bare surfaces have transformed this airy long-time favourite into a smart (for Llanberis) café/bar with a short menu of pub favourites, plus real ales. Popular with locals and visitors, it's usually the liveliest place in town. Daily 11am–11pm.

Vaynol Arms Nant Peris, 2 miles east of Llanberis ☎ 01286 872672. Slate-floored pub with good beer, hearty bar meals (£8) and plastered with mountain and slate-mining photos. Always alive with locals midweek, and with climbers and campers at weekends. Mon–Fri 5–11pm, Sat–Sun noon–11pm.

Snowdon

The highest British mountain south of the Scottish Grampians, the **Snowdon** massif (3560ft) forms a star of shattered ridges with three major peaks – Crib Goch, Crib-y-ddysgl and Y Lliwedd – and the summit, **Yr Wyddfa**, crowning the lot. If height were its only quality, it would be popular, but Snowdon also sports some of the finest walking and scrambling in Wales. Its Welsh name, Eryri, is derived from either *eryr* (land of eagles) or *eira* (land of snow); since the eagles have long gone, the latter is more appropriate, with winter snows lingering well into April.

Some outdoor enthusiasts dismiss Snowdon as overused, and it certainly can be crowded. A thousand visitors a day press into the postbox-red carriages of the Snowdon

ACTIVITIES AROUND LLANBERIS

By far the most popular activities around Llanberis are hiking (particularly on Snowdon) and rock climbing (on the crags of Llanberis Pass and elsewhere), but there's an abundance of other things to do.

Aerial obstacle course High Ropes Adventure Centre, by the slate museum (☏01286 872310, ☰ropesand ladders.co.uk). Spend a couple of hours with an instructor helping you push your boundaries on a course constructed from wooden poles. Adults £25, children £20.

Cruises A diminutive lake steamer, the *Snowdon Star* (☏07974 716418, ☰snowdonstar.co.uk), operates 40min narrated cruises on Llyn Padarn (daily: May–June & Sept 12am–5pm; July–Aug 11am–5pm; £6) from a small jetty near the slate museum.

Guided climbing and scrambling High Trek Snowdonia, Tal y Waen, Deiniolen (☏01286 871232, ☰climbing-wales.co.uk). One of several guides in the area, which offers everything from straightforward hillwalking to scrambling, rock climbing (all abilities), navigation and winter climbing to those not equipped or confident enough to get out on the rock alone.

Mountain biking The Llanberis Path up Snowdon (see box, p.354) is designated a bridleway, making it, the Snowdon Ranger Path and the Pitt's Head Track to Rhyd-Ddu accessible to cyclists; note that bikes are banned from summit tracks between 10am and 5pm from May to September. There are loads of other much easier rides in the area: ask at Llanberis Bike Hire, 34 High Street (☏01286 872787), which rents out bikes for £24 a day or £15 a half-day.

6

Mountain Railway (see p.349), while another fifteen hundred pound the well-maintained paths, making this Britain's most-climbed mountain. Opprobrium is chiefly levelled at the train for its mere existence, and at **Hafod Eryri** ("dwelling place atop Snowdon") café and bar on the summit for selling the country's highest pint of beer. But at least there's a warm place for walkers to rest, and those unable to walk up have the chance (the notoriously fickle weather permitting) of seeing the **view** over most of north Wales – and even across to Ireland on exceptionally clear days.

Brief history

The Welsh for the highest point of Snowdon, Yr Wyddfa, means "The Burial Place" – near proof that people have been climbing the mountain for millennia. More recently, early ascents were for botanical or geological reasons – 500-million-year-old fossil shells can be found near the summit from when Snowdon was on the sea bottom – but the Welsh naturalist Thomas Pennant came up here mainly for pleasure, and in 1773 his description of the dawn view from the summit in *Journey to Snowdon* encouraged many to follow. Some were guided by the Snowdon Ranger, Evan Roberts, from his house on the south side (now a YHA hostel), but the rapidly improving facilities in Llanberis soon shifted the balance in favour of the easier Llanberis Path, a route later followed by the railway. This remains one of the most popular routes, though many prefer the three shorter and steeper ones from the Pen-y-Pass car park at the top of the Llanberis Pass. By far the most dramatic, if also the most dangerous, is the wonderful Snowdon Horseshoe, which calls at all four of the high peaks.

The Llanberis Pass and Pen-y-Pass

The steady Llanberis Path, which grinds up Snowdon's gentlest ascent, may be the most popular single route up the mountain, but more walkers start from the lofty saddle at the top of the **Llanberis Pass**, the deepest, narrowest and craggiest of Snowdonia's passes, running five miles east from Llanberis itself. This is the Welsh home of **rock climbing**, and if you stop and look for a while you'll almost always see the dots of climbers inching their way up the various crags.

At the head of the pass is the YHA hostel, café and car park that make up **PEN-Y-PASS**, the base for the Miners' Track, the Pig Track and the demanding Snowdon Horseshoe (see box, p.354), which all leave from the car park.

WALKS UP SNOWDON

All the following paths are easy to follow in good weather, but the 1:25,000 OS Explorer OL17 map ("Snowdon & Conwy Valley") is still recommended.

LLANBERIS PATH

The easiest, longest and least interesting route up Snowdon, the **Llanberis Path** (5 miles to summit; 3hr; 3200ft ascent) follows the rail line. Victoria Terrace runs off the A4086 opposite the *Royal Victoria Hotel* and becomes a path that soon passes the *Pen-y-Ceunant* tearoom (see p.352). The summit comes into view towards the midway point and *Halfway House Café* (generally June to early Sept daily 10am–5pm; Easter–June & mid-Sept to Dec weekends only). From here there are views of Clogwyn Du'r Arddu (The Black Cliff, or "Cloggy" to its friends), a sheet of rock that frames a small lake. The path passes Clogwyn station, then gets steeper, passing the remains of stables where mule trains used to rest. Bwlch Glas (Green Pass) is marked by the "Finger Stone" where the Snowdon Ranger Path (see opposite) and three routes coming up from Pen-y-Pass join the Llanberis Path for the final ascent to Yr Wyddfa.

THE MINERS' TRACK

The **Miners' Track** (4 miles to summit; 2hr 30min; 2400ft ascent) is the easiest of the three routes up from Pen-y-Pass. Leaving the car park, a broad track leads south then west to the former copper mines in Cwm Dyli. Dilapidated remains of the crushing mill perch on the shores of Llyn Llydaw, a tarn-turned-reservoir with one of the worst eyesores in the national park, an overground pipeline slicing across Snowdon's east face to the power station in Nantgwynant. Skirting around the right of the lake, the path climbs more steeply to the lake-filled Cwm Glaslyn, then again to Upper Glaslyn, from where the measured steps of those ahead warn of the impending switchback ascent to the junction with the Llanberis Path.

THE PIG TRACK

The stonier **Pig Track** (3.5 miles to summit; 2hr 30min; 2400ft ascent) is really just a shorter and steeper variation on the Miners' Track, leaving from the western end of the Pen-y-Pass car park and climbing up to Bwlch y Moch (the Pass of the Pigs), which gives the route its name. Ignore the scramble up to Crib Goch (part of the Snowdon Horseshoe) and traverse below the rocky ridge looking down on Llyn Llydaw and those pacing the Miners' Track, content that you're already 500ft up on them. They'll soon catch up, as the two tracks meet just before the zigzag up to the Llanberis Path. The path is also known as the PYG track, supposedly after the nearby *Pen Y Gwryd Hotel*: no one seems able to agree on the matter.

SNOWDON HORSESHOE

Some claim that the **Snowdon Horseshoe** (8 miles round; 5–7hr; 3200ft ascent) is one of the finest ridge walks in Europe. The route makes a full anticlockwise circuit around the three glacier-graven cwms of Upper Glaslyn, Glaslyn and Llydaw. Not to be taken lightly, it includes the knife-edge traverse of Crib Goch. Every summer's day, dozens of people find themselves straddling the lip, empty space on either side, and wishing they weren't there. In winter

---

ARRIVAL AND DEPARTURE   PEN-Y-PASS

By bus The often-packed car park at Pen-y-Pass costs £5 for up to 4hr and £10 all day, so consider using the bus. Park at the park-and-ride at the bottom of the pass close to the *Vaynol Arms* (£5 all day) then ride the frequent #S1 & #S2

Snowdon Sherpa buses (£1; 7 daily; 10min) to Pen-y-Pass. Destinations Beddgelert (5 daily; 20min); Betws-y-Coed (6 daily; 15min); Capel Curig (6 daily; 10min); Llanberis (hourly or better; 15min); Porthmadog (4 daily; 45min).

ACCOMMODATION AND EATING

★**Pen-y-Gwryd Hotel** 1 mile east of Pen-y-Pass ☎ 01286 870211, ⊕ pyg.co.uk. This wonderful place of ageing furniture and magnificent Edwardian bathrooms is legendary as the hotel from which the successful Mount Everest team trained before its 1953 ascent. Edmund Hillary has signed the ceiling (as have Chris Bonington and

Portmeirion designer Clough Williams-Ellis) and donated mementoes of his trip for the splendid "Smoke Room". Edwardian rooms (some en suite) are priced per person, though all are doubles (the price for two people in a double is listed below). Expect lots of solid cooking (£25 for a 3-course meal, £30 for 5) and a congenial bygone

conditions, an ice axe and crampons are the minimum requirement. The path follows the Pig Track to Bwlch y Moch, then pitches right for the moderate scramble up to **Crib Goch**. If you baulk at any of this, turn back. If not, wait your turn, then painstakingly pick your way along the sensational ridge to Crib-y-ddysgl (3494ft), from where it's an easy descent to Bwlch Glas and on to Yr Wyddfa. Having ticked off Wales's two highest peaks, turn southwest for a couple of hundred yards to a marker stone where the Watkin Path (see below) drops away to the east. Follow it down to the stretched saddle of Bwlch-y-Saethau (Pass of the Arrows), then on to the cairn at Bwlch Ciliau from where the Watkin Path descends to Nantgwynant. Ignore that route, continuing straight on up the cliff-lined northwest ridge of Y Lliwedd (2930ft), then descend to where you see the scrappy but safe path down to Llyn Llydaw and the Miners' Track.

6

SNOWDON RANGER PATH

Many of the earliest Snowdon climbers engaged the services of the Snowdon Ranger, who led them up the comparatively long and dull but easy **Snowdon Ranger Path** (4 miles to summit; 3hr; 3100ft ascent), on the now unfashionable south side of the mountain. The path starts from the *YHA Snowdon Ranger Hostel* (see p.364) on the shores of Llyn Cwellyn, five miles northwest of Beddgelert. To the left of the hostel, a path leads up a track then ascends steeply, flattening out to cross sometimes boggy grass and eventually skirting to the right of the impressive Clogwyn Du'r Arddu cliffs. Another steep ascent eventually brings you to the Llanberis Path at Bwlch Glas. Use the Welsh Highland Railway or the #S4 bus for the return journey.

RHYD DDU TRACK

The **Rhyd Ddu Track** (4 miles to summit; 3hr; 2900ft ascent) has two branches, one starting from Pitt's Head Rock, two and a half miles northwest of Beddgelert, the other from the national park car park in Rhyd Ddu, a mile beyond that. They join up after less than a mile's walk across stony, walled grazing land, and after crossing a kissing gate continue to the northwest up to the stunning final section along the rim of Cwm Clogwyn and the south ridge of Yr Wyddfa. Use the Welsh Highland Railway or the #S4 bus to turn this into a loop.

WATKIN PATH

The most spectacular of the southern routes up Snowdon, the **Watkin Path** (4 miles to summit; 3hr; 3350ft ascent) is also the one with the greatest height gain. From Bethania Bridge, three miles northeast of Beddgelert in Nantgwynant, the path starts on a broad track through oaks opening up to long views of a series of cataracts. Ascend beside these to a disused inclined tramway where the track narrows before reaching the natural amphitheatre of Cwm Llan. The ruins of the South Snowdon Slate Works only briefly distract you from Gladstone Rock, at which, in 1892, the 83-year-old Liberal statesman, then in his fourth term as British prime minister, officially opened the route. A narrower path wheels left around the base of Craig Ddu, then starts the steep ascent past Carnedd Arthur to Bwlch Ciliau, the saddle between Y Lliwedd (see Snowdon Horseshoe opposite) and the true summit (Yr Wyddfa), then turning left for the final climb to the top.

atmosphere. Two-night minimum at weekends. Weekends only Jan & Feb; closed Nov & Dec. **£86**
YHA Pen-y-Pass ☎ 0845 371 9534, ✉ penypass@yha .org.uk. The only accommodation at Pen-y-Pass recently underwent a £1.3m renovation to update what was already

a renowned walkers' hostel into a hugely comfy modern-rustic stay. Previously there was 24hr access, limited free parking, a few two-bunk rooms, a bar licence and good meals. Dorms **£18**

Caernarfon and around

Caernarfon, superbly set at the southern entrance to the Menai Strait, has a lot going for it. Its distinctive polygonal-towered **castle** is an undoubted highlight, the **Welsh Highland Railway** now connects the town with the slopes of Snowdon and Porthmadog, and the modern marina development adds **Galeri Caernarfon**, a modest but interesting arts centre. There's also the sheer pleasure of simply meandering

6

KING ARTHUR AND SNOWDON

From the departure of the Romans until the tenth century, Welsh history is pervaded by legends of **King Arthur** (see box, p.74), **Gwrtheyrn** (Vortigern) and **Myrddin**, otherwise known as Merlin (see box, p.145). Arthur's British (as opposed to Anglo-Saxon) blood gives him a firm place in Welsh hearts, and while Caerleon in southeast Wales lays a powerful claim to being the site of Arthur's court, Snowdon is often held to be his home.

It was atop Dinas Emrys, the seat of Gwrtheyrn's realm near Beddgelert, that the most potent symbol of Welsh independence, the Red Dragon, earned its colours. The Celtic king, Gwrtheyrn, was trying to build a fortress to protect himself from the Saxons, but each night the earth swallowed the masonry. Myrddin divined this to be caused by two dragons sleeping underground: one white, the other red. When woken, they fought unendingly, symbolizing the Red Dragon of Wales's perpetual battle with the White Dragon of the Saxons.

Arthur's domain was higher up the mountain. Llyn Llydaw aspires to being the lake into which Bedivere cast Arthur's sword, Excalibur, after Arthur was mortally wounded by an arrow while on the point of vanquishing his nephew Modred at Bwlch-y-Saethau (The Pass of the Arrows), thirteen hundred feet above the lake.

among the seventeenth- and eighteenth-century buildings in the knot of streets wedged between the **town walls**.

Renovation in 2014 transformed the quayside below the castle from car park to waterside **promenade** beneath the town walls (as complete as those at Conwy). Sadly there remains no way to access the walls themselves. Factor in some great accommodation and Caernarfon makes a great, central base for exploring both sides of Snowdon, the Llŷn and even Anglesey.

Caernarfon is a town with ardent support for **Plaid Cymru** and a local **dialect** that is barely intelligible even to other Welsh-speakers. It is also the county town of Gwynedd, and one of the oldest continuously occupied settlements in Wales, once the site of the Romans' most westerly legion post.

Caernarfon Castle

Entrance on Castle Ditch • March–June, Sept & Oct daily 9.30am–5pm; July & Aug daily 9.30am–6pm; Nov–Feb Mon–Sat 10am–4pm, Sun 11am–4pm • £6.75; CADW • ☏ 01286 677617

In 1283, Edward I started work on **Caernarfon Castle**, the strongest link in his Iron Ring (see box, p.404) and the decisive hammerblow to any Welsh aspirations of autonomy. Until Beaumaris Castle was built to guard the other end of the Menai Strait, Caernarfon was the ultimate symbol of Anglo-Norman military might and political wrangling. With the Welsh already smarting from the loss of their Prince of Wales, Edward reputedly rubbed salt in their wounds by justifying his own infant son's claim to the title, having promised them "a prince born in Wales who could speak never a word of English", and subsequently presenting them with the newborn baby that had arrived after his pregnant wife had been forced to take up residence in the castle. The story is almost certainly apocryphal, since Edward's son, though born at Caernarfon, wasn't invested until seven years later.

However, Edward attempted to woo the Welsh with gestures to certain local legends. The Welsh had long associated their town with the eastern capital of the Roman Empire: Caernarfon's old Roman name, Caer Cystennin ("Fort of Constantine"), alludes to the emperor after whom Constantinople was named, and there are even some dreamers who claim that Constantine himself was born here. Edward's architect, James of St George, exploited this connection in the distinctive limestone and sandstone banding and polygonal towers, both reminiscent of the Theodosian walls still standing in Istanbul.

The castle is in an excellent state of repair, thanks largely to a nineteenth-century reconstruction, carried out after Richard Wilson and J.M.W. Turner painted Romantic images of it.

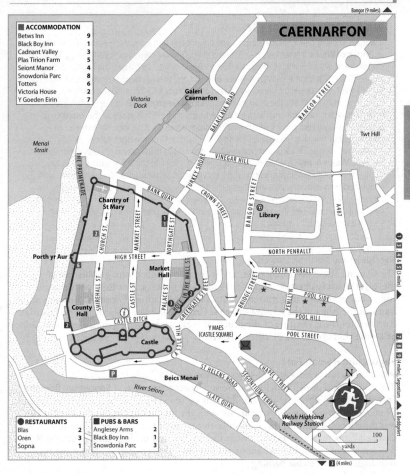

ACCOMMODATION

Betws Inn	9
Black Boy Inn	1
Cadnant Valley	3
Plas Tirion Farm	5
Seiont Manor	4
Snowdonia Parc	8
Totters	6
Victoria House	2
Y Goeden Eirin	7

RESTAURANTS

Blas	2
Oren	3
Sopna	1

PUBS & BARS

Anglesey Arms	2
Black Boy Inn	1
Snowdonia Parc	3

The King's Gate

As you enter the **King's Gate**, the castle's strength is immediately apparent. Indeed, as a military monument of its time, it is supreme, and still has an imperious presence. Seized only once, before it was finished, it then withstood two sieges by Owain Glyndŵr with a complement of only 28 men-at-arms.

Between the octagonal towers, embrasures and murder-holes cover no fewer than five gates and six portcullises once you've crossed the moat. Inside, the huge lawn gives a misleading impression, since both the wall dividing the two original wards crumbled away and all the wooden buildings that filled the wards disappeared long ago.

The Eagle Tower

The walls and towers are in a much better state than the interior, linked by such a honeycomb of wall-walks and tunnels that a tour can be exhausting. The Eagle Tower at the western end is the loftiest and most striking, its three slender turrets adorned with heavily eroded eagle sculptures affording superb views of the town. On the lower floors, displays and a short film outline the castle's history and its importance in the context of Edward I's Iron Ring.

6

WHAT PRINCE OF WALES?

It was in Caernarfon in 1969 that Charles, the current heir to the throne, was theatrically invested as **Prince of Wales**, a ceremony that reaffirmed English sovereignty over Wales in the midst of one of the most nationalist of Welsh-speaking regions. Since 1282, when the English defeated Llywelyn ap Gruffydd, the last Welsh Prince of Wales, the title has been bestowed on heirs to the English throne, usually in a ceremony held either at Windsor Castle or in Westminster Abbey in London. However, in 1911, the machinations of **Lloyd George** – MP for Caernarfon, Welsh cabinet minister and future prime minister – ensured that the investiture of the future King Edward VIII would take place in the centre of his constituency: a paradoxical move for a nationalist, but one that undoubtedly helped to advance Lloyd George's career.

By the time it was Charles's turn, nationalism was on the rise and two extremist members of the **Free Wales Army** blew themselves up trying to blow up the Prince's train. In many ways, such acts had a detrimental effect on the nationalist cause, wrongly linking extremism with the more moderate and constitutional methods of the party. Charles's 25-year commemorative return visit in 1994 was a far more low-key affair, remembered, if at all, for the local constabulary ruling that the local joke shop risked committing a public-order offence by selling "wingnut" ears and Prince Charles masks.

The Queen and Northeast towers

The Queen's Tower is entirely taken up by the numbingly thorough **Museum of the Royal Welch Fusiliers** detailing the victories of Wales's oldest regiment through collections of medals, uniforms and a brass howitzer captured from the Russians at the Battle of the Alma in the Crimea in 1854. Crossing the upper ward, you pass the slate dais used for the investiture of the Prince of Wales, a pageant expanded on in the **Prince of Wales Exhibition** in the Northeast Tower.

Segontium Roman Fort

A4085, 0.3 miles east towards Beddgelert • 12.30–4.30pm; closed Mon • Free; CADW

The western end of the Roman road from Chester terminated at **Segontium Roman Fort**, a five-acre hilltop site that the Romans occupied for three centuries from around 78 AD, though most of the remains are from the final rebuilding after 364 AD. This was the base of Maximus, the Spanish-born pretender to the imperial throne who was declared Emperor by his British troops in 383 AD, and made a failed march on Rome. The remains of Segontium are about as impressive as his march, seldom more than shin-high and somewhat baffling.

Greenwood Forest Park

B4366, 3 miles northeast of Caernarfon, just west of the village of Bethel • Daily: late March–Aug 10am–5.30pm; Sept & Oct 10am–5pm; Nov–Feb half-term 10am–5.30pm (playbarn only) • £11.95, £42.20 family pass; reduced off-peak prices • ☎ 01248 670076, ⓦ greenwoodforestpark.co.uk

A sort of eco fun park, **Greenwood Forest Park** provides a mini-rollercoaster, zipwires, slides, longbow shooting, tree houses, adventure playgrounds and the like. Underlying everything is a conservation message and almost all activities are human-powered: even that roller coaster is powered by the energy you expend walking up to the start.

Inigo Jones Slateworks

Groeslon, A487 6 miles south of Caernarfon • Daily 9am–5pm • Tours £5 • ☎ 01286 830242, ⓦ www.inigojones.co.uk

The Lôn Eifion bike path runs south from Caernarfon right by the **Inigo Jones Slateworks**, where slate has been fashioned in road-side sheds since 1861. The factory was started by one Inigo Jones, a local man apparently unrelated to the seventeenth-century architect. Many of the inscribed slate plaques on public buildings around north Wales were cut here, ample excuse for an interesting calligraphy exhibition in a 45-minute self-guided audio tour. You can even try your hand at chiselling a few random chips of slate.

Parc Glynllifon

Off A499, 6 miles south of Caernarfon • Daily 9am–5pm • Craft workshops and café free; grounds £4 • ☎01286 830222

Parc Glynllifon occupies the grounds of nineteenth-century Glynllifon Hall (not open to the public), once home of Lord Newborough. Easy trails weave through a pleasant woodland garden complete with arboretum, but look too at the former workshops, now given over to well-respected craftspeople including one of Wales's top artistic blacksmiths, Ann Catrin Evans.

Dinas Dinlle

7 miles south of Caernarfon, 1 mile west of A499 • Open access • Free; NT

The sea is doing its best to erode the still substantial remains of **Dinas Dinlle**, a 150yd-diameter **Iron Age hillfort** built 2500 years ago. The Romans also occupied this now-grassy site and presumably would have enjoyed the same wonderful views along the Llŷn and back to Snowdonia.

ARRIVAL AND DEPARTURE — CAERNARFON

By bus National Express and local buses stop on Pool Side, east of central Y Maes (Castle Square).
Destinations Bangor (Mon–Sat hourly, Sun 6 daily; 25min); Beddgelert (Mon–Sat 7 daily; 30min); Llanberis (Mon–Sat hourly, Sun 5 daily; 25min); Porthmadog (Mon–Sat 6 daily; 40min); Pwllheli (Mon–Sat roughly hourly, Sun 3 daily; 45min).

INFORMATION AND GETTING AROUND

Tourist office The TIC is on Castle Street (Easter–Sept daily 9.30am–4.30pm; Oct–Easter Mon–Sat 10am–3.30pm; ☎01286 672232, ✉caernarfon.tic @gwynedd.gov.uk).
Internet Free at the library on Bangor Street (Mon, Tues, Thurs & Fri 9.30am–7pm, Wed & Sat 9.30am–1pm), and free wi-fi at the *Anglesey Arms* (see p.360).
Bike rental Beics Menai, 1 Slate Quay (☎01286 676804, ⊕beicsmenai.co.uk). All sorts of bikes (at £15 for 2hr up to £22 for 8hr, plus tandems for a little more).

ACCOMMODATION

HOTELS AND GUESTHOUSES

★ **Betws Inn** Betws Garmon, A4085, 5 miles southeast ☎01286 650324, ⊕betws-inn.co.uk. Slate floors and whitewashed stone walls add rustic charm to the three stylish rooms of this luxury B&B, a former drovers' inn (some parts from 1620) with an inglenook fireplace in the guest lounge. Breakfasts are excellent and three-course dinners are available by arrangement (£18–25). **£80**
Black Boy Inn Northgate St ☎01286 673604, ⊕black-boy-inn.com. Low-beamed rooms in what is said to be the town's oldest building (bar the castle), plus newer rooms in an adjacent house, all including breakfast and free parking. Dynamic pricing system. **£95**
Plas Tirion Farm Llanrug, A4086, 3 miles east of Caernarfon ☎01286 673190, ⊕plas-tirion.co.uk. Welcoming, traditional B&B in a stone farmhouse, furnished with antiques and with some choice rural views. Two nights minimum in August. **£70**
Seiont Manor A4086, 3 miles east of Caernarfon towards Llanberis ☎0845 072 7550, ⊕handpicked .co.uk. Rustic edifice that has been converted into a rather grand hotel furnished with antiques, and complete with

---

EXPLORING BY THE WELSH HIGHLAND RAILWAY FROM CAERNARFON

We've covered the **Welsh Highland Railway** in detail under Porthmadog (see box, p.370). Steam- or diesel-hauled trains run from the small station in Caernarfon on St Helen's Road, some of them going the full 25 miles to Porthmadog. The following train routes are good ways to explore the railway and the wonderful scenery hereabouts:
Train to Waunfawr Visit the *Snowdonia Parc* pub and a pleasant campsite (35min).
Train to Snowdon Ranger One-hour hike up the Snowdon Ranger path (p.355) followed by a stay at the YHA hostel (see p.364).
Train to Rhyd Ddu Hike the Rhyd Ddu track to Snowdon's summit; peak season timetables give you up to 7hr for the hike.
Train to Dinas Walk the three miles back along Lôn Eifion.

6

MOUNTAIN BIKING

There's good family-oriented off-road riding in the **Beddgelert Forest** a mile out on the Caernarfon road and a mile uphill from the *Beddgelert Forest Campsite* (see p.364). Spend half a day pootling around the trails, including a six-mile signposted loop.

---

indoor pool, good restaurant, sauna and even fishing within the hotel grounds. **£136**

★**Victoria House** 13 Church St ☎01286 678263, ⓦthevictoriahouse.co.uk. Our favourite B&B in Caernarfon now has a comfortable lounge and a town wall terrace with views over the Menai Straits. Otherwise, it remains a fine stay of immaculate Victorian-styled (but modern) en-suites (all doubles, no twins), all with flatscreen TV/DVD, free wi-fi and complimentary drinks. Great value. **£70**

★**Y Goeden Eirin** Dolydd, 4 miles south of Caernarfon ☎01286 830942, ⓦygoedeneirin.co.uk. There's effortless, personal style in this classy B&B that's equal parts hospitable Welsh farmhouse and a stay full of art, literature and poetry; its owners are university lecturers. Expect eco credentials and beautifully curated decor, whether in a spacious loft or two rooms in the outbuildings. Good dinners on request too. There's also a self-catering beach cottage sleeping five a few miles away. Cash/cheque only. Doubles **£80**; cottage **£300–550**

HOSTEL AND CAMPING

Cadnant Valley Llanberis Rd, 1km east of Y Maes ☎01286 673196, ⓦcwmcadnantvalley.co.uk. Pleasant wooded campsite with lots of flat ground that feels more rural than the location – 15min walk east of the centre, near the start of the A4086 to Llanberis – suggests. Closed Nov–Feb. Pitches **£12**

Snowdonia Parc Waunfawr, 4 miles southeast on A4085 ☎01286 650409, ⓦsnowdonia-park.co.uk. Attractive year-round campsite, right by a station of the Welsh Highland Railway. Steam trains aside, its appeal is the location among mountains and next to a good microbrewery. Free showers. Pitches **£18**

★**Totters** Plas Porth Yr Aur, 2 High St ☎01286 672963, ⓦtotters.co.uk. Caernarfon's only backpacker hostel is one of the best in Wales: centrally located in an airy, modernized house, with friendly owners, clean modern dorms and inviting communal spaces. There's also a great attic en-suite double with sea views (£47.50) and *The Townhouse*, a self-contained house opposite that sleeps six. Rates include continental breakfast. Dorms **£17**, rooms **£40**, *The Townhouse* per person from **£20**

EATING AND DRINKING

RESTAURANTS

★**Blas** 23–25 Hole in the Wall St ☎01258 677707, ⓦblascaernarfon.co.uk. Excellent cooking such as *conchiglioni* with mushroom ragu and crushed hazelnuts have seen this sweet modern bistro embraced by Caernarfon locals. Lunches (£7–10) include the likes of tasty home-made lamb burgers or club sandwiches. Evening menus (mains £12–18) up the ante. Either way local ingredients star. Tues–Sat 10.30am–3pm & 6–9pm, Sun noon–3pm.

Oren 26 Hole in the Wall St ☎01286 674343. A delightfully eclectic little basement restaurant run by a Welsh-speaking Dutchman, which feels less dining out than a hosted meal. There's limited choice – home-cooked menus change weekly, typically with a theme (French, Thai, Buddhist vegetarian, Greek/Turkish) – but that allows the quality of seasonal local produce to shine. Ideal for culinary adventurers and good value at £16.50 for three courses. Reservations required. Fri–Sat from 7pm, other evenings on request.

Sopna Felin Wen, Pontrug, A4086, 2 miles east ☎01286 675222, ⓦsopna.co.uk. Quality award-winning Bangladeshi tandoori restaurant that is something of a local legend for its wide range of spicy balti dishes and delicately flavoured vegetable sides. Mains mostly around £9; £7 to take away. Daily 6–11pm.

PUBS AND BARS

Anglesey Arms The Promenade ☎01286 672158. While the pub is nothing to quicken the pulse, the sea wall outside makes this unbeatable on sunny afternoons. It offers standard pub grub (average main £10), real ales and live music on Fridays. Daily 11am–11pm.

Black Boy Inn Northgate St ☎01286 673604, ⓦblack-boy-inn.com. The closest Caernarfon comes to an old-fashioned British pub, all low beams and swirly carpets, with a choice of two wonderfully characterful low-beamed bars and the best bar meals in town: expect dishes like lamb shank with mash or pan-fried scallops (£9–15). Daily 11am–11pm.

Snowdonia Park Waunfawr ☎01286 650409, ⓦsnowdonia-park.co.uk. Rural pub four miles southeast of town by Waunfaur station on the Welsh Highland line. All about the range of beers brewed on site, ideal to wash down decent pub grub like Welsh steak and ale pie (£8–12). Bus #S4 to Beddgelert goes right by. Daily 11am–11pm.

ENTERTAINMENT

Galeri Caernarfon Victoria Dock ☎01286 685222, ⓦgalericaernarfon.com. Modern arts and entertainment complex which puts on a wide range of plays, shows mainstream and more arty films (mainly Wed evenings) and includes gallery space and a café/bar.

Beddgelert and around

At the confluence of the Glaslyn and Colwyn rivers on the south flank of Snowdon, **BEDDGELERT** is the picture-postcard village of central Snowdonia. Though tiny, it ticks all the boxes for charm: a few dozen grey houses, their window boxes bursting with flowers, a pretty bridge over a burbling river, cafés, crowds… Such is the number of tourists on sunny summer days, parking can be tricky – consider making a day of it by visiting from Caernarfon or Porthmadog on the Welsh Highland Railway. Yet even the occasional coach tour can't spoil a pleasant spot for lunches, ice creams and strolls – jolly holidays in a nutshell.

Gelert's Grave

Most visitors to Beddgelert stroll 400yd south, along the right bank of the Glaslyn, to the spot that gives the village its name, **Gelert's Grave** (*bedd* means "burial place"). Actually, the story behind this railed-off enclosure is more interesting than the site itself. They say it marks the final resting place of Prince Llywelyn ap Iorwerth's faithful dog, Gelert, who was left in charge of the prince's infant son while he went hunting. On his return, the child was gone and the hound's muzzle was soaked in blood. Jumping to conclusions, the impetuous Llywelyn slew the dog, only to find the child safely asleep beneath its cot and a dead wolf beside him. Llywelyn hurried to his dog, which licked his hand as it died. In fact, the story is an eighteenth-century invention by a local publican, though it's succeeded in luring punters ever since. The real source of the name is probably the grave of Celert, a sixth-century British saint who supposedly lived hereabouts.

WALKS FROM BEDDGELERT

Two fine hikes up Snowdon start near **Beddgelert**, and there are a couple of good ones closer to town: all are covered by the OS 1:25,000 OL17 Explorer map ("Snowdon & Conwy Valley") and 1:50,000 115 Landranger map ("Snowdon/Yr Wyddfa").

ABERGLASLYN GORGE

(3 miles return; 2hr; 100ft ascent). This fairly easy walk follows the Glaslyn as it tumbles and cascades through the madly picturesque Aberglaslyn Gorge. Cross a footbridge over the Glaslyn River in the village and follow the left bank downstream until you meet the Welsh Highland Railway. Continue between the railway and the river on the **Fisherman's Track** as the train line ducks through two tunnels. The path meets the road at Pont Aberglaslyn – the tidal limit before The Cob was built at Porthmadog – from where you can retrace your steps.

MOEL HEBOG RIDGE

(8-mile loop; 5hr; 2800ft ascent). West of Beddgelert, the lumpish **Moel Hebog** (Bald Hill of the Hawk; 2569ft) is the highest point on a fine panoramic ridge walk that also takes in the lesser peaks of **Moel Lefn** and **Moel yr Ogof** (Hill of the Cave). The final forest section can be a bit disorientating, even in good weather, so be sure you have a compass.

Start half a mile northwest of the centre of Beddgelert on the A4085, where Pont Alyn crosses the river to Cwm Cloch Isaf Farm. Follow the signs to a green lane, which soon leads up onto the broad northeast ridge, all the time keeping left of the Y Diffwys cliffs. The summit cairn is joined by two walls, the one to the northwest leading down a steep grassy slope to Bwlch Meillionen, from where you can ascend over rocky ground to Moel yr Ogof. From the top of Moel yr Ogof, it's a clear route north to Moel Lefn, then down to a cairn from where you can plan your descent. The easiest line is to Bwlch Cwm-trwsgl, near the highest point of the Beddgelert Forest, then through the forest to the A4085 and back to Beddgelert.

EXPLORING BY THE WELSH HIGHLAND RAILWAY FROM BEDDGELERT

Since 2011 Beddgelert has been linked to both Caernarfon and Porthmadog by the Welsh Highland Railway (wfestrail.co.uk), which we've detailed more fully under Porthmadog. Here are a few ways to explore the line.

Take advantage of the new Lon Gwyfrai cycle and walking track: walk to Rhyd Ddu (4.5 miles) or **rent a bike in Beddgelert** (see below) then cycle to Waunfaur (9 miles) then catch the train back (£3 bikes). Views are splendid. The track starts at the railway station.

Ride the train to Rhyd Ddu (1hr round trip; £9.70) climbing the steepest part of the route. Trains pass at Rhyd Ddu, so there is almost always a train waiting on the other side of the platform for the return trip.

Train through the tunnels of the Aberglaslyn Gorge to Pont Croesor request stop (seasonal osprey viewing) then return on a later train (£15.40 return).

Train to Nantmor (£4.50 one-way) then walk back to Beddgelert along the Fisherman's Path (1hr).

Sygun Copper Mine

Almost 1 mile northeast on A498 • Daily: British Summer Time 9.30am–5pm, otherwise 10am–4pm; closed mid-Nov to Dec except Christmas • £8.95 • ☎ 01766 890595, w syguncoppermine.co.uk

Given its pretty planted terraces, it's hard to imagine this hillside north of central Beddgelert was mined for ore by the Romans, then nineteenth-century prospectors. The **Sygun Copper Mine** showcases what was once the valley's prime source of income on a family-oriented 45-minute self-guided **tour** through the multiple levels of restored tunnels and galleries (cool at 9°C). En route, the disembodied voice of a miner describes his working life. Afterwards, you're free to potter around the ore-crushing and separation equipment, or to have a go at gold panning or using a metal detector (both £2.50).

ARRIVAL AND DEPARTURE   BEDDGELERT

By bus Beddgelert is on two bus routes: the #S4 Snowdon Sherpa from Caernarfon and the #S97 between Pen-y-Pass and Porthmadog. Services stop on the main street from Caernarfon (Mon–Sat 8 daily; 30min), Pen-y-Pass (4 daily; 20min) and Porthmadog (Mon–Sat 7 daily, Sun 3 daily; 30–50min).

INFORMATION AND ACTIVITIES

Tourist information On our last visit the TIC on the A498 in the village centre seemed set to close (previously Easter–Oct daily 9.30am–5.30pm; Nov–Easter Fri, Sat & Sun 9.30am–4.30pm; ☎ 01766 890615, w beddgelerttourism.com).

Mountain biking There's good family-oriented off-road riding in the Beddgelert Forest a mile out on the Caernarfon road and a mile uphill from the *Beddgelert Forest Campsite* (see p.364). Spend half a day pootling around the trails including a six-mile signposted loop. Beddgelert Bikes (☎ 01766 890434, w beddgelertbikes.co.uk), located beside the Welsh Highland Railway train station in Beddgelert, has bikes available to rent (£15 for 2hr, £28 for 8hr, less for kids' bikes).

ACCOMMODATION

HOTELS AND GUESTHOUSES

Colwyn Stryd Smith (opposite bridge) ☎ 01766 890276, w beddgelertguesthouse.co.uk. Central 300-year-old cottage guesthouse with comfortable (if somewhat cosy) renovated rooms, a beamed lounge and an open fire. There's a two-night minimum stay at weekends. **£65**

Plas Tan y Graig Stryd Smith (opposite bridge) ☎ 01766 890310, w plas-tanygraig.co.uk. Central and well-managed B&B that's been refurbished into a homely stylish stay. Mod cons in the seven rooms include a small fridge, flatscreen TVs and some CD/DVD players. Free wi-fi throughout, honesty bar, a drying room and packed lunches (on request) plus free flask refills. Minimum 2 nights. **£86**

★ **Sygun Fawr** 0.7 miles northeast off A498 ☎ 01766 890258, w sygunfawr.co.uk. This partly seventeenth-century country house, the smartest of the local hotels, specializes in peace (no TVs in rooms) and views of the latter stretch to Snowdon from some comfy country-styled rooms. Two- and three-night dinner deals in the restaurant (see p.364) are worth investigating. Closed Dec to mid-Feb. **£85**

6

HOSTELS AND CAMPING

Beddgelert Caravan & Campsite A498, 1 mile northwest ☎01766 890288, ⓦcampingintheforest .co.uk. Excellent, family-friendly forest campsite with a kids' play area, laundry service, decent on-site shop and a host of other facilities – not least its own (request) stop on the Welsh Highland Line. **£22.50**

Cae Du Camping 10min walk towards Capel Curig on A498 ☎01766 890345, ⓦcaeducampsite.co.uk. Spacious and peaceful site that is immaculately maintained without affecting the natural beauty of the area; there are some lovely stream-side pitches. Good facilities, too: hot showers, some power hook-ups and a small shop. Closed Oct–Feb. **£18.50**/pitch

★**Hafod y Llan** Nantgwynant, A498, 4 miles north ☎01766 510129. One for camping purists, this simple tent-only site by the start of the Watkin Path up Snowdon is on a National Trust farm, which is managed to enhance the landscape for conservation. Highly scenic, campfires are permitted, and there is a drier. Closed Nov–March. Showers 50p. **£7**/person

Llyn Gwynant Campsite A498, 5 miles northeast ☎01766 890853, ⓦgwynant.com. Large lakeside site in a gorgeous valley beneath Snowdon, which can host over 400 tents at peak times. Still, it retains its natural appeal. You can access the Watkin Path directly from the site, rent kayaks and canoes (June–Sept), and hot showers are free. Radios are banned, mobile phones don't work and bookings are not required. Closed Nov to mid-March. **£9**/person

YHA Bryn Gwynant A498, 4 miles northeast ☎0845 371 9108, ⓔbryngwynant@yha.org.uk. Beautifully sited in a former mansion in Nantgwynant, this is now looking rather tired, yet it's cheap and handy for the Watkin Path. Offers dorm beds and private rooms, plus meals are available and the hostel is licensed. Check in from 5pm. Closed Nov to early Feb. Dorms **£18.50**; doubles **£35**

YHA Snowdon Ranger Rhyd Ddu, 5 miles northwest on A498 ☎0845 371 9659, ⓔsnowdon@yha.org.uk. A former inn at the foot of the Snowdon Ranger Path. Bunks are mostly in two- and four-bed rooms, meals are available and the place is licensed. Closed Sept–March; call for exact times. Dorms **£18**; doubles **£43**

EATING AND DRINKING

CAFÉ & RESTAURANTS

Glaslyn Ices/Cafe Glyndŵr On the south side of the river bridge ☎01766 890339, ⓦglaslynices.co.uk. One of the UK's finest ice-cream makers, this small outfit produces three dozen flavours plus fruit sorbets on site to take away; mango sorbet, cinder toffee and a rich chocolate have won gongs in recent years. A good family-friendly restaurant behind offers tasty fresh baguettes, great pizzas and specials like home-made chilli con carne (£10). School and bank holidays daily 9.30am–8.30pm, otherwise Mon–Fri & Sun 10am–5pm, Sat 9.30am–8pm.

★**Hebog Caernarfon Road** ☎01766 890400, ⓦhebog-eatandsleep.co.uk. Opened in 2014, this rustic-chic bistro ticks all the boxes. It offers a good-value menu prepared from local ingredients – superb full Welsh breakfasts, jacket potatos, Welsh beef ciabattas or larger mains like home-made meatballs, fishcakes with chilli sauce or duck confit (£9–12) – outside tables beside the river and takeaway fish and chips. Daily 8am–10pm.

Sygun Fawr 0.7 miles northeast off A498 ☎01766 890258, ⓦsygunfawr.co.uk. Slow-cooked Welsh lamb shank with red wine jus or chicken in prosciutto in a tarragon sauce (mains £13–16) are typical of the à la carte dishes freshly prepared in this hotel restaurant, which is open to non-residents. Meals are served in a snug dining room with antiques or a conservatory with mountain views. Bookings recommended. Closed Dec to mid-Feb. Tues–Sun 6–10pm.

PUB

Tanronnen Inn ☎01766 890347, ⓦtanronnen.co.uk. The best of the three pubs in the village, this old inn feels more like a front room in its tiny bar with just five or so tables and a few ales on tap. Daily noon–11pm.

Blaenau Ffestiniog and around

Snowdonia's most southerly major settlement, **BLAENAU FFESTINIOG**, is spread beneath thousand-foot mountains strewn with splintered slate. The town attracts some of Snowdonia's worst weather and when clouds hunker low in the great cwm and rain lashes the grey roofs, it glowers fabulously. On days when every tourist office in north Wales is packed with wet visitors wondering what to do, Blaenau Ffestiniog looks its most dramatic.

Thousands of tons of slate a year were once hewn from caverns beneath the town, and exported worldwide. They made the first part of their journey on the Ffestiniog Railway to the ships at Porthmadog, thirteen miles away. Now, only two mines tick over (one aided by earnings from tours) and the town's population has dropped to less than half its 1910 peak of twelve thousand. For years the local economy leaned on a so-so mine tour and a location at the junction of two of the finest train journeys in Wales: the narrow-gauge **Ffestiniog Railway** and the **Conwy Valley Railway** (see box, p.341). No longer. Blaenau Ffestiniog today is quietly transforming itself into the adrenaline capital of Wales, with a world-first **zip wire** and superb **mountain biking** initiatives. Today, younger visitors are replacing the coach-tour brigade. Who'd have imagined that slate could be so much fun?

Brief history

When Snowdonia National Park was created in 1951, it formed a massive doughnut around Blaenau Ffestiniog. The town's heaps of waste slate were deemed incompatible with a national park. For years, Blaenau Ffestiniog has been in sad decline and as part of a push to make it more of a tourist destination there is now a movement to have the town brought into the park. In 2010, the national park authority voted "in principle" to include the town within the park, but that still needs the approval of the Countryside Council for Wales, then a referendum of locals, so it is likely to be a long process.

Llechwedd Slate Caverns

A470, 1 mile north of town • Daily 9.30am–5.30pm, last tour 4.30pm • Tour £14.95 • ☎ 01766 830306, ⓦ llechwedd-slate-caverns.co.uk

It's hard to get a feeling of what slate means to Blaenau Ffestiniog without a visit to **Llechwedd Slate Caverns**, which presents entertaining insights into the life of a miner in the industry's Victorian heyday. There's no charge to watch slate being split, shaped and engraved. To visit some of the 25 miles of tunnels and sixteen working levels, however, you need to take a fairly pricey one-hour tour.

On the **Victorian Mine Tour** you descend into the deepest parts of the mine on the steepest cable railway in Britian, a precipitous 1–1.8-inch incline. After donning waterproofs and headgear, you head off into the tunnels, guided by the disembodied voice of a "Victorian miner" who does a good job of explaining the working and social life of the miners who never saw daylight in winter, taking their breaks in a dank underground shelter known as a *caban*. The long caverns angling back into the gloom become increasingly impressive, culminating in one filled by a softly lit, limpid pool. The site was the setting for the first ever Welsh-language film, *Y Chwarelwr* (*The Quarrymen*), in 1935.

Antur Stiniog bike park

A470, 1 mile north of town • Thurs–Sun 9am–5.30pm, except daily during school holidays • £27.50 full day, £16 half day; rental from £30/50 for a half/full day • ☎ 01766 238007, ⓦ anturstiniog.com

Launched in 2012, **Antur Stiniog**, the newest mountain bike centre in Wales is almost as popular as the slate mine next door. It's an ambitious downhill and freeride park with five trails – a family-friendly blue grade trail for novices plus two red and two black runs. The latter's rock sections and big jumps were deemed sufficiently challenging to host the British Mountain Biking Championships in 2014. All trails offer good views if you can find time to look up while ripping downhill before catching an uplift (transport that carries you and the bike back to the top) back up to the trail heads. Small wonder this is popular – while walk-up visitors are accommodated, it's worth booking ahead to guarantee a slot. Bike hire and food in a small café is available at the centre.

THE CURSE OF THE RHODODENDRON

It is against the pervasive greyness of Blaenau Ffestiniog that Snowdonia's **rhododendron** (specifically *Rhododendron ponticum*) invasion is most evident. Come in May or June and many of Snowdonia's valleys are a riot of lilac and purple blooms. There's no doubting their aesthetic appeal, but these Turkish natives are high on ecologists' hate lists. The dense canopy cuts out so much sunlight that nothing can grow underneath – a major threat to native birds and insects that thrive in more open scrub. Volunteer action groups periodically target particular areas, blitzing a valley by digging out all the plants, but the rhododendron is proving difficult to contain.

6

THE WELSH SLATE INDUSTRY

Slate is as much a symbol of north Wales as coal is of the fabled Valleys south: it too peaked around the beginning of the twentieth century and shaped society throughout the period of British mass industrialization, drawing thousands from the impoverished hills to the relative wealth of the new towns which sprang up around the quarries.

Slate derives its name from the Old French word *esclater*, meaning "to split" – a perfect description of its most highly valued quality. Six hundred million years ago, what is now north Wales lay under the sea, gradually accumulating a thousand-foot-thick layer of fine-grained mud which metamorphosed into the purplish Cambrian slates of the Penrhyn and Dinorwig quarries and the blue-grey Ordovician slates of Ffestiniog.

The Romans used it as a cheap and durable **roofing material** for the houses of Segontium in Caernarfon, while Edward I used it extensively in his Iron Ring of castles around Snowdonia. Demand really took off with urbanization during the Industrial Revolution, and during the nineteenth and early twentieth centuries millions of tons of slate were shipped around the globe. Hamburg was re-roofed with Welsh slate after its fire of 1842 and it is the same material that still gives that rainy-day sheen to interminable rows of English mill-town houses.

By 1898, Welsh quarries – run by the English, like the coal and steel industries of the south – were producing half a million tons of dressed slate a year (and ten times as much slate waste), almost all of it from Snowdonia. At Penrhyn and Dinorwig, mountains were hacked away in terraces, with teams of **workers** negotiating with the foreman for the choicest piece of rock and the selling price for what they produced. They often slept through the week in damp dormitories on the mountain, and tuberculosis was common, exacerbated by slate dust. At Blaenau Ffestiniog, the seams required mining underground, with miners having to buy their own candles. Few workers were allowed to join the Quarrymen's Union, and in 1900, the workers in Lord Penrhyn's quarry at Bethesda went out on **strike**. For three years they stayed out – one of Britain's longest-ever industrial disputes – but failed to win any concessions. Those who got their jobs back were forced to work for even less money as a recession took hold, and although the two world wars heralded mini-booms as bombed houses were replaced, the industry never recovered its nineteenth-century prosperity, and most quarries and mines closed in the 1950s.

Welsh slate was firmly established as the finest in the world at the 1862 London Exhibition, where one skilled craftsman produced a sheet 10ft long, 1ft wide and a sixteenth of an inch thick – so thin it could be flexed. Slate is now produced worldwide, and although none beats the quality of north Wales's product, half-priced Spanish slate is imported while Welsh slate lies in the ground and unemployed quarrymen kick their heels. The remaining quarries produce relatively small quantities, much of it used for floor tiling, road aggregate or an astonishing array of ashtrays and coasters etched with mountainscapes.

More memorable are the roadside fences made from lines of broken, wafer-thin slabs, the beautifully carved slate fire surrounds and mantelpieces occasionally found in pubs and houses, as well as Westminster Abbey's memorial to Dylan Thomas, which is made entirely of **Penrhyn slate**.

ZipWorld Titan

A470, 1 mile north of town • Booking centre 9am–6pm • £50 • ☎ 01248 601444, ⓦ zipworld.co.uk

Billed as the million-pound project to transform Blaenau Ffestinog into north Wales's adrenaline capital, this project in former slate quarries is not just the longest zip line course in the world (thanks to its three runs), but also the only one that allows you to share the experience. The course sees you fly downhill alongside family or friends on three tracks – 890m, 630m and 450m – at speeds up to around 70mph. Enjoy the panorama of Cadair Idris and Snowdon from the top because all else is a blur afterwards. For more family fun, the ticket takes you into an underground cavern filled with netting to bounce around in. Reservations are essential and there are restrictions on weight, height and age. Note too that the weather can affect your ride and that ZipWorld offers rescheduling not refunds.

> **EXPLORING WITH THE FFESTINIOG RAILWAY**
> We've covered the **Ffestiniog Railway** in detail under Porthmadog (see p.370). Here are some suggested trips:
> - Make the whole return trip to Porthmadog with a couple of hours to explore the town.
> - Ride the train to Minffordd, walk the mile or so to visit Portmeirion then get the train back.
> - Drive to Tan-y-Bwlch and follow our Vale of Ffestiniog walk (see box, p.368).

Dolwyddelan Castle

A470, 6 miles north of Blaenau Ffestiniog • April–Sept Mon–Sat 10am–5pm, Sun 11.30am–4pm; Oct–March Mon–Sat 10am–4pm, Sun 11.30am–4pm • £2.80; CADW • ☎ 01690 750366

Dolwyddelan Castle commands the head of the Lledr Valley, over the Crimea Pass from Blaenau Ffestiniog. It appears a lonely site today, but was a strategic one on the important route from Aberconwy to the north and Ardudwy to the south. Llywelyn ap Iorwerth "the Great" (see p.434) may well have been born here, since his father was reputedly responsible for its construction at the end of the twelfth century. Yet the castle was soon turned against him when Edward I seized it as a base from which to further subdue the Welsh. By the end of the fifteenth century, it lay abandoned. The Wynns of Gwydyr created its appearance today with a typical Victorian reconstruction featuring fanciful battlements and a new roof. Today, it shelters only a small exhibition on native Welsh castles, but gives a panoramic view of Snowdonia from between its castellations.

Vale of Ffestiniog

Slate waste surrounds Blaenau Ffestiniog on three sides, but the fourth drops away into the bucolic **Vale of Ffestiniog**, best explored using the Ffestiniog Railway, or on a walk (see box, p.368). Activity is focused on the railway's Tan-y-Bwlch station (5 miles southwest of Blaenau Ffestiniog) where there is a café and woodland play area. Nearby you'll find Snowdonia National Park's study centre, **Plas Tan y Bwlch**, which runs numerous courses throughout the year (see p.52), and the *Oakeley Arms*.

ARRIVAL AND DEPARTURE   BLAENAU FFESTINIOG

By train The central train station serves both the Ffestiniog Railway, and mainline services to Betws-y-Coed (6 daily; 30min), Llandudno Junction (6 daily; 1hr) and Llandudno (6 daily; 1hr 20min).

By bus Buses stop outside the train station or along High Street.

Destinations Barmouth (3 daily; 1hr 10min); Betws-y-Coed (Mon–Sat 8 daily; 25min); Harlech (Mon–Sat 3 daily; 40min); Llandudno (Mon–Sat 8 daily; 1hr 10min); Porthmadog (Mon–Sat hourly; 30min).

INFORMATION

Tourist information The Artur Stiniog mountain bike information centre (☎ 01766 832214; Mon–Sat 9am–5pm) on Church Street in the heart of town centre doubles as a TIC.

ACCOMMODATION

On our last visit, the **CeLLB** arts centre (see p.368) on Park Square had won planning permission to create a 20-bed bunkhouse, thereby providing accommodation for bikers and hikers in the town centre.

★**Bryn Elltyd** 1 mile from Blaenau in Tanygrisiau ☎ 01766 831356, ⓦ accommodation-snowdonia.com. The former slate mine manager's house beside the Ffestiniog Railway is now Wales's only carbon-neutral B&B thanks to the efforts of its passionate (and helpful) environmentalist owner – if you want to know about eco living this is the place. Accommodation is in homely rooms or sweet cabins in the garden. **£76**

Bryn Tirion Farm A470, 6 miles north ☎ 01690 750366,

ⓔ price768@btinternet.com. The only camping and bunkhouse option nearby is this hospitable farm B&B run by the custodian of the Dolwyddelan Castle; think basic but cosy in a tiny self-catering bunkhouse (open all year), with bedding supplied if required (£2). Closed Nov–Feb. Dorms **£15**; camping **£5**/person

Cae Du Signposted off A470, 1.5 miles south ☎ 01766 830847, ⓦ caedu.co.uk. Very comfy, immaculately maintained guest rooms in a sixteenth-century beamed

6

A WALK DOWN THE VALE OF FFESTINIOG

4–5 miles; 2–3hr; descent only; 1:25,000 OS Explorer map OL18 ("Harlech, Porthmadog & Y Bala").
This gentle walk follows a gorgeous section of the **Vale of Ffestiniog** and completes the loop using the Ffestiniog Railway. Start at Tan-y-Bwlch station and take the train up to Tanygrisiau to start the walk. Turn right out of the station then take the second left – not the road beside the reservoir but the next one following the footpath signs. Cross the train line and pass a car park on your left before turning left down a track and skirting behind the powerhouse. The path then sticks closely to the railway tracks (occasionally crossing them), following the train line to its 360-degree loop, through sessile oak woods and past several cascades all the way to Tan-y-Bwlch, offering some great views south to the Rhinogs and west to the Glaslyn estuary en route. Even when there are several paths, you can't go far wrong if you keep the train lines in sight. Recover at the historic *Oakeley Arms* inn near Tan-y-Bwlch station.

farmhouse that is beautifully situated in open country at the end of a long drive. A bargain at this price. **£58**
Cae'r Blaidd A470, 3 miles south ☎01766 762765, ⓦwww.caerblaidd.fsnet.co.uk. Victorian country house set in four acres of woodland with just three spacious country-style rooms, two with fabulous views of the Moelwyn mountains. Sustaining breakfasts and table d'hôte dinners (£19.50 for 3 courses) are excellent and the hosts run an extensive array of guided hiking, climbing and scrambling trips. **£85**
Isallt Guest House Church St ☎01766 832488, ⓦisallt.com. Central B&B in a solid Victorian house right by the train station with six rooms – double, family, twin and single – and a DVD library. **£60**

ENTERTAINMENT

CeLL B Park Square ☎01766 832001, ⓦcellb.org. Community arts centre in a former police station with gigs, occasional cinema nights (featuring a different country each month) and an informal café/bar with mountain views, good coffee and free wi-fi. Being a community enterprise, the hours are very flexible.

Cor Y Brythoniaid Ysgol Y Moelwyn school on the A470 ☎01766 830435, ⓦcorybrythoniaid.com. The area's best male voice choir practises at this school on the A470 at the south end of town; visitors are welcome to listen. Usually Thurs 7.30pm.

Porthmadog and around

In a region stuffed with wonderful views, **PORTHMADOG**, at the crook of the Cambrian Coast and the Llŷn, has some of the finest – up the Vale of Ffestiniog and across the estuary of the Glaslyn River to the mountains of Snowdonia. The bustling town itself makes little of its wonderful position, but the legacy of its one-time status as north Wales' busiest slate port makes this a great base for exploring.

Wales's obsession with heritage railways reaches its apogee here. As well as the standard-gauge Cambrian Coast line, Porthmadog has three tourist-oriented narrow-gauge railways. The most established is the peerless **Ffestiniog Railway** that originally carried slates from Blaenau Ffestiniog. Its Harbour Station is also the terminus for the **Welsh Highland Railway**, a stunning route that connects Porthmadog via Beddgelert and the Aberglaslyn Pass to Caernarfon. Confusingly, there's also the family-oriented **Welsh Highland Heritage Railway** at the northern end of town.

If steam trains don't toot your whistle, spend at least half a day at the strange but wonderful Italianate folly of **Portmeirion**, walk beside the estuary to pretty **Borth y Gest**, have a **swim** at Morfa Bychan or spy on **ospreys** at Glaslyn.

Brief history

Porthmadog would never have existed without the entrepreneurial ventures of Lincolnshire MP, **William Alexander Madocks**. He named the town and its elder brother Tremadog, a mile to the north, after himself and the Welsh Prince Madog, who some say sailed from the nearby Ynys Fadog (Madog's Island) to North America in 1170. In 1805, Madocks fancied he could get himself some good grazing land by draining a thousand acres of estuarine mud flats here; he bought Ynys Fadog, built an earth embankment, then started on Tremadog. The town prospered and, buoyed by its success, Madocks embarked on a project to enclose a further 7000 acres by sealing off the Glaslyn estuary with a mile-long embankment known as **The Cob**, southeast of present-day Porthmadog. Madocks died before the project came to fruition, but the Glaslyn River was rerouted and soon scoured out a deep watercourse close to the north bank, ideal for a slate wharf. This was the first of several which, boosted by the completion of the Ffestiniog Railway in 1836, spread along a waterfront thick with

6

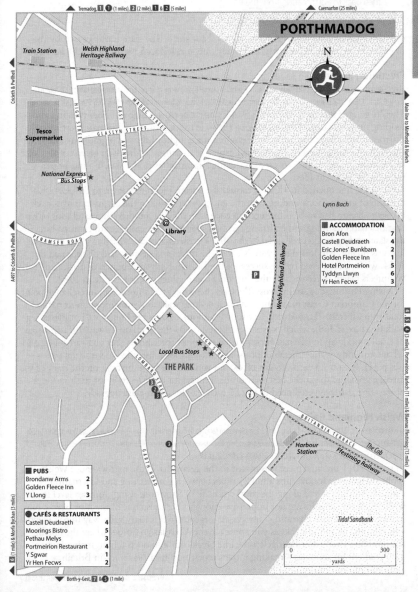

PORTHMADOG

Tremadog, 1, 1 (1 mile), 2 (2 mile), 1 & 2 (5 miles) — Caernarfon (25 miles)

Train Station

Welsh Highland Heritage Railway

Cricieth & Pwllheli

Main line to Minffordd & Harlech

Tesco Supermarket

HIGH STREET · EAST AVENUE · MADOC STREET · GLASLYN STREET

National Express Bus Stops

NEW STREET

A497 to Cricieth & Pwllheli

PENAMSER ROAD

CHAPEL STREET

@ Library

MADOC STREET

SNOWDON STREET

Lynn Bach

HIGH STREET

Welsh Highland Railway

■ ACCOMMODATION
Bron Afon	7
Castell Deudraeth	4
Eric Jones' Bunkbarn	2
Golden Fleece Inn	1
Hotel Portmeirion	5
Tyddyn Llwyn	6
Yr Hen Fecws	3

P

BANK PLACE

LOMBARD STREET

HIGH STREET

Local Bus Stops

THE PARK

GARTH ROAD

PEN CEI

Harbour Station

BRITANNIA TERRACE

Ffestiniog Railway

The Cob

4, 5, 4 (3 miles); Portmeirion, Harlech (11 miles) & Blaenau Ffestiniog (13 miles)

■ PUBS
Brondanw Arms	2
Golden Fleece Inn	1
Y Llong	3

● CAFÉS & RESTAURANTS
Castell Deudraeth	4
Moorings Bistro	5
Pethau Melys	3
Portmeirion Restaurant	4
Y Sgwar	1
Yr Hen Fecws	2

Tidal Sandbank

0 — 300
yards

6 (1 mile) & Moris Bychan (3 miles)

▼ Borth-y-Gest, 7 & 5 (1 mile)

6

TRIPS ON THE WELSH HIGHLAND RAILWAY

Timetables will affect how much you can do in one day, but here are a few suggestions for trips on the **Welsh Highland Railway**:

- Do the full Porthmadog–Caernarfon round trip: a full five hours on the train but only an hour in Caernarfon.
- Drive to Pont Croesor (where most trains currently start and there's free parking) and ride to Beddgelert from there.
- Ride to Beddgelert then walk down the Aberglaslyn Pass to Nantmor (1hr) and catch the train back to Porthmadog from there.

---

orderly heaps of slate and the masts of merchant ships. The slate traffic ceased by the middle of the twentieth century and today only a few dozen yachts grace the harbour.

Ffestiniog Railway

Glaslyn Bridge • April–Oct 4–8 services daily; Nov–March services several days a week • Sample fares: return day ticket £21; return to Tan-y-Bwlch £13.50; single fares two-thirds of a return; one child under 16 travels free with an adult • ☎ 01766 516024, ⓦ festrail.co.uk

The 2ft-gauge **Ffestiniog Railway** is Wales's finest narrow-gauge rail line, twisting and looping up 650ft from Porthmadog to the slate mining town of Blaenau Ffestiniog, thirteen miles away. The gutsy little engines make light of the steep gradients and chug through stunning scenery, from broad estuarine expanses to the deep greens of the Vale of Ffestiniog, only fading to grey on the final approaches to the slate-bound upper terminus at Blaenau Ffestiniog.

When the line opened in 1836, it carried slates from the mines down to the port with the help of gravity, horses riding with the goods before hauling the empty carriages back up again. Steam had to be introduced to cope with the one hundred thousand tons of slate that Blaenau Ffestiniog was churning out each year in the late nineteenth century, but after the slate-roofing market collapsed in the 1920s, passengers were carried instead, until the line was finally abandoned in 1946. Most of the tracks and sleepers had disappeared by 1954, when, encouraged by the success of the Talyllyn Railway, a bunch of dedicated volunteers began to reconstruct the line, only completing the entire route in 1982.

Leaving Porthmadog, trains cross The Cob then stop at Minffordd, an interchange point for the Cambrian Coast main line and the mile-long walk to Portmeirion. Short **nature trails** spur off from Tan-y-Bwlch (the fourth station), as does the longer Vale of Ffestiniog walk (see box, p.368), which passes Dduallt station by the spiral on its way to Tanygrisiau. The full round trip to Blaenau Ffestiniog takes almost three hours, but you can get on and off as frequently as the timetable allows, and the journey is included in some rail passes (see p.31). It costs £3 each way for **bikes**, but you need to book first. Sit on the right of the carriage going up to get the best view of the scenery; for more legroom or to sit in the observation carriage you'll need to pay £6 each way for a **first-class** upgrade.

Welsh Highland Railway

Glaslyn Bridge • Late March to Oct 2–4 trains daily • Sample return fares: to Beddgelert £19.20; to Caernarfon £35; to Waunfawr £11.50. First-class tickets cost an additional £8–10 each way depending on distance travelled; one child under 16 travels free with an adult, and single fares are two-thirds of a return • ☎ 01766 516000, ⓦ festrail.co.uk

In spring 2011 the final piece was placed in the jigsaw that is the narrow-gauge **Welsh Highland Railway**. It now runs a full 25 miles between Porthmadog and Caernarfon, through Beddgelert and along the southern flank of Snowdon, rising from sea level to 650ft. As if the statistics are not impressive enough, this is also one of the most scenic lines in a land packed with charming railways. A gorgeous river estuary gives way to oak woods which crowd in on the tracks as you approach the **Aberglaslyn Gorge**, where the line hugs the tumbling river. After Beddgelert the line breaks out into open terrain maintaining a 1:40 gradient for six miles – making it the steepest non-funicular track in Britain.

OPPOSITE HILL WALKER IN SNOWDONIA (P.354) >

6

EASY WALKS AROUND PORTHMADOG

The Cob (2 miles return; 1hr; flat). If the weather is fine, and particularly towards sunset, you can't go far wrong wandering around the harbour then strolling along The Cob, with the occasional steam-hauled Ffestiniog Railway service adding atmosphere to views up the estuary towards Snowdon.

Borth-y-Gest (2 miles return; 1hr; flat). This easy walk beside the Glaslyn Estuary makes a particularly nice summer evening stroll and is a good way to get to your table at *Moorings Bistro* (see p.375). Follow Pen Cei south from Porthmadog below the cliffs of Moel-y-Gest.

The reopening is the culmination of fifteen years of volunteer struggle and over £28 million expenditure, much of it from Millennium lottery and Welsh Assembly sources. It was also a tangled legal story with hurdles put up by farmers with land along the route (and the ramblers who regularly walked it). The original Welsh Highland Railway from Porthmadog to Caernarfon only ran for fourteen years (until 1937) and was pulled up decades ago, but the Welsh love affair with restoring railways as steam-driven tourist attractions kicked in and two organizations began running trips on short sections of track, one from Caernarfon and one from Porthmadog. The feats of engineering needed to reopen the old line were staggering: over twenty bridges have been rebuilt; walking and cycling paths were rerouted; four tunnels down the Aberglaslyn Gorge near Beddgelert needed extensive safety work; and most of the route lies within a national park, with its rigorous planning restrictions. Part of the justification has always been the line's transport benefits, but with the steep gradients and twisting route of the WHR, it's not a journey fast enough to satisfy the needs of commuters.

Welsh Highland Heritage Railway

Signposted off Madog St • Late March to Oct 5–6 services daily • £7.50 ticket valid all day • ☎ 01766 513402, ⓦ whr.co.uk

Don't be confused by the name, which is similar to the more epic rail journey that starts at the other end of town – the 24in-gauge **Welsh Highland Heritage Railway** is a shorter, cheaper and more child-oriented affair. It runs along almost a mile of track with a stop at the loco sheds where you get to see how a steam engine works. Fans over 18 can ride the footplate (£15 extra) or have a go at driving the train on Saturday evening or full-day sessions (3hr £75; full day £330).

Tremadog

William Madocks' original village of **Tremadog**, founded in 1805, lies just a mile north of Porthmadog. Though really just the intersection of three streets, it is a barely altered example of early town planning with a central square overlooked by an attractive (though currently empty) town hall.

Glaslyn Osprey Project

Pont Croesor on B4410, 4 miles northeast of Porthmadog • Late March to Aug • Free • ⓦ glaslynwildlife.co.uk

When there are **ospreys** on the nest, this small centre opens up with displays on these fine fish-eating eagles, replica nests and excellent archive footage of the birds. There are hopes of establishing a significant population in the area but currently there is just one breeding pair. Telescopes allow you to see the distant nest, but most will appreciate the live CCTV link from a camera just 3ft above the nest. Depending on the time of year, you may see the adults tending the eggs, watch the eggs hatch or see the chicks learning to fly.

Borth-y-Gest

The small former boat-building village of **Borth-y-Gest** envelops a picturesque harbour a mile south of Porthmadog, with a semicircle of Victorian houses lining the beach. There's nothing to do here but enjoy the estuary views from one of the waterfront cafés, maybe stay at *Bron Afon* (see p.374) and eat at the delectable *Moorings Bistro* (see p.375).

Morfa Bychan

If all the sand and water around Porthmadog leaves you hankering for a swim, **Black Rock Sands**, almost three miles southwest of Porthmadog at **Morfa Bychan**, is the best beach: a two-mile swath of golden sands with sublime views down to Harlech and up to the peaks of Snowdonia. At low tide you can explore the rock pool and even some caves.

Portmeirion

3 miles east of Porthmadog • Daily 9.30am–7.30pm • £10; free afternoon entry if you pre-book a meal at *Hotel Portmeirion* or have lunch at *Castell Deudraeth*; £2 entry Nov–March with downloaded voucher; free 20min guided tours daily 10.30am–5pm • ☎ 01766 770000, ⓦ portmeirion-village.com • Without your own transport you can walk to the site in an hour from Porthmadog or catch the #1b bus, main-line or Ffestiniog trains to Minffordd, from where it's a signposted 25min walk

If there's one time-honoured must-see hereabouts, it's **Portmeirion**. Set on a small rocky peninsula in Tremadog Bay, three miles east near Minffordd, the Italianate private village was the brainchild of eccentric architect **Clough Williams-Ellis** whose dream was to build an ideal village to enhance rather than blend in with its surroundings, using a "gay, light-opera sort of approach". The result is certainly theatrical: a stage set with a lucky dip of unwanted buildings arranged to distort perspectives and reveal tantalizing glimpses of the sea or the expansive sands behind. Portmeirion is perhaps best known as "The Village" in the 1960s British cult TV series *The Prisoner*.

In the 1920s, Williams-Ellis began scouring Britain for a suitable island – he believed only an island could provide the seclusion for his project – but having found nothing he could afford, he was gratified to be offered a piece of wilderness four miles from his home, Plâs Brondanw, at Garreg (see p.374). A Victorian house already on the site was turned into a hotel, the income from which provided funds for Williams-Ellis's "Home for Fallen Buildings". Endangered buildings from all over Britain and abroad were broken down, transported and rebuilt, every conceivable style being plundered: a neoclassical colonnade from Bristol; Siamese figures on Ionic columns; a Jacobean town hall; a Buddha; and the Italianate touches, a campanile and a pantheon. Williams-Ellis designed his village around a Mediterranean piazza, piecing together a scaled-down nest of loggias, grand porticoes and tiny terracotta-roofed houses, and painting them in pastels: turquoise, ochre and buff yellows. Continually surprising, with hidden entrances and cherubs popping out of crevices, the ensemble is wildly eclectic, yet never quite inappropriate.

More than three thousand visitors a day come to ogle the place in summer, when it can be a delight; fewer appear in winter, when it's just plain bizarre. Much of your time will be spent outside wandering around the buildings or popping into the shops selling *Prisoner* memorabilia or florally embellished Portmeirion pottery. Guests and visitors can eat at the expensive hotel-restaurant (see p.375), but most will be content with one of several cafés – better still, bring a picnic and find a spot on the paths that wind through the exotic forest that backs Portmeirion.

Hotel Portmeirion

Sometimes dismissed as the grandest folly of all and a symbol of Britain's fascination with eccentrics, Portmeirion at least supports Williams-Ellis's guiding principle that

---

THE PRISONER CONVENTION AND FESTIVAL NO.6

For one weekend in April, Portmeirion hosts **The Prisoner convention** (ⓦ portmeiricon.com) when fans book the place out to re-enact scenes as best they can – though, as much of the series was shot in the studio, the juxtaposition of Portmeirion's buildings doesn't match that of "The Village".

In a similar vein, **Festival No.6** (ⓦ festivalnumber6.com), named after the number given to the hero of *The Prisoner*, uses the village's venues to good effect in September during an eclectic festival of music, art and culture, usually pulling in major international names; Pet Shop Boys and Beck in 2014.

natural beauty and profitable development needn't be mutually exclusive. Architectural idealism aside, it was always intended to be self-sustaining, much of the finance coming from lovely waterside *Hotel Portmeirion* (see below), which also utilizes many of the cottages in the village. In the evening, when the village is closed to the public, guests see the place at its best: peaceful, even ghostly.

Plâs Brondanw

Signed off A4085 just north of Garreg • Easter–Sept daily 10am–5pm • £3.50 • ☎ 01766 772772, ⊛ brondanw.org

Most of the money Clough Williams-Ellis earned went directly to the gardens of his ancestral home **Plâs Brondanw**, four miles northeast of Portmeirion. "A cheque of ten pounds would come in and I would order yew hedging to that extent, a cheque for twenty and I would pave a further piece of terrace", he said to explain the whimsical topiary around his solid Welsh stone house. The house is closed to the public, leaving only the gardens and some of the grounds, visited by following the "To the Tower" sign opposite the entrance. A ten-minute woodland walk brings you to the outlook tower, with expansive views of Porthmadog and the Moelwyns.

ARRIVAL AND INFORMATION

BY TRAIN
The mainline train station and the Welsh Highland Heritage Railway station are at the north end of the High Street, near Tesco. The Ffestiniog and Welsh Highland railways' station is down by the harbour, about half a mile south. The following exclude Ffestiniog and Welsh Highland services. Destinations Aberdyfi (7 daily; 1hr 30min); Barmouth (7 daily; 50min); Criccieth (8 daily; 10min); Harlech (8 daily; 20min); Machynlleth (7 daily; 1hr 50min); Pwllheli (8 daily; 25min).

BY BUS
Pwllheli-bound National Express buses from London, Manchester and Liverpool stop outside Tesco on High Street: get tickets from the TIC. Note that Dolgellau buses

PORTHMADOG AND AROUND

go inland through Coed-y-Brenin: take the train if you want to stick to the coast.
Destinations Bangor (Mon–Sat 6 daily; 1hr 20min); Beddgelert (8 daily; 25min); Blaenau Ffestiniog (Mon–Sat hourly; 30min); Borth-y-Gest (#99, hourly Mon–Sat); Caernarfon (Mon–Sat 6 daily; 40min); Criccieth (Mon–Sat every 30min, Sun 7 daily; 15min); Dolgellau (3–4 daily; 50min); Pen-y-Pass (4 daily; 45min); Pwllheli (Mon–Sat every 30min, Sun 7 daily; 40min).

INFORMATION
Tourist information The TIC is at the southern end of the High Street (Easter to mid-Oct daily 10am–5pm; late Oct–Easter Mon–Sat 10am–3.30pm; ☎ 01766 512981, ⊛ visitsnowdonia.info).

ACCOMMODATION

HOTELS, GUESTHOUSES AND SELF-CATERING
Bron Afon Borth-y-Gest, 1 mile southwest of Porthmadog ☎ 01766 513918, ⊛ bronafon.co.uk. Occupying the finest location in this pretty village, on a corner of the bay, this place has fresh, bright en-suite rooms, the best at the front with fabulous views across the estuary to the mountains. Also offers separate self-catering accommodation. Closed Nov–Feb. **£60**
★ **Castell Deudraeth** Portmeirion ☎ 01766 772400, ⊛ portmeirion-village.com. Chic designer hotel in a remodelled Victorian "castle" decorated in muted tones and modern streamlined furnishings. Only a 10min walk from Portmeirion village, where you're free to roam and use the heated outdoor pool. **£189**
Golden Fleece Inn Tremadog, 1 mile north of Porthmadog ☎ 01766 512421, ⊛ goldenfleeceinn.com. The best bet for pub accommodation hereabouts, with small but stylish, simply furnished rooms above the pub or larger

rather theatrical Executive rooms (£90) in the Royal Madoc annexe nearby. Breakfast included. Also does excellent bar food and bistro meals (see opposite). **£65**
★ **Hotel Portmeirion** Portmeirion ☎ 01766 770000, ⊛ portmeirion-village.com. The spirit of Clough Williams-Ellis remains in styling that's equal parts grand and eccentric; quirky architectural and decorative elements remain in the main waterside hotel and cottages throughout Portmeirion village. Though lacking the wow factor of public areas, rooms are excellent and all different, many with beautiful views. Former guests include H.G. Wells, George Bernard Shaw and Noël Coward. The hotel also lets luxurious self-catering cottages by the week (or half-week Nov–March) that sleep up to eight people. **£174**
Yr Hen Fecws 16 Lombard St ☎ 01766 514625, ⊛ henfecws.com. While compact, the en-suite rooms in this B&B are immaculate and comfortable, with fabrics in tasteful shades of dove grey, and ruby and exposed stone

walls in many. Breakfast is served in the owners' café next door. The best value in the town centre. **£75**

BUNKHOUSE AND CAMPING

Eric Jones' Bunkbarn Tremadog, A498 to Beddgelert 2 miles north of Porthmadog, opposite *Eric Jones' Café* ☎01766 512199, ⓦericjones -tremadog.co.uk. Intended for rock climbers, this provides basic accommodation in a stone bunkhouse:

bring sleeping bags. Showers £1. The owner's café opposite rustles up breakfast. Dorms **£7.50**; camping **£6**/person

Tyddyn Llwyn Black Rock Rd ☎01766 512205, ⓦtyddynllwyn.com. Beyond the caravans is a family campsite on a grassy hillside, with clean facilities and a pub with a restaurant on site. It's a 15min walk along the road to Morfa Bychan following Bank Place southwest off High Street. Closed Nov–Feb. **£20**/pitch

EATING, DRINKING AND ENTERTAINMENT

CAFÉS AND RESTAURANTS

Castell Deudraeth Portmeirion ☎01766 770400. Beautiful conservatory brasserie that's flooded with light and fuses classical elegance with modern style. Start with cocktails in the panelled bar then choose from a Modern British menu: lunches such as potato and herb galette or bangers and mash, evening dishes like gilthead bream on garlic mash or pea and mint risotto (mostly £13 at lunch, £15–20 for dinner). Daily noon–2.30pm & 6–9.30pm.

Moorings Bistro 4 Ivy Terrace, Borth-y-Gest, 1 mile south of Porthmadog ☎01766 513500, ⓦmoorings bistroborthygest.com. Great little bistro, not least for the estuary views from its terrace, which specializes in local seafood dishes (circa £14), but also serves vegetarian dishes like mushroom, cranberry and brie Wellington, Welsh Black beef pies and cheap light lunches (£6–11). June–Sept Mon–Tues & Thurs–Sat 9am–9pm, Wed 6.30–9pm, Sun 5–9pm; other months Wed–Sun 10am–4.30pm plus some evenings (call to confirm).

Pethau Melys 10 Pen Cei ☎07881 806960, ⓦpethaumelys.co.uk. The name means "sweet things" and this cute vintage-styled café certainly is, with seating inside and out by the quay. Come for outstanding home-made pizza (£9), freshly baked cakes, bara brith and coffee (soy milk available) and to check out the owners' pottery and textiles. Tues–Sun 10am–6pm.

Portmeirion Restaurant Hotel Portmeirion ☎01766 770480. Delightful, slightly formal hotel restaurant with views across the Traeth Bach sands and an inventive modern menu; sea bass with Aberdaron crab raviloi, lamb shoulder with braised potato, wild garlic and aubergine (two courses £30). Alternatively just come for lunch on the terrace. Reservations required for dinner; dress up. Daily noon–3pm & 6.30–9.30pm.

Y Sgwar The Square, Tremadog ☎01766 515451, ⓦysgwar-restaurant.co.uk. Well-prepared and presented meals at a casual stylish restaurant – good for home-made steak-and-ale pies at lunch (average £12) or dinners of Welsh Black steak or seabass with a seafood sauce (average £17). The 3-course early-bird special (Mon–Fri 6–7pm) is excellent value at £19. Daily noon–2pm & 6–9pm.

Yr Hen Fecws 16 Lombard St ☎01766 514625. Cosy licensed daytime café that's all stone walls, wooden floors and sofas. Come for fresh home-made bistro dishes – fish chowder or local goat's eggs cheese on bruschetta – and a relaxed ambience. Mon–Sat 8am–4pm.

PUBS

Brondanw Arms Garreg, 5 miles northwest of Porthmadog ☎01766 770555. Choose from a beer garden cupped in mountains or a cosy wood-pannelled slate-floored bar in this traditional inn, known locally as *Y Ring*. It has real ales on tap, decent bar meals like gammon and eggs (£6–14), occasional live music and a great atmosphere. Daily noon–11pm.

Golden Fleece Inn Tremadog ☎01766 512421. An ancient coaching inn on Tremadog's main square with a cramped "cave bar" serving meals (£9–10) and excellent ales around the fire or in the courtyard. There's also a bistro out the back (generally Thurs–Sat) where you can expect fresh daily pies or salmon with chilli sauce (mains £10–19). Also has some accommodation (see opposite). Mon–Fri noon–3pm & 6–10pm, Sat & Sun noon–10pm.

Y Llong (The Ship) 14 Lombard St ☎01766 512990. The best pub in town is all low ceilings and walls covered with old photos of the harbour. It has a stock of real ales and a lively atmosphere. Above average pub grub like lamb shank (£12) gets the nod from locals too. Mon–Fri noon–2pm & 5–11pm, Sat–Sun noon–11pm.

The Llŷn

An undulating spur from Snowdonia's mountainous heart, the **Llŷn** takes its name from an Irish word for "peninsula", an apt description for this most westerly part of north Wales, which until the fifth century had a significant Irish population and still maintains an atmosphere reminiscent of parts of western Ireland. Nowhere in Wales feels more remote than the tip of the Llŷn or is more staunchly Welsh. In most local shops you'll only hear Welsh spoken, and Stryd Fawr is used instead of High Street.

The Llŷn is approached through either Porthmadog or Caernarfon, towns linked by the A487, which forms an effective boundary between Snowdonia proper and this cliff-and-cove-lined finger of land that juts out south and west, separating Cardigan and Caernarfon bays.

It's the beaches that lure most people to the Llŷn, specifically to the south-coast family resorts of **Criccieth**, **Pwllheli** and **Abersoch**. Yet tiny undeveloped **Aberdaron**, from where ancient pilgrims once sailed for the burial grounds of **Ynys Enlli** (Bardsey Island), probably has most charm. Alternatively, make for the quiet coves punctuating the north coast, notably gorgeous **Porth Oer** and the pub at **Porth Dinllaen**. Ancestors of those last Irish inhabitants may have been responsible for the numerous hillforts and cromlechs on the Llŷn, particularly the hut circles of the **Tre'r Ceiri** hillfort above the Welsh Language Centre at **Nant Gwrtheyrn**.

One of the greatest changes on the Llŷn is its discovery by walkers, who circuit along both coasts like a mini Pembrokeshire thanks to the Wales Coast Path.

ARRIVAL AND DEPARTURE
THE LLŶN

By train Trains and National Express buses serve both Criccieth and Pwllheli, leaving an extensive network of infrequent buses to cover the rest.

By bike Better still, bring your bike and explore the peninsula's quiet narrow lanes and rolling pastures.

Criccieth and around

CRICCIETH, five miles west of Porthmadog, clusters around its castle, magnificently sited on a small hillock commanding the bay. The castle is firmly Welsh but much of the rest of the town has long been dependent on the English: it's still smarter and more anglicized than its neighbouring towns. When sea-bathing became the Victorian fashion, English families descended on Criccieth's sweeping sand-and-shingle beach and built long terraces of guesthouses (many now retirement homes). These days, beach-bound holiday-makers go further west, leaving a quietly amiable resort that makes a convenient touring base for the peninsula and Porthmadog. The best view in town is from the hill behind **Marine Terrace**, from where you see the hulking castle set against the backdrop of the Cambrian Coast and the Rhinog mountains.

At **Llanystumdwy**, a mile west, a small museum is dedicated to the intriguing life of native son and British prime minister, David Lloyd George.

MAINTAINING TRADITIONS ON THE LLŶN

During the 1980s, north and west Wales witnessed a spate of **arson attacks** conducted by the shadowy **Meibion Glyndŵr**, or "Sons of Glyndŵr". Though their campaign against selling homes to wealthy English weekenders petered out by the 1990s, nationalists are very keen to preserve Welsh ways and maintain the vigour of the Welsh language. **Incomers** are encouraged to learn Cymraeg, thanks partly to groups like Cymuned (literally "Community"; Ⓦ cymuned.org), a pressure group formed in 2000. It advocates a minimum ten-year residency clause for home buyers, planning permission to turn a permanent dwelling into a second home, investment in schemes to help residents buy property locally, and a Welsh-learning requirement for residents. Some argue that communities might do better embracing incomers, exploiting any economic spin-off and using that to help preserve the culture and language.

Much of the peninsula falls within the **Llŷn Area of Outstanding Natural Beauty** (AONB) whose managers are endeavouring to improve the physical appearance of the landscape. Excessive road signage is being removed, traditional iron waymarkers are replacing modern ones, and old-style kissing gates and field gates have been fashioned by a local blacksmith.

GIRALDUS CAMBRENSIS AND HIS JOURNEY THROUGH WALES

Through his books *The Journey Through Wales* and *The Description of Wales*, Norman–Welsh **Giraldus Cambrensis** (Gerald of Wales, or Gerallt Cymro) has left us with a vivid picture of life in Wales in the twelfth century. Gerald worked his way up the ecclesiastical hierarchy, but failed to achieve his lifelong goal, the bishopric of St Davids, mainly because of his reformist ideals.

Gerald's influence in Wales made him the first choice when Baldwin, the Archbishop of Canterbury, needed someone to accompany him on his 51-day tour around Wales in 1188, preaching the Cross and recruiting for a third Crusade, designed to dislodge the Muslim leader Saladin from Jerusalem. During the tour, Gerald amassed much of the material for his books, where he sensitively portrayed the landscape and its people, judging that "Welsh generosity and hospitality are the greatest of all virtues", but warning "if they come to a house where there is any sign of affluence and they are in a position to take what they want, there is no limit to their demands". But on the whole, he shows sympathy for the Welsh, coming up with a conclusion that has an oddly contemporary ring: "if only Wales could find the place it deserves in the heart of its rulers, or at least if those put in charge locally would stop behaving so vindictively and submitting the Welsh to such shameful ill-treatment".

Criccieth Castle

Castle St • April–Oct daily 10am–5pm; Nov–March Mon–Sat 9.30am–4pm, Sun 11am–4pm • £3.50, free Nov–March Mon–Thurs; CADW • ☎ 01766 522227

Criccieth's only real sight is the battle-worn **Criccieth Castle**, dominating the coastline with what remains of its twin, D-shape towered gatehouse. The castle was started by Llywelyn ap Iorwerth in 1230, but strengthened and finished by Edward I, who took it in 1283. During his 1404 rebellion, Owain Glyndŵr grabbed it back, only to raze it and leave little remaining besides an outline of broken walls and the gatehouse. Nowadays, it's a great spot to sit and look over Cardigan Bay to Harlech or down the ripples of the Llŷn coast in the late afternoon, but leave time for the workaday exhibition on Welsh castles and a wonderful animated cartoon based on the twelfth-century Cambrian travels of Giraldus Cambrensis (see box above) in the ticket office.

Lloyd George Museum

Llanystumdwy, 1.5 miles west of Criccieth • Easter & July–Sept daily 10.30am–5pm; May Mon–Fri 10.30am–5pm; June Mon–Sat 10.30am–5pm; Oct Mon–Fri 11am–4pm • Last admission one hour before closing • £5 • ☎ 01766 522071

Though born in Manchester, the Welsh nationalist, Liberal statesman, social reformer and British prime minister David Lloyd George (1864–1945) lived in his mother's home village until 1880, when he was 16. He grew up in Highgate House, the home of his uncle, the village cobbler, which is now part of the **Lloyd George Museum**. It kicks off with an informative thirty-minute film on the life of this witty and powerful orator, described by Churchill as "a man of action, resource and creative energy, [who] stood, when at his zenith, without a rival". An extensive collection of gifts and awards attests to the great man's popularity, and the displays are full of anecdotes and little-known facts about him. Read between the lines to get a sense of the betrayal felt by many Welsh nationalists as his interest turned from the politics of Wales to those of Westminster.

Rustic late nineteenth-century beds and dressers furnish Lloyd George's wooden-floored two-up, two-down house, with a garden laid out much as it would have been in his day. Lloyd George is buried here under a memorial beside the River Dwyfor – a boulder and two simple plaques designed by Portmeirion's creator Clough Williams-Ellis.

Penarth Fawr

Off A497, 5.5 miles west of Criccieth • Daily 10am–5pm • Free • NT

Signposts point off the A497 down a tiny lane half a mile inland towards **Penarth Fawr**, a compact fifteenth-century hall house built to a common standard for the Welsh gentry. Constructed in 1416, the rare aisle truss hall was originally heated by a huge

6

central hearth, replaced in the seventeenth century by the large fireplace you see today. Alterations at that time included the insertion of an upper floor – a dismantled beam from this work is on display, bearing the date 1656.

ARRIVAL AND INFORMATION   CRICCIETH

By train Trains serve: Porthmadog (8 daily; 10min) and Pwllheli (8 daily; 15min).

By bus Both National Express buses from the north Wales coast and local buses stop at Y Maes.

Destinations Llanystumdwy (every 30min; 5min);

Porthmadog (Mon–Sat every 30min, Sun 7 daily; 15min); Pwllheli (Mon–Sat every 30min, Sun 7 daily; 25min).

Tourist information The nearest TICs are at Porthmadog and Pwllheli.

ACCOMMODATION

Bron Eifion 0.5 miles west on A497 ☏01766 522385, ⓦ broneifion.co.uk. Upmarket stay in the Grade II-listed mansion of a Victorian slate magnate set in five acres of grounds; he exported to the US and imported the Oregon pine for his hall pannelling. The room decor nods to that heritage but adds statement wallpapers and the obligatory luxuries. All in all a hugely relaxing stay. **£145**

★**Glyn y Coed** Porthmadog Rd, 100yd along A497 ☏01766 522870, ⓦ glynycoedhotel.co.uk. Sea views at the front and ample space make the ten rooms of this stylishly relaxed small hotel fine places to stay; those views cost £10 extra. Tasty breakfasts use locally sourced bacon

and the owners are charming. **£82**

Mynydd Du A497, 1 mile east ☏01766 522294, ⓦ mynydddu.co.uk. There are lots of caravans at this campsite (though there's a tents only field too), but what a view of Snowdonia and the sea from its sloping fields. Clean modern(ish) shower block. **£18**/pitch

Tyddyn Morthwyl Farm and Caravan Park On the Caernarfon Rd, 1.5 miles north of Criccieth ☏01766 522115. Not the closest campsite and we've heard mixed reports about the shower block. Still the views are good and there's a spacious bunkhouse in converted farm buildings: bring a sleeping bag. Dorms **£8**; **£12**/pitch

EATING AND DRINKING

Cadwalader's Castle St ☏01766 523665. The founding outlet of this regional ice-cream empire has an airy café and great sea views. Come for the rich ice creams (from £1.90) in dozens of flavours, coffee, smoothies and tasty pies. Daily: winter 10am–5pm; summer 10am–6pm, except late July–Aug 10am–10pm.

The Feathers Inn Llanystumdwy, 1.5 miles west ☏01766 523276, ⓦ tafarnyplu.com. Classic and very Welsh local pub with a snug bar and hearty, home-cooked meals (around £10) using local produce such as Caernarfon Bay crab, a changing roster of Welsh ales and a garden bar. Daily 6–11pm; food served 6–9pm.

Poachers 66–68 High St ☏01766 522512, ⓦ poachersrestaurant.co.uk. The locals' choice for a

good-value relaxed meal in the centre, this family-friendly place prepares honest bistro cooking at good prices (2 courses £16.50). Expect local fish plates, local pork with sauteed mushrooms or home-made Welsh Black beef lasagne. Mon–Sat 6–9.30pm.

★**Tir A Môr** 1–3 Mona Terrace ☏01766 523084, ⓦ tiramor-criccieth.co.uk. Delightful understated small restaurant with some of Criccieth's best meals, all prepared with care. Go à la carte to choose dishes like cod with coconut cream, ginger and chilli, or duck with star anise (mains around £15), or from Tues–Fri save with a set menu (£21.50 for 2 courses), served with a glass of one of five house wines. Booking strongly advised. Tues–Sat 6–10pm.

Pwllheli and around

The "capital" of the Llŷn, **PWLLHELI** (pronounced something like "Poothl-heli") is a solid little place that fails to live up to its seaside location nor its illustrious history. Although the town appears largely Victorian, Pwllheli's market charter dates back to 1355: Wednesday and Sunday **markets** still take place on Y Maes. It was also here at the *Maesgwyn Temperance Hotel* (now a pet shop marked with a plaque) in August 1925 that six people met to form Plaid Cymru. Even in the height of summer, you'll hear far more Welsh spoken here than English.

Notwithstanding the Victorian high street, the only real tourist attraction here is a **boat trip** to the tip of the Llŷn.

ARRIVAL AND DEPARTURE PWLLHELI

By train The central train station serves Criccieth (8 daily; 15min), Porthmadog (8 daily; 25min) and other stations down the Cambrian Coast line.

By bus National Express and local buses pull in at Y Maes. Destinations Aberdaron (Mon–Sat 9 daily; 45min);

Abersoch (Mon–Sat 10–11 daily, Sun 4 daily; 15–30min); Caernarfon (Mon–Sat roughly hourly, Sun 3 daily; 45min); Criccieth (Mon–Sat every 30min, Sun 7 daily; 25min); Nefyn (Mon–Sat roughly hourly, Sun 4 daily; 15min); Porthmadog (Mon–Sat every 30min, Sun 7 daily; 40min).

INFORMATION AND TOURS

Tourist information The TIC is in the foyer of the library, Neuadd Dwyfor, on the main street Penlan Street (May–Sept Mon–Sat 10am–5pm; Oct–April Mon–Sat 10am–3pm; ☎ 01758 613000, ✉ pwllheli.tic@gwynedd.gov.uk).

Internet Free at the library on Penlan Street.

Boat tours The Shearwater (Easter–Oct; ☎ 01758 613000, ☎ 01758 612251) sails on morning, lunchtime and

evening cruises (2–3hr; £28–39) along an impressive section of coast past St Tudwal's island to Hell's Mouth, often accompanied by dolphins and sometimes grey seals. The booking office is at Firmhelm chandlery in the town's marina, half a mile east of the centre. The meeting point is in front of the main marina building.

ACCOMMODATION AND EATING

While there's nothing to detain you overnight in Pwhelli itself, the **surrounding area** includes some of the finest accommodation on the peninsula, with a central location that makes all three coasts easily accessible.

The Old Rectory A497 at Boduan, 4 miles northwest ☎ 01758 721519, ☎ theoldrectory.net. Lovely country house in a wonderfully relaxed setting midway between the north and south coasts, with bright elegant en-suite rooms and great breakfasts. Well positioned for exploring the tip of the peninsula. **£75**

Penlan Fawr 3 Penlan St ☎ 01758 612864. For a bite or something to drink, head to this four-hundred-year-old slate-floored pub, a great barn of a building with cosy corners and sofas around a fireplace. There are so-so burgers, grills and veggie meals (mostly £5–10) on the menu and it morphs into the liveliest place in town at weekends. Daily 11am–11pm.

★**Plas Bodegroes** Efailnewydd, A497, 2 miles north of Pwllheli ☎ 01758 612363, ☎ bodegroes.co.uk. The

emphasis is very much on the food, but this is still probably the finest stay on the Llŷn, set in a Georgian country house surrounded by wonderful parkland. Rooms are contemporary country in style and the service is attentive but relaxed. The restaurant meanwhile ranks among Wales's finest for its modern interpretations of traditional dishes: starters like guineafowl, pistachio and apricot ballotine and mains such as local seabass with crab, ginger and pak choi (£45 for three courses). Sunday lunch costs a modest £20. Hotel: closed Sun & Mon; restaurant: Tues–Sat 7–10pm, Sun 12.30–2pm. **£130**

Taro Deg A497 near the train station ☎ 01758 701271, ☎ tarodeg.com. Comfortable daytime café that prepares a soup and quiche each day as well as sandwiches, Welsh rarebit and cake. Free wi-fi. Mon–Sat 9am–4.30pm.

Llanbedrog

LLANBEDROG, four miles southwest of Pwllheli, is a delightful village, worth visiting for a wonderful beach with Wales's cutest line of beach huts and one of Wales's oldest public art galleries.

Oriel Plas Glyn-y-Weddw

Llanbedrog • May–Sept daily 10am–5pm; Oct–Dec & Feb–May Wed–Mon, daily during school holidays • Free • ☎ 01758 740763, ☎ oriel.org.uk

Solomon Andrews, the Cardiff entrepreneur who built Pwllheli's West End, bought the Victorian Gothic **Plas Glyn-y-Weddw** in 1896 and turned it into a genteel centre for the arts, with pleasure gardens and legendary tea dances. All rooms peel off a

WAKESTOCK

Activity peaks in Pwllheli in early July for **Wakestock** (Ⓦwakestock.co.uk), when twenty thousand spectators arrive for a celebration of wakeboarding, skateboarding, BMX and music.

6

spectacular galleried hallway under a huge stained-glass window and a gorgeous hammerbeam oak roof, topped with a lantern. The exhibitions combine pieces from the gallery's permanent collection with touring works, often with a Welsh theme. There's also a very pleasant conservatory **café** in which to sit and gaze out to the distant sea.

Traeth Llanbedrog

Llanbedrog • Open access • Free access but £4 car park; NT

It's a short stroll from the village down to **Traeth Llanbedrog**, a sheltered beach lined with primary-hued beach huts. From the southern end of the beach, a steep, fairly rough **path** climbs through a wooded glen onto a towering headland known as Mynydd Tir-y-Cwmwd, where the sweeping views are shared by the **Iron Man**, a modern wrought-iron sculpture designed and built locally to replace an 8ft ship's figurehead erected there in 1919.

Abersoch and around

After the distinctly Welsh feel of Pwllheli, **ABERSOCH**, seven miles southwest, is a surprise. This former fishing village, pitched in the middle of two golden bays, is a largely anglicized resort, catering to yachties and holidaying families, with an abundance of cafés and restaurants.

The beaches

One reason for Abersoch's popularity is its beaches. It's only five minutes' walk to the closest, **Abersoch Bay**, a long, clean strand lined by colourful beach huts. The pale sands vanish beneath beach towels at busy times, although a short walk along the shore leaves most of the crowds. There's more space a mile north at **The Warren**, a fine stretch of beach backed by a holiday park. Surfers make for **Porth Neigwl** (Hell's Mouth), two miles to the southwest, which can be one of the finest **surf** beaches in Wales near high tide if powerful storms push swell north – beware of the undertow if you're swimming.

ARRIVAL AND DEPARTURE   **ABERSOCH**

By bus Buses from Pwllheli (Mon–Sat 10–11 daily, Sun 4 daily; 20–30min) loop through the middle of Abersoch, stopping on Lôn Pen Cei. To continue to Aberdaron by bus, you must take a Pwllheli-bound service as far as Llanbedrog, then change onto the #17.

INFORMATION

Tourist office The TIC is in The Vestry on Lôn Engan in the town centre (June–Sept daily 10.30am–3.30pm; Oct–May Sat & Sun 11am–2pm; ☎01758 712929, ⓦ abersochtouristinfo.co.uk).

ACCOMMODATION

Accommodation can be tight over **summer** and at **weekends** during spring and autumn. Almost all the **campsites** in villages around Abersoch are family-oriented places, so groups need to look reputable to be admitted.

Angorfa Lôn Sarn Bach ☎01758 712967, ⓦ angorfa .com. Bare boards and white linen characterize this superior budget B&B. The two attic rooms have the best view and breakfast is served in the daytime café downstairs. Note that the business was for sale at the time of writing. **£85**

Goslings at the Carisbrooke Lôn Sarn Bach ☎01758 712526, ⓦ goslingsabersoch.co.uk. Friendly B&B with a relaxed, homely atmosphere and sea views from some of its en-suite doubles; also has family rooms and a couple of self-catering flats nearby. Note that the business was for sale on our last visit. **£85**

★ **Porth Tocyn** 2.5 miles south of Abersoch, on the road through Sarn Bach and Bwlchtocyn ☎01758 713303, ⓦ porthtocynhotel.co.uk. Relaxed country-house hotel brimming with style, yet which also caters for families. Several rooms are interconnecting and there's a play room for kids to use while parents dine, plus an outdoor heated pool. All rooms are different (we like number 2) and many have great views of Cardigan Bay. The

coast path goes past the backdoor. Closed Nov to mid-March. **£165**

Rhydolion Llangian, 1 mile northwest of Abersoch ☎01758 712342, ⓦ rhydolion.co.uk. Small tent and caravan site that accepts groups, 15min walk from Porth Neigwl beach and 20min across fields from the pub at Llanengan. It also has 4 very well-appointed, self-contained units. Closed Nov–Feb. **£8**/person

Sgobor Unnos Tanrallt Farm, Llangian, 2 miles west of Abersoch ☎01758 713527, ⓦ tanrallt.com. Though fairly scruffy, this self-catering bunkhouse in Llangian is the only one in the area. Rates for bunkhouse include a continental breakfast. Take bus #18 from Pwllheli or Abersoch; 4 daily. Dorms **£18**; camping **£8**/person

Venetia Lôn Sarn Bach ☎01758 713354, ⓦ venetiawales.com. Apart from the view from a couple of rooms, you barely know you're at the seaside at this urban chic boutique hotel with five individually styled rooms and plush bathrooms. All are above an excellent restaurant. **£128**

EATING AND DRINKING

Coconut Kitchen Lôn Pont Morgan (main road opposite harbour) ☎01758 712250, ⓦ coconutkitchen .co.uk. The best Thai place for miles, with dishes served from an open kitchen. As well as classics like beef Massaman or green chicken curry (around £12), it features local fish and seafood in dishes like local prawn and pollack fishcakes, and offers Songkla dishes from south Thailand (£15). Takeaways available. Daily 5.30–10pm.

The Dining Room Lôn Sarn Bach ☎01758 740709, ⓦ thediningroomabersoch.co.uk. Casual wood-floored dinner-only bistro (plus some outside seating) with a short menu plus daily specials, all simply cooked from fresh ingredients. Mains (mostly £14–17) might include hake rarebit with crisp Anglesey bacon and plum tomato jellies or ribeye steak with black pepper and brandy sauce. Fish specials on Fridays. Daily 7–10pm; closed Mon–Wed in winter.

Porth Tocyn 2.5 miles south of Abersoch, on the road through Sarn Bach and Bwlchtocyn ☎01758 713303,

ⓦ porthtocynhotel.co.uk. One of Abersoch's best restaurants for ages thanks to its light modern British cooking. Set menus might include pan-fried scallops or monkfish with Mediterranean vegetables (£45.50 for 3 courses), but a lighter supper menu includes fresh fish pies and pasta (£10–14). Closed Nov to mid March.

Venetia Lôn Sarn Bach ☎01758 713354, ⓦ venetiawales.com. Grilled bream with creamed kale and pancetta or cannelloni of butternut squash – the chef's Italian heritage and local fruits of the sea (often straight from the boat) determine the seasonal Modern British menu in this smart award-winning modern restaurant. Everything is superbly presented, staff are excellent. Most mains £13–17. Wed–Sun 6.30–10pm.

Zinc Lôn Pen Cei ☎01758 712880, ⓦ zincabersoch .com. Metropolitan cool in a bar with a relaxed ambience and a wonderful terrace overlooking the inner harbour. Daily 9am–3pm & 6–11pm or later in summer.

Aberdaron and around

At the lime-washed fishing hamlet of **ABERDARON**, two miles short of the tip of the Llŷn, you really feel you're at the end of Wales. For the best part of a thousand years, up to the sixteenth century, the inn and church here were the last stops on a pilgrim

6

R.S. THOMAS

The reclusive, Cardiff-born poet **R.S. (Ronald Stuart) Thomas** (1913–2000) was something of a Welsh anti-hero. He worked as a minister in rural parishes throughout Wales, most famously in Aberdaron where he spent his last couple of working decades and much of his retirement. It was Thomas's fourth volume of poetry, published in 1955, that brought him lasting recognition, something consolidated with his best-known collections – *The Bread of Truth* (1963) and *Not that he brought Flowers* (1968).

R.S. Thomas's poetry is dark and spartan, illuminated with shafts of vision and clarity. Common themes include religion (Christianity in particular), rural and pastoral strands, and the eternal poetic topic of love in human relationships. However, it's in his Welsh-themed work that Thomas most savagely and thrillingly hits the mark.

I never wanted the drab rôle
Life assigned me, an actor playing
To the past's audience upon a stage
Of earth and stone; the absurd label
Of birth, of race hanging askew

About my shoulders. I was in prison
Until you came; your voice was a key
Turning in the enormous lock
Of hopelessness. Did the door open
To let me out or yourselves in?

A Welsh Testament

trail to Ynys Enlli or Bardsey Island, around the headland. Otherwise, Aberdaron is simply a charming low-key sort of place, with a long spread of pebbly beach to enjoy.

Porth y Swnt

At car park beside bridge • Daily: March & Oct–Dec 10am–4pm; Apr–June & Sept 9am–5pm; July–Aug 9am–6pm • £2; NT • ☎ 01758 703814

The name translates as "gateway to the sound", yet this rather undersells **Porth y Swnt**, a new National Trust attraction in the village centre. Instead, this small centre with art and traditional crafts states the case of Aberdaron as the cultural wellspring of the peninsula. Meagre exhibits in the three rooms are brought to life by audio guides, with most exhibits accompanied by an interview with geologists, artists, gardeners, walkers, poets or farmers. The result is an oral history that subtly reveals something of the unique character of the Llŷn peninsula. Take your time and it's impressionistic, even spiritual.

Church of St Hywyn

On main road as you enter Aberdaron from east • Daily: Easter–Oct 9am–6pm; Nov–Easter 10am–4pm • Free

The twelfth-century **church of St Hywyn** on the cliffs behind the stony beach still serves its original purpose and was ministered by one of Wales' greatest modern poets, R.S. Thomas (see box above). Displays on Thomas have pride of place in a beautifully simple twin-naved interior, beside material on Enlli and its pilgrims, and a pair of Latin-inscribed sixth-century gravestones – among the earliest Christian artefacts in Wales.

Plas yn Rhiw

B4413, 5 miles east of Aberdaron • Late March to May & Sept Mon & Thurs–Sun noon–5pm; June to mid-July daily except Tues noon–5pm; Aug daily noon–5pm; Oct Thurs–Sun noon–4pm • £5; NT • ☎ 01758 780219 • Pwllheli to Aberdaron bus #17b (2 daily) passes the gate

In the early years of his retirement, R.S. Thomas lived in a cottage in the grounds of **Plas yn Rhiw**, a Regency manor house on Tudor foundations at the western end of Porth Neigwl. The house was derelict in 1938 when it was bought by Thomas' moneyed friends, the Keating sisters, who restored it with the help of Portmeirion architect Clough Williams-Ellis, whose offbeat touch is evident in the flattened arches and a Gothic doorway rescued from a demolished castle. This is a manageable and relaxed place, filled with rustic furniture like a 1920s oil stove used by Honora Keating until her death in 1981, and her accomplished watercolours. The upstairs sitting room is notable for its 6ft-thick wall containing a fireplace, a spiral staircase and a window nook overlooking gorgeous gardens, all clipped box hedges, fuchsias, hydrangeas, roses and wild flowers.

Mynydd Mawr

2 miles southwest · Open access · Free; NT

Having made your way out as far as Aberdaron, it's worth exploring narrow lanes west to the end of the peninsula, **Mynydd Mawr**, the hill overlooking Bardsey Sound. Just as the road begins to climb up the hill, stop at **Braich-y-Pwll**, a headland from where a short path heads down the cliffs to the ruins of St Mary's church, the crossing point at the end of the Pilgrim's Way. The road continues from here to the top of Mynydd Mawr, the tip of the Llŷn, with footpaths to take or just gorgeous seascapes across the sound to Bardsey Island to savour.

Porth Oer

2 miles north of Abersoch · Open access · Free; parking £4; NT

The best beach hereabouts is **Porth Oer**, known as "Whistling Sands" for the white sands, which squeak as you walk on them. It is a memorable spot hemmed in by rocky promontories with easy walks either way along the coast. The only facilities are toilets and a small beach shop that's only open in mid-summer.

ARRIVAL AND DEPARTURE   ABERDARON

By bus The #17 bus comes here from Pwllheli (Mon–Sat 8 daily; 40min).

ACCOMMODATION AND EATING

Mynydd Mawr Llanllawen Fawr, 2 miles southwest ☎ 01758 760223, ⓦ aberdaroncaravanandcampingsite .co.uk Just a couple of peaceful grassy fields right by the entrance to Mynydd Mawr, yet this is something of a legend among camping afficionados for its sense of escapism as much as views across to Ynys Enlli. Hot showers and electricity hook-up available. Closed Nov–Feb. **£15**/pitch

The Ship ☎ 01758 760204, ⓦ theshiphotelaberdaron .co.uk. The cheaper of the village's two hotels, but a good array of ales and the better restaurant, serving the likes of local dressed crab starters (£8) and a range of meat and vegetarian mains like home-made lasagne or wild mushrooms with home-made pasta (£10–14). Daily noon– 2pm & 6.30–9pm. **£89**

Tŷ Newydd ☎ 01758 760207, ⓦ gwesty-tynewydd .co.uk. There's one good reason to choose this modernized hotel – beach and sea views from the front rooms (which are slightly pricier), the best with mini baconies. Nice touches like iPod docks and super king beds make up for decor that's acceptable but bland. Local crab and lobster as well as pub favourites like chilli con carne and fish and chips (£9) are served in the beachside restaurant. Daily: noon– 2.30pm & 6–8.30pm. **£110**

Y Gegin Fawr ☎ 01758 760359. The fourteenth-century stone "Big Kitchen" once served as the pilgrims' final gathering place before the treacherous crossing to Ynys Enlli. It now operates as a simple café serving crab sandwiches, home-made cream teas and cakes, and Llŷn Peninsula ice cream. Daily: Easter–Oct half-term 10am–6pm.

Ynys Enlli (Bardsey Island)

Bardsey Island or **Ynys Enlli** (The Island of the Currents) rises out of the ocean two miles off the tip of the Llŷn, separated from it by a strait of churning, unpredictable water. This national nature reserve has been an important pilgrimage site since the sixth century, when St Cadfan set up the first monastery here: three visits were proclaimed equivalent to one pilgrimage to Rome. Legend claims Ynys Enlli as "The Isle of Twenty Thousand Saints", most likely remembering the huge numbers of pilgrims who came to die at this holy spot. By the twelfth century, Giraldus Cambrensis was already claiming that "no one dies there except in extreme old age, for disease is almost unheard of".

BIRDWATCHING ON YNYS ENLLI

Interesting though the abbey ruins and later buildings are, most visitors come to Ynys Enlli watch **birds**. Among the dozen or so species of nesting sea birds are Manx shearwaters, fulmars, and guillemots, and an amazing number of vagrants turn up after being blown off course by storms. There are hides dotted around the island and **seals** all over the rocks at low tide.

Numerous other stories tell of the burial place of Myrddin (Merlin) and the former Bishop of Bangor, St Deiniol, but the only hard evidence is the crumbling **bell tower** of the thirteenth-century Augustinian Abbey of St Mary and a few Celtic crosses scattered around it. After the dissolution of the monasteries in 1536, piracy became the focus of the island's economy for over a century, gradually giving way to agriculture and fishing.

ARRIVAL AND INFORMATION   YNYS ENLLI

By boat Boats to Ynys Enlli are dependent on sea conditions and a viable load of passengers: be as flexible as possible. The cheapest crossings are with Bardsey Boat Trips (£30 return; ☎07971 769895, ⓦ bardseyboattrips.com), which flash across from Porth Meudwy, a tiny cove a mile south of Aberdaron, in around 15min; Aberdaron village shop serves as an unofficial office. Enlli Charters (☎0845 811 3655,

ⓦ enllicharter.co.uk) runs from Pwllheli (£40) and trips take an hour, seeing more of the coast. Both trips give around four hours on Enlli.

Services Apart from a dozen seasonal researchers, the island now has just one resident farming family who sell tea, coffee and snacks (11am–1pm); bring your own lunch.

ACCOMMODATION

Bardsey Island Trust ☎0845 811 2233, ⓦ bardsey .org. The island's owners rent out eight spartan but substantial electricity-free houses by the week, mostly to

birders, but also for yoga retreats, photography workshops or just as getaways. Mid-April to mid-Oct only, Sat to Sat. **£210**/week

The north Llŷn coast

Scalloped by small coves and sweeping beaches between rocky bluffs, the **north Llŷn coast** is a dramatic contrast to the busier south. It has few settlements of any size and lots of quiet little beaches. The most popular (though seldom thronged) is **Porth Dinllaen** with its pub gorgeously sited beside the sand. A rockier coastline is accessible from the Welsh language school at **Nant Gwrtheyrn**, which is overlooked by the heights of **Tre'r Ceiri** with its prehistoric hillfort remains. The road northeast from Tre'r Ceiri towards Caernarfon now bypasses one of north Wales' finest churches, the austere church of St Beuno at **Clynnog Fawr**.

Nefyn and Porth Dinllaen

There isn't much to recommend **NEFYN**, the largest of the peninsula's northern communities, but neighbouring **MORFA NEFYN**, a mile to the west, and the adjacent shoreline hamlet of **PORTH DINLLAEN**, both benefit from having lost the 1839 battle to become the terminus for ferries to Ireland. Now owned by the National Trust, Porth Dinllaen is just a pristine sweeping bay backed by a handful of houses and the popular waterside *Tŷ Coch Inn*. Easiest access is to walk half a mile along the beach from the National Trust's Porth Dinllaen car park in Morfa Nefyn.

GETTING AROUND AND INFORMATION   NEFYN AND PORTH DINLLAEN

By bus Even at the best of times, bus services are infrequent and badly timed, so you'll struggle without your own car or bike.

Services Amenities are also thinly scattered hereabouts – a few campsites dotted around, and the odd shop and pub in a village.

ACCOMMODATION AND EATING

Natural Retreats Pistyll, 1 mile north of Morfa Nefyn ☎0843 6367193, ⓦ naturalretreats.com. Renovated buildings of a former farm now offer an excellent stay in one- to three-bed cottages. Rustic beams and stone walls as well as modern rugs and natural fibres soften the modern streamlined style. The sea views from the front cottages are gorgeous. Minimum 3 nights in high season. **£177**
Penrallt Coastal Campsite Tudweiliog, 6 miles

southeast of Morfa Nefyn ☎01758 770654, ⓦ penrallt .co.uk. One of the best north Llŷn campsites, perched just behind the clifftops with separate fields for families and small tents – sunsets are astonishing when the weather allows. It also offers wooden "pods" that sleep up to four (own sleeping bags required; minimum two nights except for coast path hikers) and a yurt (mid July–mid Sept), plus direct access to the coast path (and nearby beaches), hot showers, freezer and laundry. The *Lion Inn* in Tudweiliog is a two-mile walk away. Closed Oct–Easter. Pitches £11; pods for two £25; yurt £45

Tŷ Coch Inn Porth Dinllaen ☎01758 720498, ⊛tycoch .co.uk. Forget the overpriced bar meals (jacket spuds, sandwiches and panini). Come instead to this village pub

hung with tankards for a drink: grab a pint and sit outside on the sea wall with sand between your toes and views of moutains. Perfect. June–Aug and bank holidays Mon–Sat 11am–10pm, Sun 11am–5pm; rest of the year Mon–Thurs 11am–3pm, Fri–Sat 11am–3pm & 6–10pm but worth calling to check.

6

Nant Gwrtheyrn

Northeast of Nefyn the mountains of Yr Eifl rise steeply only to plunge into the sea along **Nant Gwrtheyrn** (Vortigern's Valley), an impressively steep cleft in the hills, its edges chewed away by granite quarries. This is supposed to be the final resting place of the Celtic chieftain Vortigern, who was responsible for inviting the Saxons to Britain after his magician, Myrddin (Merlin), had seen the struggle of the two dragons – the red of the ancient Britons and the white of the Saxons.

Nant Gwrtheyrn: The Welsh Language and Heritage Centre

1.5 miles north of Llithfaen, 3 miles northeast of Nefyn • Daily 9.30am–4.30pm • Free • ☎01758 750334, ⊛nantgwrtheyrn.org

Vortigern should be pleased to know that his valley is now doing its best to atone for his error, by keeping the ancient British language alive at **Nant Gwrtheyrn: The Welsh Language and Heritage Centre**. A precipitously steep road corkscrews down to the centre, set in rows of converted cottages built in the late nineteenth century when the valley had three granite quarries. Though primarily for residential courses entirely in Welsh, the valley is also a beautiful spot to spend a couple of hours exploring, either along the Llŷn Coastal Path or around the old mine workings and piles of rock waste; a free leaflet outlines a 3-mile **walk**.

To put it all into context, visit the **Heritage Centre** in the original chapel, and the **Quarryman's Cottages**, two rooms set up to look as they might have been in 1910 with dresser, needlework sampler and Bible all in pride of place around the hearth.

A good licensed **café** provides sustenance, and there's even self-catering **accommodation** in the cottages (three-night minimum).

Tre'r Ceiri

Open access • Free

Yr Eifl is a trio of mountains that top out at 1850ft. The second highest is crowned by **Tre'r Ceiri** or "Town of the Giants" hillfort, easily the finest prehistoric remains on the Llŷn. A massive tumble of rocks is mostly formed into the waist-high walls of about 150 dry-stone hut circles, surrounded by a rampart 12ft high in places. The site is Bronze Age, but the huts are probably only a couple of thousand years old. Locals refer to them as *Cytiau Gwddelod* or "Irishmen's Huts", possibly recalling the Irish immigrant population on the Llŷn in the first few centuries AD, when five hundred people lived on this inhospitable site. Today, the ruins command a stunning **view** over the whole peninsula.

The summit is reached by a steep **path** (4km return; 2hr; 800ft ascent) which starts at a lay-by half a mile southwest of Llanaelhaearn.

Church of St Beuno

Clynnog Fawr, just off A499, 4 miles northeast of Llanaelhaearn • Easter–Oct daily, usually 10am–5pm

Light streams in through the clear windows of the large and airy, early sixteenth-century **church of St Beuno**, built on foundations laid by Saint Beuno in the sixth century. This monastic settlement is rich in ancient spiritual connections and would have been an important stop for pilgrims bound for Ynys Enlli, ensuring a hefty income that probably financed this impressive church. The interior combines spartan whitewash and limestone flags with wealthier flourishes like the fine hammerbeam roof with ornamental bosses, fine choir stalls and an imposing chancel.

The road to Caernarfon passes a turn-off to Dinas Dinlle, the gates of Parc Glynllifon, and close by the Inigo Jones Slateworks (see p.358).

The north coast and Anglesey

BRITANNIA BRIDGE AND MENAI BRIDGE,
MENAI STRAIT

The north coast and Anglesey

Wales' North Coast and its natural extension, Anglesey, encompass both the geographical and social extremities of the country. In the brash resorts of the northeast, street signs are the only indication that you are in Wales. Further west, there are places where English is seldom spoken other than to visitors. Two major forces have shaped the region. The might of thirteenth-century English king Edward I crushed the Welsh princes by means of dramatically situated castles. Then, in the nineteenth century English mill-town factory workers began holidaying here by the trainload. The set-up isn't so different today, but cars have largely taken over from the train, caravans are as popular as guesthouses and amusement arcades rule.

7

Wales's northern seaboard elicits strong reactions. Many return annually to the cheap and cheerful holiday resorts at its eastern end. Others hurry quickly past to the attractions further west. Either way, the initial strip of the **north coast** proper is not the prettiest in Wales due to its busy caravan parks and amusements scattered along the promenades and beachfronts. If they seem designed to keep you off the beaches it may be wise counsel – the sea here is none too clean.

The fast A55 highway largely bypasses **Deeside**, a wedge of former mining communities set between the salt marshes of the Dee estuary and the Clwydian Range. Divert to visit **Flint Castle**, the first link in Edward I's Iron Ring of castles, and understated **Holywell**, whose quiet attractions include St Winefride's Well, a pilgrimage site of varied fortunes during the last thirteen hundred years.

Uninspiring **Prestatyn** is notable mainly as the starting, or finishing, point of the Offa's Dyke Path. Nearby, loud and tacky **Rhyl** offers good budget accommodation and is close to several inland attractions, specifically the nuggety castle at **Rhuddlan**, the Victorian portrait gallery at **Bodelwyddan** and **St Asaph**, home to Britain's smallest cathedral. Further west, **Colwyn Bay** is smarter than Rhyl, but pales next to its western neighbours, Llandudno and Conwy.

Victorian **Llandudno** was always a posher resort and remains a cut above the rest. This queen of the north Wales coast, with its four-storey terraced beachfront, hunkers below the massive limestone hummock of the **Great Orme**, climbed by cable car and tram, and ringed by the scenic Marine Drive. With no real beach, **Conwy** is a different proposition, packing more sights than the rest of the coast put together in a lovely small town girdled by seven hundred-year-old town walls, which spur off from the mighty castle.

The A55 expressway is held tightly to the coast by the northern fringes of Snowdonia's Carneddau range for the final fifteen miles to **Bangor**, home to north Wales' only university, and consequently its liveliest town.

If it's beaches you're after, head across the treacherous channel of the **Menai Strait** to the island of **Anglesey**, a patchwork of rural communities dotted with burial chambers,

PLAS MAWR, CONWY

Highlights

❶ Llandudno The paragon of a Victorian seaside resort with a truly splendid pier and the neighbouring rugged limestone hummock of the Great Orme; getting there by tram or cablecar is half the fun. **See p.398**

❷ Conwy The pick of north Wales's towns with its imposing castle and intact ring of medieval walls enclosing a fascinating centre. **See p.403**

❸ Menai Strait Look back from Anglesey across the swirling tidal races of the Menai Strait, with the great bridges framing long views of Snowdonia. **See p.417**

❹ Beaumaris A picture-postcard castle plus a Georgian townscape make this small town a

lovely base for exploring Anglesey's beaches and Neolithic remains. **See p.418**

❺ Penmon Priory Lovely twelfth-century church containing ancient stonework, hidden in an almost forgotten corner of Anglesey. **See p.419**

❻ Newborough Warren Easy strolls through ecologically important dune systems to the remote-feeling peninsula known as Llanddwyn Island. **See p.423**

❼ South Stack Wheeling sea birds, stunning sea cliffs, a picturesque lighthouse on a small island and some great coastal walking. **See p.425**

HIGHLIGHTS ARE MARKED ON THE MAP ON PP.390–391

standing stones and Wales' greatest concentration of Neolithic remains. There's yet another stupendous castle at **Beaumaris**, built to a highly advanced concentric design. The southwestern resorts of **Rhosneigr**, **Rhoscolyn** and **Trearddur Bay** are the favoured spots for swimming and watersports, but in scenic terms there's much to be said for the extensive dune system of **Newborough** and the sea cliffs around **South Stack**, both great for birdwatching. Lastly, the ferries from **Holyhead**, at the western end of the island, provide the fastest route to Dublin and Dun Laoghaire in Ireland.

GETTING AROUND

THE NORTH COAST AND ANGLESEY

By train The train links the coastal resorts all the way to Bangor, then across to Anglesey for the run to Holyhead.

By bus With the exception of National Express bus services from Manchester, Liverpool and other English cities to Bangor and Holyhead, bus travel is much more piecemeal, although services are fairly frequent and come listed in excellent timetable booklets available free at tourist offices. Check Basics for discount fares (see p.31).

By car The A55 dual carriageway allows you to drive from the Welsh border just south of Liverpool through Anglesey to Holyhead in little over an hour, bypassing all the coastal towns and skirting the northern reaches of Snowdonia.

Deeside

The industrial hinterland that spreads over the English border from Chester can be avoided by heading directly for **Deeside**, flanking the River Dee estuary. Yet with your own transport a detour off the A55 offers a few modest sights – castle ruins at Flint, healing waters at **Holywell** and the Celtic cross of **Maen Achwyfaen**.

THE NORTH COAST & ANGLESEY

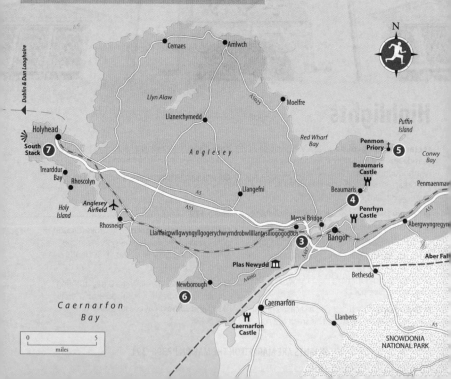

Flint Castle

Access from Castle Dyke Street • Daily 10am–4pm • Free; CADW

Otherwise missable, **Flint Castle** represents a warm-up act for the fortresses west. Its sandstone ruin was begun in 1277 as the first of Edward I's Iron Ring of fortresses (see box, p.404) to stand guard over shipping lanes into Chester. Ten-foot thick walls with towers at all corners except the southeast, where a small moat and drawbridge separate a well-preserved Great Tower, the castle's main accommodation and ultimate fall-back, show just how important the trade route was. Its demise came during the Civil War in 1647. Republican General Mytton so effectively dismantled the castle that only six years later it was practically buried in its own ruins.

ARRIVAL AND DEPARTURE FLINT

By train Trains pass every 30min running to Chester (15min), Llandudno Junction (40min) and Prestatyn (15min).

By bus Buses, from outside the train station, serve: Chester

(Mon–Sat roughly hourly, Sun 4 daily; 50min); Mold (Mon–Sat hourly, Sun 4 daily; 20min); Prestatyn (Mon–Sat hourly, Sun 4 daily; 50min).

7

Holywell and around

A place of pilgrimage for thirteen hundred years, **HOLYWELL** (Treffynnon) four miles northwest of Flint is fancifully billed as "The Lourdes of Wales", albeit without the tacky souvenir stalls selling Virgin Mary lighters. Instead, Holywell is a quiet little town that modestly plays down its ancient appeal.

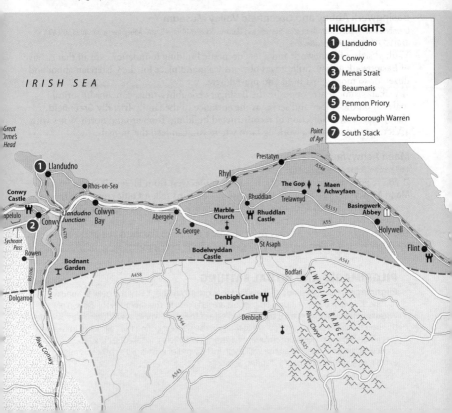

HIGHLIGHTS

1. Llandudno
2. Conwy
3. Menai Strait
4. Beaumaris
5. Penmon Priory
6. Newborough Warren
7. South Stack

IRISH SEA

St Winefride's Well

Greenfield Rd • Daily: April–Sept 9am–5pm; Oct–March 10am–4pm • 80p • Museum: daily April–Sept Wed, Sat & Sun noon–4pm • Free •
☎ 01352 713054, ⊕ saintwinefrideswell.com

Never mind that the Romans used the healing waters of **St Winefride's Well** to relieve rheumatism and gout. A seventh-century legend claims that the virtuous Winefride (Gwenfrewi in Welsh) was decapitated after resisting the advances of Prince Caradoc. The well is said to have sprung up where her head fell and when St Beuno, her uncle, placed her head beside the body, prayer and the waters revived her, setting her on track to serve as an abbess at Gwytherin Convent near Llanrwst.

Richard I and Henry V provided regal patronage, ensuring a steady flow of believers to what became one of the great shrines of Christendom even if pilgrimages became more clandestine after the Reformation, when the well became a focal point of resistance to Protestantism. A century and a half later, the Catholic king of England, James II, came here to pray for a son and heir.

Pilgrims spent the night praying in the Gothic **St Winefride's Chapel**, which encloses three sides of the well. Henry VII's mother, Margaret Beaufort, paid for the construction and earned herself a likeness among the roof bosses that depict the life of St Winefride in the ornate, Gothic fan-vaulted crypt that surrounds the well, their columns etched with graffiti dating from the 1500s.

The former custodian's house contains a small **museum** with painted banners, priests' vestements, the skeletal remains of Reformation martyrs (one of whose heads clearly ended on a spike as a warning to others) and a beautiful silver reliquary designed to display Holywell's relic – part of Winefride's thumb bone.

Basingwerk Abbey and Greenfield Valley Museum

Greenfield Valley • Abbey: daily 10am–4pm; museum: mid-March to Oct daily 10am–4.30pm • Abbey: free; museum: £5.50; CADW •
☎ 01352 714172, ⊕ greenfieldvalley.com

Vaulted slabs of stonework and a few domestic building foundations are all that survive of **Basingwerk Abbey**. Still, it was obviously a grand place for the Cistercian abbot and dozen or so monks that lived and prayed here.

A small visitor centre opposite the Basingerwerk abbey ruins contains historical material on the Abbey and serves as the entrance to the family-friendly **Greenfield Valley Museum**, a collection of reconstructed buildings from around north Wales with a Victorian school and a working farm where you can feed the animals.

Maen Achwyfaen

4 miles west of Holywell • Open access • Free; CADW

If you've got your own transport, head four miles west from Holywell to the impressive **Maen Achwyfaen** or "Stone of Lamentation", Britain's tallest **Celtic cross**. The thousand-year-old shaft, incised with interwoven latticework, is over 10ft high and crowned with a wheel cross. To get there, take the A5026 almost three miles northwest from Holywell and turn right onto the A5151. After almost a mile take the third exit at the first roundabout and follow signs to Trelogan for a little over a mile.

PILGRIMAGES AND RITUAL BATHING

Pilgrimages to St Winefride's Well mainly focus on St Winefride's Day, the nearest Sunday to June 22, when over five hundred pilgrims are led through the streets by the Bishop of Wrexham. The procession ends by the open side of the crypt where a few dozen faithful wade through the waters of a calm pool three times in the hope of curing their ailments. Immersion isn't limited to the procession: anyone, whatever their beliefs, can take the cure, albeit in a shallow stone pool rather than the well itself. Just a word of warning: it's chilly. This might explain why summer is know as "Curing Season".

GREENFIELD VALLEY HERITAGE PARK STROLL

St Winefride's Well and Basingwerk Abbey are just a mile apart, linked by a woodland trail along the track of an old pilgrims' train line. Paths weave past five mill ponds, a series of water races and the preserved remains of copper works and cotton mills, which once manufactured Queen Victoria's underwear, apparently. Together they form the **Greenfield Valley Heritage Park**. About 200yds down the Greenfield Road from the Well, take the footpath behind the factory then follow whichever paths take your fancy.

ARRIVAL AND DEPARTURE

HOLYWELL

By bus Buses along the coast call frequently at the bus station at the southern end of High St. They serve Flint (every 30min; 15min) and Rhyl (every 30min; 1hr).

ACCOMMODATION AND EATING

Blue Bell Inn B5123 in Halkyn, 4 miles southeast ☎ 01352 780309, ⓦ bluebell.uk.eu.org. A fine rural pub that's the heart of the village – it even houses the Post Office – and provides an ever-changing range of real ales and ciders, interesting malt whiskies and great views over the Dee Estuary. Mon & Wed–Fri 5–11pm, Sat & Sun noon–11pm.

Glan-yr-Afon Inn Dolphin, Milwr ☎ 01752 710052, ⓦ glanyrafoninn.com. Sixteenth-century country pub that feels a world away from Holywell. It has fourteen modern(ish) en suites, along with tasty pub grub such as slow-braised lamb shank in red wine (£12) and real ales. Follow the A5026 southwest of town then onto Milwr Road (1.2 miles in all). Food served daily noon–2.30pm & 6–9pm (till 8pm Sun). **£75**

The Mill on the Hill Greenfield Rd ☎ 01352 711004. Decent daytime tearoom right by St Winefride's Well. The bacon or sausage butties, Welsh rarebit and *bara brith* are nothing fancy, but are well made and cheap at around £3 each, and there's free wi-fi. Tues–Fri 10am–5pm, Sat–Sun 10am–4pm.

7

Prestatyn to Colwyn Bay

The cause of any vituperative comments aimed at the north Wales coast is this twenty-mile stretch of amusement arcades, caravan sites and negligible beach. Of the resorts, the best known is **Rhyl** – brash and ballsy in high summer, but there are erudite attractions nearby like the cathedral at tiny **St Asaph**, one of Edward I's castles at **Rhuddlan** and a collection of Victorian portraits and furniture at **Bodelwyddan Castle**. Chosing between neighbouring **Prestatyn** and **Colwyn Bay**, the latter is marginally the nicest of the main resorts. Don't get too excited though.

Prestatyn and around

A small-fry resort, **PRESTATYN** is pleasant enough, though really only of interest as the northern terminus of the 177-mile **Offa's Dyke Path** (see box, p.239). More committed walkers traditionally start at least ankle-deep in the water, then cross the beach beside the sculpture *Dechrau a Diwedd* (*Beginning and End*). If you're thinking of embarking on a section, be warned that you won't come across any of the Offa's Dyke earthworks until the path gets south of the River Dee. Still, you can walk out of the centre into the Clwydian Range for tremendous views – head up the High Street to the pub **Cross Foxes**, from where acorn-marked signs guide you into the hills behind.

The Gop

Trelawnyd, 4 miles southeast of Prestatyn • Open access • Free

If you've got your own transport, visit the **Gop**, Britain's second-largest artificial Neolithic mound after Silbury Hill in Wiltshire. The Gop was constructed on top of an existing hill, crowning an already splendid viewpoint with a mysterious mound. Prehistoric remains have been found both in the mound itself and in the caves directly below the hill. The superb **views** over the Clwydian hills from the top are accessed via a path from above the village of **Trelawnyd**, on the A5151. In Trelawnyd, park about 200yd up High Street and walk along a narrow gravel lane on the left following the discrete discs to the Gop – about fifteen minutes' walk in all.

ARRIVAL AND DEPARTURE
PRESTATYN

By train North coastline trains stop in the centre of town, serving Flint (every 30–60min; 15min) and Llandudno Junction (every 30–60min; 25min).

By bus Buses stop close to the train station with services to Holywell (Mon–Sat hourly, Sun 4 daily; 40min) and Rhyl (Mon–Sat hourly, Sun 4 daily; 20min).

ACCOMMODATION

Beaches Hotel Beach Rd East ☎01745 853072, ⓦthebeacheshotel.com. Beachfront hotel with comfy modern rooms, its own restaurant, a bar with outside seating and an indoor pool. Dynamic pricing means rates fluctuate according to demand. **£86**

Morgans B&B 2 miles southwest in Axton, half a mile south of Llanasa ☎01745 570981, ⓦmorgansbedand breakfast.co.uk. It's hard to think of a finer reward after Offa's Dyke path (a few miles away) than this village B&B, an effortless blend of homely crafts and modern style. **£75**

Nant Mill Gronant Rd ☎01745 852360, ⓦnantmilltouring.co.uk. Grassy, family-orientated campsite a mile east along the A548; simple but pleasant and only half a mile from the beach. Closed mid-Oct to mid-March. Pitches **£14**

Plas Ifan 17 Ffordlas, near the Cross Foxes pub ☎01745 887883, ⓦplasifan.com. Welcoming B&B that's popular with Offa's Dyke walkers: the path passes by practically a street away. Three en-suite rooms, spacious grounds and packed lunches on request. Doubles **£65**

Rhyl and around

There's nothing subtle about **RHYL** (Y Rhyl). Raw and raucous, this seaside resort three miles west of Prestatyn is a minor assault on the senses along a two-mile-long promenade of amuseuments. While no one would claim that run-down Rhyl is a sophisticated tourist destination, it is a decent option for a cheap, cheerful holiday with kids: all Punch and Judy, fish and chips and uncomplicated fun.

RHUDDLAN, three miles to the south, and essentially a suburb of Rhyl, is home to **Rhuddlan Castle** on the banks of the Clwyd River (Afon Clywedog).

SeaQuarium

East Parade • Daily: March–Oct 10am–5pm; Nov–Feb 10am–4pm • £8.98 • ☎01745 344660, ⓦseaquarium.co.uk

Though nothing to make Sea World in Florida quake, this aquatic zoo is a good option for a rainy day with the kids. It features an assortment of coastal environments plus a shipwreck zone with a shark tunnel with dogfish, basking sharks and eels. The day's highlight is feeding time – seals are fed at noon – plus fifteen minute shows at the sea-lion cove (1pm & 3pm).

Rhuddlan Castle

Rhuddlan, 3 miles south of Rhyl • April–Oct daily 10am–5pm • £3.40; CADW • ☎01745 590777

Rhuddlan Castle, now an impressive hollow ruin, was constructed between 1277 and 1282 by Edward I during his first phase of castle-building. It was designed as both a garrison and royal residence, commanding a canalized section of the then strategic river. **Gillot's Tower**, by the dock gate, provided protection for the supply ships, while the concentric plan allowed archers on both outer and inner walls to fire simultaneously. This innovation become irrelevant by 1648, when Parliamentary forces took the castle during the Civil War and demolished it.

ARRIVAL AND INFORMATION
RHYL AND AROUND

The **train and bus stations** are adjacent, near the intersection of the A548 (Russell/Wellington roads) and Bodfor/ Queen streets, which run to the sea.

By train Trains serve: Bangor (25 daily; 40min); Holyhead (23 daily; 1hr 10min–1hr 30min); Llandudno Junction (every 20–30min; 20min).

By bus Buses serve: Denbigh (Mon–Sat hourly, Sun 3 daily; 40min); Llandudno (Mon–Sat every 30min, Sun 6 daily; 1hr 10min); Prestatyn (every 30min; 20min);

Rhuddlan (Mon–Sat every 30min, Sun 6 daily; 10min); St Asaph (Mon–Sat hourly, Sun 6 daily; 25min).

Tourist information The TIC is on the seafront at West Parade, near the SeaQuarium (Easter–Sept daily 9.30am–4.30pm; Oct–Easter Mon–Fri 9.30am–4.30pm; ☎01745 355068, ✉rhyl.tic@denbighshire.gov.uk).

ACTIVITIES

Marsh Tracks Marsh Rd ☎01745 353335, ⓦmarshtracks.co.uk. BMX riding is the mainstay here, cycled on an Olympic-grade course, but this bike centre also has a 1.3km road-race circuit and mountain bike trails in the surrounding countryside. Bike hire is £5/2hr.

Pro Kitesurfing East Parade ☎07926 943421,

ⓦprokitesurfing.co.uk. Provides accredited kitesurfing lessons either off Rhyl beach or nearby, depending on conditions. One-day tasters cost £80, two-day beginner courses are £150. It also runs half-day paddleboarding sessions (£65).

ACCOMMODATION AND EATING

Barratt's Ty'n Rhyl, 167 Vale Rd ☎01745 344138, ⓦbarrattsoftynrhyl.co.uk. Rhyl's oldest house provides the venue for smart dining. "Fresh", "local ingredients" and "home-cooked" are watchwords for dishes such as duck in apple and Cognac sauce or sea bass with garden chard. Two-course menus cost £35. Reservations required. Tues–Sat 6.30–10pm, Sun noon–3pm.

Les & Rita's Fish Bar 28 Wellington Rd ☎01745 342315. Not just the best chippy in a resort stuffed with them, but the best in North Wales according to a regional

newspaper. It's cheap, too: fish and chips, a slice, peas and tea for £4.95. Mon–Sat 11.30–6.30pm.

★ **The Promenade** 38 Marine Drive ☎01745 334444, ⓦthepromenaderhyl.co.uk. The only four-star B&B in Rhyl is the smartest by a long shot. In an airy, tastefully modernized Victorian house, it offers two cheaper rooms with shared bathrooms and superb Premier en suites with sea views; all lofty and spotless. Factor in free wi-fi and parking, and it's a bargain. **£57.50**

St Asaph and around

Because of its cathedral, diminutive **ST ASAPH**, six miles south of Rhyl, ranks as a city; St Davids in Pembrokeshire is a slightly less populous "city", but St Asaph has the country's smallest **cathedral** – an edifice no bigger than many village churches. There's little else to detain you in town, but a couple of other sights lie in the surrounding area, including **Marble church** and the **National Portrait Gallery**.

St Asaph Cathedral

High St • Daily 9am–6.30pm • Free • ⓦstasaphcathedral.org.uk

Though dedicated to St Asaph, its second bishop after St Kentigern (the church's 570 founder), the cathedral in St Asaph is often associated with **William Morgan** (see box, p.396). From 1601 until his death in 1604, the creator of the Welsh bible held the bishopric here and his work is commemorated by an octagonal monument in the churchyard. Morgan's grave under the presbytery has been unmarked since George Gilbert Scott's substantial restoration of the thirteenth-century structure in the 1870s. Around a thousand Morgan Bibles were printed, of which only nineteen remain: one of them is displayed in the south transept along with Elizabeth I's 1549 copy of *The Book of Common Prayer*. There's also a collection of Psalters and prayer books, and in the north transept a sixteenth-century ivory Madonna said to have come from the Spanish Armada.

The church also contains a Welsh–Greek–Hebrew dictionary compiled by nineteenth-century polyglot Richard Robert Jones (usually known as **Dic Aberdaron**, after the fishing village where he was born). He lived more or less as a tramp while acquiring command of fifteen languages (along with smatterings of another twenty) and is buried in the parish church at the bottom of the hill.

WILLIAM MORGAN AND THE FIRST WELSH BIBLE

Until 1588 only English Bibles had been used in Welsh churches, a fact which rankled Welsh-born preacher **William Morgan**, who insisted: "Religion, if it is not taught in the mother tongue, will lie hidden and unknown". This was the professed reason behind Elizabeth I's demand for a translation, though her subjects' disaffection could be most conveniently controlled through the Church. Four clergymen took up the challenge, but it is Morgan who is remembered: working away in Llanrhaeadr-ym-Mochnant, he so neglected his other duties that he needed an armed guard to get to his services and was said to preach with a pistol at his side.

The eventual translation was so successful that the Privy Council decreed that a copy should be allocated to every Welsh church. Though it was soon replaced by a translation of the Authorized Version, Morgan's Bible differs little in style from the latest edition used in Welsh services today. More than just a basis for sermons, The **Welsh Bible** (Y Beibl) served to codify the language and set a standard for Welsh prose. Without it the language would probably have divided into several dialects or even followed its Brythonic cousin, Cornish, into history.

Marble church

Bodelwyddan, off junction 25 of A55, 2 miles west of St Asaph • No set times, usually daily May–Sept 9am–6.30pm • Free

At Bodelwyddan, the slender 202ft limestone spire of **Marble church** stands as a beacon over the flat coastal plain. The spire's finely worked Gothic tracery is its most impressive feature, and is continued inside where fourteen types of marble – Italian, Irish, Welsh – gave the church its name.

Bodelwyddan Castle: the National Portrait Gallery

Bodelwyddan, off junction 25 of the A55, 2 miles west of St Asaph • Generally open to April–Oct Wed–Sun, plus Mon & Tues in school holidays 10.30am–5pm; Nov to mid-April Sat & Sun 10.30am–4pm. See website for full opening times • £6.95 including audio tour and grounds, grounds only £4.20 • ☎ 01745 584060, ⓦ bodelwyddan-castle.co.uk

Bodelwyddan Castle is essentially a nineteenth-century country mansion, its Victorian interiors re-created during restoration in the 1980s. It now houses one of three provincial outposts of the **National Portrait Gallery**, specializing in works contemporary with the castle. That said, much of the castle is occupied by a hotel chain: cue piped muzak, cafés and the inevitable giftshop. The landscaped grounds provide some escape, with a deer park, walled garden, maze, adventure playground, and even some World War I trenches dug to train up troops before the front.

The gallery

Most of the hundred paintings are on the ground floor, approached through the "Watts Hall of Fame", a corridor lined with portraits of eminent Victorians by G.F. Watts. In the Dining Room, two portraits highlight the Pre-Raphaelite support for social reform: William Holman Hunt's portrayal of the vociferous opponent of slavery and capital punishment Stephen Lushington; and Ford Madox Brown's double portrait of Henry Farell, prime mover in the passing of the 1867 Reform Bill, and suffragette Millicent Garrett. Works by John Singer Sargent and Hubert von Herkamer also adorn the room, which, like the others, is furnished with pieces from the Victoria and Albert Museum in London.

More worthy Victorians line the library, which leads on to the Ladies' Drawing Room, with paintings of nineteenth-century society ladies. A grand staircase leads up to further examples of nineteenth-century portraiture and an interesting exhibit on the castle's time as Lowther College.

ARRIVAL AND DEPARTURE	**ST ASAPH AND AROUND**
By bus St Asaph is on the #51 bus route from Rhyl to Denbigh, which also comes within a minute's walk of the Marble Church and Bodelwyddan Castle. Buses all stop outside the cathedral.	Destinations Denbigh (every 30min; 15min); Rhuddlan (Mon–Sat hourly, Sun 5 daily; 15min); and Rhyl (Mon–Sat every 30min, Sun 4 daily; 25min).

ACCOMMODATION AND EATING

Bach Y Graig Tremeirchion, 4 miles northeast of Denbigh along the A543 ☎01745 730627, ⓦbachygraig.co.uk. A relaxed and welcoming farmstay inside a sixteenth-century house on a working dairy farm. It has a woodland trail and self-catering cottages (minimum one-week stay in summer). __£65__

★**Kinmel Arms** St George, 4 miles west of St Asaph ☎01745 832207, ⓦthekinmelarms.co.uk. A historic inn in a pretty hamlet, which offers fine Modern British dining without a fuss: expect the likes of woodpigeon, duck with honey and cardamon or Menai mussels (mains £12–25). As good a reason to come are its four suites, an effortless blend of modernity and relaxed comfort. Food served Tues–Sat noon–2.30pm & 6.30–9.30pm (pub till 11pm). __£135__

★**Tan-yr-Onnen** Waen, 2 miles east ☎01745 583821, ⓦnorthwalesbreaks.co.uk. Excellent six-room rural B&B set among the green fields of the Vale of Clwyd, just off the Offa's Dyke Path. Rooms, all en suite, are comfortably stylish, finished in calming natural shades, with free wi-fi and fluffy bathrobes as standard. __£95__

Colwyn Bay and around

The seamless towns of **COLWYN BAY** (Bae Colwyn) and **RHOS-ON-SEA**, twelve miles west of Rhyl, have marginally more charm than their eastern neighbour, with a hilly setting, an architecturally intact Victorian main street and not an amusement arcade in sight.

7

Welsh Mountain Zoo

Old Highway, 2 miles inland from Colwyn Bay • Daily: April–Oct 9.30am–6pm; Nov–March 9.30am–5pm • £10.95 • ☎01492 532938, ⓦwelshmountainzoo.org

Head steeply uphill to reach the **Welsh Mountain Zoo**, which boasts Californian sea lions, snow leopards and free-flying raptor displays. A free shuttle bus runs every twenty minutes (Easter & May to mid-Sept) between the zoo and the town's train station.

Harlequin Puppet Theatre

The Promenade, Rhos-on-Sea • School holidays daily 3pm • £5.50 • ☎01492 548166, ⓦpuppetshow.info

To catch one of the very few remaining marionette acts in the British tradition, held in its first- (and last-) built dedicated marionette theatre (a cute little venue with muralled walls), visit the ninety-minute daytime shows at the **Harlequin Puppet Theatre**, which are pitched firmly at younger kids.

St Trillo's chapel

Marine Drive, Rhos Point, Rhos-on-Sea • Generally Sun at 11am (check the sign outside) • Free

Half a mile north of the Harlequin Puppet Theatre, the minuscule **St Trillo's chapel** has seating for just six worshippers, so may have standing room only during services. More stone shed than religious building, the chapel stands over an ancient healing well and was reputedly the launch point of Prince Madoc ap Owain Gwynedd's voyage to America in 1170 – Welshmen and -women the world over like to claim that he was the first European to visit the New World.

ARRIVAL AND DEPARTURE   COLWYN BAY AND AROUND

By train Trains stop centrally on Victoria Ave and serve: Bangor (every 20–30min; 25min); Llandudno Junction (every 20–30min; 5min); Rhyl (every 20–30min; 10min).

By bus Buses stop centrally on Rhos Road and serve: Llandudno (every 10–20min; 15min); Rhyl (every 10–20min; 45min).

By bike The nicest way to explore town is by heading along the Prestatyn to Rhos-on-Sea cycle path which mostly follows the shoreline – you can rent bikes from West End Cycles, 121 Conwy Road (£13/half-day, £18/day; ☎01492 530269; Mon–Sat 9am–5.30pm).

ACCOMMODATION AND EATING

★**Ellingham House** 1 Woodland Park West ☎01492 533345, ⓦellinghamhouse.com. A considerable amount of care and attention goes into the running of this five-star B&B. There are three vast rooms and two smaller upper rooms, all furnished with antiques – one with a great view to the sea. __£79__

★**Pen-y-Bryn** Pen-y-Bryn Rd; follow Kings Drive a mile inland ☎01492 533360, ⓦpenybryn-colwynbay.co.uk.

An excellent menu of dishes like salmon fishcakes (mains £11–17), a continually changing selection of ales and a relaxed but stylish atmosphere combine into an award-winning formula in this modern country pub on the hill behind town. There are great views too. Mon–Sat 11am–11pm, Sun noon–10.30pm; food served 11am–9pm.

ENTERTAINMENT

Theatr Colwyn Abergele Rd ☏ 01492 577888, ⦿ www .theatrcolwyn.co.uk. Check out Wales' oldest theatre and the UK's oldest cinema (screening flicks since 1909), which has recently undergone an revamp. See the website for films, gigs and shows.

Llandudno

The twin limestone hummocks of the 680ft **Great Orme** and its southern cousin the Little Orme provide a dramatic frame for the gently curving Victorian frontage of **LLANDUDNO**, Wales's most enduring archetype of the genteel British seaside resort. The town occupies a low isthmus between two beachfronts: Llandudno Bay, with its promenaders and once-grand hotels, and the less developed West Shore. And despite the fun-seekers, Llandudno retains a dignified air, bolstered by its ever-improving hotels and restaurants.

Llandudno is a supremely easy place in which to wander. On a sunny day it is pure traditional seaside, all Victorian pier, sandcastles on the beach and holidaymakers wetting an ankle – simple, wholesome pleasures that seem in keeping with its origins as a purpose-built Victorian resort. "A fine and handsome place", said Bill Bryson, declaring it his favourite British seaside resort. For culture focus on the **Llandudno**

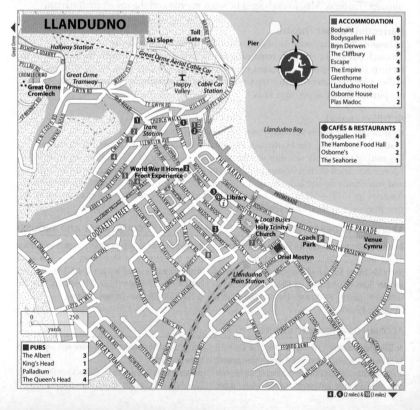

Town Trail, a series of panels full of interesting nuggets: pick up a free leaflet from the tourist office (see p.401).

Brief history

St Tudno built the monastic cell that gives Llandudno its name on the **Great Orme** in the sixth century. When Victorian copper mines in the area seemed exhausted, local landowner Edward Mostyn exploited the craze for sea bathing, with a resort for the upper middle classes.

Within fifty years of its foundation in 1854, Llandudno had become synonymous with the Victorian ideal of a refined resort, drawing music stars such as opera singer Adelina Patti and Jules Rivière, a French conductor who sat in a gilded armchair facing the audience as he waved a bejewelled ivory baton. Mostyn Street was said to have some of the finest shops outside London, patronized by the likes of Napoléon III, Gladstone and Queen Elizabeth of Romania, who stayed here for five weeks in 1890 and reputedly gave the town its motto **Hardd, haran, hedd**, meaning "beautiful haven of peace".

The pier

Daily: summer 9am–11pm, winter 9am–6pm • Free

Once the embodiment of Llandudno's ornate Victoriana, the **pier** remains a splendid affair and is the longest in Wales at just under half a mile. Of course, it's overrun in high summer – all kids and candyfloss, and mums and dads in deckchairs while the sound of a Wurlitzer whirls overhead – but that's all part of the fun.

Oriel Mostyn

12 Vaughan St • Tues–Sun 10.30am–5pm • Free • ☎ 01492 879201, ⓦ mostyn.org

The elaborate brick facade gives little clue to the raw, concrete interior of the refurbished **Oriel Mostyn** gallery. The revamp has breathed new life into the region's premier contemporary art gallery, named after Lady Mostyn, for whom it was originally built in 1901. Five rooms show exhibitions often by leading Welsh artists, supplemented by international touring exhibitions. There's also a good shop.

World War II Home Front Experience

New St • Mid-March to Oct Mon–Sat 10am–4.30pm, Sun 10am–2pm • £3.25 • ☎ 01492 871032, ⓦ homefrontmuseum.co.uk

The **World War II Home Front Experience** pays a nostalgic visit to early 1940s Britain, with wartime shopfronts, wardens' huts, bomb shelters and the like all packed into one small room, where ration books and children's toys are displayed alongside evocative treatment of the Women's Land Army.

Great Orme and around

The views from the top of the **Great Orme** (Y Gogarth) are magical, stretching out over the seascapes to the shores of Anglesey and the northern limits of the Carneddau range, where Snowdonia plunges into the sea.

Formed three hundred million years ago, this huge lump of carboniferous limestone was developed in the Bronze Age as people began to smelt malachite-rich ore to supply copper throughout Europe. The Celts further exploited the ore, but the Vikings did not. Their legacy is the name: Orme derives from Old Norse, meaning "worm" or "sea serpent", which is just how the Great Orme might have appeared from sea.

Walking aside, there are three ways to get on to the Orme – the **Marine Drive**, the **Great Orme Tramway** and the **cable car**. Once there, go for a stroll. You might spot some of the rare or endangered maritime botanical species – goldilocks aster, spotted cats-ear and spiked speedwell – or see fulmars wheel on updraughts. The feral **cashmere goats** that roam all over the mountain are usually easier to find, especially if you ask the staff at the visitor centre.

Marine Drive

Always open • Free for walkers and cyclists; driving toll (£2.50) applies in summer (roughly 9am–8pm; winter 9am–4pm)

The easiest way to get a feel for the skirts of the Great Orme, this four-mile circuit cuts into the rock high above the coast. The one-way loop road starts near Llandudno's pier with stops at various viewing points and a café at the tip, with a summit road a quarter of the way around.

Great Orme Tramway

Church Walks • Daily: Easter–late Oct 10am–6pm; late Oct till Easter 10am–5pm • £4 single, £6 return • ☎ 01492 879306, Ⓦ greatormetramway.co.uk.

The most atmospheric means of reaching the Great Orme's summit are the vintage **Great Orme Trams** which creak along a one-mile route to the top, much as they have since 1902. Cars leave every 20min to a Halfway Station, where you change to a second tram.

Great Orme Aerial Cable Car

Happy Valley • Easter–Sept daily, roughly 10am–5pm, depending on the weather • £8 single, £8.50 return • ☎ 01492 877205

Near the base of the pier and close to the start of Marine Drive, a **cable car** lifts people up to the summit when it isn't too windy in open four-seater cabins above the formal gardens of **Happy Valley**.

Great Orme Country Park

Visitor centre: Easter–Oct daily 10am–5.30pm • Free

However you arrive, all routes converge on the flat summit of the **Great Orme Country Park**, where there's a car park (small fee), gift shop, uninspiring café/bars and a visitor

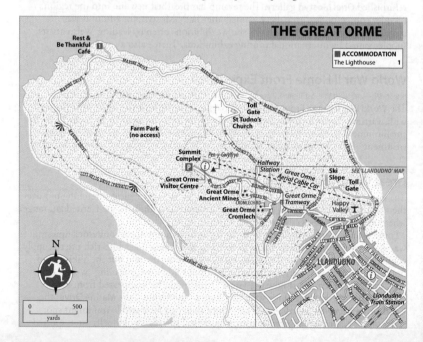

THE GREAT ORME

■ ACCOMMODATION
The Lighthouse   1

centre with display boards on flora and fauna, including the Kashmiri goats descended from a pair given as a gift to George IV. **Walks** are well signposted and easy to piece together using our map: either loop around the walls of the farm park (2-mile loop; 1hr), or head down to St Tudno's church (1 mile return; 30min).

St Tudno's church

St Tudno's Rd • April–Oct daily 9am–5pm; Nov–March Wed, Sat & Sun 9am–5pm • Free

Small and pretty, **St Tudno's** is the area's original church (after which Llandudno was named) and now stands isolated, though it was once part of a substantial village. The oldest parts are twelfth-century, with later extensions and considerable restoration in the nineteenth century.

Great Orme Ancient Mines

Bishop's Quarry Rd, 400m west of Halfway Station or 500m east of Visitor Centre • Mid-March to Oct daily 10am–5pm • £6.75 •
☎ 01492 870447, ⓦ greatormemines.info

From the Great Orme Tramway's Halfway Station, it's a five-minute walk to the long-disused **Great Orme Ancient Mines**. The earliest workings here were assumed to be Roman, until excavations in 1987 uncovered four-thousand-year-old animal bones that had been used as scrapers 200ft down. This is one of the few sites in Britain where mineral veins were accompanied by dolomitization, a rock-softening process which enabled copper to be extracted using the simple tools available in the Bronze Age, and which led to the Great Orme becoming the pre-eminent copper mine in Europe.

After an explanatory film, the **self-guided tour** peeks into some of the four miles of tunnels uncovered – enough to get a feel for the cramped working conditions. Topside, you can get an idea of how the ore was smelted to make tools.

Great Orme Cromlech

At end of Cromlech Rd, off St Beuno's Rd, 300yd from Great Orme Tramway Halfway Station • Open access • Free

Tucked away in a small field at the end of a residential road, the **Great Orme Cromlech** (Liety'r Filiast) is a five-thousand-year-old Neolithic burial chamber and one of the most impressive remants of the Orme's rich prehistory. It would originally have been within an earth mound; no burials were found within it.

ARRIVAL AND DEPARTURE   LLANDUDNO

By train Direct services to Llandudno's forlorn train station arrive from Betws-y-Coed and Chester; for all other services change at Llandudno Junction, near Conwy.
Destinations Bangor (12 daily; 40min); Betws-y-Coed (4 daily; 40min); Blaenau Ffestiniog (6 daily; 1hr 20min); Chester (roughly hourly; 1hr 10min); Holyhead (18 daily; 1hr 20min); Llandudno Junction (every 30min; 10min).
By bus Local buses stop on either Mostyn Street or

Gloddaeth Street, while National Express buses from Chester, Bangor and Pwllheli (bookings at the TIC) stop at the Coach Park on Mostyn Broadway.
Destinations Bangor (every 40min; 1hr); Betws-y-Coed (8 daily; 50min); Blaenau Ffestiniog (9 daily; 1hr 10min); Conwy (hourly; 20min); Llanrwst (every 30min; 35–50min); Rhyl (every 20min; 1hr 10min).

INFORMATION

Tourist information The TIC is in the Library Building, Mostyn Street (Easter–Sept Mon–Sat 9am–4.30pm, ☎ 01492 577577, ✉ llandudnotic@conwy.gov.uk, ⓦ visit llandudno.org.uk). Stocks a free map of Great Orme footpaths.

Internet There's free access at the library on Mostyn Street (Mon, Tues & Fri 9am–6pm, Wed 10am–5pm, Thurs 9am–7pm, Sat 9.30am–1pm). There's s also free wi-fi at *Café Lux* in Oriel Mostyn and other cafés around town.

GETTING AROUND

By bike The nearest bike rental is in Colwyn Bay (see p.397).
By bus Alpine run an open-top double-decker bus looping from Llandudno to Conwy and back, which is perfect for a

day-trip (first Sat in March to October hourly 10am–4pm, every 30min first weekend in May–August; £8 for 24hr; ☎ 01492 879133).

SKIING AND TOBOGGANING

Llandudno Ski & Snowboard Centre on Wyddfyd Rd (generally Mon–Fri 10am–10pm, Sat & Sun 10am–6pm; ☎01492 874707, ⒲jnlllandudno.co.uk) offers a couple of hours on the dry slopes (including all equipment) for £13.50, or you can make a run down the 700yd-long, snow-free Toboggan Run (£5).

ACCOMMODATION

Although Llandudno has several hundred **hotels**, book ahead in high summer, especially for bank holidays. Competition keeps **prices** low and rates are often cheaper if you stay for two or more nights. The best general areas for inexpensive accommodation are St Davids Road and Deganwy Ave, each of which has almost a dozen guesthouses. The nearest tent **camping** is at Conwy (see p.408).

Bodnant 39 St Mary's Rd ☎01492 876936, ⒲llandudno-bedandbreakfast.co.uk; map p.398. Comfortable six-room guesthouse (including two singles), its homely style pepped by modern statement wallpapers, on a tree-lined street. **£76**

Bodysgallen Hall A470, 3 miles south of town ☎01492 584466, ⒲bodysgallen.com; map p.398. This award-winning National Trust-owned country hotel is in a partly seventeenth-century house in 200 acres of parkland. Accommodation is reassuringly traditional – think floral curtains in antique-filled rooms and blankets, not duvets, in the manor – and there are two restaurants (see opposite) and a spa on site. **£189**

Bryn Derwen 34 Abbey Rd ☎01492 876804, ⒲www.bryn-derwen.co.uk; map p.398. Sumptuous, traditionally styled small hotel at the foot of the Orme, with huge Victorian common areas but mod cons like wi-fi throughout, plus off-street parking. Closed Dec & Jan. **£80**

★The Cliffbury 34 St Davids Rd ☎01492 877224, ⒲thecliffbury.co.uk; map p.398. Stylish wallpaper, sparkling white bathrooms, free wi-fi (naturally) and dedicated hosts define this classy B&B on a quiet street with six individually decorated rooms. Superior rooms are bigger and come with DVD player and robes. Breakfast ingredients are locally sourced where possible. Generally two-night minimum stay. **£65**

The Empire Church Walks ☎01492 860555, ⒲empirehotel.co.uk; map p.398. Proper hotel facilities like air con, swimming pools and a spa in a proper 54-room hotel, sensitively renovated to bring modern interior design to its Victorian heritage. The cheapest budget rooms face onto the inner courtyard, otherwise town views come as standard. **£105**

★Escape 48 Church Walks ☎01492 877776, ⒲escapebandb.co.uk; map p.398. One of the most celebrated B&Bs in North Wales, this is effortlessy chic, with nine individually designed rooms that combine clean-lined modernism, retro or antique pieces, yet is playful rather than po-faced; book online to select your room. Free wi-fi, great breakfasts, a guest lounge with honesty bar and lovely hosts complete the package. **£90**

Glenthorne 2 York Rd ☎01492 879591, ⒲glenthorne-guesthousellandudno.co.uk; map p.398. Very good Welsh-speaking guesthouse with seven recently refurbished rooms and a welcoming atmosphere. This is a relaxing home from home with evening meals available on request. Minimum two night stay. **£64**

The Lighthouse Marine Drive ☎01492 876819, ⒲www.lighthouse-llandudno.co.uk; map p.400. Wonderfully eccentric and escapist B&B that boasts vast seascapes. Fabulously located in a former lighthouse at the tip of the Great Orme, every room is different, though they all have sea views and a cosy nautical appeal. Not cheap but unique. **£170**

Llandudno Hostel 14 Charlton St ☎01492 877430, ⒲www.llandudnohostel.co.uk; map p.398. Family-run, forty-bed hostel in the centre of town with dorm beds, twin rooms, a family room and a friendly atmosphere. Sheets, towels and a continental breakfast are supplied, but there's no self-catering kitchen. Often full with school groups during term time, so call ahead. Dorms **£18**; twins **£50**

★Osborne House 17 North Parade ☎01492 860330, ⒲osbornehouse.com; map p.398. Enjoy the flamboyance of this seafront place – there are antique beds and marble bathrooms in the six enormous suites, yet it remains elegant not kitsch. Some rooms overlook the Promenade, plus there's a very good restaurant attached. **£145**

Plas Madoc 60 Church Walks ☎01492 876514, ⒲plasmadocguesthouse.co.uk; map p.398. Comfortable guesthouse at the base of the Great Orme with five rooms in calm shades of cream and white, and a superior room with bath and good views over the town. Full breakfasts include vegan and gluten-free options. Free wi-fi. **£67.50**

EATING AND DRINKING

As a major resort, Llandudno offers a good choice of restaurants. Most are around Mostyn Street where numerous pubs cater to most tastes. The liveliest bars are along Upper Mostyn Street which can be crowded at weekends.

CAFÉS AND RESTAURANTS

★**Bodysgallen Hall** A470, 3 miles south of town ☎01492 584466, ⓦbodysgallen.com. A refined address for some of the finest dining around (smart(ish) dress required). Modern British menus (£29 for two courses) may include Orme lobster or lamb with pea and chive crème fraîche. Alternatively, go for club sandwiches or chicken and sweet chilli salads in the relaxed, modern bistro *1620*, located in the former coach house (Mon–Fri 2-course lunches £14 if booked in advance). Restaurant Tues–Sun 12.30–2.30pm & 5–10pm; bistro Mon–Sat 12.30–3pm & 5.30–9pm.

The Hambone Food Hall 3 Lloyd St ☎01492 860084. Good deli and eat-in bistro that produces made-to-order sandwiches – from stilton, cranberry and bacon to simple ham salad for around £3 – and home-made soups, along with a range of meat pies, pâtés and salads (to go or eat in). Daily 9am–4pm.

Osborne's 17 North Parade ☎01492 860330, ⓦosbornehouse.co.uk. Opulent café and restaurant lit by chandeliers, with modern dishes like herb-crusted salmon and lemon butter (£12.95) or slow-roast lamb. Lunch menus of sandwiches or home-made fishcakes are lighter. Come early for a cocktail or an excellent afternoon tea (£13). Mon–Thurs & Sun 10.30am–9.30pm, Fri & Sat 10. 30am–10pm.

The Seahorse 7 Church Walks ☎01492 875315, ⓦthe -seahorse.co.uk. This two-in-one dinner-only restaurant – intimate and smarter upstairs, a sociable brasserie in the cellar – remains one of the town's best options. The menu is predominantly fish and seafood (£28 for 2 courses):

expect the likes of haddock chowder, fresh seafood or Parma ham-wrapped monkfish. Daily 4.30–10pm.

PUBS

The Albert 56 Madoc St ☎01492 877188, ⓦalbertllandudno.co.uk. What looks like a standard issue pub provides one of the finest pub-menus in town – blackboard specials like seafood spaghetti or salmon with pea and asparagus risotto (£10–14) plus great Sunday roasts – as well as several fresh local ales. Daily 11.30am–10pm or later; food served noon–9pm.

King's Head Old Rd ☎01492 877993, ⓦkingshead llandudno.co.uk. Llandudno's oldest pub – a snug cocoon of Victorian wood beside the tram terminus – serves substantial bar meals, like beef burgers and home-made pies and pastas (mains £9–13). Mon–Thurs & Sun noon–11pm, Fri & Sat noon–midnight.

Palladium 7 Gloddaeth St ☎01492 863920. Wetherspoon chain pub, so expect uninspiring reheated meals and discounted beer, but what a building – the fabulous surrounds of an old theatre, still with its stalls and wonderful ceiling. Daily 9am–midnight or later.

The Queen's Head Glanwydden (off A470), 3 miles southeast ☎01492 546570, ⓦqueenshead glanwydden.co.uk. Welsh Pub of the Year recently, this is a fine spot for a drink, but excels most in a seasonal menu which includes open sandwiches, asparagus and broad-bean risotto, home-made pies, and local seafood (mains £10–19). Book ahead for Sunday lunch (£12). Food served Mon–Fri noon–2pm & 6–9pm, Sat & Sun noon–9pm.

7

ENTERTAINMENT

Venue Cymru The Promenade ☎01492 872000, ⓦvenuecymru.co.uk. North Wales's premier live

entertainment centre, this modern 1500-seat theatre lures touring companies and occasional international acts.

Conwy and around

Though small in size, **CONWY** affords a huge amount to see and do. Its belt of town walls encloses not just a stunning early medieval castle but some fascinating glimpses into the past of north Wales. With its marvellous setting and abundant accommodation, this is the ideal base for a few days spent exploring the Lower Conwy Valley and the coast around its estuary. It's easy to make a day-trip to Llandudno, and there's a sprinkling of attractive diversions within a few miles. Thousands come here specifically to see **Bodnant Garden** and tiny **Rowen** has a low-key appeal.

Conwy remains one of the highlights of the north coast, its setting on the Conwy estuary, backed by a forested fold of Snowdonia, irresistible to painters and photographers ever since Englishman Paul Sandby published his *Views of North Wales* in 1776. And don't let castle-weariness put you off. Nothing within Conwy's core of medieval and Victorian buildings is more than 200yds from the town walls, which makes Conwy wonderfully easy to potter around. You can easily visit the castle, Elizabethan townhouse Plas Mawr or cutesy treats like Britain's smallest house in one day. But don't be surprised if you want to stay longer.

Brief history

For centuries the Conwy estuary provided a good living for the families who had held mussel-gathering rights on the sands while the Cistercian monastery of **Aberconwy**, established in 1172, attended to spiritual needs. Then a century later the monastery was moved eight miles upriver to Maenan, near Llanrwst, to make way for the strongest link in Edward I's chain of fortresses.

During incursions along Wales's north coast, Edward I's Anglo-Norman ancestors never managed to establish a bridgehead west of the Conwy River. Accordingly, once over the river in 1283, Edward established another of his bastide towns, from which the Welsh were mostly excluded for well over a century.

Conwy Castle

Rose Hill St · Daily: March–June, Sept & Oct 9.30am–5pm; July & Aug 9.30am–6pm; Nov–March 10am–4pm · £6.75; joint ticket with Plas Mawr £8.75; CADW · ☎ 01492 592358

Edward I chose a strategic knoll at the mouth of the Conwy River for the site of **Conwy Castle**, built in just five years by James of St George. Overlooked by a low hill, the castle appears less easily defensible than others along the coast, but James constructed eight massive towers in a rectangle around two wards separated by a drawbridge and portcullis, and added turrets atop the four eastern towers.

Bar a brief siege during the Welsh uprising of 1294, the castle saw little action until 1399, when Richard II stayed there on his return from Ireland. He was lured from safety by the Earl of Northumberland, Bolingbroke's vassal. Northumberland swore in the castle's chapel to grant Richard safe passage, but imprisoned him at Flint, enabling Bolingbroke to become Henry IV. From the fifteenth century, the castle fell into disuse, but was refortifed for the Civil War. At the restoration of the monarchy in 1665, the castle was stripped of all its iron, wood and lead, and left as it is today.

The interior

Strolling along the ramparts, you can look down onto something unique among the Iron Ring fortresses, a roofless but largely intact interior. The outer ward's 130ft-long

---

THE IRON RING

Dotting the north Wales coast, a day's march from each other, Edward I's fearsome **Iron Ring** of castles represents Europe's most ambitious and concentrated medieval building project, designed to prevent the recurrence of two hugely expensive military campaigns (see p.435). After Edward's first successful campaign in 1277, he was able to pin down his adversary, **Llywelyn ap Gruffydd** ("the Last"), in Snowdonia and Anglesey, gaining space and time to build the now largely ruined castles at **Flint**, **Rhuddlan**, **Builth Wells** and **Aberystwyth**, and consolidate his grip by confiscating and upgrading several Welsh castles.

Although Llewellyn's second uprising (1282) also failed, Edward was determined not to have to fight a third time for the same land, and set about extending his Iron Ring in an immensely costly display of English might, which – together with the Treaty of Rhuddlan (1284) – effectively crushed Welsh resistance. **Harlech**, **Caernarfon** and **Conwy** are nearly contemporaneous, yet manifest a unique progression towards the later, highly evolved concentric design of **Beaumaris**. All these castles (and the town walls of Caernarfon and Conwy) were built by **James of St George d'Espéranche** – the master military architect of his age – whose work at Conwy, Caernarfon, Harlech and Beaumaris is now recognized with **UNESCO World Heritage Site** status.

Each castle was integrated with a **bastide town** – an idea borrowed from Gascony in France, where Edward I was duke – the town and castle being mutually reliant on each other for protection and trade. The bastides were always populated with English settlers, and the Welsh were only permitted to enter during the day, but not to trade and certainly not to carry arms. It wasn't until the eighteenth century that the Welsh would have towns they could truly call their own.

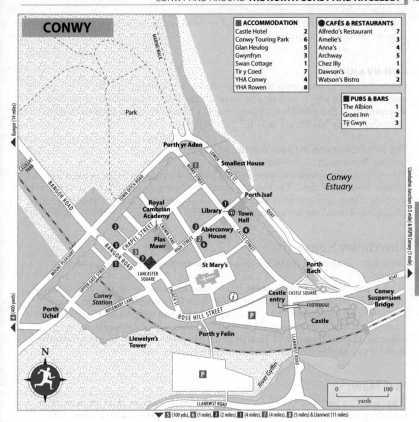

CONWY

■ ACCOMMODATION	
Castle Hotel	2
Conwy Touring Park	6
Glan Heulog	5
Gwynfryn	3
Swan Cottage	1
Tir y Coed	7
YHA Conwy	4
YHA Rowen	8

● CAFÉS & RESTAURANTS	
Alfredo's Restaurant	7
Amelie's	3
Anna's	4
Archway	5
Chez Illy	1
Dawson's	6
Watson's Bistro	2

■ PUBS & BARS	
The Albion	1
Groes Inn	2
Tŷ Gwyn	3

▼ **5** (100 yds), **6** (1 mile), **2** (2 miles), **3** (4 miles), **7** (4 miles), **8** (5 miles) & Llanrwst (11 miles)

Great Hall and the King's Apartments are well preserved, but the only part of the castle to have kept its roof is the **Chapel Tower**, named for the small room built into the wall whose semicircular apse still shows some heavily worn carving. The floor below holds a small exhibition on religious life.

Conwy Suspension Bridge

Mid-March to Oct daily 11am–5pm • £1; NT • ☎ 01492 573282

Anchored to the castle walls as if it were a drawbridge, Thomas Telford's slender **Conwy Suspension Bridge** was actually part of an 1826 road improvement scheme. Contemporary with his Menai Strait bridge, it mimics the crenellations of the battlements above to compensate for spoiling the view of the castle immortalized by J.M.W. Turner. The bridge was used until 1958 and now serves as a footbridge linking the town to a **tollhouse**, furnished as it would have been circa 1900.

The town walls

The 30ft-high **town walls** branch out from the castle into a three-quarter-mile-long circuit around Conwy's core. Inaccessible from the castle they were designed to protect. The walls are punctuated by 21 evenly spaced horseshoe towers, as well as twelve latrines that bulge out from the wall-walk. Only half of the distance can be walked

– the best section being from Porth Uchaf to Porth yr Aden – with great views over the town to the castle and estuary beyond.

Conwy Quay

Conwy's river and town walls meet beside the boats at **Conwy Quay**. It's a lively spot on sunny days, with people sipping a beer outside the *Liverpool Arms*, eating locally made ice cream from *Parisella's* kiosk or preparing to embark on regular harbour cruises (May–Sept every 30min; £6; ☎07917 343058).

The smallest house in Great Britain

Conwy Quay • Easter to mid-Oct daily 10am–5pm • £1

The self-proclaimed **smallest house in Great Britain** is wedged between two terraces, one of them now demolished. The two tiny rooms combined are only 9ft high and 6ft wide, the door taking up a quarter of the frontage. Most people will have to duck to get in, a problem that vexed the last resident, a 6ft 3in-tall fisherman, until he left around 1900.

Aberconwy House

Castle St • March–June & Sept–Oct daily 11am–5pm; July–Aug daily 10am–5pm; Nov–Dec Sat–Sun noon–3pm • £3.40; NT • ☎ 01492 592246

Timber and stone **Aberconwy House** is the oldest house in Conwy and its sole surviving medieval building, dating from about 1300. Built for a wealthy merchant, it saw service as a bakery, antique shop, sea captain's house and temperance hotel – various incarnations which are re-created in rooms furnished with a simple yet elegant collection of rural furniture on loan from the Museum of Wales. Tours start with an introductory film in the attic then finish in the kitchen.

Plas Mawr

20 High St • April–Sept daily 9am–5pm; Oct Tues–Sun 9.30am–4pm • £5.75, joint ticket with castle £8.75; CADW • ☎ 01492 580167

Conwy's grandest residence is the splendid **Plas Mawr**, or "great mansion", one of the best-preserved Elizabethan town houses in Britain. It was built in a Dutch style for Robert Wynn of Gwydir Castle, who was one of the first native Welsh to live in the town, returning to the area after mixing at European courts. The main part of the house dates from 1576, with features such as the gatehouse added some ten years later to augment the grand effect. In the Great Hall, the plaster overmantel was designed to impress visitors with Wynn's noble credentials – especially his descent from the Princes of Gwynedd – and much of the superb plasterwork throughout the house relates to the Wynn dynasty. The exception is the Great Chamber, presumably so as not to upstage visiting royalty. The tour – aided by an excellent recorded commentary – concludes with an exhibition about contemporary attitudes to cleanliness that's compulsively gory and hilariously scatological.

WALKS AROUND CONWY

Conwy Mountain (2 miles return; 1hr; 650ft ascent). One of Conwy's best short walks heads onto the gorse-, bracken- and heather-covered slopes of Conwy Mountain, and the 800ft Penmaenbach and Alltwen peaks behind, all giving fantastic views right along the coast. The walk starts at a small car park on Mountain Road, reached by following Cadnant Park off Bangor Road just outside the town walls.

Marine Walk (800yd return; 20min; flat). It is hard to beat a simple stroll along the Conwy Estuary. Start at the northern end of Conwy Quay and simply follow the path to a local nature reserve, Coed Bodlondeb, a peaceful woodland around what was a Victorian mansion surrounded by an unusual array of trees among which you might see nuthatches and jays.

SNOWDONIA, SURF CENTRAL

Think Snowdonia, think mountains. Yet an audacious project aims to turn the lush Conwy valley south of Rowen into a prime surfing destination. On our last visit, the world's first public surfing lagoon, **Surf Snowdonia** (Wsurfsnowdonia.co.uk), was about to begin construction in the otherwise unremarkable village of Dolgarrog, seven miles south of Conwy. Generated by a sort of underwater snowplough, the waves in the 1000ft-pool will be from head- to waist-high. Equipment hire and instant video replays are available, and a café and accommodation will be on-site. The site is scheduled to open in summer 2015.

Royal Cambrian Academy Art Gallery

Crown Lane • Tues–Sat 11am–5pm • Free • ☎01492 593413, Wrcaconwy.org

The **Royal Cambrian Academy Art Gallery** just behind Plas Mawr is home to the Royal Cambrian Academy, a group aiming to foster art in Wales. At its best during the annual summer exhibition, the airy, well-lit galleries display work by the Academy members, almost all of them Welsh or working in Wales.

7

RSPB Conwy

Off the A55, 1 mile east of Conwy, near Llandudno Junction • Daily 9.30am–5pm; free guided walks Sat 11am, plus May–Aug Wed 7pm • £3 • ☎01492 584091, Wrspb.org.uk/conwy

It is hard to imagine that in the early 1990s this RSPB wetland reserve was a 3000-ton heap of silt dumped from the creation of the A55 Expressway tunnel. What you'll see depends on the season, but you might spot Canada geese, shelducks, bitterns, lapwings, stoats, dragonflies and much more. The lakes are a tidal roost, so there's usually more birdlife when high tide forces birds off the adjacent estuary. The traffic noise near the visitor centre is just another reason to borrow a free pair of binoculars and stroll along the boardwalks, spending quiet time in the hides; the longest two-mile trail provides great views. Or at least hang out in the café with its big windows overlooking the lake and reed beds, and telescopes trained on whatever is interesting that day – there's a great playground for kids just outside.

Rowen

Five miles south of Conwy on the eastern slopes of the Carneddau range, the tiny mountainside hamlet of **ROWEN** is one of the prettiest in the area, composed of a few cottages, a post office, a chapel and the excellent **Tŷ Gwyn** pub (see p.410). The adjacent public telephone box contains leaflets of walks in the area. If you don't mind the short drive into Conwy, **Tir y Coed** and the *YHA Rowen* hostel (see p.410) make a great base for the area.

Bodnant Garden

Tal-y-Cafn, off the A470, 8 miles south of Conwy • March to mid-Oct daily 10am–5pm (till 8pm Wed May–Aug); late Oct–Feb daily 10am–4pm • £9.50, £4.54 in winter; NT • ☎01492 650460 • #25 bus from Llandudno and Llandudno Junction roughly every hour

During May and June, the 160ft laburnum tunnel blooms and rhododendrons are in flower all over Wales's finest formal garden and one of the loveliest in Britain. Laid out in 1875 around Bodnant Hall (closed to the public) by its then owner, English industrialist Henry Pochin, the garden spreads over eighty acres of the Conwy Valley. Divided into an upper terraced garden and lower Pinetum and Wild Garden, shrubs and plants provide a blaze of colour throughout the opening season, but autumn is a perfect time to be here, with hydrangeas still in bloom and fruit trees shedding their leaves. You'll need a minimum of two hours to fully appreciate the place.

Bodnant Welsh Food Centre

On the A470, 9 miles south of Conwy • March–Sept Mon–Sat 9.30am–6pm, Sun 10am–4pm • ☎ 01492 651100, ⓦ bodnant-welshfood .co.uk • #25 bus from Llandudno and Llandudno Junction roughly every hour

For foodies, a reason to go south to the Bodnant estate is the **Bodnant Welsh Food Centre** a mile to the south. It was opened in 2014 to showcase regional produce in a superb delicatessen – there's also an outlet of the National Beekeeping Centre of Wales here. This is an excellent option to stock up for a picnic or self-catering.

ARRIVAL AND DEPARTURE

CONWY AND AROUND

By train Llandudno Junction, less than a mile east across the river, serves as the main train station for services from Chester to Holyhead, as well as for trains heading south to Betws-y-Coed and Blaenau Ffestiniog. Only slow, regional services stop in Conwy itself (on request).
Destinations Bangor (11 daily; 20min); Holyhead (11 daily; 1hr); Llandudno Junction (11 daily; 4min).

By bus Local buses stop either on Lancaster Square or outside the town walls on Town Ditch Road. National Express coaches go from Llandudno.
Destinations Bangor (every 20min; 45min); Llandudno (every 20min; 20min); Llanrwst (hourly; 35min); Rowen (8 daily; 15min).

GETTING AROUND

By bus Alpine runs an open-top double-decker bus service looping from Conwy to Llandudno and back (10am–4pm: first Sat in March, April, Sept & Oct hourly; first weekend in

May–August every 30min; £8 for 24hr ticket; ☎ 01492 879133) – perfect for a day-trip.

INFORMATION AND ACTIVITIES

Tourist information Near the castle on Rosehill Street (June–Aug Mon–Fri 9.30am–5.30pm, Sat–Sun 10am–5pm; Sept–May Mon–Fri 9.30am–5pm, Sat–Sun 10am–4pm; ☎ 01492 577566, ⓔ conwytic@conwy.gov.uk).
Internet At the library, Castle Street (Mon, Thurs & Fri 10am–5.30pm, Tues 10am–7pm, Sat 10am–1pm).

Green Dragon Activities Conwy Quays Marina ☎ 07900 266353, ⓦ greendragonactivities.co.uk. The organizer of the World Bathtubbing Championships also runs stand-up paddleboarding lessons (six minimum, or call to join groups), plus trips on bike-powered catamarans.

ACCOMMODATION

HOTELS AND GUESTHOUSES

Castle Hotel 5 High St ☎ 01492 582800, ⓦ castlewales .co.uk. A renovated central coaching inn that positively creaks with historic character. All 28 rooms have been renovated with contemporary styling without abandoning the hotel's appeal. Free central parking for guests and a great restaurant (see p.410). Look online for cheap rates. **£144**
Glan Heulog Llanrwst Rd ☎ 01492 593845, ⓦ conwy -bedandbreakfast.co.uk. Toile and modern wallpapers, country charm and friendly owners make this one of Conwy's best small guesthouses. A Victorian house with six en suites, including one family room, it's half a mile out on the B5106 Trefriw road. **£72**
★ **Gwynfryn** 4 York Place ☎ 01492 576733, ⓦ gwynfrynbandb.co.uk. A modern country ambience makes this central B&B a fine choice. Its five decorated rooms – mostly en suite, one with a separate private bathroom – have a small fridge and DVD player, and access to a film library and free wi-fi. "Superiors" have more space, views and bathtubs. **£70**
Swan Cottage 18 Berry St ☎ 01492 596840,

ⓦ swancottageconwy.com. While some rooms are small and modern decor trends have yet to arrive, this B&B is friendly and central. There are three en-suite rooms – two with great estuary views, one in the attic. **£60**
Tir y Coed Rowen ☎ 01492 650219, ⓦ tirycoed.com. This has bags of style and luxury to spare, whether in cosy standard doubles or the large Rowen Suite, yet remains as relaxed as you'd hope of a small country five-star hotel. Nor will you go hungry – the in-house restaurant is excellent. **£135**

HOSTELS AND CAMPSITES

Conwy Touring Park ☎ 01492 592856, ⓦ conwytouringpark.com. Though fully equipped (if a little dated in the toilet blocks), nature rules in this campsite spread over several fields. It lies just over a mile south along the B5106 (bus #19) and is linked by a footpath into Conwy. Closed Oct–March. Pitches **£20**
YHA Conwy Lark Hill ☎ 0845 371 9732, ⓔ conwy@yha .org.uk. Spacious, modernized hostel in a purpose-built block a fifteen-minute walk uphill from the centre. Offers bright two- and four-bunk rooms, all en suite, and great

views to the castle. It serves good-value meals (including an excellent £5 buffet breakfast), is licensed and is often booked up, so reservations are recommended. Check-in afternoons only. Dorms £21; twins £35

YHA Rowen Rowen, half a mile up a steep hill above the village ☎0845 371 9038. A recently refurbished retreat – all silence and views across the Conwy valley – in a former farmhouse on the flanks of the Carneddau range. Self-catering only. Also has space for two tents. Reach it by turning right 200yd past the pub. Closed Oct–April. Dorms £17.50

EATING AND DRINKING

CAFÉS AND RESTAURANTS

Alfredo's Restaurant Lancaster Square ☎01492 592381. A throwback to the 1970s decor-wise, but no one seems to care in this always-busy Italian restaurant. A reliable spot for good-value pizza and pasta (£9–10), and respectable mains like steak in a creamy mushroom sauce (£17). Daily 6–10pm.

Amelie's 10 High St ☎01492 583142. Relaxed upstairs café for home-made soups, light lunches of salmon and spinach fishcakes (£9), or just coffee and a slice of home-made poppy and lemon cake. Evening meals at weekends have a French accent with the likes of chicken cassoulet (£14). Tues–Thurs 10am–4.30pm, Fri–Sat 10am–9pm.

Anna's 9 Castle St ☎01492 580908. Traditional Victorian-styled tearoom above an outdoors shop. Offers the requisite afternoon tea and cakes, but also serves breakfasts and home-made lunches such as lasagne, fish pie or quiche (£8). Daily 10am–5pm.

Archway 12 Bangor Rd ☎01492 592458. Quality fish and chip restaurant that also does award-winning pies (mains average £7). Everything is cooked to order to eat in the modern café-style restaurant or take away – perfect for the Quay on a summer evening. Mon–Thurs 11.30am–2pm & 4.30–8pm, Fri–Sun 11.30am–8.30pm.

Chez Illy High St ☎01492 547012. A tiny bolthole of a café with a limited range of food – paninis and sandwiches mostly, but also the best coffee in town. A good pit stop. Daily 9am–5pm.

Dawson's Castle Hotel, 5 High St ☎01492 582800, ⓦcastlewales.co.uk. Quality ingredients well cooked and served without fuss in a quality hotel restaurant. Start with an aperitif in the bar then browse the Modern British menu, which has dishes like twice-cooked Denbeighsire pork, and salmon on pea and leek risotto (average £17). Daily 8am–11pm.

★**Watson's Bistro** Chapel St ☎01492 596326, ⓦwatsonsbistroconwy.co.uk. The best eating in town, locals say, and no wonder with dishes like pan-roasted hake with prawns and samphire (£18). Local ingredients feature strongly and vegetarian options are excellent, plus there are bargain set lunch and early dinner menus (£11 for two courses) and a terrace beneath the town walls. Mon–Tues 5.30–8pm, Wed–Sun noon–2pm & 5.30–8pm (Fri & Sat till 9pm).

BARS AND PUBS

★**The Albion Ale House** Corner of Uppergate St ☎01492 582484, ⓦalbionalehouse.weebly.com. Four local breweries, including the excellent Conwy Brewery, joined forces to run this Grade II listed pub. There's no muzak and no TVs, just eight ales on tap, bar snacks like local pies, open fires and the charm of a 1920s wooden interior that's as shiny as a conker. Mon–Thurs & Sun noon–11pm, Fri–Sat noon–midnight.

Groes Inn Tyn-y-Groes, 2 miles south on B5106 to Llanrwst ☎01492 650545, ⓦgroesinn.com. Good food and cask ales in a wonderfully pub dating to 1573 – it's said to be the oldest licensed house in Wales. Mains like pork chops with black pudding or local lamb with mash cost £10–15. Mon–Thurs noon–3pm & 6.30–11pm, Fri–Sat noon–3pm & 6.30pm–midnight, Sun noon–6pm; food served Mon–Fri noon–2pm & 6.30–9pm, Sun noon–2.30pm. Closed Mon Nov–Feb.

★**Tŷ Gwyn** Rowen, 4 miles south of Conwy ☎01492 650232. Life doesn't get much better than a sunny evening spent sitting outside this lovely village pub. There's a friendly atmosphere, home-cooked meals such as cod goujons and chips and a pretty small beer garden with a stream. Daily: June–Sept Mon–Wed 4pm–midnight, Thurs–Sun noon–midnight; Oct–May Mon–Fri 4pm–midnight, Sat–Sun noon–midnight.

Bangor

After a few days in mid-Wales or the mountains of Snowdonia, **BANGOR** comes on like a city. In fact, it's not big, but as the largest town in Gwynedd and home to **Bangor University**, which dominates the skyline, it passes for cosmopolitan in these parts. Aside from a couple of sights or perhaps a trip to the shops (don't get excited), there's little to detain you – Bangor only receives a trickle of summer visitors. In contrast to the largely English-speaking resorts on the north coast, Bangor is overwhelmingly Welsh-speaking.

The cathedral

Cathedral Close • Daily 9am–5pm • Free

Bangor's **cathedral** boasts the longest continuous use of any in Britain. A hint of its ancient origins can be gleaned from the blocked-in window dating from the Norman rebuilding of 1071. The rest of the structure is the result of reconstructions after being sacked by King John (1211), Edward I (1277) and Owain Glyndŵr (1402), with heavy-handed touches by George Gilbert Scott in 1866.

The spacious interior houses the sixteenth-century wooden **Mostyn Christ**, depicted bound and seated on a rock. Look, too, for the arched tomb in the south transept said to contain the remains of Owain Gwynedd, although the story goes that after being posthumously excommunicated for incest with his first cousin the Bishop of Bangor was asked to remove his body from the cathedral.

Bangor Museum and Art Gallery

Ffordd Gwynedd • Tues–Fri 12.30–4.30pm, Sat 10.30am–4.30pm • Free • ☎ 01248 353368

Standard regional museum exhibits are enlivened by a collection of traditional costumes and an archeology room containing the most complete Roman sword found in Wales. Other rooms hold a set of furniture from a moderately wealthy Criccieth farm, and cover three hundred years of acquisitions, from heavy Welsh dressers to fine

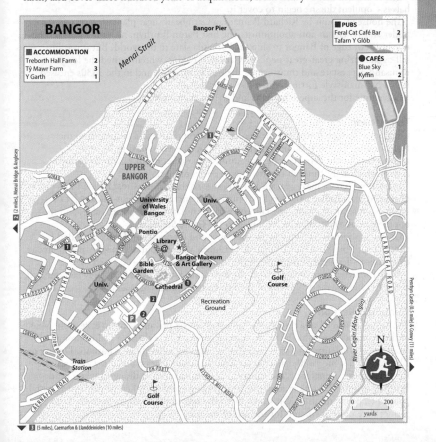

Italian pieces. There's also a detailed model of Telford's Menai bridge and an art gallery concentrating on Welsh contemporary works.

Bangor Pier

End of Garth Rd • Mon–Fri 8.30am–dusk, Sat & Sun 10am–dusk • 50p

North of the centre, there's a fine view of Telford's bridge from Bangor's pristine **Victorian pier**, which juts 1550ft into the Menai Strait – over halfway across to Anglesey. Though it's a fifteen-minute walk from the town centre, it feels many miles removed – a good place to watch the world drift by.

Penrhyn Castle

A5 at Llandygai, 2 miles east of Bangor • House: March–Oct daily 11am–5pm, Nov–Dec Sat–Sun noon–3pm; gardens & railway museum: March–Oct daily 11am–5pm, Nov–Feb daily noon–3pm • £10.35, grounds & railway museum only £6.75; NT • ☎ 01248 363219 • Buses #5, #6, #67 and #75 run frequently from Bangor to Penrhyn's gates, though it's still a mile to the house

The awkward truth of **Penrhyn Castle** is that it's testament to the Anglo–Welsh gentry's oppression of the rural Welsh. Built on the huge profits of a Welsh slate mine, this nineteenth-century neo-Norman fancy is a testament to hubris in its three hundred luxurious rooms. Still, it also shows the Victorians in their pomp did nothing by halves – opulent doesn't begin to cover it.

The house was built by Richard Pennant, a Caribbean sugar plantation owner, slave trader and vehement anti-abolitionist. The first Baron Penrhyn, he built a port on the northeastern edge of Bangor to ship his Bethesda slate to the world. But it was his self-aggrandizing great-great-nephew, George Dawkins, who inherited the forty-thousand-acre estate and transformed the neo-Gothic hall and in the 1830s encased it in a Norman-style fortress with a five-storey keep.

Leave time for the superb **gardens** and the excellent **café**.

The interior

Overblown though it may be, the decoration is impressive and fairly true to the Romanesque. Dawkins' architect, Thomas Hopper, even looked to Norman architecture for the furniture, but succumbed to mod cons for a central heating system which went through twenty tons of coal a month.

Everything is on a massive scale and no more so than in the **Great Hall** with its pair of stained-glass zodiac windows by Thomas Willement. Three-foot-thick oak doors separate subsequent rooms: the **Library**, with its full-size slate billiard table, and the oppressive **Ebony Room**, which leads onto the **Grand Staircase**.

Upstairs, original William Morris wallpaper and drapes around the King's Bed contrast with the Slate Bed, designed for Queen Victoria but declined by her in favour of a Hopper-designed four-poster in the **State Bedroom**.

Away from the pomp you can visit the enormous **kitchens**, convincingly laid out as if about to cater for the 1894 visit of the Prince and Princess of Wales.

Painting collection

The family managed to assemble the country's largest private **painting collection**. Much of this remains, especially in the two dining rooms, where there's a Gainsborough landscape, Canaletto's *The Thames at Westminster* and a Rembrandt portrait. During the Blitz of 1940, some 1800 masterpieces from London's National Gallery were sent here for safekeeping. Apparently, the gallery's curators had second thoughts when Lord Penrhyn stumbled drunk among the canvases one evening. When he demanded rental payments, prime minister Winston Churchill ordered the treasures be moved to a former slate mine at Manod for the rest of the war.

7

Industrial Railway Museum

Open 1hr before castle • Entry included in castle or grounds tickets

The castle's stable block houses the **Industrial Railway Museum**, packed with gleaming rolling stock once used on the estate's quarry-to-port rail line. Look out for the 1848 *Fire Queen*, a very early loco built for the Padarn Railway in Llanberis and retired in the 1880s.

ARRIVAL AND DEPARTURE
BANGOR

By train All trains on the north coast line between Chester and Holyhead stop at Bangor's train station on Station Road, at the south end of Holyhead Road.
Destinations Chester (21 daily; 1hr); Conwy (11 daily; 20min); Holyhead (22 daily; 30–40min); Llandudno (18 daily; 40min); Rhosneigr (9 daily; 25min); Rhyl (25 daily; 40min).
By bus National Express and local buses stop in the centre

of town on a short spur off Garth Road.
Destinations Beaumaris (every 30min; 20–35min); Caernarfon (every 15min; 25min); Conwy (every 20min; 45min); Holyhead (hourly; 1hr 15min); Llanberis (hourly; 45min); Llandudno (every 15min; 1hr); Llanfairpwll (every 30min; 15min); Llangefni (every 30min; 35min); Menai Bridge (every 30min; 20min).

INFORMATION

Tourist information There is no TIC, but limited tourist information is available from the Bangor Museum.
Internet Free access at the library, on Ffordd Gwynedd

(Mon, Tues, Thurs & Fri 9.30am–7pm, Wed & Sat 9.30am–1pm) and at *Blue Sky* (see below).

ACCOMMODATION

Bangor doesn't have a huge choice of accommodation and there's little reason to stop overnight. Most of the cheaper options are at the northern end of **Garth Road**, a 20min walk from the train station.

Treborth Hall Farm A487, 1.8 miles southwest of upper Bangor between the two Menai Strait bridges ☎01248 364104, ⍟treborthleisure.co.uk. The nearest campsite to town is a relaxed spot, partly in an old walled garden. There are coin-operated showers (£1) and everything is well kept. The #5 bus service passes the entrance. Closed Nov–March. Pitches **£12**
Tŷ Mawr Farm B4366, 5 miles southwest of Bangor and 0.5 mile east of Llanddeiniolen ☎01286 670147,

⍟tymawrfarm.co.uk. Cosy B&B on a working farm with views of Snowdonia from its floral rooms and good home-made food on request. Quality, well-equipped self-catering cottages also available for short lets outside the school holidays. Doubles **£110**; cottages from **£390**/week
Y Garth Garth Rd ☎01248 362277, ⍟thegarthguest house.co.uk. Probably the best value in the centre of town, this decent B&B has ten en-suite rooms and does a full breakfast ("you won't eat till tea-time", they promise). **£60**

EATING AND DRINKING

★Blue Sky Rear of 236 High St ☎01248 355444, ⍟blueskybangor.co.uk. Bangor's finest daytime café by a long shot occupies a small hall with exposed rafters and mismatched wooden tables. The casual feel belies delicious food, most created from local and organic ingredients, and often gluten-free. Expect breakfasts, sandwiches and sharing platters, plus daily soups and blackboard specials like welsh lamb meatballs with fusilli or mushroom rarebit (priced £5–8). Also has occasional evening gigs and films; check the website. Mon–Sat 9.30am–5.30pm.
Feral Cat Café Bar 161 High St ☎01248 370445. While the food is average – student-friendly burgers and salmon-and-broccoli pasta (£7) – this spacious pub is less rough

around the edges, and a relaxing spot for a drink. The rear deck also gets afternoon sun. Daily 10am–10pm.
Kyffin 129 High St ☎01248 355161. A sweet little vegetarian and vegan café with Fairtrade coffee and a warm atmosphere that makes you want to stick around for home-made light lunches such as spicy lentil lasagne or broccoli and apple tart (mostly under £6). Mon–Sat 9.30am–5pm.
Tafarn Y Glôb 7 Albert St, Upper Bangor ☎01248 362095. Good predominantly Welsh-speaking pub in a residential area that's popular with students in term-time and locals year-round. Poor choice of real ales, though. Daily 11.30am–10pm or later.

ENTERTAINMENT

Pontio Deiniol Rd ⍟pontio.co.uk. Pontio, an "Arts and Innovation Centre" with a 450-seat theatre, outdoor amphitheatre and slew of dining areas and bars, this new

centre seems destined to become the major performance hub for north Wales, with comedy, theatre and cabaret, some in Welsh – visit the website for listings.

Anglesey

The island of **Anglesey** (Ynys Môn) is a world apart, its green ripple of fields and farms a far cry from the mountains and hemmed-in settlements of Snowdonia. Seen from the four-lane A55, which speeds across Anglesey towards Holyhead, the island can look dull. It's only the smaller roads that reveal gentle pace and superb coastal scenery, not to mention Wales's greatest concentration of pre-Christian sites.

Traditionally, Anglesey was known as **Mam Cymru**, "The Mother of Wales", attesting to the island's former importance as the country's breadbasket. In the twelfth century, Giraldus Cambrensis noted that "When crops have failed in other regions, this island, from its soil and its abundant produce, has been able to supply all Wales". The land remains predominantly agricultural, with small fields, stone walls and white houses reminiscent of parts of Ireland and England. Linguistically and politically, though, Anglesey is intensely Welsh, with over seventy percent of its population using Welsh as their first language. Most residents will at least understand the lines of one of Anglesey's most famous poets, Goronwy Owen, whose eulogy on his homeland translates as "All hail to Anglesey/ The delight of all regions/ Bountiful as a second Eden/ Or an ancient paradise". Those who visit the sandy coves and rocky headlands would proabaly agree – the island is superb for **sea kayaking**.

The tourist hotspot is **Beaumaris** thanks to its wonderful setting and castle. Following the south coast clockwise there's a string of minor sights and lovely beaches until you reach **Holy Island** (Ynys Gybi), an hourglass of land just a few yards off the northwest coast of Anglesey, and connected by road and rail bridges. The more ancient and picturesque approach turns west at Valley, and passes close to the fine beaches at **Rhoscolyn** and **Trearddur Bay** before reaching Holyhead (ferry port for Ireland) and the impressive sea-bird cliffs around **South Stack**.

The north and west coasts of Anglesey are quieter, with just a smattering of minor sights and some highly rewarding stretches of the 125-mile **Anglesey Coast Path**.

Brief history

The earliest people on Anglesey were Mesolithic hunters who arrived between 8000 and 4000 BC. Around 2500 BC, a new culture developed among the small farming communities, giving rise to the many henges and stone circles on the island, which held sway until the Celts swept across Europe in the seventh century BC, led by their priestly class, the druids. Anglesey – well positioned at the apex of Celtic sea traffic – became the most important druidic centre in Europe. The druids were so firmly established that Anglesey was the last place in Wales to fall to the Romans, in 61 AD.

The vacuum left by the Romans' departure in the fifth century was soon filled by the greatest of all Welsh dynasties, the Princes of Gwynedd, who held court at **Aberffraw**. Under Rhodri Mawr, in the ninth century, their influence spread over most of Wales as he defeated the encroaching Vikings, earning thanks from Charlemagne for his efforts. Anglesey again fell to outsiders towards the end of the thirteenth century when Edward I defeated the Welsh princes, sealing the island's fate by forging the final link in his Iron Ring of castles at **Beaumaris**, nowadays by far the most absorbing town on the island.

ARRIVAL AND GETTING AROUND ANGLESEY

By train The train line from Bangor crosses the Menai Strait, stopping at the station with the longest name in the world – usually abbreviated to Llanfairpwll – before continuing to meet the ferries at Holyhead.

By bus Buses fill in the gaps left by trains – all detailed in the free Ynys Môn public transport timetable. One of the most useful is #42 which links Bangor, Menai Bridge and Llanfairpwll before looping around the south coast to Aberffraw then inland to Llangefni. Number #62 from

Bangor tracks the east coast from Red Wharf Bay to Ceamaes Bay. Note that services are sketchy on Sunday.

By bike If you've come with a bike, Anglesey is crisscrossed by a spider's web of routes: download route maps from ⓦ visitanglesey.co.uk.

On foot Ynys Môn is ringed by the 125-mile Anglesey Coastal Path (ⓦ angleseycoastalpath.com). Most people set aside twelve days for the complete circuit.

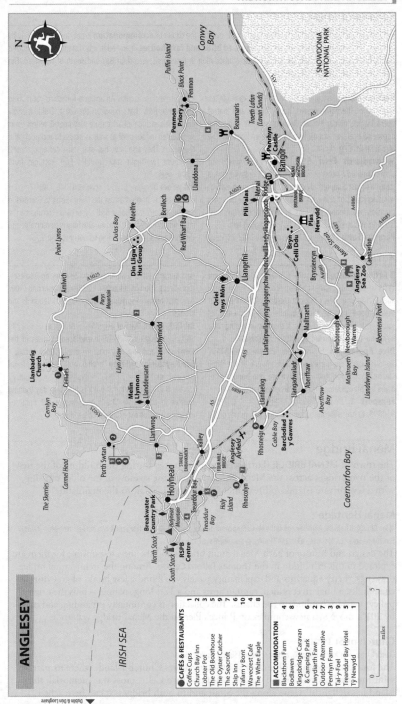

ANGLESEY

IRISH SEA

Dublin & Dun Laoghaire ▲

Conwy Bay

SNOWDONIA NATIONAL PARK

7

● **CAFÉS & RESTAURANTS**
Coffee Cups	1
Church Bay Inn	2
Lobster Pot	3
The Old Boathouse	5
The Oyster Catcher	9
The Seacroft	7
Ship Inn	6
Tafarn y Bont	10
Wavecrest Café	4
The White Eagle	8

■ **ACCOMMODATION**
Blackthorn Farm	4
Bodlawen	8
Kingsbridge Caravan & Camping Park	6
Llwydiarth Fawr	2
Outdoor Alternative	7
Penrhyn Farm	3
Tal-y-Foel	9
Treaddur Bay Hotel	5
Tŷ Newydd	1

0   miles   5

7

ACCOMMODATION

The island is so compact that if you have your own transport, the choice of **accommodation** is not goverened solely by location. There are some excellent, moderately priced **B&Bs and farmhouses**, many relatively distant from recognized sights, but no less appealing for it. We list accommodation in Beaumaris, Trearddur Bay and south of Holyhead. The following provide rural alternatives.

Bodlawen Brynsiencyn ☎01248 430379, ⓦanglesey farms.com. The name means "happy home" and that of opera-singing owner Marian Roberts is: think traditional decor and a relaxed atmosphere in a modern house on the Menai Strait. **£70**

★**Llwydiarth Fawr** B5111, 0.5 mile north of Llanerchymedd ☎01248 470321, ⓦangleseyfarms .com. Not just a supremely comfortable stay in an award-winning B&B, but one with class, in a handsome Georgian mansion set among the hills of a working farm. Self-catering also available. Doubles **£85**; cottages **£100**

Penrhyn Farm Penrhyn, Llanfwrog ☎01407 730134,

ⓦangleseyfarms.com. An antique-furnished yet relaxed farmhouse B&B that's bang on the coast. Child- friendly credentials include an adventure playground, tennis court and heated indoor pool as well as access to rockpools and the beach. They also have five-star self-catering cottages. Minimum two-night stay. Doubles **£60**, cottages from **£300**/week

Tal-y-Foel Dwyran, Brynsiencyn ☎01248 430977, ⓦtal -y-foel.co.uk. If views across the Menai Strait to Caernarfon appeal, this nice farmhouse B&B is your place. Fortunately the large simply furnished rooms are also hugely comfortable and there's access to the horseriding school next door. **£75**

ACTIVITIES

B-Active@Rhoscolyn Outdoor Alternative, Rhoscolyn ☎01407 860469, ⓦb-active-rhoscolyn.co.uk. A small agency based at the campsite Outdoor Alternative that makes good use of the fabulous indented coast of southwest Holy Island. Trips include coasteering and kayaking, the latter including wildlife watching.

Dive Anglesey 1 Church Terr, Holyhead ☎01407 764545, ⓦdiveanglesey.co.uk. The wreck of the 1880 steamship *Missouri* and Rhoscolyn are two popular sites dived by this operator with decades of experience.

Funsport 1 Beach Terrace, Rhosneiger ☎01407 810899, ⓦfunsportonline.co.uk. Right before one of the

best surfing, wind- and kitesurfing beaches on Anglesey, this offers tuition (windsurfing £20/hour, kitesurfing £100/ day) plus rental of surfboards, stand-up paddleboards and kayaks.

RibRide Porth Daniel near Menai Bridge ☎0333 1234 303, ⓦribride.co.uk. Wildlife and scenic cruises in the Menai strait and Anglesey coast (from £24); book ahead.

Sea Kayaking Anglesey Porth Daniel, Water St, Menai Bridge ☎07973 172632, ⓦseakayakinganglesey .co.uk. Half-day tasters for novices plus two-day training courses in the Menia Straits and even a full Anglesey circumnavigation for experienced paddlers.

Menai Bridge

The town of **MENAI BRIDGE** (Porthaethwy) was created during the building of the first of the two bridges across the Menai Strait. It sits in the shadow of the older crossing, with a few private islands to break the view across the strait to the mainland.

Menai Heritage

Mona Rd, 200yd from the Anglesey end of the Menai Suspension Bridge • Easter, late July–late Sept & autumn half-term Mon–Thurs & Sun 10am–5pm • £3, kids free • ☎01248 715046, ⓦmenaiheritage.co.uk

The design and history of both Menai Strait bridges and the men responsible for them are explored in this exhibition in the **Thomas Telford Centre**. Among the architectural bridge drawings, pretty aquatints and explanatory panels you'll find a few hunks of grey iron – chain links, a huge rivet punch, capstan arms and a 12ft-long spanner – plus the original pulleys used for hauling up the chains. The collection is continually expanding and may, by 2015, move to a new complex on Prince's Pier on the Menai Bridge waterside.

Church of St Tysilio

Church Island • Mid-July to Aug daily, and for occasional Sunday services • Free

The fourteenth-century **Church of St Tysilio** occupies Church Island, where its patron saint founded his cell around 630 AD. Topped by a Celtic cross war memorial, the island has delightful views along the Strait and to both bridges. It can be reached

SPANNING THE MENAI STRAIT

Two bridges – both engineering marvels of their time – link Anglesey to the mainland over the **Menai Strait**, a fourteen-mile-long tidal race that in places narrows to 200yd wide, forcing the current up to eight knots as it rushes between Conwy and Caernarfon bays. The **best views** are from the Anglesey shore, where you can look over the rocky mid-channel islets to the heartland of Snowdonia: make for the lay-by on the A5, a mile east of Llanfairpwll.

For centuries before the bridges were built, drovers used the Strait's narrow stretches to herd Anglesey cattle to market in England. Travellers had to wait for low tide to cross Lafan Sands, northeast of Bangor, then find a boat to take them to Beaumaris, guided only by the sound of church bells in foggy weather. So it's not surprising that Irish MPs, needing transport to Westminster and a faster mail service, pushed for a fixed crossing.

MENAI SUSPENSION BRIDGE

The first permanent link, in 1826, was Telford's **Menai Suspension Bridge**, the world's first large iron suspension bridge, spanning 579ft between piers and 100ft above the water to allow high-masted sailing ships to pass. Almost everything about the project was novel, including the process of lifting the sixteen 23-ton chains into place, which involved a pulley system and 150 men kept in time by a fife band. One man celebrated their achievement by running across the nine-inch-wide chain from Anglesey to the mainland.

BRITANNIA TUBULAR BRIDGE

In 1850, Robert Stephenson also made engineering history with his **Britannia Tubular Bridge**, which carried trains across the Strait in twin wrought-iron tubes. It was severely damaged by fire in 1970, however, leaving only the limestone piers that now support the twin-deck A5/A55 road and rail bridge to Llanfairpwll and Holyhead.

7

through the woodland behind the car park on the approach to the Menai Bridge itself, or from the town along a causeway and waterside promenade named **Belgian Walk** (having been built by refugees during World War I).

EATING AND DRINKING   MENAI BRIDGE

Tafarn y Bont Telford Rd ☎01248 714864, ⓦtafarnybont.com; map p.415. Shame it's beside a roundabout by the Menai Suspension Bridge, yet this modernized pub and restaurant remains a popular spot for a beer out the front in the afternoon sun or to tuck into quality pub meals like Welsh lamb cottage pie (lunches £6–9; dinner mains £14–18). Mon–Sat 6–11pm, Sun noon–11pm; food served Thurs–Sat 6–9pm, Sun noon–3pm.

Beaumaris and around

With its attractive setting on the Menai Strait, air of relaxed prosperity, handsome looks and plenty to see, **BEAUMARIS** (Biwmares) is happy holidays writ large. Inevitably, it draws the summer crowds, although evenings are far more peaceful. And at any time the views across to the Snowdonian mountains are superb.

The original inhabitants were evicted by Edward I to make way for the construction of his new castle and bastide town, dubbed "beautiful marsh" in a ploy to attract English settlers. Today the place can still seem like the small English outpost Edward intended, with a smart Georgian terrace (designed by Joseph Hansom, of cab fame) and more English accents than you'll have heard for a while. Many of their owners come by yacht, an echo of the port's fleet of merchant ships, which disappeared with the Menai bridges and growth of Holyhead.

While you can lose a happy half day simply mooching around Beaumaris's giftshops and galleries, drinking in views across the Strait, the main attractions – the **castle**, **court** and **gaol** – each offer their own angle on Welsh history. For a jaunt afterwards, there's a cruise out around **Puffin Island** or a wander along the nearby coastline close to **Penmon Priory** may suit better.

7

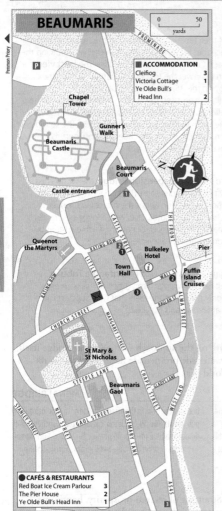

BEAUMARIS

PROMENADE
Penmon Priory

P

ACCOMMODATION
Cleifiog — 3
Victoria Cottage — 1
Ye Olde Bull's
Head Inn — 2

Chapel
Tower

Gunner's
Walk

Beaumaris
Castle

Beaumaris
Court

Castle entrance

Queenot
the Martyrs

RATING ROW

Town
Hall

Bulkeley
Hotel

Pier

THE FRONT

WALL ST

Puffin
Island
Cruises

CASTLE STREET

LITTLE LANE

ALMA STREET

RAGLAN ST

BARRAS ROW

CHURCH STREET

MARGARET STREET

St Mary &
St Nicholas

STEEPLE LANE

Beaumaris
Gaol

CHAPEL STREET

GLADAS LANE

WESTEND

STANLEY STREET

NEW STREET

GAOL STREET

ROSEMARY LANE

A545

CAFÉS & RESTAURANTS
Red Boat Ice Cream Parlour — 3
The Pier House — 2
Ye Olde Bull's Head Inn — 1

Beaumaris Castle

Castle St • March–June, Sept & Oct daily 9.30am–5pm; July & Aug daily 9.30am–6pm; Nov–Feb Mon–Sat 10am–4pm, Sun 11am–4pm • £5.25; CADW • ☎ 01248 810361

The town's central feature is **Beaumaris Castle**, the most picturesque of Edward's gargantuan fortresses with its water-filled moat and loop-holed ramparts. It was built in response to Madog ap Llywelyn's capture of Caernarfon in 1294, architect James of St George producing a symmetrical octagonal form, his finest and most highly evolved expression of concentric design. Lacking the domineering majesty of Caernarfon, Conwy or Harlech, its low outer walls seem almost welcoming – belying the deadly ingenuity of its design.

Sited on flat land at the edge of town, the castle is approached over a moat and through Moorish-influenced staggered entries at the huge towers of the Gate Next the Sea and the South Gatehouse. The moat originally linked the castle to the sea (now well over a hundred yards away), with a shipping channel allowing boats of up to forty tons to tie up at the iron rings hammered into a protective spur of the outer defences, **Gunner's Walk**. Supplies could be brought in, including the corn that was fed into a mill, still visible immediately below.

The battlements

Despite over thirty years' work and plans for a lavish palace, the castle was never quite finished, leaving most of the inner ward empty, and the corbels and fireplaces unused. You can explore around half of the inner and outer **walls**, from which archers could fire simultaneously from the inner and outer defences. Then wander through miles of internal passages in the walls, finding your way to the first floor of the **Chapel Tower**, with a small lime-washed chapel. An exhibition below catalogues the "Castles of Edward I".

When put to the test, the castle failed to withstand Owain Glyndŵr – who took it in 1403 and held it for two years – but during the Civil War, its Royalist defenders held out against General Mytton and 1500 Parliamentarian troops until 1646. After Charles II's accession, the castle was returned to the Bulkeley family, only to be left to fall into ruin before twentieth-century restoration returned some of its glory.

Beaumaris Court

Castle St • April–Sept 10.30am–5pm, closed Fri; October & half-terms Sat–Sun 10.30am–5pm • £3.60 • ☎ 01248 811691,
ⓦ visitanglesey.co.uk

Fittingly, Beaumaris Castle overshadows the juridical instruments of English rule, the
Jacobean **Beaumaris Court**. From 1614 until 1971, it hosted the quarterly Assize Courts.
These were traditionally held in English, giving the jury little chance to follow the
proceedings, and Welsh-speaking defendants none against judges notorious for slapping
heavy penalties on relatively minor offences. Undoubtedly they sympathized with the
sentiments embodied in **The Lawsuit**, a plaque in the main courtroom depicting two farmers
pulling the horns and tail of a cow as a lawyer milks it. A good free audio tour fills in the
details. For visuals ask about the theatrical re-enactments of court cases staged within several
times a month in high season (£5.50), followed by a twilight visit to the gaol (see below).

Beaumaris Gaol

Steeple Lane • April–Sept 10.30am–5pm, closed Fri; October & half-terms Sat–Sun 10.30am–5pm • £4.50 • ☎ 01248 810921,
ⓦ visitanglesey.co.uk

Many local citizens were transported from the court to the colonies for their felonies;
others wound up in **Beaumaris Gaol**. When it opened in 1829, this was considered a
model prison, with running water and toilets in each cell, and an infirmary. Women
prisoners did the cooking and were allowed to rock their babies' cradles in the nursery
above by means of a pulley system. Advanced perhaps, but nonetheless this is a gloomy
place: witness the windowless punishment cell, the stone-breaking yard and the treadmill
water pump. The least fortunate inmates were marched along a first-floor walkway
through a door in the outer wall to the gibbet, where they were publicly hanged.

Penmon Priory

4 miles northeast of Beaumaris • Open access • Free; parking £2.50; CADW • Bangor–Beaumaris bus #57 runs to Penmon, Mon–Sat
roughly hourly

Penmon Priory's original wooden buildings were razed by the Danes in the tenth
century. Their replacements, the twelfth-century church and the thirteenth-century
south range of the cloister, are still standing. Only the **church** is in good repair and still
used, the serene, lime-washed nave housing an unusual Norman pillar-piscina – a font
gouged from the plinth of a pre-Norman cross still used for Sunday services – and the
Penmon Cross, moved here to prevent a thousand years of Welsh weather completely
scouring off its plait and fret patterns. There's more patterned stonework in the south
transept, approached through a magnificent chevron- and chequerboard-patterned arch.

The church's site was chosen for its proximity to the refreshing waters of **St Seiriol's
Well**, which now feeds a calm pool and is reached by either the path behind the church,
or another opposite the distinctive domed **dovecote**, built around 1600 to house one
thousand pairs of birds.

Black Point and Puffin Island

The parking fee for Penmon Priory also covers you for the toll road that runs three-
quarters of a mile beyond the dovecote to **Black Point**, the easternmost point of
Anglesey. A short strait separates you from **Puffin Island**, known in Welsh as Ynys
Seiriol, recalling Penmon's St Seiriol, whose original Augustine community was on the
island. It is now home to nesting razorbills, guillemots and puffins, all once permissible
food during Lent. Cruises around Puffin Island leave from Beaumaris seafront
(Easter–October; £8.50).

ARRIVAL AND INFORMATION   BEAUMARIS

By bus There are regular buses (#53, #56, #57 and #58)
from Bangor (every 30min; 20–35min), Menai Bridge
(every 30min; 15min) and Penmon (11 daily; 15min).

Tourist information A desk in the foyer of the Town Hall
on Castle Street stocks leaflets and sometimes has
volunteers in attendance.

ACCOMMODATION

★**Cleifiog** Townsend ☎01248 811507, ⓦcleifiog bandb.co.uk; map p.418. There are just three rooms – cosy wood-pannelled "Pattern" and larger "Tapestry" with plenty of light are our favourites – in this mostly Georgian town house. Views across the Menai Strait to Snowdonia are great and it's a struggle to leave the lovely guest lounge when the fire is lit and the hospitality is so welcoming. Two-night minimum at weekends. **£90**

Kingsbridge Caravan & Camping Park Llanfaes, 2 miles northeast of Beaumaris ☎01248 490636, ⓦkingsbridgecaravanpark.co.uk; map p.415. Spacious well-maintained campsite with separate family areas, campervan hookups and four-berth static caravans for hire. Pitches **£23**; **£250**/week

★**Victoria Cottage** Victoria Terrace ☎01248 810807, ⓦvictoriacottage.net; map p.418. One of Anglesey's finest B&Bs, tucked behind the waterfront terrace, offers sleigh beds in two spacious en-suite rooms and a loft family suite which occupies the entire top floor. Charm, great views and fine breakfasts come as standard. **£90**

Ye Olde Bull's Head Inn 18 Castle St ☎01248 810329, ⓦbullsheadinn.co.uk; map p.418. The ancient coaching inn that was General Mytton's headquarters during the Civil War and housed Dr Johnson and Charles Dickens is now the best hotel in Beaumaris. Accommodation is either in very comfortable antique-styled rooms in the main building, or larger more chic and modern rooms and suites across the road in *The Townhouse*. All include an excellent breakfast. **£105**

EATING

The Pier House The Front ☎01248 811055. On a sunny day, there is nowhere better for a bite or coffee than this waterfront bistro with picture-postcard views across the Strait. On the menu are breakfasts, sandwiches, fish and chips, and larger mains like local *moules marinière* or steak and ale pie (average £8–10). Daily 9am–9pm.

Red Boat Ice Cream Parlour 34 Castle St ⓦredboatgelato.com. Cheerful, vintage-style decor and a superb, ever-changing selection of superb gelati and sorbets, all freshly made on the premises, tap into the happy holidays ambience of Beaumaris. There are also panini, home-made soups (£4), coffees, cakes and smoothies. Daily 10am–6pm.

★**Ye Olde Bull's Head Inn** 18 Castle St ☎01248 810329, ⓦbullsheadinn.co.uk. Beaumaris's top hotel hits the button for eating and drinking. For tradition there's a cosy bar, while for more modern dining the conservatory *Brasserie* has the likes of fish tagine or duck with puy lentils, as well as fresh home-made burgers (mains average £14). And for fine dining there's the superb restaurant *Loft*, Welsh restaurant of the year in 2013 due to inventive seasonal dishes featuring island produce (£47.50 for 3 courses). Bar Mon–Sat 11am–11pm, Sun noon–10.30pm; Brasserie daily noon–2pm (till 3pm Sun) & 6–9pm; Loft Tues–Sat 7–9.30pm.

Llanfairpwllgwyngyllgogerychwyrndrobwllllantysiliogogogoch and around

When Robert Louis Stephenson wrote "to travel hopefully is a better thing than to arrive" he might have been thinking of **LLANFAIRPWLL**, the village with the longest place name in Britain and little else except a wool shop and a small train station (request stop only) bearing the famed sign **Llanfairpwllgwyngyllgogerychwyrndrobwllllantysiliogogogoch**. Sadly, "St Mary's church in the hollow of white hazel near a rapid whirlpool and the Church of St Tysilio near the red cave" is no authentic Welsh tongue twister, but the fabrication of a Menai Bridge tailor in the 1880s. He added to the original first five syllables in an attempt to draw tourists – as indeed it has.

There's no reason to linger after the obligatory photo at the train station, so push on around the south coast for: Whistler's mural at **Plas Newydd**; the burial mound of **Bryn Celli Ddu** and **Barclodiad y Gawres**; the **Anglesey Sea Zoo** with its ecological approach to the region's sealife; the wild dunes of **Newborough Warren**; and the pretty beaches and coves around **Rhosneigr**.

Marquess of Anglesey's Column

A5, 0.5 mile east of Llanfairpwll • Daily 9am–5pm • £1.50

You can hardly miss the bronze figure atop the 91ft-high Doric **Marquess of Anglesey's Column**. The apocryphal story has him declaring to Wellington, on having a leg blown off at Waterloo, "Begod, sir, there goes me leg", to which Wellington dryly replied,

"Begod, sir, so it do". There hadn't been much love lost between them since the Marquess ran off with Wellington's sister-in-law some years previously. You can climb the 115 steps up to the Marquess to share his view across the Strait to Snowdonia, and see his replacement leg at Plas Newydd.

ARRIVAL AND INFORMATION   LLANFAIRPWLL

Public transport The only issue hereabouts is public transport. No bus loops around the south-west coast, so that travel without your own wheels becomes a matter of constantly backtracking to source another connection; central Llangefni (see p.429) provides a useful transport hub.

Tourist office The TIC here (July–Aug Mon–Sat 9.30am–5.30am, Sun 9.30am–4.30pm; Sept–June Mon–Sat 9.30am–5pm, Sun 9.30am–4.30pm; ☎ 01248 713177, ⓦ visitanglesey.co.uk) is effectively the tourist office for the whole island.

Plas Newydd

A4080, 1.5 miles southwest of Llanfairpwll • House: Early to mid-March Sat–Sun 11am–3pm, mid-March to early Nov Sat–Wed; free guided tours 11–noon, self-guided tours noon–4.30pm • Gardens: Jan–Feb Sat–Sun 11am–4pm, March–June & Sept to early Nov Sat–Thurs 10.30am–5.30pm, July–Aug daily 10.30am–5.30pm • £9.35, garden only £7.35; NT • ☎ 01248 715272 or ☎ 01248 714795

Plas Newydd is the ancestral home of the marquesses of Anglesey, as it has been since the eighteenth century. A house has stood here, overlooking the Menai Strait, since the sixteenth century, but it was the First Marquess's huge profits from Anglesey's Parys Mountain and other ventures that paid for its transformation by James Wyatt and Joseph Potter into a Gothic mansion in the late eighteenth century.

The **Gothic Hall**, with its Potter-designed fan-vaulted ceiling, leads to the finest room in the house, the Music Room, originally the great hall, covered with oil paintings, including portraits of the First Marquess and his wife. There's a transition to neoclassical in the Staircase Hall and a gallery lined with portraits of monarchs and family members; those of the Sixth Marquess and his sister are the work of Rex Whistler, who spent two years here in the 1930s.

Whistler's masterwork is a 58ft-long trompe l'oeil **mural** of a fantastical seascape towards the Snowdonia mountains and beyond. Portmeirion is there, as are the Round Tower from Windsor Castle and the steeple from St Martin's-in-the-Fields in London. Whistler himself appears as a gondolier and as a gardener in one of the two right-angled panels at either end. The **Cavalry Museum** beyond exhibits the world's first articulated leg, designed for the First Marquess, who lost his at Waterloo.

Save time for the grounds, which were landscaped by Humphrey Repton in the early nineteenth century, and the tiled **tearoom** (open daily year-round) in the former milking parlour.

Bryn Celli Ddu

0.5 mile north of A4080, about 2.5 miles southwest of Llanfairpwll • Open access • Free; CADW • The #42 bus passes within half a mile; otherwise it's an hour-long walk from Llanfairpwll

Atmospheric **Bryn Celli Ddu**, the "Mound of the Dark Chamber", is one of Anglesey's most significant prehistoric features, built four thousand years ago on the site of a Neolithic henge. Archeological digs have shown it to be an extensive religious site, but all you can see today is a well-proportioned henge and stone circle, later built over to turn it into a passage grave beneath an earthen mound. The original entrance stone was whisked off to the National Museum in Cardiff, but a replica gives an idea of its carved spiral patterns. In the last chamber you'll find an impressive, smooth monolith beneath a far less impressive concrete beam.

Anglesey Sea Zoo

Brynsiencyn, 7 miles southwest of Llanfairpwll • Feb half-term–Oct half-term daily 10am–5pm • £7.50 • ☎ 01248 430411, ⓦ angleseyseazoo.co.uk

Facing Caernarfon across the Menai Strait, the **Anglesey Sea Zoo** is somewhere to entertain the kids on a wet day. In its small aquarium, local marine environments

– tidal flats, quayside, wrecks and kelp forest – are re-created in wave tanks and shallow pools. Expect to see plaice, turbot and dogfish camouflaged against the shingle bottom.

Newborough Warren

Newborough, 3 miles west of the Sea Zoo • Open access • Free, parking £3

The southwestern end of the Menai Strait is marked by Abermenai Point, a huge sand bar backed by the 600-acre **Newborough Warren**, one of the most important dune systems anywhere in Britain. Since 1948, much of the land has been clad in pines, which stabilize the ground and provide habitat for goldcrests, warblers and rare native red squirrels, justifying the Warren's designation as a national nature reserve. Thick-horned **Soay sheep**, Britain's oldest native breed, are also common. From the small town of Newborough (Niwbwrch), head a couple of miles to the main car park.

Llanddwyn Island

Beyond the car park at Newborough Warren a short well-marked trail weaves through the pines to the beach and **Llanddwyn Island**, a glorious peninsula of rocky coves and sandy beaches. On it stands Tŵr Mawr (the Great Tower), built in 1800 to warn the ships in Caernarfon Bay, later supplanted by the disused lighthouse, built in 1873 in the style of an Anglesey windmill. There's also a row of restored cottages and the ruined thirteenth-century **Church of St Dwynwen**, dedicated to the patron saint of lovers in Wales. In the fifth century, after her abortive affair with Welsh prince Maelon, Dwynwen became a nun at Llanddwyn and requested that hopeful lovers who make a supplication to God in her name should receive divine assistance. Certainly the location has heavenly scenery – even more so at sunset. You can also reach the beach from free forest car parks a mile north of Newborough. From each, well-marked trails, none more than an hour or two's stroll – go through the trees until you emerge to one of the most spectacular views in Wales.

Llangadwaladr church

A4080, 4 miles northwest of Newborough • Often closed except Sun mornings • ☏ 01407 840282

The area around tiny Llangadwaladr was once the seat of the great ruling dynasty of the Princes of Gwynedd who from the seventh-century reign of Cadfan until Llywelyn ap Gruffydd's death in 1282 controlled northwest Wales, and often much of the rest of the country. Evidence lies in **Llangadwaladr church**, built in the thirteenth century, with a memorial plaque, carved in Latin in about 625, incorporated into an inside wall. It reads "Cadfan the King, wisest and most renowned of all kings".

Barclodiad y Gawres

Scheduled visits Sat & Sun noon–4pm from the Wayside Stores, 1 mile north in Llanfaelog • Free; CADW • Call ahead ☏ 01407 810153

Cable Bay (Porth Trecastell) was the eastern terminus of the first telegraph cable to Ireland, though it is now better known for its good sandy beach. On the headland to the south, the heavily reconstructed remains of the five-thousand-year-old **Barclodiad y Gawres** (the Giantess's Apronful) burial chamber are more dramatic than Bryn Celli Ddu, with chevrons and zigzag patterns.

WORTH ITS SALT?

With provenance being key in foodie circles, **Halen Môn**, which sources the sea water for its salts from the Menai Strait beside the Sea Zoo, is on a roll. Some of the world's top restaurants use it, and their smoked sea salt is an important ingredient in Barack Obama's favourite chocolates, apparently. Quality food shops around Wales stock the white stuff along with flavoured varieties such as vanilla and celery. Or you can pick it up direct from the producer's on-site shop beside the Anglesey Sea Zoo (see above) in Brynsiencyn (Mon–Fri 10am–4pm; ☏ 01248 430871, ⊚ halenmon.com).

Rhosneigr

Not so long ago **RHOSNEIGR** was just another peaceful Edwardian seaside town on the southwest coast. It remains justifiably popular with holiday-makers as a small-fry beach resort spread across several small bays. Yet, in recent years, Rhosneigr has been re-energized as Anglesey's watersports capital. It offers some of the best **windsurfing** and **kitesurfing** conditions in Wales, with both waves and flat water in winds from the north, through west to south, plus occasional surfing waves. Kitesurfing is best on the north beach, surfing on the southern Broach Beach. Either way, the backdrop of Snowdonia is spectacular. See our activities section (see p.416) if you feel like joining in.

EATING AND DRINKING   RHOSNEIGR

The Oyster Catcher 0.5 mile north of centre on A4080 link road ☎01407 812829, ⓦoystercatcher anglesey.co.uk; map p.415. This hip glass-walled box shows the direction Rhosneigr is heading. It's both an informal restaurant above, serving the likes of fish pie, local mussels and lamb loins (mains £9–16), as well as a popular design-led bar that's always buzzing in summer. Food Mon–Fri noon–2.30pm & 6–9pm, Sat–Sun noon–9pm, bar till 11pm; school holidays food daily noon–9pm, bar till 11pm.

Holy Island

At the western extremity of Anglesey is **HOLY ISLAND**, though you'll barely notice you've changed island as you cross a small inlet at Four Mile Bridge (via Valley). While its focus, **Holyhead**, is barely worth a visit, there are some good sights around the island if you have your own transport or a bike – particularly the birdlife at **South Stack** and the lovely beach resorts of **Trearddur Bay** and **Rhoscolyn** further south.

Holyhead

Drab **HOLYHEAD** (Caergybi; pronounced in English as "holly-head") is Anglesey's largest town and the terminus for ferry routes to Ireland. Built on the site of a Roman fort and former hermitage of the sixth-century Saint Cybi, who put the "holy" into the name, it's really only of interest for ferry passengers. If you have time to kill you could visit the thirteenth-century **Church of St Cybi** beside the port (June–Sept Mon–Sat 11am–3pm; free) to see stained glass by Edward Burne-Jones and William Morris.

Holyhead Maritime Museum

Beach Rd • Mid-April to Oct daily 10am–4pm • £3.50 • ☎01407 769745, ⓦholyheadmaritimemuseum.co.uk

Tucked into Wales' oldest lifeboat station beside the Newry Beach seafront, the **Holyhead Maritime Museum** contains memorabilia of local maritime disasters along with models of lifeboats through the years, and the ferries that have plied the Ireland route over the centuries. Far more fun are the whale's eardrums, which show a passing resemblance to a human head and face. For no apparent reason, two on display have been carved to portray Mussolini and Hitler.

ARRIVAL AND DEPARTURE   HOLYHEAD

By train The train station is in the town centre and is linked by Arriva trains to north Wales destinations and inter-city Virgin trains as far as London.
Destinations Bangor (22 daily; 30–40min); Chester (23 daily; 1hr 30min–2hr); Conwy (11 daily; 1hr); Llandudno (18 daily; 1hr 20min); Llanfairpwll (9 daily; 30min).
By bus Local and National Express bus stops are by the passenger ferry terminal.

Destinations Amlwch (Mon–Sat 7 daily; 50min); Bangor (Mon–Sat hourly; 1hr 15min); Cemaes (Mon–Sat 7 daily; 45min); Llanfairpwll (Mon–Sat hourly; 1hr); Llangefni (Mon–Sat hourly; 45min); Menai Bridge (Mon–Sat hourly; 1hr); Rhoscolyn (Mon–Sat 3 daily; 15min); Trearddur Bay (Mon–Sat 4 daily; 10min).
By ferry For ferries to and from Ireland see Basics (see p.27).

7

ACCOMMODATION

Yr Hendre Porth-y-Felin Rd ☎01407 762929, ⓦyr-hendre.net. The best beds in central Holyhead are the three in this very comfy B&B with three country-modern floral rooms and a generous welcome, set in a charming ex-manse. **£65**

EATING AND ENTERTAINMENT

Canolfan Ucheldre Mill Bank ☎01407 763361, ⓦucheldre.org. Anglesey's premier centre for the performing arts and exhibitions, fashioned from a former convent chapel. Presents recent films three nights a week and has the daytime café *Gegin Ucheldre* (noon–2pm; closed Sun morning) where everything is home made.

Harbourfront Bistro Newry Beach ☎01407 763433, ⓦharbourfrontbistro.co.uk. Offers sandwiches and toasted baguettes, cakes and coffee, or mains of Welsh lamb or seared tiger prawns (£10), all served in front of good harbour views – the terrace is a fine spot to wait for a ferry. Reservations required for dinner. Wed & Sun noon–2.30pm, Thurs–Sat noon–2.30pm & 6–9pm.

South Stack and around

You need your own transport to get to **South Stack** (Ynys Lawd), two miles west of Holyhead, where you can watch sea birds, visit a dramatic lighthouse and follow a path (45min) to the top of the 700ft **Holyhead Mountain** (Mynydd Twr).

Ellin's Tower Seabird Centre

South Stack • Easter–Sept daily 10am–5pm; visitor centre daily 10am–5pm • Free • ☎01407 762100, ⓦrspb.org.uk/wales

Views of the cliffs around South Stack are best from the RSPB-run **Ellin's Tower Seabird Centre** perched on the cliff edges. From April until the end of July, binoculars and closed-circuit TV give an unrivalled opportunity to watch up to three thousand birds – razorbills, guillemots and a few puffins – nesting on the nearby sea cliffs while choughs and peregrines wheel outside the tower's windows. You'll find it just below the RSPB-run **South Stack Visitor Centre**, a café-cum-interpretive centre on the road.

South Stack Lighthouse

South Stack • Easter–Sept Sat–Thurs 10.30am–5pm • £5.15

A twisting path with over four hundred steps leads down from the South Stack car park to a suspension bridge over the surging waves, once the keeper's only access to the now fully automated pepper-pot **lighthouse**, built in 1809. Views on to the cliffs are stupendous as you climb down to the island and, once there, you'll find exhibitions on local wildlife and can take a tour of the lighthouse itself. Tickets are issued at the visitor centre (see above).

Cytiau'r Gwyddelod

Across the road from South Stack Kitchen • Open access • Free; CADW

Nineteen low stone circles comprise the **Cytiau'r Gwyddelod** hut circles, which are probably late Neolithic or early Bronze Age. There seem to have originally been fifty buildings, formed into eight distinct farmsteads separated by ploughed fields.

Caer y Twr

Open access • Free; CADW

The summit of Holyhead Mountain is ringed by the remains of the seventeen-acre **Caer y Twr**, one of the largest Iron Age sites in north Wales. Seemingly, it was only used during times of war, as no signs of permanent occupation have been unearthed, just a 6ft-high dry-stone wall enclosure around the ruins of a Roman beacon.

Trearddur Bay

At the waist of Holy Island's hourglass shape, **TREARDDUR BAY** (Bae Trearddur) is moderately smarter and more centred than its neighbour Rhosolyn. At its heart is a deeply indented bay with a fine beach and, beyond it, rocky coves. It's emerged as something of a minor resort (it's a far nicer base than Holyhead) with a good, clean swimming beach.

ARRIVAL AND DEPARTURE   TREARDDUR BAY

By bus The #23 bus service goes from Holyhead (Mon–Sat 5 daily; 7–15min).

ACCOMMODATION AND EATING

Blackthorn Farm 2 miles northwest ☎ 01407 765262, ⓦ blackthornleisure.co.uk; map p.415. A farm holiday resort with comfy B&B in eight en-suite rooms, plus a well-maintained campsite (closed Nov–Feb) with a good shower block. Doubles **£75**; camping **£10**/person

The Seacroft Ravenspoint Rd ☎ 01407 860348, ⓦ theseacroft.com; map p.415. Modern, stylish restaurant and bar with a brisk nautical feel and a constant stream of visitors. Expect the likes of dressed Anglesey crab or oven-roast cod with Welsh rarebit (£14) as much as

burgers with chunky chips (£10) and pizzas (£8–10), to eat in the restaurant or bar areas. Daily 11.30am–10pm or later; food served Mon–Fri noon–2pm & 5–9pm, Sat–Sun noon–9pm.

Trearddur Bay Hotel Behind bay off Lon Isallt ☎ 01407 860301, ⓦ trearddurbayhotel.co.uk; map p.415. Glass balconies overlook the main bay in the best rooms and there's a heated indoor pool moments behind the beach – just what you need from a bright modern holiday hotel with 42 rooms. **£155**

Rhoscolyn

At the southern tip of Holy Island lanes wander to the tiny, scattered seaside settlement of **RHOSCOLYN**. With a couple of exquisite sandy beaches, lots of rocky outcrops and coastal walking, this is the ideal place to spend a day or two chilling out. Kayakers love the place, though you'll require your own equipment or need to join a tour (see p.416).

ARRIVAL AND DEPARTURE   RHOSCOLYN

By bus The #23 bus service runs here from Holyhead (Mon–Sat 3 daily; 15min).

ACCOMMODATION AND EATING

Outdoor Alternative Circa 800m south of centre, off through road ☎ 01407 860469, ⓦ outdooralternative .co.uk; map p.415. Relaxed, small and simple campsite with an eco-ethos not far from the beach. Caters to activity groups (kayakers, climbers, walkers etc) – it also has its own activities agency (see p.416). Phone in advance for directions. **£6**/person

★**The White Eagle** Village centre ☎ 01407 860267,

ⓦ white-eagle.co.uk; map p.415. Excellent gastropub offering some of the best eating on Holy Island – cuisine such as slow-braised ox cheek or Tuscan bean stew (mains mostly £11–14) – and excellent cask ales. The huge deck with long views of the indented coastline is a great spot for a pint or two beforehand. Be warned: it's busy and reservations are for large groups only. Mon–Sat noon–11pm, Sun noon–10.30pm.

Northern, eastern and inland Anglesey

The **northern and eastern sides of Anglesey** are quieter than the south and west; their settlements cluster behind sheltered coves that, with the odd rocky headland, form an appealing (if seldom dramatic) coastline. This is primarily family holiday country, albeit of a gentle bygone rural style – just a few caravan sites and not an amusement arcade for miles.

GETTING AROUND   NORTHERN, EASTERN AND INLAND ANGLESEY

By bike or on foot Towns are well spaced along (or just off) the A5025, making cycling between them, or walking the coastal path, an ideal way to get around.

By bus Relying on buses is possible, though less

rewarding. The #62 runs from Bangor to Amlwch via Red Wharf Bay and Moelfre (twice hourly Mon–Sat), and on to Cemaes (4 daily Mon–Sat).

Melin Llynnon

Llanddeusant • Easter–Sept Sat–Thurs 10.30am–5pm • £3.60 • ☎ 01407 730797, ⓦ visitanglesey.co.uk

A few miles inland from the A5025, signposts tempt you towards **Melin Llynnon**, Anglesey's sole working, traditional windmill. At one time, around fifty mills on

Anglesey ground away to feed north Wales; most are either rotting in fields or are converted into barns and houses. Restored from dereliction, Melin Llynnon is now canvas-sailed and again producing flour. Everything in the mill is wind-powered, even the hoists that lift the grain through trapdoors, and milling skills have been re-learnt by modern millers, who now demonstrate the process and sell the result from a good café.

This was originally the site of an Iron Age village, something recalled in the two 30ft-diameter, thatched **round houses** built here in 2007.

Porth Swtan

The highlight of the northwest coast is **PORTH SWTAN** (Church Bay), a gesture of a settlement gathered around a sweep of sand and backed by yellow rocks dating from the pre-Cambrian era, some 570 million years ago. There's limited free parking.

Swtan

Just back from the beach at Porth Swtan • Easter–May Fri–Sun & June–Sept Tues–Sun all noon–4pm • £3.50 • ☎ 01407 730186, ⓦ swtan.co.uk

Swtan is the only surviving thatched cottage on Anglesey and the story of its restoration is told in a short film. There's occasionally a fire burning in the inglenook fireplace in the tiny stone-flagged kitchen dining room, and the thatch construction can be easily seen in the roof of the hen house.

ACCOMMODATION AND EATING	PORTH SWTAN

Church Bay Inn Church Bay, 0.5 miles back from the beach ☎ 01407 730867; map p.415. A friendly pub that not only has real ales but is about the only place in these parts with a beer garden looking towards the setting sun. Mon–Fri 4–10pm, Sat–Sun noon–10pm or later.

The Lobster Pot Church Bay ☎ 01407 730241, ⓦ lobsterpotrestaurant.co.uk; map p.415. Rather dated in decor and not cheap, this is the only option for restaurant-style dining in the village. There's lobster of course, thermidor or grilled (£24), plus local mussels and a tasty fisherman's pie (£15). Easter–Oct Tues–Sat noon–2pm & 6–9pm (same times Mon & Sun on bank

holidays); Nov–Easter Sat–Sun noon–2pm & 6–9pm.
Tŷ Newydd Church Bay ☎ 01407 730060; map p.415. Simple, low-key camping – effectively just a field attached to a farm opposite *The Lobster Pot* – that serves tents and a few caravans. There are hot showers, though. £6/person
Wavecrest Café Church Bay ☎ 01407 730650; map p.415. Sweet and simple little beach café with sea views from picnic tables on a grass bank. Come for the straightforward home-made baguettes and salads (£5–9), but leave space for the best cream-and-strawberry-filled scones (£4). Easter–Sept Thurs–Mon 10am–4.30pm; Oct–Easter Sat–Sun 10am–4.30pm.

Cemaes

The harbourside village of **CEMAES** is wedged between several dozen **windfarm** towers and the bulk of the **Wylfa Nuclear Power Station** (decommissioned but still there). Nonetheless, Cemaes is a charming spot with one of the most attractive harbours on the north coast, occupied by the odd trawler and boatloads of yachties.

Llanbadrig Church

On the headland at the eastern side of Cemaes Bay • May–Sept daily 9am–noon & 2–4pm • Free

The mainly fourteenth-century **Llanbadrig Church** is one of only two Welsh churches dedicated to St Patrick. Its origins date back to the fifth century, when Ireland's patron saint is supposed to have been shipwrecked and made his way to a cave below the site of the present church. The current building was restored in the nineteenth century by Lord Stanley of Alderley, Bertrand Russell's grandfather, a Muslim who used Islamic imagery in the stained glass.

EATING	CEMAES

Coffee Cups The Heritage Centre, 36 High St ☎ 01407 710004; map p.415. A sweet little café with a pretty garden behind. On the menu are toasties filled with cheese and

caramelized onion or ginger jam, apple and cheese (£3.50), sandwiches and salads, plus home-made cakes and tea in vintage crockery. Mon–Sat 11am–4pm, Sun 1–4pm.

Amlwch and around

AMLWCH, five miles east of Cemaes, would be just another tiny fishing village but for Parys Mountain (Mynydd Parys), once the world's largest source of **copper**. Neolithic and Roman miners were followed by industrial production in the eighteenth century when Amlwch boomed. Pollution had become a problem, but people noticed that the iron hulls of ships didn't corrode in the copper-laced harbour waters, fuelling a demand for protective copper sheathing that boosted the market for Parys copper (and coined the term "copper-bottomed" to mean reliable). International competition virtually killed the mines in the early nineteenth century.

Copper Kingdom

In the harbour • April–Oct Tues–Sun 11am–5pm • £5 • ☎ 01407 830298, ⓦ copperkingdom.co.uk

On the wharf in the old copper bins, the new **Copper Kingdom** museum relates the story of how little Amlwch became the copper capital of the world in the first half of the 1700s. Using interactive exhibits and touchscreen displays, it narrates that mine's history yet covers the social side as much as the economic, allowing visitors to track the lives of miners, a copper lady or a mine assayer to see what the mine meant to each of them.

Sail Loft Visitor Centre

Above the harbour • Easter then Whitsun–Oct Tues–Sun 11am–4.30pm • Free • ☎ 01407 832255, ⓦ copperkingdom.co.uk

The former Watch House beside Amlwch's pretty port houses the **Sail Loft Visitor Centre**, full of material covering Amlwch's maritime past, including artifacts from shipwrecks around the Anglesey coast, on the intentionally sloping floor of a former sail loft. The centre distributes a free **Porth Amlwch Heritage Trail** leaflet and can direct you to walks along a rewarding stretch of the Anglesey Coast Path.

Parys Mountain

Visit the ruined pumping mill on top of **Parys Mountain** by a path from the car park on the B5111. A box at the car park has leaflets for the Industrial Heritage Trail that leads around Parys' ravaged moonscape, made all the more bizarre by the derelict remains, multicoloured rocks, coppery pools of water and patches of scrubby heather and gorse.

Moelfre and around

MOELFRE's branding as Anglesey's maritime village explains the number of anchors rusting around the village. It has a reputation for shipwrecks – they say the remains of the **Hindlea** can be seen at very low tides off a northern headland after it went down in October 1959, exactly a century after the 2700-ton **Royal Charter** foundered, with the loss of four hundred lives and nearly £400,000-worth of gold – though wandering around the peaceful grey-pebbled cove on a sunny day it seems unlikely. A kilometre north of the centre, Traeth Lligwy is a lovely scimitar of white sand tailormade for summer picnics.

Din Lligwy Hut Group

1 mile west of Moelfre, off A5025 • Open access • Free; CADW

The late Neolithic **Din Lligwy Hut Group** forms the centrepiece of a site spanning three thousand years of human occupation. A five-sided walled enclosure contains the foundations of several circular and rectangular buildings dated to the second and fourth centuries which, along with the hut group on Holy Island, give the best indication of how these people actually lived, rather than how they buried their dead. To the northeast of the main enclosure stands **Capel Lligwy**, a ruined twelfth-century church, and a short distance to the south is the **Lligwy Burial Chamber** with a 28-ton capstone.

Red Wharf Bay

A few miles south of Moelfre, **Red Wharf Bay** (Traeth Coch) forms a broad sweep of golden sand that never gets too crowded. Most people head for the northern side where facilities are concentrated.

EATING   **RED WHARF BAY**

The Old Boathouse Red Wharf Bay ☎01248 852731, ⓦboathouserestaurantanglesey.co.uk; map p.415. This garden café-restaurant has a great location overlooking the bay. Expect fish dishes or steak and ale pies, sharing platters of home-made pâtés and terrines (£15), burgers and sandwiches, and paninis (£6). Daily: Feb–Easter 10am–4pm; Easter–June & Sept–Oct 10am–7pm; July & Aug 9.30am–9pm; Nov–Dec 10am–7pm.

★**Ship Inn** Red Wharf Ba ☎01248 852568, ⓦshipinnredwharfbay.co.uk; map p.415. Ancient inn with tables outside opposite the bay – a lovely spot for real ales and meals like grilled lemon sole with dill cream, Anglesey crab (£12–16 mains) or Welsh ham and chutney sandwiches. Mon–Fri noon–2.30pm & 6–9pm, Sat–Sun noon–4.30pm & 5.30–9pm.

Llangefni

The main reason to venture inland on the island is to visit **LLANGEFNI**, Anglesey's low-key county town and the second largest on the island after Holyhead. A solid little farming centre, it's a bastion of Welsh, which is spoken every day by ninety per cent of the inhabitants, and also home to the **Oriel Ynys Môn** gallery.

7

Oriel Ynys Môn

0.5 mile north of Llangefni on B5111 • Daily 10.30am–5pm • Free • ☎01248 724444, ⓦorielynysmon.info

The combined museum and art gallery, **Oriel Ynys Môn**, provides an excellent overview of the factors in the island's turbulent history, from pre-Christian sites and the dynastic lines of the Princes of Gwynedd to exhibits about conservation, shipwrecks and the Welsh language. One corner of the gallery is devoted to the life and works of **Charles Tunnicliffe** who spent thirty years from 1947 painting wildlife from his Shorelands home in Malltraeth, near Newborough Warren. A separate room is dedicated to works by exalted Llangefni-born landscape painter **Kyffin Williams** (1918–2006), who returned to paint Anglesey in his later years.

ARRIVAL AND DEPARTURE   **LLANGEFNI**

By bus Llangefni is 5 miles west of Llanfairpwll, and on the #4 bus route between Holyhead (hourly; 50min) and Bangor (hourly; 35min).

DYLAN THOMAS

Contexts

History

Before the end of the last Ice Age around ten thousand years ago, Wales and the rest of Britain formed part of the greater European whole, while the early migrant inhabitants eked out a meagre existence on the tundra or a better one among the oak, beech and hazel forests in the warmer periods. Most lived in the southeast of Britain, but small groups foraged north and west, leaving 250,000-year-old evidence in the form of a human tooth in a cave near Denbigh in north Wales and a hand axe unearthed near Cardiff.

It wasn't until the early part of the **Upper Paleolithic age** that significant communities settled in Wales, those of the Gower peninsula interring the "Red Lady of Paviland" around 24,000 BC. This civilization remained on Europe's cultural fringe as the melting ice cut Britain off from mainland Europe around 5000 BC. Migrating Mesolithic peoples had already moved north from Central Europe and were followed by **Neolithic colonists**, whose mastery of stone and flint working found its expression in over a hundred and fifty cromlechs (turf-covered chambered tombs) dotted around Wales, primarily Bryn Celli Ddu and Barclodiad y Gawres on Anglesey, and Pentre Ifan in Mynydd Preseli. Skilled in agriculture and animal husbandry, the Neolithic people also began to clear the lush forests covering Wales below 2000 feet, enclosing fields, constructing defensive ditches around their villages and mining for flint.

The earliest stone circles – more extensive meeting places than cromlechs – were built at this time. As the Neolithic period drifted into the **Bronze Age** around 2000 BC with more sophisticated use of metals, social structures became well organized. The established aristocracy engaged in much tribal warfare, as suggested by large numbers of earthwork forts built around this period – the chief examples being at Holyhead Mountain on Anglesey and the Bulwalks at Chepstow.

The Celts

Celtic invaders spreading from their central European homeland settled in Wales in around 600 BC, imparting a great cultural influence. Familiar with Mediterranean civilization through trading routes, they introduced superior methods of metalworking, forging iron into weapons and coins. Gold was used for ornamental works – the first recognizable Welsh art – heavily influenced by the symbolic, patterned **La Tène** style still thought of as quintessentially Celtic.

The Celts are credited with introducing the basis of modern Welsh (see p.465). This highly developed language was emblematic of a sophisticated social hierarchy headed by **druids** (see p.432). Yet the Celts were unable to maintain an organized civic society to match that of their successors, the Romans.

250,000 BC	**2000 BC**	**600 BC**	**78 AD**
Earliest evidence of human existence in Wales.	Bronze Age settlers arrive from the Iberian peninsula.	Celts reach the British Isles bringing their ritual priests, the druids.	Roman conquest of Wales completed as Agricola kills druids of Anglesey.

THE DRUIDS

During Celtic times, the **druids** were a ritual priesthood with attendant poets, seers and warriors. Through a deep knowledge of ritual, legend and the mechanics of the heavens, the druids maintained their position between the people and a pantheon of over four thousand gods. Most of these were variations of a handful of chief gods worshipped by the great British tribes: the Silures and Demetae in the south of Wales, the Cornovii in mid-Wales and the Ordovices and Deceangli in the north.

The Romans in Wales

Life in Wales, unlike that in most of England, was never fully Romanized, the region remaining under legionary control throughout its three-hundred-year occupation. **Julius Caesar** made cross-Channel incursions in 55 and 54 BC, kicking off a century-long but low-level infusion of Roman ideas which filtered across to Wales. After the full-scale invasion in 43 AD the Romans swept across southern England to the frontier of south Wales. Expansionism fomented anti-Roman feeling along the frontier between the Lowland Zone (southern and central England) and the Highland Zone (northern England, Scotland and Wales). Traditionally insular Welsh hill tribes united with their Brythonic cousins in northern England to oppose the Romans, who forced a wedge between them. The Roman historian **Tacitus** recorded the submission of the Deceangli near Chester, providing the oldest written mention of a Welsh land. The Romans sent an expeditionary force against the Silures and the toughest nut, the druid stronghold of Anglesey, but were kept at bay until around 75 AD, when legionary forts were built at Deva (Chester, England) and Isca Silurium (Caerleon).

By 78 AD, Wales was under Roman control, its chief fortresses at Deva, Isca Silurium and Segontium (Caernarfon) boasting all the trappings of imperial Roman life: bath houses, temples, mosaics and underfloor heating. Through three centuries of occupation, the Celtic people sustained an independent existence, though elements of Roman life filtered into the Celtic culture: agrarian practices improved, Christianity was partly adopted, the language adopted Latin words (pont for "bridge", ffenestr for "window") and the prevailing La Tène artistic style took on classical Roman elements.

The Roman Empire was already in decline when **Magnus Maximus** (Macsen Wledig) led a campaign to wrest control of the western empire from Emperor Gratian in 383 AD. Maximus' rule was short-lived but Wales was effectively free of direct Roman control by 390.

The age of the saints

Historical orthodoxy views the departure of literate Latin historians, skilled stonemasons and an all-powerful army as heralding the **Dark Ages**. In fact, a civic society probably flourished until a century later, when the collapse of trade routes was hastened by the dramatic spread of Islam around the Mediterranean, and Romanized society gave way to a structured form of **Celtic society**. For the next few centuries, **Teutonic barbarian tribes** struggled for supremacy in the post-Roman power vacuum in southern and eastern England but had little influence in Wales where Irish incursions took place against a background of increasing religious energy (see box opposite).

80–100	**early 4th C**	**5th–6th C**	**c.589**
Construction of Caerleon amphitheatre completes the trappings of Roman life.	Roman departure from Wales.	Age of Saints.	Saint David (Dewi Sant) dies after a life of miracles. He later becomes Wales' patron saint.

KING ARTHUR MUDDIES THE WATERS

The fourth and fifth centuries AD were marked by the establishment of the main dynastic kingdoms that were set to steer Wales through the next seven hundred years. The already sketchy history of this period was further muddied in 1136, when Geoffrey of Monmouth published his *History of the Kings of Britain*, portraying **King Arthur** as a feudal king with his court at Caerleon. Victorian Romantics embellished subsequent histories, making it practically impossible to extract much truth from this period.

Between the fifth and the sixth centuries the **Celtic Saints**, ascetic evangelical missionaries, spread the gospel around Ireland and western Britain, promoting the Middle Eastern eremitical tradition of living a reclusive life. Where their message took root, they founded simple churches within a consecrated enclosure, or llan, which often took the saint's name, hence Llanberis (Saint Peris), Llandeilo (Saint Teilo) and numerous others. In south Wales, **Saint David** (Dewi Sant) was the most popular (and subsequently Wales' patron saint), dying around 589 after a miracle-filled life, during which he established the religious community at St Davids, which had become a place of pilgrimage by the twelfth century.

The Welsh kingdoms

Towards the end of the sixth century the **Angles** and **Saxons** in eastern Britain began to entertain designs on the western lands. The inability of the independent western peoples to unify against this threat left the most powerful kingdom, Gwynedd, as the centre of cultural and political resistance. The weaker groups were unable to hold the invaders, and after the battle at Dyrham, near Gloucester in 577, the Britons in Cornwall were separated from those in Wales, who became similarly cut off from their northern kin in Cumbria after the battle of Chester in 616.

The eighth-century construction of **Offa's Dyke** (Clawdd Offa) – a linear earthwork demarcating, rather than defending, the boundary between Wales and the kingdom of Mercia – gave the Welsh a firm eastern border and allowed them to concentrate on unifying the patchwork of kingdoms as their coasts were being harried by **Norse and Viking invaders**.

Rhodri Mawr (Rhodri the Great) killed the Viking leader off Anglesey, helping the country's rise towards statehood through his unification of most of Wales. By this stage, England had developed into a single powerful kingdom, and though the various branches of Rhodri's line went on to rule most of Wales down to the late thirteenth

IRELAND INVADES WALES

In the fifth century, the Irish (Gwyddyl), who had a long tradition of migrating to the Llŷn and parts of mid-Wales, attacked the coast and formed distinct colonies, but were soon expelled from the north by Cunedda Wledig, the leader of a Brythonic tribe from near Edinburgh, who went on to found the royal house of Gwynedd, consolidating the Brythonic language and naming regions of his kingdom – the modern Ceredigion and Meirionydd – after his sons. In the southwest, the Irish influence was sustained; the kingdom of Dyfed shows clear Irish origins.

616	**c.784**	**c.900–1050**	**1066**
Battle of Chester – Wales isolated from rest of Britain.	The completion of Offa's Dyke physically separates England from Wales.	Hywel Dda largely reunifies Wales and codifies the Law of Wales.	Normans invade England and set up Lords Marcher to control the Welsh borderlands.

> **WELSH BY ANY OTHER NAME**
>
> Bonded by their resistance to the Saxons, the Welsh started to refer to themselves as Cymry (fellow-countrymen), rather than the Saxon term "Welsh", which is generally thought to mean either foreigners or Romanized people.

century, the princedoms were frequently forced to swear fealty to the English kings. Defensive problems were exacerbated by the practice of partible inheritance, which left each of Rhodri's sons with an equal part of Wales to control.

Rhodri Mawr's grandson **Hywel Dda** (Hywel the Good) largely reunified the country from southwest Wales. He added Powys and Gwynedd to his domain, but his most valuable legacy is his codification and promulgation of the medieval **Law of Wales** (see box below). After Hywel's death in 950, anarchy and internal turmoil reigned until his great-great-grandson, **Gruffydd ap Llywelyn**, seized power in Gwynedd in 1039. He unified all of Wales, taking the coronation of the weak English king, Edward the Confessor, as an opportunity to annex some of the Marches in Mercia. Edward's successor, Harold, wasn't having any of this and killed Gruffydd, heralding a new phase of political fragmentation.

The arrival of the Normans

In 1066, the **Normans** swept across the English Channel and stormed England. Though Wales was unable to present a unified opposition to the invaders, the Norman king, William, didn't attempt to conquer Wales. The **Domesday Book** – commissioned in 1085 to record land ownership as a framework for taxation – indicates that he only nibbled at parts of Powys and Gwynedd. Instead, he installed a huge retinue of barons, the **Lords Marcher**, along the border to bring as much Welsh territory under their own jurisdiction as possible. Despite generations of squabbling, the barons managed to hold onto their privileges until Henry VIII's Act of Union over four hundred years later.

A lack of English commitment or resources allowed the Welsh to claw back their territory through years when distinctions between English, Normans and Welsh were beginning to blur, which helped form three stable political entities: Powys, Deheubarth and Gwynedd. The latter, led by Owain Gwynedd from his capital at Aberffraw on Anglesey, now extended beyond Offa's Dyke and progressively gained hegemony over the other two. Owain Gwynedd's grandson, Llywelyn ap Iorwerth (the Great), incorporated the weaker territories to the south into his kingdom and captured several Norman castles to reach the peak of the Welsh feudal pyramid. After tussling with England's King John, Llywelyn won a degree of Welsh autonomy, though this largely fell apart after his death.

> **THE LAW OF WALES**
>
> Around 930 at modern-day Whitland in southern Carmarthenshire, Hywel Dda codified the progressive and enlightened **Law of Wales**. Women were allowed to initiate divorce proceedings, people weren't punished for stealing food that kept people alive, and there was parity between children born in and out of wedlock. These laws held sway until forcibly abandoned under the 1536 Act of Union with England, though many elements survived in common-law practice.

1180–93	1188	1196–1240	1246–82
St Davids Cathedral built.	Archbishop Baldwin (accompanied by Giraldus Cambrensis) recruits for the Third Crusade.	Llywelyn ap Iorwerth (the Great) rules as Prince of Gwynedd and later most of Wales.	Llywelyn ap Gruffydd (the Last) intermittently rules large parts of Wales.

Edward I's conquest

Most of the work of regrouping Wales around one standard fell to Llywelyn the Great's grandson, **Llywelyn ap Gruffydd** (Llewellyn the Last). In the 1250s, he won control of Gwynedd, then pushed the English out of most of Wales. The English king Henry III was forced to ratify the **Treaty of Montgomery** in 1267, thereby recognizing Llywelyn as "Prince of Wales" in return for his homage. The English monarchy's war with the barons allowed Llywelyn time to politically consolidate his lands, which now stretched over all of modern Wales excepting Pembrokeshire and parts of the Marches.

The tables turned when Edward I succeeded Henry III and began a crusade to unify Britain. With effective use of sea power, Edward had little trouble forcing the already weakened Llywelyn back into Snowdonia. Peace was restored with the **Treaty of Aberconwy**, which deprived Llywelyn of almost all his land and stripped him of his financial tributes from the other Welsh princes, but left him with the hollow title of "Prince of Wales".

Edward now set about surrounding Llywelyn's land with castles at Aberystwyth, Builth Wells, Flint and Rhuddlan. After a relatively cordial four-year period, Llywelyn's brother Dafydd rose against Edward, inevitably dragging Llywelyn along with him. Edward didn't hesitate and swept through Gwynedd, crushing the revolt and laying the foundations for the remaining castles in his **Iron Ring**, those at Conwy, Caernarfon, Harlech and Beaumaris. Llywelyn, already battered by Edward's force, was captured and executed at Cilmeri in 1282.

Throughout the fourteenth century, famine and the Black Death plagued Wales. The Marcher lords appropriated the lands of defaulting debtors, while royal officials clawed in all the income they could from towns around the castles. These factors and the pent-up resentment of the English sowed seeds of a rebellion led by the tyrannical but charismatic **Owain Glyndŵr** (see box, p.283).

The Tudors and union with England

During the latter half of the fifteenth century, the succession to the English throne was contested in the **Wars of the Roses** between the houses of York (white rose) and Lancaster (red rose). Welsh allegiance lay broadly with the Lancastrians, who had the support of the ascendant north Welsh Tewdwr (or Tudor) family. Henry Tudor escaped from besieged Harlech Castle to Brittany when Yorkist Richard III took the English throne in 1471. Fourteen years later, Henry returned to Wales, defeating

---

THE STATUTE OF RHUDDLAN

The **Statute of Rhuddlan** in 1284 set down the terms by which the English monarch was to rule Wales: much of it was given to the Marcher lords who had helped Edward I, the rest was divided into administrative and legal districts similar to those in England. Though the treaty is often seen as a symbol of English subjugation, it respected much of Welsh law and provided a basis for civil rights and privileges. Many Welsh were content to accept and exploit Edward's rule for their own benefit. In 1294, however, a rebellion led by Madog ap Llywelyn gripped Wales and was only halted by Edward's swift and devastating response. Most of the privileges enshrined in the Statute of Rhuddlan were rescinded.

1270–1320	1277	1277–83	1284
Tintern Abbey built.	Llywelyn humiliated. Signs Treaty of Aberconwy at the end of the First War of Welsh Independence.	Edward I begins Aberystwyth, Flint, Rhuddlan, Caernarfon, Conwy and Harlech castles.	Statute of Rhuddlan signed by Edward I.

Richard at the Battle of Bosworth Field, so becoming **Henry VII** and sealing the Lancastrian ascendancy.

For the most part Henry lived up to the high Welsh expectations, removing many of the restrictions on land ownership imposed at the start of Glyndŵr's uprising, and promoting many Welshmen to high office. Still, Wales had been largely controlled by the English monarch since the Statute of Rhuddlan.

Just as Henry VIII's decision to convert his kingdom from Catholicism to Protestantism was borne more from his desire to divorce his first wife than from any religious conviction, it was his need for money which brought about the **Dissolution of the Monasteries** in 1536 – ultimately resulting in a more studied approach to religion and learning in general. Under the reign of Elizabeth I, Jesus College was founded in Oxford for Welsh scholars, and the Bible was translated into Welsh for the first time by a team led by Bishop **William Morgan** (see p.396).

The Dissolution hastened the emergence of the Anglo-Welsh gentry, a group eager to claim a Welsh pedigree while promoting the English language and the legal system.

The Civil War and the rise of Nonconformism

A direct descendant of the Tudors, **James I** came to the throne in 1603 to general popular approval in Wales. Many privileges granted to the Welsh during the Tudor reign came to an end, but the idea of common citizenship was retained, the Council of Wales remaining as a focus for Welsh nationalism. James, fearful of both Catholicism and the new threat of Puritanism – an extreme form of Protestantism – courted a staunchly Anglican Wales and curried the favour of Welsh ministers in the increasingly powerful Parliament. Though weak in Wales, Puritanism was gaining a foothold, especially in the Welsh borders, where William Wroth and Walter Cradock set up Wales' first dissenting church at Llanfaches in Monmouthshire in 1639.

The monarchy's relations with the Welsh were strained by **Charles I**, who was forced to levy heavy taxes and recruit troops, but the gentry were mostly loyal to

---

ACT OF UNION

Sovereignty was finally fixed in Henry VIII's 1536 **Act of Union** (and a subsequent act of 1543). It's a misleading title, and one that was not used to describe the Act until the twentieth century, for it implies a level of equality between the two nations that did not exist. Unlike the Acts of 1707 and 1800 that brought Scotland and Ireland into the Union – and were the decisions of independent parliaments in Edinburgh, Dublin and London – the 1536 Act was a unilateral decision by Westminster, which had no Welsh representation. It decreed that English was to be the only language of the courts and other official bodies, effectively creating a two-tier Wales of English-speaking lords and masters and a Welsh-speaking proletariat. At the same time the Marches were replaced by shires (the equivalent of modern counties), the Welsh laws codified by Hywel Dda were voided, and partible inheritance (equal among all offspring) gave way to primogeniture, the eldest son becoming the sole heir. This period set in stone the struggles and the injustices that are still playing out nearly five hundred years later.

1301	1400–12	1485	1536–38
Edward I revives title of "Prince of Wales" and bestows it on his son, Edward II.	Owain Glyndŵr's revolt ushers in a third War of Welsh Independence. Glyndŵr dies in hiding in 1416.	Henry VII ascends the throne after landing from exile at Pembroke and beating Richard III at Bosworth.	Henry VIII suppresses monasteries.

the king at the outbreak of the **Civil War**, which saw the Parliamentary forces install **Oliver Cromwell** as the leader of the **Commonwealth**. The Puritan support for Parliament didn't go unnoticed, and after Charles' execution, they were rewarded with the livings of numerous parishes and the roots of Puritan Nonconformism spread in Wales.

As Cromwell's regime became more oppressive, the Anglican majority welcomed the successful return of the exiled **Charles II**, and the monarchy was restored, thereby suppressing Nonconformity. The Baptists, Independents and Quakers who made up the bulk of Nonconformists continued to worship in secret, until **James II** passed the **Toleration Act** in 1689, finally allowing open worship, but still banning the employment of dissenters in municipal government, a limitation which remained in force until 1828.

The rise of Methodism

The propagation of Nonconformism led to a welter of new religious books in Welsh in the late seventeenth century, but with most people still illiterate, religious observance remained an oral tradition. In 1699, the **Society for Promoting Christian Knowledge** established schools where the Bible, along with reading, writing and arithmetic, was taught in Welsh as well as English. This met with considerable success in middle-class anglicized towns, but failed to reach rural areas where children couldn't be spared from farm duties. The next big reformist push came in 1731, when **Griffith Jones** organized reading classes in the evenings and quieter winter season, so farmers and their families could attend. Within thirty years, half the Welsh population could read.

By the middle of the eighteenth century, a receptive and literate populace was ready for what became the **Methodist Revival**, driven by a strong belief in a resurgent Welsh nation. In contrast to the staid Anglican services, the Methodists held evangelical meetings. Meanwhile, improved schooling brought about a literary revolution, and Wales re-established itself as the language for a vast body of literature.

In 1811, the Calvinist Methodists broke from the framework of Anglicanism. As the gentry remained with the Established Church, the chapel became the focus of social life, discouraging folk traditions considered incompatible with puritanical thrift and temperance. Political radicalism was also discouraged and since only property owners were eligible to vote, established dynasties were perpetuated.

Wales and the Industrial Revolution

Small-scale mining and smelting had taken place in Wales since the Bronze Age, but agriculture remained the mainstay of an economy centred on meat, wool and butter. The enormous rise in grain prices in the early nineteenth century forced Welsh farmers to diversify and adopt the more advanced English farming practices of crop rotation, fertilizing and stock breeding. Around the same time, acts of Parliament allowed previously common land to be "enclosed", the grazing rights often being assigned solely to the largest landowner in the district. Inevitably, this forced smallholders to migrate to the towns where ever more workers were required to

1536–43	1588	1639	1646
Acts of Union unite Wales and England, conferring equal rights but with government conducted wholly in English.	The complete Bible is translated into Welsh for the first time, chiefly by William Morgan.	First Puritan congregation in Wales convened at Llanfaches, Gwent.	Harlech and Raglan besieged during the Civil War. Harlech, the last Royalist castle, falls in 1647.

mine the seams and stoke the furnaces, fuelling the **Industrial Revolution**. In the north, **John Wilkinson** started his ironworks at Bersham and developed a new method of boring cylinders for steam engines; while in the south, foundries sprang up in the valleys around Merthyr Tydfil under English ironmasters. Gradually the under-educated, impoverished chapel-going Welsh began to be governed by rich, church-going, English industrial barons.

Improved materials and working methods enabled the exploitation of deeper coal seams, particularly in the south Wales valleys, not just to supply the iron smelters but for domestic fuel and to power locomotives and steamships. South Wales' rural valleys were ripped apart and quiet hamlets turned into long rows of terraced houses snaking up the valley sides, roofed in north Wales slate. Transportation of huge quantities of coal and steel was crucial for continued economic expansion, initially on the roads and canals built in the early nineteenth century, then by train as the 1850s rail boom took hold.

In mining towns, working conditions were atrocious, with men and women toiling incredibly long hours in dangerous conditions; children as young as 6 worked alongside them, until this was outlawed by the Mines Act in 1842. Pay was low and often in a currency redeemable only at the poorly stocked, expensive company (Truck) shop. The **Anti-Truck Act** of 1831 improved matters, but a combination of rising population, fluctuating prices and growing need for political change brought calls for reform. The 1832 **Reform Bill** fell far short of the demands for universal suffrage by ballot and the removal of property requirement for voters. This swelled the ranks of the Reformist Chartist movement, and when a petition with over a million signatures was rejected by Parliament, the **Chartist Riots** broke out in northern England and south Wales. The Newport demonstration was disastrous, the marchers walking straight into a trap laid by troops, who killed over twenty men and captured their leader, **John Frost**. Chartism continued in a weakened form for twenty years, buoyed by the **Rebecca Riots** in 1839–43, when guerrilla tactics put an end to tollgates on south Welsh turnpikes.

1850 to World War I

During the latter half of the nineteenth century the radical reformist movement and religion slowly became entwined, with the Nonconformists petitioning for **disestablishment** of the Church in Wales. Eventually, as a consequence of the 1867 Reform Act, industrial workers and small tenant farmers got the vote, giving a long-awaited strong working-class element to the electorate. The following year, **Henry Richard** was elected as Liberal MP for Merthyr Tydfil, becoming the first Welsh member of what soon became the dominant political force and bringing the ideas of Nonconformity – land reform, disestablishment and the preservation of the Welsh language – to Parliament for the first time.

The 1872 Secret Ballot Act and 1884 Reform Act enfranchised farm labourers and further freed up the electoral system, although the Anglican Church was only disestablished in 1920. The Nonconformist Sunday Schools offered primary education for the masses, supplemented by a number of secondary schools, as well as Wales' first major tertiary establishment in Aberystwyth in 1872, followed by colleges at Cardiff (1883) and Bangor (1884). Until they were federated into the University of Wales in 1893, voluntary contributions garnered by Nonconformist chapels supported the

1759	1782	1794	1839–43
Dowlais Ironworks started, followed by Merthyr Tydfil iron industry.	Beginning of north Wales slate industry with the opening of Pennant's Penrhyn slate quarry at Bethesda.	Cardiff to Merthyr canal completed.	Rebecca Riots put an end to tollgates on turnpikes.

colleges. The apotheosis of "Chapel power" came in 1881 with the passing of the Welsh Sunday Closing Act, enshrining Nonconformism's three basic tenets: observance of the Sabbath, sobriety and Welshness.

Industry and the rise of trade unionism

The rise in Welsh consciousness (see box, p.440) paralleled the rise in importance of the **trade unions**. The 1850s were a prosperous time in the Welsh coal fields, but by the end of the 1860s the Amalgamated Union of Miners was forced to call a strike (1869–71), which resulted in higher wages.

A second strike in 1875 failed and the miners' agent, **William Abraham** (**Mabon**), ushered in the notorious "sliding scale", which fixed wage levels according to the selling price of coal. This brought considerable hardship to the Valleys, which became insular worlds with strictly ordered social codes and a rich vibrancy borne from the essential dichotomy of the chapel and the pub. Meanwhile, annual coal production doubled in twenty years. By 1913, 57 million tons were being extracted each year by a quarter of a million people. Similarly punitive pay schemes were implemented in the north Wales slate quarries where membership of **Undeb Chwarelwyr Gogledd Cymru** (The North Wales Quarrymen's Union) was all but outlawed by the slate barons. Things came to a head in 1900 when the workers at Lord Penrhyn's quarry at Bethesda started one of Britain's longest-ever industrial disputes, lasting three years.

From 1885, the vast majority of Welsh MPs were Liberals who helped end the sliding scale in 1902 and brought in an eight-hour day by 1908. The start of the twentieth century heralded the birth of a new political force when **Keir Hardie** became Britain's first Labour MP, for Merthyr Tydfil.

World Wars I and II

World War I (1914–18) was a watershed for Welsh society. The Welsh identified with the plight of defenceless European nations and rallied to fight alongside the English and Scots. At home, the state increasingly intervened in people's lives: agriculture was controlled by the state, rationing food, and industries, mines and railways were under public control. The need for Welsh food and coal boosted the economy and living standards rose dramatically. Many were proud to be led through the war by Welsh lawyer **David Lloyd George** (see p.444), who rose to the post of Minister of Munitions, then of War, becoming Prime Minister by 1916. By the time conscription was introduced, patriotic fervour had waned. Many miners, reluctant to be slaughtered in the trenches and resentful of massive wartime profits, welcomed the 1917 Bolshevik

---

RAIL, STEAM AND SPEED

Britain's greatest nineteenth-century **engineers** made their names in Wales: **Thomas Telford** built canal aqueducts and successfully spanned the Menai Strait with one of Britain's earliest suspension bridges; **Isambard Kingdom Brunel** surveyed the Merthyr–Cardiff train line, then pushed his Great Western network almost to Fishguard; and **Robert Stephenson** speeded the passage of trains between London and Holyhead on Anglesey for the Irish ferry connection.

1845–50	**1872**	**1884**	**1900**
Britannia Tubular Bridge built across the Menai Strait.	University College of Wales opens in Aberystwyth, followed by Cardiff (1883) and Bangor (1884).	Reform Act. Farm labourers and small tenant farmers get the vote for the first time.	Britain's first Labour MP, Kier Hardie, elected for Merthyr Tydfil.

THE RISE IN WELSH CONSCIOUSNESS

Immigration to the coal fields from England meant that English became the language of commerce and the route to advancement, Welsh being reserved for the home and chapel life of seventy percent of the population. Welsh was still being spoken in Nonconformist schools when, in 1846, they were inspected by three English barristers and seven Anglican assistants. The inspectors' report – known as **The Treason of the Blue Books** – declared the standards deplorable, largely because of the use of the Welsh tongue. The public defence of Welsh that ensued failed to prevent the introduction of the notorious "Welsh Not", effectively a ban on speaking Welsh in school.

As the nineteenth-century Romantic movement took hold throughout Britain, the London Welsh looked to their heritage. The ancient tales of *The Mabinogion* were translated into English, the **Welsh Language Society** was founded in 1885, eisteddfodau were reintroduced as part of rural life, and the ancient bardic order, the **Gorsedd**, was reinvented. But disestablishment remained the *cause célèbre* of Welsh nationalism. Perhaps the greatest advocate of both separatism and Welsh nationalism was **Michael D. Jones** (see box, p.322), who helped establish a Welsh homeland in **Patagonia**.

By 1907 Wales had a national library at Aberystwyth, and a national museum was planned for Cardiff, by now the largest city in Wales.

Revolution, and though Communism never really took hold, the socialist Labour Party caught the postwar fallout.

Similar dramatic changes were taking place in rural areas, where Welsh farming was embracing new machinery and coming out of nearly a century of neglect. High wartime inflation of land prices and the fall in rents forced some landowners to sell off portions of major estates to their tenants in the so-called "green revolution".

After the postwar boom came the Depression. All of Wales' mining and primary production industries suffered, and unemployment reached 27 percent, worse than in England and Scotland. South Wales soon became the **Labour movement**'s stronghold in Britain. This was challenged by Lloyd George's newly resurgent Liberal Party, but his Westminster-centred politics were no longer trusted in Wales and Labour held firm, seeking to improve workers' conditions: the state of housing was still desperate, and health care and welfare services needed boosting. The Labour Party effectively became the hope that had previously been entrusted to the chapels, though nationalists were drawn to a new party, **Plaid Cymru** (see box opposite).

Some relief from the Depression came with re-armament in the lead-up to **World War II**, but by this stage vast numbers had migrated from south Wales to England, leaving the already insular communities banding together in self-reliant groups centred on local co-ops and welfare halls. The demands of the war saw unemployment all but disappear and the Welsh economy gradually restructured, with more people switching from extractive industries to light manufacturing, a process which continues today.

The postwar period

Any hopes for a greater national identity were dashed by the Attlee Labour government from 1945 to 1951, which nationalized transport and utilities with little regard for

1925	1926	1936	1951
Plaid Genedlaethol Cymru (Welsh National Party) formed.	Miners' strike and General Strike.	Saunders Lewis and nationalist colleagues burn building materials on the Llŷn.	Minister for Welsh Affairs appointed.

national boundaries. However, under the direction of Ebbw Vale MP, **Aneurin Bevan**, the postwar Labour government instituted the National Health Service, dramatically improving health care in Wales and the rest of Britain, and providing much-improved council housing.

The nationalized coal industry, now employing less than half the number of twenty years before, was still the most important employer at nationalization, but a gradual process of closing inefficient mines saw the number of pits drop from 212 in 1945 to 11 in 1989, and none today. Sadly, the same commitment wasn't directed at cleaning up the scars of over a century of mining until after 1966, when one of south Wales' most tragic accidents left a school and 116 children buried under a slag heap at **Aberfan**.

The Labour Party remained in overwhelming control during the 1960s and 1970s, though the party's reluctance to address nationalist issues allowed Plaid Cymru to become a serious opposition for the first time. Attlee had thrown out the suggestion of a Welsh Secretary of State in 1946, and not until Plaid Cymru fielded numerous candidates in the 1959 election did the Labour manifesto promise a cabinet position for Wales.

The position of **Secretary of State for Wales** was finally created in 1964 by Harold Wilson's Labour government, who also created the **Welsh Development Agency** and moved the Royal Mint to Llantrisant in south Wales. With Plaid Cymru's appeal considered to be restricted to rural areas, Labour was shocked by the 1966 Carmarthen by-election, when **Gwynfor Evans** became the first Plaid MP. It wasn't until 1974 that Plaid also won in the constituencies of Caernarfon and Meirionydd, and suddenly the party was a threat, forcing Labour to address the question of devolution (see box, p.442).

PLAID CYMRU: THE EARLY YEARS

By 1925, a new sense of nationalism emerged and champions of Welsh autonomy formed **Plaid Genedlaethol Cymru** (the National Party of Wales), often known as Plaid. In September 1936, in one of the first modern separatist protests, its president **Saunders Lewis** joined two other Plaid members (the Rev. Lewis Valentine and D.J. Williams) and set fire to the construction hut of a new aerodrome being built on the Llŷn as part of Britain's build-up to the war. They immediately reported themselves to the nearest police station, attracting huge publicity in the process. Interest in the ensuing trial electrified Wales, causing howls of outrage when the government decided to divert it from sympathetic Caernarfon to the Old Bailey in London. Even recalcitrant nationalist Lloyd George was outspokenly critical of the English decision. The three men were duly imprisoned for nine months, becoming Plaid Cymru's first heroes. Lewis spent the rest of his life immersed in literary criticism, becoming one of Wales' greatest modern writers.

Similar public displays and powerful nationalist rhetoric won over an intellectual majority, but the voting majority continued to fuel the Labour ascendancy in both local and national politics. Plaid Cymru were less enthusiastic about World War II, remaining neutral and expressing unease at the large number of English evacuees potentially weakening the fabric of Welsh communities. However, the war saw the formation of a Welsh elementary school in Aberystwyth and Undeb Cymru Fydd, a committee designed to defend the welfare of Wales.

1955	1966	1967	1982
Cardiff declared capital of Wales.	Gwynfor Evans, first Plaid Cymru MP, elected for Carmarthen. Aberfan disaster.	Welsh Language Act passed. Limited recognition of Welsh as a formal, legal language.	Welsh-language TV channel S4C begins broadcasting.

Modern Wales

The Conservative government of **Margaret Thatcher** came to power in 1979, winning an unprecedented 31 percent of Welsh votes. The referendum that year effectively sidelined the home-rule issue and Thatcher was able to implement her free-market policies. With 43 percent of the Welsh workforce as government employees, privatization had a dramatic impact. The number of jobs in the steel industry, manufacturing and construction all plummeted, doubling unemployment in five years. Despite this, the Conservatives increased their tally of MPs at the 1983 election, while Labour saw their lowest percentage since 1918.

The resulting breakdown of traditional Valley communities and successive anti-union measures failed to break the solidarity of south Welsh workers during the year-long **Miners' Strike** (1984–85). Meanwhile, the Welsh continued to turn away from the established religions and the chapel ceased to be the focal point of community life. Something like two-thirds of the country's six thousand chapels have since closed.

During the 1980s, support for Plaid Cymru shifted back to the rural areas, enthusiasm for the Welsh language increased and a steady decline in numbers of Welsh-speakers was reversed. New Welsh-only schools opened even in predominantly English-speaking areas, learners' classes sprouted everywhere and in 1982 S4C, the first **Welsh-language television channel**, began broadcasting.

When Tony Blair and "New" Labour won a huge majority in 1997, one of the central policy proposals was the **devolution** of some degree of power from London to a parliament in Scotland and a **National Assembly for Wales** – the first all-Wales tier of government for six hundred years. The proposal was endorsed by the Welsh people only by the most slender of margins in a referendum. The first of the four-yearly elections to the Assembly took place in 1999, when a huge swing to Plaid Cymru denied the Labour party its assumed overall majority. Labour has remained the largest party ever since, with **Rhodri Morgan**, a committed supporter of Welsh devolution, as First Minister for most of that time. **Carwyn Jones** took over as leader of Labour and First Minister in 2009, a position he still holds.

In the National Assembly 2007 election, after more than eighty years in opposition, **Plaid** helped form the government, but in the 2011 elections, its support dropped dramatically and it recorded its worst showing at an assembly election (it currently has just eleven seats) – so low that the Conservatives became the major opposition.

In 2006 the Government of Wales Act affirmed that the Queen would, for the first time, appoint Welsh ministers and sign Welsh orders in Council. As the Assembly moved into a snazzy new building on the waterfront of Cardiff Bay, the Welsh Government really began to enmesh itself into the fabric of Welsh life. The 2006 Act also made provision for a **referendum** on further devolution of powers. In March 2011

NO TO SELF-GOVERNMENT

In 1978 Labour tabled the **Wales Act**, promising the country an elected assembly to act as a voice for Wales, but with no power to legislate or raise revenue. In the subsequent **referendum** in 1979, eighty percent of voters opposed the proposition, with even the nationalist stronghold of Gwynedd voting against it.

1984–85	1992	1997	1999
Miners' strike.	Welsh Language Bill gives Welsh equal status with English in public bodies.	Referendum on Welsh Assembly. Only half the country votes, of whom 50.3 percent vote yes, a majority of just 6000 nationwide.	First Welsh Assembly elections. Assembly begins sitting. Wales hosts the Rugby World Cup.

a "Yes" vote finally allowed the Welsh Government to create primary legislation (ie "Welsh laws") without consulting Westminster. Almost two-thirds of voters supported the change, with Monmouthshire the only county to vote "No".

It's not just in the political arena that the country has grown up: there has been a significant surge of national confidence and self-expression, particularly in the cultural and sporting arenas. In 2014, the one hundredth anniversary celebrations of Dylan Thomas' birth did much to boost national self-esteem, while the entrance of football clubs Swansea and Cardiff into the Premier League for the first time has led to a much greater profile for the country in general; the continued success of the Welsh rugby team, meanwhile, is always a source of keen celebration.

That is not to say that everything is rosy: farming lurches along in a state of semi-paralysis, and poverty and ill health still dog many old working-class communities. But these are interesting times in Wales: there is the undeniable feeling that this small country is facing a brighter future than many would have dared predict even one generation ago.

2006	**2011**	**2014**
The new Welsh Assembly building (the Senedd) opens on St Davids Day. Government of Wales Act gains Royal Assent.	Wales emphatically votes for primary law-making powers.	Wales celebrates the centenary of Dylan Thomas' birth.

Modern Welsh nationalism

Plaid Cymru – the Welsh nationalist political party – was formed in 1925, but the political impetus that gave birth to the new movement had been bubbling for decades, if not centuries.

The Welsh identity had always been culturally rich, but was politically expressed only as part of the great Liberal tradition: in the dying years of the nineteenth century, 25 or 30 Welsh Liberal MPs often voted en bloc, making their voice heard. The fiery Welsh patriot **David Lloyd George** (1863–1945; prime minister 1916–22) had embodied many people's nationalist beliefs, although his espousal of greater independence for Wales came unstuck when, ever the expedient politician, he realized the potential difficulty of translating this ideal into hard votes in the industrialized, anglicized south of Wales. During Lloyd George's premiership, the Irish Free State was established, drawing inevitable comparisons with the Home Rule demands being less stridently articulated in Scotland and Wales. But the Liberal Party was in sharp decline, nowhere more markedly than in the industrialized Valleys, which had deserted them in favour of new socialist parties. With the urban slide of Liberalism, Welsh nationalism was gradually honed into the embryonic Plaid Cymru (see box, p.441).

Postwar Wales

Prewar Liberal tradition was still strong in rural Wales, though by the 1951 election this had become just three parliamentary seats out of 36. The **Labour party** was now the establishment in Wales, winning an average of around sixty percent of votes in elections from 1945 to 1966. Two Welsh Labour MPs, Megan Lloyd George, daughter of the great Liberal premier, and S.O. Davies, spearheaded new parliamentary demands for greater Welsh independence, presenting a 1956 petition to parliament demanding a Welsh assembly. Massive popular protests against the continued flooding of Welsh valleys and villages to provide water for England shook the establishment.

The 1963 formation of the boisterous Cymdeithas yr Iaith Gymraeg – the **Welsh Language Society** – attracted a new youthful breed of cultural and linguistic nationalists. The ruling Conservatives offered the sop of nominating a part-time Welsh Minister, confirming Cardiff as the capital and making the red dragon the official Welsh flag. Meanwhile, the Labour party formed a Welsh Council where Labour MPs, trade unionists and ordinary party members began to articulate the need for greater independence.

In the **general election of 1964**, the party stood on a more nationalistic platform than ever before. As usual, they swept the board in Wales, and finally won throughout the UK as a whole. The post of **Secretary of State for Wales**, backed by a separate Welsh Office, was created, although with fewer powers than the Scottish equivalent.

Plaid Cymru starts to win

Plaid Cymru scored its first hit when its president, Gwynfor Evans, won a by-election in Carmarthen in July 1966. In the heart of socialist south Wales, Plaid ran the Labour government astonishingly close in two by-elections – in Rhondda West (1967) and Caerphilly (1968) – and the party saw swings of over 25 percent to cut Labour majorities of over twenty thousand to just a couple of thousand. It seemed that Plaid's time had come. Its traditional vote in the north and west was soaring and it appeared that the party had finally overcome its single-issue status around the Welsh language.

Despite amassing 176,000 votes (eleven percent of the poll in Wales) in the **1970 general election**, Plaid failed to take any new seats and even lost their place in Carmarthen.

Gwynfor Evans was returned in Carmarthen in 1974, but Plaid's earlier success in the industrialized south had evaporated, and they once again became a party of rural Wales.

The new Labour government now set up the **Wales Development Agency**, devolved the huge responsibilities of the Department of Trade and Industry in Wales to the Welsh Office in Cardiff, and even supported a referendum on devolution.

The 1979 referendum and beyond

On St Davids Day 1979, the Welsh people made their feelings known, when a four-to-one majority rejected the devolution proposal. People feared being swamped by (toothless) bureaucracy, and a large number of the eighty percent of the country who did not speak Welsh feared that a Welsh assembly would be the preserve of a new "Taffia", a *Cymraeg* elite. Both north and south Walians worried about potential domination by the other.

The shock waves were great. Weeks later, the Labour government fell and **Margaret Thatcher**'s first Conservative administration was ushered in. Political nationalism seemed to have gone off the boil, and Plaid Cymru were back to just two MPs in the northwest. In the early 1980s Britain's manufacturing base collapsed and unemployment rose, particularly in south Wales, where mines and foundries closed. Welsh nationalism was suffering an identity crisis, typified by Plaid Cymru's controversial 1981 rewriting of its own constitution to fight for an avowedly "Welsh socialist state", causing some of its more conservative members to quit the party. Basing itself as a republican, left-wing party would, it was believed, bring greater fruit in the populated south.

Like so many other political affiliations and ideals in the 1980s, Welsh nationalism underwent something of a sea change. Plaid Cymru began to broaden its base with a firmly socialist, **internationalist outlook**. The party matured, developing serious policies on all aspects of Welsh life, from traditional rallying calls of language and media to sophisticated analyses of economic policy, the Welsh legal framework and the country's role in the European Union. But Welsh devolution ceased to be the preserve of Plaid Cymru alone. Both Labour and the Liberal Democrats evolved devolutionary strategies for Wales and Scotland. Even the ruling Conservatives devolved more decision-making out to the Welsh Office in Cardiff. This, ironically, strengthened the nationalist hand. Plaid and the other parties pointed out that a huge swath of government existed in Wales, not overseen by any all-Wales authority. The call for a Welsh assembly to oversee this vast array of public expenditure was consistently supported by huge majorities in opinion polls, and formed the basis of the Labour Party's manifesto for Wales throughout the 1990s.

Labour government and a new referendum

The **1997 general election** changed everything. The Conservatives were spectacularly swept from power, failing to keep any seats in Wales. Labour – or "New" Labour as the party was styled under Tony Blair – won hugely, denting any further Plaid progress.

A CHANNEL FOR WALES

Plaid President and former MP Gwynfor Evans was single-handedly responsible for the most high-profile activity of Welsh nationalism in the early 1980s. The Conservative party had fought the 1979 election on a manifesto that included a commitment to a Welsh-language TV channel. When plans for the new UK Channel 4 were drawn up, this promise had been dropped. Evans decided to fast until death, if necessary, as a peaceful protest. The huge publicity quickly forced the Thatcher government to make its first U-turn, and **Sianel Pedwar Cymru** (S4C) was born in 1982. Perhaps the Tories realized the political advantage of bringing Welsh nationalism into the legitimate fold, for the Welsh media industry dissipated many angry and impassioned arguments for national self-determination. Certainly, many of the most heartfelt radicals ended up in prominent positions within Wales' media.

Within six months of Blair's election, referenda took place in Wales and Scotland on the devolution proposals. Scotland voted for its parliament; in Wales, the proposals barely scraped through. Although this was potentially the first piece of self-government for Wales in six hundred years, many nationalists felt that it fell far short of expectations and was not worth supporting. Plaid Cymru's own stance mirrored this ambivalence: initially unenthusiastic and only coming out for the Assembly in the latter stages of the campaign. Wales itself was split in half by the devolution vote. The border areas and Pembrokeshire, true to their historical anglicization, voted no, while Plaid's west coast strongholds and the "Old" Labour bastions of the industrial Valleys were just enthusiastic enough to swing the ballot.

The National Assembly for Wales

When it came to voting for the Welsh Assembly, Plaid Cymru achieved spectacular gains, taking Labour strongholds like Rhondda, Islwyn and Llanelli. The Plaid share of the vote, at nearly thirty percent, was enough to deny Labour – once the absolute party in Wales – an overall majority. So far, this has proven to be Plaid's high-water mark.

One of Plaid's main drawbacks in recent years had been confusion, and disillusion, over its leadership, particularly in the Assembly under the lacklustre Anglesey AM Ieuan Wyn Jones. In 2012, however, he stood down and the party elected a new (and the first female) leader, Leanne Wood. She is now heading an impressive new generation in Plaid, who, if given half the chance, should be able to restore some status to the party; how much progress has been made will be one of the more fascinating aspects of the 2016 National Assembly elections.

Since the arrival of the Assembly, it's hard for even the most ardent of nationalists to argue that Wales' system of government is the most pressing issue facing the nation. With farming in crisis, one of the poorest standards of living in the UK, and job opportunities limited, there are plenty of meatier matters to chew on. If the Assembly can be seen to make a difference to these issues, its reputation will soar.

However, in the early years of the twenty-first century, it's safe to say that the majority of Welsh people are fairly happy with things as they are. Despite the gradual decline in the number of Welsh-speakers – according to the 2011 census, nineteen percent of the population speak Welsh (though this is not much below the level in the 1970s) – the feeling of Welsh identity appears to be growing, with 66 percent of the population calling themselves Welsh.

This general sense of Welshness has been much augmented in recent years, as much by sporting achievements (particularly rugby) and rock music (notably the Manic Street Preachers) as by any politician. Wales is more and more happily, and very easily, calling itself a nation. The question that still hangs in the air is simply this: to be a nation, does Wales really need to be a state?

NATIONALISM AWAY FROM THE ASSEMBLY

With Plaid Cymru having to play it as a sober democratic party, much of the more interesting aspects of Welsh nationalism are to be found away from party politics. Regular dust-ups over patronizing English attitudes still periodically ignite the media, while debates rage on about English in-migration and the purchase of second homes in the heartlands of the Welsh language and culture. In a journalistic atmosphere that has at times been decidedly febrile and ill-tempered, the first casualty has been proper debate, with everything reduced to hysterical soundbites. Out of this environment has come the pressure group **Cymuned** ("Community"; Ⓦcymuned.org), whose slogan "Dal dy dir!" ("Hold your ground!") is seen daubed all around Wales. Cymuned is slick, modern and thoughtful, and could well prove to be the intellectual driving force for modern Welsh nationalism, especially as Plaid Cymru continues to struggle.

Natural history of Wales

Whole bookshelves are devoted to Wales' landscapes, land use, flora and fauna. What follows is a general overview of the effects of geology, human activity and climate on the country's flora, fauna and land management. It must be remembered that nowhere in Wales is untouched, almost every patch of "wilderness" being partially the product of human intervention, thoroughly mapped, mined and farmed. Still, Wales is covered with a wide array of sites deemed to be of national or international importance (see box, p.448). Nor is anywhere free from pollution: the conurbations of England are too close, power stations and factories dot the countryside, and the sea is in a poor state. That said, several clean-air-loving lichen species – found in few other places in Britain – abound in Wales. The country also supports 1100 of Britain's 1600 native plants, with ferns and other moisture-loving species particularly well represented.

Geology

Wales' mountain ranges often provide the best insight into the country's geological history. Between 600 and 400 million years ago, **Snowdonia** was twice submerged for long periods in some primordial ocean where molten rock from undersea volcanoes cooled to form igneous intrusions in the sedimentary ocean-floor layers. Snowdon, Cadair Idris and the Aran and Arenig mountains are the product of these volcanoes, with fossils close to the summit of Snowdon supporting the theory of its formation on the sea floor.

After Silurian rocks had been laid down, immense lateral pressures forced the layers into concertina-like parallel folds with the sedimentary particles being rearranged at right angles to the pressure, giving today's vertically splitting sheets of **slate**, the classic metamorphosed product of these forces. The folded strata that rose above the sea bore no resemblance to today's mountains; the cliff face of Lliwedd on Snowdon shows that the summit was at the bottom of one of these great folds between two much higher mountains.

In the very recent geological past from 80,000 to 10,000 years ago, these mountains were shaped by the latest series of **Ice Ages**, with glaciers scouring out hemispherical cirques divided by angular ridges, then scraping down the valleys, gouging them into U-shapes, with waterfalls plunging down their sides.

Snowdonia is linked by the long chain of the **Cambrian Mountains** to the dramatic north-facing scarp slope of the **Brecon Beacons**, south Wales' distinctive east–west range at the head of the south Wales coal field. Erosion of the ancient rocks which once covered what is now northern Britain washed down great river systems, depositing beds of old red sandstone from 350–400 million years ago. These **Devonian** rocks lay in a shallow sea where the molluscs and corals decayed to form limestone, which in turn was overlaid by more sediment forming millstone grit. Subsequent layers of shale and sandstone were interleaved with decayed vegetable matter, forming a band known as **coal measures**, from which the mines once extracted their wealth. The whole lot has since been tilted up in the north, giving a north-to-south sequence which runs over a steep sandstone ridge (the Brecon Beacons), then down a gentle sandstone dip-slope arriving at the pearl-grey limestone band where any rivers tend to dive underground into **swallow holes**. They reappear as you reach the gritstone, often tumbling over waterfalls into the coal valleys.

WALES' PROTECTED AREAS

3 National Parks Snowdonia, the Brecon Beacons and the Pembrokeshire Coast comprise almost twenty percent of Wales. All are outstanding, though they do contain towns, accommodation and even industry.

5 Areas of Outstanding Natural Beauty (AONBS) The Anglesey coast, the Llŷn coast, the Clwydian Range and Dee Valley, the Gower peninsula and the Wye Valley (partly in England) collectively encompass two percent of Wales.

72 National Nature Reserves (NNRS) Smaller areas (from a few acres to large chunks of the Cambrian Mountains) with specific habitats such as lowland bogs, sweeping sand dunes or ancient woodlands. They're widely promoted, usually posted with information boards and threaded with easy, well-signed walking trails.

1000 Sites of Special Scientific Interest (SSSIS) Generally small areas singled out for special protection. Most are on private land with no right of access.

Land settlement and usage

During the last interglacial period, Wales was warm enough to support hippos and lions, but humans, pressed for space by the expanding ice sheets, killed them off, leaving bears and boars, which in turn were dispatched by human persecution.

After the last ice sheet drew back from Wales around ten thousand years ago, the few plant species which had survived on the ice-free peaks were in a strong position to colonize, producing an open grassland community. Over several thousand years, forests of birch, juniper and hazel became mixed deciduous woodland with oak, elm and some pine, and in wetter areas damp-loving alder and birch.

Early settlement

The Neolithic tribes began to settle on the upland areas, using their flint axes to clear the forests. The discovery of bronze and later iron hastened the process, especially since wood charcoal was required for **smelting** iron ore. And so began the spiralling devastation of Wales' native woodlands. As the domestication of sheep and goats put paid to any natural regeneration of saplings, more land became available for arable farming. Thin, acidic mountain soils and a damp climate made **oats** – fodder for cattle and horses – about the only viable cereal crop, except in Anglesey which, by the time the Romans arrived in the first century AD, was already recognized as Wales' most important **wheat**-growing land.

Meanwhile, some of the last beaver lodges in Britain dammed the Teifi in the twelfth century, while half a millennium later, wolves disappeared from the land.

Cattle droving

Until the sixteenth century, Cistercian monasteries kept extensive lands, cleared woods and developed sheep and cattle farms which subsequently became part of the great estates which still take up large tracts of Wales. By contrast, the less privileged were still smallholders living simple lives. In the 1770s the travel writer Thomas Pennant noted in his *Tours in Wales* that the ordinary people's houses on the Llŷn were "very mean, made with clay, thatched and destitute of chimneys". The poor state of housing had much to do with the right to build (Tŷunnos) on common land with common materials.

In the eighteenth century, **droving** reached its peak. Welsh black cattle, fattened on Anglesey or the Cambrian coast, were driven to market in England, avoiding the valley-floor toll roads by taking highland routes that can still be traced. Nights were spent with the cattle corralled in a halfpenny field (so called because this was the nightly rate per animal) next to a lonely homestead heralded by three Scots pines, which operated as an inn. It was a hard journey for men and cattle, but tougher still for the geese, whose webbed feet were toughened for the long walk with tar and sand.

At home, women ground the wheat, aided by mills driven by fast-flowing streams which later provided power for textile mills, especially around Ruthin, Denbigh,

Newtown, Llandeilo and along the Teifi Valley. The Cistercians had laid the foundations of the **textile industry** for both wool and flannel, but it had generally remained in the cottages, with nearly every smallholding keeping a spinning wheel next to their harp.

The Industrial Revolution

The next major shift in land use came with a wave of **enclosure acts** from 1760 to 1820, which effectively removed smallholders from upland common pasture and granted the land to holders of already large estates. The people were deprived of their livelihood, and access to open country was denied.

The mountain building processes discussed above have left a broad spectrum of minerals under Wales. **Copper** had been mined since the Bronze Age and the Romans dabbled in **gold** extraction, but mining became big business in the latter half of the eighteenth century with the extraction of **slate** (see box, p.366) in north Wales and **coal** (see box, p.108) in the south.

Forests

Until five thousand years ago, birch, juniper, hazel, oak and elm covered the mountainsides, but devastating forest clearances and a wetter climate have left only a few pockets of native woodland in the valleys. **Pengelli Forest** in Pembrokeshire represents one of Wales' largest blocks of ancient woodland, comprising **midland hawthorn** and **sessile oak**, the dominant tree in ancient Welsh forests. Parts of the Severn and lower Wye valleys are well wooded, as is the Teifi Valley, where oak, ash and sycamore predominate. You can still occasionally see evidence of **coppicing** – an important and ancient practice common a century ago – where trees are cut close to the base to produce numerous shoots harvested later as small-diameter timbers. Under the canopy, **bluebells** and **wood sorrel** are common, and in the autumn look out for the dozens of species of **mushroom**, especially the delicious but elusive **chanterelle**, found mainly under beech trees.

It is a delight to wander in relict stands of the ancient oak woodlands, and along the streams where the **dipper** and **kingfishers** flourish. On sheltered water you might also find shelduck, Canada geese and three species of swan.

A far greater area of Wales is smothered in gloomy forests of planted **conifers** (predominantly sitka spruce) which are too shaded and acidic for wildflowers and are forbidding to most birds. But elusive **pine martens** thrive there, where their diet of small rodents is readily available. Both pine martens and the more common **polecats** are found in wild corners throughout Wales. **Foxes** are widespread, along with **brown hares**, **stoats** and **weasels**. **Rabbits** seem to be everywhere, and the North American **grey squirrel** has all but dislodged the native red squirrel from its habitat.

Thanks to its protected status, the elusive **badger** is increasingly common. There have been contentious attempts to have an official cull to combat the spread of TB in cattle, though its likely efficacy is still subject to a scientific investigation.

With Welsh red dragons dying out along with King Arthur, much smaller lizards and two species of snake are all that remain of Wales' reptiles. The venomous, triangular-headed **adder** is sometimes spotted sunning itself on dry south-facing rocks, but, except in early spring when it is roused from hibernation, it frequently slithers away unnoticed. The harmless **grass snake** prefers a wetter environment and is equally shy. Easily mistaken

---

TOP 5 WILDLIFE VIEWING SPOTS

Skomer, Skokholm and Grassholm Pembrokeshire. Sea birds. See p.178
Ramsey Island Pembrokeshire. Sea birds and dolphins. See p.186
Bwlch Nant-yr-Arian Rheidol Valley. Red kites. See p.278
Newborough Warren Anglesey. Red squirrels, soay sheep. See p.423
South Stack, Holyhead. Sea birds. See p.425

COUNTRYSIDE AND WILDLIFE ORGANIZATIONS

Campaign for the Protection of Rural Wales Ⓦ cprw.org.uk.
Friends of the Earth: Cymru Ⓦ foe.co.uk/cymru.html.
National Wetland Centre Ⓦ wwt.org.uk/llanelli.
Natural Resources Wales Ⓦ naturalresourceswales.gov.uk.
Royal Society for the Protection of Birds (RSPB) Ⓦ rspb.org.uk/wales.
Wildlife Trust of South and West Wales Ⓦ welshwildlife.org.

---

for a snake, the **slowworm** is actually a legless lizard and is common throughout Wales, as are **toads** and **frogs** – though the rare **natterjack toad** is only found in a few locations.

Open moorland and mountains

Much of the Welsh high country is grazed, both by farmed sheep and (in Snowdonia) by **goats** which are descended from domesticated escapees. Generally welcomed by farmers, they forage on the precipitous ledges, thereby discouraging sheep from grazing ventures beyond their capabilities. On the Carneddau in Snowdonia and on the Brecon Beacons you might also see shy herds of feral **ponies**.

Grazing makes forest regeneration impossible as animals munch on fresh seedlings. It looks like only grass survives, but open moorlands are also home to **arctic alpines**, which cling to small pockets of soil among the high crags and gullies of Snowdonia and the Brecon Beacons (their southernmost limit in Britain). Their range hasn't changed since they were discovered by seventeenth-century botanists such as Thomas Johnson and Welshman Edward Lhuyd, who found *Lloydia serotina*, a glacial relic more popularly known as the **Snowdon Lily**, actually a spiderwort that looks not unlike a small off-white tulip. In Britain, it is found only around Snowdon and then only rarely seen between late May and early June, when it blooms.

Cwm Idwal in the Ogwen Valley is a great place to spot some of the more common species, in particular the handsome **purple saxifrage**, whose tightly clustered flowers often push through the late winter snows, later followed by the starry and mossy saxifrages and spongy pink pads of **moss campion**. The star-shaped yellow flowers of **tormentil** are typical of high grassy slopes, and you may also find **mountain avens**, distinguished by its glossy oak-like leaves, and, when it blooms in June, by its eight white petals. From June to October, purple heads of **wild thyme** cover the ground, providing food for a small beetle unique to Snowdonia.

Poor acid soils on the igneous uplands foster the growth of lime-shy bracken, bilberry and purple **heather** which combine with decayed **sphagnum moss** in wetter areas to form peat bogs. These support the **bog asphodel**, which produces its brilliant yellow spikes in late summer, often in company with the **spotted orchid** and less frequently the tiny **bog orchid**. Insectivorous plants such as **butterwort** and **sundew** both gain nutrients that their poor surroundings cannot provide by digesting insects trapped on the sticky hairs of their leaves.

The high country supports **red kites** (see box, p.452) and large populations of **kestrels**, usually seen hovering motionless before plummeting onto an unsuspecting mouse or vole. Golden-brown **buzzards** gently wheel on the thermals on the lookout for prey which can be as big as a rabbit. Buzzards and peregrine falcons are as happy picking at carrion, but have to compete with sinister black **ravens** that inhabit the highest ridges and display their crazy acrobatics, often banding together to mob the bigger birds.

Acidic heather uplands provide habitats for **grouse**, whose laboured flight is in complete contrast to the darting zigzag of its neighbour, the **snipe**. On softer grassland, expect to find the **ring ouzel**, a blackbird with a white cravat, and the **golden plover**, a bird still common, but being threatened, like many others, by the spread of conifer forests.

Rivers, estuaries and wetlands

Wales' clean, fast-flowing rivers make ideal conditions for the **brown trout**, a fish managed for sport throughout the country. **Salmon** are less common, found mainly in the Wye (where it is important as game fish) and the Usk. Along with **roach**, **perch** and other coarse fish, the depths of Bala Lake (Llyn Tegid) claim the unique silver-white **gwyniad**, an Ice Age relic not dissimilar to a small herring, said never to take a lure.

Otters almost became extinct in Wales some years back, but a concerted effort on the part of the Otter Haven Project has seen their numbers climbing in the Teifi and some of the rivers in Montgomeryshire, though they are seldom seen.

Wales' rivers spawn estuarine "meadows", which in summer are carpeted with bright violet **sea lavender** and mauve **sea aster**. An unusual coastal feature is the dam-formed string of **Bosherston Lakes**, south of Pembroke, where the fresh water supports rafts of **white-water lilies**. Further west, the Pembrokeshire coast is a blaze of colour in early summer, with white-flowered **scurvy grass** and **sea campion**, yellow **kidney vetch** and **celandine**, and blue **spring squill**. **Bluebells** and **red campion** cloak Pembrokeshire's islands, while the majority of species mentioned can be found in abundance in Newborough on Anglesey.

The mud flats and saltings of Wales' estuaries provide rich pickings for wintering waders. The **Dee estuary**, on the northern border with England, plays host to Europe's largest concentration of **pintail** as well as **oystercatchers**, **knot**, **dunlin**, **redshank** and many others. Numerous terns replace them in the summer months. Commercially viable beds of **cockles** still exist on the north coast of the Gower and families still own rights to musselling the sands of the Conwy estuary.

The coast

The long Welsh coast is thick with **sea birds**, thanks partly to the profusion of islands and its position on the main north–south migratory route. The islands off the Pembrokeshire coast are incomparable for sea-bird colonies, the granite pinnacle of **Grassholm**, eight miles offshore, hosting the world's third-largest Atlantic gannet colony with 39,000 pairs. Nearby, **Skokholm** and **Skomer** between them support 3500 pairs of **storm petrels** and an internationally significant population of 150,000 pairs of the mainly nocturnal **Manx shearwater**, which spend their winter off the coast of South America. Burrows vacated by rabbits on the islands also provide nests for puffins, while **razorbills**, **guillemots** and **kittiwakes** nest on the cliffs. Since the eradication of the rats that previously deterred burrow-nesting birds, Manx shearwaters are also now colonizing nearby **Ramsey Island**. In the north, make for **Ynys Enlli** (Bardsey Island) off the Llŷn coast, and the wonderful **South Stack Cliffs** on Anglesey which, especially from May to July, are alive with breeding guillemots, razorbills and puffins.

THE ROCKS OF WALES

Geologists puzzled over the forces that shaped the Welsh landscape for centuries before early nineteenth-century geologist **Adam Sedgwick** and his collaborator (and later rival) **Roderick Murchison** began to unravel their secrets. They explained the source of the shattered, contorted and eroded rocks that form the ancient peaks of Snowdonia and gave the rock types names associated with the land where their discoveries took place.

Anglesey, the Llŷn and Pembrokeshire all have older **pre-Cambrian** rocks, while those around St Davids are some of the most ancient in the world.

The **Silurian** period (400–440 million years ago) is named after the ancient south Welsh tribe, the Silures, while the Celtic Ordovices who occupied mid- and north Wales gave their name to the **Ordovician** period (440–500 million years ago), and the **Cambrian** period (500–600 million years ago) is named after the Roman name for Wales.

RED KITE RECOVERY

Like many other raptors, fork-tailed **red kites** were traditionally persecuted by gamekeepers and suffered from the use of pesticides, which caused thinning of eggshells. Before the banning of DDT in the 1960s Welsh red kite numbers were down to a handful of breeding pairs, mostly in the Elan Valley. But with careful management numbers have been on the increase for years and there are now over six hundred breeding pairs. Their once narrow range has expanded as far south as Pembrokeshire, and they are now even seen far across the border into parts of England.

Though best observed in their natural environment hunting or simply wheeling on thermals, for a real spectacle, head to one of the **feeding sites**: Bwlch Nant yr Arian, near Aberystwyth (see p.278); Llandeusant Red Kite Feeding Station, in the Brecon Beacons (Ⓦ redkiteswales .co.uk); or Gigrin Farm, near Rhayader (see p.233).

In the water, dolphins can often be seen: the coast of mid-Wales is notable for **bottlenose dolphins**. The same territory has also seen occasional visits by **leatherback turtles**, particularly in late summer. Perhaps global warming is attracting new species to Wales just as it threatens others.

Ecology and the future

With smokestack industries now largely absent from Wales, and the Valleys mostly devoid of working coal mines, nature is struggling to claw its way back. A verdure inconceivable forty years ago now cloaks the hillsides, and already the industrial remains are being cherished as cultural heritage; as much a valid part of the "natural" landscape as the mountain backdrops. If you need convincing, climb up to the disused slate workings behind Blaenau Ffestiniog or walk the old ironworks tramways around Blaenafon.

In other areas, much remains to be done to restore the ecological balance. The increasing commercialization of farming has led not just to the damaging application of pesticides and excessive use of nitrogen-rich fertilizers, but to the wholesale removal of **hedgerows** and **dry-stone walls**, ideal habitats for numerous species of flora and fauna. Conservation groups promote the skills needed to lay hedges and build dry-stone walls, but for every success, another chunk of farmland is paved over with a new bypass, or a meadow is turned over to **conifers**, which are clear-felled every thirty years or so.

The largest forest owner, the Forestry Commission, is keen to shake off its monoculture image and is bordering its forests with a mix of broad-leaved trees and conifers of different ages. As an extended public relations exercise it also welcomes mountain bikers in some forests.

Far from being areas where nature is allowed to take its course, the **national parks** can be their own worst enemies, attracting thousands of people a day. Some attempt is being made to control the effects of tourism through path management and the promotion of public transport, but this is more than outweighed by the increasingly aggressive promotion of these regions.

Paradoxically, and for all the wrong reasons, **military zones** – Mynydd Eppynt and most of the Castlemartin peninsula, for example – have become wildlife havens away from the worst effects of human intervention.

Environmental groups are also keeping a weather eye on offshore **oil** and **gas** exploration off the west Wales coast, while in south Wales there has been considerable resistance to developments in Milford Haven where, since 2009, huge liquefied natural gas-carrying ships from Qatar have been offloading their cargo and feeding it into Britain's gas network.

One success in recent years has been the decision not to press ahead with the **Usk Barrage**, which was planned to create a freshwater lake on the outskirts of Newport by damming the estuary, forcing otters and other protected species to abandon the river.

Music in Wales

Dylan Thomas' observation that "We are a musical nation" is as relevant as ever. Despite the near-obliteration of the mining industry, male voice choirs (see box, p.118) remain a feature of Welsh life, with many choirs opening their practice sessions to the public. But Welsh music extends far beyond the dwindling chapels, into the country's village halls, clubs, festival sites and pubs. In quieter venues, harp players repay their musical debt to ancestors who accompanied the ancient bards (traditional poets and storytellers), while modern folk music draws directly from the broader Celtic musical tradition.

Welsh-language rock musicians have traded commercial success for unabashed nationalism, spanning styles from punk to hip-hop. Some bands sing in both English and Welsh, and there is a fast-growing scene in English-language Welsh rock, building on the success of outfits like the Manic Street Preachers. These days, Wales continues to punch above its weight, churning out a phenomenal amount of good music for a country its size.

Folk

The Welsh *gwerin* has a much wider meaning than its English counterpart "folk". At a Welsh *gŵyl werin* (folk festival), you're as likely to encounter the local rock band as the local dance team – with the entire community turning out, too.

Welsh folk song has always remained close to the heart of popular culture, conveying political messages and social protest. After centuries of political and religious suppression, traditional Welsh music and dance have fought back from near extinction. Unlike their Celtic cousins in Ireland, Scotland and Brittany, many folk musicians in Wales have learnt their tunes from books and manuscripts rather than from older generations of players.

As you travel around, scan posters for the word *twmpath* – the equivalent of a barn dance or ceilidh, and used when Welsh dances are the theme of the night. Calling (dance instructions) could be in Welsh or English, depending on where you are in the country. *A Noson Lawen*, literally "a happy night", usually offers a harpist, perhaps some dancers and a repertoire of Welsh standards.

History

The bardic and **eisteddfod** traditions have played a key role in Welsh culture. Often the **bard**, who held an elevated position in Welsh society, was the non-performing composer, employing a harpist and a *datgeiniad*, whose role was to declaim the bard's words. The first eisteddfod appears to have been held in Cardigan in 1176, with contests between bards and poets and between harpers, pipers and *crwth*-players (see p.454). Henry Vlll's **Act of Union** in 1536 was designed to anglicize the country by stamping out Welsh culture and language, and the eisteddfod tradition degenerated over the next two centuries.

In the eighteenth and nineteenth centuries, the rise of **Nonconformist religion**, with its abhorrence of music, merry-making and dancing, further hammered Welsh traditions. **Edward Jones**, *Bardd y Brenin* (Bard to the King), observed sorrowfully in the 1780s that Wales, which used to be one of the happiest of countries, "has now become one of the dullest". Folk music only gained some sort of respectability when London-based Welsh people, swept along in a romantic enthusiasm for all things Celtic, revived it at the end of the eighteenth century.

In the heartland of the Welsh language around mid- and northwest Wales, folk music can be heard in many of the same **venues** that stage rock events. The language is considered more important than musical categories, and the folk club concept is alien to Welsh speakers, who never saw the need to segregate music that was a natural part of their cultural life. Folk clubs are found in the anglicized areas and only a few of them feature Welsh music.

The harp

Historically the most important instrument in the folk repertoire, the **harp** has been played in Wales since at least the eleventh century, although no instruments survive from the period before the 1700s. The only surviving ancient music is the manuscript of **Robert ap Huw**, written about 1614 in a strange tablature that has intrigued music scholars: five scales were used, but no one has yet defined satisfactorily how they should sound.

The simple early harps were superseded in the seventeenth century by the rich-sounding **triple harp**, with its complicated arrangement of two parallel rows of strings sounding the same note, with a row of accidentals between them. The nineteenth-century swing towards classical concert music saw the invasion of the large **chromatic pedal harps** that dominate today, but the triple, always regarded as the traditional Welsh harp, was kept alive by gypsy musicians who preferred to play something portable. One Welsh harp performance that's well worth catching is the **Cerdd Dant**, where the harpist leads with one tune, accompanying soloists and groups take a counter-tune, and they all end up together on the final note. Wales even has a royal harpist, a position reinstated in 2000 after almost a century and currently held by Hannah Stone from Swansea.

In recent years craftsmen have re-created the *crwth* (a stringed instrument which may have been either plucked or bowed), the *pibgorn* (a reed instrument with a cow's horn for a bell) and the *pibacwd* (a primitive Welsh bagpipe), championed by masters such as Ceri Rhys Matthews.

Folk musicians

The country's foremost triple harpist, **Robin Huw Bowen**, has revived interest in the instrument with appearances throughout Europe and North America, and also makes unpublished manuscripts of Welsh dance music widely available through his publishing company. The lineage of North Wales triple harpist **Llio Rhydderch** stretches back centuries. For a more contemporary take on the instrument, poet/musician **Twm Morys** (son of writer Jan Morris) blends modern Welsh and Breton influences. One of Wales' most well-known harpists is **Elinor Bennett**, who has accompanied some of Wales' biggest rock acts. But these days, it's her daughter-in-law, **Catrin Finch**, who is the country's (if not Britain's) foremost harpist. Official Harpist to the Prince of Wales for four years, Finch's wonderful recent collaborative album, *Clychau Dibon*, with Senegalese koro player Seckou Keita, earned her the Songlines Magazine Award for best cross-cultural album of 2014. In a similar vein, listen out, too, for young blues-folk harp songwriter **Georgia Ruth Williams**, whose 2013 album, *Week of Pines*, is sublime.

The father of Welsh folk, politician/songwriter **Dafydd Iwan**, remains as hugely popular and prolific as ever with charismatic performances and powerful albums such as 2007's *Man Gwyn* (featuring songs about the early Welsh emigration to Patagonia and North America). Songwriter **Meic Stevens** (often referred to as the "Welsh Bob Dylan") straddles folk and acoustic rock; if you get the chance to see him live, grab it. Singer/harpist **Siân James**, from mid-Wales, has found fame for her spine-tingling voice and exquisite tunes. Other female pacesetters include the Cardiff-born veteran singer **Heather Jones**, and the soulful **Julie Murphy**, born in Essex but now a fluent Welsh-speaker and part of Welsh cultural ambassadors, **Fernhill**.

There are now some terrific young bands to watch out for, including **Mabon**, a high-energy five-piece led by Celtic accordionist Jamie Smith. Likewise, **Elin and the**

GIGS AND FESTIVALS

VENUES

Listed approximately from south to north Wales.

Newport Folk Club Newport Fugitives Athletic Club, High Cross Rd, Rogerstone, Gwent (☎01633 897923, ⓦnewportfolkclub.co.uk). Sessions Thurs at 8.45pm plus occasional gigs.

Llantrisant Folk Club Pontyclun Athletic Club, Castan Road, Pontyclun (☎01443 226892, ⓦfolkwales.org.uk). International guest list mixed with local sessions centred on Welsh tunes. Wed at 8.30pm.

Castle Folk Club Glenbrook Inn, Coldbrook Road East, Barry (☎01446 402822, ⓦcastlefolk.com). All are welcome to perform. Second Tues of the month at 8.30pm.

Pembrokeshire Folk Fishguard Sessions at the Royal Oak, Fishguard (☎07934 418186, ⓦpembrokeshire-folk-music.co.uk). Tues at 8pm.

Pontardawe Acoustic Club Pontardawe Inn, 123 Herbert St, Pontardawe (☎01792 865087). Mainstay of the Welsh folk scene, good for anything from very traditional stuff to modern folk-rock. Wed at 8.30pm.

Halfpenny Folk Club The Greyhound, Oldwalls, nr Llanrhidian, Gower (☎01792 850803, ⓦhalfpenny folkclub.com). Designer clientele rub shoulders with the chunky jumper brigade. Sun at 8.30pm.

Llangollen Folk Club Sun Inn, 49 Regent St, Llangollen (☎01978 860233). Cheerful session and open mic. Wed at 8.30pm.

Conwy Folk Club Royal British Legion, Rosehill St, Conwy (☎01492 877324, ⓦconwyfolkclub.org.uk). Mon at 8pm.

FESTIVALS

Listed in chronological order.

Cwlwm Celtaidd Porthcawl ⓦcwlwmceltaidd.org. Fantastic, increasingly high-profile Celtic festival of pan-Celtic music and partying over a long weekend in early March.

Cadi Ha Holywell. Small traditional dance event. First weekend in May.

Tredegar House Festival Newport, Gwent ⓦtredegarhousefestival.org.uk. A laidback and enjoyable long weekend at the country house, good for session players and dancers. Mid-May.

Fishguard Folk Festival Pembrokeshire ⓦpembrokeshire-folk-music.co.uk. Small, traditional event with a good spread of international performers and plenty of busking. Late May.

Gower Folk Festival Greyhound Inn, Oldwalls, Gower peninsula ⓦgowerfolkfestival.co.uk. Varied and

high quality line-up in beautiful surroundings. Mid-June.

Gŵyl Ifan Cardiff ⓦgwylifan.org. Wales' biggest and most spectacular folk-dance festival, with hundreds of dancers giving displays throughout the city centre. Mid-June.

Sesiwn Fawr ("Big Session") Dolgellau ⓦsesiwnfawr .co.uk. This once-huge rock-fest returns to its Celtic roots with gigs over a week. Mid-July.

Pontardawe International Festival Pontardawe. One of Britain's flagship folk events, with an ambitious line-up of international performers heading for the Swansea Valleys town each year. Mid-August.

Green Man Festival Near Crickhowell ⓦgreenman .net. Wales' largest music festival, this fantastic three-day happening in the Brecon Beacons offers everything – including folk, new folk and Americana. Mid-August.

FOLK MUSIC RESOURCES

Cob Records ⓦcobrecords.com. Extensive mail-order business.

Cwmni Fflach ⓦfflach.co.uk. Great label, with indie, rock, pop, folk and choral releases.

Cymdeithas Genedlaethol Ddawns Werin Cymru (Welsh National Folk Dance Society) ⓦdawnsio .com/en. A useful source of events information with access to heaps of CDs, DVDs and dance pamphlets.

Sain ⓦsainwales.com. The major Welsh recording company.

St Fagans National History Museum Near Cardiff (see p.95). A vibrant museum and a vital centre for research and collecting work.

Taplas ⓦtaplas.co.uk. English-language bimonthly magazine of the folk scene in Wales; a great source for current events, with back editions archived on its website.

Tŷ Siamas Dolgellau ⓦtysiamas.com. The National Centre for Welsh Folk Music.

Tribalites and **Calan** feature a mix of Welsh and Irish traditions with a contemporary edge. All three bands regularly play high-profile festivals, garnering increased nationwide attention on the way.

English-language Welsh pop

The historic lack of international pop artists to emerge from Wales long blamed on the music-industry dominance of London-based labels and media – has changed utterly in the last couple of decades, at least for English-language groups. It started with the Manic Street Preachers in the early 1990s, who spawned an unprecedented interest in contemporary Welsh rock. London A&R reps descended on Cardiff and Newport in search of the next big thing, accelerating the careers of bands like the Super Furry Animals, Catatonia and the Stereophonics. Their widespread success has meant bands from Wales no longer feel hampered by their provenance, and there is a wealth of fine new talent coming through.

The early years

The most enduring name in English-language Welsh pop is 1960s sex symbol **Tom Jones**, now in his 70s and still pulling in crowds around the world. Similarly, Cardiff-born singer **Shirley Bassey** has carved out a hugely successful career since the mid-1950s, particularly with the immortal theme song to the 1964 James Bond film *Goldfinger*, and, in 1972, *Diamonds Are Forever*; her most recent crowning glory, however, came in 2007 when, aged 70, she played to a rapturous Glastonbury crowd.

Cardiff musician-turned-record-producer **Dave Edmunds**, whose first band Love Sculpture scored a UK hit in 1968, has had his hands on many a hit record since then – both as a producer and a solo performer – during the 1970s and 1980s. Classically trained pianist **John Cale** went to America in 1963 and found fame alongside Lou Reed with the **Velvet Underground**, one of the most influential avant-garde rock bands of the 1960s. Following his departure from the band, he worked as a producer and collaborator, working with the likes of Nick Drake and Brian Eno. In addition, he has recorded numerous solo records, his latest being the enjoyably odd *Shifty Adventures in Nookie Wood* (2012).

The 1980s music scene was generally pretty dire, though not just in Wales. Welsh rock music was personified by Rhyl's rabble-rousing rock fundamentalists **The Alarm**, fronted by Mike Peters, while Swansea's husky-toned rocker **Bonnie Tyler** was still building on the huge commercial success begun in the late 1970s. Possibly the most surprising Welsh success story of the 1980s was Fifties rock'n'roll impersonator **Shakin' Stevens**, who had a string of massive, nostalgia-driven hits.

The Welsh renaissance

It all changed in the 1990s following the emergence of South Wales rock nihilists the **Manic Street Preachers**. The band's first two albums merely set the scene for the industrial art-rock masterpiece that was *The Holy Bible* (1994), a record as thrilling and as visceral as any produced in the 1990s, and one that still resonates today. The 1995 disappearance, and presumed suicide, of fractured, anorexic guitarist Richey Edwards remains the band's defining moment, but they returned as a three-piece a year later, displacing their bedsit rock/punk for the anthemic *Everything Must Go* (1996), their most successful album to date, which also features their most famous song, the rousing *A Design for Life*. Their follow-up album, *This Is My Truth, Tell Me Yours* (1998), continued their progress to megastardom, though it took several patchy records before they discovered a return to form with the blistering *Journal for Plague Lovers*, the album featuring lyrics left to the band by Edwards. Their fine output has continued in recent years with the gorgeous, largely acoustic *Rewind the Film* (2013) and the heavy rock blast of *Futurology* (2014).

The now legendary Welsh bands compilation album *Dial M for Merthyr* (1995) showcased the Manics alongside many who subsequently became huge, all united by a tendency towards clever, zeitgeist lyrics and Welsh loquaciousness. Most exciting among them are the **Super Furry Animals**, whose fusion of Seventies psychedelia with new millennium clubland quirkiness and techno-geekery has created a niche all of their own.

Their ten albums to date range from poignant ballads to thumping raw rock, proving them to be masters of many genres and true innovators; their all-Welsh language album

Mwng (2000) became the best-selling work ever in Welsh. On sabbatical at the time of writing, a couple of the band members have undertaken solo projects, including the ever-prolific frontman, **Gruff Rhys**, whose two most recent releases, *Hotel Shampoo* (2011) and *American Interior* (2014), are typically off-kilter affairs, the latter a combined album/film project. Check out, too, Rhys' side-project, Neon Neon, and their two releases to date, *Stainless Style* (2008) and *Praxis Makes Perfect* (2013). Meanwhile, the Super Furries' keyboard player **Cian Ciaran** has also released two albums, the latest being the excellent *They Are Nothing Without Us* in 2013.

In a similar vein, indie-psych band **Gorky's Zygotic Mynci** were responsible for a handful of marvellously quirky records, such as the folksy *Barafundle* (1997) and the gorgeous *The Blue Trees* (2000), before splitting in 2006. Lead singer **Euro Childs** has gone on to carve out a similarly prolific solo career, his latest offering, *Situation Comedy* (2013), a piano-pop delight.

A more mainstream sound came from the likes of now-defunct **Catatonia**, whose Welsh-accented frontwoman **Cerys Matthews** was responsible for some wonderful lyrics; the most memorable of these feature on their best-selling album *International Velvet* (1998), whose title track contains the chorus "every day, when I wake up, I thank the Lord I'm Welsh" – still something of an unofficial national anthem. Yet another lead singer turned solo artist, Matthews' subsequent output has ranged from US-inspired country/folk to an album of traditional Welsh songs, *Hullabaloo* (2013).

Another of the big 1990s Welsh bands was Valleys outfit the **Stereophonics**, whose distinctive sound was shaped around singer Kelly Jones' rasping voice. Still recording, and regulars on the festival circuit, their 1997 debut *Word gets Around* remains their best record to date.

The new millennium

While the likes of the Manics and the SFA continue to produce exciting records, there has been a new generation of bands whose influence has come more from the thrashier elements of post-millennial American rock. South Wales has been a particularly fertile breeding ground for this angst-ridden wall of noise, producing some of the genre's most celebrated protagonists, notably Bridgend rockers **Funeral for a Friend** and **Bullet for My Valentine**. Spearheading the charge from North Wales, meanwhile, are **The Joy Formidable**, a powerful, guitar-heavy trio, whose ferocious 2013 album *Wolf's Law* demonstrates this to great effect.

Back in the mainstream, one of the major Welsh success stories has been **Duffy** (Aimee Anne Duffy); her debut album *Rockferry* (2008) showcased her big soulful voice to great effect, and also spawned saw the number one single *Mercy*, making Duffy the first Welsh female to achieve a number one pop single in a quarter of a century. Other bands making waves on the indie-rock and pop front include the ebullient Cardiff collective **Los Campesinos!**, and the poppier **Marina and the Diamonds**, fronted by the Abergavenny-born singer Marina Diamandis.

More offbeat is psych-folk singer **Cate Le Bon**, who first came to prominence providing guest vocals on albums by Neon Neon and the Manic Street Preachers.

EISTEDDFOD

The National Eisteddfod Society was formed in the 1860s, and today, three major week-long competitive events are held every year: the **Llangollen International Eisteddfod** (ⓦ international-eisteddfod.co.uk) in July; the **National Eisteddfod** (ⓦ eisteddfod.org.uk) in the first week of August; and the Urdd Eisteddfod (ⓦ urdd.org), Europe's largest youth festival, at the end of May. The National and the Urdd alternate between venues each year.

The competitions' rules have meant that eisteddfodau have helped formalize Welsh culture. Such parameter-defining is naturally alien to the free evolution of traditional song and music, but eisteddfodau have played a major role in keeping traditional music, song and dance at the heart of national expression.

ESSENTIAL LISTENING

Catatonia & Cerys Matthews *Way Beyond Blue* and *Hullabaloo*
Gorky's Zygotic Mynci & Euro Childs *The Blue Trees* and *Situation Comedy*
Los Campesinos! *Romance is Boring*
Manic Street Preachers *The Holy Bible* and *Journal for Plague Lovers*
Super Furry Animals *Rings around the World* and *Radiator*

Another who sings in both English and Welsh, she's now a bona fide star in her own right; seek out the slightly bonkers but utterly charming *Mug Museum* (2013).

There's a thriving **dance music** scene, too, in all its fragmented glory. Tongue-in-cheek Newport rappers **Goldie Lookin' Chain** had a mammoth following for a while. Rural west Wales is the base for dub gurus **Zion Train**, doing spliffed-up remakes of classic new wave tracks. Big beatz'n'breaks come from Cardiff's **Phantom Beats**. **Vandal** is a local hero in the dance music realm, as is James Hannam who operates as **Culprit One**.

Welsh-language rock

While English-language Welsh bands have usually enjoyed success by making their nationality an irrelevance, Welsh-language bands have highlighted their strong national identity, fostering a unique, self-propagating Welsh-language rock scene. Boundaries are now increasingly blurred: many bands choose to sing in both Welsh and English, simply because it's the way most of their members use both languages. Indeed, established English-language artists like the Super Furry Animals' frontman **Gruff Rhys** has raised the profile of Welsh-language music to new heights. But this is only a recent phenomenon and remains largely outside the mainstream.

The roots of this thriving, youthful and innovative scene owe much to the punk explosion of 1976 which kicked over many of rock's statues, partly thanks to the anarchic fervour of London bands like The Clash and the Sex Pistols, but also by virtue of its strong DIY ethic. The home-grown Welsh-language pop scene consolidated when in 1983 Caernarfon punk band **Anhrefn** (Disorder) set up **Recordiau Anhrefn**, churning out what it called "dodgy compilations of up-and-coming left-field weirdo Welsh bands". Throughout the 1980s, any band that couldn't get some sort of record deal would simply press their own vinyl and sell their records at gigs. From this era, perhaps the most enduring legacy is the band **Datblygu**, most often described as a Welsh version of spectacularly misanthropic The Fall. Meanwhile North Walians **Llwybr Llaethog** (Milky Way) were ploughing their anti-establishment furrow.

Such DIY efforts were boosted by Radio One DJ **John Peel** – to many, the standard-bearer for underground pop in the UK. Peel became aware of the growing number of Welsh-language bands and began playing their records on air and inviting them in for sessions. This introduced Welsh music to a Europe-wide audience and proved an important catalyst to new Welsh bands. By the 1990s, Welsh-language pop music had established a solid infrastructure of bands, labels and venues that continues to this day. One of the most prolific, eclectic and innovative of these labels is **Ankstmusik**, releasing Welsh-language pop of varied styles, best seen in some wonderful compilation albums, including *S4C Makes Me Want To Smoke Crack*. On the same label, former Tystion rapper Gruff Meredith has metamorphosed to great acclaim into **MC Mabon**.

Other major promoters of Welsh-language pop are the Caernarfon-based **Crai Records**, a subsidiary of the more folk-oriented **Sain Records** and the **Fflach** label in Aberteifi (Cardigan), and their subsidiary **Rasp** for dancier artistes and projects.

The grassroots Welsh **gig circuit** is also healthy, with a lively local pub and club scene. University student unions also regularly put on Welsh bands. Welsh-language pop bands can also be found at the **National Eisteddfod** (see box, p.457), and at local bars and clubs.

Film

Wales' wonderful scenery has formed the backdrop to many a film – from low-budget local efforts to *Lawrence of Arabia* and even Bollywood blockbusters. However, few of the big films have Welsh themes, and those that do have tended to be at the budget end of the spectrum, often playing on a slightly whimsical view of Wales. There's no doubting, though, that Wales has produced some of Britain's finest actors over the years, not least Richard Burton and Sir Anthony Hopkins; of the modern crop, A-listers include the likes of Christian Bale, Rhys Ifans, Ioan Gruffudd, Matthew Rhys and Michael Sheen. While such stellar names haven't necessarily helped the domestic industry, the Film Agency for Wales was established in 2006 with a charter "to ensure that the economic, cultural and educational aspects of film are effectively represented in Wales, the UK and the world".

This commitment to a viable and sustainable Welsh film industry was further boosted in 2014 when the famous Pinewood Studios set up studios in Cardiff. BBC Wales is also now very prominent down in Cardiff Bay, thanks to the hugely impressive Roath Lock Drama Village, where several of the BBC's flagship programmes are filmed, most notably *Doctor Who* (its spin-off, *Torchwood*, was also filmed here) and *Casualty*. Location-seekers should check out ⍵doctorwholocations.net, ⍵moviemapnorthwales .co.uk and ⍵visitwales.com/things-to-do/attractions/tv-film-locations.

American Interior (2014). Super Furry Animals frontman, Gruff Rhys, traverses the continent in this spontaneous docu-film in which he retraces the steps of his eighteenth-century relative, the explorer John Evans.

The Edge of Love (2008). Jealously threads this fairly limp exploration of the relationships between Dylan Thomas (Matthew Rhys), his wife (Sienna Miller) and his childhood sweetheart (Keira Knightley). Partly filmed in Thomas's old haunts on the Cambrian coast around New Quay.

First Knight (1995). Sean Connery stars as King Arthur, with Richard Gere as Sir Lancelot, in this patchy action film filmed largely in Snowdonia.

Happy Now (2001). Distinctly oddball thriller, filmed in and around Barmouth, which becomes the mysterious Welsh seaside town Pen-y-Wig.

Hedd Wyn (1992). First Oscar-nominated Welsh-language film, about the north Wales poet who went off to fight in World War I and never returned.

House of America (1997). Dark and depressing tale of secrets and yearning in a family stuck on a mouldering farm in west Wales.

How Green was my Valley (1941). None of it was filmed in Wales, but this Oscar-winning version of the classic Welsh book came to define the world image of Wales for generations.

Human Traffic (1999). Feelgood E-culture film, with a superb performance from John Simm, as well as a star cameo by Welsh drug-trafficking guru Howard Marks; fine soundtrack too. Filmed in Cardiff.

Inn of the Sixth Happiness (1958). Snowdonia puts in a fine performance as northern China in this Ingrid Bergman-led classic tale of self-discovery.

King Arthur (2004). Big-screen epic, with huge battles and a rather less sensational account of the "real" king of the Britons than had gone before. Ioan Gruffudd shines as Sir Lancelot.

Kyun! Ho Gaya Na Pyaar (2004). Translating as "It has happened – love", this is a big-budget Bollywood production, with former Miss World, Aishwarya Rai, as the love interest. Large sections were filmed in mid-Wales and Snowdonia.

On the Black Hill (1987). Hauntingly beautiful adaptation of the downbeat Bruce Chatwin novel about twin brothers growing up in the Black Mountains.

Patagonia (2011). Romantic road movie starring Matthew Rhys with parallel stories following both a Cardiff couple visiting Welsh Patagonia and two Patagonians travelling through Wales. Not entirely successful, but sumptuously shot and includes an odd cameo by Duffy.

Pride (2014). Delightful film recalling the true story of how a group of gay and lesbian activists decided to raise money for the families of miners in a Welsh village during the 1984 Miners' Strike.

The Prisoner (1971). Big-screen version of the enigmatic cult TV series, also filmed largely at the fantasy village of Portmeirion.

Sleep Furiously (2008). This tender documentary tells about the slow decline of Trefuerig, the tiny Ceredigion farming village where director, Gideon Koppel, grew up after his parents sought refuge from Nazi Germany there.

Solomon a Gaenor (1998). Filmed in both Welsh and English versions, this Oscar-nominated weepie is a *Romeo and Juliet* tale set in the Valleys in Edwardian times.

Submarine (2011). Richard Ayoade's quirky, funny and warm-hearted coming-of-age drama is set in 1980s Swansea. Wonderfully offbeat.

Tiger Bay (1959). Cardiff Bay provides a suitably gritty backdrop to this engrossing British crime drama, starring John and Hayley Mills, the latter starring in her film debut.

Twin Town (1997). Entertaining drug-fuelled romp set in Swansea that introduced Rhys Ifans to the world, who actually stars here with his brother, Llyr.

Under Milk Wood (1972). Phantasmagoric take on the classic Dylan Thomas "play for voices", with an all-star cast including Richard Burton and Elizabeth Taylor. Filmed partly in Fishguard.

Very Annie Mary (2001). Offbeat tale of love and singing in the Valleys, with Ioan Gruffudd and Matthew Rhys camping it up to the nines as the only gays in the village.

Books

Some of the books listed here are published by small local presses, and you're unlikely to find them in bookshops outside Wales, though most can be ordered online. The Welsh Books Council website (@gwales.com) sells a huge selection, and you'll often be able to pick up rare and out-of-print titles by scouring the many independent or secondhand bookshops in Wales – Hay-on-Wye is particularly good for the latter.

For information on readings and literary events throughout the year, check out Literature Wales (@literaturewales.org), while The New Welsh Review (@newwelshreview.com) is an excellent resource for all the latest book releases. Welsh fiction is undergoing something of a renaissance; look out for works by the current leading crop of Welsh wordsmiths, spanning a wide range of styles and subject matters. Ones to watch include English-language writers such as Trezza Azzopardi, Kitti Harri, Rachel Tresize and Dannie Abse, and Welsh-language authors including Tony Bianchi, Gwyn Jenkins, Ceri Wyn Jones and Alan Llwyd. A good place to start for fans of fiction is *Rarebit, New Welsh Fiction*, an anthology of short stories.

TRAVEL AND IMPRESSIONS

★**George Borrow** *Wild Wales*. Highly entertaining and easy-to-read account of the author's walking tour of Wales in 1854.

Giraldus Cambrensis (Gerald of Wales) *The Journey Through Wales* and *The Description of Wales*. Learned ruminations and unreserved opinions form the basis of two witty and frank books in one volume, written in Latin by the quarter-Welsh clergyman after his 1188 tour around Wales recruiting for the Third Crusade. *The Journey* "through our rough, remote and inaccessible countryside" contains anecdotes and ecclesiastical point-scoring, while *The Description* covers rural life.

★**Gwynfor Evans** *Eternal Wales* (published as *Cymru o Hud* in Welsh). With magnificently moody photography by Marian Delyth, this is a passionate and erudite tour de force through some of Wales' lesser-known corners.

Peter Finch *Real Cardiff, Real Cardiff Two* and *Real Cardiff Three*. Compelling ambles around the Welsh capital, full of oddball nuggets and with a terrific sense of context and place.

Jon Gower and Jeremy Moore *Wales at Water's Edge*. Beautifully produced coffee-table book documenting – both verbally and visually – the wonderful Welsh coastline, published to coincide with the opening of the All Wales Coastal Path in 2012.

Jeremy Moore and Nigel Jenkins *Wales, The Lie of the Land*. A gorgeous, glossy tome that combines the luscious photography of Jeremy Moore and the musings of poet Nigel Jenkins. Spirited, passionate and a fine souvenir of contemporary Wales.

★**Jan Morris** *Wales: Epic Views of a Small Country*. Prolific half-Welsh travel writer Jan Morris immerses herself in the country that she evidently loves. Highly partisan and fiercely nationalistic, the book combs over the origins of the Welsh character and describes the people and places of Wales with precision and affection.

H.V. Morton *In Search of Wales*. Learned, lively and typically enthusiastic snapshots of Welsh life in the early 1930s. A companion volume to his *In Search of England*.

★**Mike Parker** *Neighbours from Hell?* English émigré Parker holds few punches as he rips into English attitudes to Wales, the Welsh and all things Cymric. A hugely entertaining romp through history, politics, the nature of Welsh tourism, sex and the royal family.

★**Jim Perrin** *Snowdon, The Story of a Welsh Mountain*. Dense, riveting and highly personal account of the iconic mountain, placed within the wider context of the region's history, language and folklore. Great footnotes, too.

Pamela Petro *Travels in an Old Tongue*. An American woman comes to Wales to study, is bewitched by the place, attempts to learn Welsh and then sets off on a global pursuit of Welsh enclaves and speakers from Japan to Norway, Germany and Patagonia. Funny, informative and extremely perceptive about the language and its wider cultural significance.

Peter Sager *Wales*. A passionate and fabulously detailed 400-page celebratory essay on Wales, and especially its people, by a German convert to the cause of all things Welsh.

Meic Stephens *A Most Peculiar People: Quotations About Wales and the Welsh*. Varied volume of quotations going back to the century before Christ and up to 2000. As a portrait of the nation, with all of its frustrating idiosyncrasies and endearing foibles, it is a superb example.

HISTORY, SOCIETY, ART AND CULTURE

Jane Aaron et al (ed) *Our Sisters' Land: The Changing Identities of Women in Wales*. A series of challenging and well-written essays that delve deep into male-dominated Welsh society, from the home to the political system. Includes personal testimonies and some startling facts about just how entrenched bigotry still is within much of the Welsh establishment.

Richard Booth *My Kingdom of Books*. Typically bullish autobiography by the man who made Hay-on-Wye the world's biggest secondhand bookshop. Some interesting stuff on his tussles with authority and his semi-serious declaration of Hay as an independent country.

Janet Davies *The Welsh Language*. Very readable history and assessment of one of Europe's oldest living languages. Packed full of maps showing the demographic and geographic spread of Welsh over the ages.

★**John Davies** *A History of Wales*. Exhaustive run through Welsh history and culture from the earliest inhabitants to the twenty-first century. This is clearly written and very readable, but at 700 pages, it's hardly concise.

Gwynfor Evans *Land of My Fathers* and *For the Sake of Wales*. Plaid Cymru's late elder statesman first produced the former tome in Welsh, translating it into English for publication forty years ago. It's a thorough and polemical history of the country. The latter work, his autobiography, covers Welsh political and social life from World War II to the National Assembly. Hugely readable and inspirational.

Geoffrey of Monmouth *History of the Kings of Britain*. First published in 1136, this is the basis of almost all Arthurian legend. Writers throughout Europe and beyond used Geoffrey's unreliable history as the basis of a complex corpus of myth.

Jon Gower *The Story of Wales*. Gower's book is a spin-off from the television series – he's a former BBC Wales Arts and Media correspondent – but it's no worse for that; concise and well structured, the coverage of the country's recent history is particularly lucid.

★**Ron Jones and Joe Lovejoy** *The Auschwitz Goalkeeper: A Prisoner of War's True Story*. Written with the football correspondent of the *Guardian* newspaper, this is Welshman Jones' extraordinary account of his incarceration in Auschwitz following his capture in North Africa; the aftermath of Auschwitz is no less gruelling, including the infamous death marches.

Alan Llwyd *Cymru Ddu/Black Wales: A History*. A long and insightful look at the history of multi-racial Wales in both Welsh and English.

Peter Lord *The Visual Culture of Wales*. Lavishly produced and beautifully illustrated three-volume overview of the art and architecture of Wales, from the early industrial society to the present day.

Elizabeth Mavor *The Ladies of Llangollen*. The best of the books on Wales' most celebrated lesbian couple traces the ladies' inauspicious beginnings in Ireland, their spectacular elopement and the way that their Llangollen home, Plas Newydd, became a place of pilgrimage for dozens of influential eighteenth-century visitors.

Owen Sheers *Calon*. Written by the Welsh Rugby Union's poet in residence, this is not only a riveting account of one year spent with the national team, but also goes to the heart of what rugby means to the Welsh. Check out, too, his non-fiction narrative, *The Dust Diaries*, set in Zimbabwe.

LITERATURE

Enid Blyton *Five Get Into a Fix*. In this, the seventeenth of Blyton's timeless series of kids' adventure novels, Julian, Dick, Anne, George and Timmy the dog unearth secret passageways to rescue an old woman from a sinister tower in the snowy Welsh mountains. Vintage "Famous Five".

Bruce Chatwin *On the Black Hill*. This entertaining and finely wrought novel follows the Jones twins' eighty-year tenure of a farm on the mid-Wales border with England. Chatwin casts his sharp eye for detail over both the minutiae of nature and the universal human condition, providing a gentle angle on Welsh–English antipathy.

★**Alexander Cordell** *The Fire People*. Set against the backdrop of the Merthyr Tydfil riots of 1831, this is a feisty fictionalization of the life and unjust death of Dic Penderen, the "first Welsh Martyr of the working class". The same author's *Rape of the Fair Country*, *Hosts of Rebecca* and *Song of the Earth* form a dramatic historical trilogy in the bestseller tradition, partly set in the cottages on the site of the Blaenafon ironworks during the lead-up to the Chartist Riots. *This Sweet and Bitter Earth* immortalizes Blaenau

Ffestiniog in a lusty slate epic.

Lewis Davies *Work, Sex and Rugby*. Perennially popular novel that tells you all you need to know (and much you don't) about Valleys men.

Richard John Evans *Entertainment*. Scabrous roller-coaster ride through Rhondda living and loving, guaranteed to offend and cause maximum hilarity.

Thomas Firbank *I Bought a Mountain*. One of the few popular books set in north Wales, in which Anglo–Canadian Firbank spins an autobiographical yarn of his purchase of most of the Glyder range and subsequent life as a Snowdonian sheep farmer during the 1930s.

Iris Gower *Copper Kingdom*, *Proud Mary*, *Spinners' Wharf*, *Black Gold*, *Fiddler's Ferry*, *The Oyster Catchers* – the list goes on. Romantic novels by Wales' most popular author, who died in 2010, mostly set in and around Swansea and the Gower (from which she took her pen name).

★**Niall Griffiths** *Grits*, *Sheepshagger*, *Kelly + Victor*, *Stump*, *Wreckage*, *Runt*. Arguably the best dissector of darkness, drugs, comradeship and hopelessness in modern

Britain, Griffiths' panoply of novels set between Aberystwyth and Liverpool are suffused with a metaphysical sense of culture and landscape.

Emyr Humphreys *The Gift of a Daughter*. The mood and landscape of Anglesey is beautifully evoked by perhaps the greatest living Welsh novelist. His final publication, a collection of short stories called *The Woman at the Window*, shows that the nonagenerian has lost none of his powers.

Siân James *Not Singing Exactly*. Dazzling and diverse short-story collection from one of Wales' premier romantic novelists. In *The Sky over Wales*, she recalls her childhood days in the 1930s in a series of charming vignettes.

★ **Cynan Jones** *The Long Dry*. Set in coastal west Wales over the course of one hot summer's day, this is an engaging tale of one farmer's struggle with life on the land. The rural theme is continued to even more thrilling effect in *The Dig*, a tense short story which explores the fate of a recently widowed farmer and his relationship with a badger-baiter.

Glyn Jones *The Island of Apples*. Set in south Wales and Carmarthen in the early years of the twentieth century, this is an artful portrayal of a sensitive Valleys youth's enthralment in the glamour of the district's new arrival.

Gwyn and Thomas Jones (trans) *The Mabinogion*. Welsh mythology's classic, these eleven orally developed heroic tales were finally transcribed into *The White Book of Rhydderch* (around 1300–25) and *The Red Book of Hergest* (1375–1425). Originally translated by Lady Charlotte Guest between 1838 and 1849 at the beginning of the Celtic revival.

Lewis Jones *Cwmardy*. Longtime favourite socialist novel, written in 1937 and portraying life in a Rhondda Valley mining community in the early years of the twentieth century. Followed by its sequel, *We Live*.

Tia Jones *The Moss Gatherers*. Two rural communities either side of the Irish Sea provide the backdrop to this atmospheric story of family intrigue and betrayal.

Richard Llewellyn *How Green Was My Valley, Up into the Singing Mountain, Down Where the Moon is Small* and *Green, Green My Valley Now*. Vital tetralogy in eloquent and passionate prose, following the life of Huw Morgan from his youth in a south Wales mining valley through emigration to the Welsh community in Patagonia and back to 1970s Wales. A bestseller during World War II and still the best introduction to the vast canon of "valleys novels", *How Green Was My Valley* captured a longing for a simple, if tough, life, steering clear of cloying sentimentality.

★ **Caradoc Pritchard** *One Moonlit Night*. Dense, swirling tale of a young boy's emotional and sexual awakenings in an isolated north Wales village. Full-blooded Welsh prose at its most charged.

Malcolm Pryce *Aberystwyth Mon Amour*. Surprise bestseller in the shape of this furious, funny black comedy set in an Aberystwyth overlaid with film-noir surrealism and dastardly twists of plot. Follow-ups *Last Tango in Aberystwyth, The Unbearable Lightness of Being in Aberystwyth* and *Don't Cry for me Aberystwyth* are just as entertaining.

Kate Roberts *The Living Sleep* and *Feet in Chains*, among others. Penned by the pre-eminent Welsh-language writer of the twentieth century, these two novels, available in English translation, tell tales of life in a north Wales slate village.

★ **Dylan Thomas** *Collected Stories*. All of Thomas' classic prose pieces: *Quite Early One Morning*, which metamorphosed into *Under Milk Wood*, the magical *A Child's Christmas in Wales* and the compulsive, crackling autobiography *Portrait of the Artist as a Young Dog*. In all of Thomas' works, the language still burns bright.

★ **Dylan Thomas** *Under Milk Wood*. Thomas' most popular play tells the story of a microcosmic Welsh seaside town (modelled on New Quay) over a 24-hour period. Ideally, obtain a recorded version of the play to absorb its rich poetry (or, as Thomas himself described it, "prose with blood pressure").

Alice Thomas Ellis (ed) *Wales – An Anthology*. A beautiful book, combining poetry, folklore and prose stories rooted in places throughout Wales. All subjects, from rugby and mountain-climbing to contemporary descriptions of major events, are included in an enjoyably eclectic mixture of styles. Excellent introduction to Welsh writing.

Rachel Trezise *In and Out of the Goldfish Bowl*. Now firmly established as one Wales' brightest authors, Rachel Trezise's unsparing account of one girl's life growing up in the Rhonnda is a great read. Her latest offering, *Cosmic Latte*, is a fine collection of short stories, featuring an array of wonderfully disparate characters.

★ **Charlotte Williams** *Sugar and Slate*. Humorous and unstintingly honest memoir of mixed identity: the author is the daughter of a black Guyanese father who grew up in a Welsh-speaking community.

John Williams *The Cardiff Trilogy*. Omnibus of Williams' contemporary low-life Cardiff crime writing containing: *Five Pubs, Two Bars and a Nightclub*, a very funny short-story collection that inspired the E-culture hit film *Human Traffic*; *Cardiff Dead*, a full-length novel that packs in the Welsh cultural references effortlessly and to great effect; and *Temperance Town*, a novella in the same vein.

Raymond Williams *Border Country*. 1960 novel that perfectly captures the sense of change overwhelming rural Welsh life in that era. A timeless classic.

TOP 5 WELSH READS

Jan Morris *Wales: Epic Views of a Small Country*
Mike Parker *Neighbours from Hell?*
Niall Griffiths *Grits*
Caradoc Pritchard *One Moonlit Night*
R.S. Thomas *Selected Poems*

POETRY

★**Dannie Abse** *Welsh Retrospective* and *Arcadia, One Mile*. Two superb collections from one of Wales' most prolific twentieth-century poets, showing his huge range of intellectual interests and warm, beguiling style of writing. Now in his 90s, his latest work, *Speak, Old Parrot*, reflects on his Jewish upbringing, among other subjects.

John Barnie *The City* and *The Confirmation*. One of Wales' best contemporary writers, notable mainly for his combination of poetry and prose styles, narration and description. Evocative tales of wartime childhood and stifling parenting, leading to a poignant search for love.

Gillian Clarke *Collected Poems*. A good introduction to the nature-inspired and homely poetry of one of Wales' leading contemporary writers and the current National Poet. Her latest work, *Ice*, is a delightful set of poems on a distinctly wintery theme.

Dafydd Johnston *Iolo Goch: Poems*. All of the surviving poems of Owain Glyndŵr's court bard are shown in translation and context. A fascinating insight into courtly medieval Wales at a time of great national resurgence.

Gwyneth Lewis *Keeping Mum*. Wales' first-ever National Poet shows her verbal power and dexterity with this 2003 collection, especially when combing over the irregularities of bilingual existence.

Robert Minhinnick *Selected Poems*. Overview of the early career of one of Wales' finest poets: best when picking over his English-speaking south Walian youth in rich, impassioned imagery.

Meic Stephens (ed) *New Companion to the Literature of Wales*. A customarily thorough volume of Welsh prose, spanning the centuries from the folk tales of *The Mabinogion* to modern-day writings.

Dylan Thomas *Collected Poems*. Though Thomas is renowned for his dense and difficult poems, look out for lighter works which resound with perfect metre and precise structure. Classics include *Do Not Go Gentle Into That Good Night*, a passionate yet calm elegy to his dying father.

★**R.S. Thomas** *Selected Poems*. Thomas wrote poetry that tugs at issues such as religion (he was an Anglican priest), Wales ("brittle with relics") and the family. His passion shines throughout this book, probably the best overview of his prolific work.

★**Harri Webb** (ed Meic Stephens) *Collected Poems*. Fine collection of 350 works by a modern-day patriot and poet of biting satire and eloquent expression.

WILDLIFE AND THE ENVIRONMENT

Douglas Botting *Wild Britain: A Traveller's Guide*. Not much use for species identification but plenty of information on access to the best sites and what to expect when you get there. Excellent photos.

Collins Field Guides Series of thorough, pocket-sized identification guides. Topics include insects, butterflies, wildflowers, mushrooms and toadstools, birds, mammals, reptiles and fossils.

★**William Condry and Jeremy Moore** *Heart of the Country*. Jeremy Moore's gorgeous photography is the perfect accompaniment to the late William Condry's Country Diary entries from the *Guardian*.

David Saunders *Where to Watch Birds in Wales*. Enthusiasts' guide to Wales' prime birding locations, along with a bird-spotting calendar and a list of English–Welsh–scientific bird names. Not an identification guide.

OUTDOOR PURSUITS

Cicerone Guides *The Ridges of Snowdonia, Hill Walking in Snowdonia, Ascent of Snowdon, Welsh Winter Climbs, Scrambles in Snowdonia* and others. Clearly written pocket guides to the best aspects of Welsh mountain activities.

Ordnance Survey National Trail Guides Large paperback editions full of instructive descriptions and additional side-walks from *Offa's Dyke North, Offa's Dyke South, Glyndŵr's Way* and *Pembrokeshire Coast Path*.

★**Carl Rogers** *Mountain and Hill Walking in Snowdonia*. Superb pocket hikers' guide in two volumes, the first covering Snowdon and its environs, the second detailing southern Snowdonia. Beautifully produced with great photos, detailed colour maps, and info on the best parking spots and even some of the easier scrambles.

Welsh

The Welsh language, Cymraeg, is spoken widely throughout the country and as a first language in many parts of the west and north. Its survival and resurgence is remarkable considering that the heart of English culture and its language – the most expansionist the world has ever seen – lies right next door.

Brief history

The Welsh language can be traced back to the sixth century. Celtic inscriptions on stones, a section of written Welsh in the eighth-century **Lichfield Gospels**, the tenth-century codified laws of Hywel Dda in neat Welsh prose, and the twelfth- and thirteenth-century **Mabinogion** folk tales (believed to have been collated from earlier Welsh writings) show that Welsh was a thriving language for centuries. Moreover, the early language is still identifiable and easily comprehensible for any modern-day Welsh-speaker.

English domination since the Norman era has been mirrored in the fate of the Welsh tongue. The Norman lords were implanted in castles throughout Wales to subjugate the natives, with official business conducted in their native French.

Real linguistic warfare came with the 1536 **Act of Union** (see box, p.436), which legitimized the growing practice of imposing English lords and churchmen on the restless, but effectively cowed, Welsh. It is likely that the language would have died out, but William Morgan's 1588 **translation of the Bible** into Welsh brought Welsh into the everyday public arena, ultimately ensuring its survival. Certainly, new and Nonconformist religious movements from the seventeenth century onwards embraced the language.

In the first half of the nineteenth century, over ninety percent of the country's population spoke Welsh, with English dominant in pockets of Pembrokeshire and along the English border. But as the **Industrial Revolution** progressed, mine owners and capitalists from England came into the rapidly urbanizing southeastern corner of Wales, substantially diluting the language.

In 1854, **George Borrow** undertook his marathon tour of Wales and noted the state of the native tongue throughout. As a natural linguist, he had mastered Welsh and fired questions at people he encountered as to their proficiency in both Welsh and English. The picture he paints is of poorer people tending to be monolingual Welsh-speakers, wealthier people and those near the border bilingual.

Discouragement of Welsh continued in many guises, most notably in it being forbidden in schools in the latter half of the nineteenth and early twentieth centuries. Anyone caught speaking in Welsh had to wear a "**Welsh Not**", a piece of wood on a leather strap that would only be passed on if someone else was heard using the language. At the end of the school day, the child still wearing the Welsh Not was soundly beaten. It is hardly surprising that use of the language plummeted.

The politics of the language

Welsh has survived thanks to those who campaigned to save it, principally the eisteddfod revivalists of the eighteenth century and the political movements of the twentieth century. The formation of **Plaid Cymru**, the Welsh National Party, in 1925 was largely around the issue of language, as indeed its politics have been ever since.

Concerns about the language reached a zenith with the 1962 radio broadcast *Tynged yr iaith* (The Fate of the Language) by the Plaid founder member, Saunders Lewis. This became a rallying cry that resulted in the formation of Cymdeithas yr Iaith Gymraeg, the **Welsh Language Society**, the following year. One of the most high-profile early campaigns was the daubing of monoglot English road signs with their Welsh translations. Nearly all signs are now in both languages. A 1967 Welsh Language Act allowed many forms of officialdom to be conducted in either language, stating that Welsh, for the first time in over four hundred years, had "equal validity" with English.

Welsh-medium education also blossomed, with bilingual teaching in all primary schools and for at least a year in all secondary schools. In traditionally Welsh-speaking areas students got five years of Welsh, and since 2000 all Welsh schools much teach Welsh up to age 16. Increasing numbers of schools all over the land educate their students in all subjects through the Welsh language. Early objections from some non-Welsh-speaking parents that their children were being "forced" to learn a "dead" language have now largely abated. Welsh-language university courses are also becoming more popular, so, for pretty much the first time in Wales' history, it is possible to be educated in Welsh from nursery to degree level.

The other modern cornerstone for developing Welsh has been **broadcast media**. The BBC Welsh-language Radio Cymru began in the late 1970s, to be joined – after a considerable battle – by the S4C TV station in 1982. Together, they have sponsored and programmed popular Welsh learners' programmes and given the old language greater space than it has ever enjoyed before.

The situation today

Welsh-language classes are now offered right across the country, as well as outside the country in language centres across Britain, and universities in Europe and North America.

The Welsh language is both one of Wales' key strengths and its key drawbacks in the quest for some sort of national emancipation. There is still suspicion towards the Welsh-speaking "elite" who are seen to control the media and local government in the

THE FALL AND RISE OF CYMRAEG

According to the first British census of 1851, 90 percent of Welsh people spoke Welsh. Every decade thereafter the figures dipped quite spectacularly – 49.9 percent in 1901, 37.1 percent in 1921, 28.9 percent in 1951 and 18.9 percent in 1981. Then, in 1991 and again in 2001, the percentage of Welsh-speakers rose slightly. The proportion still hovered around the one-fifth mark but the most marked increase was among the lower age groups, those most able to ensure its future.

From the sharp decline of the mid-twentieth century, it's a dramatic turnabout and testament to bold policies, particularly in education and mass media. National TV and radio stations broadcast in Welsh, road signs are written in both Welsh and English, official publications, many tourist brochures and even restaurant menus are bilingual, Welsh-medium schools are everywhere, books in Welsh are published at a growing rate of around four hundred every year, and magazines, newspapers and websites in the old language are mushrooming.

WHERE WELSH IS SPOKEN

According to the 2011 census, nineteen percent of the population speak Welsh, but the spread is far from even, with a far lower percentage of speakers in the populous and anglicized regions of Gwent and around Cardiff; that said, this is one of the few areas where the language is actually growing in popularity. Although it is unusual to hear Welsh regularly in the border counties, it is commonly understood throughout most of West Glamorgan, Carmarthenshire, the northern half of Pembrokeshire and around Cardigan Bay. The northwestern corner, centred on Snowdonia, Anglesey and the Llŷn, is the real stronghold of Welsh, reflected in these areas' steadfast political affiliation to Welsh nationalism.

THE CELTIC LANGUAGE FAMILY

The original Celtic tongue was spoken over a wide area, gradually dividing into two forms which, although there are occasional similarities, have little in common. Goidelic (or Q-Celtic) is now spoken in the Isle of Man, Ireland and Scotland; **Brythonic** (P-Celtic) is spoken in Wales, Cornwall (where it is barely hanging on), and Brittany.

country. Welsh nationalism is so defined by the language that Plaid Cymru has nearly always had great difficulty in appealing to those who speak only English, particularly in the urban southeast. Nonetheless, the Welsh language continues to flourish. The **Welsh Language Board** was formed in 1994, and with the arrival of the **National Assembly** in 1999, with around half of its members proficient in Welsh, the language has gained a number of firm footholds in official life. In 2010 the Welsh Assembly unanimously passed the **Welsh Language Measure**, which puts Welsh on equal footing with English, though some contend it still doesn't make Welsh an official language in all cases. Still, its other provisions should ensure that Welsh continues to flourish. Increasingly, Wales is developing as a model bilingual entity, in which there is room for both languages to thrive together.

Speaking Welsh

Although Welsh words, place names in particular, can appear bewilderingly incomprehensible, the rules of the language are far more strictly adhered to than in English. Thus, mastering the basic constructions and breaking words down into their constituent parts means that pronunciation need not be anywhere near as difficult as first imagined.

The Welsh alphabet

The Welsh **alphabet** is similar to the English, though there are no letters j, k, v, x and z in Welsh, except in occasional words appropriated from other languages. As well as the five English vowels, Welsh has y and w. Most vowels have two sounds, long and short: a is long as in car, short as in fat; e long as in there, short as in pet; i long as in sea, short as an tin; o long as in more, short as in dog; u roughly like a Welsh i; w long as in soon, short as in look; y long as in sea and short as in bun or pin. A circumflex over any vowel lengthens its sound. **Adjoining vowels** are pronounced as the two separate sounds, with the stress generally on the first.

Welsh **consonants** are pronounced in similar ways to English, except c and g are always hard as in cat and gut (never soft as in nice or rage), and f is always pronounced as v as in vine. Additional consonants are ch, pronounced as in German or as in loch, dd, pronounced as a hard th as in those, ff and ph as a soft f as in five, and si as in shoe. The Welsh consonant that causes most problems is ll, featured in many place names such as Llangollen. This has no direct parallel in English, although the tl sound in Bentley comes close. The proper way to pronounce it is to place the tongue firmly behind the top row of teeth and breathe through it without consciously making a voiced sound.

Some Welsh words also **mutate**, where a word affects the beginning of a following one, principally to ease pronunciation. Prepositions commonly mutate the following word, turning an initial B into F or M, an initial C into G or Ngh, a D into Dd or N, F into B or M, G into Ngh or the initial letter being dropped altogether, Ll into L, M into F, P into B, Mh or Ph, T into Th, D or Nh. Thus, "in Cardiff (Caerdydd)" is "yng Nghaerdydd" (note that the "yn" also mutates to ease pronunciation) and "from Bangor" is "o Fangor". Mutated words are extremely common in the component parts of place names.

WELSH VOCABULARY

mouth of a river; confluence of two rivers	Aber	literally "curved stone", generally used to refer to megalithic burial chambers	Cromlech
river	Afon	valley	Cwm
Scotland	Alban	public	Cyhoeddus
museum	Amgeuddfa	society	Cymdeithas
son of	Ap (ab)	Welsh	Cymraeg
open	Ar Agor	Welshness	Cymreictod
closed	Ar Gau	Wales	Cymru
for sale	Ar Werth	the Welsh people	Cymry
slow	Araf	good	Da
small, lesser	Bach	south	De
bread	Bara	Saint David	Dewi Sant
good morning	Bore da	no (as an instruction), nothing	Dim
morning	Bore	fort	Din or dinas
slope of a hill	Bron	thank you	Diolch
hill	Bryn	end	Diwedd
mountain pass	Bwlch	over	Dros
table	Bwrdd	black	Du
bus	Bws	water	Dŵr
stronghold, chair	Cadair	day	Dydd
fort	Caer	vale	Dyffryn
song	Cân	man (men)	Dyn (-ion)
centre	Canol	church	Eglwys
hundred	Cant	festival	Eisteddfod
chapel	Capel	ridge	Esgair
stone	Carreg	small, lesser	Fach
home	Cartref	big, greater	Fawr
castle	Castell	farm	Fferm
national	Cenedlaethol	road	Ffordd
meadow	Clun	forest	Fforest
gate, perch	Clwyd	garden	Gardd
red	Coch	blue	Glas
forest, woodland	Coed	valley	Glyn
rock	Craig	hotel	Gwesty
artificial island on a lake	Crannog	white	Gwyn
craft	Crefft	temporary summer-house	Hafod
welcome	Croeso	half	Hanner
rood screen	Croglen		

RESOURCES FOR WELSH LEARNERS

Acen ☎ 029 2030 0800, 🌐 acen.co.uk. Cardiff-based, S4C-originated company providing a multimedia Welsh course, a Welsh-learners' magazine and copious numbers of useful contacts.

Cymdeithas Madog (Welsh Studies Institute in North America) 🌐 madog.org. Runs an annual week-long residential language course in the US or Canada, plus a directory of resources.

Cymdeithas yr Iaith (Welsh Language Society) ☎ 01970 624501, 🌐 cymdeithas.org. Campaigning and political organization dedicated to improving the status of the Welsh language.

Nant Gwrtheyrn ☎ 01758 750334, 🌐 nant gwrtheyrn.org. Residential national language centre on the coast of the Llŷn (see p.52).

National Language Unit of Wales ☎ 029 2026 5000, 🌐 wjec.co.uk/nlu. Provides a comprehensive guide to Welsh teaching provision.

today	Heddiw	good afternoon	P'nhawn da
police	Heddlu	vale	Pant
old	Hen	park	Parc
road	Heol	football	Pêl-droed
longing, yearning	Hiraeth	head, top (as of a valley)	Pen
spirit	Hwyl	village	Pentre(f)
lower	Isaf	the Party of Wales	Plaid Cymru
language	Laith	hall, mansion	Plas
sacred enclosure, early church	Llan	bridge	Pont
lodging place, B&B	Llety	port, gateway	Porth
England	Lloegr	hill	Rhiw
path	Llwybr	English language	Saesneg
book	Llyfr	Englishman	Sais
lake	Llyn	saint	Sant
place, court	Llys	Parliament	Senedd
stone	Maen	hello	Shwmae
field	Maes	shop	Siop
market	Marchnad	county, shire	Sir
big, greater	Mawr	street	Stryd
mill	Melin	how are you?	Sut ydych chi? (formal)
woman	Menyw		or Sut ywt ti? (informal)
burial place of saint	Merthyr	office	Swyddfa
mile	Milltir	post office	Swyddfa'r Post
bare or rounded mountain	Moel	pub	Tafarn
sea	Môr	beach	Traeth
coastal marsh	Morfa	town	Tref
mountain	Mynydd	tower	Tŵr
valley, stream	Nant	house	Tŷ
hall	Neuadd	uppermost, highest	Uchaf
new	Newydd	the	Y, Yr or 'r
to swim	Nofio	island	Ynys
good night	Nos da	hospital	Ysbyty
good evening	Noswaith dda	school	Ysgol
please	Os gwelwch chi'n dda		

WELSH NUMBERS

1	un	20	dau-ddeg
2	dau (fem. dwy)	21	dau-ddeg-un
3	tri (fem. tair)	22	dau-ddeg-dau
4	pedwar (fem. pedair)	30	tri-deg
5	pump	40	pedwar-deg
6	chwech	50	pum-deg
7	saith	60	chwe-deg
8	wyth	70	saith-deg
9	naw	80	wyth-deg
10	deg	90	naw-deg
11	un-deg-un	100	cant
12	un-deg-dau	200	dau gant
13	un-deg-tri	1000	mil

Small print and index

A ROUGH GUIDE TO ROUGH GUIDES

Published in 1982, the first Rough Guide – to Greece – was a student scheme that became a publishing phenomenon. Mark Ellingham, a recent graduate in English from Bristol University, had been travelling in Greece the previous summer and couldn't find the right guidebook. With a small group of friends he wrote his own guide, combining a highly contemporary, journalistic style with a thoroughly practical approach to travellers' needs.

The immediate success of the book spawned a series that rapidly covered dozens of destinations. And, in addition to impecunious backpackers, Rough Guides soon acquired a much broader readership that relished the guides' wit and inquisitiveness as much as their enthusiastic, critical approach and value-for-money ethos.

These days, Rough Guides include recommendations from budget to luxury and cover more than 120 destinations around the globe, as well as producing an ever-growing range of ebooks.

Visit **roughguides.com** to find all our latest books, read articles, get inspired and share travel tips with the Rough Guides community.

Rough Guide credits

Editors: Alison Morris, Natasha Foges, Emma Gibbs, Melissa Graham
Layout: Jessica Subramanian
Cartography: Lokamata Sahu
Picture editor: Rhiannon Furbear-Williams
Proofreader: Susannah Wight
Managing editor: Mani Ramaswamy
Assistant editor: Payal Sharotri
Production: Emma Sparks

Cover design: Nicole Newman, Rhiannon Furbear-Williams, Jessica Subramanian
Photographers: Diana Jarvis, Scott Stickland, Paul Whitfield
Editorial assistant: Rebecca Hallett
Senior pre-press designer: Dan May
Programme manager: Helen Blount
Publisher: Joanna Kirby
Publishing director: Georgina Dee

Publishing information

This eighth edition published March 2015 by
Rough Guides Ltd,
80 Strand, London WC2R 0RL
11, Community Centre, Panchsheel Park,
New Delhi 110017, India
Distributed by Penguin Random House
Penguin Books Ltd,
80 Strand, London WC2R 0RL
Penguin Group (USA)
345 Hudson Street, NY 10014, USA
Penguin Group (Australia)
250 Camberwell Road, Camberwell,
Victoria 3124, Australia
Penguin Group (NZ)
67 Apollo Drive, Mairangi Bay, Auckland 1310,
New Zealand
Penguin Group (South Africa)
Block D, Rosebank Office Park, 181 Jan Smuts Avenue,
Parktown North, Gauteng, South Africa 2193
Rough Guides is represented in Canada by Tourmaline
Editions Inc. 662 King Street West, Suite 304, Toronto,
Ontario M5V 1M7
Printed in Singapore
© Rough Guides, 2015

Maps © Rough Guides
Contains Ordnance Survey data © Crown copyright and
database rights 2015
No part of this book may be reproduced in any form
without permission from the publisher except for the
quotation of brief passages in reviews.
480pp includes index
A catalogue record for this book is available from the
British Library
ISBN: 978-1-40935-662-2
The publishers and authors have done their best to
ensure the accuracy and currency of all the information
in **The Rough Guide to Wales**, however, they can accept
no responsibility for any loss, injury, or inconvenience
sustained by any traveller as a result of information or
advice contained in the guide.
1 3 5 7 9 8 6 4 2

Help us update

We've gone to a lot of effort to ensure that the eighth
edition of **The Rough Guide to Wales** is accurate and up-
to-date. However, things change – places get "discovered",
opening hours are notoriously fickle, restaurants and
rooms raise prices or lower standards. If you feel we've got
it wrong or left something out, we'd like to know, and if
you can remember the address, the price, the hours, the
phone number, so much the better.

Please send your comments with the subject line
"**Rough Guide Wales Update**" to ✉ mail@uk.roughguides
.com. We'll credit all contributions and send a copy of the
next edition (or any other Rough Guide if you prefer) for
the very best emails.
Find more travel information, connect with fellow
travellers and plan your trip on ⓦ roughguides.com.

ABOUT THE AUTHORS

Tim Burford studied languages at Oxford University and worked briefly in publishing. In 1991 he began writing hiking guides to east-central Europe and then Latin America. Somewhat randomly, he also works on the Rough Guides to Romania and Alaska, and leads hiking groups in Europe's mountains. He lives in Cambridge, loves train travel in Europe, and flies only across oceans and as rarely as possible.

Norm Longley Having spent most of his life writing Rough Guides to countries in eastern Europe and the Balkans, Norm has now turned his hand to the UK, having researched guides to Scotland, Ireland and Wales. He lives in Bath and can occasionally be seen erecting marquees on the Rec.

James Stewart (@jamesstewart.biz) is a freelance journalist and the author of over fifteen guidebooks, including Rough Guides' Germany, Australia and Bali and Lombok. He has previously written guidebooks to Wales's best campsites and budget accommodation.

Acknowledgements

Tim Burford: Thanks as ever to Freddie and Robbie in Haverfordwest, to Jane Harris at Visit Wales and Sara Whines at Four bgb, to Katy and Norm, and to Mani, Natasha, Melissa, Alison and all at Castell Rough Guides.

Norm Longley: Thanks to Alison, Natasha and Emma for their diligent and enthusiastic editing. A very special thanks to Sara Whines at Four bgb and Jane Harris at Visit Wales for their invaluable assistance throughout the course of this book. Thanks are also due to my colleagues Tim and James, and most importantly, to Christian, Luka, Patrick and Anna.

Readers' updates

Thanks to all the readers who have taken the time to write in with comments and suggestions (and apologies if we've inadvertently omitted or misspelt anyone's name):

Richard Brock, Andrew Cameron, Hilary Fender, Anne Fowler, William Fraatz, Helen Hale, John Matthews, Richard Reast, Mitchell Sandler, Rhiannon Scutt, Simon Sleight, Mark Woodall, Rachel and Martin Wright

Photo credits

Index

Maps are marked in grey